SELECT PROCEEDINGS OF THE EUROPEAN SOCIETY OF INTERNATIONAL LAW

This is the fourth in the Series of Select Proceedings of the European Society of International Law (ESIL) featuring the most important and interesting papers presented at the Fifth Biennial Conference on 'Regionalism and International Law', organised by ESIL and the University of Valencia in 2012. As usual, the best papers from that conference have been re-written, edited and drawn together by the two editors to present a perspective on what is a flourishing forum for the discussion of new ideas and scholarship on international law.

Select Proceedings of the European Society of International Law

Fourth Volume

Regionalism and International Law
Valencia, 13–15 September 2012

Edited by
Mariano J Aznar
and
Mary E Footer

·HART·
PUBLISHING
OXFORD AND PORTLAND, OREGON
2015

Published in the United Kingdom by Hart Publishing Ltd
16C Worcester Place, Oxford, OX1 2JW
Telephone: +44 (0)1865 517530
Fax: +44 (0)1865 510710
E-mail: mail@hartpub.co.uk
Website: http://www.hartpub.co.uk

Published in North America (US and Canada) by
Hart Publishing
c/o International Specialized Book Services
920 NE 58th Avenue, Suite 300
Portland, OR 97213-3786
USA
Tel: +1 503 287 3093 or toll-free: (1) 800 944 6190
Fax: +1 503 280 8832
E-mail: orders@isbs.com
Website: http://www.isbs.com

Hart Publishing is an imprint of Bloomsbury Publishing plc.

British Library Cataloguing in Publication Data
Data Available

ISBN: 978-1-84946-532-8

Typeset by Compuscript Ltd, Shannon
Printed and bound in Great Britain by
Lightning Source UK Ltd

Avant-Propos/Foreword

ANNE PETERS[1] ET LAURENCE BOISSON DE CHAZOURNES[2]

A l'invitation du Professeur Mariano J Aznar et de l'Université de Valence, la Société européenne de droit international (SEDI) a tenu sa cinquième Conférence biennale.

Cette Conférence a permis que l'année 2012 entre dans la mémoire collective de la SEDI comme *annus mirabilis* pour l'histoire du droit international, après 1492, année dans laquelle les rois Isabella et Fernando I ont réalisé la Reconquista de Granada et ont financé le voyage de Cristóbal Colón aux « Indes » ... Le thème de la Conférence était lié à la reconnaissance du fait que—pour le meilleur et pour le pire—l'Europe a historiquement été le centre du monde à partir de l'ère moderne, en créant différentes périphéries qui ont dû adopter la foi, l'organisation sociale et les systèmes juridiques européens. L'influence de l'Europe sur les autres continents est un fait historique qui méritait d'être revisité d'un point de vue juridique. L'une des idées de la Conférence était aussi d'évaluer les réactions, pour ainsi dire, des autres régions envers l'Europe et leurs approches du droit international.

L'Espagne—et à nouveau pour le meilleur et pour le pire—a eu une influence à l'échelon régional. Est-ce que le futur du droit international est « régional »—pour paraphraser le titre d'un article d'Anne-Marie Slaughter de 2006 (qui d'ailleurs portait le sous-titre : « The European way of international law »)? Et est-ce que ce régionalisme reflète l'évolution du droit international qui est usuellement relaté comme la propagation des règles développées dans les ordres internes des États européens depuis le XVIème siècle, un « droit public de l'Europe » (comme l'appelait Gabriel Bonnot de Mably en 1746) qui s'est après étendu sur d'autres continents, et enfin sur le globe entier ?

A travers des organisations régionales, des traités bilatéraux de libre-échange, les opérations régionales de maintien de la paix, des mécanismes de règlement de différends régionaux, le droit international peut sans doute acquérir une sorte de réalité et mise en œuvre effective. De ce point de vue, le régionalisme serait un progrès désirable, dépassant une focalisation excessive et étroite sur l'État national et évoluant dans la direction d'un système « plus » international. Toutefois, le régionalisme est aussi susceptible de menacer l'aspiration à un système universel de droit international, précisément parce que son succès pourrait résulter en la fragmentation du droit international. Chacun de ces deux points de vue antagonistes portent un grain de vérité en lui-même : l'idée d'un droit international régional peut former un pont

[1] Présidente de la SEDI, 2010–12.
[2] Présidente de la SEDI, 2012–14.

entre l'État souverain et le droit international, mais elle peut aussi être source de cloisonnement. Ce caractère ambivalent du régionalisme est l'une des raisons du choix par les organisateurs de ce thème fascinant pour la cinquième Conférence biennale de la SEDI.

Cette Conférence fut un grand succès, réunissant de très nombreux participants, universitaires et praticiens, provenant d'Europe et d'autres régions du monde. Le présent ouvrage compte une sélection des communications très stimulantes présentées lors de cette Conférence. Elles portent sur les facettes normatives, institutionnelles et juridictionnelles du phénomène régional dans l'ordre international, dans une perspective historique et contemporaine. Les débats et échanges furent riches et le présent ouvrage en est le reflet. Il témoigne également de la vitalité de la Société européenne de droit international en tant qu'espace de réflexion et d'échanges d'idées.

Nous exprimons notre profonde gratitude au Professeur Mariano J Aznar et à son équipe pour avoir organisé la cinquième Conférence biennale et pour avoir permis que les communications présentées puissent être accessibles dans un ouvrage. Nos remerciements vont également à la Professeure Mary Footer qui a co-dirigé cet ouvrage.

Contents

Introduction

MARIANO J AZNAR* AND MARY E FOOTER†

THE QUESTION OF how regionalism is relevant to, and interacts with, international law lay at the heart of the fifth Biennial Conference of the European Society of International Law, held in Valencia, Spain, from 13 to 15 September 2012. Critical to that question were two others: 'Why Regionalism?'—And does regionalism still matter in our global society?

Our programme outline on *Regionalism and International Law/Régionalisme et droit international* suggested that Europe—for better or for worse—has historically been at the centre of the world from the Modern era onwards, creating different spaces for the adoption of European faiths, social organisation and legal systems. Similarly, Europe's influence on other continents called for a re-evaluation from a legal point of view. Thus, 'feedback' from other regions about Europe and the European approach to international law, if there is one, was important to us.

And there were other reasons for scrutinising the relationship between regionalism and international law, not least because it allowed us to revisit one of the leitmotifs of the Society, which is the unity and fragmentation of international law. Having already analysed this theme from a specialist, a theoretical and a judicial perspective in previous biennial conferences, a regional perspective was added to our research *acquis*.

Instead of adopting a 'horizontal' view in its analysis of regionalism, the fifth Biennial Conference examined regionalism to discern the existence of new centres and peripheries. The focus shifted from economic development to access to technology, from new generations of human rights to the immaterial concepts of groups and ethnicity, as well as taking into account other variables so as to foster new approaches to regionalism and its impact on international law. At Valencia there were eight fora and eight agorae, each with their unique approach, to examining the relationship between regionalism and international law.

The conference proceedings delve into many different aspects of *Regionalism and International Law*, beginning in Part I with *The History and Concept of Regionalism*. Louise Fawcett introduces the concept of regionalism and its historical evolution, prior to focusing on some regional aspects of peace operations, terrorism and weapons of mass destruction. Liliana Obregón provides us with a short history of Latin American law, with a sweep of events commencing in 1795 through to the contemporary era. Bernardo Sepúlveda-Amor gives his insightful comments on these

* Professor of Public International Law and Director of *Centro de Estudios de Derecho y Relaciones Internacionales* (CEDRI), Universitat Jaume I de Castellón.

† Professor of International Economic Law and Co-director of the Nottingham International Law and Security Centre (NILSC), University of Nottingham School of Law.

two contributions, while Jean Salmon offers his reflections on the concept of regionalism and the separate notion of 'region'.

Part II examines *Regionalism and the Unity of International Law*. André de Hoogh provides a *tour d'horizon* of the topic from a positivist perspective, while Dirk Pulkowski dwells on notions of regionalism, international law as a unified legal order, and the challenge of regionalism to the unity of international law. Both chapters are critiqued by Mathis Forteau, before Philippa Webb closes this Part with her views on regional challenges to the law of state immunity.

Part III addresses the issue of *Regionalism, International Organisation and Integration*, with contributions from Jean-Marc Sorel on the problem of integration in international organisations, dependent upon whether they are universal or regional in character, while Santiago Villalpando examines the relationships between the UN Charter and regional organisations. Karel Wellens offers his comments on both contributions.

Part IV moves on to examine *Regionalism and Globalisation*. Ana Peyró Llopis portrays a world in which globalisation acts as a brake on the development of 'supranational' international law, and a global legal order is emerging, José Manuel Pureza reflects on the juxtaposition of new regionalism and the emergence of global constitutionalism, and Antonio Remiro Brotóns offers his comments.

Part V focuses on *Allocating Interests: States' Legal Policies between Universalism and Regionalism*, with contributions by Anders Rönquist on the challenge for states of universal and regional cooperation, Daphne Shraga on the balance of power that has seemingly been struck in the different relationships between universalism and regionalism concerning human rights, international criminal justice and peace operations, and Dorothy Estrada-Tanck on the concept of human security and universal human rights in the context of undocumented migrants.

Part VI is devoted to *Regionalism, Peace and Security*, with contributions by Olivier Corten in which he questions the role of the African Union (AU) in seemingly removing itself from the UN Security Council's authority, and Ana Salinas de Frías who questions the extraterritorial application of the European Convention on Human Rights in matters of peace and security; both with comments by Mohamed Bennouna. This Part is completed by Juan Jorge Piernas López, who reflects on the specific role of the AU in South Sudan, while Alma Corina Borja Monroy examines regional practice before the International Criminal Court, based on the cases of Northern Uganda and Sudan.

Part VII offers us *Regional Integration: Some Perspectives on Trade, Investment and Development*, with a contribution by Irene Blázquez-Navarro on public interest in EU foreign investment policy after the Treaty of Lisbon; she is joined by Ousseni Illy, who examines African regional economic arrangements. Gabrielle Marceau comments on both chapters, with reference to the institutional setting for regional trade arrangements in the WTO—in principle and in practice. In concluding this Part, Nitish Monebhurrun provides us with an analysis of the contemporary notion of development in international investment law and overlooked regional realities.

Part VIII on *Regionalism and Human Rights* is introduced by Theodore Christakis, who examines the judicial activism of some regional human rights treaty bodies and state sovereignty, and whose contribution is commented on by Djamchid Momtaz.

Meanwhile Antonio Cançado Trinidade offers his thoughts on the regional system of human rights protection.

Finally, Part IX brings together *Universal and Regional Responses to the Environment and Our Common Heritage*, with a chapter by Géraud de Lassus St-Geniès on articulating universal and regional approaches to climate change, while a set of contributions from Yoshinobu Takei and Claudia Cinelli examine the potential for the convergence of the Polar regions and the delimitation process in the central Arctic, respectively.

The 2012 ESIL Biennial Conference was held under the Presidency of Honour of Her Majesty the Queen Sofia of Spain, organised by the Universitat de Valencia and the *Centro de Estudios de Derecho internacional y de Relaciones internacionales* (CEDRI), and sponsored by the *Confédération Suisse*, the Universitat Jaume I of Castellón, the Spanish Ministry of Economy, the Regional Government of Valencia, the Fine Arts Museum of Valencia, Broseta LLP and Éditions Bruylant.

July 2015

Part I

The History and Concept of Regionalism

1

Regionalism: From Concept to Contemporary Practice

LOUISE FAWCETT*

I. INTRODUCTION

THE GROWTH OF regionalism, expressed as formal regional organisation, has received a great deal of scholarly attention since the Second World War. From its early days, regionalism has been much debated, and alternatively praised for its potential and criticised for its ill-defined nature and limited capacity. However, by the start of the twenty-first century, if not earlier, regionalism was well established in the vocabulary of international relations scholars and practitioners, such that it would be hard to imagine a world without it. Moreover, regionalism has become an integral part of the multilateral architecture, a position set out in the UN Charter and more recently emphasised in the European Union's Security Strategy, adopted in 2003:

> In a world of global threats, global markets and global media, our security and prosperity increasingly depend on an effective multilateral system. The development of a stronger international society, well-functioning international institutions and a rule-based international order is our objective.[1]

Though the European experience has been central to the story of regionalism, both history and contemporary practice show that this is not the only example to draw upon. South American states were early advocates of regionalism, following their independence in the nineteenth century; by the latter part of that century, South American regionalism was fused with a wider pan-Americanism. The twentieth century saw the emergence of the flagship regionalisms of the European Community (later the European Union) and the North Atlantic Treaty Organization—models which were widely imitated elsewhere. In the twenty-first century, African states under the umbrella of the African Union foster ever more elaborate integrative schemes and have been path-breakers. An example of this is their adoption of the

* Professor of International Relations, Wilfrid Knapp Fellow and Tutor in Politics, St Catherine's College, University of Oxford.

[1] European Union, 'A Secure Europe in a Better World', European Security Strategy (Brussels, 12 December 2003) 9.

principle of 'Responsibility to Protect', which was embodied in article 4(h) of the Constitutive Act of the African Union[2] (even before its final adoption in the United Nations World Summit Outcome Document of 2005).[3] More recently, organisations in the Middle East, despite their sovereignty-loving charters, appear to have followed suit, embracing interventionist policies in response to the events of the so-called 'Arab Spring'. Worldwide, leading states are active in the promotion of regionalism, and most states in most parts of the world are members of multiple regional organisations.

Regional organisations are treaty- and charter-based, giving them formal status in international law. This status is enhanced—critically—through the recognition and status accorded to regional organisations by the United Nations and other multilateral organisations such as the World Trade Organization. It will be a particular concern of this chapter to track the evolution and complex features of this relationship.

However, regional organisations also derive legitimacy through the articulation and implementation of distinctive regional norms and practices. The Arab League, for example, derives legitimacy through its very 'Arabness', drawing on a rich common culture and history. The states of Southeast Asia are known for their articulation of what has been called the 'ASEAN way', which is a consensus-based approach based upon strict observance of sovereignty.[4] Today the ASEAN way has become the 'Asian way', extending the idea to a broader and still developing concept of East Asian regionalism.[5]

Though the advent of 'new regionalisms', particularly since the end of the Cold War, has seen the expansion and revision of the early idea of regionalism to include new organisations, actors and issue areas,[6] the original concept of regionalism: that of the policies and practices of state-based permanent organisations, with membership confined to a limited geographical area, retains extraordinary importance. This is demonstrated not only by the continuing development and complexity of existing organisations and their constitutional arrangements, but by the take-up of the concept by new and emerging powers, for which regionalism is seen increasingly as an important policy tool and a demonstration of their influence on the regional, but also global stage. China's approach to regionalism is illustrative in this respect (once a sceptic, but now an active player in a number of regional fora like the ASEAN Regional Forum (ARF) or Shanghai Cooperation Organization (SCO). Consider also tiny Qatar's recent role in influencing regional responses to the Arab Spring uprisings that started late in 2010, through the Gulf Cooperation Council. Given regionalism's growing importance and multidimensionality, it is an appropriate moment to review the history and concept of this phenomenon in world politics,

[2] Constitutive Act of the African Union (adopted 11 July 2000, entered into force 26 May 2001) 2158 UNTS 3, art 4(h).

[3] UNGA Res 60/1 (24 October 2005) UN Doc A/RES/60/1, paras 138–39.

[4] A Acharya, *Constructing a Security Community in South East Asia: ASEAN and the Problem of Regional Order*, 2nd edn (New York, Routledge, 2009).

[5] R Stubbs, 'ASEAN Plus Three: Emerging East Asian Regionalism' (2002) XLII/3 *Asian Survey* 453–54.

[6] See generally, B Hettne, A Inotai and O Sunkel (eds), *Studies in the New Regionalism*, Vols I–V (London, Macmillan, 1999–2001); L Fawcett and A Hurrell, *Regionalism in World Politics: Regional Organizations and International Order* (Oxford, Oxford University Press, 1995) 1–4.

and to assess its significance in regulating and framing contemporary debates about international order.

While investigating the nature and diverse uses of the concept, this chapter takes a broad and comparative historical perspective towards regionalism in practice, arguing that such an overview is essential to understanding its present trajectory, and its wider implications and ramifications for international relations and international law. The following two sections of the chapter deal accordingly with the concept and history of regionalism; Section IV focuses on some contemporary examples of regionalism in the security field and considers their wider implications.

II. THE CONCEPT OF REGIONALISM

The concept of regionalism has a complex history because of its essentially contested and flexible nature[7] and because of a divergence of views as to whether or not regionalism is an effective or desirable organising mechanism in international politics.

In respect of the concept itself there has been considerable debate (perhaps too much debate) about what constitutes a region, how a region is operationalised, and consequently, what is regionalism? Theoretically the problem has been compounded by the variety of qualitative and quantitative approaches on offer, which seek to both measure and understand the process.[8] A related issue is the inherent flexibility and evolving nature of the concept: regions and regionalisms share common features, but these are subject to adaptation and change. The UN Charter contributes to this flexibility, avoiding precise definitions of regional agency, to allow for the possibilities of multiple partnerships.[9] Another good example of this conceptual flexibility lies in the very debate about old and new regionalism, with old regionalism characterised mainly by the state-based regional organisations of the post-Second World War era, and new regionalism by both formal and informal interactions between state and non-state actors. Old regionalisms were focused (mainly) around examples provided by a European/North American core. New regionalisms have a more global reach and greater autonomy from the core, embracing emerging regions from the former 'South'.

Regionalisation is a related term, which is sometimes used interchangeably with regionalism, but it refers rather to an increase of regional interaction and activity: regionalism refers to policies and projects, regionalisation refers to processes.

Given this flexibility and the expansion of regional level activity, particularly since the Cold War, it is important to employ a definition broad enough to accommodate change in direction and purpose, yet narrow enough to ensure that the concept retains cohesion and can be approached with analytical rigour. This discussion may be likened to that over new versus traditional security issues. At the end of the Cold

[7] L Van Langenhove, *Building Regions: The Regionalization of World Order* (London, Routledge, 2011) 1–2.

[8] F Söderbaum and T Shaw, *Theories of New Regionalism* (London, Palgrave Macmillan, 2003) 5–6.

[9] D Sarooshi, *The United Nations and the Development of Collective Security: The Delegation by the UN Security Council of its Chapter VII Powers* (Oxford, Oxford University Press, 1999) 1–2, 142–46.

War, while some scholars called for the broadening of the concept to embrace a far wider understanding of security, others advocated retaining a more parsimonious concept, without which a discussion of security might become too elastic to be analytically useful.[10] Arguably, debates about 'new regionalism' have also suffered from this ambiguity driven by the ballooning of definitions whereby any activity at any regional level, whether supra-state, sub-state or trans-state, may be called regionalism.

With some adaptation, Joseph Nye's older (and tighter) definition of a region as a limited number of states linked by geography and interdependence, and of regionalism as the formation of and policies pursued by inter-state groups based around regions, has stood the test of time.[11] This is not to ignore the effects of globalisation and non-state actors on the processes of regionalism, a point emphasised by scholars of new regionalism like Björn Hettne,[12] but to highlight the fact that the state remains regionalism's 'gatekeeper', and as such the most vital and enduring reference point in the practice and regulation of regionalism.[13] This is borne out not only by looking at state responses to global crises, but also by considering the regional policies of emerging global players, like Russia or China, which prioritise state-based regionalisms and state regulation of regional processes. The state has not 'retreated', at least not in the manner predicted by Susan Strange.[14] Regional integration—the union of previously disparate parts and the creation of supranational authority—is a narrower subset of activity that comes under the category of regionalism. Its progress, outside the European institutions, has hitherto been very limited.

In respect of the second point as to whether or not regionalism is effective or desirable, the first question to be posed is: effective or desirable in relation to what? Regionalism has been judged in terms of its relationship with other multilateral institutions notably those relating to trade and finance (the Bretton Woods institutions) and security (the United Nations system). This debate dates back to the very foundations of modern regionalism. Early architects of the post-war institutions favoured a 'universal' over a particularist or regional approach to problem-solving.[15] This was the age of global 'constitutions'.[16] Regionalism, as understood in the 1930s, had acquired a bad name: marked by the aggressive and expansionist politics of powerful states like Germany or Japan, with their pan-European and pan-Asian projects respectively. The belief, informed by utopian post-war thinking, upheld that only a universal or near-universal collective of states could offer the best guarantee of international order. However, there was also recognition that states would wish to conduct their economic, political and security affairs within defined regional and geographical contexts, as already evidenced in the Americas, in the

[10] M Ayoob, 'The Security Problematic of the Third World' (1991) 43(2) *World Politics* 259.
[11] J Nye (ed), *International Regionalism* (Boston, Little Brown and Co, 1968) vii.
[12] B Hettne, 'Globalization and the New Regionalism: the Second Great Transformation' in B Hettne, A Inotai and O Sunkel (eds), *Globalism and the New Regionalism* (London, Macmillan, 1999) 6–11.
[13] BM Russett and John O'Neal, *Triangulating Peace* (New York, WW Norton & Co, 2001).
[14] S Strange, *The Retreat of the State: The Diffusion of Power in the World Economy* (Cambridge, Cambridge University Press, 1996).
[15] C Schreuer, 'Regionalism v Universalism' (1995) 6 *European Journal of International Law* 477–99.
[16] HH Koh, 'Why do Nations Obey International Law?' (1996–97) 106 *Yale Law Journal* 2599, 2614.

Inter-American system, and indeed in Europe itself where a so-called 'concert' of powers had regulated nineteenth-century regional relations. The UN's own organisation clearly reflects this, for example in the establishment of regional economic commissions and voting procedures.[17] As regards regions and their roles outside the UN system, it was only after considerable discussion at the San Francisco conference and elsewhere, and with pressure from parties with an interest in empowering regions, that the principle of regionalism was accommodated by the UN Charter (as it had been, though only minimally, by the League of Nations),[18] though within an institutional and legal hierarchy that clearly favoured universalism.

The provisions for regional agencies and their relationship within the UN are mostly clustered in Chapter VIII, Articles 51–54 of the UN Charter, but with important references elsewhere. Article 52 UN, for example, offers regional arrangements a formal role in contributing to international peace and security in the post-war world. The tone, unequivocally, is UN-first with insistence on reference and deference to Security Council decision-making. Hence Article 53 UN asserts that 'the Security Council shall, where appropriate, utilise such regional arrangements or agencies for enforcement action under its authority'. This hierarchy is reinforced by article 103 UN, which emphasises the primacy of UN obligations over 'any other international agreement'. Not all regional organisations are considered fully consistent with the purposes of Chapter VIII UN: the North Atlantic Treaty Organization (NATO) is one example. There are currently 14 Chapter VIII entities identified as attendees at regular high-level meetings of the UN Secretary General: five in Africa, two each in the Middle East, Europe, Asia-Pacific and the Americas.[19] Similarly in respect of the General Agreement on Tariffs and Trade (GATT) and later the World Trade Organization (WTO), whose agreements embody the spirit of a multilateral trading system, there is a provision, in article XXIV, for regional trade arrangements provided these are 'non-discriminatory' in nature.

The debate about regionalism and universalism has been a very important one and has informed both the history and concept of regionalism. The relationships anticipated by the UN Charter failed to materialise in the Cold War, as discussed below, because of the emergence of bipolarity and defensive alliance systems, which were contrary to the spirit of the Charter. Regional actors did not feature prominently in the UN's new peacekeeping roles. However, a possible framework for such relationships—and their reinterpretation—was laid down at the end of the Cold War, which saw the growth and expansion of regional organisations. The potential of regionalism was clearly highlighted in former UN Secretary General Boutros-Ghali's *Agenda for Peace*,[20] a post-Cold War milestone for the institution, in simultaneously addressing peace-keeping, peacemaking and preventive diplomacy—tasks which

[17] K Graham, 'The Regional Input for "Delivering as One"' in P De Lombaerde, F Baert and T Felicio (eds), *The United Nations and the Regions* (Dordrecht, Heidelberg, London, New York, Springer, 2012) 189, 194–97.

[18] Covenant of the League of Nations (adopted 29 April 1919, entered into force 10 June 1920) art 22. See R Zimmern, *The League of Nations and the Rule of Law* (London, Macmillan, 1945) 522.

[19] Graham, 'Regional Input for "Delivering as One"' (n 17) 197–98.

[20] B Boutros-Ghali, *An Agenda for Peace: Preventive Diplomacy, Peacemaking and Peace-keeping* (New York, United Nations, 1992).

regional institutions were invited to share. Later, in *An Agenda for Democratization* he spoke of the new regionalism, not as 'resurgent spheres of influence' but as a 'healthy complement' to internationalism.[21] Under Boutros-Ghali a further precedent was set when he and his successor, Kofi Annan, convened the first of what would be seven meetings with the heads of 11 regional organisations to discuss ways to further enhance cooperation and consultation. Though the last of these meetings was held in 2007, both the UN Security Council and member states have demonstrated 'growing interest in the process and making it more concrete'.[22] The present UN Secretary General, Ban Ki-Moon, has continued the effort, but choosing to focus instead on partnerships with the AU, highlighting the security situation of the African continent.

Though the relationship between the UN and regional institutions has clearly widened in interpretation and scope, some of the early reticence and ambiguity remains.[23] The relationship has been competitive as well as complementary, with organisations like the Economic Community of West African States (ECOWAS) in Liberia, and NATO in the former Yugoslavia operating outside the strict remit of the Charter, though this itself has been the subject of different interpretations. The key issues are timely action in grave international crises and establishing the appropriate remit for regionally based activity within a Charter-friendly framework which enhances cooperation and avoids duplication. Limited capacity and resources, partiality and over-dominance by strong states are problems frequently identified with regional organisation.[24] While so-called regional hegemons may provide necessary leadership, an abuse of power may be seen to delegitimise regional agency. Despite efforts to resolve tensions in the relationship, such issues have not been fully resolved, and scholars and policy makers continue to work on models designed to achieve a more equitable and integrated system. One example of such efforts is reflected in the 2006 Report of the High Level Panel on UN System Wide Coherence which contains, inter alia, recommendations for the streamlining of UN relationships with regions and regional structures to create a 'coherent regional institutional landscape'.[25]

Overall, there has been an important and unmistakable trend towards emphasising the importance of a supportive and complementary relationship between the UN and regional institutions; one that has been recognised by the UN and other actors, even if the details of this relationship have not been worked out. This has been borne out, for example, by recent events connected with the Arab Spring, where

[21] B Boutros-Ghali, *An Agenda for Democratization* (New York, United Nations, 1996) 33.

[22] L Van Langenhove, T Felicio and A Abass, 'The UN and Regional Organisations for Peace: Tracking a Slippery Partnership' in P de Lombaerde, F Baert and T Felicio (eds) (n 17) 91, 98.

[23] See J Lepgold, 'Regionalism in the Post-Cold War Era: Incentives for Conflict Management' in PF Diehl and J Lepgold (eds), *Regional Conflict Management*, (Oxford, Rowman & Littlefield, 2003) 9, 12–14.

[24] L Fawcett, 'The Evolving Architecture of Regionalization' in M Pugh and WPS Sidhu (eds), *The United Nations and Regional Security: Europe and Beyond* (Boulder CO, Lynne Rienner, 2003) 11, 21–23; R Tavares, *Regional Security: The Capacity of International Organizations* (London, Routledge, 2009).

[25] 'Delivering As One', Report of the Secretary General's High Level Panel on United Nations Systems-wide Coherence in the areas of development, humanitarian assistance and the environment (20 November 2006) UN Doc A/61/583, 10; Graham, 'Regional Input' (n 17) 190–93.

the legitimacy of international action in enforcing the no-fly zone over Libya, and the condemnation of incumbent regimes for human rights and other violations, was greatly enhanced by the support by relevant regional institutions—the League of Arab States (LAS), the Gulf Cooperation Council (GCC) and the Organization of the Islamic Conference (OIC). These are just the latest among numerous examples to demonstrate how the concept of regionalism has been firmly established in the new and expanded vocabulary of peace operations.

III. THE HISTORY OF REGIONALISM

A better understanding of the concept of regionalism and its contemporary importance in international relations and international law can be arrived at by reviewing its history. As helpful as offering a snapshot of their current activities is observing the different stages and incremental growth of regional organisation and activity. In this respect it is useful, to borrow a recent term from democratisation studies, to take a 'historical turn' in analysing regionalism.[26] Doing so allows us not only to track the life cycles of different organisations but also to note the key processes, events and 'turning points' that have impacted on their development. Regionalism is far from being a linear or uniform process; rather it has emerged in stages, shaped by a variety of external and internal factors alike.

In what can only be a brief survey, for the purposes of this chapter we consider regionalism across what we might call the 'long twentieth century', or from the late nineteenth to the early twenty-first century.[27] Though 1945 is often taken to be a starting point in the development of formal organisation, there are significant prior histories of regionalism which deserve mention, since these informed early institution-building, and arguably continue to inform regional processes today. For example Arabism, born of the late Ottoman and European colonial experiences, has closely informed the development of regional institutions, notably the LAS, but also the GCC. Hence Arab Congresses pre-dated formal organisation. Though constitutionally the LAS (and the GCC) was an organisation that placed state sovereignty first, the influence of Arabism in decision and alliance-making was marked, particularly in respect of Arab-Israel relations and the question of Palestine.[28]

Different parts of the Americas, as already noted, had already developed their own unique perspective of regionalism with a distinctive 'regional idea' based on anti-colonialism and independent statehood.[29] Indeed South American states sought to embed their ideas of sovereignty, independence and equality into international

[26] G Capoccia and D Ziblatt, 'The Historical Turn in Democratization Studies: A New Agenda for Europe and Beyond' (2010) 43 *Comparative Political Studies* 934.

[27] *cf* EJ Hobsbawm, *The Age of Extremes: The Short Twentieth Century, 1914–1991* (London, Michael Joseph, 1994).

[28] MN Barnett, *Dialogues in Arab Politics: Negotiations in Regional Order* (New York, Columbia University Press, 1998).

[29] L Fawcett, 'The Origins and Development of Regional Ideas in the Americas' in L Fawcett and M Serrano (eds), *Regionalism and Governance in the Americas* (London, Palgrave Macmillan, 2005) 30–35.

law particularly in respect of non-intervention. The merging of different regional ideas around the concept of pan-Americanism in the late nineteenth century was an important development marking US ascendency, but it remained incomplete. Since 1945, different South American states have advocated alternative routes to regionalism, of which the Southern Cone Common Market (MERCOSUR), and most recently the Union of South American Nations (UNASUR) and the Bolivarian Alternative for the Americas (ALBA), are examples. In these cases and in those of Asia and Africa, where the influence of pan-Africanism on ideas about the region and statehood were significant, it is not difficult to see how old and new regional concepts are merged in current institutional frameworks. Hence we can see how the 'pan-' idea provides legitimacy in a variety of institutional settings.

Despite such antecedents, the post-1945 starting point for a study of contemporary regionalism remains compelling because of the novelty of *formal* international institutions, the expansion of the international arena through decolonisation, and the first attempt to set out the parameters for a regional-multilateral relationship in the United Nations and other bodies. Indeed, as argued, it is impossible to understand the evolution of regionalism without a consideration of this relationship. Regionalism is often described as proceeding in waves,[30] and the Cold War and its ending are often seen as providing a dividing line between regionalism's first and second waves. The reality is more complex, with arguably more waves and less distinction than this simple division allows. However, it is the case that the post-Cold War expansion of regionalism, across different regions and issue arenas, had a powerful impact on its status in international relations and international law. Again the influence of European institutions in this expansion process is striking, but ultimately Europe provided only one of a number of examples of 'new regionalism'.[31]

Early post-war regionalisms were clustered around three main types: those focusing on security regionalism (like NATO, South East Asian Treaty Organization (SEATO), Central Treaty Organization (CENTO)), those concentrated on economics (European Community (EC) later to become the European Union (EU), North American Free Trade Area, Pacific Free Trade Area) and more multipurpose organisations (Organization of American States, Organization of African Unity or League of Arab States).[32] The first two types, despite appearances, were not unconnected; economic regionalism—like that of the EC—had an evident security rationale. Security regionalisms also reflected economic and other forms of interdependence. The record of early regionalism, outside the European experiments and the quasi-regionalism of NATO, was not judged to be particularly successful. This was true if measured through economic criteria or security cooperation. Indeed both CENTO and SEATO (associated with external powers but without internal legitimacy) failed

[30] ED Mansfield and HV Milner, 'The New Wave of Regionalism' (1999) 53 *International Organization* 589–627.

[31] M Telo, 'Introduction: Globalization, New Regionalism and the Role of the European Union' in M Telo (ed), *European Union and New Regionalism*, 2nd edn (London, Ashgate, 2007) 1–18.

[32] This section draws on L Fawcett, 'Exploring Regional Domains: A Comparative History of Regionalism' (2004) 80 *International Affairs* 432–34; L Fawcett, 'Regionalism and Global Governance' in P de Senarclens and A Kazancigil (eds), *Regulating Globalization: Critical Approaches to Global Governance* (Tokyo, UNU Press, 2007) 150–76.

to survive. In a Cold War environment, reflected in the composition of the Security Council, the envisaged relationship between the UN and regional organisations did not materialise. Nor did a new legal basis for regionalism emerge.

However, in a wider sense, the concept and practice of regionalism were more firmly established. With the evident constraints on the United Nation system, peace, security and economic development were delivered regionally by the institutions on both sides of the East-West divide. And different regional actors, despite their relative weakness and dependence on the superpowers, were slowly empowered. The EC is the most obvious example, but it is not alone. These, above all, were learning years for regional institutions, with lessons in economic integration, institutional development, power balancing, non-alignment and the development of security communities. Not only had a raft of new regional institutions emerged, but they also learned to adapt, survive and develop in a changing regional and global environment, and this was important in terms of facing future challenges.

The later Cold War period saw a further period of institution-building at the regional level, which again provided some new and important precedents for later activity. Though the influence of the Cold War was still apparent, the emergence of these newer organisations was a reflection of the changing security and economic priorities and the desire of regional actors to manage their local environment. Some examples are ASEAN, ECOWAS, the South Asian Association for Regional Cooperation, and the GCC. The GCC, for example, was founded in a hostile and difficult security environment characterised by the Iranian Revolution (1978–79) and the Iran-Iraq War, which started in 1980. All had a security as well as economic orientation, though their charters often emphasised more politically neutral economic agendas—the GCC is a case in point. Rather different in terms of geographical reach and orientation were the Conference of Security and Cooperation in Europe (later OSCE) and the Organization of the Islamic Conference. Founded between 1967 and 1986, all these institutions marked a change in regionalism: a move away from the Europe-focused economic regionalisms and the NATO-type security alliances, though both these remained relevant. Despite their Cold War foundations and limited initial scope (ASEAN provides a good example), all remain relevant today and many have significantly expanded their remit and activities in the new post-Cold War security architecture.

Viewed in retrospect, the Cold War had proved to be an arena for selective growth and consolidation of regionalism. Against this backdrop, a second wave of regional expansion commenced around and soon after its ending. Displaying novel features in terms of its scope and multidimensionality, there were also elements of continuity. The EU, for example, had already entered a new phase of region-building, formalised in the Maastricht Treaty of 1992. International system change, as in the early Cold War, in particular the removal of 'superpower overlay', transformed the international security environment, making regions more vulnerable and regionalism more attractive.[33] Regions and their accompanying institutions accordingly

[33] B Buzan and O Waever, *Regions and Powers: The Structure of International Security* (Cambridge, Cambridge University Press, 2003).

grew in importance: there were a number of new organisations, including the Asia Pacific Economic Conference (APEC), the ASEAN Regional Forum (ARF), the Arab Maghreb Union (AMU), and the Commonwealth of Independent States (CIS), while older organisations expanded their memberships as well as taking on different tasks and activities. Yet initially, as after the two world wars, there was also a revival of hopes for universalism, expressed in the reinvigoration of the United Nations system, which many considered—and some early evidence supported this—had the chance to operate as its founders and Charter intended. There were great expectations of a new era for the UN, supported by a string of early post-Cold War successes, which peaked around the time of the Gulf War of 1991. President George Bush Sr saw UN action at this time as being at the centre of his hopes for a 'New World Order'.

Very quickly, however, a series of disappointments and failures, of which the cases of Rwanda and Somalia are two prominent examples, revealed the continuing limitations of UN action. Continuing and ever more complex global crises led to a significant re-evaluation of the possibilities of regionalism in theory and practice, and with it an increasing recognition that regionalism, if not an alternative, could, indeed should, provide at least an important supplement to multilateralism. Thomas Weiss noted how 'the logic behind Chapter VII' was brought back by the over-extension of the UN.[34] This had already found expression in the statements and actions of former UN Secretary-General Boutros-Ghali, noted above. In 2000, after a troubled peacekeeping decade, a UN Panel chaired by Lakhdar Brahimi conducted a comprehensive review of peacekeeping operations,[35] preparing the ground for the subsequent High Level Panel on Threats, Challenges and Change, which highlighted more explicitly the importance of partnership. The High Level Panel's report, 'A More Secure World. Our Shared Responsibility', acknowledged that the Security Council had 'failed to make the most of the potential advantages' of working with regional institutions, and that the UN had much to learn from organisations that had taken the lead in setting normative standards to guide preventative efforts. Enhancing the role of regional institutions was identified as one of four pillars of any future security architecture, and a way of closing the North-South divide as regards security provision.[36]

The combined result of the post-Cold War explosion of new regionalisms, and the new legitimacy bestowed upon them by states, the UN and pre-existing multilateral institutions, has certainly raised their international profile In terms of this 'explosion', a couple of points can be made in summary. In quantitative terms there has been major growth and expansion of regional arrangements, both in terms of new organisations and new memberships of existing organisations, and these are tracked in various databases, including that of the United Nations University Institute on Comparative Regional Integration Studies (UNU-CRIS), a leading centre for regional integration studies founded in 2001, whose very existence reflects the

[34] T Weiss, *Beyond UN Sub-contracting: Task Sharing with Regional Security Arrangements* (London, Palgrave MacMillan, 1998) xii.

[35] Report of the Panel on United Nations Peace Operations (21 August 2000), UN Doc A/55/305–S/2000/209 (the 'Brahimi Report').

[36] 'A More Secure World: Our Shared Responsibility', Report of the High Level Panel on Threats, Challenges and Change (2 December 2004) A/59/565.

importance attached to new regionalisms.[37] Qualitatively there have also been significant changes, characterised by an expansion of tasks and activities, and importantly constitutional change. In this process, African organisations, under the umbrella of the reformed AU in 2001[38] with its novel institutions like the Pan-African Parliament and Court of Justice, stand out. Normative change, whether the empowering of institutions in respect of peace operations and other security provisions, or the promotion and protection of democratic practices and human and minority rights, can also be seen in institutions in the Americas (OAS and MERCOSUR) and Europe (both the EU but also the OSCE). The ASEAN Charter (2008), may be seen as an important 'constitutional moment' providing the institution with a more formal, legal framework to achieve deeper economic and security cooperation.[39] Plans, with consequences as yet unclear, for the deeper consolidation and integration of the GCC were put forward at the end of 2011 by Saudi Arabia's King Abdullah.

In short, since 1945 regionalism has both survived and adapted well to new international system challenges. In considering some aspects of the novelty and increasing scope of the 'new' regionalism we can appreciate how this process has contributed to its further consolidation and reconsideration by the wider international community and global institutions like the UN. In a more multipolar international system in which emerging states seek to influence the norms of global governance, regionalism is enjoying an enhanced role. Cross-regional learning has taken place—and here the phenomenon of inter-regionalism or cooperation between regional groups (of which the Asia-Europe Meeting, ASEM, is one example) has a place.[40] Importantly also, recognition by the UN and other multilateral institutions has paved the way for a much more robust involvement of regional institutions. As explored further in the next section in respect of new security regionalism, the relationship remains a complex one and the idea of a more unified system has not materialised. But history and experience show that regional institutions have established a new legitimacy in international relations and the partnerships established between the EU and the UN,[41] or the AU and the UN (cooperating since 2008 in a joint peacekeeping operation in Darfur, for example) are exemplary in this respect.

IV. CONTEMPORARY REGIONALISMS: SOME CONSIDERATIONS

This section reviews in more detail some of the areas where regional institutions have made an impact on the contemporary security arena,[42] including peace operations and humanitarian intervention, anti-terror activities and non-proliferation

[37] See for more information about UNI-CRIS: www.cris.unu.edu.

[38] For details of the African Union, see above n 2.

[39] SSC Tay, 'The ASEAN Charter: Between National Sovereignty and the Region's Constitutional Moment' (2008) 12 *Singapore Year Book of International Law* 151, 152.

[40] H Hanggi, Roloff and J Ruland, *Interregionalism and International Relations* (London, Routledge, 2006).

[41] The EU is the largest financial contributor to the UN and has special 'participant' status in a number of UN conferences. See for further information: www.eu-un.europa.eu.

[42] D Lake and P Morgan (eds), *Regional Orders: Building Security in a New World* (Pennsylvania PA, Pennsylvania State University Press, 1997).

(the last two in particular have assumed new salience on the agenda of regional organisations since 2001). All these areas have important implications for assessing the capacity and legitimacy of regionalism and its relationship to multilateral treaties and international law. They were central to the 2003 European Security Strategy and have addressed not only European, but also a wide range of regional institutions.

A. Peace Operations

Peace operations, broadly conceived, are a good example of the regionalisation of security provision, its motivation, impact and potential. Regional actors, both formal and more ad hoc informal regional institutions, have been increasingly active in a variety of solo and combined peace operations, many in conjunction with the UN.[43] This provides a contrast to the Cold War period, when regional organisations and actors played relatively minor roles. In 2010, for example, as recorded by the Centre on International Cooperation, of a total of some 40 peacekeeping operations, nearly half were conducted by regional organisations.[44] And of some 50 political (civilian) missions, again just under half were carried out by regional organisations.[45] The range—and geographical reach—of these operations is wide: from enforcement missions, like those of NATO in Afghanistan, or more recently Libya, to election monitoring or institution-building, like those of the EU or OSCE in Bosnia-Herzegovina.

The continuing high demand for peace operations and the multiple challenges facing the UN system have encouraged regional organisations to take on much more active roles in this area. Though such operations draw on a UN Chapter VIII model, they display considerable variation. Early African operations (like those of ECOWAS in the Liberian conflict), for example, while influenced by the neglect of pressing humanitarian crises in the continent, were also criticised for failing to apply the UN standards in respect of humanitarian intervention. Other operations, like that of NATO in Kosovo, bypassed UN deliberations and were initiated without obtaining prior Security Council authorisation.[46] Despite such regional differences and practices, as the changing discourse of multilateralism illustrates, regional actors are regarded as increasingly significant players. In the words of former UN Secretary-General Kofi Annan, 'multilateral institutions and regional security organisations have never been more important'.[47]

[43] TJ Farer, 'The Role of Regional Collective Security Arrangements' in TG Weiss (ed), *Collective Security in a Changing World* (Boulder CO, Lynne Rienner, 1993) 153–86; J Morris and H McCoubrey, 'Regional Peacekeeping in the Post-Cold War Era' (1999) 6(2) *International Peacekeeping* 129–51.

[44] Centre on International Cooperation, *Global Review of Peace Operations 2010* (Boulder CO, Lynne Rienner, 2011).

[45] ibid.

[46] For a discussion see, B Simma, 'NATO, the UN and the use of force: legal aspects' (1999) 10 *European Journal of International Law* 1–22.

[47] 'Regional Security Organizations never more important than today, says Secretary-General to European Security Organization Meeting', message from the UN Secretary-General Kofi Annan to the Organization for Security and Cooperation in Europe (OSCE) Ministerial Council (9 December 2002) SG/SM/8543.

There have been fluctuations in the numbers of regional peacekeepers and operations in the first decade or so of the twenty-first century. Overall however, there has been a pattern of sustained growth, demonstrated by the start-up of new missions in Africa and parts of Central Asia, and the expansion and reinforcement of NATO and EU operations in Afghanistan and the Democratic Republic of Congo, respectively. Though there are significant gaps in regional security provision, with some regions falling outside the direct remit of regionally led activity (notably East Asia and the Middle East), the involvement of regional institutions in more, and ever more complex, peace operations looks set to continue. This situation is partly the result of incremental growth, development and learning of institutions in the post-Cold War period. It also reflects the severity of regional security concerns and the absence of other security providers, generating a high demand for regional action. Core regional states, aware of the opportunities of shaping regional security policy, have been increasingly willing to provide leadership.

If this regionalisation of peace operations has taken place, what have been its wider effects on multilateralism? Here the conclusions, as suggested, remain mixed. First the results are patchy not all regions conduct their own peace operations, though this could change. Second, continuing doubts are expressed inside the United Nations and in the wider policy-making community about issues of leadership and legitimacy in respect of regional actors.[48] Where regional organisations and actors have diverged from UN practice or conducted operations without prior authorisation of the UN Security Council, as in the cases of ECOMOG and NATO, there are evident consequences for UN legitimacy and authority.

Third, and not unconnected with the above, questions have been asked about impartiality, or the tendency of strong regional powers to impose their own security agendas without sufficient regard to fellow members, making regional operations a vehicle for hegemony rather than participation. Examples cited are Russia in the CIS, Nigeria in ECOWAS, Australia's role in the Pacific Islands Forum or the East Timor intervention, and the US in NATO. Fourth, accepting the precedent of the regionalisation of peace operations could encourage the policy of excluding areas like Africa from UN-led peace operations.[49] All these are real concerns. Yet given the present, more multipolar international environment and the limited capacity of older multilateral frameworks like the UN, the search for regional solutions, greater ownership of regional problems and the tendency for regional institutions and actors to play more active roles in peace operations look set to continue. The constitutional changes or new instruments designed to support these activities should also be noted.

The types of peace operations described above represent one element of the new security agenda of regional institutions in the twenty-first century and are an indicator of their emerging roles as multilateral actors. Another measure of security regionalisation is the (re)securitisation of issues like terrorism or the spread of weapons

[48] BL Job, 'The UN, Regional Organizations, and Regional Conflict: Is there a Viable Role for the UN?' in RM Price and MW Zacher (eds), *The United Nations and Global Security* (London, Palgrave Macmillan, 2004) 227–43.

[49] R Bellamy and P Williams, 'Whose Keeping the Peace? Regionalization and Contemporary Peace Operations' (2005) 29(4) *International Security* 157–95.

of mass destruction (WMD) and their take up by regional institutions. Such security issues are not new: their novelty lies in the way that they have been classed as core security threats by dominant states and institutions—in particular the US and Europe—following the series of international terrorist attacks between 2001 and 2005 and the growing aspirations of states like Iran and North Korea to nuclear status. Terrorism and WMD are today at the centre of contemporary security debates, and demand appropriate institutional responses. They have posed new challenges to security institutions, already in the process of readjustment after the Cold War.

B. Terrorism

'Terrorism', variously defined, has been adopted as a key security issue by many regional organisations. In contrast to peace operations, however, the UN has been slower to provide an obvious model for regions to follow.[50] Long unable to agree a common definition or policy on terrorism, the UN's Global Counter Terrorism Strategy, adopted in 2006,[51] represented an important breakthrough. However, it depends heavily on member states for implementation and underspecifies the potential role of regional bodies.[52] This leaves open the possibility of a variety of regional interpretations and practices. While a number of groups have moved to endorse the UN's initiative, regional responses differ significantly, reflecting the particular situation of each region, the robustness of its institutional arrangements and its relationship and exposure to different terrorist threats.

A number of well-established regional institutions—NATO, the OAS, MERCOSUR, the OAU and the EU, for example—already had anti-terrorist provision in place to deal with longstanding local threats. Since the Cold War, but particularly since 9/11, these organisations have upgraded this provision. Regions are arguably well positioned to react to, monitor and deter terrorist activity, by sharing police and military intelligence for example, and most regional organisations have responded to terrorist attacks by incorporating new institutional mechanisms. The OAS and MERCOSUR have established the Inter-American Committee against Terrorism and the Terrorism Working Group, respectively.[53] The AU has adopted an additional protocol on the prevention and combating of terrorism. The founding document of the Shanghai Cooperation Organization singled out terrorism, separatism and extremism as 'three evils' to confront, reflecting concerns of members like Russia and China. Through the establishment of a Regional Anti-Terrorist Structure (RATS), based in Tashkent, it has continued to develop its capacity in this area. NATO for its

[50] J Boulden and T Weiss (eds), *Terrorism and the UN: Before and After 9/11* (Bloomington IN, Indiana University Press, 2004).

[51] UNGA Res 60/288 (8 September 2006), UN Doc A/RES/60/288.

[52] See Eric Rosand et al, 'The UN Global Counter-Terrorism Strategy and Regional and Sub-Regional Bodies: Strengthening a Critical Partnership', Centre on Global Counterterrorism Cooperation (2008) www.globalct.org/wp-content/uploads/2008/10/strengthening_a_critical_partnership.pdf.

[53] A Oelsner, 'Consensus and Governance in Mercosur: The Evolution of the South American Security Agenda' (2009) 40(2) *Security Dialogue* 191–212.

part in 2002 endorsed a new Military Concept for Defence against Terrorism;[54] the EU in 2005 adopted a broader counter-terrorism strategy.[55]

The potential for regional organisations to act in this area is highlighted by the longstanding difficulty faced by the UN in articulating a common position on terrorism. Despite the Common Strategy, which a number of institutions have signed up to, the results are mixed. Dealing with terrorism, even defining terrorism, is an issue that is particularly prone to agenda-setting by core states, and it remains to be seen to what extent states will wish to entrust such delicate 'homeland security' concerns to international institutions. This may reinforce a preference for more unilateral, bilateral, or informal small group action. The cases of NATO and the EU are both illustrative in this respect: individual states' capabilities are not matched at the formal institutional level.[56] Further, some states' interpretations of terrorism and the terrorist threat—that of the SCO, for example—may not conform to the UN's wider counter-terrorism strategy.

The securitisation of terrorism is only partially regionalised, and is a reminder of the way in which core states can still dominate and constrain security options worldwide. Different states and regions also react differently to terrorism depending on their own perception and experience of terrorist threats and the local security culture. This can both enable and disable concerted regional action, as the examples of Palestine and Colombia show. In both cases different regional (and extra-regional) actors disagree on the definition and thus the policy that should be adopted in dealing with such threats. In this way an emerging, if still contested, multilateral norm is subject to considerable local interpretation, change and even dilution.

C. Weapons of Mass Destruction

The issues regarding WMD share some of the above characteristics, though this has long been the domain of multilateral action and treaties and much less of regional agencies, the lynchpin being the Non-Proliferation Treaty of 1968.[57] Since the end of the Cold War both the UN and a range of regional actors have entered the field, with a new dimension to WMD provided by the terrorist threat above, since a particular concern of policy makers is the possible use of WMD by terrorist groups. Security regionalisation, such as has occurred in this area, may be regarded as more of a top-down process, driven by existing multilateral regimes and the desire of core states to restrain nuclear proliferation. Informal arrangements, like the Six-Party Talks

[54] See NATO's military concept for defence against terrorism, available at www.nato.int/cps/en/natolive/topics_69482.htm.

[55] See 'The European Union Counter-Terrorism Strategy', Council of Europe, Brussels (November, 2005), available at http://register.consilium.eu.int/pdf/en/05/st14/st14469–re04.en05.pdf.

[56] See further D Keohane, 'The Absent Friend. EU Foreign Policy and Counter Terrorism' (2008) 46 *Journal of Common Market Studies* 125–46.

[57] Treaty on the Non-Proliferation of Nuclear Weapons, International Atomic Energy Agency (opened for signature 1 July 1968, entered into force 5 March 1970) 729 UNTS 161, available at www.iaea.org/Publications/Documents/Treaties/npt.html.

and the Proliferation Security Initiative,[58] or the EU-3,[59] formed to kerb the nuclear aspirations of North Korea and Iran respectively, have played important, though hitherto largely unsuccessful roles, in attempting to uphold the non-proliferation regime.

Many regional institutions today publicise commitments to non-proliferation and uphold the enforcement of existing multilateral treaty regimes. The EU, for example, since 2003 has had in place an anti-proliferation policy to strengthen and universalise the existing multilateral system and sustain a viable non-proliferation regime, even though two EU states are themselves nuclear powers.[60] ASEAN, South Pacific and Latin American states also support nuclear-free zones through long-standing treaties. Twenty-four Latin American countries in 1967 signed the Latin American Nuclear Free Zone Treaty at Tlatelolco establishing an 'early commitment to prohibit and prevent the use, manufacture, production or acquisition of nuclear weapons in the region, turning Latin America into the sole continent free from nuclear war competition'.[61] ASEAN's summit in 1995 saw the signature of the Bangkok Treaty, or Treaty on the Southeast Asia Nuclear Weapon-Free Zone (SEANWFZ), establishing a moratorium on the production of nuclear weapons between the 10 member states.[62] The Pelindaba Treaty establishing a nuclear weapons-free zone among African states came into effect in 2009.[63] While there are rational balance of power arguments supporting such cooperation for the regions in question, one might also ask what role in enforcing these regimes has been played by powerful external actors (like the US or China, for example), and whether or not regional regimes alone could ever be fully effective in restraining the ambitions of an aspiring nuclear state. However, a weak regional regime is certainly a hindrance to non-proliferation: in the regional security complex that is the Middle East, it has proved impossible to restrain Israel's (or, for many years, Iran's) nuclear ambitions, notwithstanding the longstanding call by Arab states for a nuclear-free region.

Though the issue of WMD, like terrorism, could represent a new growth area, with great possibilities for security cooperation and a good multilateral-regional mix of initiatives, evidence shows that in this high politics arena, proliferation issues are still more likely to be handled outside formal regional organisations—by the

[58] J Bajoria and B Xu, 'The Six-Party Talks on North Korea's Nuclear Program' September 2013, available at www.cfr.org/proliferation/six-party-talks-north-koreas-nuclear-program/p13593; Proliferation Security Initiative (PSI), for which see, www.psi-online.info/.

[59] Comprising Britain, France and Germany; see 'Iran's Nuclear Programme', European Union External Action Services at http://eeas.europa.eu/iran/nuclear_en.htm.

[60] European Security Strategy, 2003, above n 1.

[61] Treaty for the Prohibition of Nuclear Weapons in Latin America (done at Tlatelolco, 14 February 1967, entered into force 25 April 1969) 634 UNTS 281 (LANWFZ or Tlatelolco Treaty), available at www.iaea.org/Publications/Documents/Treaties/tlatelolco.html; see also, D Tussie, 'Latin America: Contrasting Motivations for Regional Projects' (2009) 35 *Review of International Studies* 169, 170.

[62] Treaty on the South East Asia Nuclear Weapon Free Zone (done at Bangkok, 15 December 1995, entered into force 28 March 1997) 35 ILM 635 (SEANWFZ or Bangkok Treaty), available at http://cns.miis.edu/inventory/pdfs/aptbang.pdf.

[63] The African Nuclear Weapon Free Zone Treaty (done at Pelindaba 11 April 1996, entered into force 15 July 2009) 35 ILM 698 (Pelindaba Treaty), available at www.au.int/en/content/african-nuclear-weapon-free-zone-treaty-pelindaba-treaty.

P-5, strong regional powers, ad hoc groupings and existing multilateral frameworks. While declaratory statements and confidence building measures of the sort described here have a role to play, non-proliferation in the current international environment is often deemed too dangerous to be left to weak regional organisations and it is precisely the case that the two longstanding nuclear challengers have operated outside the domain of regional or formal organisation (the July 2015 P5+1 agreement on Iran's nuclear programme was brokered under UN auspices). On the other hand, scholars have noted a trend towards legalisation even in the more informal environment of Southeast Asian regionalism, as exemplified by the ASEAN Charter. For example, the NFZ treaty referred to above includes, in article 21, the right of referral of a dispute to the International Court of Justice.[64]

This brief analysis of the performance of regional institutions in three core security areas by no means exhausts their range of security activities, but offers an illustration of their developing roles in a multilateral context. For any issue area chosen, there will be a different regional response, depending on local security priorities and conditions, the level of regional consensus and existing multilateral provision. The above analysis shows how major and contentious security agendas, particularly in respect of terrorism and WMD, are still set and partly managed by powerful states, often in an ad hoc or informal way or by utilising existing multilateral frameworks like the UN. Indeed in assessing the growth of regionalism in security affairs it is important to note how the UN still acts as lynchpin of any regional security system. However, there is increasing, if still uneven, involvement by regional actors in these and other areas, both in policy initiatives and agenda setting.

V. CONCLUSION

This chapter has sought to show how the evolution of the concept as well as the historical record of regionalism deserves careful consideration to appreciate its contemporary importance in international relations and international law. Regionalism, against the views of early sceptics, has established itself as an integral part of the multilateral architecture and vocabulary of international relations. Though regionalism has presented itself in a diversity of forms and its position in respect of the UN and WTO has been contested and ambiguous at times, the importance of a robust and interdependent relationship is widely acknowledged. The importance of such a relationship has been demonstrated by a consideration of three core contemporary security issues.

Regionalism has come a long way since its limited empowerment in the League Covenant, and the constrained environment in which it operated (UN provision notwithstanding) in the Cold War: it now has global reach, incorporating an increasingly important Southern dimension. But despite this take up by a growing number of actors and extension into new issue areas, it is not a substitute for states or global institutions. Rather it should be seen as part of a hybrid multilateral system.

[64] For the SEANNFZ Treaty, see above n 62, art 21; E Mansfield and E Solingen, 'Regionalism' (2010) 13 *Annual Review of Political Science* 146–63.

Thus, the world of regional councils envisaged by the British Prime Minster, Winston Churchill, in 1945, the regional coalitions for developing countries proposed by the Indian scholar Rajni Kothari, or the 'Peace in Parts' idea explored by US scholar Joseph Nye, while providing formulas for thinking about how regions might organise the world, have not materialised.[65] Such ideas, like more contemporary understandings of world order based around 'a world of regions',[66] do not provide an alternative, but an important complement, to a world of states supported by global institutions, imperfect as these may be. It is indeed a hybrid system of global governance, still underpinned by universal institutions like the UN, but with regions playing an important role, that states aspire to.

[65] R Kothari, *Footsteps into the Future*, (New Delhi, Longman, 1974); J Nye, *Peace in Parts. Integration and Conflict in Regional Organization* (Boston, Little Brown and Co, 1971).

[66] PJ Katzenstein, *A World of Regions, Asia and Europe in the American Imperium* (Ithaca NY, Cornell University Press, 2005) 1.

2

Regionalism (Re-)constructed: A Short History of a 'Latin American International Law'

LILIANA OBREGÓN*

I. INTRODUCTION

IN 1912, MANOEL Alvaro de Souza Sa Vianna (1860–1924) published a book arguing that 'a Latin American International Law does not exist, nor can exist.'[1] The Brazilian diplomat was responding to the Chilean lawyer, Alejandro Álvarez's (1868–1960) paper on the 'Origin and Development of American International Law,' presented at the Third Latin American Scientific Congress held in Rio de Janeiro five years earlier.[2]

This was not the first time that a debate on the existence of a Latin American international law came up. Forty years before, when the Argentine diplomat and lawyer, Carlos Calvo (1842–1902) published *Derecho Internacional teórico y práctico de Europa y América*[3] another Argentine lawyer and scholar, Amancio Alcorta (1842–1902), wrote a review on Calvo´s book complaining that he did not mention the possibility of a Latin American international law.[4] Calvo responded that a regional approach was impossible because international law dealt with general principles and did not provide solutions to specific problems.[5]

* Associate Professor of Law, Universidad de los Andes, Bogotá, Colombia.

[1] MA de Souza Sá Vianna, *De la non existence d'un droit international americain: dissertation presentée au Congres cientifique Latino-Américain (Premier Pan-Américain)* (Rio de Janeiro, L Figueredo, 1912) 11.

[2] This article was later modified and published as A Alvarez, 'Le droit international américain, son origine et son évolution' (1907) XIV *Revue Générale de Droit International Public* 393–405.

[3] C Calvo, *Derecho Internacional teórico y práctico de Europa y América* (Paris, Amyot/Durant et Pedone-Lauriel, 1868).

[4] A Alcorta, 'La ciencia del derecho internacional. A propósito de la obra de Calvo' (1883) VII *Nueva Revista* 464–83, 636. The debate is also cited by JM Yepes, *Alejandro Alvarez, créateur du droit international américain. La notion de l'universalité du droit des gens en rapport avec les conceptions internationales américaines* (Paris, Les Éditions internationales, 1938) 1–31, and HB Jacobini, *A Study of the Philosophy of International Law as Seen in the Works of Latin American Writers* (The Hague, Martinus Nijhoff, 1954). For a contemporary analysis of the Calvo-Alcorta debate, see A Becker Lorca, 'International Law in Latin America or Latin American International Law? Rise, Fall, and Retrieval of a Tradition of Legal Thinking and Political Imagination' (2006) 47 *Harvard International Law Journal* 283–305.

[5] C Calvo, 'Polémica Calvo-Alcorta' (1883) 8 *Nueva Revista de Buenos Aires* 629–31.

The Calvo—Alcorta debate did not close the issue for Álvarez who took on the challenge of arguing for a 'Latin American international law' as its self-proclaimed first theorist. Álvarez stated that his predecessors had never presented a comprehensive study on the emergence or content of such a law.[6] So, for half a century, Álvarez embraced the role of the main advocate for Latin American international law with a significant following of other lawyers in the region who wrote, claimed and argued for its existence. However, as the economic and political scenario in Latin America changed and coinciding with Álvarez´s death in 1960, the invocation of a Latin American international law fell into disuse and oblivion until, I argue, a recent revival of Latin American approaches to international law 'from below.'

Though we can establish that the promotion of Latin American international law surged as a response to geopolitical, economic and strategic factors in relation to global power players, rather than from a natural or shared historical source, what is important for the purpose of this chapter is when and how claims of a homogenous identity to promote regional projects of legal unification surged. More recently, the question would be how those identity claims excluded as much as they included to fit into the description of what is 'Latin America' under international law.

Thus this chapter disregards the limited question of the existence (or not) of a Latin American international law, and prefers to review the moments when a Latin American identity was invoked in regionalist projects, according to three different stages: initiation of that identity (nineteenth century); its theorization and emergence (first half of the twentieth century); and its fall (second half of the twentieth century). The chapter concludes with a brief description of the twenty-first century resurgence of different forms of regional collaboration and a reconstruction of Latin American identity from a broader and more pragmatic contemporary vision.

II. THE EARLY NINETEENTH CENTURY: THE BIRTH OF AN AMERICAN PERSPECTIVE ON THE LAW OF NATIONS

Immanuel Kant´s publication 'On Perpetual Peace' in 1795 argued for a confederation of states as a plausible legal solution to the problem of war. Though Kant was aware of the utopian character of his proposal, he imagined that a union of states would progress only in Europe and would be led by European states. However, the idea of a union of states as a means for "perpetual peace" was quickly appropriated by independence leaders of the new Spanish American states, with Simón Bolivar as its main proponent.[7]

[6] A Alvarez, *Le droit dnternational américain: son fondement, sa nature: d'apres l'histoire diplomatique des états du nouveau monde et leur vie politique et économique* (Paris, A Pedone, 1910), 267 ff. For an analysis of Alvarez' oeuvre see the articles by A Becker Lorca, JL Esquirol, C Landauer, L Obregón, and K Zobel in the 'Special Issue: Alejandro Álvarez' (2006) 19 *Leiden Journal of International Law*.

[7] I González Niño, *Simón Bolívar, precursor del derecho internacional americano* (Bogotá, Instituto Colombiano de Estudios Latinoamericanos y del Caribe, 1985) 1–131; M Mackenzie, *Los ideales de Bolivar en el derecho internacional americano* (Bogotá, Biblioteca del Ministerio de Gobierno: Colección Bolivariana, 1955) 1–548; A de la Peña y Reyes, *El Congreso de Panamá y algunos otros proyectos de unión hispano-americana* (México, Publicaciones de la Secretaría de Relaciones Exteriores, 1926) 1–262; SB Planas Suárez, *La doctrina de Monroe y la doctrina de Bolivar: los grandes principios de la política*

As early as 1815, in a text known as the *Jamaica Letter*, Bolívar expressed the idea of regional integration. It was only after several former Spanish territories were recognised as independent states by Spain that Bolívar decide to proceed with the organisation of a congress in Panamá that would lead to a 'union, league and confederation' of the new American states. Bolívar's congress has been praised as the starting point of a Latin American international law,[8] despite the literature that also exists concerning its failure.[9]

Bolívar argued that the Isthmus of Panamá was an ideal site for regional integration because it was ´midway between Mexico City and Buenos Aires´; it had symbolic value as the centre of the world, 'looking to Asia and Africa on the one hand and Europe on the other'; and the Isthmus of Panama was a geographic and political parallel to the ancient Greek congress held at the Isthmus of Corinth.[10] The invitations for the Congress sent in 1824 proclaimed the urgency of bringing the former Spanish colonies together in an effort to consolidate an 'eternal' government, celebrate the power of Columbus's world, make diplomatic alliances and international treaties[11] and provide advice and mediation for regional conflicts in a 'society of sister nations.'[12] Bolívar wrote in his diary that the congress was 'destined to form the widest, most extraordinary or strongest league ever appeared to this day on earth ... The relations of political societies will receive a code of public law that will rule universal behaviour ... the New World will be constituted by independent nations, bound together by a common law defined by their external relations.'[13] The union envisaged by Bolívar also sought to protect the fragility of a newly won independence in the face of a still-threatening Spain and the uncertainty about the rest of Europe´s support for the new states.

Organising the congress meant overcoming problems of distance and communications as well as recognizing new leaders that were managing sovereign units made up of a vast diversity of peoples, inheritors of three hundred years of a complex caste system of political, legal and social stratification. By the time of independence,

internacional americana (Habana, El Siglo XX, 1924) 1–111; GA de la Reza, *El Congreso de Panamá de 1826 y otros ensayos de integración latinoamericana en el siglo XIX: estudio y fuentes documentales anotadas* (Mexico, UNAM-Azcapotzalco y Ediciones y Gráficos Eón, 2006); JM Torres Caicedo, *Unión latino-americana, pensamiento de Bolívar para formar una liga americana. Su origen y sus desarrollos ...* (Paris, Rosa y Bouret, 1865) 1–385; E Vieira Posada, *La integración de América Latina: del Congreso Anfictiónico de Panamá en 1826 a una comunidad Latinoamericana o Sudamericana de Naciones en el año 2010* (Bogotá: Editorial Univ. Javeriana, 2004); JM Yepes, *Del Congreso de Panamá a la Conferencia de Caracas, 1826–1954: el genio de Bolívar a través de la historia de las relaciones interamericanas* (Caracas, Cromotipo, 1955).

[8] ibid.

[9] GA de la Reza, 'El Congreso Anfictiónico De Panamá. Una hipótesis complementaria sobre el fracaso del primer ensayo de integración latinoamericana' (2003) *Araucaria Revista Iberoamericana de Filosofía, Política y Humanidades* 5, 10.

[10] S Bolívar, *Coleccion de documentos relativos a la vida pública del libertador de Colombia y del Perú para servir a la historia de la independencia del suramérica: Tomo Tercero* (Carácas, Impresa de Devisme Hermanos, 1826) 178.

[11] ibid, 175.

[12] Vieira Posada, *La Integración De América Latina* 43.

[13] GA de la Reza, 'Simon Bolivar: Un pensamiento sobre el Congreso Anfictiónico de Panamá, Lima Febrero 1826 in *Documentos sobre el Congreso Anfictiónico de Panamá* (Carácas, Fundación Biblioteca Ayacucho/Banco Central de Venezuela, 2010) 84–5.

a population of about 17 million people lived in the former Spanish colonies, composed of approximately 7.5 million Indians, 5 million castes (or *mestizos*, 'mixed' peoples), 3 million Creoles (or 'whites'),[14] and 800,000 slaves.[15] The representation dilemma is best summarised in Bolívar's well-known phrase:

> We ... are not Indians nor Europeans, but a middle species between the legitimate owners of the country, and the Spanish usurpers, in short, we being Americans by birth, and our rights derived from Europe, we have to dispute this land against the natives of this country and against the invaders ... so we are in the most extraordinary and complicated case.[16]

Bolívar viewed the Creole minority as natural leaders, did not recognise the legal existence (as citizens) of the *mestizo* (mixed race)[17] and black majority, put the Indians as litigious opponents of land rights, and presented Europeans in opposition. Thus, a union based on the idea of a common origin, customs and language was an extraordinary challenge in face of the vast diversity of the majority population. In any case, Bolívar sent invitations to the Great Colombia, the United States of Mexico, the Republics of Central America, Peru, Chile and the United Provinces

[14] During the colonial period the legal and political elite was composed of Spanish and *Criollo* functionaries. *Criollo* was a term that began to be applied by the Spanish conquerors as early as the sixteenth century to designate a person born in America of Spanish parents. Thus, the Spaniards saw Criollos with suspicion, as impure or defective Europeans who were suspect of having been mixed with the local population. Notwithstanding, because of the interactive and dialogic character of the Criollo's identity it is constraining and misleading to describe the Criollo as a monolithic subject or as a homogenous elite. Because defining Criollos according to racial categories is confusing and misleading, I treat the Criollo as a social and legal standing rather than a strictly biological one. Criollos, like other social subjects during the colonial period, were defined in legal terms through separate jurisdictions, privileges and restrictions. As Spanish Americans (*españoles americanos*), however Criollos were part of a minority that had access to education, were landowners and belonged to the ´Republic of the Spanish´ if other social conditions were met, such as honour, purity of blood, legitimacy of birth, connections, etc. Criollos were automatically esteemed worthier than the *castas* (mixed peoples), the Indians (who belonged to a separate and distinct legal and social sphere designated as the ´Republic of Indians´), and slaves or free blacks. The Spanish term *Criollo* should not to be confused with the understanding of the English or French usage of *Creole* in Louisiana and in the Caribbean. In both of these regions, where a black presence has been central to the emergence of public political culture, Creole means free people of African descent. In most of Spanish America, with the possible exception of Cuba, the term Criollo posed a presumption of cultural and physical ´whiteness´. It is a deeply ambivalent and profoundly unstable social category as it rested on assumptions of racial purity despite the fact that by the nineteenth century Criollos were, in fact, largely miscegenated. The original connotation was purposely pejorative as earlier versions of the term distinguished those slaves born in America from those born in Africa. See L Obregon, 'Between Civilisation and Barbarism: Creole interventions in international Law' (2006) 27(5) *Third World Quarterly* 818–819.

[15] M Lucena Giraldo, *A los cuatro vientos: las ciudades de la América hispánica* (Madrid, Ambos Mundos, Fundación Carolina Centro de Estudios Hispánicos e Iberoamericanos, Marcial Pons Historia, 2006), 245. These numbers should be viewed with great caution, as there are limitations on how the information was taken and how the groups resisted being identified under racial categories. See also DJ Robinson (ed), 'Social Fabric and Spatial Structure in Colonial Latin America', Dellplain Latin American Studies, No 1 (Department of Geography, Syracuse University, 1979) 17–22. Bolívar and other Creole leaders formed part of a minority that was not representative of the vast majority.

[16] S Bolívar, 'Contestación de un americano meridional (es el jeneral Bolivar) a un caballero de esta isla (Jamaica)' in *Coleccion de documentos relativos à la vida pública del libertador de Colombia y del Perú para servir a la historia de la independencia del suramérica: Tomo Vigésimo Primero* (Carácas, Impresa de GF Devisme 1830) 21.

[17] The term *mestizo*, meaning mixed, was a racial category used in Spanish America during the colonial period to describe people of mixed (white, indigenous, african) ancestry.

of Río de la Plata as well as the new state of Bolivia and the Empire of Brazil.[18] The United States was invited, but its representative could not participate in the discussions and agreements.[19] Great Britain and the Netherlands were invited as European observers.[20]

However, the question of Haiti's participation in the Bolivarian project presents a view of what sort of identity was constructed in view of legal unity. By 1824, the slave revolt in Haiti was three decades old, and ten years had lapsed since its declared independence, constituting it as the first sovereign state in the hemisphere after the United States. The first Haitian President, Alexandre Petion, contributed to Bolívar's independence project in 1816 with men, ships, money, guns, gunpowder and a printing press, and asked him in return to grant freedom to 'all those who are still under the yoke of slavery'.[21] Bolívar's vow turned into an opportunity to recruit slaves for his army in exchange for their liberty,[22] but three months later Bolívar, defeated by Spanish forces (also composed of former slaves), went back to Haiti to request more support. For the second time, Petion provided supplies and volunteers, after which Bolívar won the final battle for independence in Carácas. In gratitude, Bolívar sent Petion one of his favourite swords; after Petion's death in 1818, Bolívar honoured him as 'the author of our independence',[23] but never complied with the promise of liberating all slaves.[24]

In response to Haiti's generous support, the Haitian government anticipated an invitation to Panama, hoping their presence would lead to diplomatic recognition by the new Spanish American states. However, the governments of the United States, Great Colombia and Peru refused to invite Haiti, in fear of implied recognition and promotion of similar uprisings across the continent.

[18] D Bushnell, *Simón Bolívar: hombre de Caracas, proyecto de América: una biografía* (Buenos Aires, Editorial Biblos, 2002) 130.

[19] Letter of Henry Clay, Secretary of State, to Richard C Anderson, United States Minister to Colombia, in WR Manning (ed), *Diplomatic Correspondence of the United States Concerning the Independence of the Latin-American Nations*, (New York, Oxford University Press, 1925) Document 145, 253. For a story on the discussion of the United States' participation in Panama, see JJ Malanson, 'The Congressional Debate over U.S. Participation in the Congress of Panama, 1825–1826: Washington's Farewell Address, Monroe's Doctrine, and the Fundamental Principles of U.S. Foreign Policy' (2006) 30 *Diplomatic History* 813–38.

[20] J Schoonhoven and C Tymen De Jong, 'The Dutch Observer at the Congress of Panama in 1826' (1956) 36 *The Hispanic American Historical Review* 28–37. Bolívar conceived of the British government as a constituent member in supporting the union and argued that Americans would benefit from British 'character and habits', while in return the British would receive commercial domain, equal citizenship and geographical centrality to further their relations with Asia. De la Reza, 'Simon Bolivar: Un Pensamiento Sobre El Congreso Anfictiónico' 84.

[21] S Bolívar, 'Latin-American Correspondence Author(s): Simon Bolívar and Alexandre Sabes Petion' (1946) 7(2) *Phylon* 196.

[22] S Bolívar, 'Decreto sobre libertad de los esclavos—Carúpano, 2 de junio de 1816' in V Lecuna (ed), *Bolívar, Simón: Proclamas y discursos del Libertador, 1811–1830* (Los Teques, Biblioteca De Autores y Temas Mirandinos, 1983) 148–49.

[23] S Bolívar, 'Latin-American Correspondence'.

[24] Only Chile, which was invited to Panama but declined to attend, had abolished slavery before 1826. None of the states represented in the Panama Congress had abolished slavery. The abolition of the slave trade was a long and controversial process that lasted for most of the nineteenth century. Mexico abolished slavery in 1829, Colombia (Panama), Ecuador and Venezuela between 1851 and 1854, with payment of compensation by the state to the slave owners, Argentina in 1853, Peru in 1855, and finally the imperial government of Brazil in 1888.

In 1832, four years after the Congress of Panama, when it was evident that an American perspective did not include Haiti, Andrés Bello published the first international law treatise of the Americas under the title *Principios del Derecho de Jentes* and later as *Principios del Derecho Internacional* in its second (1844) and third (1864) editions. Bello appropriated European and US texts and rewrote, edited and organised in a first treatise, written in Spanish, with an 'American perspective' as part of the draft agenda for the American states in the region.[25] Bello's publication inspired the writing of other texts, but his was the most reprinted, distributed and taught in the nineteenth century. His work also inaugurated the teaching of international law in the new republics, anticipating similar courses later given in Europe and the United States.[26]

The efforts on the part of Bolívar, Bello and others could be understood as belonging to a 'Creole legal consciousness', or a set of ideas about the law shared by Creole lawyers in the post-independence period. As this was a large population, in a vast region, over a period of political and social instability, two concepts were part of that consciousness: one was a unified American legal identity and the other the 'desire to attain civilisation'. Legal consciousness is 'a particular form of consciousness characteristic of advocates of a social group at a given time'.[27] In most of the former Spanish colonies a 'Creole' was a person of Spanish descent born in the Americas with a presumption of white racial culture and physical presence, and a sense of belonging to the American continent (Creole patriotism).[28] However, as an ambivalent and unstable category it is better to think of the Creole from a social and legal subject position, rather than as a biological marker.[29]

Therefore, the American legal identity (as part of Creole consciousness) is characterised by: a regional legacy of Indian law and Spanish law; a common understanding of the historical (and 'civilised') roots of the law in the region as being

[25] See I Jaksic, *Andrés Bello: la pasión por el orden* (Santiago de Chile, Editorial Universitaria/ Imagen De Chile, 2001) 323, L Obregón, 'Construyendo la región americana: Andrés Bello y el derecho internacional' in B González Stephan and J Poblete (eds), *Andrés Bello y los estudios latinoamericanos* (Pittsburgh, Instituto Internacional de Literatura Iberoamericana, 2009).

[26] In France, Germany and England the first international law courses began to be taught (as individual courses) during the second half of the nineteenth century. In the United States, the first international law courses were delivered at Yale in 1846, Harvard in 1863 and Columbia University in 1865. By 1907, only 10 of the 81 law schools in the United States taught international law, a course that was considered a 'luxury', and continues to be an elective course in the curriculum of most US law schools. See M Koskenniemi, *The Gentle Civilizer of Nations: The Rise and Fall of International Law 1870–1960* (Cambridge, Cambridge University Press, 2001); JM Raymond and BJ Frischholz, 'Lawyers Who Established International Law in the United States,1776–1914' (1982) 76 *American Journal of International Law* 802–29.

[27] D Kennedy, 'Toward a Historical Understanding of Legal Consciousness: The Case of Classical Legal Thought in America 1850–1940' (1980) 3 *Research in Law and Sociology* 3–24, 23.

[28] On the construction of the category of the Creole; see EA Kuznesof, 'Ethnic and Gender Influences on "Spanish" Creole Society in Colonial Spanish America' (1995) 4 *Colonial Latin American Review* 153–68; B Lavalle, Las promesas ambiguas: ensayos sobre el criollismo colonial en los Andes (Lima, Pontificia Universidad Católica, 1993); JA Mazzotti (ed), Agencias criollas: la ambigüedad 'colonial' en las letras hispanoamericanas (Pittsburgh, Instituto Internacional de Literatura Iberoamericana, 2000).

[29] For this reason, for example honour would be a more important factor than race to determine the position of the Creole in society, especially for lawyers. See VM Uribe Urán, *Honorable Lives: Lawyers, Family, and Politics in Colombia 1789–1850* (Pittsburgh, University of Pittsburgh Press, 2000) 276.

Roman law; a European heritage transformed into a practice of law believed to be American; and the use of foreign sources to solve local problems by Creole lawyers who understood themselves to be superior to the rest of the native population.[30]

Moreover, with the birth of new nations in the Americas, Creole lawyers appropriated the discourse of civilisation spread in Europe during the French Revolution, expressing the idea of progress and the perfectibility of man as a universal fact achieved through the law and institutions.[31] The term 'civilisation' was understood as a collective achievement of unity and perfection synthesised in Europe. Its opposite, barbarism, had no framework outside of Europe. In order not to be excluded from the rights assigned (by Europe) to members of the 'community of civilised nations', the Creoles showed a 'desire to attain civilisation', as one of the shared ideals within Creole legal consciousness that appeared in the constitutions and laws of Latin American countries, and gave prevalence to economic, religious, educational and social policies geared towards improving an already existing 'civilisation'.[32]

III. THE SECOND HALF OF THE NINETEENTH CENTURY: FROM AMERICANS TO LATIN AMERICANS, FROM THE LAW OF NATIONS TO INTERNATIONAL LAW

The global scenario had changed since the Congress of Panama and the publication of Bello's text. The nineteenth-century Creole elite's patriotic Americanism included the United States as a model of successful autonomy which inspired new constitutions and forms of government.[33] The Congress of Panama adopted U.S. President Monroe´s doctrine of 1823 as a useful principle against frequent European

[30] L Obregón, 'Completing Civilization: Creole Consciousness and International Law in Nineteenth-Century Latin America' in A Orford (ed), *International Law and Its Others* (Cambridge, Cambridge University Press, 2006) 247–64.

[31] The French word *civilisation* comes from the use of the words *civilité* (civility) and *poli* (refined, emitting prudent laws). For a more extensive description using the concept of civilisation in international law, see L Obregón, 'The Civilized and the Uncivilized in the History of International Law' in Bardo Fassbender and Anne Peters (eds), *Oxford Handbook on the History of Public International Law* (Oxford, Oxford University Press, 2012) 917–39.

[32] J Armada y Losada and Marqués de Figueroa, *Civilización Hispanoamericana su carácter, sus perspectivas* (Madrid, Unión Ibero-Americana, 1927) 46 pp; JR Goberna Falque, *Civilización: historia de una idea* (Santiago de Compostela, Universidade de Santiago de Compostela, 1999) 277 pp; RH Pearce, *The Savages of America: a Study of the Indian and the Idea of Civilization* (Baltimore, Johns Hopkins Press, 1965) 260 pp; D Ribeiro, *Las Americas y la civilización: proceso de formación y causas del desarrollo desigual de los pueblos americanos* (Mexico, Editorial Extemporaneos, 1977) 630 pp; C Rojas, *Civilization and Violence: Regimes of Representation in Nineteenth-Century Colombia* (Borderlines MI, University of Minnesota Press, 2001); D Faustino Sarmiento, *Civilización i barbarie, vida de Juan Facundo Quiroga. I aspecto físico, Costumbres, i abitos de la República Arjentina* (Santiago, Impresa del Progreso, 1845) 3–324.

[33] US constitutionalism spread through the work by A de Tocqueville, *De la démocratie en Amérique* (Paris, 1836), with a first translation into Spanish by DA Sánchez de Bustamante, under the title *De la democracia en América del Norte*, in 1837. This text had a broad circulation among the Creole elites; see H Fix Zamudio, 'Función del poder judicial en los sistemas constitucionales Latinoamericanos' in H Fix Zamudio (ed), *Latino América: constitucion, proceso y derechos humanos* (México, Porra, 1988) 223.

interventions.[34] By the mid-nineteenth century, however, the Latin America´s claimed a violation of the Monroe doctrine when the United States' intervened in the region, such as the U.S. incursion and war in Mexico in 1848 and its appropriation of the territories of California and Texas, and William Walker's 1855 invasion of Nicaragua where he sought to reinstate slavery and annex it to the United States.[35]

Thus, the concept of a '*Latin* America' emerged in the second half of the nineteenth century as a Creole adaptation of French 'Latinism' in response to the expansionist policy of the United States. Pan-latinism emanated from the works of the French economist Michel Chevalier (1806–79), an official of Napoleon III, and Ernest Renan (1823–92), who promoted union among 'Latin' states, based on nineteenth-century ethnic and cultural categories of European historicism. Pan-latinism projected France's opposition to the continental domination of the Anglo-Saxon nations (Great Britain and the United States). At the same time it was another geo-ideological model, used to legitimise France's expansionist economic interests and cultural patronage.[36] Chevalier divided the world into two natural families: a progressive (European) Western civilisation, and an Eastern civilisation (Japan and China), that advanced in opposite directions.[37]

European civilisation, as described by Chevalier, was subdivided into two 'natural' families according to their historical and geographical origins: a Northern *Germanic* Europe, of Protestant religion, and a Catholic *Latin* Europe. According to Chevalier, the two families were correspondingly reproduced in America: in the north, the Germanic family and to the south, the descendants of Latin Europe. He argued for the need to counter the advance of the 'Anglo-Saxon race' over the 'Latin race' because of the power imbalance due to disproportionate Anglo-Saxon progress.[38] It was important for the future of the human race that the Anglo and Latin races should return to a balance in their domination of the American continent and avoid the advancement of Western and Eastern civilisations. Not surprisingly, Chevalier argued that France was the only country that could balance the Latin presence on the continent.[39]

Although Chevalier's pan-latinism defended France's imperial role, his description of the former Spanish colonies as part of the 'Latin family' found resonance among the Creole elite living in Paris. Apparently, the Chilean diplomat and lawyer, Francisco Bilbao, was the first to use the term '*Latin* America' and 'Latin-Americans',

[34] The first American Congress led by Creole independence leader, Simón Bolívar, and held in Panama in 1826, proposed the unification of the new states into one, the adoption of the U.S President Monroe´s Doctrine of 1823 as a regional principle of non-intervention and for the first time suggested the idea of a unified international law in an effort to defend the new-born American republics against the imperial intentions of the monarchies and autocracies of Europe.

[35] See A Bolaños Geyer, *William Walker: The Gray-Eyed Man of Destiny* (Lake Saint Louis MI, Privately published, 1988); N Bertram Gerson, *Sad Swashbuckler: The Life of William Walker* (Nashville, T Nelson, 1976).

[36] See JL Phelan, *El origen de la idea de América* (Mexico, Universidad Nacional Autónoma de México, 1979).

[37] According to Chevalier, both civilisations would soon meet and mix; see M Chevalier, 'Sobre el progreso y porvenir de la civilización' (1853) 1 *Revista Española De Ambos Mundos* 1–10.

[38] For Chevalier, race was a cultural and ethnic concept, rather than a matter of skin colour.

[39] Chevalier, 'Sobre el progreso y porvenir de la civilización'.

in a lecture titled the 'Idea of a Federal Congress of Republics' presented to the diplomatic community in Paris on 22 June 1853. Bilbao used the concept of 'Latin American', as opposed to 'Anglo American', in a manner similar to Chevalier's description of the two races on the continent, but he did not give France or any other European nation a role against US expansionism. Bilbao's solution was to revive the proposal for a union of 'Latin' peoples of the Americas against the United States, which had gone from being an ideal model for the region to a threat.[40]

The conference at which Bilbao spoke, like Chevalier's books and articles, had a major impact among other Creoles such as the Colombian diplomat José María Torres-Caicedo. Torres-Caicedo has also been credited with coining the term 'Latin America', or at least was its most active promoter. After Bilbao realised that Torres-Caicedo used a term that legitimised French expansionist political agenda and French cultural patronage, he stopped using it. Torres-Caicedo separated the term from its connotation with French imperialism and used it, as Bilbao had, in opposition to US imperialism to build the idea of a regional project of unification.[41]

In Torres-Caicedo's 1856 poem 'Las dos Américas´ ('The Two Americas'), he compares 'Latin America' and the Saxon race, in the context of William Walker's invasion of Nicaragua. Torres-Caicedo glorified the unification of the former Spanish colonies (which he based on a community of language, religion, law and traditions), in contrast to the threat of US imperialism.[42] He circulated a manifesto among the Parisian Creole community defending the project of a confederacy, union or league to join Central and South America in one great and autonomous nationality. These principles were: a) a common nationality with the same civil and political rights, regardless of place of birth; b) the adoption of the rule *uti possidetis* of 1810 to define the territorial limits; c) the use of same codes, dimensions, weight and money; d) the establishment of a single supreme court of justice; e) a uniform system of postal conventions; f) the compulsory validity of all contracts celebrated in America, be they the product of public or private acts; g) a liberal system of trade and customs; h) a uniform and compulsory education system; i) freedom of conscience and religious tolerance; j) the modern law of extradition; k) the training of armed forces for the common defence; l) uniform principles applied to commercial treaties, conventions, consular conventions and the nationality of the children of foreigners; m) a legitimate government is not responsible for damage caused to foreigners during civil wars or riots, at a greater rate than it is for damage caused to its own nationals; n) active advertising against the slave trade, whether they be black, yellow or white; and o) the establishment of a French news chapter to defend American interests and represent the laws, resources, institutions, geography and topography of the states of Latin America.[43]

[40] M Bilbao (ed), *Obras completas de Francisco Bilbao* (Buenos Aires, Imprenta de Buenos Aires, 1866), vol 1, 293.

[41] Phelan, *El origen de la idea de América.*

[42] The complete poem can be found in AJ Rivadeneira Vargas, *El bogotano JM Torres Caicedo (1830–1889): La multipatria latinoamericana* (*Colección Lecturas De Bogotá*) (Bogotá, Academia Colombiana de Historia, Alcaldía Mayor de Bogotá, 1989) 61–73.

[43] Torres Caicedo's text is transcribed in ER Pérez Calvo and LR Pérez Calvo, *Vida y trabajos de Carlos Calvo: Los Calvo en el Río de la Plata* (Buenos Aires, Ediciones Dunken, 1996) 152, fn 11. Calvo argued that the text contained many of his ideas. Calvo published his collection of treaties in 1862 as C Calvo,

Carlos Calvo began to use the term '*Latin* America' in common defence of sovereignty and independence among the nations of the region. In 1862, after Calvo's publication of a treaty compilation, José María Samper, a Colombian native,[44] published a review of Calvo's book in an article entitled 'Latin American public law'. In a similar way to Bilbao, Samper described the presence of two European races in America, but read them in reverse: the North was the result of a vital, vigorous and free race, and the South was the legacy of the degenerate Spanish race. Due to this legacy, Samper argued that the creation of a regional international law was of utmost importance 'as an element of civilization … the truthful symbol, the synthesis, the most complex manifestation and the highest form of being of a people.'[45]

Bilbao, Torres-Caicedo and Samper's writings illustrate the early Latin American elite's appropriation of international legal discourse. Like many Europeans of their time, Latin American lawyers were convinced that international reform could result from their society, history, human nature and institutional modernity. They were critical of European interventions but in favour of imperialist actions inside their own borders. They rejected European and US interventions in Latin America, but at the same time, through the civilising discourse they justified the appropriation of indigenous lands in their own countries and supported European colonisation of Africa in the late nineteenth century.

IV. THE FIRST HALF OF THE TWENTIETH CENTURY: FROM LATIN AMERICANS TO PAN-AMERICANS

A century after Bolívar's failed attempt and many other proposals, projects and conferences seeking legal and political integration, the Chilean lawyer, Alejandro Álvarez, began promoting the recognition of a Latin American international law.[46] Both adherence and opposition to the Álvarez project followed almost immediately. On the one hand, lawyers like Manóel Álvaro de Souza Sá Vianna opposed the

Colección completa de los tratados, convenciones, capitulaciones, armisticios y otros actos diplomáticos: de todos los estados de la América Latina: comprendidos entre el golfo de Mejico y el cabo de Hornos: desde el año de 1493 hasta nuestros días precedidos de una memoria sobre el estado actual de la América, de cuadros estadísticos, de un diccionario diplomático y de una noticia histórica sobre cada uno de los tratados más importantes (Paris, A Durand, 1862) xxx. Torres Caicedo published his ideas on the origin and future of the Latin American Union in JM Torres Caicedo, *Unión latino-americana.*

[44] JM Samper, *Ensayo sobre las revoluciones políticas y la condición social de las Repúblicas Colombianas (Hispano Americanas) con un apéndice sobre la geografía y población de la confederación granadina* (Paris, E Thunot y Co, 1861) 83. JM Samper, 'Derecho público latino-americano' in *Miscelánea ó colección de artículos escogidos de costumbres, bibliografía, variedades y necrología* (Paris, Eugene Vanderhaeghen, 1869) 350–59, originally published in 1862 in *El Comercio de Lima.*

[45] Samper, 'Derecho público latino-americano' 351.

[46] A Álvarez, 'Origen y desarrollo del derecho internacional americano' in *Tercer Congreso Científico Latino Americano* (Rio de Janeiro, 1905); A Álvarez, 'Le droit international américain, son origine et son évolution' (1907) XIV *Revue Générale de Droit International Public* 393–405; A Álvarez, *American Problems in International Law* (New York, Baker, 1909) 1–102; Alejandro Álvarez, *Le droit international américain: son fondement, sa nature: d'après l'histoire diplomatique des états du nouveau monde et leur vie politique et économique* (Paris, A Pedone, 1910) 1–386.

regional project, arguing that common problems or historical experience shared by a group of countries did not constitute a sufficient basis for an autonomous or separate sphere of international law, because international law was based on principles, laws and rules observed by the international society.

Others, following Álvarez, justified international law in terms of American regionalism as he did for the first time in 1905.[47] For half a century, Álvarez defended the need to recognise a regional version of international law in relation to Europe and America. In 1909, he published the 'American Problems in International Law' and 'Latin America and International Law' and the following year he published the book, *Le droit international américain*. Before the First World War, Álvarez published a book on the Monroe doctrine and its impact on the American nations. During the First World War, he published *Le droit international de l'avenir*, a book proposing the renewal of the failed international law, backed by the moral force of a Latin American perspective. In the inter-war period, Álvarez also published several essays and articles on the American need to codify international law.

From 1916 to 1918, Álvarez spoke in more than thirty US universities to promote the unification of what he called the Pan-American school. In Latin America he promoted his theory in scientific meetings and managed to push a motion at the First Pan- American Scientific Congress for all research in the social sciences to be done from 'an American point of view'.

In one of his most representative texts, he used three arguments to identify Latin American legal unity: 1) differences between American and European nations, 2) the idea of a regional homeland with its civilising origins in Europe, and 3) the idea that Latin American nations were civilised like their European counterparts.[48] Thus, according to Álvarez, the New World had a different point of view and *sui generis* problems unknown in the Old World.[49] For Álvarez, American characteristics appeared in other disciplines such as political science, philosophy and literature.[50]

With regard to law, Álvarez noted that freedom and sovereignty were understood differently in the two continents. The Europeans had no conception of continental solidarity, according to Álvarez, because they did not come from the same origins, nor did they have the same cultures or problems. On the other hand, Latin America solidarity came from the help the new states gave each other to achieve their independence and the same moral, geographical, material influences, needs and problems.[51] Álvarez noted the Latin American intellect had been influenced by

[47] The essay was later modified and published as 'Le Droit International Américain, son origine et son évolution' (1907) XIV *Revue Générale de Droit International Public* 393. In the revised edition, the geography was broadened to include the United States, and 'Latin America' was changed to 'America', to include the entire continent.

[48] A Álvarez, 'International Law and Related Subjects from the Point of View of the American Continent: a Report on Lectures Delivered in the Universities of the United States, 1916–1918, Under the Auspices of the Carnegie Endowment for International Peace, Including a Comparative Study of the Universities of Latin America and the United States' Pamphlet, Carnegie Endowment for International Peace, Division of International Law (1922) vii.

[49] ibid, 25.

[50] ibid, 30.

[51] ibid.

Europe producing a 'Latin American soul' that was 'less altruistic, but with greater reverence for literature and the arts, more idealistic, imaginative and cosmopolitan than the Anglo-American.'[52] The Latin had, in regard to institutions, 'a spirit of solidarity', which helped to forget the 'fights and wars ... unfortunately that had taken place between them'.[53] The American nations, including the United States, had a 'liberal and democratic spirit' based on equality and universal suffrage, while Europe represented the 'unstable and dangerous' concepts of 'individualism, the balance of power, alliances and armed peace.'[54]

After the Second World War, Álvarez continued to believe it was necessary to place the American continent at the head of international law, and expressed these ideas in several of his dissenting votes as a judge of the International Court of Justice. When the US began promoting the Pan American Congress, Álvarez, like others in the Creole tradition, recognised the inequalities of power in international life, but did not wish to present the American states as backward. Instead, he preferred to designate them as more advanced than the Europeans during the most critical moments of the two world wars, whereupon Álvarez reversed the civilisation-barbarism dichotomy and asserted the moral authority of Latin American and American proposals.

V. THE SECOND HALF OF THE TWENTIETH CENTURY: FALL AND OBLIVION OF LATIN AMERICAN INTERNATIONAL LAW

With the emergence of the United Nations and other international organisations in the second half of the twentieth century, the gradual fragmentation of international law into specialised problem areas, Álvarez's death in 1960, and a growing global polarisation, the promotion and belief in a Latin American international law fell into abandonment and oblivion.

After the emergence of the Organization of American States (OAS) in 1948 the unifying approach was predominantly an economic one. This was expressed in the establishment of other organisations such as the Latin American Free Trade Association (1960), the Central American Common Market (1960), the Andean Community of Nations (1969) the Cartagena Agreement (1980) and Mercado Común del Sur (MERCOSUR) (1986). Latin American lawyers continued to participate in international law institutions, such as those related to the law of the sea, during the 1980s, and with human rights and international environmental law in the 1990s. However, the lawyers participating in these efforts were fragmented and no longer promoted a united front in promotion of a Latin American international law as in the first half of the twentieth century.

[52] ibid, 79.
[53] ibid, 28.
[54] ibid, 14.

VI. CONCLUSION: THE EARLY TWENTY-FIRST CENTURY: THE COMEBACK OF INTERNATIONAL LAW *IN* LATIN AMERICA?

Since colonial times, Americans have thought about issues of difference and identity and have used exceptionalism as a discourse of response to external domination.[55] This continuous reconstruction of identities has allowed for economic, educational, cultural, and artistic projects of the most varied political and social trends. Many self-identified Latin Americans pushed for inclusion in a Eurocentric discourse because their ambition was to participate in the construction of knowledge that they considered universal and interdependent.[56]

Legal scholars have also wanted to be recognised as outstanding participants and contributors to the project of international law. Since the nineteenth century, multiple projects, institutions, and studies attempted to define a regional international law. However, the perspective of identity differed in every age and was derived from a geopolitical realignment in accordance with the global and regional context.

The most recent efforts of Latin American integration, such as the Community of Latin American and Caribbean States (CELAC), are illustrative of the strength and continuity of Latin American discourse adapted to regional and global circumstances. In 2011, 33 heads of state met in a conference in a manner that would have disturbed their nineteenth-century predecessors: two heads of state were women, three proclaimed Indian ancestry, the United States and Canada were excluded, and Haiti's contribution to Latin America was recognised. CELAC's constitutive document, the Declaration of Caracas,[57] recalled the Congress of Panama as foundational to Latin American and Caribbean unity and discussed continental 'sovereignty, the destiny of peace, development and social transformation'.[58] The declaration proposed a path of progress 'outlined by the liberators of Latin America and the Caribbean for more than two hundred years' and 'effectively commenced with the independence of Haiti in 1804.'[59] It also recalled the forgotten assistance of Alexandre Petion to Simón Bolívar, as the 'participation of indigenous peoples and Afro-descendants in the struggle for independence' and 'their contributions moral, political, economic, spiritual and cultural in shaping our identities and the construction of our nations and democratic processes.'[60]

The new CELAC proposes the union's origins in the formation, multicultural, multinational nature of the Latin American and Caribbean identity, the geographical differences as a factor of wealth and the right of each nation to build its own

[55] E Dussel, 'Philosophy in Latin America in the Twentieth Century: Problems and Currents' in E Mendieta (ed), *Latin American Philosophy Currents, Issues, Debates* (Bloomington, Indiana University Press, 2003) 15.

[56] J Lund, 'Barbarian Theorizing and the Limits of Latin American Exceptionalism' (2001) 47 *Cultural Critique* 54–90, 76.

[57] Declaration of Caracas, adopted by Heads of State and Governments of the countries of Latin America and the Caribbean at the CELAC Summit, Caracas, Bolivarian Republic of Venezuela, 3 December 2011, available at: www.pnuma.org/forodeministros/19-reunion%20intersesional/documentos/CARACAS%20DECLARATION.pdf.

[58] ibid, art 16.

[59] ibid, art 13.

[60] ibid, art 17.

political and economic system. The proposed objective of CELAC is 'to become a space that protects the rights of all cultures and ethnic groups of the region to existence, preservation and coexistence, as well as the multicultural character of our countries, and plurinational of some of our countries, especially of the native communities recreating and promoting their historical memory, their ancestral knowledge and experience.'[61]

The declaration repeats some of the principles once identified as Latin American: 'the peaceful settlement of disputes, prohibition of use and threatened use of force, respect for self-determination, respect for sovereignty, respect for territorial integrity, non-interference in the internal affairs of each country and the protection and promotion of all human rights and democracy.'[62]

This does not mean governments in the region have reached the utopia of the development of international law, as it remains one of the regions where solidarity ends when certain economic or political issues are affected (such as the relationship with Cuba, the United States, or free trade agreements). It is also a region whose nations represent the greatest disparity in the distribution of wealth in the world, and problems of discrimination on the bases of gender, race or ethnicity still abound.

Perhaps, then, the best way to think about the relationship of international law in the region is to promote neither its essence nor its exceptionalism but rather to look at what initiatives use international law as a privileged tool of integration. Some recent academic projects seek a critical reflection on the past instead of the traditional admiration for it, while others assess the present with an optimistic view of the possibilities offered by international law to challenge common problems in this region.[63] The question remains: is this a new way of thinking about regionalism and international law in Latin America, or is it more of the same?

[61] ibid, art 22.

[62] ibid, art 23.

[63] A Becker Lorca, 'International Law in Latin America or Latin American International Law? Rise, Fall, and Retrieval of a Tradition of Legal Thinking and Political Imagination' (2006) 47 *Harvard International Law Journal* 283–305 and A Becker Lorca, 'Universal International Law: Nineteenth-Century Histories of Imposition and Appropriation' (2010) 51 *Harvard International Law Journal* 475–552; J Esquirol, 'Can International Law Help? An Analysis of the Colombian Peace Process' (2000) *Connecticut Journal of International Law* 23–92; JL Esquirol, 'Writing the Law of Latin America' (2008) 40 *George Washington International Law Review* 693–732 and J Esquirol, 'Latin America' in A Peters and B Fassbender (eds), *Oxford Handbook on the History of Public International Law* (Oxford, Oxford University Press, 2012) 553–77; O Guardiola-Rivera, *What If Latin America Ruled the World?: How the South Will Take the North Through the 21st Century* (London, Bloomsbury Press, 2010) 1–472; L Obregón, 'The Colluding Worlds of the Lawyer, the Scholar and the Policymaker: A View of International Law from Latin America' (2005) *Wisconsin International Law Journal* 145–72; L Obregón, 'Completing Civilization'; L Obregón Tarazona, 'Latin American International Law' in JD Armstrong and J Brunée (eds), *Routledge Handbook of International Law* (London, Routledge, 2009) 154–64; C Rodriguez Garavito (ed), *El derecho en américa latina: un mapa para el pensamiento jurídico del siglo XXI* (Bogotá, Siglo XXI Editores, 2011).

3

Comments on Fawcett and Obregón

BERNARDO SEPÚLVEDA-AMOR*

THE PRESENTATIONS BY Liliana Obregón and Louise Fawcett address the concept and history of regionalism from very different angles and will surely spark a lively discussion on the past virtues and failures of regionalism, and its prospects for the future.

From my side, I would like to contribute to the debate by sharing some thoughts on the importance of the notion of regionalism in the Latin American context. In terms of law-making and institution-building, regionalism has been central to the Latin American experience since the emergence of the young American republics as fully fledged members of the international community.

The promotion of regional solutions through regional institutions and legal rules has been crucial to the advancement of the distinctively political interests of Latin American countries, interests which have not infrequently been at odds with those of the Great Powers. Two aspects stand out in this on-going process. First, these countries' ability to influence the content of general international law. Second, their contribution to the regional dimension of peace and security. I shall briefly address both aspects in these remarks.

With regard to the first question, it is not my intention to revisit here the old debate as to the existence or non-existence of a distinct 'Latin American international law', as claimed by Alejandro Álvarez in the early twentieth century. What interests me about the way Latin American countries have influenced general international law, is what this process tells us about the relationship between regionalism and universalism, and the notion of regionalism itself: Whereas the adoption of particular legal rules may be required in order to advance regional interests, the latter may be even better served through the universalisation of those very rules. At least, this is how I understand the rationale for some of the legal rules advocated for the first time by Latin American countries in their relations among themselves and with third states.

Remarkably, some of the doctrines and rules that originated in this region in the nineteenth and twentieth centuries were regarded in many quarters, at first, as extravagant and contrary to the laws of civilised nations. Ultimately, however, some of them came to be embraced as part and parcel of general international law.

The *uti possidetis juris* principle is a paradigmatic example. Originally invoked in connection with the process of decolonisation in Latin America in the early nineteenth

* Judge of the International Court of Justice.

century, it is nowadays not considered 'a special rule which pertains solely to one specific system of international law. It is a general principle, which is logically connected with the phenomenon of the obtaining of independence, wherever it occurs'.[1] The International Court of Justice (ICJ) has frequently relied upon this principle in cases involving territorial delimitation in Latin America and Africa.[2]

In the context of diplomatic protection, the Calvo doctrine, already more than one hundred years old, is still very much a part of contemporary international law. Calling for the equal treatment of nationals and foreigners, this doctrine has found legal expression in the rule of customary international law requiring the exhaustion of local remedies as a precondition to the exercise of diplomatic protection (Article 14, ILC Draft Articles on Diplomatic Protection).[3]

The so-called Drago doctrine, formulated in 1903 against the backdrop of various instances of 'gun-boat diplomacy' by European powers and the United States, was instrumental in banning the use of force as a legitimate means of enforcing the recovery of debts as between states. Originally formulated by former Argentine Foreign Minister, Luis María Drago, this doctrine made its way into conventional law (outside the Americas) through the adoption of the 1907 Hague Convention Respecting the Limitation of the Employment of Force for the Recovery of Contract Debts,[4] that is, well before the use of force in international relations was generally prohibited by the Pact of Paris of 1928[5] and the UN Charter of 1945.[6] The Drago doctrine may thus be viewed as a precursor to contemporary international law standards on counter-measures and the use of force.

The system of Inter-American Conferences, which pre-dated the establishment of the Organization of American States (OAS),[7] played a crucial role in the codification and progressive development of international law, including through the formulation of international rules that are nowadays part of the law of nations. A particularly

[1] *Frontier Dispute (Burkina Faso v Republic of Mali)* [1986] ICJ Rep 565, para 20.

[2] The International Court of Justice has stated that there can be 'no doubt about the importance of the *uti possidetis juris* principle as one which has, in general, resulted in certain and stable frontiers throughout most of Central and South America' (*Land, Island and Maritime Frontier Dispute (El Salvador v Honduras: Nicaragua intervening)* [1992] ICJ Rep 386, para 41. In a previous case, the Court noted that: 'the principle of *uti possidetis* seems to have been first invoked and applied in Spanish America, inasmuch as this was the continent which first witnessed the phenomenon of decolonization involving the formation of a number of sovereign States on territory formerly belonging to a single metropolitan State.' It added that the principle 'has kept its place among the most important legal principles ... Indeed it was by deliberate choice that the African States selected, among all the classical principles, that of *uti possidetis*' (*Frontier Dispute* [1986] ICJ Rep 565 and 567, paras 20 and 26).

[3] Articles on Diplomatic Protection, Report of the International Law Commission adopted at its 58th Session (1 May to 9 June and 3 July to 11 August 2006) and submitted to the General Assembly, UN Doc A/61/10.

[4] Convention Respecting the Limitation of the Employment of Force for the Recovery of Contract Debts (signed at The Hague, 18 October 1907, entered into force 26 January 1910) (1907) 187 CTS 250.

[5] Treaty between the United States and Other Powers Providing for the Renunciation of War as an Instrument of National Policy (signed at Paris, 27 August 1928) 94 LNTS 57 (the Pact of Paris—also known as the Kellogg-Briand Pact).

[6] Charter of the United Nations (adopted at San Francisco, 26 June 1945, entered into force 24 October 1945) 1 UNTS xvi.

[7] Charter of the Organization of American States (adopted at Bogotá, Colombia on 30 April 1948, entered into force 13 December 1951) 119 UNTS 3.

important achievement in this regard was the adoption, within the framework of the 1933 Montevideo Conference, of the Convention on the Rights and Duties of States,[8] enthusiastically promoted by the Latin American states and, to the surprise of many, signed and later ratified by the US.

The Montevideo Convention encapsulates the main principles advocated by the Latin American states since their independence. Many of them are nowadays recognised as part of general international law. Amongst them, we may mention the principle of non-intervention, the principle of sovereign equality and the definition of the constituent elements of the state *qua* legal person (territory, population, government and capacity to conduct international relations).

The modern law of the sea is another field that has been very much influenced by Latin American countries. Whereas 60 years ago the 200-mile territorial sea claimed by several Latin American states was flatly rejected by many maritime powers, the fact is that a modified rule of the 200-mile concept has come to be accepted through the recognition of a 12-mile territorial sea with full sovereignty, and a 'patrimonial sea'—to use the terminology coined by Latin American countries—involving a 200-mile exclusive economic zone and a continental shelf where sovereign rights are exercised.[9]

In relation to the law of treaties, the Inter-American Conferences took a liberal and flexible approach to the question of reservations, advocating the abandonment of the rigid unanimity rule with regard to the acceptance of reservations to multilateral treaties.[10] The inter-American approach was subsequently endorsed by the ICJ in its 1951 Advisory Opinion on reservations to the Genocide Convention, where the Court took the view that 'a State which has made and maintained a reservation which has been objected by one or more of the parties to the Convention but not by others, can be regarded as being a party to the Convention if the reservation

[8] Convention on the Rights and Duties of States (signed at Montevideo, 26 December 1933, entered into force 26 December 1934) 165 LNTS 19.

[9] See J Castañeda, 'Negotiations on the Exclusive Economic Zone in the Third UN conference on the Law of the Sea' in J Makarczyk (ed), *Essays in Honour of Judge Manfred Lachs*, Institute of State and Law of the Polish Academy of Science (The Hague, Martinus Nijhoff, 1984), 605–23.

[10] Havana Convention on Treaties (adopted on 20 February 1928 at the Sixth Inter-American Conference), Article 6, paragraph 3, reads as follows: 'In international treaties celebrated between different States, a reservation made by one of them in the act of ratification affects only the application of the clause in question in the relation of the other contracting States with the State making the reservation.' (Reservations to the Convention on the Prevention and Punishment of the Crime of Genocide (Written Statement by the Organization of American States, 14 December 1950) [1951] ICJ Pleadings 15–20, 15.) In a progressive development of the 1928 principle, in 1932 the Governing Board of the Pan-American Union added the following rules with respect to the legal effect of reservations:

'1. The treaty shall be in force, in the form in which it was signed, as between those countries which ratify it without reservations, in the terms in which it was originally drafted and signed.
2. It shall be in force as between the governments which ratify it with reservations and the signatory States which accept the reservations in the form in which the treaty may be modified by said reservation.
3. It shall not be in force between a government which may have ratified with reservations and another which may have already ratified, and which does not accept these reservations' (ibid, 17). These rules were approved by the 1938 Lima Conference of American States. It was said that the procedure followed by the Pan-American Union is the best adapted to secure the ratification of multilateral treaties by as many states as possible. It makes it unnecessary at the time a treaty is drafted to eliminate from the text all those elements likely to give rise to reservations (ibid at 18).

is compatible with the object and purpose of the Convention'.[11] Subsequently, the 1969 Vienna Convention on the Law of Treaties incorporated,[12] in articles 20 and 21, rules similar to those recognised by the Inter-American Conferences and the ICJ, respectively.

Turning to the realm of foreign policy, a word is warranted on the so-called Estrada doctrine, formulated by the Mexican Foreign Secretary as early as 1930 in connection with the recognition of foreign governments, a practice considered offensive and a means of illegitimate intervention on the part of the Great Powers. According to the Estrada doctrine, Mexico would keep or withdraw its diplomatic agents as well as continue to accept foreign diplomatic agents without passing judgment upon changes of government in foreign countries. The Estrada doctrine was based on the premise that a change of government was an internal matter for each State. Two of the more outspoken critics of this doctrine, the US and the United Kingdom, ultimately embraced it by the late 1970s, when they stated publicly that they would no longer accord recognition to governments and would instead focus on the question of whether they wished to entertain diplomatic relations with the new governments.[13]

Let me now turn briefly to regionalism in connection with peace and security, an area where, historically, Latin American states have exhibited a strong preference for regional arrangements over universal mechanisms for conflict management and settlement. The introduction of Chapter VIII in the UN Charter very much responds to the concern of Latin American states to accommodate regional arrangements within the UN institutional framework.

As regards collective security, the relationship between Latin American countries and universalism as embodied in the UN Charter has undergone an important evolution over the years. Cold War-related conflicts on the continent put Latin America's regional penchant to the test, raising the question whether the OAS had absolute primacy and exclusivity in resolving political disputes within the inter-American system, or whether states were entitled to resort directly to the UN (and thus bypass the hegemonic power of the US in the area), thereby opening the door to a balance of political influences through the intervention of the universal organisation.

[11] *Reservations to the Convention on the Prevention and Punishment of the Crime of Genocide* (Advisory Opinion) [1951] ICJ Rep 26.

[12] Vienna Convention on the Law of Treaties (done at Vienna, 23 May 1969, entered into force 27 January 1980) 1155 UNTS 331, arts 20 and 21.

[13] In 1977 the Estrada doctrine was vindicated by the US, which indicated that it would 'avoid the use of recognition in cases of changes of governments and ... concern ourselves with the question of whether we wish to have diplomatic relations with the new governments ... The Administration's policy is that the establishment of relations does not involve approval or disapproval but merely demonstrates a willingness on our part to conduct our affairs with other governments directly.' (For the full text see DJ Harris, *Cases and Materials on International Law*, 7th edn (London, Sweet & Maxwell, 2010) 143.) In 1980 Lord Carrington, the British Foreign Secretary, stated in the UK House of Lords: 'there are practical advantages in following the policy of many other countries in not according recognition to Governments. Like them, we shall continue to decide the nature of our dealings with régimes which come to power unconstitutionally in the light of our assessment of whether they are able of themselves to exercise effective control of the territory of the State concerned, and seem likely to continue to do so.' (For the full text, see ibid 139.)

The 1954 Guatemalan *coup d'état*, the 1965 occupation of the Dominican Republic by the US, the Cuban missile crisis and the Central American conflicts of the 1980s brought to the forefront the existing tension between regionalism and universalism in the Latin American context. The situation was resolved in favour of universalism when the OAS Charter was amended in 1985,[14] so as to allow member states to decide for themselves whether to submit an international dispute to the peaceful procedures set forth in the OAS Charter or to the consideration of the UN.

Of course, this does not mean that all the problems surrounding the relationship between the UN Charter and regional arrangements have disappeared. In connection with the 1965 US armed intervention in the Dominican Republic, the question posed itself as to whether a regional organisation such as the OAS was empowered to adopt enforcement measures without Security Council authorisation under Chapter VII of the UN Charter.

As we all know, this is a question that is still very much present in the political and legal debate in connection with regional organisations worldwide. With regard to the 1965 events, what originally was a unilateral coercive measure was magically converted into a peace-keeping operation by the OAS without any reaction on the part of the UN.

In the field of security, Latin America's regional stance against nuclear weapons is noteworthy, particularly in times of nuclear proliferation. The 1967 Tlatelolco Treaty[15] is the first example of a region—the whole of Latin America—declaring itself free of nuclear weapons. Other regions have taken similar measures, but many others should follow suit. Conflict-prone areas such as the Middle East require the implementation of effective measures to abandon a risky nuclear arms race in the very near future.

To conclude, I would like to make some general remarks on the general state of health of regional institutions in Latin America today. I shall start by noting that, in its institutional dimension, regionalism is currently facing a number of problems in this part of the world. One of them relates to the obvious weakness of the OAS, for which member states are the only ones to blame

In general, it seems accurate to say that the inter-American system is currently immersed in a deep political crisis. It no longer has the power to cement together all the states of the system. There is also a process of institutional fragmentation, characterised by the presence of a number of exclusive sub-regional organisations, some of which are incompatible with one another and very much ideologically orientated.

The inter-American system of human rights is perhaps the strongest asset of the OAS. However, the role of the Commission and the Court is being seriously challenged. Venezuela has recently announced its withdrawal from the Inter-American

[14] Protocol of Amendment to the Charter of the Organization of American States (approved at Cartagena de Indias, 5 December 1985, entered into force 16 November 1988) OAS Treaty Series No 66 (1986) 25 ILM 527.

[15] Treaty for the Prohibition of Nuclear Weapons in Latin America and the Caribbean (signed at Tlatelolco, Mexico City 14 February 1967, entered into force 22 April 1969) 634 UNTS 281 (Treaty of Tlatelolco).

Convention of Human Rights.[16] Other states are also questioning the need to comply with the decisions and judgments of the Commission and the Court. By weakening the role and functions of these two organs, there is at present a clear danger to the integrity of the system as a whole.

Latin America, in the past a powerful advocate of regionalism, is in urgent need of reconstructing its regional identity in accordance with its original values. Only by acting as a collective force will Latin America be able to have an influence in the international arena.

[16] American Convention on Human Rights (signed at San José, Costa Rica, on 22 November 1969, entered into force 18 July 1978) 1144 UNTS 123 (*Pacto de San José* establishing the Inter-American Court of Human Rights); El Ministro de Poder Popular para Relacciones Exteriores de la República de Bolivariana de Venezuela, [Ministry of the Popular Power for Foreign Affairs of the Bolivarian Republic of Venezuela] Note 000125 p 9, para 2 (6 September 2012), available at www.oas.org/dil/esp/Nota_Republica_Bolivariana_de_Venezuela_al_SG_OEA.PDF (Spanish original).

4

Quelques réflexions sur des concepts de régionalisme et de region

JEAN SALMON*

I

LES RÉFLEXIONS QUE je voudrais formuler à propos des concepts de régionalisme et de région me sont dictées non tant par l'intitulé du présent forum que par ceux de l'ensemble des forums et agora de ce congrès.

En effet, les mots du langage courant ne prennent un sens juridique qu'à travers un contexte saisi par le droit. Dans le langage courant le mot « régionalisme » est défini, dans le dictionnaire Robert, comme « une tendance à conserver ou à favoriser certains traits particuliers d'une région, d'une province ... ». On est ainsi renvoyé au concept de « région » qui selon le même dictionnaire se définit principalement comme suit : « Territoire relativement étendu, possédant des caractéristiques physiques et humaines particulières qui en font une identité distincte des régions voisines ou au sein d'un ensemble qui l'englobe ».

L'utilisation de ce terme en droit ne lui enlève aucune de ses caractéristiques du langage commun. Une région est en principe une *zone géographique* qui *fait partie d'un ensemble plus étendu*. Mais cette région elle-même possède une *identité distincte* par rapport aux régions voisines ou par rapport à l'ensemble qui l'englobe.

Ainsi pour reprendre l'exemple dont il a été question dans les exposés précédents la région ayant pris la forme d'une organisation internationale sous le nom d'Organisation des États américains faisait partie d'un ensemble plus étendu les Nations Unies et se trouve être distinct d'autres régions comme l'Europe, par exemple.

Dans ce cas-ci la région de base est formée d'un ensemble d'éléments—des États—qui sont liés par des liens de solidarité les uns avec les autres et souhaitent réaliser des intérêts communs. Ce sont ces valeurs ou objectifs communs—réels ou fantasmés—qui font leur singularité et les distinguent de l'ensemble plus étendu ou des régions voisines.

* Professeur émérite de l'Université libre de Bruxelles. Membre de l'Institut de droit international.

II

Les organisations internationales régionales peuvent être très variées ainsi que l'exposé de Mme Louise Fawcett l'a montré.

En particulier du fait de la malléabilité d'une variable qui est au cœur du concept de région : la « tendance à conserver ou à favoriser certains traits particuliers » comme le dit le dictionnaire Robert ou pour le dire d'une autre manière la tendance à conserver ou à favoriser: *les liens de solidarité au sein de ladite région et le désir de réaliser des intérêts communs.* Ces derniers sont particulièrement divers et malléables. Une organisation régionale n'est pas l'autre.

On a pu s'en rendre compte à propos des ententes régionales prévues par les propositions de Dumbarton Oaks à la Conférence de San Francisco. Les tenants du panaméricanisme entendaient conserver une spécificité culturelle et une autonomie d'action assez vaste par une organisation régionale *préexistante aux intérêts les plus variés.* Les Européens entendaient, au travers de ce concept mettre au point une organisation régionale *future chargée d'assurer la sécurité collective* de leur continent notamment par l'exercice collectif du droit de légitime défense.

Les liens de solidarité qui justifient la création de régions sous forme d'organisations internationales ou d'ententes peuvent être très variés : linguistiques, religieux (souvenons nous du *cujus regio, eius religio* de la renaissance), ethniques, nationalistes, idéologiques, politiques, sociaux, sécuritaires, stratégiques ou économiques (néolibéraux ou socialistes), etc. Différents objectifs peuvent être cumulés par une organisation déterminée.

Mais, tout aussi bien, un État peut être membre d'organisations régionales différentes ayant des objets distincts auxquels il est attaché. Et être ainsi, par exemple, membre de la Ligue arabe en même temps que du Conseil de coopération du Golfe, de la Conférence islamique et de certaines organisations économiques arabes.

III

Le second élément au cœur de la définition de « région » est *l'élément géographique.* En principe, qui dit région suppose une zone territoriale, où existe une continuité géographique des membres du groupe. Par exemple l'Union Européenne, le Conseil de l'Europe ; le panaméricanisme, la zone euro, le Benelux, etc.

Dans certains cas cependant un lien de solidarité d'une autre nature prime la base géographique, l'OECD, l'Organisation de la conférence islamique internationale, etc. sont des regroupements où les membres ne relèvent pas tous d'une même zone géographique. Pour l'OTAN, on a élargi la base géographique de départ, additionnant les Etats-Unis et le Canada à une partie de l'Europe pour en faire ce que l'article 5 du Pacte atlantique appelle la « région de l'Atlantique nord ».

IV

La promotion des intérêts d'une région peut toutefois prendre d'autres formes que celle d'une organisation internationale.

Ainsi la base géographique prime même si elle ne se définit plus comme un regroupement d'États mais comme une zone géographique qui est l'objet de leur intérêt commun : ainsi les régions dénucléarisées ou zones de paix par exemple l'Océan indien).[1]

On rencontre encore des *zones ne relevant d'aucune souveraineté* : zone du Traité sur l'Antarctique ; Déclaration de Rio de 1992 (principe 2), qui exprime la conviction commune des États concernés qu'ils ont le devoir « de faire en sorte que les activités exercées dans les limites de leur juridiction ou sous leur contrôle ne causent pas de dommages à l'environnement dans d'autres États ou dans les régions [zones] ne relevant d'aucune juridiction nationale ».

Même attitude à l'égard de l'espace extra-atmosphérique défini, lui aussi, comme une région.[2] La protection de l'environnement procède de même fréquemment en prenant des régions comme objet de ses soins : ainsi en matière de changement climatiques.[3]

V

On parle aussi de régions géographiques spécifiques en cas de situation conflictuelle où deux États se disputent la souveraineté d'une zone particulière (par exemple délimitation maritime « *dans la région* du Golfe du Maine » ou « dans la région située entre le Groënland et Jan Mayen »). « Le Conseil de sécurité … Autorise les États membres qui coopèrent avec le Gouvernement koweïtien … à user de tous les moyens nécessaires pour … rétablir la paix et la sécurité internationales *dans la région* » (S/Rés 678 (1990) du 29 novembre 1990). « Constatant qu'il existe une rupture de la paix *dans la région* des îles Falkland (Malvinas) » (S/Rés 502 (1982) du Conseil de sécurité du 3 avril 1982 à propos des îles Falkland/Malvinas).

VI

Il se peut aussi que le droit international constitue des régions avec des éléments territoriaux appartenant à plusieurs États différents. La notion de région frontalière est évidemment centrale dans les conventions relatives à la coopération transfrontalière.

La protection de l'environnement couvre fréquemment des *régions transfrontières* ayant des caractéristiques physiques que l'on entend préserver sur le territoire de

[1] « L'Assemblée générale … demandant … à tous les États de considérer et de respecter l'Océan indien comme une zone de paix d'où seraient exclues les rivalités et la compétition entre grandes puissances ainsi que les bases conçues dans le contexte de ces rivalités et de cette compétition, et déclarant que *cette région* doit également être exempte d'armes nucléaires » (AG Rés 2832 (XXVI), 16 décembre 1971).

[2] « L'espace extra-atmosphérique, y compris la Lune et les autres corps célestes, peut être exploré et utilisé librement par tous les États sans aucune discrimination, dans des conditions d'égalité et conformément au droit international, toutes les régions des corps célestes devant être librement accessibles » (traité sur les principes régissant les activités des États en matière d'exploration et d'utilisation de l'espace extra-atmosphérique, 27 janvier 1967, art 1 § 2, RTNU, vol 610, p 205.

[3] « Toutes les parties … établissent, mettent en œuvre, publient et mettent régulièrement à jour des programmes nationaux *et, le cas échéant, régionaux* contenant des mesures visant à atténuer les changements climatiques » (art 4 § 1(b) de la convention de New York (1992) sur les changements climatiques).

plusieurs États : (bassin fluvial, forêt tropicale, zone aride, zone humide, région maritime ou région d'habitat d'une espèce déterminée).

L'Union européenne s'occupe intensément des politiques régionales des pays membres. Mais ceci peut aussi concerner les organes de l'ONU. Exemple : Respect de la politique anti apartheid dans les régions.[4]

VII

Le droit international prend aussi, de diverses manières, *les régions dans les régions*, ne fut-ce que pour déterminer la portée de leurs engagements sur le plan international ou pour assurer un effet direct aux obligations qui les concernent.

Sans trop bien savoir où les classer, on s'en voudrait de ne pas retenir l'intérêt que porte le droit international aux *régions habitées par des peuples autochtones* et autres *peuples premiers*. Les efforts à l'OIT et ailleurs sont particulièrement notoires.[5]

VIII

Allions nous oublier un classique du régionalisme et de tous les manuels de droit international : les coutumes régionales ou les conventions régionales?[6]

IX

Il découle des réflexions qui précèdent et qui se bornent à des illustrations superficielles et aléatoires, que l'extension et la compréhension des concepts de régionalisme et de région est étendue et se présente sous des formes différentes selon la manière dont ils sont saisis par le droit. C'est donc pour chaque forme du concept que se pose la passionnante évolution de son histoire individuelle. Celle-ci variera et évoluera selon la prise de conscience des liens de solidarité et des intérêts communs dans chaque hypothèse retenue. Ceci a été fort bien montré par les exposés de Mme Obregon, de Mme Fawcett et de Monsieur le juge Sepulveda pour le concept de régionalisme (latino ou pan) américain.

[4] « Les États inciteront *toutes leurs autorités régionales* ... pour assurer la stricte observation des dispositions de la présente déclaration » (AG Rés 32/105, 14 décembre 1977: Déclaration internationale contre l'apartheid dans les sports, art 10).

[5] « La présente Convention s'applique aux peuples dans les pays indépendants qui sont considérés comme indigènes du fait qu'ils descendent des populations qui habitaient le pays, ou une région géographique à laquelle appartient le pays, à l'époque de la conquête ou de la colonisation ou de l'établissement des frontières actuelles de l'État, et qui, quel que soit leur statut juridique, conservent leurs institutions sociales, économiques, culturelles et politiques propres ou certaines d'entre elles. » (convention de l'OIT n° 169 concernant les peuples indigènes et tribaux dans les pays indépendants du 27 juin 1989).

[6] « Les engagements internationaux tels que les traités d'arbitrage, et les ententes régionales comme la doctrine de Monroë, qui assurent le maintien de la paix ne seront considérés comme incompatibles avec aucune disposition du présent Pacte » (Pacte de la SDN, art 21).

Part II

Regionalism and the Unity of International Law

5

Regionalism and the Unity of International Law from a Positivist Perspective

ANDRÉ DE HOOGH*

I. INTRODUCTION

FOR THE LAST decade or so, an animated discussion has been raging over concerns about the fragmentation of international law. Fragmentation may come about as a result of different legal (treaty) regimes being set up by states, the lack of coordination between such regimes and hence the potential for conflict; it may also occur due to the proliferation of international courts, tribunals and bodies, charged with monitoring compliance or deciding disputes over interpretation, application and violation.[1] Within this discussion, the regionalism factor does not take pride of place, except perhaps in the field of international trade law as regards customs unions or free trade agreements, since quite a few of those are regionally organised.[2] The rationale for the debate among WTO scholars is that the purpose of the agreements in question is to provide advantages to some WTO members but not to others, which will of necessity be inconsistent with the prescriptions related to most favoured nation treatment.[3]

Speaking of 'regionalism and the unity of international law' a certain opposition, tension or conflict seems to be implied. In view of the terminology involved, some might even suggest that the former could rise to the level of an existential threat to the latter. Certainly this has been the gist of certain authors over time, and not just

* Associate Professor in International Law, University of Groningen, the Netherlands. My thanks to Jörg Kammerhofer, Abel Knottnerus and Antenor Hallo de Wolf for their detailed comments on earlier drafts; final responsibility for this chapter is mine alone.

[1] See Report of the Study Group of the International Law Commission (ILC), finalised by Martti Koskenniemi, 'Fragmentation of International Law: Difficulties arising from the Diversification and Expansion of International Law', UN Doc A/CN.4/L.682, 13 April 2006.

[2] See RE Baldwin and T Carpenter, 'Regionalism: Moving from Fragmentation towards Coherence', in T Cottier and P Delimatsis (eds), *The Prospects of International Trade Regulation: From Fragmentation towards Coherence* (Cambridge, Cambridge University Press, 2011) 136–65.

[3] For instance art I:1 of the General Agreement on Tariffs and Trade 1947, 55 UNTS 1947 (GATT 1947). The possibility of concluding such agreements was envisaged and found regulation in art XXIV GATT 1947.

in the recent past.[4] And yet the relationship between regional law and international law generally could also be seen in a much more positive light, by focusing on the inspiration and influence that regional arrangements or organisations have had on the (progressive) development of international law at large; or, vice versa, the way in which international law has pushed the creation of regional rules.

After some preliminary observations on the meaning of regionalism and the question of unity of international law (section II), this contribution will continue by considering regionalism and certain questions of validity in relation to the primary sources of international law (section III). Finally, some issues concerning the (non-) application by regional authorities of other norms or obligations of international law will be broached by reference to first, the disagreement between the African Union (AU) and International Criminal Court (ICC) over the arrest warrant against President al-Bashir and his immunity, and second, the clash over the compatibility of targeted sanctions of the Security Council (SC) with fundamental rights protected under EU law (section IV).

II. REGIONALISM AND THE UNITY OF INTERNATIONAL LAW

When it comes to the meaning of the word regionalism, the *Oxford English Dictionary* suggests 'the theory or practice of regional rather than central systems of administration or economic, cultural or political affiliation'.[5] From a geographical perspective it is certainly possible to identify various regions, though the lines of separation are not always altogether obvious. For purposes of this contribution one may further recall, pointing to the dictionary meaning quoted above, that various forms of cooperation have been established in many regions, political as well as legal, and these can be termed systems of administration or may involve economic, cultural and political affiliations or associations. Forms of cooperation and the resulting affiliations or associations are most commonly legally organised via the conclusion of treaties.[6]

In the International Law Commission (ILC) 'Report on Fragmentation of International Law', finalised by Martti Koskenniemi, the ILC study group distinguished three meanings for regionalism: first, a set of approaches and methods for examining international law; second, a technique for international law-making; and third, the pursuit of geographical exceptions to universal rules of international law.[7] These three approaches or methods will be briefly recounted.

The first meaning discussed by the ILC Fragmentation Report recalls that various orientations of legal thought and culture have expressed themselves in approaches or

[4] For example, CW Jenks, 'Regionalism in International Judicial Organization' (1943) 37 *American Journal of International Law* 314–20.

[5] See for a definition of regionalism, the *Oxford English Dictionary*, available on-line at www.oxforddictionaries.com/definition/english/regionalism?q=regionalism.

[6] A notable exception, at least initially, was the Helsinki Final Act, which was stipulated to be ineligible for registration under art 102 of the UN Charter. Conference on Security and Co-operation in Europe, Final Act, 1975, p 59, available at www.osce.org/mc/39501.

[7] ILC, Fragmentation Report 103–5, paras 199–204; 106–8, paras 205–10; and 108–12, paras 211–17, respectively.

doctrines, such as the Anglo-American, continental, Soviet, Third World, European, (Latin) American, African and Asian traditions or perspectives.[8] The Report considers that the influence these approaches or doctrines have had lies in the impact they (may) have had on the development of international law generally. Rules developed in a regional context may have lost their geographical limitation and contributed to the development of universal rules of international law.[9] Indeed, the Report notes that there is a strong presumption among the legal profession that international law itself is universal in character, that regionalism in this sense does not necessarily claim any normative content, and that in many cases the approach or perspective taken is not reflective of any 'regional' property in the geographical sense, but rather of a certain 'convergence of interests, values and political objectives'.[10]

Considering the second meaning, the Report notes that regionalism can be seen as a 'privileged forum for international law-making'.[11] The idea behind this observation points to the likely homogeneity of interests, which ensures greater legitimacy and possibilities of enhanced efficiency and implementation at the regional level.[12] According to the Report, various studies concerning theories of interdependence and international regimes have shown that it may be advantageous to govern through larger or regional units.[13] Concluding, the Report again comments that regionalism perceived through the prism of cooperation and rational choice is to be seen from a functional perspective, and to be approached as part of the problem of special regimes.[14]

The Report goes on to discuss a third meaning, with regionalism referring to two possible normative aspects: 'a rule or principle with a geographical sphere of validity or a regional *limitation* to the sphere of validity of a universal rule or principle.'[15] The first is taken to mean that a rule or principle would be binding only for states of a certain region, whereas the second amounts to a claim that states within a certain region would not be subject to the binding force of an otherwise universal rule or principle.[16] The Report proposes, among others suggestions, that there is very little support for drawing normative consequences from the concept of regionalism, other than those that might flow from the (proven) existence of a regional rule of customary international law.[17] Essentially, it will be this third meaning, namely of geographical exceptions to universal rules of international law, that is explored further in the present contribution. It is only when normative consequences are drawn from regionalism that any tension or conflict between regionalism and the unity of international law may be said to exist.

Moving to the topic of unity, the first issue that arises is what exactly one means by positing the unity of international law, as opposed to, for instance, the fragmentation

[8] ibid 103–4, paras 199–200.
[9] ibid 104, para 201.
[10] ibid 105, paras 202 and 204.
[11] ibid 106, para 205.
[12] ibid.
[13] ibid 106–7, para 207.
[14] ibid 107–8, para 208.
[15] ibid 108, para 211.
[16] ibid.
[17] ibid at 111, para 215.

of that law. The on-line Oxford dictionary defines unity as 'the state of being united or joined as a whole'.[18] The dictionary traces back the word in English via the French *unité* to the Latin *unitas*, and this in turn from *unus*, meaning one.[19] The question may thus be raised whether international law is *united or joined as a whole* or *one*. Fragmentation is defined in the US English dictionary as 'the process or state of breaking or being broken into small or separate parts'.[20] To the extent that regionalism would indeed entail normative consequences, international law could be said to be broken into (regional) parts.

Starting with the question of whether international law is *one*, reference was made in the past especially to traditions or approaches such as Marxist or Soviet (opposed to bourgeois), Third World, Islamic, European, Latin American, Anglo-American (opposed to continental), Arab, Asian or African international law.[21] Yet at the same time, claims made in this respect did not amount to a rejection *in toto* of international law, but rather of specific norms related to specific fields.[22] In fact, in other respects states caught up in any particular ideology, religion or region tended to strongly affirm certain specific norms, especially those related to the protection of sovereignty, equality and territorial integrity, the principle of non-intervention, and the right of self-determination of peoples.[23]

More particularly, seeing unity in terms of the primary subjects of international law—*ratione personae* as it were—the times that participation in the international community, diplomacy and the creation of international law was reserved to (circles of) Christian, European or civilised states, have long gone with the demise of the constitutive theory of recognition and (European) colonialism and imperialism.[24]

[18] *Oxford English Dictionary*, available on-line at www.oxforddictionaries.com/definition/english/unity?q=unity.

[19] ibid.

[20] ibid, available on-line at www.oxforddictionaries.com/definition/american_english/fragmentation. The American meaning is preferred because the British meaning in its definition uses the noun 'fragment' instead of 'part'.

[21] See I Brownlie, 'Problems Concerning the Unity of International Law' in *Le Droit international à l'heure de sa codification: études en l'honneur de Roberto Ago* (*International Law at the Time of Its Codification: Essays in Honour of Roberto Ago*) (Milan, Giuffrè, 1987) vol I, 153–62, 154–55, 159; ILC, Fragmentation Report 103–5, paras 199–204.

[22] In particular those rules that gave protection to foreign control over natural resources and foreign investments, and those that seemed to favour the markets of industrialised states. See W Wengler, 'La crise de l'unité de l'ordre juridique international' (trans Girard) in *Mélanges offerts à Charles Rousseau: La communauté internationale* (Paris, Pedone, 1974) 329–40, 335–36.

[23] See for example, E Riedel, 'The Progressive Development of International Law at the Universal and Regional Level' in R Wolfrum (ed), *Strengthening the World Order: Universalism v. Regionalism, Risks and Opportunities of Regionalization* (Berlin, Duncker & Humblot, 1990) 115, 117–18; RY Jennings, 'Universal International Law in a Multicultural World' in M Bos and I Brownlie (eds), *Liber Amicorum for The Rt Hon Lord Wilberforce, PC, CMG, OBE, QC* (Oxford, Clarendon Press, 1987) 39, 44–45, 49.

[24] See Convention on the Rights and Duties of States (signed at Montevideo, 26 December 1933) 165 LNTS 19, arts 3 and 6–7. Note that the Montevideo Convention was drawn up as part of the Inter-American system. See also Brownlie, 'Problems concerning the Unity of International Law' 156–57; G Abi-Saab, 'International Law and the International Community: The Long Road to Universality' in RStJ McDonald (ed), *Essays in Honour of Wang Tieya* (Dordrecht, Martinus Nijhoff, 1994) 31, 36–40; O Elias, 'Regionalism in International Law-Making and the Westphalian Legacy' in C Harding and CL Lim (eds), *Renegotiating Westphalia: Essays and Commentary on the European and Conceptual Foundations of Modern International Law* (The Hague, Kluwer Law International, 1999) 25–44, 33–36.

The advent of universal, political international organisations contributed to this, as especially the rise in membership in the United Nations shows.[25] What is more, those political entities which are not states or are not recognised as such, like Taiwan, Somaliland, Kosovo and Palestine, aspire to acquire the status of a state.[26]

In effect, no state rejects the existence and binding character of international law,[27] and even those states that have shown particular disregard for (some rules of) international law under certain governments have not done so.[28] Suggestions by some states that certain states or regimes are rogue, or outlaws, or even part of an axis of evil,[29] have been put forward as part of a political or policy agenda.[30] This has been done for a specific purpose rather than as a general proposition that the states or regimes concerned would not be subject to the law or that international law would not be applicable in the relations with such states at all.[31]

While we may therefore claim that international law is one in the sense that its primary subjects have been identified or are identifiable,[32] the same cannot be easily said

[25] See for the list of UN Members, available at www.un.org/en/members/growth.shtml.

[26] Sometimes evidenced by application for membership in the United Nations, which according to art 4 of the UN Charter is open to peace-loving states. See for example, the application by the Republic of China (Taiwan), Letter 13 August 2007, A/62/193, Annex 1, available at www.un.org/en/documents/ods/. See Jennings, 'Universal International Law' 44–45.

[27] P-M Dupuy, 'L'unité de l'ordre juridique international: cours général de droit international public (2000)' 297 *Receuil des cours* (Hague Academy of International Law and Martinus Nijhoff Publishers, 2002) 9, 90. Jennings, 'Universal International Law' 40–41. He also noted that the early inclination of newly independent states to reject customary international law, and to insist on being able to pick and choose which treaties of a predecessor state to be bound by, has long been abandoned (though he also points to the strong influence of such positions on the law of state succession); ibid 46–48. However, note importantly that Islamic states increasingly adhere to Shari'a as the foundation or inspiration of positive law, and this leads Prost to point to their different attitude towards international law in the sense that they appear to posit, or accept, a kind of Islamic *Grundnorm*. M Prost, *The Concept of Unity in Public International Law* (Oxford, Hart Publishing, 2012) 115–25.

[28] Paradoxically one might put both Afghanistan under the Taliban government (1996–2001) and the USA under President Bush (2001–09) in this category. See G Simpson, *Great Powers and Outlaw States, Unequal Sovereigns in the International Legal Order* (Cambridge, Cambridge University Press, 2004) 319–48; P Sands, *Lawless World* (London, Penguin books, 2006) 143–257.

[29] National Security Strategy of the United States 2002, section V, available on-line at http://georgewbush-whitehouse.archives.gov/nsc/nss/2002/; and National Security Strategy of the United States 2006, section III, V-VI, on-line available at http://georgewbush-whitehouse.archives.gov/nsc/nss/2006/index.html; USA, President Bush, State of the Union, 29 January 2002, available on-line at www.edition.cnn.com/2002/ALLPOLITICS/01/29/bush.speech.txt. See Simpson, *Great Powers and Outlaw States*, 278–316.

[30] The ICJ pointed out that grounds provided by US authorities for intervening in another state for reasons of that state's domestic or foreign policy, ideology or armaments were 'statements of international policy, and not the assertion of existing rules of international law.' *Military and Paramilitary Activities in and against Nicaragua* (*Nicaragua v United States of America*) (Merits) [1986] ICJ Rep 14, 109, para 207.

[31] Note that Simpson claims that such states have been subjected to far-reaching measures, mostly through Security Council action, that evidence the application of an alternative legal domain than the one that applies to democratic, liberal states, Simpson, *Great Powers and Outlaw States*, 311–16. See also J Vidmar, 'Norm Conflicts and Hierarchy in International Law: Towards a Vertical International Legal System' in E de Wet and J Vidmar (eds), *Hierarchy in International Law: The Place of Human Rights* (Oxford, Oxford University Press, 2012) 13–41, 38–40.

[32] Though this latter issue of 'identification' is much more difficult considering that the traditional qualifications set forth in art 1 of the Montevideo Convention do not help us much when the status of a political entity is in dispute.

with respect to the multitude of norms that make up international law. Approaching the matter from a *ratione materiae* perspective, would it not in fact be better to speak of international laws in the plural?[33] This in view of the fact that each treaty is an island of its own and that rules of customary international law may in certain ways be grouped together in a functional sense—the law of the sea, the law of outer space, etc—but with little attempt made to enhance the coherence between such fields.[34] Or in other words, can it be said that the rules, the norms of international law are *united or joined as a whole*? And if so, what constitute the bonds or the glue that hold(s) all such rules together?

For some authors what makes international law unitary in character lies in its nature as a coercive legal order, entailing that for each substantive norm international law envisages the application of a sanction in case of its breach.[35] However, this particular argument was intended to show, mostly, that international law is *true* law. As such, the argument was levelled against the Austinian type of claim that international law, being the result of opinions of nations, is not law properly styled and constitutes no more than positive morality; this in turn was based on that author's more general claim that law constitutes a species of the command of a sovereign and is enforced through application of a sanction (an evil).[36] As a characteristic necessary for a norm to be considered law in the first place, and hence not particular to international law per se, it provides an insufficient basis to explain the unity of international law.

A less restrictive and more fruitful approach can be seen in the distinction made between primary and secondary rules, credited to a large extent to HLA Hart.[37] Primary rules in Hart's view were concerned with the actions that individuals must or must not do, and secondary rules with those that specify how primary rules may be 'ascertained, introduced, eliminated, varied, and the fact of their violation conclusively determined.'[38] According to Hart, the latter category of rules was subdivided into rules of recognition that allow for the identification of primary rules, rules of change that allow identification of those that may introduce new or eliminate old primary rules, and rules of adjudication allowing for the determination of violations of primary rules and the application of sanctions.[39]

[33] Dupuy observed that the unity of international law is a rather recent development; he speaks of the international legal orders, in the plural, before being federated into one general international legal order. To this may be added his claim that special or partial international legal orders are subordinated to the general international legal order. Dupuy, 'L'unité de l'ordre juridique international' 86–91.

[34] See H Golsong, 'Le développement du droit international régional' in *Régionalisme et universalisme dans le droit international contemporain: Colloque de la Société Française pour le Droit International* (Paris, Pedone, 1977) 221, 223, 233; Riedel, 'The Progressive Development of International Law' 116. Note, however, the section on conflict clauses in the ILC, Fragmentation Report 135–51, paras 267–94.

[35] Wengler, 'La crise de l'unité de l'ordre juridique international' 329–35. See H Kelsen, *Principles of International Law* (New York, Rinehart & Co, 1952) 3–18 and also 18–89; and discussion in Dupuy, 'L'unité de l'ordre juridique international' 67–69.

[36] J Austin, *The Province of Jurisprudence Determined*, 2nd edn (New York, Burt Franklin, 1861) 119–29. See also discussion in HLA Hart, *The Concept of Law*, 2nd edn (Oxford, Oxford University Press, 1994) 227–32.

[37] ibid 80–81, 94.

[38] ibid 94.

[39] ibid 94–99.

In principle then it may be possible to argue that international law is unified, largely, through its secondary rules.[40] A complicating factor with respect to the categories of primary and secondary rules is that international law lacks a centralised, higher authority empowered to make or change rules, to adjudicate or to determine the existence of violations, and to apply sanctions.[41] This led Hart to deny international law its unity and to put forward the proposition that international law, lacking even a basic rule of recognition, consists merely of a set or of sets of primary rules rather than being unified as a legal system.[42] As Dupuy noted, Hart failed to discuss such secondary rules as do quite clearly exist in international law, such as those related to the law of treaties and of international responsibility.[43] In the end, the unity of international law cannot be negated and lies with the common understanding of the political communities in the world as to the nature and necessities of the international legal system, general agreement on the sources of international law and on the rules to determine violations and the permissible responses thereto.

III. VALIDITY AND SOURCES OF INTERNATIONAL LAW AND OBLIGATION

In considering more closely the question of the bonds or the glue that tie(s) various parts of international law together, first an excursion will be made into the topic of validity. Robert Jennings, for instance, observed that international law possesses the quality of universality, which is the recognition that it is valid and binding in all states irrespective of all kinds of differences that may exist between them.[44] He continued by stating:

> All this is not to say, of course, that there is no room for variations, perhaps even in matters of principle ... Universality does not mean uniformity. It does mean, however, that such a regional international law, however variant, is a part of the system as a whole and not a separate system, and it ultimately derives its validity from the system as a whole.[45]

Although today this particular point on validity can be argued persuasively, as a matter of principle it can be questioned. If a number of political entities within a region, one might call them states, were to come to (either tacit or express) agreement that they would be bound by rules established by covenants or by practice recognised as law, such regional law would not of necessity need to rely for its validity on some overarching (global) legal system. To put it differently, the regional system

[40] See to this effect Dupuy, 'L'unité de l'ordre juridique international' 39, who makes reference to secondary rules in terms of formal unity and to the Charter of the United Nations in terms of material, ie substantive, unity. One may note that Hart, *The Concept of Law* 79–99, refers in the title of his fifth chapter to the 'law as the union of primary and secondary rules'. On this aspect and its relation to sources, see also critically Prost, *The Concept of Unity* 83–105.

[41] Noted by Hart, ibid 214.

[42] ibid 232–37.

[43] Dupuy, 'L'unité de l'ordre juridique international' 76. See also O Casanovas y La Rosa, transl from the Spanish by F Barrett, *Unity and Pluralism in Public International Law* (The Hague, Martinus Nijhoff, 2001) 15–18, 65–67, 249–50.

[44] Jennings, 'Universal International Law' 40–41.

[45] ibid 41.

could be the whole rather than a part, and therefore would not find a legal basis in an all-embracing, universal legal system. Of course Jennings would have realised as much, since the explanation he provided for this claim was that:

> This must be so if only because States within a particular region or system must also live with other States of the world society. There must always be some basic universal element—some general fabric of law—that binds all mankind.[46]

As some have pointed out, the existence of a society generates the existence of law, *ubi societas ibi jus*.[47] Today, international society encompasses most political entities and international law purports to cover all that occurs in all the lands and seas of the world (and even beyond this '*3rd rock from the sun*'). However, the pretension of the universality of contemporary international law is the result of its expansion both *ratione personae* and geographically. Before this occurred only natural law, in the words of Jennings perhaps suitable as a 'general fabric of law', could provide a basis for universality. In the absence of both natural law and international law, all (positive) law and legal systems that developed in earlier times possessed independent validity.

This brings us to the second point to be made, and that is that with respect to international law it is widely accepted that most, if not quite all, of its norms are dispositive in character.[48] This claim has been supported by the ICJ, when it observed:

> Without attempting to enter into, still less pronounce upon any question of *jus cogens*, it is well understood that, in practice, rules of international law can, by agreement, be derogated from in particular cases, or as between particular parties, ...[49]

In other words, states are entitled to adopt specific norms that are divergent from rules of (universal) customary international law and from treaties, at least to the extent that these do not infringe the rights of other states bound by such rules or treaties. In this respect Jörg Kammerhofer has claimed that the presumption is that all law is compelling (*jus cogens*) and that therefore the dispositive character of law (*jus dispositivum*) must be stipulated by and within the law itself.[50]

Although persuasive as a proposition with respect to national systems of law—where the subjects of law are subordinated to and bound by law ordinarily made by

[46] ibid.

[47] Eg Abi-Saab, 'International Law and the International Community' 31.

[48] See ILC, Fragmentation Report 45–47, paras 79–84; 56, para 103; 83, para 154; and 181–82, para 361; also ILC, 'Conclusions of the Study Group on the Fragmentation of International Law: Difficulties arising from the Diversification and Expansion of International Law' in Report of the International Law Commission adopted at its 58th Session (1 May to 9 June and 3 July to 11 August 2006), A/61/10, 407–23, 409, points 8–9.

[49] *North Sea Continental Shelf Cases* (*Federal Republic of Germany v Denmark; Federal Republic of Germany v The Netherlands*) Judgment [1969] ICJ Rep 3, 42, para 72. Earlier on, however, the Court had observed: 'speaking generally, it is a characteristic of purely conventional rules and obligations that, in regard to them, some faculty of making unilateral reservations may, within certain limits, be admitted;—whereas this cannot be so in the case of general or customary international law rules and obligations which, by their very nature, must have equal force for all members of the international community, and cannot therefore be the subject of any right of unilateral exclusion exercisable at will by any one of them in its own favour.' Ibid 38–39, para 63.

[50] See J Kammerhofer, *Uncertainty in International Law: A Kelsenian perspective* (London, Routledge, 2011) 177–78 (see also pp 135–37 and 154).

a discrete institution made up of a select group of individuals and characterised by a hierarchically layered legal system (*Stufenbau*)—international law presents certain features that may account for a different position. For one, there is, or at least there used to be, complete identity of those subjects of law that are bound by international law and those that possess the authority to make it.[51] Another feature peculiar to international law is that it recognises the sovereignty of states, in effect the independence of decision-making of territorially limited political communities, and which signifies the lack of subordination to any higher authority.[52]

These two features combined may account for the assumption that rules of international law may be derogated from by common accord. Basically this boils down to the proposition that states may adopt valid norms diverging from or in opposition to an existing, valid norm of conventional or customary law.[53] The ICJ has claimed as much, though from a different angle, when it observed:[54] 'In general, treaty rules being *lex specialis*, it would not be appropriate that a State should bring a claim based on a customary-law rule if it has by treaty already provided for means of settlement of such a claim.' But if treaty rules are, in general, special law in relation to general (customary) international law, then regional treaties may without the need for any further justification regulate any topic differently.[55] Nevertheless, the proposition that the dispositive character of international law has its basis in or results from the fact that general law may be modified by special law, endorsed by the ILC Study Group on Fragmentation,[56] appears to miss the mark. In fact, in many cases the choice made in a treaty is not motivated by a desire to tailor a general rule to the specific topic, theme or situation at hand, but is simply a preference for a different rule that is brought to life by sovereign states through a(n) (collective) act of will.

Relevant to the topic of this contribution, the ICJ has recognised, though somewhat implicitly, that the development of a rule of regional or local customary international law is indeed possible. Responding to a claim to this effect by Colombia, it investigated the (Latin American) state practice and *opinio juris* put forward by Colombia regarding an alleged right of diplomatic asylum, but came to the conclusion that no

[51] The omission of the words 'subordinated to' in the sentence preceding this footnote is deliberate, since states as sovereign entities create and contribute to international law voluntarily: 'International law governs relations between independent States. The rules of law binding upon States therefore emanate from their own free will as expressed in conventions or by usages generally accepted as expressing general principles of law and established in order to regulate the relations between these co-existing independent communities or with a view to the achievement of common aims. Restrictions upon the independence of States cannot therefore be presumed.' *Case of the S.S 'Lotus'* (*France v Turkey*) PCIJ Series A No 10, 4, 18.

[52] ibid. See generally, A de Hoogh, 'The Sovereigns are Dead, Long Live the Sovereigns—Reflections on State Sovereignty and International Law' in E Rieter and H de Waele (eds), *Evolving Principles of International Law, Studies in Honour of Karel C. Wellens* (Leiden, Martinus Nijhoff Publishers, 2012) 169–85.

[53] ILC, Fragmentation Report 45–47, paras 79–84; 56, para 103; 83, para 154; 181–82, para 361; 151–65, paras 295–319. See in this respect Vienna Convention on the Law of Treaties (done at Vienna, 23 May 1969, entered into force 27 January 1980) 1155 UNTS 331, art 41.

[54] *Military and Paramilitary Activities* case 137, para 274.

[55] To this effect, ILC Fragmentation Report 109, para 212, which distinguishes this from *normative* regionalism that suggests that even those states in the region, or outside of it, that do not accept the rule in question are bound by it. See more broadly, ibid 109–11, paras 213–15.

[56] ILC, Conclusions of Study Group on Fragmentation at 409, points 8–9.

such rule had developed.[57] This particular right of diplomatic asylum would constitute a derogation of the territorial sovereignty of a state, since it withdraws a person from the jurisdiction of that state.[58] As such it would constitute, in the words of the ILC Fragmentation Report,[59] a (rather limited) regional exception to an otherwise universal rule of customary international law, namely the exclusive authority and control a state possesses over its territory.[60]

A much stronger version of a claim of regional preference would be where the regional rules of international law would be opposable to all states within and outside the region. This view was put forward by Alvarez, who argued in 1950 that American international law was binding on all states of the New World, and on states of other continents if an issue affects America (referring to immigration and American security zones in times of war).[61] Insofar as treaties are concerned, their invocation against any particular state will capsize on the fundamental precept that treaties require consent in order to be binding, and do not create any obligations for third states without their consent.[62] Hence the ICJ gave short shrift to Colombia's attempt to invoke the 1933 Convention on Political Asylum, since Peru had not ratified it.[63]

Moreover, Colombia's claim that American international law allowed it to qualify unilaterally and definitively the conduct of a person seeking asylum as a political offence foundered in view of inconsistent practice and strong political expediency.[64] Eventually, the ICJ put the final nail in the coffin for Alvarez's argument that all states in the New World are bound by American international law. Alvarez had argued that a custom need not be accepted by all states of the New World to be part of American international law. However, the ICJ claimed that, even if such a custom existed between certain Latin American states, it could not be invoked against Peru, since that state had repudiated the custom by not ratifying the most directly relevant

[57] Colombian-Peruvian a*sylum case (Colombia v Peru)* (Merits) [1950] ICJ Rep 266, 276–78. On the possibility of local custom, see *Case concerning Right of Passage over Indian Territory* (Merits) [1960] ICJ Reports 6, 39 and more broadly 40–44. Crawford notes that the ICJ paid scant attention to regional considerations and saw the issues very much 'through the prism of general international law'. JR Crawford, 'Universalism and Regionalism from the Perspective of the Work of the International Law Commission', *International Law on the Eve of the Twenty-first Century: Views from the International Law Commission* (New York, United Nations, 1997) 99, 113–14.

[58] *Asylum* case, 274–75 and Dissenting Opinion Alvarez, ibid 290, 292, who claimed that in Latin American countries asylum is a consequence of the extraterritoriality of the diplomatic premises. Therefore the grant of asylum constitutes the legitimate exercise of a prerogative that does not constitute interference with, or a limitation of, the sovereignty of the territorial state.

[59] ILC, Fragmentation Report 108–09, para 211.

[60] Vienna Convention on Diplomatic Relations (done at Vienna, 18 April 1961, entered into force 24 April 1964) 500 UNTS 95, arts 1, 4–8, 10–11, 21–22 and 29–31.

[61] *Asylum* case, Dissenting Opinion Alvarez, 294. Alvarez claimed: 'A principle, custom, doctrine, etc., need not be accepted by all of the States of the New World in order to be considered as a part of American international law. The same situation obtains in this case as in the case of universal international law.' See also discussion in Casanovas y La Rosa, *Unity and Pluralism* 31–33.

[62] Vienna Convention on the Law of Treaties, arts 2(g–h), 11–17, and 34–35.

[63] *Asylum* case, 276; the 1933 Convention on Political Asylum (adopted at Montevideo on 26 December 1933 by the Seventh International Conference of American States, entered into force 28 March 1935) OAS Treaty Series No 34. Ironically Peru proceeded to ratify this treaty in 1960: see www.oas.org/juridico/english/sigs/a-37.html.

[64] *Asylum* case, 276–77.

treaties.[65] The Court's observations on this point can be read as acceptance of what we would now call persistent objection, but in a regional setting.[66]

It may be, however, that a regional body would take a less conservative perspective, and an example of this is the Inter-American Commission on Human Rights (IACHR) on the question of imposition of the death penalty on persons who have committed a crime as a minor. In its ground-breaking decision *Roach and Pinkerton* in 1987 the Commission accepted, on the one hand, that there did not exist a rule of customary international law barring the imposition of the death penalty on minors, and that in any case the United States (persistently) objected to any such rule,[67] while, on the other hand, it appeared to argue that this obstacle and the (persistent) objection of the United States could be overcome if a rule of *jus cogens* existed to the same effect.[68] Coming to a conclusion, it next found that:

> in the member States of the OAS there is recognized a rule of jus cogens which prohibits the State execution of children. This norm is accepted by all States of the Inter-American system, including the United States. The response of the U.S. government to the petition in this case affirms that '[A]ll states, moreover, have juvenile justice systems; none permits its juvenile courts to impose the death penalty'.[69]

Likening 'the imposition of the death penalty on juveniles' to 'the execution of children', the decision is noteworthy for its acceptance of the concept of *jus cogens* and for positing, so it seems, a rule of regional *jus cogens* prohibiting both. As a matter of principle, there seems to be no objection to recognising the possibility that a rule of regional *jus cogens* could emerge.[70] However, the concept of *jus cogens* has developed at the universal level, and one cannot simply assume that it would apply within a regional context. Yet the IACHR did not trace whether (the concept of) *jus cogens* as such was accepted by states generally, nor even for that matter whether American states had done so.[71] Moreover, the concept of persistent objection to an emerging

[65] ibid 277–78. Crawford criticises the ICJ for imposing a stricter standard of proof than it would have imposed if the case had concerned an alleged rule of general international law. His argument is that the ICJ in investigating regional and local custom treated the issue as bilateral, and that mere abstention (refraining from ratifying a treaty containing the rule) could not be considered clear and convincing evidence of persistent objection. Crawford, 'Universalism and Regionalism' 115. While agreeing substantially on the latter point of criticism, the former ignores the fact that the ICJ had first found regional practice to be inconsistent and *opinio juris* to be absent.

[66] See also *Fisheries case* (*United Kingdom v Norway*) (Judgment) [1951] ICJ Rep 116, 131.

[67] *Roach and Pinkerton v United States* (Case 9647), Resolution No 3/87, *Annual Report of the Inter-American Commission on Human Rights 1986–1987*, OEA/SerLN/II71, Doc 9, Rev 1 (22 September 1987), available at www.cidh.org/annualrep/86.87eng/EUU9647.htm, paras 60 and 54.

[68] ibid para 54.

[69] ibid para 56.

[70] Commissioner Dr MG Monroy Cabra in his dissenting opinion on *Roach and Pinkerton*, pointing to the requirement that peremptory norms must be accepted by the international community *as a whole*, claimed that there cannot be any question of regional *jus cogens*, ibid at point 4. See D Shelton, 'Normative Hierarchy in International Law' (2006) 100 *American Journal of International Law* 291, 313–14; and also Vidmar, 'Norm Conflicts and Hierarchy' 21–22, who suggests that the prohibition of the death penalty may constitute regional *jus cogens* and possibly take precedence over an obligation under the Charter.

[71] The Commission referred to authors and cases instead: *Roach and Pinkerton*, IAHCR Case 9647, para 55.

rule of customary international law was accepted without further comment, and the Commission posited that such a rule would nevertheless be binding on a protesting state if the rule had acquired the status of *jus cogens*.[72]

More recently the IACHR has claimed that a rule of customary international law prohibiting the imposition of the death penalty on minors has emerged (arguing that it is 'inconsistent with prevailing standards of decency').[73] It once more accepted the possibility of persistent objection, but unconvincingly suggested that the United States could not be considered a persistent objector.[74] Not surprisingly it now claims that a rule of *jus cogens* to this effect is in existence that binds all states and hence, of course, the United States,[75] and that: 'The norm cannot be validly derogated from, whether by treaty or by the objection of a state, persistent or otherwise'.[76] It is to be noted, however, that the Commission shies away from appealing to American international law, and invokes universal rules rather than regional ones, and once again brings into play *jus cogens* in an attempt to circumvent the persistent objection.

So far the discussion has focused on regional international law binding states within the region concerned, but Alvarez also argued that states outside the region would be bound if the matter affected America.[77] In international law there does not appear to be any matter of principle militating against the possibility of a purely regional rule becoming binding on states outside the region. A similar kind of construction has been suggested with respect to so-called objective regimes, concerned with certain topics or territorial spaces covered by a treaty that purportedly would be opposable to non-parties.[78] However, the process by which any regime would become binding on third states is one of acceptance, recognition or acquiescence, and not by virtue of a (sovereign) decision of the parties or states involved. Indeed, this could hardly be any different considering the sovereignty and equality of states, the requirement of consent to be bound to treaties, and the inability of any state to bind another in the absence of a (treaty) commitment to that effect.

However, the sentiments recorded are not necessarily a thing of the past, when considering the claim of Ecuador when it stated that its 'sovereign' decision to grant Julian Assange—who had sought refuge in the Ecuadorian embassy in London—diplomatic

[72] ibid para 54.

[73] IACHR, *The Death Penalty in the Inter-American Human Rights System: From Restrictions to Abolition*, 31 December 2011, OEA/Ser L/V/II Doc 68, available at www.oas.org/en/iachr/docs/pdf/deathpenalty.pdf, 71 and 75.

[74] ibid 75–76, pointing among others things to federal practice setting the minimum age for imposition of the death penalty at 18 years and ignoring the United States' reservation to the International Covenant on Civil and Political Rights (adopted 16 December 1966, entered into force 23 March 1976) 999 UNTS 171 (ICCPR).

[75] IACHR *The Death Penalty in the Inter-American Human Rights System* 75–76.

[76] ibid 76.

[77] *Asylum* case, Dissenting Opinion Alvarez, 294.

[78] See generally B Simma, 'The Antarctic Treaty as a Treaty Providing for an Objective Regime' (1986) 19 *Cornell International Law Journal* 189–209; M Fitzmaurice, 'Third Parties and the Law of Treaties' (2002) 6 *Max Planck Yearbook of UN Law* 37–127, 44, 66–136. See also ILC, Fragmentation Report 75, para 140, and 123–24, para 240.

asylum should be respected by the United Kingdom.[79] UK Foreign Secretary William Hague struck back that very same day by affirming that:

> We will not allow Mr Assange safe passage out of the UK, nor is there any legal basis for us to do so. The UK does not accept the principle of diplomatic asylum. It is far from a universally accepted principle: the United Kingdom is not a party to any legal instruments which require us to recognise the grant of diplomatic asylum by a foreign embassy in this country. Moreover, it is well established that, even for those countries that do recognise diplomatic asylum, it should not be used for the purposes of escaping the regular processes of the courts.[80]

This situation, of course, does not witness a specific appeal to a regional rule, and the press report cited instead sees Ecuador invoking sovereignty. An appeal to American international law would most likely not benefit Ecuador, as the grant of asylum to Assange is not a matter that concerns Latin America.[81] Assange is an Australian, present in the United Kingdom, facing extradition to Sweden, with the possible prospect of further extradition to the United States. The Ecuadorian decision itself in fact refers far more strongly to universal rules, and suggests a duty for the United Kingdom to cooperate in the protection of human rights based on the UN Charter.[82] Moreover, Ecuador claims that the right to asylum as a human right creates obligations *erga omnes* and belongs to *jus cogens*.[83]

In raising once more the topic of *jus cogens* the question of validity takes a different turn and the question of hierarchy of sources may be raised. First and foremost, the concept of *jus cogens* per se cannot be traced back to the theoretical construct of Kelsen where each norm derives its validity from a higher norm.[84] Though it is claimed at times that *jus cogens* norms are hierarchically higher (superior) to other, ordinary norms, the validity of such other norms does not derive from peremptory norms of international law. Peremptory norms can be a source of invalidity, but they cannot be the source of validity of other norms. Though quite a few attempts are made to establish peremptory norms as superior to others and to present them as norms against which all others can be tested, recently the ICJ rebuffed such efforts by pointing to the substantive nature of the norms of *jus cogens* and by positing that only rules in conflict with the underlying substantive norms, as opposed to conduct

[79] BBC, 'Julian Assange: Ecuador grants Wikileaks founder asylum', 16 August 2012, available at www.bbc.co.uk/news/uk-19281492.

[80] UK, 'Foreign Secretary statement on Ecuadorian's Government decision to offer political asylum to Julian Assange', 16 August 2012, available at www.gov.uk/government/news/foreign-secretary-statement-on-ecuadorian-government-s-decision-to-offer-political-asylum-to-julian-assange.

[81] Alvarez's observations pertaining to asylum only concerned Latin American states. *Asylum* case, Dissenting Opinion Alvarez, 292.

[82] Statement of the Government of the Republic of Ecuador on the asylum request of Julian Assange, News Release No 042, at http://cancilleria.gob.ec/statement-of-the-government-of-the-republic-of-ecuador-on-the-asylum-request-of-julian-assange/?lang=en.

[83] ibid.

[84] Kelsen, *Principles of International Law* at 408–19; H Kelsen, *Reine Rechtslehre*, 2nd edn (Wien, Franz Deuticke, 1960) 196–97.

or rules hindering the enforcement of *jus cogens* norms, would bring into play the legal consequences attached to the concept.[85]

All states accept international law and share a common understanding of its sources.[86] The validity of regional conventional and customary law does not depend specifically on the existence of an overarching legal system. As most international law is conceived of as *jus dispositivum*, regional rules do not (necessarily) challenge the universality of its (primary) rules. However, it may be that the application of regional rules or decisions causes a conflict with the application of other or universal norms. This will be considered next in the light of two situations of (outright) confrontation that have arisen in a regional context.

IV. (NON-)APPLICATION OF INTERNATIONAL LAW IN A REGIONAL CONTEXT

Among others, two conflicts have erupted as a result of a confrontation between regional and (potentially) universal bodies that may be instructive. The first involves the conflict between the African Union and the International Criminal Court over the (lack of) immunities of President al-Bashir of Sudan. The second concerns a conflict between the European Union and the United Nations Security Council over sanctions targeted at specific individuals and their compatibility with fundamental rights protected under EU law. These two situations will be discussed consecutively.

A. The International Criminal Court and the African Union

It may be recalled that the situation of Darfur was referred to the International Criminal Court in 2005 by the UN Security Council, in Resolution 1593,[87] acting under Chapter VII of the UN Charter, pursuant to article 13 of the Statute of the International Criminal Court.[88] On the application of the Prosecutor for an arrest warrant against President al-Bashir, Pre-Trial Chamber I decided to grant the request and issue an arrest warrant, which was circulated to all states parties to the Statute and to members of the Security Council that are not parties.[89] As the arrest warrant was directed at an incumbent head of state of a non-party to the Statute,[90] the Pre-Trial Chamber appeared to consider, in a rather cursory manner, whether President al-Bashir enjoyed immunity. It rather bluntly claimed that: 'the Chamber considers

[85] *Jurisdictional Immunities of the State* (*Germany v Italy: Greece intervening*) (Judgment) 3 February 2012, paras 92–97, available at www.icj-cij.org/docket/files/143/16883.pdf. See also Vidmar, 'Norm Conflicts and Hierarchy' 33–38; and earlier Shelton, 'Normative Hierarchy' 306–09.

[86] *Contra* Prost, *The Concept of Unity* 91–105.

[87] UNSC Res 1593 (31 March 2005) UN Doc S/RES/1593, para 1.

[88] Rome Statute of the International Criminal Court (done at Rome on 17 July 1998, entered into force on 1 July 2002) 2187 UNTS 91.

[89] ICC, Pre-Trial Chamber I, *Decision on the Prosecutor's Application for a Warrant of Arrest against Omar Hassan Ahmad al Bashir*, ICC-02/05-01/09, 4 March 2009, available at www.icc-cpi.int/iccdocs/doc/doc639096.pdf.

[90] Up-to-date information concerning ratification of the Rome Statute is available at https://treaties.un.org/pages/ViewDetails.aspx?src=TREATY&mtdsg_no=XVIII-10&chapter=18&lang=en.

that the current position of Omar Al Bashir as Head of a state which is not a party to the Statute, has no effect on the Court's jurisdiction over the present case.'[91] In coming to this conclusion the Pre-Trial Chamber pointed to article 27(2) of the Statute, stipulating that immunities do not bar the Court's exercise of jurisdiction,[92] without however considering the effect that article 98(1) might have in this respect.

For this reason the decision was quickly and severely criticised in the literature,[93] but more importantly states, including parties to the Rome Statute, failed to act on the arrest warrant when President al-Bashir visited their territory.[94] This eventually led Pre-Trial Chamber I to issue two decisions on the failure of Malawi[95] and Chad[96] to arrest and surrender President al-Bashir, in which it motivated why he did not benefit from immunity under article 98(1) of the Statute. The Chamber determined that Malawi and Chad ought to have consulted with the ICC on the matter of immunities pursuant to articles 86, 87 and 89, that they had failed to cooperate with the ICC by not arresting and surrendering President al-Bashir, and it had its decisions on these issues transmitted to the Security Council and to the Assembly of States Parties of the ICC.[97]

In its observations Malawi invoked its Immunities and Privileges Act to accord immunities to President al-Bashir but the Chamber denied this claim and held, pointing to article 27 of the Vienna Convention on the Law of Treaties, that Malawi could not invoke its internal law to escape from its obligation to cooperate with the ICC.[98] More significant, for the purposes of this contribution, is that both Malawi[99] and Chad[100] invoke(d) the position of the African Union (AU), which is that current heads of states of non-parties to the Statute are entitled to immunity. Rather than investigating the legal effect of the decisions taken by the Assembly of the African Union, the Pre-Trial Chamber continued to argue the substantive issue. It concluded by stating that customary international law contains an exception to the

[91] *Al Bashir Arrest Warrant* decision, 15, para 41.

[92] ibid, para 43.

[93] Generally P Gaeta, 'Does President Al Bashir Enjoy Immunity from Arrest?' (2009) 7 *Journal of International Criminal Justice* 315–32; D Akande, 'The Legal Nature of Security Council Referrals to the ICC and Its Impact on Al Bashir's Immunities' ibid 333–52.

[94] See D Akande, 'Denmark Invites Sudanese President Bashir to Climate Change Conference' in *EJILTalk!* 19 November 2011, available at www.ejiltalk.org/denmark-invites-sudanese-president-bashir-to-climate-change-conference/; D Akande, 'ICC Reports Kenya and Chad to the UN Security Council over Bashir's Visits' in *EJILTalk!* 28 August 2010, available at www.ejiltalk.org/icc-reports-kenya-and-chad-to-the-un-security-council-over-bashirs-visits/; and JD Van der Vyver, 'Prosecuting the President of Sudan: A Dispute between the African Union and the International Criminal Court' (2011) 11 *African Human Rights Law Journal* 683–98, 684–87.

[95] ICC, Pre-Trial Chamber I, *Decision Pursuant to Article 87(7) of the Rome Statute on the Failure of the Republic of Malawi to Comply with the Cooperation Requests Issued by the Court with Respect to the Arrest and Surrender of Omar Hassan Ahmad Al Bashir*, ICC-02/05-01/09, 12 December 2011, available at www.icc-cpi.int/iccdocs/doc/doc1287184.pdf 12–20, paras 22–46.

[96] ICC, Pre-Trial Chamber I, *Decision Pursuant to Article 87(7) of the Rome Statute on the Refusal of the Republic of Chad to Comply with the Cooperation Requests Issued by the Court with Respect to the Arrest and Surrender of Omar Hassan Ahmad Al Bashir* (transl), ICC-02/05-01/09, 13 December 2011, available at www.icc-cpi.int/iccdocs/doc/doc1384955.pdf 6–8, paras 12–14.

[97] ICC, *Malawi* decision, 21; ICC, *Chad* decision, 8.

[98] ICC, *Malawi* decision, 9, para 13; 12, paras 19–21.

[99] ibid 9–10, paras 13–15.

[100] ICC, *Chad* decision, 6–7, paras 12–13.

immunities of a head of state before international courts in the case of international crimes; consequently article 98(1) of the Rome Statute was simply considered to be inapplicable.[101]

The resolutions of the AU Assembly are straightforward in calling upon the Security Council to defer the proceedings against President al-Bashir pursuant to article 16 of the Rome Statute, and in deciding in 2009 that AU Members shall not cooperate in the arrest of President al-Bashir, pursuant to article 98 of the Rome Statute.[102] In 2010, however, the AU Assembly called on Members to 'balance, where applicable, their obligations to the AU with their obligations to the ICC.'[103]

In response to the Chamber's decisions on Malawi and Chad, the AU reiterated its understanding of article 98(1) of the Rome Statute that this provision had been included to safeguard the immunities of officials from non-states parties, out of recognition that the Rome Statute could not remove such immunities.[104] The AU Assembly was also looking at the possibility of requesting an advisory opinion of the ICJ as to the immunities of (senior) state officials (of non-states parties to the Rome Statute) under international law.[105] The Assembly has even gone as far as to refer to article 23(2) of the Constitutive Act of the African Union,[106] which authorises it to impose sanctions on a Member that fails to comply with decisions and policies of the Union.[107] A recent novelty concerns the African Union encouraging African states, which are parties to the Rome Statute, to conclude bilateral agreements with African non-states parties on the immunities of their senior officials under article 98(2) of the Rome Statute.[108]

Clearly then the AU is on a collision course with the ICC and intends to drive its views and convictions home. What is surprising is that the 33 African parties to the

[101] ICC, *Malawi* decision, 20, para 43. For a critical comment, see D Akande, 'ICC Issues Detailed Decision on Bashir's Immunity (... At long Last ...) But Gets the Law Wrong' in *EJILTalk!* 15 December 2011, available at www.ejiltalk.org/icc-issues-detailed-decision-on-bashir%E2%80%99s-immunity-at-long-last-but-gets-the-law-wrong/.

[102] African Union (AU) (Assembly) 'Decision on the Report of the Commission on the Meeting of African States Parties to the Rome Statute of the International Criminal Court' (AU, Sirte, Libya, 1–3 July 2009), Doc Assembly/AU/13(XIII), Assembly/AU/Dec 245(XIII) Rev 1, paras 9–10. The Assembly also decided that AU Members should not comply with the arrest warrant against Colonel Qadhafi. AU (Assembly) 'Decision on the Implementation of the Assembly Decisions on the International Criminal Court' (AU, Malabo, Equatorial Guinea, 30 June–1 July 2011), Doc EX/CL/670(XIX), Assembly/AU/Dec 366(XVII), para 6.

[103] AU (Assembly) 'Decision on the Progress Report of the Commission on the Implementation of Decision Assembly/AU/Dec 270(XV) on the Second Ministerial Meeting on the Rome Statute on the International Criminal Court (ICC) (AU, Kampala, Uganda, 25–27 July 2010), Doc Assembly/AU/10(XV), Assembly/AU/Dec 296(XV), paras 5–6.

[104] For a more elaborate justification of the AU position, see AU (Commission) Press Release N° 002/2012 (9 January 2012), available at www.au.int/en/sites/default/files/PR-%20002-%20ICC%20 English.pdf.

[105] AU (Assembly) 'Decision on the Progress Report of the Commission on the Implementation of Assembly Decisions on the International Criminal Court (ICC)' (Addis Ababa, Ethiopia, 29–30 January 2012), Doc EX.CL/710 (XX), Assembly/AU/Dec 397(XVIII), paras 6, 8 and 10; and AU (Assembly), 'Decision on the Implementation of the Decisions on the International Criminal Court (ICC)' (Addis Ababa, 15–16 July 2012), Doc EX.CL/731 (XXI), Assembly/AU/Dec 419(XIX), para 3.

[106] AU (Assembly) 'Decision on Progress Report, 29–30 January 2012', para 8.

[107] Constitutive Act of the African Union (done at Lomé, Togo, 11 July 2000, entered into force 26 May 2001) 2158 UNTS 33.

[108] AU (Assembly) 'Decision on Implementation of ICC Decisions, 15–16 July 2012', para 7.

Rome Statute went along so easily with decisions of the Assembly,[109] knowing that this would create a conflict of obligations for them from which they cannot extricate themselves, except perhaps by either not receiving President al-Bashir, or by withdrawing from the Rome Statute (article 127).[110] The Assembly decisions, which have been cited, breathe an air of frustration concerning the lack of attention to, and consideration of, African views about the necessity of preserving the peace and leaving open the possibility of political compromise.

Having the UN General Assembly request an advisory opinion of the ICJ on the matter of immunities may seem like an attractive option considering the conservative position taken by the ICJ in the *Arrest Warrant* case.[111] However, it is unlikely to yield the desired result. Setting up the ICJ as arbiter of the legality of decisions of the ICC will probably not be to the liking of the ICJ in view of the express power in the Rome Statute (article 119(1)), which states that disputes in regard to the judicial function of the ICC shall be settled by the decision of the ICC itself.[112] The aforementioned possibility, to refer a dispute on interpretation or application of the Rome Statute to the ICJ, is available only if the dispute arises between two or more states parties to the Statute. In the situation discussed here the dispute relates to the interpretation and application of the Rome Statute by the ICC itself, in other words it is a dispute between (African) states and the ICC.

Although the African states may be right about the interpretation of article 98(1) of the Statute,[113] the only way forward for them would be to work through the procedures of the Rome Statute, which would require them to use the extant (appeals) procedures to their fullest extent. Indeed, one may wonder how the conduct of African states parties to the Rome Statute, in allowing the Assembly of the African Union to impose on them an obligation of non-cooperation with the ICC regarding the arrest of President al-Bashir, can be squared with the primordial maxim of *pacta sunt servanda*. This maxim requires them to perform their obligations under the Rome Statute in good faith.[114]

However, while African states parties may be reproached for not playing their part, the ICC may be admonished, *a fortiori*, for not raising the question of immunities at the appropriate time. Thus the Pre-Trial Chamber did not even mention

[109] See K Mills, '"Bashir is Dividing Us": Africa and the International Criminal Court' (2012) 34 *Human Rights Quarterly* (2012) 404–47, 423–26.

[110] See D Akande, 'Africa and the International Criminal Court', *EJILTalk!* 8 June 2009, available at www.ejiltalk.org/africa-and-the-international-criminal-court/; and D Akande, 'Is Kenya Pushing for a Mass African Withdrawal from the ICC?' in *EJILTalk!* 14 January 2011, available at www.ejiltalk.org/is-kenya-pushing-for-a-mass-african-withdrawal-from-the-icc/. The National Assembly of Kenya has voted to urge the government to withdraw from the ICC: BBC, 5 September 2013, available at www.bbc.com/news/world-africa-23969316. For comment see C Jalloh, 'Kenya Should Reconsider Proposed Withdrawal from the ICC', available at www.ejiltalk.org/kenya-should-reconsider-proposed-withdrawal-from-the-icc/.

[111] *Arrest Warrant of 11 April 2000 (Democratic Republic of the Congo v Belgium)* [2002] ICJ Rep 3, 21–26, paras 51–61.

[112] For a more positive view, see D Akande, 'The African Union's Response to the ICC's Decisions on Bashir's Immunity: Will the ICJ Get Another Immunity Case' in *EJILTalk!* 8 February 2012, available at www.ejiltalk.org/the-african-unions-response-to-the-iccs-decisions-on-bashirs-immunity-will-the-icj-get-another-immunity-case/.

[113] *Contra* Van der Vyver, 'Prosecuting the President of Sudan' 687–93.

[114] Vienna Convention on the Law of Treaties, art 26.

article 98(1) of the Statute in its decision to issue the arrest warrant, and only came up much later with a rather unpersuasive argument.[115] The Appeals Chamber could have tackled the topic in its decision concerning the charge of genocide—admittedly quite a different topic—and it should have raised it in view of the overwhelming need to provide clarity on such a controversial issue.[116] This all the more so because immunities are a legal issue that must be decided, as the ICJ has held, as a preliminary matter and *in limine litis*.[117]

In the end the Pre-Trial Chamber did no more than take up one particular substantive issue underlying the African discontent and failed to address the conflict of obligations that had arisen. That conflict of obligations cannot, unfortunately, be solved, for two interrelated reasons.

First, in the absence of any established (formal) hierarchy between and within the sources of international law and obligation,[118] precedence of one over the other cannot be based on any normative foundation.[119] The fact that one obligation derives from a binding decision authorised by treaty (the obligation to cooperate with the ICC) and another from a rule of customary international law (the obligation to respect immunities) does not determine which of the two should give way; there is no choice possible as to which is *lex superior* and which *lex inferior*, there is no *Stufenbau*.[120] Moreover, that one obligation derives from a decision authorised by a (potentially) universal treaty and another from a decision authorised by a regional treaty does not prejudge the choice either; both are binding upon the states addressed.

Second, there might be no problem if the treaty constitutes a departure from the customary international law rule, but this is precisely what is in dispute between the ICC and the AU. If we take as a starting position that (most) rules of international law are *jus dispositivum*, then immunities for heads of states could be set aside by treaty but then only for heads of states of parties to the treaty. Article 27 of the ICC Statute makes sense for officials of parties, whereas article 98 of the Statute makes sense for officials of non-parties, and dividing them up in this way accords with the law of treaties.[121] The claim of the Pre-Trial Chamber, to the effect that an exception exists under customary international law regarding the immunities of heads of states prosecuted for international crimes before international courts, solves this problem. At the same time, it creates another one in that a large part of article 98(1) of the Statute would be made redundant and without practical effect.

[115] See Akande, 'ICC Issues Detailed Decision on Bashir's Immunity'.

[116] D Akande, 'Should the ICC Appeals Chamber have made a decision on Bashir's Immunity?' in *EJILTalk!* 13 February 2010 available at www.ejiltalk.org/should-the-icc-appeals-chamber-have-a-made-a-decision-on-bashirs-immunity/.

[117] *Difference Relating to Immunity from Legal Process of a Special Rapporteur of the Commission on Human Rights* (Advisory Opinion) [1999] ICJ Rep 62, 88, para 63.

[118] See M Akehurst, 'The Hierarchy of Sources of International Law' (1974–75) 47 *British Year Book of International Law* 273–85, 273–80; A Pellet, 'Article 38' in A Zimmerman, C Tomuschat, K Oellers-Frahm (eds), *The Statute of the International Court of Justice, A Commentary* (2006) 677–792, 773–77; Shelton, 'Normative Hierarchy in International Law' 291–92 and 294–95; and Vidmar, 'Norm Conflicts and Hierarchy' 13.

[119] See Shelton, ibid 293–94; A Tzanakopoulos, 'Collective Security and Human Rights' in De Wet and Vidmar, *Hierarchy in International Law* 42–70, 44–48.

[120] For an excellent discussion of the theoretical problems, see Kammerhofer, *Uncertainty in International Law* 139–94.

[121] Vienna Convention on the Law of Treaties, art 34.

Noticeable in this regard is the claim by the AU Commission that the Pre-Trial Chamber is ignoring the AU Assembly decision not to cooperate with the arrest of President al-Bashir, binding upon AU members, and that it would be wrong to force Malawi and Chad to violate their obligations towards the AU.[122] The rationale of the AU Commission is based on its view of the state of international law at large (the provisions of the Rome Statute, customary international law, and relevant SC decisions) and also its concerns over peace and security in Africa. However, its claim is that an AU decision should be given precedence over one adopted by the ICC, and therefore goes much further than the Assembly, as it asserts:

> The African Union will continue the fight against impunity as required by Article 4 of the Constitutive Act and the relevant Assembly decisions and shall oppose any ill-considered, self-serving decisions of the ICC as well as any pretensions of double standards that become evident from the investigations, prosecutions and decisions by the ICC relating to situations in Africa.[123]

Yet why the African Union's *regional* decisions ought to *legally* prevail over those of the ICC, to which African states have freely subscribed, cannot be ascertained.

B. The Security Council and the European Union

We now move on to another example where compliance with international legal obligations has been upset by a decision of a regional institution: the *Kadi and Al Barakaat* case of 2008.[124] In that case the Court of Justice of the European Community (Grand Chamber) (ECJ) annulled Council Regulation (EC) 881/2002[125] insofar as it concerned Kadi and the Al Barakaat International Foundation. In its reasoning the ECJ found that the freezing of assets of Kadi and the Foundation unjustifiably violated their fundamental rights, in particular the right of defence and to be heard, the right to an effective legal remedy, the principle of effective judicial protection, and the right to property.[126] The freezing measures imposed against Kadi and the Foundation by Council Regulation 881/2002 were the direct result of the implementation of Security Council Resolutions 1267, 1333 and 1390, which contained the obligation for UN Members to impose the measures on persons placed on the Consolidated List by the sanctions committee (the 1267 Committee) should they be found in their territory.[127]

[122] AU (Commission) Press Release N° 002/2012 (9 January 2012).

[123] ibid.

[124] Joined Cases C402/05 P and C415/05 P, *Yassin Abdullah Kadi and Al Barakaat International Foundation v Council of the European Union and Commission of the European Community* [2008] ECR I-06351.

[125] Council Regulation (EC) 881/2002 of 27 May 2002 imposing certain specific restrictive measures directed against certain persons and entities associated with Usama bin Laden, the al-Qaida network and the Taliban, [...] [2002] OJ L139/9. For judgment of the Court of First Instance, see Case T-315/01, *Yassin Abdullah Kadi v Council of the European Union and Commission of the European Communities* [2005] ECR II-03649.

[126] *Kadi and Al Barakaat* case, paras 333–71.

[127] UNSC Res 1267 (15 October 1999) UN Doc S/RES/1267, paras 3 and 4(b); UNSC Res 1333 (19 December 2000), Doc S/RES/1333, para 8; UNSC Res 1390 (28 January 2002), Doc S/RES/1390, paras 2–3. See generally on the 1267 Committee, www.un.org/sc/committees/1267/aq_sanctions_list.shtml.

In this respect it is to be noted that the issue is not purely a conflict for the European Community on the one hand to respect fundamental rights and on the other hand to respect Security Council decisions. Fundamental rights, according to the ECJ, are an integral part of the general principles of Community law, and all acts of that Community can be fully tested as to their lawfulness even when the act concerned implements a SC resolution adopted under Chapter VII of the Charter.[128] However, Security Council resolutions that impose binding obligations are not as such binding on the European Union, since the EU is an international organisation, possesses legal personality[129] separate from its Member States, and can only be bound by a treaty if it has consented thereto.[130] The ECJ therefore did not review the lawfulness of the resolution as such, and it specifically denied that it had the power to do so (even if limited to the question of compatibility with *jus cogens*).[131]

Although the ECJ observed that the European Community must respect international law when exercising its powers (and interpret measures and limit their scope in the light of relevant rules of international law), this cannot be read to amount to an admission that the Community is bound by binding Security Council decisions.[132] In this respect it may be noted that the ECJ ignored the pronouncement made in the annexed declarations to the Lisbon Treaty that:

> the European Union and its Member States will remain bound by the provisions of the Charter of the United Nations and, in particular, by the primary responsibility of the Security Council and of its Members for the maintenance of international peace and security.[133]

Horst Krenzler and Oliver Landwehr quite astutely observe that the ECJ avoided the issue as to whether the EU is bound by the Charter or SC decisions.[134] The situation then is rather different from that of the EU with respect to, for instance the United Nations Convention on the Law of the Sea[135] or the Agreement establishing the World Trade Organization,[136] to which it is a party in its own right.[137]

[128] *Kadi and Al Barakaat* case, paras 283–85 and 326.

[129] Consolidated Version of the Treaty on European Union [2010] OJ C-83/13, art 47.

[130] Vienna Convention on the Law of Treaties, art 34; and Vienna Convention on the Law of Treaties between International Organizations or between International Organizations and States (done at Vienna, 21 March 1986, not yet in force), art 34.

[131] *Kadi and Al Barakaat* case, para 287 (see also para 286).

[132] ibid at para 291. Note however Streinz, who in referring to para 296 raises the question as to how this can be harmonised considering that the Court held that the Community 'is bound by the EC Treaty (now TFEU) itself to take the necessary measures to implement Security Council resolutions?' R Streinz, 'Does the European Court of Justice keep the Balance between Individual and Community Interest in *Kadi*?' in U Fastenrath et al (eds), *From Bilateralism to Community Interest, Essays in Honour of Judge Bruno Simma* (Oxford, Oxford University Press, 2011) 1118–31, 1126.

[133] Declarations Annexed to the Final Act of the Intergovernmental Conference which adopted the Treaty of Lisbon, signed on 13 December 2007, para 13. 'Declaration concerning the common foreign and security policy, third recital' [2010] OJ C-83/335, 343.

[134] HG Krenzler and O Landwehr, '"A New Legal Order of International Law": On the Relationship between Public International Law and European Union Law after *Kadi*' in Fastenrath et al, 1004–23, at 1020–21.

[135] United Nations Convention on the Law of the Sea (concluded at Montego Bay on 10 December 1982, entered into force 16 November 1994) 1833 UNTS 397.

[136] Agreement Establishing the World Trade Organization (done at Marrakech on 15 April 1994, entered into force 1 January 1995) 1867 UNTS 154.

[137] On these two international agreements and their position in EU law, see Krenzler and Landwehr, 'A New Legal Order of International Law' 1011–17.

If indeed the EU were bound, as a legal person, to the Charter and SC decisions, it would be barred from invoking its own, autonomous legal order to justify non-performance of its international obligations. That norm applies analogously to the rules established under both the Vienna Conventions on the Law of Treaties[138] and the customary international law of state responsibility.[139] As for responsibility, the International Law Commission provided in its draft on the Responsibility of International Organizations that the characterisation of an act of an international organisation as internationally wrongful is governed by international law.[140] It is, however, a matter of regret that the Commission declined to introduce specific language into the draft text, similar to that in its draft on state responsibility, which affirms that this characterisation is not affected by a state's internal law. The Commission opined that, since the rules of an international organisation are part of international law, they cannot be sharply differentiated from (other) international law.[141] Yet, this aspect had not prevented it from proposing a provision that was to become article 27(2) of the 1986 Vienna Convention on the Law of Treaties, admittedly with qualifications,[142] stipulating that an international organisation may not invoke the rules of that organisation to justify non-performance of a treaty.

The ECJ seems to treat the matter as one related to the hierarchy of sources within the EU's own legal order, finding that the status of both the Charter and SC decisions as given effect by the Regulation ranked lower than the primary law, but higher than secondary legislation.[143] Hence it was allowed to engage in a full review of the Regulation as to its consistency with 'higher' fundamental rights.[144] Essentially, the ECJ ignored the status of SC decisions under international law and their relationship to EU law more generally by claiming, somewhat disingenuously:

> However, any judgment given by the Community judicature deciding that a Community measure intended to give effect to such a resolution is contrary to a higher rule of law in the Community legal order would not entail any challenge to the primacy of that resolution in international law.[145]

[138] 1969 Vienna Convention on the Law of Treaties, art 27 and 1986 Vienna Convention on the Law of Treaties with and between International Organizations, art 27.

[139] Articles on Responsibility of States for Internationally Wrongful Acts in ILC, 'Report of the International Law Commission on the Work of its 53rd Session' (23 April to 1 June and 2 July to 10 August 2001), UN GAOR, 56th Sess, Supp No 10, p 43, UN Doc A/56/10, annexed to UNGA Res 56/83 (12 December 2001) as corrected by UN Doc A/56/49(Vol I)/Corr4.

[140] Responsibility of International Organizations in ILC, 'Report of the International Law Commission on the Work of its 66th Session' (26 April to 3 June and 4 July to 12 August 2011), UN GAOR, 66th Sess, Supp No 10 (A/66/10) 54–68, art 5.

[141] Commentary on art 5 of the Articles on the Responsibility of International Organizations ibid, 82, paras 3–4.

[142] See Articles on the Law of Treaties between States and International Organizations or between International Organizations, YBILC (1982), Vol II, Pt Two, with respect to art 27 and Commentary at 38, paras 2–4; see also the discussions on arts 27, 30 and 46 at Official Records of the United Nations Conference on the Law of Treaties between States and International Organizations or between International Organizations, held in Vienna, from 18 February to 21 March 1986, A/CONF.129/16, Documents of the Conference (vol I) 115–19, 119–22 and 129–39 respectively.

[143] *Kadi and Al Barakaat* case, paras 305–08; see Krenzler and Landwehr, 'A New Legal Order of International Law' 1020–21.

[144] *Kadi and Al Barakaat* case, paras 281–84 and 316–17.

[145] ibid para 288.

It then proceeded to support this conclusion by arguing that:

> It must however be noted that the Charter of the United Nations does not impose the choice of any particular model for the implementation of resolutions adopted by the Security Council under Chapter VII of the Charter, *since they are to be given effect in accordance with the procedure applicable in that respect in the domestic legal order of each Member of the United Nations*. The Charter of the United Nations leaves the Members of the United Nations a free choice among the various possible models for transposition of those resolutions into their domestic legal order.
>
> It follows from all these considerations that *it is not a consequence of the principles governing the international legal order under the United Nations that any judicial review of the internal lawfulness of the contested regulation in the light of fundamental freedoms is excluded by virtue of the fact that that measure is intended to give effect to a resolution of the Security Council adopted under Chapter VII of the Charter of the United Nations*.[146]

This dualistic approach to the relationship between SC decisions and EU law has not gone unnoticed in the doctrine,[147] yet these observations of the ECJ do misrepresent the amount of freedom left to (monist and dualist) states regarding the implementation or fulfilment of international obligations.[148] That international law does not impose any choice of model of implementation or fulfilment of obligations does not lead to the consequence drawn by the ECJ that this *therefore* allows for the review of implementing measures as to their conformity with constitutional or fundamental rights, or with obligations and rights under other (human rights) treaties. The freedom that international law leaves to states is always subject to the basic premise and condition that an international obligation will indeed be fulfilled. Moreover, it has long been established that a state cannot invoke its internal law, including its constitution, to justify non-performance of its international obligations.[149]

As the EU is an entity that is in a sense closer to a federal state than an international organisation, the rules against invoking its own, internal and constitutional legal order should acquire, if only analogously, full force.[150] Yet, by invoking the fundamental rights of its own legal order and the power to review the Security Council's freezing of assets implemented by Regulation 881/2002, as to its consistency with such rights, the ECJ is invoking precisely the European legal order in order to escape from international obligations. As such it is quite difficult to see how its review of the Regulation that implements the resolution(s) and its finding that it is

[146] ibid paras 298–99 (emphasis added).

[147] See especially Krenzler and Landwehr, 'A New Legal Order of International Law' 1018–21.

[148] In this sense Tzanakopoulos, 'Collective Security and Human Rights' 58–59.

[149] 1969 Vienna Conventions on the Law of Treaties, art 27 and 1986 Vienna Convention on the Law of Treaties with and between International Organizations, art 27; Articles on State Responsibility, arts 3 and 32; Articles on Responsibility of International Organizations, art 31(2); *Treatment of Polish Nationals and Other Persons of Polish Origin or Speech in the Danzig Territory* (Advisory Opinion) PCIJ Rep Series A/B, No 44, 4, 24. See earlier A de Hoogh, 'The Relationship between National Law and International Law in the Report of the Georgia Fact-Finding Mission', *EJILTalk!* 4 January 2010 available at www.ejiltalk.org/the-relationship-between-national-law-and-international-law-in-the-report-of-the-georgia-fact-finding-mission/.

[150] *Contra* Krenzler and Landwehr, 'A New Legal Order of International Law' 1022, who claim that the EU is not a state and that it is problematic to apply concepts to it developed in relation to sovereign entities.

contrary to a higher rule of law would not pose, as the ECJ suggests, 'any challenge to the primacy of that resolution in international law'.[151]

However, much of the foregoing is in fact not pertinent (yet), as the EU cannot be considered bound directly to either the Charter or to SC decisions. Basically the ECJ ignores the real problem, which is that its decision presents the EU member states, all of them UN members that have agreed to accept and carry out SC decisions (article 25 Charter), with a conflict of obligations and one that according to the Charter must be solved in favour of obligations under the Charter (article 103).[152] An actual and immediate conflict of obligations was averted by creatively using the space offered by the Court to remedy some of the violations found.[153] But this did not change the basic facts underlying the situation, as Kadi was still to be found on the Consolidated List of the 1267 Committee after 2008, and no judicial review of the freezing measures was introduced at the UN level.[154]

It therefore comes as no surprise that Kadi once again brought the case before (what is now) the General Court, which in 2010 annulled Commission Regulation 1190/2008,[155] finding that his right of defence, right to effective judicial review and protection, and right to property had been violated.[156] Although the General Court seemed sympathetic to criticisms voiced against the ECJ's judgment, noting also that it was not bound by that prior decision, it declined to act upon such criticisms and held that it would be for the ECJ to provide answers.[157] It rejected in particular a suggested limitation of the full review adopted by the ECJ, since this would amount to no review at all, and this had been ruled upon by the ECJ to be vitiated by an error of law.[158] Although the General Court ruled in his favour, Kadi remained on the Consolidated List of the 1267 Committee and was only delisted by the Security Council on 5 October 2012.[159]

[151] See Streinz, 'Does the European Court of Justice Keep the Balance' 1125–26, who notes that the control exercised by the Court could lead to non-implementation of the resolution.

[152] To similar effect, 1986 Vienna Convention on the Law of Treaties with and between International Organizations, art 30(6).

[153] See Streinz, 'Does the European Court of Justice Keep the Balance' 1127–29; F Stenhammar, 'United Nations Targeted Sanctions, the International Rule of Law and the European Court of Justice's Judgment in *Kadi* and *al-Barakaat*' (2010) 79 *Nordic Journal of International Law* 113–40, 133.

[154] In 2009 the Security Council created the Office of the Ombudsperson to assist the 1267 Committee in assessing requests for de-listing (replacing the function of the Focal Point established by UNSC Resolution 1730 with respect to the Consolidated List); see UNSC Res 1730 (19 December 2006) Doc S/RES/1730, paras 1–2 and Annex; SC Res 1904 (17 December 2009) Doc S/RES/1904, paras 20–32 and Annex 2. Generally L Boisson de Chazournes and P J Kuijpers, 'Mr Kadi and Mrs Prost: Is the UN Ombudsperson Going to Find Herself between a Rock and a Hard Place?' in Rieter and de Waele, above n 52, 71.

[155] Commission Regulation 1190/2008 of 28 November 2008 amending for the 101st time Council Regulation (EC) 881/2002 imposing certain specific restrictive measures directed against certain persons and entities associated with Usama bin Laden, the al-Qaida network and the Taliban [2008] OJ L322/25.

[156] Case T-85/09 *Yassin Abdullah Kadi v Commission* [2010] ECR II-05177, paras 171–95.

[157] ibid paras 112 and 121 (more broadly paras 112–51).

[158] ibid paras 123–26, adding (para 123) that it would be for the ECJ to reverse this 'precedent'.

[159] See SC/10785, 5 October 2012; the Al Barakaat International Foundation was delisted on 22 October 2009, SC/9773, both available at www.un.org/sc/committees/1267/pressreleases.shtml. Consolidated List, updated 19 August 2013, at www.un.org/sc/committees/1267/1267.pdf.

The member states of the EU and the UN may eventually be confronted with a conflict of obligations,[160] and the Court's reluctance to grant precedence to obligations under the Charter and SC decisions, required under article 103 of the Charter,[161] may be seen as no more than an assertion of autonomy of the EU legal order vis-à-vis the UN legal order or international law at large. Crucially, bodies and institutions established by treaty are bound by, and bound to apply, the particular law that created them.[162] They therefore display a strong allegiance to their own legal regime and, in the absence of regulation to the contrary, will deny application of *foreign* law if this cannot be accommodated within, or if it conflicts with, their own primary and/or secondary law. However, in asserting the autonomy of the EU legal order, the ECJ and the General Court ignore such indications as may exist that, in case of conflict of obligations under the Charter and under other treaties, the former should prevail over the latter.

V. CONCLUDING OBSERVATIONS

The concept of regionalism was addressed in the ILC Fragmentation Report, in which it was concluded that very few normative consequences could be drawn from it other than possibly establishing a regional rule of customary international law. Drawing upon Hart's distinction between primary and secondary rules, notwithstanding his reluctance to qualify international law as a (unified) legal system, the unity of international law was found to lie with the common understanding of the political communities of the world as to the nature and necessities of the international legal system and their general agreement on the sources of international law, the rules to determine violations and the permissible responses thereto.

Venturing into the relationship between regional and universal international law, it was found that rules of regional international law do not necessarily depend on the system as a whole for their validity. The integration of regional international law into the international legal system is rather the result of international law's expansion *ratione personae* and geographically. This perspective is, moreover, strengthened by the widely held view that (most) rules of customary and conventional international law are dispositive in character and may be replaced between certain States only, by virtue of their sovereignty, by equally valid rules provided they apply *inter se*. Hence, regional treaties and regional rules of customary international law may come into existence and be applied without being held to violate other rules of international law.

[160] Cuyvers notes that an actual conflict of obligations depends on the question whether a removal from the European list would bar EU Member States from implementing their obligations under the relevant SC decisions directly by placing Kadi on their national lists; A Cuyvers, 'The Kadi II Judgment of the General Court: The ECJ's Predicament and the Consequences for Member States' (2011) 7 *European Constitutional Law Review* 481–510, 505–09.

[161] See Stenhammar, 'United Nations Targeted Sanctions' 125–27 and 137–38, pointing out that this entails precedence for a binding SC decision over Community law.

[162] See Streinz, 'Does the European Court of Justice Keep the Balance' 1118–19 and 1130, who observes that courts and judges must apply the law and constitutions by which they are created.

However, as the *Asylum* case shows, the creation of regional rules of international law is subject to certain limitations provided by international law at large. Regional treaties only bind their parties and do not create obligations or rights for third states (article 34 of the Vienna Convention on the Law of Treaties). The existence of a regional rule of customary international law must be established, in the same manner as universal rules, by reference to state practice and *opinio juris* (article 38(1)(b) Statute ICJ), although persistent objection is considered possible and such rules are not opposable to states outside the region.

In its *Roach and Pinkerton* decision the Inter-American Commission on Human Rights seemed to claim the existence of a regional rule of *jus cogens* that prohibits the death penalty for juvenile offenders in order to overcome the persistent objection of the United States to such a rule. In more recent times, however, the Commission's claim is that a universal rule of customary international law exists, prohibiting the imposition of the death penalty for offences committed by minors, subject to persistent objection, but also that a universal rule of *jus cogens* to this effect exists, which is not subject to persistent objection. In a similar vein one sees Ecuador invoking its sovereign decision to grant diplomatic asylum to Assange and relying on universal rules for the protection of human rights, rather than claiming the existence of a singularly (Latin) American rule that is opposable to the UK.

Two concrete situations have been investigated in which a conflict (may) exist(s) between obligations imposed under international law generally and those established under a regional treaty. With respect to the arrest warrant issued by the ICC against President al-Bashir, the AU has decided that its members, both parties and non-parties to the Rome Statute, shall not cooperate in executing that arrest warrant. As to the targeted sanctions imposed by decisions of the Security Council, the ECJ has held that the EC Regulation implementing them violates fundamental rights protected under EU law. In view of the lack of hierarchy between and within the sources of international law and obligation, a (potential) conflict cannot be solved a priori by granting precedence to one or the other. A complicating factor is that the regional organisations concerned are not directly bound by the decisions of the international body and claim autonomy of decision-making based on their own legal order.

As such, the suggested tension between regionalism and the unity of international law may be re-cast in terms of the lack of hierarchy and the rudimentary relationship between domestic or regional legal orders and the international legal order. The claim by the ILC Study Group on Fragmentation is that there is a strong presumption against normative conflict and that there exists a principle of harmonisation and a principle of systemic integration in the context of treaty interpretation.[163] However, the Study Group also observed that there is a definite limit to harmonisation in cases of *genuine* conflict.[164] The two situations discussed have shown considerable conflict, a lack of (political) will to come to a solution, and further confrontation therefore seems likely.

[163] ILC, Fragmentation Report 25–28, paras 37–43; ILC, Conclusions of Study Group on Fragmentation 408, point 4, and 413–16, points 17–23.

[164] ILC, Fragmentation Report 27, para 42. See also Tzanakopoulos, 'Collective Security and Human Rights' 50–52.

6

Theoretical Premises of 'Regionalism and the Unity of International Law'

DIRK PULKOWSKI*

I. INTRODUCTION

A PRINCIPAL CONCERN of international lawyers in the twentieth century was to ensure that international law would evolve from a selective *jus publicum europaeum* to a universal international legal order. The modern multilateral convention as a paradigm of global lawmaking, open for accession by any state, was no doubt one of the driving forces of the globalisation and universalisation of international law. Bruno Simma has thus called multilateral treaties the 'workhorses of community interest'.[1]

Yet universalisation appears to have given rise to a countervailing trend, as the Conference organisers observe: the development of plurilateral forms of international law at the regional level. The title of the Conference's initial agora, 'Regionalism and the Unity of International Law', subtly implied a threefold premise. First, the empirical proposition that regional lawmaking has resulted in regionalist approaches to international law. Secondly, the jurisprudential proposition that international law should be conceived as a unified international legal order. Thirdly, the proposition that the theoretical foundation of the unity of international law is being affected by regional approaches to international law.

This chapter is intended to probe each of these premises, focusing in particular on theories of unity within the legal order. Based on the argument that ambitious conceptions of legal unity are not suitable for international law, the chapter reaches the tentative conclusion that regional lawmaking (benign or malign as it may be for other reasons) is unlikely to damage the fabric of international law.

* Senior Legal Counsel, Permanent Court of Arbitration, The Hague. The views set out in this chapter are those of the author alone. The discussion of theories regarding the unity of international law is based on Chapter 5 of the book *The Law and Politics of International Regime Conflict* (Oxford, Oxford University Press, 2014).

[1] B Simma, 'From Bilateralism to Community Interest' 250 *Recueil de cours* (The Hague, Hague Academy of International Law and Martinus Nijhoff, 1994) 234, 322.

II. REGIONAL AND REGIONALIST INTERNATIONAL LAW

Today's international legal order is composed of norms of varying scope of application. At one end of the spectrum is general international law, typically of a customary nature, which applies to all states. At the other end of the spectrum is the bilateral treaty, applying only to the signatories of the instrument. In between these extremes are a variety of (typically, treaty-based)[2] norms applying to a more or less significant cross-section of the state community. Such norms range from plurilateral treaties with limited adherence, to quasi-universal multilateral conventions. Thus, there is nothing unusual in the fact that some (if not most) norms of international law apply selectively to some states only—a phenomenon that is also denoted as 'particular' international law.

In essence, regional international law is nothing more than a geographically confined form of particular international law. Examples of regional lawmaking include: in the area of trade law, the evolution of regional trade agreements to complement the more universal regime of the World Trade Organization (WTO); in the area of investment, the evolution of bilateral and plurilateral investment agreements as substitutes for a multilateral investment agreement, which was previously unsuccessfully promoted under the auspices of the Organization for Economic Cooperation and Development (OECD); in the area of international security, the negotiation of regional security or arms control treaties to complement the UN Charter prohibitions on the use of force, the Geneva Conventions, or global arms control treaties; and in the area of human rights, the creation of regional systems of human rights protection that apply in addition to the international covenants.

The fact that there is no shortage of regional lawmaking, however, is not yet a proof of regionalism. As the suffix suggests, regionalist international law conveys a particular expression of affiliation to a region, in deliberate contradistinction to central forms of authority or more universally held values. There is no automatic equation of regional rules with regionalist intentions; and regional rules and global rules are not necessarily in conflict with one another. Some examples include the following.

Regional norms may be enacted precisely to support and strengthen global norms. This appears to be the rationale of the ECOWAS Convention on Small Arms and Light Weapons.[3] Regional lawmaking may also represent a first step toward, or a replacement for, global lawmaking. Bilateral and plurilateral investment treaties, often similar in content, which serve as a permanent 'stand-in' for a multilateral investment treaty would fit under that category.[4]

[2] While regional customary international law is also conceivable, its practical relevance is limited and will therefore not be discussed in detail in this chapter. The International Court of Justice (ICJ) considered that regional customary international law was established in the *Right of Passage over Indian Territory Case (Portugal v India)* (Merits) [1960] ICJ Rep 6, paras 39–40. By contrast, the ICJ did not find proof of the existence of such regional custom in the *Asylum Case (Colombia v Peru)* (Merits) [1950] ICJ Rep 266, para 276.

[3] See D Garcia, 'Arms restraint and regional international law making: the case of the Economic Community of West African States' (2009) 18 *African Security Review* 78.

[4] A number of plurilateral—typically, regional—investment agreements have recently been negotiated, including: the 2012 China-Japan-Korea Trilateral Investment Treaty; the 2009 ASEAN Comprehensive

Moving toward less harmonious relationships, regional (hard or soft) lawmaking processes may represent attempts to reinterpret global norms. Some regional human rights treaties, or the (soft-law) declarations under the auspices Organization of Islamic Cooperation,[5] might be understood in that way.[6]

Finally, regional lawmaking can occur as a deliberate counter-movement against more universal law and express expectations of state conduct or values that diverge from global norms. The inclusion of a 'cultural exception' within the North American Free Trade Area (NAFTA) may be seen as such a counter-movement, spearheaded by Canada, vis-à-vis the more limited exceptions available within the WTO system. Other examples would include certain investment treaties by Latin American states that provide for 'just' compensation in the event of expropriation, as opposed to 'prompt, adequate and effective compensation' as would be the case under general international law.

III. INTERNATIONAL LAW AS A UNIFIED LEGAL ORDER?

While regional lawmaking is not necessarily an expression of regionalism, some international law clearly *is* regionalist, enacted with the intention of contesting universal norms. To what extent does such regionalist law pose a challenge—or threat—to the unity of the international legal order? At the most fundamental level, the question presupposes that international law can meaningfully be conceptualised as a unified system. However, what constitutes the unity of international law (if indeed there is such a thing)?

A. Unity of the Legal Order as a Validity Condition for Norms?

According to one approach, the integration of a rule into a coherent and unified whole is a condition for the *validity* of that rule. Paradigmatically, that approach is present in Hans Kelsen's *Stufenbau* of legal norms, whereby higher-ranking norms specify the validity conditions for lower-ranking norms. The Kelsenian normative pyramid culminates in an (imagined) *Grundnorm,* which constitutes the basic rule of recognition of all other rules of the system. The *Grundnorm* unifies the legal

Investment Agreement; the 2009 ASEAN-Australia-New Zealand Free Trade Agreement; the 2007 Investment Agreement for the COMESA Common Investment Area; the 2006 Bolivarian Alliance for the Peoples of Our America—Peoples' Trade Treaty (ALBA-TCP); and the 2004 Dominican Republic-Central America-United States Free Trade Agreement (DR-CAFTA). Currently, negotiations for a Trans-Pacific Partnership Agreement and negotiations among members of the Union of South American Nations (UNASUR) are ongoing.

[5] See revised Charter of the Organisation of the Islamic Conference (done at Dakar, 14 March 2008), available at www.oic-oci.org/is11/english/Charter-en.pdf.

[6] See AE Mayer, 'Universal versus Islamic Human Rights: A Clash of Cultures or a Clash with a Construct?' (1993/1994) *Michigan Journal of International Law* 307 and A Tadjdini, 'The Organisation of Islamic Cooperation and Regional Challenges to International Law and Security' (2012) 4 *Amsterdam Law Forum* 36.

order into a single system. In Kelsen's earlier writings, the question of validity is thus inseparable from the idea of an orderly hierarchy of legal rules.[7]

From a legal theory perspective, there is a lot to be said both for and against the apparent link between the legal existence (that is, validity) of a norm and its integration into a unified legal order. Ultimately, I would submit that the equation of legal coherence and validity is unconvincing. First, it does not conform to our experience as practising lawyers. The 'law out there' sometimes recognises as valid certain norms that contradict other norms. Joseph Raz made that point clear when he observed that law

> is the result of the rough-and-tumble of politics ... and reflects the vagaries of pragmatic compromises, or changing fortunes of political forces, and the like. Their law, therefore, does not form a coherent body of principle and doctrine. But it makes sense to accept it and regard it as binding.[8]

Secondly, while conflicting rules may be undesirable, they are not inconceivable. The assumption that a higher norm cannot logically endorse both the validity of the legal consequence x and the contrary of that legal consequence, $\neg x$, simply is not correct. A legal rule is valid if it satisfies the criteria or validity conditions specified in the rule of recognition—no more and no less. To illustrate this point, it suffices to imagine a rule of recognition that bestows with legality any prescription that emanates from a specified legislative process. If the legislator chooses to enact two contradictory rules, without repealing one of them, the result may be a dysfunctional legal order; it may have troubling consequences and appear irrational; but it is not an 'illogical' or inconceivable legal order.

For international law, the point is well illustrated by a longstanding debate concerning so-called 'illegal treaties': are there any consequences for the validity of norms if a treaty conflicts with a previously concluded agreement? In the International Law Commission's deliberation concerning the draft articles on the law of treaties, then Special Rapporteur, Sir Hersch Lauterpacht, suggested that a treaty should enjoy no legal validity 'if its performance involves a breach of a treaty obligation previously undertaken'.[9] However, the International Law Commission ultimately declined to follow Lauterpacht's approach. In its draft of what later became the Vienna Convention on the Law of Treaties, the Commission considered that both of two conflicting treaties should be considered equally valid. Non-performance of one of them would trigger the international responsibility of the state.[10] Hence, the view that conflicting rules can be valid within one and the same legal system has prevailed in the doctrine of international law.

Accordingly, no special threat to legal unity can arise from regionalist international law as a result of its refusal to recognise the primacy of universal international

[7] H Kelsen, *Reine Rechtslehre*, 2nd edn (Wien, Franz Deuticke, 1960) 209 et seq; 228.

[8] J Raz, 'The Relevance of Coherence' in J Raz (ed), *Ethics in the Public Domain* (Oxford, Clarendon Press, 1994) 282–83.

[9] Yearbook of the International Law Commission, 1953, vol II, A/CN 4/63; and ibid, 1954, vol II, A/CN 4/87.

[10] See also, WM Reisman and D Pulkowski, 'Nullity' in R Wolfrum (ed), *The Max Planck Encyclopedia of Public International Law* (2008).

law. International law does not require all norms of the system to be seamlessly integrated with each other in order to recognise them as valid.

B. Unity as a Substantive Principle of Law

A second theory that warrants exploration is whether regionalist lawmaking is potentially inconsistent with substantive principles of international law that mandate coherence and unity. While there is no *conceptual necessity* for international law to be a unitary order, unity may be a result of the application of *substantive principles* of law.

In domestic law, it has often fallen to constitutional courts to endorse substantive principles of legal unity of constitutional rank. For example, the German *Bundesverfassungsgericht* relied on the principle that the legal order must be free of contradictions (*Widerspruchsfreiheit der Rechtsordnung*) as a structural principle (*Strukturprinzip*) of constitutional rank:

> The principle of the rule of law requires all lawmaking organs at the federal level and the *Länder* to each coordinate their regulations in such a way that the addressees of the norms are not exposed to inconsistent regulations, which would make the legal order contradictory.[11]

Yet, while the coherence requirement in domestic law can be construed as a positive legal duty based on constitutional guarantees of equal protection or the rule of law, similar foundations for a duty to achieve legal coherence are not available for international law. The 'international constitution', if one wishes to denote certain constitutive rules and processes of the international system by such a term, contains only rudimentary concepts of the rule of law and sovereign equality, which cannot reasonably be interpreted as implying a positive duty to enact and apply international law in a coherent manner. International lawyers will need to content themselves with a weaker foundation of the principle of coherence.

C. Unity as an Epistemological Postulate

A third justification for the unity of the international legal order is to qualify it as a (mere) postulate, which is necessary for epistemological reasons. In short, the argument is that unity and coherence are necessary to uphold the theoretical coherence of the *science* of law (*la jurisprudence* or *die Rechtswissenschaft*); they constitute *epistemological desiderata,* rather than an inherent property of legal norms.

On this view, to engage *lege artis* in their particular 'science', international lawyers must strive to give effect to all valid legal norms. That can be achieved through two

[11] BVerfGE 98, 106 pp 118 et seq. 'Das Rechtsstaatsprinzip verpflichtet alle rechtsetzenden Organe des Bundes und der Länder, die Regelungen jeweils so aufeinander abzustimmen, daß den Normadressaten nicht gegenläufige Regelungen erreichen, die die Rechtsordnung widersprüchlich machen.'

juridical techniques: deduction along normative hierarchies (logical coherence), or the orientation of legal norms towards commonly held values (axiological coherence).

Logical coherence is a weak model for structuring international law: one might say that, by virtue of article 103 UN, the provisions of the United Nations Charter are of a higher hierarchical rank than other international law. Moreover, peremptory norms of international law take precedence over other norms. However, these rudimentary elements of formal hierarchy cannot establish a unified legal order. The bulk of international law—regional or universal—cannot be deductively related either to the Charter or to any peremptory norms.

Hence, the question is whether the normative postulate of legal unity can be based on axiological coherence—an underlying 'value-glue'[12] (as Andreas Paulus put it). Certainly, there are trends towards a constitutionalisation of international law into a community-oriented and value-laden global order. It would seem that many seemingly technical legal rules, whether contained in universal or regional treaties, can be related to one or another globally recognised value. However, the emergence of global values with wide acceptability does not imply any universal agreement as to how to rank or prioritise them. And, in most situations, there is no international institution that could render an authoritative pronouncement as to which value should prevail as the master value in a given situation. Hence, 'the contribution' of global value catalogues 'to conflict seems as significant as their contribution to consensus'.[13]

That conclusion changes only marginally when one focuses, more narrowly, on *jus cogens*. Can the concept serve as a kind of universal systemic value glue for the international legal order? The canon of *jus cogens* rules can certainly be said to embody fundamental value judgments that are shared by all states and other relevant actors within the international order. And to the extent that its content is clear, it seems plausible to require all law-applying actors to take account of peremptory norms when interpreting specific treaty norms (whether they are regional or more universal in character). However, as a practical matter, *jus cogens* is not capable of turning the 'bric-à-brac'[14] of international law into an orderly whole. To most concrete questions arising in day-to-day treaty interpretation, *jus cogens* simply provides no guidance. Depicting *jus cogens* as a quasi-constitutional canon of values, which all other international law would refer back to, means asking for a promise that the concept cannot hold. In Paulus's words, *jus cogens* is more of a substitute to, than the kernel of, 'a truly public, quasi-constitutional order in international affairs'.[15]

[12] A Paulus, 'Commentary to Andreas Fischer-Lescano & Gunther Teubner: The Legitimacy of International Law and the Role of the State' (2004) 25 *Michigan Journal of International Law* (2004) 1047–58, 1050.

[13] FV Kratochwil, 'How Do Norms Matter?' in M Byers (ed), *The Role of Law in International Politics: Essays in International Relations and International Law* (Oxford, Oxford University Press, 2000) 35–68, 62.

[14] J Combacau, 'Le droit international: bric-à-brac ou système?' (1986) 31 *Archives de philosophie du droit* (1986) 85–105.

[15] A Paulus, 'Jus Cogens Between Hegemony and Fragmentation: An Attempt at a Re-appraisal' (2005) 74 *Nordic Journal of International Law* 297–333, 331.

D. Unity Through General International Law

Hence, both common justifications for legal unity—logical coherence and axiological coherence—appear insufficient as theoretical grounding for the unity of the international legal order. In light of these difficulties, some jurists have premised the unity of international law on something rather unique in international law: the universally applicable body of norms that we call 'general international law'. General international law acts, as it were, as a body of background norms that apply automatically to the extent that states have not derogated them, and in which all other—regional or global—treaty regimes are embedded. General international law, thus, attains a 'quasi-constitutional' status.[16] As the Chairman of the International Law Commission put it in his presentation at the Sixth Committee of the General Assembly,

> [w]hen this topic was put on the Commission's agenda, at the turn of the new millennium, it was amidst concerns that unity of international law was under threat, that the 'general' was giving too much way to the 'special'. The results of the work of the study group give us hope and fortitude that this may not be, entirely, the case. General international law remains the thread that holds relations among States together in the international legal system.[17]

General international law arguably provides a more appropriate foundation for the cohesion of the international legal order than formal hierarchies or a shared canon of values of *jus cogens* status. The concept of general international law is proper to the international order, relatively well defined, and frequently invoked in legal practice. However, the reach of the concept is limited. While general international law provides a helpful reference point for the interpretation of special secondary rules of international law, including rules defining the legal consequences of breach, it provides little guidance to the interpretation of the great majority of primary (substantive) rules in particular treaty regimes. Hence, as treaty regimes attain an ever-greater degree of technical specialisation, premising the unity of the legal order on general international law becomes less and less plausible.

IV. REGIONALIST CHALLENGES TO THE UNITY OF INTERNATIONAL LAW

It has become apparent that strong concepts of legal unity are not suitable for international law. International law is not by definition unitary, simply as a result of being law. It is not logically unified by hierarchies of norms. And it is not unified axiologically by constitutive value judgments. This is not to say that international law is mere 'bric-à-brac', to use Jean Combacau's[18] term again. There is at least a core of rules of general international law that apply universally and can serve as a focal point for interpreters who wish to make their interpretation coherent with other norms of the international legal order. That, however, may be a disappointing conclusion for

[16] T Schilling, 'On the Constitutionalization of General International Law', Jean Monnet Working Paper 06/05, available at www.centers.law.nyu.edu/jeanmonnet/archive/papers/05/050601.pdf.

[17] 18th Meeting of the Sixth Committee, UN News, 1 November 2006, GA/L/3308, available at www.un.org/News/Press/docs/2006/gal3308.doc.htm.

[18] Combacau, 'Le droit international: bric-à-brac ou système'.

jurists committed to the unity of the international legal order. It means that coherence among various norms of international law is a regulative ideal that may or may not prevail in particular interpretive efforts. While international law is amenable to unity, and offers various discursive tools to achieve it, there is no guarantee that systemic coherence will necessarily prevail.

With this sceptical conclusion on the first two premises, contained in the title of this part—as regards the amount of lawmaking that is actually regionalist and the degree of unity of the international legal order—there is relatively little to be said in relation to the third premise, namely that there are regionalist challenges to the unity of international law. Clearly, there can, and will, be situations when regional rules and universal rules of international law conflict with one another. As the author of one text book for students of international law put it: '[I]n some instances, situations arise in which obligations assumed under regional or particular international law clash with those adopted under general international law.'[19] However, such regionalist challenges are less frequent than one might think and in any event are unlikely to pose a threat to elements of unity in international law. To return briefly to the theories of legal unity sketched above, one can conclude as follows:

The existence of conflicting regional norms does not call into question the formal *validity* of universal international law. Instead, any breach of one set of norms as a result of compliance with the other set of norms is a matter of state responsibility.

Regional norms of international law do not threaten any *formal hierarchy* of norms within the international order. As explained above, international law cannot convincingly be regarded as logically unified, by virtue of hierarchical relationships between norms.

Regional international law does not threaten any *axiological unity* within the international order. Universal international law itself is internally pluralistic. While many values have received recognition in international treaties, these values cannot transform international law into a unified whole. Regional international law may add to the value pluralism within the international legal order but does not thereby qualitatively change international law into something other than it already is.

Finally, regional international law does not jeopardise legal unity by potentially setting out prescriptions that differ from *general international law*. As noted above, it is true that general international law is an important unifying element within the international legal order. Yet its diminishing practical importance is not related to regionalism, but to a desire to cooperate in the context of increasingly detailed issue-specific treaty regimes, which can be regional or global in scale.

V. CONCLUSION AND PROSPECTS FOR REGIONALISM AND THE UNITY OF INTERNATIONAL LAW

What follows from this analysis is the conclusion that regionalism does not affect legal unity in ways that are qualitatively different from other phenomena of modern

[19] A Abass, *Complete International Law: text, cases, materials* (Oxford, Oxford University Press, 2011) 10.

international lawmaking. Regional law is a sub-variant of particular international law, and as such is neither more nor less prone to creating disorder in the international system than other forms of particularism.

This is not to suggest that it would not be interesting to study regionalism, and its relationship with universal international law, in detail. The most rewarding analysis of this sort is likely to be specific and contextual (rather than theoretical). In some instances, regionalist lawmaking may reveal itself as an early stage of issue-specific differentiation of the universal legal order, starting within a regional coalition of like-minded actors. Regionalism may be a strategy for 'nurturing' special norms within a regional protected space, with the goal of eventually implanting them in the global system. In other instances, regionalism may be intended to destabilise existing norms of more universal reach. Again, in other instances, regionalism may appear as an attempt to shield a geographical community from global lawmaking processes.

Regionalism is unlikely to damage the fabric of international law. However, this reassuring conclusion merely sets the basis for an examination of what regionalist law does to universal law and, conversely, how universal norms impact regional lawmaking and law application.

7

Commentaire sur de Hoogh et Pulkowski

MATHIAS FORTEAU*

COMME LES CONTRIBUTIONS à forte ambition conceptuelle de MM. De Hoogh et Pulkowski l'ont montré, il est difficile de penser le régionalisme dans sa relation au droit international sans entrer dans des débats ontologiques relatifs à la nature même du droit international. Dans ces circonstances, le rôle du discutant me paraît devoir se limiter à formuler quelques interrogations et quelques pistes de réflexion aux fins d'orienter un débat dont il serait parfaitement vain de prétendre épuiser toute la richesse et la complexité.

Cinq commentaires paraissent de ce point de vue pouvoir être utilement faits.

I

En premier lieu, on peut se demander dans quelle mesure l'intitulé retenu par les organisateurs du colloque—que nous remercions vivement de cette belle réussite—n'est pas un peu trop orienté, ou, pour le formuler différemment, ne souffre pas d'unijambisme. Jorge Cardona Llorens a évoqué dans son discours introductif au colloque la « nécessaire unité du droit international ». Bien que, personnellement, j'adhère au credo universaliste, je me demande tout de même s'il n'y a pas là un postulat qui aurait mérité de faire lui-même l'objet d'un débat. Chacun conçoit, ne serait-ce qu'intuitivement, qu'il est des situations dans lesquelles le régionalisme menace le droit international. Mais l'inverse n'est-il pas vrai aussi? N'y a-t-il pas des cas dans lesquels c'est le droit international qui menace ce que l'on pourrait appeler, sinon l'unité, du moins l'intégrité du droit régional?

C'est ce qui semble s'être dessiné, par exemple, tout dernièrement dans le raisonnement de la Cour européenne des droits de l'homme dans l'affaire *Nada c Suisse* qui posait de nouveau la question des rapports entre résolutions du Conseil de sécurité et Convention européenne des droits de l'homme. Dans l'affaire *Al-Jedda* tranchée par la Cour une année plus tôt, la Cour avait indiqué que « lorsque doit être interprétée une résolution du Conseil de sécurité, il faut présumer que celui-ci n'entend

* Professeur à l'Université Paris Ouest, Nanterre La Défense; Membre de la Commission du droit international des Nations Unies. Le style oral de la communication a été volontairement conservé.

pas imposer aux Etats membres une quelconque obligation qui contreviendrait aux principes fondamentaux en matière de sauvegarde des droits de l'homme. »[1] Dans l'affaire *Nada* en revanche, la Cour observe qu'en l'espèce,

> contrairement à ce qui était le cas dans l'affaire *Al-Jedda* précitée ... la résolution 1390 (2002) demande expressément aux Etats d'interdire l'entrée et le transit sur leur territoire des personnes figurant sur la liste des Nations Unies. Il en découle que la présomption est renversée en l'espèce, eu égard aux termes clairs et explicites, imposant une obligation d'introduire des mesures susceptibles de violer les droits de l'homme, qui ont été employés dans le libellé de cette résolution.[2]

En termes à peine diplomatiques, la Cour reproche au Conseil de sécurité d'imposer aux membres des Nations Unies de s'écarter de leurs obligations, au premier chef régionales, en matière de droits de l'homme. C'est là un exemple—que l'on pourrait multiplier—où le droit international à vocation universelle porte atteinte au droit régional.

II

En second lieu, et toujours pour interpeller le sujet, il est légitime de se demander s'il existe véritablement des « régions » susceptibles, par leur existence, de faire naître des droits « régionaux ». Pour ne prendre que l'exemple européen, il est douteux que, *d'un point de vue juridique*, il soit possible d'isoler une région « Europe ». L'Europe du Conseil de l'Europe n'est pas celle de l'Union européenne.[3] L'Europe du Conseil de l'Europe ou de l'Union européenne n'est pas davantage celle *des* groupes régionaux européens au sens qu'en retiennent les Nations Unies.[4] Au sein même d'ailleurs du système des Nations Unies, les groupes régionaux voient leurs contours se différencier selon la nature particulière des buts de l'institution spécialisée concernée.[5] Au surplus, ces différents groupes régionaux sont fortement concurrencés par des groupes *politiques* unissant plusieurs Etats autours d'intérêts communs qui transcendent leur proximité géographique (que l'on songe, par exemple, au Groupe des 77, aux pays exportateurs de pétrole, aux BRIC, ou encore aux Etats sans littoral ou aux Etats côtiers). Il conviendrait de mesurer quel est le poids respectif aujourd'hui

[1] CEDH (Grande Chambre), *Al-Jedda c Royaume-Uni*, 7 juillet 2011, n° 27021/08 par 102.

[2] CEDH (Grande Chambre), *Nada c. Suisse*, 12 septembre 2012, n° 10593/08 par 172.

[3] Imagine-t-on que la Russie, membre du Conseil de l'Europe, rejoigne un jour l'Union européenne? Le cas de la Turquie est, quant à lui, plus ambigu, compte tenu de l'incertitude qui persiste quant à sa vocation à rejoindre l'UE, certains Etats membres paraissant s'y opposer par principe au prétexte de considérations faussement objectives (la Turquie ne serait pas géographiquement européenne, ce qui est discutable puisque, par exemple, elle est membre du Conseil de l'Europe dont le Statut prévoit en son préambule et en son article 3 que seuls des Etats « européens » peuvent en être ou en devenir membres).

[4] Il existe en effet au sein des Nations Unies un groupe d'Europe occidentale et un groupe d'Europe orientale. Le second inclut notamment la Russie. Le premier inclut quant à lui des Etats non européens comme l'Australie ou le Canada. Les sièges à attribuer au sein des organes des Nations Unies sont répartis par groupes régionaux.

[5] VM Forteau, « International Organizations or Institutions, Regional Groups », *Max Planck Encyclopedia of Public International Law* (accessible en ligne à l'adresse www.mpepil.com ou chez Oxford University Press, 2012) par 13.

de ces groupes politiques, d'une part, et des groupes régionaux, d'autre part, dans les grandes négociations internationales. Il n'est pas garanti que le « régionalisme » sorte en tête, à la seule exception, sans doute, des organisations d'intégration comme l'Union européenne dont, en principe, les positions en matière de politique étrangère lient les Etats membres.[6]

III

En admettant qu'il existe un phénomène régional dans le monde contemporain, ce que nous ne remettons finalement pas en cause au bénéfice des nuances qui précèdent, car le fait est incontestable,[7] il importe toutefois d'en distinguer deux grandes formes.

Certaines formes de régionalisme peuvent être qualifiées de « protectionnistes », de « nationalistes », ou de « défensives ». Derrière ces qualificatifs bien imprécis, il s'agit de viser les approches régionales qui entendent se soustraire aux règles universelles. Cette forme de régionalisme, jugée menaçante pour l'ordre juridique international, s'est longtemps manifestée dans le champ de la sécurité collective[8] et plus volontiers aujourd'hui dans le champ des droits de l'homme sous l'appellation du « relativisme ».[9]

Mais il faut prendre conscience qu'il existe aussi des régionalismes à caractère universaliste, tout contradictoire que puisse paraître cette formule. Le « droit international américain » apparu à la fin du 19ème et au début du 20ème siècle, comme, plus tard, le « droit international africain » ou le « droit international asiatique » ont d'abord et avant tout constitué des tentatives de s'affranchir de l'impérialisme européen. Leur conceptualisation ne visait pas à se distancier de la société internationale mais, à l'inverse, à revendiquer l'égale souveraineté des différents membres de celle-ci de manière à pouvoir y participer pleinement, sans craindre l'interventionnisme européen.[10] Aujourd'hui, cette prétention universaliste prend d'autres formes. Lorsque les juges européens revendiquent par exemple la prééminence des droits fondamentaux face aux abus qu'ils estiment être commis au travers des sanctions imposées par le Conseil de sécurité, ce qu'ils défendent en définitive, ce ne sont pas les seules

[6] V l'article 34 TUE, avec l'exception du paragraphe 2 qui réserve « les responsabilités qui ... incombent [aux Etats membres qui sont par ailleurs membres du Conseil de sécurité] en vertu des dispositions de la Charte des Nations Unies ».

[7] Ne serait-ce qu'au plan institutionnel : il existe bien des organisations ou des juridictions régionales que l'on peut aisément identifier comme telles (l'UA n'est pas l'UE, et l'une et l'autre relèvent d'un genre différent de l'ONU ; le même raisonnement peut être tenu pour les cours régionales des droits de l'homme par exemple, dans leurs relations aux juridictions universelles).

[8] Sur la problématique des « accords régionaux » dans le domaine du maintien de la paix et de la sécurité internationales et la méfiance manifestée à leur égard par les rédacteurs de la Charte des Nations Unies, v. en particulier les commentaires des articles 52 et 53 de la Charte par E Kodjo, H Ghérari et R Kolb *in* J-P Cot, A Pellet, M Forteau (éd), *La Charte des Nations Unies. Commentaire article par article*, vol II (Paris, Economica, 2005) 1367–1437.

[9] V par exemple à cet égard les contributions de P Tavernier, Ph Weckel, A Rinaldi et A-L Vaurs-Chaumette *in* SFDI, *Droit international et diversité des cultures juridiques/International Law and Diversity of Legal Cultures* (Paris, Pedone, 2008) 413–41.

[10] VM Forteau, « Regional International Law », *Max Planck Encyclopedia of Public International Law*, *op cit*, pars 2–5.

valeurs européennes mais des valeurs qu'ils estiment universelles—même si, pour ce faire, ils sollicitent sur le plan *formel* un raisonnement régionaliste.[11]

Dans ces circonstances, la portée de certaines revendications régionalistes n'est pas facile à apprécier. Traduisent-elles une volonté de repli ou au contraire le désir de contribuer, à leur niveau, à l'affermissement du droit universel? On peut s'interroger par exemple sur l'intention des Etats membres de l'Union africaine lorsqu'ils ont créé la Commission de l'Union africaine pour le droit international en 2009. L'article 4 du Statut de cette nouvelle commission lui assigne en particulier l'objectif d'

> [e]ntreprendre des activités relatives à la codification et au développement progressif du droit international sur le Continent africain, avec un accent particulier sur les lois de l'Union telles que contenues dans les Traités de l'Union, dans les décisions des organes délibérants de l'Union et dans le droit coutumier international africain émergeant de la pratique des Etats membres.[12]

Doit-on comprendre qu'il lui incombe de codifier et de développer progressivement le droit international africain, pour tenir compte des particularités de ce dernier,[13] ou bien de codifier et développer progressivement le droit international au niveau africain? La consultation des thèmes inscrits à l'ordre du jour de la Commission de même que l'intervention récente des représentants de cette nouvelle Commission devant la Commission du droit international des Nations Unies et le débat qui s'en est suivi n'ont pas véritablement permis de lever cette ambiguïté.[14]

IV

Ce dernier débat exige de déterminer dans quelle mesure l'existence, éventuelle, d'*approches* régionales du droit international se traduit effectivement par l'émergence d'authentiques *droits régionaux*. Sur ce dernier point, je suis en plein accord avec MM. de Hoogh et Pulkowski qui ont, l'un et l'autre, souligné à juste titre la grande banalité du « droit régional ». Du point de vue de la *technique juridique* en effet, le droit international contemporain ne réserve aucun traitement à part aux normes

[11] Dans l'affaire *Kadi*, la CJUE prétend se livrer à un contrôle exclusivement intra-européen (la conformité d'un acte de l'UE aux droits fondamentaux européens). Mais substantiellement, le droit fondamental en cause est de nature autant européenne qu'universelle.

[12] UA, Conseil exécutif, Quatorzième session ordinaire, janvier 2009, EX.CL/478 (XIV) a. (l'adresse du site Internet de la Commission est la suivante : http://au.int/SP/AUCIL/).

[13] Particularité en partie assumée par les rédacteurs du Statut de la Cour africaine de Justice et des droits de l'homme dont l'article 31, consacré au droit applicable, vise notamment les « principes généraux de droit reconnus universellement ou par les Etats africains » (texte et commentaire in T Barsac, *La Cour africaine de Justice et des droits de l'homme* (Paris, Cedin, Pedone, 2012) 113 et 94).

[14] V ONU, CDI, A/CN.4/SR 3146, résumé de la séance du 17 juillet 2012, pp 3 et seq (accessible sur http://www.un.org/law/ilc/). V. par exemple p 3 : l'objectif de la Commission africaine est « the codification and progressive development of international law from the African perspective ». Parmi les thèmes inscrits à son ordre du jour, certains sont propres au continent africain, d'autres sont de nature universelle (droit des immunités ou relations avec la CPI par exemple). Lors du débat au sein de la CDI, certains intervenants ont souligné la nécessité que la Commission africaine développe la « lecture africaine » du droit international, d'autres ont considéré que la tâche de cette commission était davantage d'aider les pays africains à harmoniser leurs positions dans les enceintes universelles ou à recueillir leurs pratiques nationales du droit international.

« régionales ». Celles-ci suivent le même sort que toute règle *spéciale*, qu'il s'agisse de sa formation, de son respect ou de sa sanction, ce qui m'avait conduit à défendre ailleurs l'idée que le concept de droit régional s'est purement et simplement évanoui depuis son apparition il y a plus d'un siècle en se dissolvant dans la catégorie plus large, *et la seule qui soit opératoire d'un point de vue juridique*, de la *lex specialis.*[15] Le constat vaut d'ailleurs autant pour les règles primaires que pour les règles secondaires puisque la *lex specialis* peut également se déployer par exemple en droit des traités (la convention de Vienne de 1969 n'est d'application que supplétive) ou en droit de la responsabilité.[16] Le volontarisme est passé par là. Ce dernier a en un sens permis le régionalisme (en permettant aux Etats non-européens de s'affranchir de l'impérialisme européen en adoptant les règles qu'ils *souhaitaient* librement s'imposer), mais pour mieux le faire disparaître (rien ne distingue une norme bilatérale d'une norme régionale à partir du moment où l'une comme l'autre sont voulues).

Dire cela ne revient nullement à nier l'existence de certains phénomènes indiscutables, qui sont couramment rattachés au régionalisme. Lesdits particularismes juridiques peuvent tout à fait s'expliquer néanmoins par d'autres raisons que le régionalisme. J'en entrevois deux en particulier.

D'une part, il faut tenir compte de l'avènement d'organisations internationales *d'intégration* ou *supranationales*, à l'instar de l'Union européenne. Bien sûr, les affinités régionales facilitent la mise en place de telles organisations, mais leurs particularités juridiques, les seules qui nous intéressent, trouvent leur explication non pas dans la proximité régionale, mais dans la mécanique même de l'intégration. Il est douteux d'affirmer par exemple que la désormais célèbre affaire *Kadi* aurait vu la CJUE défendre une approche régionale du droit international. Dans cette affaire, des droits fondamentaux *autant régionaux qu'universels* étaient mis en danger par une réglementation *autant régionale qu'internationale.*[17] Ce qui explique la position de la Cour tient uniquement à sa volonté de ne pas contourner l'efficacité des voies de recours qui caractérisent une organisation d'intégration. Le régionalisme, me semble-t-il, n'y prend aucune part.

D'autre part, il importe d'intégrer comme paramètre la fragmentation juridictionnelle de l'ordre juridique international. La difficulté que pose aujourd'hui le régionalisme n'est pas tant d'ordre substantiel (au sens où des *conceptions* divergentes du droit international coexisteraient et s'affronteraient sur la scène internationale). Le problème vient du fait que les Etats ont confié à des juridictions *différentes*, et notamment régionales, la mission de contrôler le respect d'obligations qui, bien souvent, sont de nature internationale et pas seulement régionale. Que la CJUE ait reçu compétence pour contrôler le respect des libertés de circulation dans le marché intérieur européen ne suscite pas la moindre difficulté, car ces règles sont propres à l'UE.

[15] VM Forteau, « Regional International Law », *Max Planck Encyclopedia of Public International Law,* op cit, pars 11 et seq.

[16] V l'article 55 des Articles de 2001 de la CDI sur la responsabilité de l'Etat pour fait internationalement illicite.

[17] Il n'est pas inutile de rappeler au demeurant que la Déclaration n° 13 annexée au traité de Lisbonne dispose que « la Conférence souligne que *l'Union européenne* et ses Etats membres *demeureront* liés par les dispositions de la Charte des Nations Unies ».

Qu'en revanche la Cour européenne des droits de l'homme,[18] la Cour interaméricaine des droits de l'homme et la Cour internationale de Justice, pour ne citer qu'elles, puissent connaître de réclamations relatives à des droits de même nature, quand bien même ceux-ci seraient inscrits dans des instruments conventionnels différents, introduit un risque inévitable de division jurisprudentielle dont la source, de nouveau, n'est pas en tant que telle le régionalisme, mais le fait même de la dispersion juridictionnelle ; c'est comme une loi de la nature en effet que plus les juridictions sont nombreuses, plus le risque de désaccord entre elles augmente. Le phénomène se constate dans tous les ordres internes et lorsqu'il se retrouve sur la scène internationale, il n'est nul besoin de convoquer le régionalisme pour l'expliquer.

V

Il reste enfin à souligner que si les avantages de ce qu'on appelle le « régionalisme » ne sont pas à négliger (laboratoire utile, forme de subsidiarité qui facilite la gestion des problèmes internationaux), il n'est pas certain que ceux-ci fonctionnent de manière réciproque. La tendance aujourd'hui est à saluer les « interactions normatives »[19] entre le niveau universel et le niveau régional. Il est heureux, par exemple, que la Cour internationale de Justice s'appuie désormais sur la jurisprudence des cours régionales, comme elle l'a fait dans l'affaire *Diallo* en 2010.[20] En irriguant le droit international, le droit « régional » participe à son affermissement. Mais la question que l'on est en droit de se poser est de savoir, en retour, si le droit international irrigue lui aussi le droit régional. L'observation de la pratique pourra laisser dubitatif à cet égard, et la raison en est à trouver je pense avant tout dans des facteurs sociologiques—de sociologie juridique pour être plus précis. En Europe en tout cas, il semble que le « profil » des praticiens du droit « régional » soit de moins en moins internationaliste et de plus en plus « interniste » ou « régionaliste ». Au fur et à mesure que les organisations d'intégration développent leurs compétences et que le droit dérivé prend de l'ampleur et envahit les ordres internes, les praticiens de la matière doivent en être des spécialistes, ce qui les éloigne nécessairement des rives internationalistes et ce qui conduit par ricochet à une prise en compte souvent insuffisante du droit international dans le droit de l'intégration. Il conviendrait d'y réfléchir dans l'organisation de nos cursus dans les facultés de droit et dans la manière dont nous enseignons le droit international. C'est une préoccupation sur laquelle, compte tenu de son objet social, la société européenne de droit international pourrait peut-être à l'avenir estimer opportun de se pencher.

[18] Rappelons qu'initialement les rédacteurs de la CEDH avaient envisagé d'en confier le respect à la Cour internationale de Justice. V.E Decaux, « Article 62 », *in* LE Pettiti et al (dir), *La Convention européenne des droits de l'homme. Commentaire article par article* (Paris, Economica, 1995) 909–11. V également le Pacte de Bogota de 1948 qui renvoie à la CIJ pour les différends entre Etats américains.

[19] V en particulier dernièrement L Burgorgue-Larsen et autres (dir), *Les interactions normatives. Droit de l'Union européenne et droit international* (Paris, Pedone, 2012) 380 p.

[20] CIJ, *Ahmadou Sadio Diallo (Guinée c Congo)*, arrêt du 30 novembre 2010, www.icj-cij.org, pars 67–68.

8

Regional Challenges to the Law of State Immunity

PHILIPPA WEBB*

I. INTRODUCTION

STATE IMMUNITY IS an area of the law where a unified, universal approach is critical to the fulfilment of its goals. Those goals are well-summarised by the 2009 Naples Resolution of the Institut de droit international, according to which immunities are:

> conferred to ensure an orderly allocation and exercise of jurisdiction in accordance with international law in proceedings concerning states, to respect the sovereign equality of States and to permit the effective performance of the functions of persons who act on behalf of States.[1]

Each of these goals requires a common understanding of the scope of state immunity. Without such an understanding, we could be faced with competing claims to jurisdiction, inter-state disputes over the limits of sovereignty, and the disruption of international relations.

There is also a normative element to be taken into account. It is not enough for the law on state immunity to be universal; it must also develop in a way that balances respect for sovereignty with commercial accountability and the desire to end impunity.

As yet there is no universal conception of the law of state immunity. In this chapter I rely primarily on judicial decisions as the 'unit of analysis', but also consider state practice as reflected in treaty negotiations and ratifications and national legislation. There is probably much practice that is hidden from view in the form of diplomatic exchanges or internal government decisions on, for example, waiver of immunity. What is obvious is that codification efforts through the two main treaties have not

* Reader in Public International Law, The Dickson Poon School of Law, King's College London. I am grateful to Amal Clooney and Ben Batros, as well as the participants at the ESIL Conference, for comments on earlier drafts. I also thank Lady Hazel Fox QC, from whom I have learned so much about this field of law.

[1] Institut de Droit International, 3ème Commission, Session de Naples, 'Resolution on the Immunity from Jurisdiction of the State and of Persons who Act on Behalf of the State in case of International Crimes', Rapporteur: Lady Fox, ('Naples Resolution'), art II(1), vol 73 *Annuaire de l'Institut de droit international [AIDI]* (Paris, Editions A Pedone, 2009) 228.

achieved widespread ratification. Further, there are indications that a trend towards greater unity during the past decade has slowed down.

This chapter will illustrate the problem of fragmentation between regions and even within a region with respect to two aspects of the law of state immunity. First, there are different regional approaches to the fundamental question of whether the doctrine of state immunity is absolute or restrictive. Second, even within regions where the restrictive doctrine is accepted, there is uncertainty as to the exceptions to state immunity, in particular, whether there is a potential exception for grave violations of human rights. I will then consider potential solutions to these regional challenges through international lawmaking mechanisms. I conclude that unity can only be achieved through customary international law. Although the existence of a 'regional custom' is possible, a universal custom is required in order to achieve the goals of the law of state immunity.

II. ABSOLUTE OR RESTRICTIVE IMMUNITY: REGIONAL DIVISIONS[2]

In examining the attitude of states to the absolute or restrictive doctrines of state immunity, it is striking that the divisions are not between civil and common law countries or between developed and developing states. Instead, they are largely along regional lines.[3]

In around 2005, it appeared that adherence to the restrictive doctrine of state immunity would become almost universal. The restrictive doctrine was clearly codified in a UN Convention on the Jurisdictional Immunities of States and their Property (UNCSI),[4] which had been negotiated with the participation of states from every region. A variety of states had signed up to the Convention, including China—the state most closely associated with the absolute doctrine of state immunity. However, as of 2015, the UNCSI had not entered into force and it was becoming viewed as a 'European' legal instrument. Meanwhile, the absolute doctrine has received reinforcement in recent court decisions, including in Hong Kong in the *FG Hemisphere* case.

As states began to engage in activities not wholly reserved to the state in the late nineteenth century, such as commercial transactions, there was a movement, originating in Europe, towards the contemporary doctrine of restrictive immunity. This doctrine drew the distinction between *acta jure imperii* (acts of governmental authority to which immunity still attached) and *acta jure gestionis*

[2] This section refers to immunity from adjudication. Immunity from enforcement is generally subject to fewer exceptions, although the restrictive doctrine also pertains to this type of immunity in many national jurisdictions.

[3] If states have not enacted legislation on immunity and have had no or few cases before their national courts, their position has to be ascertained through government statements, such as the response to surveys by the UN in 1982, the International Law Commission in 1988, and the Council of Europe in 2002; see H Fox QC and P Webb, *The Law of State Immunity*, 3rd edn (Oxford, Oxford University Press, 2013) 148–50.

[4] UN Convention on the Jurisdictional Immunities of States and their Property (UNCSI) adopted by the UNGA Res 59/38 (LIX) (2 December 2004).

(commercial or private acts in respect of which there was no longer immunity).[5] As Lord Wilberforce observed in *I Congreso*, given the willingness of states to enter into commercial or other private law transactions with individuals, '[i]t is necessary in the interests of justice to individuals having such transactions with a state to allow them to bring such transactions before the courts'.[6]

Italy and Belgium were the first states to draw a distinction between *acta jure imperii* and *acta jure gestionis,* at the turn of the twentieth century.[7] Around the same time, the mixed courts of Egypt, heavily influenced by French and English law, also drew a distinction between the public and private acts of government.[8] The restrictive doctrine slowly spread throughout Europe. The situation as of 1963 was summarised by the West German Federal Constitutional Court in the *Empire of Iran* case:

> The trend in recent decades has led to a situation in which one can now no longer point to a long-standing custom observed by the overwhelming majority of states, in conscious fulfillment of a legal obligation, whereby foreign states are immune from domestic jurisdiction even in respect of actions relating to their non-sovereign activities.[9]

In 1969 the French Cour de Cassation adopted the restrictive doctrine.[10] Spain did not adopt the restrictive doctrine until the 1990s,[11] but it has since strongly supported the doctrine and ratified the UNCSI on 21 September 2011. In the 1970s, the UK Court of Appeal endorsed the doctrine and it was codified in the State Immunity Act of 1978.[12] The UK Act in turn served as a model for many Commonwealth states.[13] The European influence thus spread to certain states in Asia, Africa and Oceania. In Africa, courts in Botswana, Kenya, Nigeria, and Zimbabwe have accepted application of the restrictive doctrine.[14]

The US has broadly followed the timeline of European developments, with the Tate Letter of 1952[15] making the restrictive doctrine the official policy of the State Department and the codification of the rule in the Foreign Sovereign Immunities Act of 1976.[16] Canada passed its State Immunity Act in 1982.[17] Europe and North America thus overwhelmingly adhere to the restrictive doctrine.

[5] *Guttieres v Elmilik* (1886), 1886-I *Foro italiano*, 913 (Court of Cassation in Florence).

[6] *I Congreso del Partido* [1983] 1 AC 244, 262.

[7] *Guttieres v Elmilik*, above n 5; *SA des Chemins de Fer Liégeois-Luxembourgeois v l'État Néerlandais*, Pasicrisie belge 1903, I 294.

[8] For a brief overview of a decision by the Egyptian Mixed Court of Appeal, 27 December 1894, see Fox and Webb, *The Law of State Immunity* 153–54; see also MSW Hoyle, 'The Mixed Courts of Egypt 1886–1895' (1986) 1 *Arab Law Quarterly* 562.

[9] *Empire of Iran*, German Federal Const Ct, 30 April 1963, BvG vol 16, 27, 45 ILR 57, noted in Fox and Webb, *The Law of State Immunity* 157.

[10] *Administration des Chemins de Fer du Gouvernement Iranien v Société Levant Express Transport*, Cass Le Civl, 25 February 1969 (1970) RGDIP 98.

[11] Spain, *Rigopoulos v Spain*, Const Ct, 10 February 1997.

[12] State Immunity Act 1978 c 33. Lord Denning had since 1958 supported the restrictive rule (see Fox and Webb, *The Law of State Immunity* 141).

[13] Fox and Webb, *The Law of State Immunity* 146.

[14] Fox and Webb, *The Law of State Immunity* 161. Cameroon has also supported the restrictive rule in reply to the questionnaire of the ILC Special Rapporteur Mr Ogiso in 1988.

[15] 19 May 1952, 26 US Department of State Bulletin 984.

[16] 28 USC §§ 1330, 1332, 1391(f), 1441(d), 1602–11.

[17] RSC 1985, c S-18.

This influence has not spread to Latin America, where UN surveys in the 1980s indicated that most Latin American countries remain opposed to the restrictive doctrine;[18] only Mexico and Paraguay have signed the UNCSI.

Among former Soviet countries, there is mixed practice. Russia has indicated some support for the restrictive doctrine in its case law and by signing the UNCSI in 2006.[19] Lithuania[20] has abandoned the absolute doctrine, and Estonia, Finland and Slovakia have also signed UNCSI. On the other hand, courts in the Czech Republic, Bulgaria, Poland and Romania continue to apply the absolute doctrine to commercial claims.[21]

In Asia, the general movement had until recently been towards the restrictive doctrine. India, Singapore, Malaysia and the Philippines have adopted the restrictive rule.[22] Japanese courts started to move away from the absolute rule in 2000 and the government ratified UNCSI in 2010, having earlier adopted national legislation that largely followed the Convention.[23]

The People's Republic of China (PRC) had for many decades supported the absolute doctrine, but there have been recent signs of openness to a modification of the doctrine in commercial matters, in particular the fact that China signed the UNCSI in 2005. Moreover, it was beyond doubt that the restrictive doctrine had applied in Hong Kong immediately prior to the handover to PRC on 1 July 1997.[24] However, a landmark 2011 judicial decision has entrenched and expanded China's adherence to the absolute doctrine. In *Democratic Republic of the Congo v FG Hemisphere Associates*, the Hong Kong Court of Final Appeal held that 'the [Hong Kong Special Administrative Region] cannot, as a matter of legal and constitutional principle, adhere to a doctrine of state immunity which differs from that adopted by the PRC. The doctrine of state immunity practiced in HKSAR, as in the rest of China, is accordingly a doctrine of absolute immunity'.[25] This result is somewhat surprising, given that China had already signed (but not ratified) the UNCSI, which clearly adopts the restrictive doctrine. The *FG Hemisphere* decision entrenches the absolute doctrine in China and may well influence other states in the region which are wavering between the two approaches, such as Indonesia. As a practical matter, arbitral awards are no longer enforceable against a foreign state's assets (including commercial assets) in Hong Kong, subject to waiver by the state in question.

The restrictive doctrine, originating in Europe, has spread to North America, Oceania, parts of Africa and Asia, and some former Soviet countries. The absolute doctrine, on the other hand, remains strong in Latin America and in China and Hong Kong. The potential for universal adherence to the restrictive doctrine—which

[18] R Higgins, *Problems and Process* (Oxford, Clarendon Press, 1994) 81.

[19] *Kalashnikova v United States*, Russian Federation Const Ct, Judgment of 2 November 2000, cited in Fox and Webb, *The Law of State Immunity* 159.

[20] *Cudak v Lithuania*, Merits and just satisfaction, App No 15869/02 [2010] ECHR 370, IHRL 159.

[21] Fox and Webb, *The Law of State Immunity* 160.

[22] ibid 146–48 and 161.

[23] ibid 163; Act on the Civil Jurisdiction of Japanese Courts over Foreign States 2009.

[24] This was on the basis of a UK statute extended to Hong Kong: *Democratic Republic of the Congo and Ors v FG Hemisphere Associates LLC*, Hong Kong Ct of Appeal [2011] HKEC 747, para 212.

[25] ibid para 183. The ruling was affirmed by the Standing Committee of the National People's Congress on 26 August 2011.

seeks to achieve the right balance between sovereignty and accountability—has been undermined by the entrenchment of the Chinese support for absolute sovereign immunity and the slow uptake of the UNCSI.

III. IMMUNITY FOR HUMAN RIGHTS VIOLATIONS: INTRA-REGIONAL TENSIONS

The issue of whether state immunity should be absolute or restrictive largely divides along regional lines. However, the question of the scope of the restrictive doctrine of immunity—in particular, whether there should be an exception for grave violations of human rights—has led to intra-regional tensions. Europe has once again been at the centre of legal developments. The courts of several European countries have taken the view that immunity should be set aside for *jus cogens* violations. Courts in Belgium, France, Italy, the Netherlands, Poland, Spain, Switzerland and the UK have been actively prosecuting state officials for international crimes.[26] However, there is an emerging division within the European region on whether this approach can be taken when the *state* itself is the object of the complaint.[27] This uncertainty in state practice is reflected in the 2009 Naples Resolution of the Institut de Droit International. The Institut was unable to agree on the existence of human rights exception, instead stating that the provisions on the immunity of persons who act on behalf of a state are 'without prejudice to the issue whether and when a state enjoys immunity from jurisdiction before the national courts of another state in civil proceedings relating to an international crime committed by an agent of the former state'.[28]

A brief survey of recent practice on state immunity illustrates the division in Europe.[29] The courts of the UK, Poland, Slovenia and Germany, as well as Greece's highest court, have held that there is no human rights exception, whereas Italian and other Greek courts have set aside immunity for claimed violations of *jus cogens* norms.

The UK House of Lords has rejected the existence of an exception to state immunity for civil claims resulting from alleged breaches of *jus cogens* norms;[30] this decision was subsequently upheld by the ECtHR.[31] The Polish Supreme Court has also

[26] See P Webb, 'Human Rights and the Immunities of State Officials' in E de Wet and J Vidmar (eds), *Hierarchy in International Law: The Place of Human Rights* (Oxford, Oxford University Press, 2012) 114.

[27] There is however some overlap in judicial approaches regarding the immunity of the State and of the official in *civil* proceedings, for which see, eg, *Jones v Saudi Arabia* [2006] UKHL 26, discussed below (refusal to set aside immunity of the state and of the officials in a civil claim concerning torture).

[28] Institut de Droit International, Naples Resolution, Art IV, AIDI, 2009, 229.

[29] This is based in part on *Jurisdictional Immunities of the State (Germany v Italy, Greece intervening)*, (Dissenting Opinion of Judge Gaja) [2012] ICJ Rep 99, para 11. See also R Pavoni, 'Human Rights and the Immunities of Foreign States and International Organizations' in de Wet and Vidmar (eds), *Hierarchy in International Law*, 71.

[30] *Jones v Ministry of Interior of the Kingdom of Saudi Arabia* [2006] UKHL 26, paras 24–28 (Lord Bingham) and 49 (Lord Hoffmann). The House of Lords also rejected an exception to the immunity of a state official in civil proceedings at para 71 (Lord Hoffmann).

[31] *Jones and Others v The United Kingdom* App Nos 34356/06 and 40528/06 (ECtHR 14 January 2014), paras 198 and 215.

found no such exception.[32] The Constitutional Court of Slovenia perceived a 'trend', but found no

> rule of international customary law, which would in the case of violations of the cogent norms of international law in the area of human rights protection as a consequence of state activities in the framework of *iure imperii* ... allow Slovenian courts to try foreign states in such cases.[33]

The German Federal Supreme Court (Bundesgerichtshof) reached the same conclusion when it was requested to enforce the Greek judgment on the merits in the *Distomo* case.[34] In the *Distomo* case, the Hellenic Supreme Court had found a *jus cogens* exception to the immunity of the German state, but the Special Supreme Court in *Margellos* repudiated that approach and, under Greek law, it is the view adopted in *Margellos* that must be followed in later cases.[35]

Support for an exception to state immunity for serious violations of human rights is found in the case law of the Italian Corte di Cassazione, particularly the judgments in *Ferrini* and *Milde*,[36] and of the lower courts in Greece. The French Cour de Cassation in 2011 pointed in its dicta to the potential existence of a restriction on state immunity when a claim concerns reparation of the breach of a *jus cogens* norm, provided that the breach consists of positive conduct (not an omission) by the foreign state.[37]

When we move beyond Europe, obviously the states in Asia, Africa and Latin America that still adhere to the absolute doctrine will not admit of any exception to human rights. In North America, however, we see a different trend where legislative action has been taken in order to set aside state immunity for terrorism-related offences, and not serious human rights violations as such.[38]

These divided views have been adjudicated at the regional and international levels, both for the moment stopping short of holding that a human rights exception

[32] *Natoniewski v Federal Republic of Germany*, Poland Supreme Ct (Civil Chamber), 29 October 2010, 30 *Polish YIL* (2010) 299

[33] Const Ct of Slovenia, Judgment of 8 March 2001, case Up-13/99, quoted in *Jurisdictional Immunities of the State* (Dissenting Opinion of Judge *Ad Hoc* Gaja), above n 29, 321, part of para 11.

[34] *Greek citizens v Federal Republic of Germany*, case No III ZR 245/98, *Neue Juristische Wochenschrift*, 2003, 3488; 129 ILR 556. *Prefecture of Voioti v Federal Republic of Germany*, case No 11/2000, 129 ILR 513 (*Distomo* case).

[35] *Jurisdictional Immunities of the State* (Judgment), [2012] ICJ Reports, 99, 134 para 76 and 136 para 83. *Margellos v Federal Republic of Germany*, Anotato Eidiko Dikastirio [AED] [Special Supreme Court] Greece, 17 September 2002, case No 6/2002, translation in 129 ILR 525 et seq.

[36] *Ferrini v Federal Republic of Germany*, Corte di Cassazione [Court of Cassation], Italy, 11 March 2004, No 5044, *Riv Dir Int* 87 (2004) 539 et seq, translation in 128 ILR 668; *Max Josef Milde* case, Tribunale Militare di La Spezia [Military Court of La Spezia], 10 October 2006 (registered on 2 February 2007).

[37] *GIE La Réunion Aérienne c La Jamahiriya Arabe Libyenne*, Cour de Cassation, France, 9 March 2011, case 09-14743, *Bull civ*, March 2011, No 49, 49.

[38] The US FSIA, s 1605(a)(7) removes immunity in respect of specified terrorism-related offences for acts committed outside the US in relation to a limited number of specified states designated as a 'State sponsor of terrorism' under federal legislation. Recent amendments to the Canadian State Immunity Act (Canadian SIA) follow the US model of designating 'State sponsors of terrorism' and introduce an even broader jurisdictional basis: Safe Streets and Communities Act 2012, which enacts the Justice for Victims of Terrorism Act and includes amendments to the Canadian SIA. See also the Alien Tort Statute 28 USC § 1350 and the Torture Victim Protection Act Pub L No 102-256, 106 Stat 73 in the US which have been invoked by courts to set aside immunity of state officials for violations of the laws of nation and torture, respectively.

applies under customary international law. In *Al-Adsani v United Kingdom*, by a majority of nine votes to eight, the European Court of Human Rights stated that it did not 'find it established that there is yet acceptance in international law of the proposition that states are not entitled to immunity in respect of civil claims for damages for alleged torture committed outside the forum state.'[39]

The influence of this judgment is limited by its closely divided set of votes and the fact that it had to examine the case through the framework of the right to access to justice under article 6(1) of the European Convention on Human Rights. The question of a human rights exception to state immunity was more clearly put in the 2012 ICJ judgment in *Jurisdictional Immunities of the State*.[40]

The case concerned an application by Germany alleging that Italy was in breach of international law because of its national courts' disregard of Germany's entitlement to immunity in claims for reparation by victims of acts of war damage committed by German armed forces in 1943–45.[41] The Court found in favour of Germany, by majorities of 12-3 and 14-1 on the various issues. The Court held that

> The rules of State immunity are procedural in character and are confined to determining whether or not the courts of one State may exercise jurisdiction in respect of another State. They do not bear upon the question whether or not the conduct in respect of which the proceedings are brought was lawful or unlawful.[42]

In consequence, the fact that a plea relates to a violation of *jus cogens* norms does not suffice to set aside a state's entitlement to immunity.[43]

In handing down its judgment the ICJ emphasised that

> it was addressing only the immunity of the State itself from the jurisdiction of the courts of other States, the question of whether, and if so to what extent, immunity might apply in criminal proceedings against an official of the State is not in issue in the present case.[44]

It also indicated a temporal limit, with its judgment reflecting the rule 'under customary international law as it presently stands'.[45] These two caveats leave the door open to the development and accumulation of state practice on a human rights exception to state immunity, but as explained below, it is more likely that the ICJ pronouncement will lead to the coalescence of views around the absence of a human rights exception.

IV. INTERNATIONAL LAWMAKING AS A METHOD OF UNIFICATION

A. Lawmaking Through Treaties

How can these divisions between and within regions be resolved in order to have a coherent approach to the law of state immunity? One method is lawmaking through

[39] *Al-Adsani v United Kingdom* [GC] ECHR (2001-XI) 101 para 66.
[40] *Jurisdictional Immunities of the State* (Judgment), above n 35.
[41] ibid 110–14, paras 21–29.
[42] ibid 140, para 93.
[43] ibid 142, para 97, and 143, para 101.
[44] ibid 139, para 91.
[45] ibid.

treaties. The 1972 European Convention on State Immunity (ECSI)[46] and the 2004 UNCSI[47] are attempts at harmonisation, but each has only had a limited impact.

As regards the 'absolute *versus* restrictive' challenge, both treaties confirm the restrictive doctrine of state immunity. They are structured in terms of stating the 'general rule' of immunity and then listing the exceptions to that rule, such as commercial transactions, employment contracts, territorial torts, and so on. The ECSI is however limited by the fact that it only considers the immunity of a contracting state from the jurisdiction of other contracting states. It has to date only received eight ratifications out of a possible 47.[48] The UNCSI is drafted as a universal convention, but over the past eleven years it has only attracted 19 out of the required 30 ratifications for it to enter into force. The majority of the states parties come from Europe.[49] For many of these European states parties, the ratification of UNCSI reflects the fact its courts have already been applying the doctrine of restrictive immunity; ratification has not therefore been a catalyst for the introduction of the restrictive doctrine.[50]

Neither the ECSI nor the UNCSI have contributed to resolving the question of a potential human rights exception to immunity. The ECSI, adopted in 1972, did not address this question. By the time UNCSI was being negotiated within the ILC and the UN General Assembly, the question of immunity for *jus cogens* violations had emerged as a significant issue. The UN General Assembly's Sixth Committee Working Group acknowledged that the question was of current interest, but 'the existence or non-existence of immunity in the case of violation by a state of *jus cogens* norms of international law' did not readily fit into the present draft nor did it seem 'ripe enough ... to engage in a codification exercise'.[51] This was not an outright rejection of such an exception, but the silence of UNCSI on the existence of an exception does not assist with unifying the disparate regional and national approaches to this question. The ICJ drew no insights from UNCSI in this regard in its 2012 judgment.

In other areas of law we have seen the unifying effect of an international convention. The 1948 Convention on the Prevention and Punishment of Genocide, for example, has facilitated a largely coherent approach to the prosecution of genocide in national and international jurisdictions. Unlike UNCSI and ECSI, that Convention is widely ratified, is relatively comprehensive in scope and has been accepted as codifying customary international law.[52] Until UNCSI attains the same status, its influence will be limited to its states parties, which are concentrated in Europe.

[46] ECSI, CETS No 074, entered into force 11 June 1976.

[47] UNSCI, above n 4.

[48] Austria, Belgium, Cyprus, Germany, Luxembourg, Netherlands, Switzerland and United Kingdom. Spain is not a party. Non-member states of the Council of Europe may also accede to the ECSI, but none have done so.

[49] Austria, Czech Republic, Finland, France, Italy, Latvia, Liechtenstein, Norway, Portugal, Romania, Spain, Sweden and Switzerland.

[50] See, eg, for Spain, C Gutierrez Espada, 'La adhesión española (2011) a la convención de las naciones unidas sobre las inmunidades jurisdiccionales de los estados y de sus bienes (2005)' 3(2) (2011) *Cuadernos de Derecho Transnacional* 145–69.

[51] ILC, Convention on Jurisdictional Immunities, Report of the Chairman of the Working Group (12 November 1999), UN Doc A/C 6/54/L 12, paras 46–48.

[52] See analysis of the Genocide Convention in *Application of the Convention on the Prevention and Punishment of the Crime of Genocide (Bosnia and Herzegovina v Serbia and Montenegro)* [2007] ICJ Rep 43.

UNCSI could be said to fit Aust's definition of a 'limping treaty': a universal treaty that has difficulty in attracting wide ratification and is unlikely ever to enter into force.[53] His 2003 survey of more than a dozen 'limping treaties' did not include the UNCSI, as it had not yet been adopted for signature, but his conclusion that the reasons for the failure to attract a greater number of ratifications can almost always be found in the 'national interest' holds true.[54] The nature and scope of state immunity remains controversial and states may be reluctant to accept UNCSI's provisions on, for example, the exceptions to immunity from enforcement or the definition of the commercial exception. They may prefer the evolving standards of customary international law. Alternatively, states with firmly established state immunity legislation, such as the UK, US and many Commonwealth countries, may be hesitant to make even small adjustments to a statutory scheme that has been interpreted and clarified by years of domestic jurisprudence.

B. Developing the Law Through Judicial Decisions

A second mechanism for developing the law of state immunity is the decisions of international courts. The ICJ Statute recognises that judicial decisions can be a source of international law (article 38(1)(d)). Only a small percentage of disputes are settled by international courts. However, the influence of these decisions on how the different states and regions understand international law is inversely proportionate to the frequency and volume of the decisions, which makes them an important unit of analysis. Despite the criticisms of international courts and cases of noncompliance with their decisions, the reputational and other consequences of ignoring these courts are factors that political actors take very seriously.[55]

Although there is a prevalent view that courts only declare the law, in my view the reality is that they can also be involved in developing the law. A shorthand way of describing this phenomenon is 'judicial lawmaking',[56] but a more apt description is of a court acting as an 'agent' in the development of international law.[57] In the *Jurisdictional Immunities of the State* case, the ICJ was confronted with diverse approaches to a legal problem, with a clear schism within the European region. The Court did not 'make' the law as such in this case; it confirmed what is apparent from

[53] A Aust, 'Limping Treaties: Lessons from Multilateral Treaty-Making' (2003) 50 *Netherlands International Law Review* 244, 244.

[54] ibid 264.

[55] JS Martinez, 'Towards an International Judicial System', (2003) 56 *Stanford Law Review* 429, 432.

[56] AM Danner, 'When Courts Make Law: How the International Criminal Tribunals Recast the Laws of War' (2006) 59 *Vanderbilt Law Review* 101; A Boyle and C Chinkin, *The Making of International Law* (Oxford, Oxford University Press, 2007) 266–69.

[57] For scholars discussing this idea in the context of the ICJ, see CJ Tams and A Tzanakopoulos, 'Barcelona Traction' 40: The ICJ as an Agent of Legal Development' (2010) 23 *Leiden Journal of International Law* 781, 784–85; F Berman, 'The ICJ as an "Agent" of Legal Development?' in CJ Tams and J Sloan (eds), *The Development of International Law by the International Court of Justice* (Oxford, Oxford University Press, 2013) 7–21; CG Weeramantry, 'The Function of the International Court of Justice in the Development of International Law' (1997) 10 *Leiden Journal of International Law* 309–40; H Lauterpacht, *The Development of International Law by the International Court* (New York, Praeger, 1958).

the majority of state practice. Judge Bennouna in his Separate Opinion urged the Court to take an active role in guaranteeing 'l'unité du droit international au service de la justice internationale':

> Cette éminente fonction ne peut se satisfaire d'une approche formaliste étroite, consistant à analyser l'immunité en elle-même, *stricto sensu,* sans souci des victimes des crimes internationaux qui demandent que justice leur soit rendue.[58]

Although I believe the ICJ reached the correct decision on the law, it cannot be overlooked that what the Court says may have a chilling effect by halting or slowing down the development of this aspect of the law of state immunity. While the Court's judgments are technically only binding on the parties to the dispute, the ICJ's status as the UN's principal judicial organ means that its pronouncements are generally treated as authoritative.

With the expansion of human rights law and the growing sense that impunity for international crimes cannot be tolerated,[59] it is possible that over time the exception to state immunity for *jus cogens* violations developed in certain Italian and Greek courts could have been taken up by other European jurisdictions, and gradually spread to North America, Latin America, Oceania, and eventually Asia and Africa. The judgment has however essentially closed off this approach. In his Dissenting Opinion, Judge Yusuf asked, 'Would it not have been more appropriate to recognise, in the light of conflicting judicial decisions and other practices of states, that customary international law in this area remains fragmentary and unsettled?'[60]

It is noteworthy that the ICJ did make an effort to pay attention to what the ECtHR had said on state immunity.[61] The ECtHR has affirmed that the grant of state immunity in civil proceedings does not violate the right of access to a court under article 6(1) of the European Convention on Human Rights (ECtHR) as long as it pursues a legitimate purpose and is proportionate. The ECtHR found the criteria of legitimacy and proportionality were met even in cases where a state was accused of serious human rights violations.[62] The ICJ judgment is consistent with the ECtHR's case law, which enhances the unity of international law as applied by these regional and international bodies.

C. Customary International Law

If the 'chilling effect' of the ICJ's judgment can be overcome, then there is the potential for national legislatures and national and regional courts to establish a human rights exception to state immunity through accumulating practice that becomes

[58] *Jurisdictional Immunities of the State* (Separate Opinion of Judge Bennouna) [2012] ICJ Rep 99, para 28.

[59] At least with respect to criminal proceedings—civil suits against individuals have tended to result in the upholding of immunity.

[60] *Jurisdictional Immunities of the State* (Jurisdiction), above n 35, 111 para 24.

[61] ibid 139, para 90.

[62] *Al Adsani v UK*, above n 39; *Fogarty v UK*, ECHR (2001) App No 37112/97, (2001) 34 EHRR 302; *McElhinney v Ireland*, ECHR (2001) App No 31253/96, (2001) 34 EHRR 323. Since confirmed in *Jones v UK*, ECHR (2014) App Nos 34356/06 and 40528/06.

customary international law. The ICJ was careful to qualify its ruling by reference to 'customary international law *as it presently stands*'.[63]

For a rule to be established as customary, the corresponding practice does not have to be in 'absolutely rigorous conformity with the rule'.[64] It need not be the majority of states, but attention must be paid to the states most affected by the potential customary rule. In the *Legality of the Threat or Use of Nuclear Weapons*, the opposition of the few nuclear-weapon states blocked the finding of a customary rule prohibiting the weapons in any circumstance even though a large majority of states favoured such a rule.[65] In the realm of immunity, the most-affected states would be those that are highly engaged in activities (including military interventions and commercial transactions) in other jurisdictions, and thus exposed to litigation in foreign courts. This would include the US, UK, and China, cutting across three different regions. If the customary rule on exceptions to state immunity is to change, it will likely have to evolve from consistent legislative, judicial or executive (eg, waiver of immunity) practice in these three states.

An alternative to a stand-alone human rights exception to state immunity would be to use the existing commercial exception to immunity to hold states accountable for human rights violations committed, for example, in an employer-employee relationship, by private military and security companies, by state-owned enterprises engaged in resource extraction.[66] The tort exception also provides an avenue, although the ICJ judgment has closed off its application to military activities during an armed conflict.

Although some regional trends in immunity can be identified, I do not believe that there is a 'regional custom' for immunity applicable only within a defined group of states. In the *Asylum* and *Haya de la Torre* cases[67] Columbia claimed a local custom recognising the right of embassies of other states in Latin America to give asylum to political fugitives. The ICJ specified that a party must provide (a) the custom is established in such a manner that it has become binding on the other party; (b) constant and uniform usage practised by the regional states; (c) this usage is an expression of a right appertaining to the state granting [the right] and a duty incumbent on the territorial state.[68] These three features are not present in any region with respect to either the absolute or restrictive doctrine or a human rights exception to immunity.

V. CONCLUSION

The law of state immunity has historically been driven by the practice of the European region. In the contemporary world, the influence of major commercial powers,

[63] *Jurisdictional Immunities of the State* (Judgment), above n 35, 139 para 91 (emphasis added).

[64] *Military and Paramilitary Activities in and against Nicaragua (Nicaragua v United States of America)* [1986] ICJ Rep 14, 98 para 186.

[65] *Legality of the Threat or Use of Nuclear Weapons* [1996] ICJ Rep 226, 255 para 73.

[66] This is an idea raised in the Fox and Webb, *The Law of State Immunity* 612.

[67] *Asylum Judgment (Colombia/Peru)* [1950] ICJ Rep 266 and *Haya de la Torre (Colombia v Peru)* [1951] ICJ Rep (1951) 71.

[68] *Asylum Judgment,* above n 67, 276. On the facts of the *Asylum* case, Peru had not adhered to the claimed regional custom and had even repudiated it.

such as China, cannot be ignored. At the same time, any attempts to create a discrete 'regional custom' on state immunity should be rejected, as this will undermine the desired goal of a coherent law that facilitates international relations. Regionalism can be a path to fragmentation or to universalism.[69] In this field of law, regionalism leads us down the fragmentation route, and must be resisted.

I believe that customary international law—the sheer accumulation of state practice accompanied by a sense of legal obligation—is the best way for a universal law of state immunity to be achieved. Such a universal law should be based on the restrictive doctrine and allow the dynamic development of an exception to immunity for the most grave violations of human rights, especially when there is no other avenue for reparation to the victims.

[69] Anne Peters, Welcome Address, ESIL 5th Annual Conference, Valencia, 13 September 2012.

Part III

Regionalism, International Organisation and Integration

9

Quelques remarques à propos de la problématique de l'intégration dans le cadre des organisations internationales à vocation universelle ou régionale: contre la dictature de la ligne droite

JEAN-MARC SOREL*

I. INTRODUCTION

SI L'ON PREND les trois mots de la problématique, on peut trouver rapidement les oppositions : le régionalisme semble s'opposer à l'universel, les organisations internationales à l'Etat et l'intégration à la simple coopération. En réalité, le plus perfectionné des logiciels n'arriverait pas à nous donner les équations parfaites entre ces oppositions. Trop de paramètres entrent en ligne de compte. Il nous semble également que la problématique des relations entre organisations universelles et régionales est déjà largement explorée, et d'une manière suffisamment complète pour qu'il soit inutile d'ajouter des banalités à ces études.[1]

Pour simplifier le débat, nous prendrons donc les trois branches de la problématique (régionalisme, organisation internationale et intégration) comme une interrogation globale sur la question de l'intégration via les organisations internationales qu'elles soient à vocation régionale ou universelle, cette réflexion débouchant sur la question de savoir si l'intégration est la voie qui doit être suivie systématiquement aussi bien dans le cadre régional qu'universel pour les organisations internationales.

Auparavant, il est sans doute utile de s'interroger sur le phénomène de « l'intégration » en lui-même. Qu'est-ce qu'intégrer ? Qui intègre ? Comment intègre-t-on ? Qu'est-ce qu'on intègre ? En effet, l'impression aujourd'hui, du moins dans le cadre de l'Union européenne, est qu'on ne s'interroge plus sur ce phénomène, on le pense acquis, et comme tout acquis, on ne le remet pas en cause. L'intégration

* Professeur à l'Ecole de Droit de la Sorbonne (Université Paris 1).

[1] Voir la communication dans ce colloque de Santiago Villalpando (« Les relations entre les Nations Unies et les organisations régionales »), ainsi que l'excellent et très complet cours de Laurence Boisson de Chazournes, « Les relations entre organisations régionales et organisations universelles » (2010) 37 *RCADI* 83–406.

est devenue une donnée incontournable dont on se dit—du moins dans les milieux politiques pro-européens—qu'elle est bénéfique sans trop savoir en quoi elle l'est.

Etre intégré, c'est a priori se fondre dans une certaine collectivité grâce à différents facteurs que des autorités peuvent faciliter ou non selon leur volonté d'intégrer. Du point de vue juridique, et selon un spécialiste de ces questions:

> l'intégration internationale est le processus par lequel les décisions qui étaient prises auparavant par des responsables d'Etats-Nations distincts sont maintenant prises par des personnes qui relèvent d'un centre nouveau (l'organisation internationale). Le fonctionnalisme international est le processus par lequel des activités spécifiques (fonctions) sont maintenant exécutées par des organisations internationales et non par différentes autorités d'Etats-Nations.[2]

Cette définition est intéressante mais est loin de couvrir tous les mystères de l'intégration. En effet, elle explique avant tout le processus, la décision prise désormais par une organisation en lieu et place d'Etats. Mais elle n'explique pas la finalité de l'intégration ni, a fortiori, si cette intégration est efficace et positive et quelles en sont les conséquences concrètes pour les populations des Etats concernés. En effet, l'intégration, c'est à la fois l'action d'intégrer mais aussi de s'intégrer dans un groupe. Plus précisément, le Dictionnaire de Droit international public nous indique que l'intégration est : « Une opération tendant à faire entrer un élément extérieur dans une entité dont il devient une partie indissociable », mais aussi que cela concerne la « Fonction d'une organisation internationale qui vise à unifier progressivement par des mécanismes appropriés, l'économie, voire le système politique des Etats membres », et que, « Par extension, on parle d'organisation d'intégration, ou d'organisation supranationale, pour désigner les organisations internationales dotées des pouvoirs nécessaires pour remplir de telles fonctions ».[3] Le mystère demeure en grande partie mais on ressent nettement que cette intégration vise avant tout l'économie et que l'Union européenne, à la fois par ses objectifs économiques et par les pouvoirs de ses organes intégrés, est le « prototype » d'une organisation d'intégration, ce qui a par ailleurs tendance à masquer, voire à faire oublier, que bien d'autres organisations, même si à un niveau moindre, peuvent prétendre à la fonction d'intégration.

Il faut donc interroger les différentes formes d'intégration (ou idées d'intégration) qui ont surgit au cours de l'histoire assez brève des organisations internationales. Même si le cheminement n'est pas uniquement historique car le phénomène de l'organisation internationale n'a pas évolué d'une manière linéaire, il s'apparente quand même à quelques phases repérables dans l'histoire.[4] L'organisation internationale étant au départ assimilée à l'Etat, on a en quelque sorte tout d'abord constaté une sorte d'intégration par opposition (II). La confrontation avec l'Etat s'avérant

[2] CF Alger, « Fonctionnalisme et intégration » (1977) XXIX/1 *RISS* 77. Voir aussi : Michel Virally, « La notion de fonction dans la théorie de l'organisation internationale », *Le droit international en devenir, Essais au fil des ans* (Paris, PUF—IHEI, 1990) 271–90 ; Ricardo Monaco, « Les principes régissant la structure et le fonctionnement des organisations internationales » (1977) III *RCADI* 79–225.

[3] *Dictionnaire de Droit international public* (sous la direction de J Salmon) (Bruxelles, Bruylant/AUF, 2001) 590–91.

[4] Les sujets ayant des points communs, les propos qui suivent empruntent à notre communication : « L'institutionnalisation des relations internationales », dans le *Traité des organisations internationales* (sous la direction de E Lagrange, et J-M Sorel) (Paris, LITEC, 2013).

aussi inutile qu'improductive, c'est l'intégration par la fonction qui a ensuite été privilégiée, type d'intégration dont l'Union européenne est encore aujourd'hui une excellente représentation (III). Mais dans nombre d'organisations, régionales ou à vocation universelle, en dehors de l'Union européenne (dont il faut rappeler le caractère unique à travers le monde), le fonctionnalisme s'est souvent illustré d'une autre manière, moins volontaire et plus évolutive, et l'intégration s'est alors faite « par défaut », non sur la base explicite d'une volonté politique, mais par l'extension des pouvoirs d'organisations qui s'imposent faute de contradiction et qui se rendent ainsi indispensables (IV). *In fine*, il apparait que l'intégration dans les domaines sensibles pour la vie des peuples ne peut se faire que par « l'acceptation » de l'autre et nécessite à la fois des décisions politiques et une sorte d'éducation à la tolérance qui en garantisse la pérennité : vaste programme, utopique certes, mais l'intégration en elle-même est tout aussi utopique (V).

Deux petites précautions s'imposent néanmoins. La première est que la littérature sur l'intégration (notamment pour l'Union européenne) est abondante et que nous ne l'ignorons pas, même si elle a été volontairement laissée de côté pour justement s'extraire de la « pression doctrinale » dans ce sens.[5] La deuxième précaution concerne les idées quelque peu provocatrices véhiculées dans cette brève présentation. Certaines vont au-delà de notre propre pensée mais il a semblé salutaire de bousculer des idées un peu trop « reçues ».

II. L'INTÉGRATION PAR L'OPPOSITION : ORGANISATION INTERNATIONALE *VERSUS* ETAT

En l'espèce, il s'agit de revenir sur un fait connu : l'organisation internationale était inclassable lors de son apparition et pendant quelques décennies. Dès lors, on lui a donné un rôle modeste dans des domaines très techniques lors de son apparition au XIXème siècle (dans une forme à peu près achevée), puis on l'a assimilée à l'Etat en la comparant à toutes les formes étatiques possibles, ce qui, à l'inverse, représentait sans doute un excès car ses compétences étaient limitées. A partir de l'après seconde guerre mondiale, c'est plutôt en tant qu'auxiliaire de l'Etat que l'organisation est ciblée, ce qui permet de la laisser fluctuer au gré des oppositions idéologiques de la guerre froide. Certains lui donnent alors des « pouvoirs inhérents » pour concurrencer l'Etat, mais cette théorie reste cantonnée finalement aux fonctions judiciaires. Il en résulte surtout que cette opposition entre l'Etat et l'organisation internationale est la marque du défaut de l'anthropomorphisme étatique, de l'obsession du modèle étatique, de la supranationalité, l'ensemble ne menant pas à une intégration positive.

[5] Outre les ouvrages généraux sur les organisations internationales, d'une manière très sélective, on peut citer : J Klabbers, *An Introduction to International Institutional Law* (Cambridge, Cambridge University Press, 2002); EU Petersmann, « Time for a United Nations 'Global Compact' for Integrating Human Rights into the Law of Worldwide Organizations : Lessons from European Integration » (2002) *European Journal of International Law* 621–50 ; BS Chimini, « International Institutions Today : An Imperial Global State in the Making » (2004) 15 *European Journal of International Law* 1–37; V Leary, « International Institutions : Towards Coherent Multilateralism », en L Boisson de Chazournes et V Gowland-Debbas (eds), *L'ordre juridique international, un système en quête d'équité et d'universalité, Liber Amicorum G. Abi-Saab* (The Hague, Martinus Nijhoff Publishers, 2001) 823–29.

Lorsque les organisations internationales apparaissent dans le courant (commissions fluviales) et vers la fin (Union administratives) du XIXème siècle, c'est essentiellement la préoccupation commerciale qui anime les Etats dans l'acte de création, le capitalisme étant en pleine essor. On a donc pu les considérer comme des enfants du libéralisme, ce qui ancre le primat économique sur les fonts baptismaux. Dès lors, l'idée est de rendre le commerce plus fluide avec une mise en commun normative, mais il n'est guère question de remplacer les Etats dans certaines fonctions. On fait simplement converger les unilatéralismes. Nous sommes loin de l'intégration, et encore plus du supranationalisme, dans une mouvance internationale dont l'horizon pour le moment indépassable est l'inter-étatisme.

Néanmoins, le phénomène intrigue et certains souhaitent pousser, au moins en théorie, beaucoup plus loin l'étude de cette entité nouvelle. Comme seul l'Etat existe sur la scène internationale, c'est vers cet unique modèle que les regards se porteront. On peut alors estimer que l'excès d'assimilation est non seulement erroné mais nuisible. On considère en effet que les unions administratives ou les commissions fluviales ressortent finalement toutes d'un même creuset menant à l'organisation internationale contemporaine et peuvent se comparer à des formes étatiques. Les logiques sont pourtant très différentes et on ne peut assimiler une logique territoriale étatique avec une logique dès l'origine fonctionnaliste. Néanmoins, que les modèles de l'union, de la confédération, voire de la fédération, aient pu servir comme base comparative pour la doctrine ne va pas rejaillir sur une montée en puissance des organisations en tant que « quasi-Etats ».

Les approches dites « réalistes » vont rapidement supplanter cette vision faussement idyllique, surtout au moment où la guerre froide enterre les élans utopistes nées de la deuxième guerre mondiale. Elles ont pour base la primauté et l'unicité de l'Etat comme seul acteur des relations internationales. Le courant réaliste, qui voit dans l'État le seul acteur important et incontournable de la vie internationale, nie à l'organisation une autonomie propre pour en faire un lieu de purs rapports de force entre les États membres. Autrement dit, aucune transcendance n'est admise, l'organisation n'étant que le reflet des intérêts contradictoires ou convergents des États qui la dominent. Hans Morgenthau aux États-Unis ou Raymond Aron en France ont illustré ce courant. Dans son prolongement, c'est la vision idéologique de l'organisation du monde qui est présente. Ainsi, les pays occidentaux, les pays socialistes ou les pays en développement ont reporté dans cette vision de l'organisation internationale leur « schéma » de l'organisation planétaire et ses conflits sous-jacents. On ne s'étonnera pas, par exemple, que les États socialistes y voyaient le lieu où se poursuit la lutte des classes. L'organisation n'est plus alors qu'un simple « auxiliaire » des Etats, quand ce n'est pas un simple « instrument ». L'intégration via l'organisation n'est plus à l'ordre du jour, sauf dans chaque camp idéologique.

En réaction à ce minimalisme fonctionnel, certains auteurs ont pu développer des théories permettant, à l'inverse, à l'organisation de s'affirmer comme un acteur intégratif puissant et autonome. Ainsi, à partir du début des années 60, la thèse des « pouvoirs inhérents » de l'organisation voit le jour.[6] Il s'agissait d'expliquer, qu'en

[6] Notamment à travers les écrits de Finn Seyersted. Voir la communication de Pierre Klein (« Les compétences et pouvoirs de l'organisation internationale ») dans le *Traité des organisations internationales*, op cit.

dépit « d'infirmités congénitales » (absence de territoires, sauf temporairement, ou de ressortissants), l'organisation est bien un sujet à part entière du droit international. Certes, le principe de spécialité et les strictes compétences d'attribution de l'organisation internationale l'empêchaient de prétendre à un rôle étendu, mais qu'à cela ne tienne, des pouvoirs « cachés », donc inhérents, existent et peuvent s'exercer si nécessaire à l'image de la plénitude de compétences des Etats. Finalement, ces fameux pouvoirs se concentreront sur les fonctions judiciaires[7] et ne seront pas, comme le souhaitaient ses initiateurs, un puissant levier caché d'intégration.[8]

Il résulte de cette brève analyse que l'intégration via l'organisation s'est faite pendant longtemps sur la base d'une opposition—comparaison avec le modèle étatique. Ce modèle a donc constitué une sorte « d'obsession », l'organisation internationale ne pouvant chercher qu'une forme de supranationalité en concurrençant et supplantant l'Etat. La réponse maladroite d'une partie de la doctrine fut de tenter de donner corps à la fonction d'intégration de l'organisation « aux forceps », avec le défaut qu'on ne quittait pas l'Etat comme point d'horizon indépassable. Le paradigme sur lequel on réagissait restait figé. Le postulat était une forme d'obsession du supranational comme objectif de l'organisation et l'idée que l'Etat et l'organisation seront forcément antagonistes.[9]

III. L'INTÉGRATION PAR LA FONCTION : PUISSANCE FONCTIONNELLE *VERSUS* VOLONTÉ POLITIQUE

Dans la saga de l'intégration, le deuxième temps (qui n'est pas chronologique) a consisté non à remplacer l'Etat mais à lui retirer certaines fonctions qu'il serait incapable de gérer. Le fonctionnalisme ainsi prôné s'éloigne d'une vision intégrative politique pour s'immiscer dans le champ des compétences dites « techniques ». Il convient de préciser que l'étude de l'intégration suppose la vision d'une fonction particulière de l'organisation, celle qui mènera l'organisation vers son caractère supranational.[10] Il s'agit par conséquent d'un axe d'étude qui s'oppose à une fonction de l'organisation beaucoup plus répandue dans la pratique : la simple coopération, qui laisse subsister la structure classique de la société internationale en États souverains.

[7] Cette technique fut notamment appliquée par la Cour européenne des droits de l'homme dans des arrêts du 14 novembre 1960 et du 7 avril 1961 (affaire *Lawless*). En l'espèce, la Cour part du caractère inhérent de sa fonction juridictionnelle pour affirmer sa compétence dans la révision de ses propres arrêts.

[8] Comme le rappelle Pierre Klein, « Ainsi que l'a relevé la Chambre d'appel du T.P.I.Y. dans l'affaire *Blaskic*, la terminologie paraît à cet égard maintenant bien fixée, l'expression 'pouvoirs implicites' s'appliquant aux pouvoirs des organes politiques des organisations internationales, alors que les 'pouvoirs inhérents' renvoient uniquement aux fonctions judiciaires par nature », op cit.

[9] Pour une contribution récente sur l'évolution des formes de l'organisation internationale, voir : M–C Runavot, « L'avenir du 'modèle intergouvernemental' de l'organisation internationale » (2011)/3 *RGDIP* 675–709.

[10] C'est un anglais, Leonard Woolf, qui, lors de la naissance de la SdN, pressentit le premier les possibilités des organisations internationales. David Mitrany, son élève, sera le premier à conceptualiser ces idées au moment de la seconde guerre mondiale et sera suivi par le courant « néo-fonctionnaliste » avec notamment Ersnt Haas ou Joseph Nye qui vont développer en continuité la logique de l'intégration. Pour la présentation la plus achevée du fonctionnalisme, voir : David Mitrany, *A Working Peace System* (London, Royal Institute of International Affairs, 1943; aussi: Chicago, Quadrangle Books, 1966).

Le fonctionnalisme n'est pas à proprement parler une théorie mais une manière d'envisager le rôle des organisations internationales. Néanmoins, face à la relative irréductibilité de l'organisation internationale à l'analyse théorique, le fonctionnalisme est souvent apparu comme la seule théorie globale et cohérente de l'organisation internationale. Or, le fonctionnalisme est directement en prise avec l'intégration selon une définition communément acceptée.[11] Si l'intégration renvoie aux normes de l'organisation qui remplaceraient les décisions prises par les Etats-Nations, le fonctionnalisme toucherait les aspects opérationnels en ce qu'une fonction spécifique serait désormais exercée par l'organisation. La « Famille des Nations Unies » fut un banc d'essai propice à cette théorie dans le schéma de l'après-guerre. En réalité, il est bien difficile de distinguer ces deux aspects, toute fonction entraînant une prise de décision qui se concrétise bien souvent sous forme de normes.

Quoi qu'il en soit, les théories qui poussent la logique du fonctionnalisme jusqu'à ses extrémités buttent le plus souvent sur les difficultés de l'intégration. Ainsi, un auteur comme Karl Deutsch a étudié, dans les années cinquante, les « réseaux de communication » pour en déduire l'existence de « communautés pluralistes » (dont les unités restent autonomes) et de « communautés par amalgame » (dont les unités se fondent dans un ensemble unique). Il en conclut que l'intégration est rarement possible car elle suppose la réunion de nombreuses conditions (similitude de puissance économique, complémentarité des élites, adaptabilité des gouvernements...). De même, l'analyse systémique, via son fondateur David Easton, procède d'une étude empirique ou le « système » est étudié comme un tout, mettant en évidence les différents niveaux d'intégration qui existent dans une communauté : l'intégration technique, l'intégration politique et l'intégration de « la vie des peuples », ce dernier niveau étant le plus difficile à atteindre.[12] C'est pourtant le seul qui vaille si l'on veut s'intéresser aux conséquences concrètes de l'intégration.

Il est indéniable que le fonctionnalisme aura une forte influence sur la construction européenne. C'est en effet à partir du Plan Schuman et de l'expérience de la CECA qu'Ernst Haas élabore sa théorie de « l'intégration fonctionnelle » dans le cadre régional.[13] Globalement, l'intégration de structures économiques doit mener à une « communauté politique » selon un processus de « dynamique ascendante ». L'analyse est aussi élargie et modifiée car la communauté politique ne découle pas naturellement de la coopération technique mais est involontairement créée sur la base de modes de vie comparables, ou du moins, conciliables. Avec Haas, le fonctionnalisme ne devient qu'un des moyens de l'intégration qui est le but ultime d'une Europe fédérale. Ce déterminisme socio-économique fera de Jean Monet un lecteur attentif de Haas mais il n'est guère évident aujourd'hui de constater une « dynamique ascendante » partant d'un rapprochement économique vers une « communauté politique », et c'est plutôt l'entente politique qui semble faire défaut pour pousser le rapprochement économique vers des modes de vie comparables.

[11] Voir la définition de CF Alger citée en introduction.

[12] Voir aussi l'analyse empirique de W Lang, « New Regionalism in a Changing World Order », en *International Law : Theory and Practice (Essays in Honour of Eric Suy)* (Leiden, Brill, 1998) 45–60.

[13] E Haas, *The Uniting of Europe, Political, Social and Economic forces, 1950–1957* (Stanford, Stanford University Press, 1958).

On mesure ainsi assez rapidement les limites du fonctionnalisme. Le fonctionnalisme suppose la séparation du technique et du politique et le primat du premier sur le second.[14] Cette séparation étanche ne correspond pas à la réalité sociale. Aucune question ne peut être traitée en dehors du champ du politique lorsqu'elle acquiert une certaine importance.[15] Il en découle une vision du politique trop simpliste car localisée au seul « pouvoir » du gouvernement. Cette simplification s'accompagne d'un optimisme exagéré car les compétences souveraines ne se laissent pas amoindrir « en douceur » mais nécessitent souvent une décision claire qui est une véritable étape.[16] D'autre part, le fonctionnalisme semble plus adapté aux organisations opérationnelles qu'à celles dont le rôle essentiel est d'ordre normatif, c'est-à-dire qui émettent des normes d'harmonisation ou de réglementation. Dans ce dernier cas, l'échelon national persiste souvent et il n'y a pas remplacement de la fonction par une organisation internationale mais simplement complémentarité. On tente plutôt d'adapter les administrations nationales au contexte international, et on les consolide plus qu'on ne les supprime. Les normes dans le domaine de l'éducation (UNESCO), de la santé (OMS) ou même de l'échange postal (UPU) en sont d'autres exemples. Cependant, une fois de plus, cette coupure peut paraître fictive, chaque organisation internationale ayant souvent à la fois une action normative et une activité opérationnelle (cette dernière découlant au départ de la production de normes). Simplement, la « fonction » exercée par une organisation est souvent plus visible lorsqu'elle se traduit par une activité opérationnelle concrète.

IV. L'INTÉGRATION PAR DÉFAUT : COMPÉTENCES D'ATTRIBUTION *VERSUS* POUVOIRS IMPLICITES

Incapable de concurrencer l'Etat qui, via son territoire et ses nationaux, garde une suprématie dans l'identité des relations internationales, et incapable de s'imposer fonctionnellement sans la puissance politique nécessaire à un centre de décision digne de ce nom, l'organisation internationale intègre « ses sujets » d'une manière qui semble presque indolore, incolore et sans saveur. On pourrait presque dire « naturellement ». Il s'agit bien de fonctionnalisme mais plutôt « par défaut ». C'est parce qu'elle se rend indispensable que l'organisation internationale intègre par ses propres compétences qu'elle étend bien souvent au-delà de ses simples compétences d'attribution via un jeu subtil entre spécialisation, subsidiarité et pouvoirs implicites.

Le principe de spécialité semble s'imposer aux organisations internationales. Partant du principe clair et non démenti que « les limitations à la souveraineté ne se présument pas », il faut admettre, qu'en cas de contestation de l'autorité de l'organisation, l'Etat risque de l'emporter, d'autant que l'organisation est un sujet

[14] Ce paragraphe reprend nos remarques dans la communication du le *Traité des organisations internationales*, op cit.

[15] Le FMI en a fait l'amère expérience en considérant ses politiques d'ajustement comme uniquement « techniques ».

[16] Le passage à la monnaie unique dans le cadre de l'Union économique et monétaire en est une illustration. La question des transferts de compétences au compte-goutte en France lors des révisions constitutionnelles en est aussi un bon exemple.

dérivé issu des Etats et qu'à ce titre l'organisation n'a qu'une « autorité d'exception » (selon l'expression de J Combacau) qui s'oppose à « l'autorité de droit commun » des Etats. Une interprétation restrictive des clauses attributives d'autorité sera donc souvent la plus conforme à la volonté des parties. De plus, l'organisation n'est qu'un sujet fonctionnel et ne peut exercer que la (ou les) fonction—mais toute la fonction—pour laquelle elle fut créée. L'organisation est donc limitée par le principe de spécialité que devra respecter son droit dérivé. Certaines organisations ont des buts très larges (ONU, UA, Conseil de l'Europe, etc) et l'on peut estimer qu'elles ont une compétence quasi-générale. C'est le chemin suivi par la Communauté européenne/Union européenne après avoir été spécialisée en matière économique. Néanmoins, aussi larges soient les buts de l'organisation, tous les actes normatifs doivent pouvoir être rattachés—plus ou moins directement—à une disposition de l'acte constitutif. C'est une précaution prise par les Etats et rappelée dans de nombreux actes constitutifs.[17] Pour bien marquer cette limite, certains actes prévoient, qu'en dehors de ces domaines, le reste est de la compétence de l'Etat. C'est l'objectif de l'article 2§7 de la Charte des Nations Unies qui énonce globalement le principe du domaine réservé de l'Etat, sauf en cas d'utilisation du chapitre VII de la Charte. Rappelons d'autre part que la CIJ est venu rappeler ce principe à l'OMS dans l'avis de 1996 sur la *Licéité des armes nucléaires*.

Néanmoins, ce principe de spécialité connait des failles de différentes manières. Le principe de subsidiarité en est une bonne illustration[18] car il inverse la proposition et permet à l'organisation d'intervenir sur la base d'une présomption favorable alors que, pour d'autres organisations, il s'agit d'une interdiction quasi-absolue. Le principe de subsidiarité élargit nettement le principe de spécialité d'autant qu'il est assez difficile de savoir ce qu'est une « compétence exclusive », par exemple de l'Union européenne.[19] De même, le principe de subsidiarité fut utilisé d'une certaine manière par l'ONU dans l'opération en Somalie pour justifier son action face à l'absence d'Etat, puis dans d'autres cadres.

Le principe de spécialité vient, par conséquent, a priori, limiter le droit dérivé mais le principe de subsidiarité l'élargit et, de plus, l'interprétation de la spécialité s'est souvent exercée en élargissant celle-ci par la magie des pouvoirs implicites.

[17] Par exemple, l'article 3 B du traité sur l'Union européenne précisait: « La communauté agit dans les limites des compétences qui lui sont conférées et des objectifs qui lui sont assignés par le présent traité ».

[18] Rappelons qu'il fut introduit en Europe par l'Acte unique de 1986 en matière de protection de l'environnement puis fut généralisé par le traité sur l'Union européenne par son article 3 B: « Dans les domaines qui ne relèvent pas de sa compétence exclusive, la Communauté n'intervient, conformément au principe de subsidiarité, que si et dans la mesure où les objectifs de l'action envisagée ne peuvent être réalisés de manière suffisante par les Etats membres et peuvent donc, en raison des dimensions ou des effets de l'action envisagée, être mieux réalisés au niveau communautaire. L'action de la Communauté n'excède pas ce qui est nécessaire pour atteindre les objectifs du présent traité ». On retrouve désormais ce principe, *mutatis mutandis*, dans l'article 5 du TUE.

[19] Rappelons également que la CJCE avait une jurisprudence à la fois extensive et fluctuante sur cet aspect. L'avis 1/94 du 15 novembre 1994 sur les compétences entre la Commission et les Etats dans les domaines de la future OMC est, à cet égard, éloquent (en l'espèce, contrairement à l'opinion de la Commission, la CJCE a reconnu qu'il existe un domaine de compétence exclusive de la Communauté pour l'accord sur le commerce des marchandises—GATT—alors que la compétence revient aux Etats pour l'accord sur les aspects des droits de propriété intellectuelle qui touchent au commerce—ADPIC—et le commerce des services lorsqu'existent des mouvements transfrontaliers de personnes).

Malgré les limites précitées, lors de conflits d'attribution de compétences entre les Etats et les organisations internationales, la solution ne penche pas forcement en faveur de l'Etat car l'on estime généralement que les organisations ne peuvent exercer que les compétences reconnues par leur acte constitutif mais qu'elles peuvent aussi exercer les compétences que l'acte constitutif implique et sans lesquelles les buts de l'organisation ne peuvent être atteints.[20] La CIJ comme la CJCE utiliseront cette notion pour « grignoter » des compétences aux Etats et les placer dans le giron des organisations internationales.[21] En ce sens, l'acte constitutif n'est pas un acte isolé mais le point de départ d'un système logique qui permet à l'organisation de fonctionner. Il s'agit tout simplement de l'application à l'organisation internationale de la technique de l'interprétation des traités, dite téléologique, c'est-à-dire en fonction des buts. A priori, ceci n'apparaît pas comme un développement exceptionnel si ce n'était le point de départ de tout le droit dérivé autonome de l'organisation internationale et d'un puissant levier d'intégration. La CIJ a souvent eu l'occasion d'appliquer cette « théorie »,[22] mais c'est sans doute la CJCE qui poussera le plus loin cette possibilité et donnera aux organes communautaires tous les pouvoirs—et même au-delà—impliquées dans le traité de Rome et les traités suivants.[23] L'équilibre entre le droit dérivé étendu par les pouvoirs impliqués et le respect des compétences de l'Etat va orienter l'organisation soit vers la coopération, soit vers l'intégration: plus le droit dérivé s'imposera, à l'exemple de la Communauté européenne/Union européenne, plus l'organisation sera intégrée. Néanmoins, comme le remarque Pierre

[20] Cette notion dite des « pouvoirs implicites » (parfois nommée « théorie des pouvoirs implicites ») ou des « pouvoirs impliqués » (correspondant mieux à la traduction de l'expression *implied powers*) trouve son origine dans le droit fédéral et plus précisément dans la jurisprudence de la Cour suprême américaine dans la célèbre affaire de 1819 *MacCulloc v Maryland*, et fut élaborée par le juge Marshall à propos de la répartition des compétences entre l'Etat fédéré et l'Etat fédéral. En l'espèce, le juge a reconnu à l'Etat fédéral la possibilité d'adopter des actes qui n'étaient pas expressément mentionnés dans la constitution : « *pourvu que les fins soient légitimes, qu'elles soient dans la sphère de la constitution; tous les moyens qui sont appropriés à ces fins, qui ne sont pas interdits, mais qui sont compatibles avec la lettre et avec l'esprit de la constitution, sont constitutionnels* ».

[21] Pour la CIJ, le point de départ est le célèbre avis du 11 avril 1949. Pour démontrer que l'ONU, dans le cadre de sa mission de maintien de la paix, pouvait légalement envoyer des agents et les protéger (protection fonctionnelle), la CIJ a dû interpréter la Charte qui n'indique rien sur cet aspect. La Cour admet que l'ONU : « doit être considérée comme possédant les pouvoirs qui, s'ils ne sont pas expressément énoncés dans la Charte, sont, par une conséquence nécessaire, conférés à l'organisation en tant qu'essentiels à l'exercice des fonctions de celle-ci ».

[22] La CIJ a une jurisprudence relativement constante concernant les pouvoirs implicites de l'ONU. En 1954, dans son avis du 13 juillet, la Cour a considéré que l'AGNU avait la capacité nécessaire pour créer un tribunal administratif chargé de régler en dernière instance les litiges entre l'organisation et ses fonctionnaires, et que cette capacité « est nécessairement impliquée par la Charte » (*Effets des jugements du TANU*, *Rec CIJ* 1954, p 46 et seq). Dans son avis de 1962 sur *Certaines dépenses des Nations Unies* (*Rec CIJ* 1962, p 151) qui touche au problème global de financement des Opérations de maintien de la paix refusé par l'URSS et la France, la Cour donne une interprétation similaire.

[23] L'exemple le plus net est sans doute le célèbre arrêt *Commission c Conseil* du 31 mars 1971 (dite affaire *AETR*, 22/70, *Rec* 1971, p 263) qui démontre une conception tout à fait extensive de cette notion en estimant qu'il convenait de se référer au « système général du droit communautaire » en l'absence de dispositions spécifiques dans le traité de Rome relatives à la négociation et à la conclusion d'accords internationaux en matière de transports. On peut constater une jurisprudence constante avec, par exemple, l'arrêt *Lütticke* du 28 avril 1971 (Aff 4/69, *Rec* 1971, p 325) ou *Charmasson* du 10 décembre 1974 (Aff 48/74, *Rec* 1974, p 1383). Dans ce dernier cas, la CJCE s'appuie sur le traité pour écarter une carence normative du Conseil, « l'effet utile » étant poussé dans ses derniers retranchements avec à l'appui un raisonnement déductif et pas seulement inductif.

Klein, la théorie des pouvoirs implicites ne remet pas en cause le principe fondamental des compétences d'attribution car l'invocation de cette théorie ne peut justifier une extension du champ de compétences matérielles de l'organisation, mais tout au plus une extension des pouvoirs ou des moyens d'action (initialement) reconnus aux organes de l'organisation pour permettre la réalisation de ses buts.[24] La réalité impose surtout de constater qu'entre la simple coopération et l'intégration réelle, une large gamme de situations apparaît. De surcroit, plus le traité est détaillé (le cas de l'Union européenne) et moins les compétences implicites sont théoriquement possibles car les compétences d'attribution officielles se suffisent à elles-mêmes.

C'est peut-être dans cet enchaînement—souvent subtil et non linéaire—qu'il faut rechercher ce qui peut apparaître comme une forme d'hégémonie (au sens gramscien) de l'organisation menant à une intégration plus poussée.[25] En effet, l'organisation semble alors opérer un processus de normalisation et de socialisation sans rupture violente. Les organisations de la famille de Bretton Woods, et particulièrement le FMI, semblent répondre à ce schéma : elles représenteraient des organisations fonctionnelles, qui peuvent mener à un certain fonctionnalisme, où l'absence de coercition (la sanction est remplacée par la non-participation) et la possibilité de pénétrer au cœur du système étatique conduisent à socialiser des attitudes vers un comportement donné. Pour aboutir à ce résultat, les deux organisations agissent toujours avec le consentement de l'Etat pour éviter l'accusation d'ingérence. L'équilibre entre la contrainte et le consentement ainsi réalisé à travers un système de valeurs culturelles imprègne, se répand, socialise et intègre un système social.

Il n'empêche que l'organisation se rend souvent indispensable lorsqu'elle gère un domaine international sans lequel l'Etat ne peut agir. Peut-on recevoir ou faire décoller un avion de son territoire sans l'OACI ? Peut-on recevoir ou envoyer du courrier ou avoir un système de télécommunication sans l'UPU ou l'UIT ? Par défaut donc, l'organisation intègre et socialise un milieu donné, même s'il ne s'agit pas d'une intégration positive, parce que voulue en quelque sorte, et admettant la capacité d'une organisation internationale de faire mieux que les Etats, et même si ceci est très variable d'une organisation à une autre et ne revêt jamais la même force normative. On reste toujours insatisfait au regard d'une véritable intégration.

V. L'INTÉGRATION PAR LA TOLÉRANCE : INTÉGRATION *VERSUS* ACCEPTATION

Face à l'impossibilité d'une théorie globale, il faut admettre que toute intégration véritable suppose une éducation à la tolérance, et donc une « acceptation » de l'autre. Dès lors, il faut abandonner l'idée de supranationalité car le nationalisme que l'on espère combattre ressurgit via le « village », soit dans un cadre communautaire, soit dans un cadre religieux (phénomène dit du « glocal » aujourd'hui bien connu), et fait de l'organisation un clone imparfait de l'Etat. De même, il faut abandonner l'espoir (stupide) de séparer droit et politique ou la « politique » et les aspects fonctionnels.

[24] Voir la communication de Pierre Klein, *Traité des organisations internationales*, op cit.

[25] Voir notre communication, *Traité des* organisations internationales, op cit.

Une organisation est une structure sociale qui peut devenir un sujet vivant et autonome selon la volonté de ses membres. C'est par l'expression de ses fonctions explicites ou latentes que l'organisation internationale se caractérisera et socialisera le milieu auquel elle est destinée. Sans doute la notion de *global governance* apparue récemment se rapproche-t-elle plus de cette réalité : il s'agit de rendre compte d'une action impliquant des intérêts très divers (privés, publics, économiques ou non ...) dans un but de coopération, sans l'idée qu'une supranationalité soit consubstantiellement nécessaire à l'accomplissement de cette action. Mais chaque théorie ou approche méthodologique peut rendre compte du phénomène organisationnel. Ainsi l'approche dite *Law and Economics* est-elle parfois privilégiée parce qu'elle semble s'adapter à l'économisme ambiant et à la nécessité d'adapter l'étude du droit aux contraintes économiques.[26] De même le « constitutionnalisme », également très en vogue, passe souvent par l'organisation internationale car celle-ci serait à même de structurer les domaines communs et les normes communes.

Le droit reste fondamentalement la résultante d'un rapport de force ou, selon la belle expression de François Gény, « Tout droit est issu de la politique. Le droit représente une politique qui a réussi. »[27] Lui faire jouer un rôle « neutre » est un leurre dont le fonctionnalisme dans la pureté de ses principes est une illustration. La politique reprend ses droits et c'est parfois le rapprochement politique qui devra précéder la coopération fonctionnelle pour lui donner l'impulsion nécessaire. L'Europe souffre sans doute de ce handicap dans certains domaines sensibles comme la politique étrangère et la défense ou, plus récemment, la question de l'harmonisation budgétaire. Isoler les progrès de l'intégration de ceux de l'entente politique reste donc fondamentalement illusoire.

Pour revenir à nos interrogations initiales : qui intègre ? Si l'on prend justement l'exemple topique de l'Union européenne, ce sont les institutions de l'Europe, mais pas à leur propre profit. Elles travaillent par une sorte de délégation pour unifier. L'organisation de l'Union européenne n'est en ce sens qu'une forme de superstructure au service d'une certaine forme d'intégration qui, dans un schéma marxiste, est au service de l'infrastructure économique. Evidence sans doute mais qu'il est bon de rappeler pour se souvenir qu'il est parfois difficile d'estimer que des peuples européens plus unis doivent passer par cette voie ô combien étroite.

Que doit-on intégrer ? Des hommes dans une Europe que l'on veut unie, des modes de vie, des institutions, ou simplement des fonctions (l'économie, la justice, la politique étrangère, les activités maritimes, l'agriculture, etc) ? Or, il semble bien que l'on ait privilégié une intégration des fonctions sur une intégration des hommes, autrement dit que l'on ait pensé qu'en alignant des fonctions communes, on parviendrait à rendre les hommes plus soudés par l'utilisation de ces fonctions. Le problème a sans doute été que, parmi ces fonctions, le guide suprême fut l'économie, ou plutôt l'économisme. Certes le rouleau compresseur du libéralisme peut apporter un semblant d'unité, mais encore faut-il qu'il corresponde à un souhait unifié. Or, au gré de la versatilité des peuples et de leurs choix via les élections, ces souhaits changent et

[26] ibid, notre communication, *Traité des organisations internationales*, op cit.

[27] F Gény, « Le droit positif, ses rapports avec la philosophie et le politique », *Mélanges Basdevant* (Paris, Pedone, 1960) 234.

les dirigeants successifs se trouvent alors confrontés eux-mêmes à des modifications dans les valeurs porteuses, certes sur une marge assez faible. Dès lors, l'intégration subit les aléas de ces variations.

L'intégration ne se décrète pas, ne s'impose pas, elle s'apprend lentement à l'aide d'une forme d'éducation de la tolérance. Mais, pour ceci, il ne faut pas avoir l'économisme comme unique horizon. Or, à l'heure actuelle, on sent bien que les organisations ont assimilé les différentes strates de l'intégration sans que se dégage un schéma clair. La structure interétatique persiste, le fonctionnalisme reste partiel car sous-tendu par une vision souvent uniquement économique, les pouvoirs de l'organisation s'étendent via leur caractère implicite mais la frontière reste mouvante en fonction des aléas politiques, et la décision politique elle-même fait souvent défaut pour donner à l'organisation un pouvoir qui lui serait véritablement « propre ».

Il en résulte souvent une intégration forcée par la crise. On a pu répéter à de nombreuses reprises que l'Union européenne a connu des phases d'intégration post-crises. Il semble bien que l'épisode du Pacte budgétaire en soit une nouvelle illustration. On peut s'en féliciter, mais on ne peut ignorer que ce n'est toujours pas une intégration positive, d'autant qu'elle est inhibée par la croyance que seule l'Union européenne est une véritable organisation d'intégration, en ignorant superbement le reste du monde.

La voie de l'intégration suivie jusqu'à présent apparaît donc bien comme étant une des possibilités parmi d'autres d'aboutir à « l'acceptation » au sens large et philosophique, que ce soit des Etats, des domaines d'intérêts ou des divers peuples ou populations concernées par une organisation internationale. Mais ce n'est pas un horizon indépassable qui doit guider les organisations comme un but ultime et unique. On ne peut oublier qu'intégration et intégrisme ont la même racine. Mais surtout, on ne sait finalement pas ce qu'est réellement l'intégration, si ce n'est, pour le moment, un exercice de style consistant à postuler l'efficacité d'une organisation.

10

L'évolution des relations entre les Nations Unies et les organisations régionales de la Charte à nos jours

SANTIAGO VILLALPANDO*

I. INTRODUCTION

LA PRÉSENTE CONTRIBUTION a pour objectif de faire le point sur le cadre institutionnel dans lequel se placent les relations entre les Nations Unies et les organisations régionales. Si cette question se trouve en amont des thèmes de fond traités par d'autres panels de ce colloque, elle n'en reste pas moins essentielle pour appréhender les succès et les défis du régionalisme en droit international. La coopération entre organisations internationales est en effet la cheville ouvrière de l'interaction entre l'universel et le régional dans des domaines aussi variés que la coopération économique, le maintien de la paix et de la sécurité internationales, la protection de l'environnement ou la promotion des droits de l'homme.[1]

Ce cadre institutionnel a d'ailleurs suivi une étonnante évolution depuis 1945. La Charte des Nations Unies et la pratique des premières décennies de l'Organisation semblaient annoncer que les relations avec les accords et organismes régionaux resteraient limitées et figées dans un cadre normatif rigide (II). La pratique contemporaine, au contraire, se caractérise par la fluidité et le dynamisme, marqués par la multiplication des acteurs et des formes de coopération (III).

II. DES RELATIONS FIGÉES SELON LA CHARTE DES NATIONS UNIES

La première constatation est que la Charte des Nations Unies consacre un chapitre entier (le chapitre VIII) aux accords régionaux.[2] Le cadre normatif rigide établi par

* Chef de la Section des traités, Bureau des affaires juridiques de l'Organisation des Nations Unies. Les opinions exprimées dans ce texte sont celles de l'auteur et ne reflètent pas nécessairement les vues de l'Organisation des Nations Unies.

[1] Pour une excellente étude des relations entre organisations régionales et organisations universelles en général, voir : L Boisson de Chazournes, « Les relations entre organisations régionales et organisations universelles » (2010) 347 *Recueil des cours de l'Académie de droit international* 79–406.

[2] Pour des commentaires aux dispositions de ce chapitre, voir notamment : W Hummer et M Schweitzer, « Article 52 » et « Article 54 », dans B Simma et al (dir), *The Charter of the United*

ce chapitre (A) a cependant mené à une pratique initiale limitative de la coopération entre l'Organisation et les accords régionaux (B).

A. Un Cadre Normatif Restrictif

Comme le montre le chapitre VIII, l'Organisation des Nations Unies ne prétend pas au monopole de l'action dans la poursuite des buts de la Charte. En soi, il s'agit là d'une affirmation importante : la création d'une organisation universelle qui se veut « un centre où s'harmonisent les efforts des nations vers ces fins communes »[3] n'exclut pas une participation de mécanismes au niveau régional pour la poursuite des valeurs partagées par la communauté internationale dans son ensemble. Ces derniers sont non seulement préférables à l'action unilatérale ou inorganique, en ce qu'ils assurent une légitimité et une meilleure coordination desdits efforts, mais ils pourraient également présenter des avantages par rapport aux mécanismes universels. Les institutions régionales peuvent, en effet, mettre à profit la solidarité plus étroite et immédiate des États d'une région, qui partagent souvent la même perception des valeurs communes et sont plus directement en relation avec la situation qui pourrait nécessiter d'une action collective sur le terrain. Cette vision était présente dans une proposition égyptienne à la Conférence de San Francisco qui, dans sa définition des accords ou organismes régionaux, identifiait la « proximité, [la] communauté d'intérêts ou [les] affinités culturelles, linguistiques, historiques ou spirituelles » des États membres comme étant à l'origine de leur responsabilité commune pour le règlement pacifique des différends, le maintien de la paix et la sécurité dans leur région et le développement de leurs relations économiques et culturelles.[4]

Cela dit, dans la Charte, cette reconnaissance du rôle des institutions régionales apparaît pour le moins frileuse. Cela ressort, tout d'abord, des travaux préparatoires. Le plan proposé par les quatre grandes puissances à Dumbarton Oaks, en 1944, n'accordait déjà qu'une place subsidiaire aux accords ou organismes régionaux.[5] Les débats à la Conférence de San Francisco montrent certainement une volonté de préserver l'action régionale, mais certaines propositions visant à en étendre le champ d'application ou à en préciser les termes (comme la proposition égyptienne mentionnée ci-dessus) furent mises de côté.

Dans l'agencement de la Charte, la référence aux accords régionaux reste par ailleurs cloisonnée au chapitre VIII. En dehors de celui-ci, les seules mentions du régionalisme se trouvent à l'article 33, qui cite le recours aux organismes ou accords

Nations: A Commentary, vol I, 2e éd (Oxford, Oxford University Press, 2002), respectivement 807–53 et 890–95; G Ress et J Bröhmer, « Article 53 » dans ibid 854–90; E Kodjo et H Gherari, « Article 52 » dans J-P Cot, A Pellet et M Forteau (dir), *La Charte des Nations Unies: Commentaire article par article*, vol II, 3e éd (Paris, Economica, 2005) 1367–1402; R Kolb, « Article 53 » dans ibid 1403–37; M Gueuyou, « Article 54 », ibid 1439–45.

[3] Art 1, par 4, de la Charte des Nations Unies.

[4] Voir *Documents de la Conférence des Nations Unies sur l'organisation internationale*, tome XII (San Francisco, 1945) 854–55 et 859–60.

[5] Voir Propositions de Dumbarton Oaks relatives à l'établissement d'une organisation internationale, chapitre VIII, section C, dans *Documents de la Conférence des Nations Unies* (n 4) 16–17.

régionaux parmi les moyens de règlement pacifique des différends, et à l'article 47, qui prévoyait l'établissement de sous-comités régionaux du Comité d'état-major, avec l'autorisation du Conseil de sécurité et après consultation des organismes régionaux appropriés. Ces deux références sont d'ailleurs étroitement liées, respectivement, aux articles 52 et 53 du chapitre VIII. En revanche, les dispositions relatives au développement de la coopération internationale dans le domaine politique, au développement progressif du droit international et sa codification, à la coopération internationale dans les domaines économique, social, intellectuel ou humanitaire, ou à la gestion des territoires non autonomes et au régime de tutelle ne font pas mention expresse de la perspective régionale.[6]

Le texte même du chapitre VIII confirme cette frilosité. L'article 52 ne montre certainement pas un grand enthousiasme lorsqu'il se limite à déclarer qu'« [a]ucune disposition de la présente Charte ne s'oppose à l'existence d'accords ou organismes régionaux ... pourvu que [ceux-ci] et leur activité soient compatibles avec les buts et les principes des Nations Unies ».[7] Certains commentateurs sont même allés jusqu'à se demander si cette disposition ne devait pas être interprétée comme sanctionnant l'invalidité des accords ou organismes régionaux qui ne se conformeraient pas à de telles conditions.[8] Quant au rôle de tels accords ou organismes, il reste étroitement encadré: (1) dans le cadre du règlement pacifique des différends (article 52), l'action des accords ou organismes régionaux est certes encouragée, mais elle se borne aux « différends d'ordre local » (à savoir probablement ceux entre États parties à des tels accords ou membres de tels organismes) et « n'affecte en rien » les fonctions de l'Assemblée générale et du Conseil de sécurité sous le chapitre VI de la Charte, qui peuvent dès lors intervenir à tout moment ; (2) dans le cadre du maintien de la paix et de la sécurité internationales (articles 53 et 54), les accords ou organismes régionaux sont conçus comme de simples instruments du Conseil de sécurité, qui ne peuvent entreprendre aucune mesure coercitive sans l'autorisation de celui-ci et doivent, en tout temps, le tenir « pleinement au courant » de toute action entreprise, ou même envisagée.

En d'autres termes, ce qui ressort de la Charte des Nations Unies, c'est un cadre normatif des relations entre l'Organisation et les accords régionaux rigoureusement axé sur la primauté de l'organisation universelle.

B. Une Interprétation Initiale Limitative

Une interprétation rigoureuse de ce cadre normatif a conduit à une pratique limitative de la coopération avec les accords et organismes régionaux dans les premières années d'activité de l'Organisation. On n'en mentionnera que quelques éléments.

6 A l'exception peut-être du « principe général du bon voisinage », auquel renvoie l'article 74, qui peut avoir une dimension régionale (voir A Hasbi, « Article 74 » dans Cot, Pellet, Forteau (n 2), notamment 1780 et 1783–89).

7 Il se place en tout cas dans la lignée de l'article 21 du Pacte de la Société des Nations selon lequel « [l]es engagements internationaux, tels que les traités d'arbitrage, et les ententes régionales, comme la doctrine de Monroë, qui assurent le maintien de la paix, ne sont considérés comme incompatibles avec aucune des dispositions du présent Pacte ».

8 H Kelsen, *The Law of the United Nations* (London, Stevens and Sons, 1950) 324.

L'adoption de la Charte a en fait précédé le développement de l'intégration régionale telle que nous la connaissons de nos jours. A l'époque, seul le système américain comptait avec une institutionnalisation bien établie. D'autres régions allaient bientôt suivre le pas. Cependant, dans les premières années, seules trois organisations régionales semblaient indubitablement relever du chapitre VIII, à savoir : l'Organisation des États américains ;[9] la Ligue des États arabes ; et l'Organisation de l'Unité africaine.

L'application de l'article 53 relatif aux mesures coercitives étant bien entendu mise de côté par le blocage de l'action du Conseil de sécurité sous le chapitre VII, on ne rencontre que quelques rares applications de l'article 52 sur le règlement pacifique des différends. Dans la résolution 199 (1964) du 30 décembre 1964, notamment, le Conseil de sécurité exprima sa conviction que l'Organisation de l'Unité africaine « doit pouvoir aider, dans le cadre de l'Article 52 de la Charte des Nations Unies, à trouver une solution pacifique à tous les problèmes et différends qui affectent la paix et la sécurité sur le continent africain ». Dans la lignée du chapitre VIII, le Conseil y encourageait en l'espèce cette Organisation « à poursuivre ces efforts pour aider le Gouvernement de la République démocratique du Congo à réaliser la réconciliation nationale », tout en tenant le Conseil « pleinement au courant de toute action qu'elle entreprendra ».

Le cadre institutionnel du chapitre VIII présentait, en outre, des difficultés dans la pratique. L'invitation adressée au Secrétaire général de la Ligue des États arabes à assister aux sessions de l'Assemblée générale en qualité d'observateur (contenue dans la résolution 477 (V) du 1er novembre 1950) fut précédée de débats dans lesquels la conformité de la Ligue à l'esprit du chapitre VIII fut mise en question, en raison autant de sa composition que de ses procédures et statuts. De même, lors des débats à l'Assemblée générale et au Conseil de sécurité, en 1962, sur des mesures prises à l'encontre de Cuba par l'Organisation des États américains, l'action de cette organisation fut contestée par certaines délégations comme étant contraire aux principes de la Charte.[10]

III. DES RELATIONS FLUIDES DANS LA PRATIQUE CONTEMPORAINE

Faisons maintenant un pas de géant jusqu'à nos jours : nous y retrouvons un paysage bien différent. Si l'un des délégués qui avaient participé à la rédaction du chapitre VIII à San Francisco voyait l'état actuel des relations entre les Nations Unies et les organismes régionaux, il serait certainement surpris, autant par la multiplication et la diversité des institutions régionales (A) que par l'intensification et la fluidité de leur coopération avec l'organisation universelle (B).

[9] L'article 1er de la Charte de l'Organisation des États américains établit d'ailleurs expressément que : « Dans le cadre des Nations Unies, l'Organisation des États américains constitue un organisme régional ».

[10] Voir Hummer et Schweitzer (n 2) 844 ; Kodjo et Gherari (n 2) 1379–80.

A. La Multiplication des Organisations Régionales

Sa première surprise viserait probablement la multiplication et l'entremêlement des organisations régionales avec lesquelles les Nations Unies maintiennent une coopération régulière. Le spectre contemporain de ces organisations régionales est loin de répondre à l'agencement ordonné qu'on aurait pu prédire en 1945, et il se caractérise au contraire par le croisement des sphères géographiques et des États membres. On rencontre des organisations inspirées non seulement par la proximité géographique de leurs membres, mais également par d'autres critères, comme la communauté de langue (voir, par exemple, l'Organisation internationale de la Francophonie ou la Communauté des pays de langue portugaise) ou de religion (par exemple, l'Organisation de la coopération islamique). Leur objectif ne se limite souvent pas au règlement des différends ou au maintien de la paix, mais couvre toutes les sphères de la coopération internationale, comme le développement économique, social, culturel ou même juridique (voir, par exemple, l'Organisation juridique consultative pour les pays d'Asie et d'Afrique). En outre, dans le langage onusien, aux côtés des organisations régionales, il est désormais couramment fait référence à la dimension « sous-régionale », ce qui témoigne d'une décentralisation croissante de l'action internationale. Loin de rester théorique, cette décentralisation connaît des exemples pratiques très concrets dont l'intervention de la Communauté économique des États d'Afrique de l'Ouest dans les conflits au Libéria et en Sierra Leone.[11]

Ce phénomène a, en soi, une conséquence directe sur l'interprétation du chapitre VIII de la Charte. Au-delà de l'Organisation des États américains, l'Union africaine et la Ligue des États arabes, il est difficile de s'accorder sur les organismes qui relèveraient de ce chapitre. Comme on le verra ci-après, d'ailleurs, la fluidité de la coopération actuelle avec les organisations régionales est telle qu'elle a enlevé de l'importance à cette question.

Le nombre et la diversité des organisations régionales est également manifeste dans la liste des institutions invitées à participer, de façon permanente, en qualité d'observateurs aux sessions et aux travaux de l'Assemblée générale. On rencontre là une myriade d'organismes à tout niveau d'intégration, dont la Communauté des Caraïbes, le Conseil de coopération des États arabes du Golfe, le Secrétariat du Commonwealth, le Système d'intégration de l'Amérique centrale, pour n'en citer que certains. L'intégration régionale, d'ailleurs, ne manque pas de soulever des défis nouveaux, comme le démontre le débat sur les modalités de la participation de l'Union européenne aux travaux de l'Organisation, à la suite de la délégation à l'Union des fonctions de représentation extérieure de certains États membres en vertu du Traité

[11] Voir la résolution 788 (1992) du 19 novembre 1992, dans laquelle le Conseil de sécurité, ayant rappelé les dispositions du chapitre VIII de la Charte, remerciait la Communauté « des efforts qu'elle a fait pour rétablir la paix, la sécurité et la stabilité au Libéria ». Voir également la résolution 1132 (1997) du 8 octobre 1997, par laquelle le Conseil de sécurité, agissant en vertu du chapitre VIII de la Charte, autorisait la Communauté, en coopération avec le gouvernement démocratiquement élu de la Sierra Leone, à veiller à la stricte application des mesures adoptées par la résolution sous le chapitre VII, et demandait à tous les États de coopérer avec la Communauté à ce sujet.

de Lisbonne. L'Assemblée générale a trouvé une solution particulière à ce problème, qui réaffirme le statut d'observateur de l'Union, tout en lui accordant certaines prérogatives spéciales.[12]

Deuxième élément de surprise : loin de se limiter à « se conformer » aux buts et principes des Nations Unies, les organismes régionaux jouent souvent un rôle pionnier dans le développement de ces derniers. L'on citera, parmi d'autres exemples, l'Acte constitutif de l'Union africaine qui, dans un amorcement précoce d'une discussion aujourd'hui très à la mode dans les cercles onusiens sous l'égide de la « responsabilité de protéger », sanctionne « le droit de l'Union d'intervenir dans un État membre sur décision de la Conférence, dans certaines circonstances graves, à savoir : les crimes de guerre, le génocide et les crimes contre l'humanité » (article 4, alinéa *h*)). On pourrait également se référer à la contribution essentielle de plusieurs organisations régionales, comme le Conseil de l'Europe, l'Organisation des États américains ou l'Organisation internationale de la Francophonie, dans la promotion des valeurs démocratiques sur le plan international.

Les organisations régionales ont d'ailleurs innové non seulement dans les règles de fond, mais également dans les mécanismes et procédures pour la poursuite des buts et principes des Nations Unies. Dans un rapport de 2009 sur la mise en œuvre de la responsabilité de protéger, le Secrétaire général mentionnait ainsi deux exemples d'« initiatives originales prises par certains organismes régionaux ou sous-régionaux [qui] mériteraient peut-être d'être imitées dans d'autres parties du monde », à savoir : l'institution, en 1992, par l'Organisation pour la sécurité et la coopération en Europe, d'un Haut-Commissaire pour les minorités nationales ayant pour mission de déceler les tensions ethniques et de tenter de les désamorcer avant qu'elles ne dégénèrent ; et le système d'alerte précoce et de réponse rapide de la Communauté économique des États d'Afrique de l'Ouest.[13]

[12] Voir la résolution 65/276 de l'Assemblée générale (Participation de l'Union européenne aux travaux de l'Organisation des Nations Unies), adoptée le 3 mai 2011. L'Assemblée y rappelle que l'Union européenne s'est substituée à la Communauté économique européenne, qui avait le statut d'observateur depuis 1974 (résolution 3208 (XXIX) du 11 octobre 1974). L'Assemblée réaffirme « qu'elle est un organe intergouvernemental dont la composition est limitée aux États qui sont Membres de l'organisation des Nations Unies » et décide d'adopter des modalités, énoncées dans une annexe à la résolution, pour la participation des représentants de l'Union européenne, en qualité d'observatrice. Elle convient, par ailleurs, « qu'à la demande d'une organisation régionale dotée du statut d'observateur, dont les États membres ont pris des arrangements autorisant ses représentants à parler en son nom et au nom desdits États membres, elle pourra prévoir pour la participation des représentants de cette organisation régionale des modalités telles que celles annoncées dans l'annexe ». Selon ces modalités, les représentants de l'Union siègent parmi les observateurs et peuvent notamment : *a*) être inscrits sur la liste des orateurs avec les représentants des grands groupes pour faire des interventions ; *b*) être invités à participer au débat général de l'Assemblée générale selon l'ordre de préséance découlant de la pratique établie pour les observateurs et le niveau de représentation ; *c*) demander que leurs communications concernant les sessions et travaux de l'Assemblée générale et les sessions et travaux de toutes les réunions et conférences internationales organisées sous son égide et des conférences des Nations Unies soient distribuées directement et sans intermédiaire, comme documents de l'Assemblée ou documents de réunion ou de conférence; et *d*) présenter oralement des propositions et des amendements convenus par les États membres de l'Union européenne; ces propositions et amendements ne pourront être mis aux voix qu'à la demande d'un État Membre.

[13] La mise en œuvre de la responsabilité de protéger, Rapport du Secrétaire général, Doc NU A/63/677 (12 janvier 2009), par 37.

B. Une Coopération Souple

Si l'on se penche sur la relation de ces institutions régionales avec l'Organisation des Nations Unies, on observe une coopération à la fois souple et omniprésente.

L'intensification de la coopération avec les organisations régionales s'est faite de manière progressive. Un bon indicateur en ce sens est de suivre l'apparition, dans l'ordre du jour de l'Assemblée générale, des points relatifs à la coopération avec les différentes organisations. L'on constate ainsi que l'Assemblée a pris l'initiative, dès 1965, d'inviter le Secrétaire général à rechercher les moyens permettant de promouvoir la coopération avec l'Organisation de l'Unité africaine,[14] et qu'elle suit les relations avec l'Organisation de la Conférence islamique depuis 1980, avec la Ligue des États arabes depuis 1981 ou avec l'Organisation des États américains depuis seulement 1987.[15]

En 2001, l'Assemblée générale a accompli un pas important aux fins d'assurer la cohérence de l'approche de l'Organisation dans ce domaine, en décidant de considérer tous les points relatifs à la coopération avec les organismes régionaux dans un débat commun, tenu tous les deux ans, sous un point unique de son ordre du jour intitulé « Coopération entre l'Organisation des Nations Unies et les organisations régionales ou autres ».[16] Le titre même de ce point annonce, d'ailleurs, la flexibilité de l'approche actuelle, la référence aux « organisations régionales ou autres » témoignant d'une volonté de ne pas s'empêtrer dans le formalisme qui caractérisait, notamment, la terminologie du chapitre VIII de la Charte.

Depuis 2004, l'Assemblée demande en outre au Secrétaire général de lui présenter des rapports biennaux de synthèse unifiés au titre de ce point.[17] La lecture de ces rapports montre jusqu'à quel point la coopération entre les Nations Unies et les organismes régionaux s'effectue dans tous les domaines d'action de l'Organisation, à tous les niveaux, et suivant les modalités les plus variées. Le rapport de 2014 décrit les activités de coopération avec 21 organisations différentes, dans toutes les régions du globe, comprenant des initiatives du Conseil de sécurité, des différents départements du Secrétariat, du Haut-Commissariat aux droits de l'homme, de tous les fonds et programmes et de plusieurs agences spécialisées. A titre d'exemple, la coopération des Nations Unies avec l'Union africaine inclut : des réunions de consultation conjointes entre le Conseil de sécurité et le Conseil de paix et de sécurité de l'Union africaine ; l'appui aux opérations de maintien de la paix déployées par l'Union africaine (notamment au Mali et en Centrafrique) ; l'assistance technique en matière politique, logistique ou diplomatique ; ou des projets spécifiques dans multiples domaines, y compris le développement, la lutte contre la criminalité, la promotion des droits de l'homme, l'agriculture, le désarmement, la météorologie ou le commerce international.[18]

[14] Voir résolution 2011 (XX) du 11 octobre 1965.

[15] Voir Étude de l'ordre du jour de l'Assemblée générale, Note du Secrétariat, Doc NU A/58/CRP 6 (24 mars 2004), annexe I, pp 7–8.

[16] Voir résolution 55/285 du 7 septembre 2001, annexe, pars 3–9.

[17] Voir résolution 58/316 du 1er juillet 2004, annexe, par 4 *l*).

[18] Voir Coopération entre l'Organisation des Nations Unies et les organisations régionales ou autres, Rapport du Secrétaire général, Doc NU A/68/228*-S/2014/560* (4 août 2014), notamment pars 4–26.

Il ne s'agit là, toutefois, que de manifestations concrètes d'un changement d'approche délibéré des Nations Unies dans la coopération avec les organisations régionales. Dès 1992, le Secrétaire général Boutros-Ghali, dans son Agenda pour la paix, insistait sur le fait que « la conception d'un projet de coopération et la division du travail à l'intérieur de ce projet doivent être adaptés selon les réalités de chaque cas, dans un esprit de souplesse et de créativité ».[19] Quant au Secrétaire général Annan, il insistait, en 2005, sur les « rôles complémentaires » que doivent jouer les Nations Unies et les organisations régionales dans l'action menée en faveur de la paix et de la sécurité internationales, proposant des mécanismes concrets pour améliorer leur coordination.[20]

Le Document final adopté par les chefs d'État et de gouvernement des États membres des Nations Unies à l'issue du Sommet mondial de 2005 contient pas moins de dix-sept références aux bénéfices découlant de l'approche régionale pour faire face aux problèmes globaux.[21] Le Document inclut la décision d'élargir la consultation et la coopération avec les organisations régionales et sous-régionales non seulement en matière de paix et sécurité, mais aussi dans les domaines économique, social et culturel.

Le concept de « responsabilité de protéger », également proclamé dans le Document final de 2005, met lui-même l'accent sur la nécessité de coopérer avec les organisations régionales compétentes.[22] Dans son rapport sur la mise en œuvre du concept, le Secrétaire général Ban reprenait cette idée non seulement dans le contexte de ce qu'il a dénommé le troisième pilier de la responsabilité—à savoir l'action collective lorsqu'un État manque à son obligation de protection—mais également pour

[19] Agenda pour la paix, Diplomatie préventive, rétablissement de la paix, maintien de la paix, Rapport présenté par le Secrétaire général en application de la déclaration adoptée par la Réunion au sommet du Conseil de sécurité le 31 janvier 1992, Doc NU A/47/277–S/24111 (17 juin 1992), par 62 (voir, en général, pars 60–65). Le supplément de l'Agenda pour la paix insistait, quant à lui, sur la nécessité de créer des mécanismes de consultation concertés (quoique non nécessairement officiels), de respecter la primauté des Nations Unies, d'assurer une division du travail clairement définie et arrêtée en commun afin d'éviter des chevauchements d'activité et des rivalités, et de toujours maintenir un souci de cohérence dans l'action universelle et régionale. Le supplément identifiait, par ailleurs, au moins cinq formes que revêt la coopération entre les Nations Unies et les organisations régionales dans le cadre du maintien de la paix, à savoir : la consultation ; l'appui diplomatique ; l'appui opérationnel ; le codéploiement ; et les opérations conjointes. Voir : Supplément à l'Agenda pour la paix: rapport de situation présenté par le Secrétaire général à l'occasion du cinquantenaire de l'Organisation des Nations Unies, Doc NU A/50/60-S/1995/1 (25 janvier 1995), pars 86 et 88.

[20] Dans une liberté plus grande : développement, sécurité et respect des droits de l'homme pour tous, Rapport du Secrétaire général, Doc NU A/59/2005 (24 mars 2005), pars 213–15. Voir également : Un monde plus sûr : notre affaire à tous, Rapport du Groupe de personnalités de haut niveau sur les menaces, les défis et le changement, Doc NU A/59/565 (2 décembre 2004), annexe, pars 270–73.

[21] Résolution 60/1 de l'Assemblée générale des Nations Unies (Document final du Sommet mondial de 2005), adoptée le 16 septembre 2005, pars 3 (mobilisation de la communauté internationale dans les domaines économique et social), 40 (coopération Sud-Sud), 54 (énergie propre et changement climatique), 56 (système mondial d'alerte rapide pour risques naturels), 65 (problèmes de pays en développement sans littoral), 68 (besoins particuliers de l'Afrique, notamment en matière de médiation et règlement pacifique des conflits), 71 (paix et sécurité collective), 82, 87 et 88 (lutte contre le terrorisme), 93 (maintien de la paix), 100 et 101 (consolidation de la paix), 127 (respect des droits de l'homme), 139 (responsabilité de protéger), 144 (promotion d'une culture de paix) et 170 (renforcement des relations entre l'Organisation des Nations Unies et les organisations régionales et sous-régionales).

[22] ibid par 139.

ce qui est du deuxième pilier—celui de l'assistance internationale et du renforcement des capacités.[23]

Le Conseil de sécurité a suivi le pas de ce mouvement. Dans sa résolution 1631 (2005) du 17 octobre 2005, il se déclarait résolu à prendre les mesures appropriées pour renforcer la coopération avec les organisations régionales et sous-régionales en vue de maintenir la paix et la sécurité internationales, conformément au chapitre VIII de la Charte des Nations Unies. Là encore, les domaines de coopération couvrent les secteurs les plus variés, y compris la prévention des conflits, la gestion des crises et le déploiement rapide des forces de maintien de la paix, la lutte contre le commerce illicite des armes légères et le terrorisme, ou le règlement pacifique des différends.[24] Dans un rapport faisant suite à cette résolution, le Secrétaire général faisait état de la mise en place d'un partenariat entre l'Organisation des Nations Unies et les organisations régionales et autres organisations intergouvernementales ayant trouvé son origine dans les années 90 et qui comprend une coopération opérationnelle avancée dans le cadre de la prévention des conflits, le rétablissement, le maintien et la consolidation de la paix, le désarmement, la protection des civils ou le secours en cas de catastrophe naturelle.[25]

IV. CONCLUSION

La réalité actuelle de la coopération avec les organisations régionales, tout en faisant encore référence au chapitre VIII de la Charte, a largement dépassé le cadre institutionnel qui était prévu à l'origine. Pour les Nations Unies, l'un des défis principaux dans ce domaine est aujourd'hui d'adopter « une approche pragmatique et souple du

[23] Rapport du Secrétaire général, Doc NU A/63/677 (n 13), respectivement aux par 11 *c*) et *b*). Voir également, pour ce qui est du deuxième pilier, ibid, par 30 (sur le rôle des mécanismes régionaux et sous-régionaux dans les bons offices et efforts diplomatiques publics), 37 (initiatives originales prises par certains organismes régionaux ou sous-régionaux pour la prévention des conflits), 38 (renforcement des capacités civiles des organisations régionales et sous-régionales) et 47 (mise en place de processus interrégionaux d'apprentissage et de prise en compte des enseignements tirés de l'expérience dans le domaine de l'aide liée à la responsabilité de protéger). Pour ce qui est du troisième pilier, voir ibid, pars 49–50 (rôle des organisations régionales ou sous-régionales dans le cadre de la réaction résolue en temps voulu), 51 (mesures non coercitives prises sous le couvert d'accords régionaux ou sous-régionaux), 56 et 58 (adoption de mesures collectives coercitives par le biais d'accords régionaux ou sous-régionaux au titre de l'article 53 de la Charte avec le consentement préalable du Conseil de sécurité), 57 (coopération avec les organisations régionales dans l'application de sanctions ciblées) et 65 (mise en place de modes de collaboration plus efficaces entre l'ONU et les accords et organismes régionaux et sous-régionaux).

[24] Par ailleurs, dans sa résolution 1809 (2008) du 16 avril 2008, le Conseil de sécurité s'est déclaré, dans le contexte de sa considération de la question de la paix et la sécurité en Afrique, « résolu à prendre des mesures efficaces pour resserrer encore les relations entre l'ONU et les organisations régionales, en particulier l'Union africaine, conformément au Chapitre VIII de la Charte des Nations Unies », et a prié le Secrétaire général de lui faire le bilan de la coopération avec les organisations régionales concernées. C'est ainsi que, depuis 2008, le rapport du Secrétaire général sur la coopération entre l'Organisation des Nations Unies et les organisations régionales ou autres est soumis à l'Assemblée générale et au Conseil de sécurité conjointement. Le Conseil reste activement saisi de la question (voir notamment sa résolution 2033 (2012) du 12 janvier 2012, dans laquelle il montre notamment sa détermination de tirer des enseignements des instances de coopération récente avec l'Union africaine (par exemple au Darfour et en Somalie) afin d'améliorer la coordination.

[25] Les possibilités et les défis que présente le partenariat dans le domaine de la sécurité sur les plans régional et mondial, Rapport du Secrétaire général, Doc NU A/61/204–S/2006/590 (28 juillet 2006).

partenariat », tout en préservant les responsabilités que la Charte confie aux organes onusiens et en assurant la cohérence et l'impartialité de l'action commune.[26]

La relation entre les Nations Unies et les organisations régionales a, en fin de compte, suivi une évolution qui n'est pas sans rappeler le phénomène de « modernité liquide » qui, selon le sociologue polonais Zigmunt Bauman, caractérise notre société contemporaine.[27] De l'état « solide » du chapitre VIII, fondé sur un cadre normatif rigide qui consacrait la primauté de l'organisation universelle, nous sommes passés à un état « liquide » de ce qu'on appelle désormais un « partenariat », qui se caractérise—dans les termes des Secrétaires généraux successifs—par la « souplesse », la « créativité » et la « complémentarité ».

Au travers de cette approche flexible, on a su dépasser l'interprétation limitative des textes constitutifs, en tirant profit de la multiplication et la diversité des institutions régionales contemporaines. Il s'agit là certainement d'un développement positif, en ce qu'il permet d'amplifier les capacités des Nations Unies dans la poursuite des buts de la Charte et de moduler l'action internationale conformément aux particularités de chaque situation.

Cela dit, cette approche n'est pas sans poser certains défis, qui découlent justement du dépassement du cadre institutionnel originel. La souplesse et le dynamisme du partenariat actuel impliquent une évolution continue des rôles respectifs de l'organisation universelle et des organisations régionales. Dans cette perspective, les décisions bien connues de la Cour européenne des droits de l'homme dans les affaires *Behrami* et *Saramati*[28] et de la Cour de Justice des Communautés européennes dans l'affaire *Kadi*[29] présentent des problèmes opérationnels très concrets, en ce qui concerne, par exemple, l'effectivité de la mise en œuvre des résolutions du Conseil de sécurité ou la mobilisation sur le terrain de forces pour le maintien ou le rétablissement de la paix et la répartition de leurs tâches. La question qui se pose est donc dans quelle mesure le dynamisme nouveau de la coopération ne donne pas lieu à une certaine insécurité découlant de la perte d'un cadre de référence stable et n'encourage pas une certaine forme de « forum shopping » entre les Nations Unies et les différentes organisations régionales. En tout état de cause, les Nations Unies ont su mettre à profit—comme elles l'ont d'ailleurs fait dans d'autres domaines, tel que celui de la sécurité collective—les atouts de ce nouvel état des relations internationales, au bénéfice de la poursuite des buts et principes de la Charte.

[26] Voir ibid pars 11 et 100.

[27] Voir, notamment, Z Bauman, *Liquid Modernity* (Cambridge, Polity Press et Blackwell Publishers, 2000).

[28] Cour européenne des droits de l'homme (Grande Chambre), *Agim Behrami et Bekir Behrami c France, requête n° 71412/01, et Ruzdhi Saramati c France, Allemagne et Norvège*, requête no 78166/01, décision sur la recevabilité (31 mai 2007).

[29] Cour de Justice des Communautés européennes (Grande Chambre), *Yassin Abdullah Kadi et Al Barakaat International Foundation c Conseil de l'Union européenne et Commission des Communautés européennes*, affaires jointes C-402/05 P et C-415/05 P, arrêt (3 septembre 2008).

11

Commentaire sur Sorel et Villalpando

KAREL WELLENS*

I. INTRODUCTION

TOUT D'ABORD J'AIMERAIS remercier de tout cœur le Conseil de la Société et en particulier les organisateurs de cette Conférence, Jorge et Mariano, amis depuis longtemps, de m'avoir invité en me donnant « the challenging task of initiating the discussion [through] the main ideas or the main critical issues raised (if any) you wish to point out ».

Ma tâche n'est pas facile, vue entre autres la qualité renommée des deux rapporteurs, le fait aussi, je cite Jean-Marc Sorel, que « 'penser' l'organisation internationale est un exercice difficile » et, last but not least, la haute qualité de l'analyse offerte, il n'y a que deux ans, par Laurence Boisson de Chazournes dans son cours à la Haye, j'y reviendrai.[1]

Voici donc mes réflexions qui pourraient stimuler le débat sous la présidence de Jean-Michel Arrighi.

II. LE SUJET DE NOTRE FORUM

Le concept de « région » a connu une évolution et « trans-regional and meta-regional bodies » se sont manifestés.[2] D'autre part, il existe aussi le régionalisme particulier des collectivités territoriales non-étatiques, bien que « la prise en compte des collectivités territoriales non-étatiques par les organisations internationales à vocation universelle »[3]—se distingue fortement d'un rôle quelconque actif, effectif et fonctionnel.

La réalite nous apprend que « regional integration is not always a path strewn with roses, and conflict among States, among private entities—be they natural or

* Professeur émérite de droit international de l'Université Radboud de Nimègue (Pays Bas).

[1] L Boisson de Chazournes, « Les Relations entre Organisations Régionales et Organisations Universelles » (2010) 347 *Recueil des Cours de l'Academie de Droit International* 79–406.

[2] G Schiavone, « International Organizations between Regionalization and Globalization at the Dawn of the 21st Century » dans *Studi di Diritto Internazionale in Onore di Gaetano Arangio-Ruiz* (Napoli, Editoriale Scientifica, 2004), Vol II, 1403–1424, 1413.

[3] J-M Sorel, dans SFDI, Journée d'études, *Les collectivités territoriales non-étatiques dans le système juridique international* (Paris, Pedone, 2002) 125–43.

legal persons—and among private individuals and national and/or regional authorities forms an integral part of regional integration ».[4]

III. LES APPROCHES CHOISIES PAR LES RAPPORTEURS

A. Le Rapport de Santiago Villalpando

Dans son rapport Santiagio Villalpando a mis l'accent, dans le cadre institutionnel, sur la coopération entre l'ONU et les institutions régionales, coopération qui, comme il vient de démontrer de manière convaincante, a subi une évolution remarquable du restrictif, pratique limitative de coopération—donnant quand même un cadre de référence stable—à la situation actuelle, caractérisée par une coopération souple et dynamique, mais de nature fluide, laissant de côté le formalisme pré-existant.

Nous connaissons les lignes directrices de l'évolution esquissée dans le rapport: un rôle « pionnier » des institutions régionales dans le développement des buts et principes des Nations Unies (l'article 4, alinéa h de l' Acte de UA)[5], promotion des valeurs démocratiques par diverses organisations régionales et dans leur mise en place de mécansimes et procédures novatrices de consultation et de coopération, y compris « l'intégration » du concept de la responsabilité de protéger.[6]

En passant il faut bien noter qu'il n'est pas du tout évident de mettre en place dans toutes les régions du monde un système régional pour le maintien de la paix et la sécurité.[7]

Il y a deux questions qui se posent à propos du rapport de Santiago Villalpando.

L'intensification de la coopération avec les organisations régionales qui actuellement caractérise tant l'attitude et les actions de l'Assemblée Générale que du Conseil de Sécurité rejoint en fait, dans une certaine mesure, les désirs des pouvoirs moyens à Dumbarton Oaks. A juste titre Santiago Villalpando a cité le rapport du Secrétaire général, qui avait identifié comme un des défis principaux pour les Nations Unies celui d' adopter « une approche pragmatique et souple du partenariat » tout en préservant les responsabilités que la Charte confie aux organes onusiens et en assurant la cohérence et l'impartialité de l'action commune.

Voici la première question qui se pose.

Quels sont les défis principaux pour les organisations régionales compte tenu de la situation actuelle de la coopération? Serait-il audacieux pour elles d'essayer de pousser plus loin, en vue de regagner une autonomie déniée? Par exemple le

[4] J AE Vervaele, « Mercosur and Regional Integration in South America » 15 (2005) *International and Comparative Law Quarterly* 387–410, 407.

[5] Dans ce contexte on pourrait révéler qu'en 1943 Winston Churchill était en faveur d'un nombre de Conseils Régionaux sous le contrôle d'un Conseil mondial, ainsi cité par N White, *The Law of International Organisations* (Manchester, Manchester University Press, 1996) 156.

[6] Sur les problèmes à cet égard voyez par exemple I Terwase Sampson, « The Responsibility to Protect and ECOWAS Mechanisms on Peace and Security : Assessing their Convergence and Divergence on Intervention » (2011) 16 *Journal of Conflict and Security Law* 507–40.

[7] D Ouhan, « Commonwealth of Independent States : is there any Chance to Establish an Effective System of Collective Security in the Region? » (2011) 15 *Max Planck Yearbook of United Nations Law* 281–328.

débat sur la mise-en œuvre de mesures coercitives du Conseil de Sécurité est bien connu : utilisation progressive des cours et tribunaux régionaux à cet effet ou se limiter à faire entendre ses voix politiques dans la phase d'élaboration des mesures? Ambivalence aussi en matière des opérations pour le maintien de la paix : « tentatives de bénéficier du système onusien (validation de l'opération régionale, légitimité, financement, structure) » et en même temps « résister à se soumettre au contrôle du Conseil de Sécurité ».[8] Est-on en route vers une relation de parité?[9] Toutes des questions pertinentes que Laurence à posées à juste titre dans son cours et qui continuent à nous préoccuper.

La deuxième question est la suivante.

« L'étendue de la marge d'appréciation dont peuvent jouir les institutions régionales dans la mise-en œuvre de mesures » coercitives[10] et la pratique judiciaire européen de « conforming interpretation »[11] se situent dans le même contexte et me conduisent à la deuxème question : est-ce qu'on se trouve là devant une nouvelle forme de dédoublement fonctionnel, cette fois-ci entre l'organisation universelle et les organisations régionales ces dernières appelées « to act on behalf of the UN legal order, aiming *specifically* at faciliating the realisation of *values* stemming from that order? ».[12]

B. Le Rapport de Jean-Marc Sorel

Jean-Marc Sorel a choisi une approche totalement différente dont il vient de mettre en exergue les points les plus saillants. Son rapport me semble essentiellement une mise en garde contre les logiciels et des théories qui ne réussiraient (jamais) à nous faire comprendre la problématique de l'intégration, moins encore à l'utiliser ou de la diriger vers sa vocation dite positive. C'est enfin le fonctionnalisme qui se manifeste et prétend comme « la seule théorie globale et cohérente de l'organisation internationale » liée au phénomène de l'intégration.

Il s'agit en fait « de deux faces d'une même réalité » comme « l'intégration se réfère aux normes de l'organisation » tandis que « le fonctionnalisme touche les aspects opérationnels ».

Il faut quand même constater avec Jean-Marc Sorel « qu'entre la simple coopération et l'intégration une large gamme de situations apparaît ».[13]

[8] Boisson de Chazournes, *supra* n 1, 346.

[9] ibid.

[10] ibid 398.

[11] L Boisson de Chazournes et Pieter Jan Kuijper, « Mr Kadi and Mrs Prost : Is the UN Ombudsman Going to Find Herself between a Rock and a Hard Place? », dans E Rieter and H de Waele (eds), *Evolving Principles of International Law. Studies in honour of Karel Wellens* (Leiden, Brill Nijhoff, 2012) 71–90, 78–79.

[12] P De Sena and M C Vitucci, « The European Courts and the Security Council : Between Dédoublement Fonctionnel and Balancing Values » (2009) 20 *European Journal of International Law* 193–228, 210.

[13] A cet égard on peut rappeler les six éléments du régionalisme qui, selon Winfred Lang, pourraient être utilisés afin de mesurer le mouvement d'un processus régional vers plus ou moins d'intégration : W Lang, « New Regionalism in a Changing World Order » dans K Wellens (ed), *International Law : theory and Practice : Essays in honour of Eric Suy* (The Hague, Brill Nijhoff, 1998) 45–60,50 : « 1) institution-building ; 2) levels of economic development ; 3) a feeling of togetherness (psychological); 4) similarity of political regimes ; 5) communications and transactions ; 6) external political environment ».

Je suis d'accord avec le rapporteur que la coupure entre le rôle essentiellement d'ordre normatif et celui de caractère opérationnel paraît plutôt fictive et de ce fait ôte au fonctionnalisme la prétention d'offrir l'avantage d'être plus adapté à la catégorie d'organisations dites opérationnelles.

Pourtant je me demande si son critique addressée au fonctionnalisme n'est pas trop sévère dans ce sens que le fonctionnalisme peut rendre service en tant qu'instrument par exemple pour limiter l'exercise des pouvoirs et compétences des organisations par le biais de régimes d'accountability et de responsabilité. On pense au débat certainement pas achévé sur la co-responsabilité d'organisations internationales universelles ou régionales et de ses Etats membres concernés pour violations des normes du droit humanitiaire dans le cadre des opérations pour le maintien de la paix, conduites conjointement ou avec autorisation.

L'efficacité du fonctionnalisme et de l'intégration ne survivrait pas la traversée des domaines peu controversés vers les vrais pouvoirs des gouvernements. A cet égard Jan Klabbers nous rappelle, à juste titre, que cette distinction « might not be overly effective » comme il y a une ligne tellement fine « between what some would appreciate as political and what others would regard as rather functional, and much may depend on one's position ».[14]

C'est une erreur de considérer les problèmes d'ordre technique comme dépassant la politique.[15]

A propos du principe de la subsidiarité, il faut bien reconnaître avec Laurence que « le principe n'est pas transposable dans tous les champs des relations entre organisations universelles et régionales ».[16]

En nous offrant « un éclairage » utile des théories diverses, y compris le fonctionnalisme, Jean-Marc Sorel a fortement amélioré notre compréhension « de la dynamique qui lie les organisations internationales à leur environnement ».

IV. L'INTÉGRATION DANS LE CADRE DES ORGANISATIONS INTERNATIONALES

Je suis d'accord avec Jean-Marc Sorel que l'intégration n'est pas nécessairement « la voie qui doit être suivie aussi bien dans le cadre régional qu'universel pour les organisations internationales », mais à mon avis la problématique de l'intégration dans le cadre des organisations internationales comprend plus que « le processus par lequel les décisions qui étaient prises auparavant par les responsables d'Etats-Nations distincts sont maintenant prises par des personnes qui relèvent d'un centre nouveau (l'organisation internationale) ».[17] La problématique de l'intégration est plus diverse à cause du « fonctionnement » de l'intégration à multiples niveaux et à travers des modalités très diverses.

[14] J Klabbers, *An Introduction to International Institutional Law* (Cambridge, Cambridge University Press, 2002) 26–27.

[15] ibid.

[16] Boisson de Chazorunes, *supra* n 1, 401.

[17] Citation de CF Alger par Jean-Marc Sorel dans son rapport, *supra* n 3.

Tout d'abord il ne faut pas négliger que la protection d'intérêts régionaux est un élément structurel parmi d'autres du processus de décision des organisations internationales comme démontré par Rudiger Wolfrum,[18] ce qui n'est pas surprenant vu le fait que « integration of all interests involved is one of the prerequisites for the acceptability of the decisions taken »[19] et qu'à cet égard des groupes régionaux peuvent servir en tant que « pre-clearance fora ».[20]

Ensuite, une approche « intégrée » tant sur le niveau des normes que dans le domaine opérationnel des aspects et des questions des droits de l'homme, le maintien de la paix et la sécurite internationales, développement, protection de l'environnement, constitue, à mon avis, une évolution plus importante du fonctionnement des organisations internationales que les aspects institutionnels,[21] ou économiques de l'intégration dans le sens traditionnel sur l'axe cooperation/intégration réelle. Cette forme d'intégration n'est pas seulement qualitativement distincte, mais en surplus elle pourrait promouvoir l'efficacité, la légitimité démocratique et le self-gouvernance des organisations internationales.[22]

La position tenue par Nigel White que « regional bodies and organisations are far more likely to be able to adopt an integrated appraoch in dealing with particular tasks »[23] reste à être vérifié par la recherche.

V. QUELQUES TRAITS COMMUNS AUX DEUX RAPPORTS

Bien que totalement différent il m'est apparu que les deux rapports possèdent un nombre, restreint bien-sûr, de traits communs.

Tout d'abord, banal de remarquer, mais réalité qui s'impose à toute réflexion sur notre sujet, n'importe quelle approche qui découpe l'analyse d'une organisation internationale, universelle ou régionale, et l'examen de leur interaction, de l'environnement ou le paysage dans lequel se situent nos questions est condamnée à l'inefficacité partielle ou totale.

Deuxièmement, la fluidité se retrouve tant dans la pratique contemporaine des relations entre L'ONU et les organisations régionales que dans les courants économiques, financiers et politiques qui sont à la base des divers modèles de simple coopération ou d'intégration relativement avancée. L'appel croissant et justifié d'une correction sociale de l'Europe economique suffit à titre d'exemple.

Les deux rapporteurs ont soulginé, de manière differente, le lien intrinsèque et tout à fait naturel entre les activités normatives et les activités opérationnelles des organisations, lien qui se manifeste surtout à travers des thèmes particuliers, appartenant au deuxième volet du programme des fora.

[18] « The Protection of Regional or other Interests as Structural Element of the Decision-Making Process of International Organisations » 1 *Max Planck Yearbook of United Nations Law* (1997) 259–82.

[19] ibid 261.

[20] ibid 282.

[21] Bien que le degré d'institutionalisation continu à être considéré comme un des critères les plus significatifs pour mesurer le poids relatif d'une organisation régionale : Giuseppe Schiavone, *supra* n 21, 1418.

[22] EU Petersmann, « Time for a United Nations 'Global Compact' for integrating Human Rights into the Law of Worldwide Organizations : Lessons from European Integration » (2002) 13 *European Journal of International Law* 621–50.

[23] N White, *supra* n 5, 138.

VI. UNE QUESTION NON SOULEVÉE

A mon avis il y a une question non soulevée par les rapporteurs—ce qui ne surprend pas vue la tâche qui leur avait été assignée—mais qui néanmoins devrait se poser.

Quelle est l'influence certaine mais peut-être difficile à déchifrer et à évaluer des diverses traditions régionales en droit international[24] sur le fonctionnement des organisations régionales et sur leur évolution hésitante vers l'intégration. Peut-être il nous faudrait approfondir cette piste de recherche.

VII. EST-ON EN VAIN À LA RECHERCHE D'UN SCHÉMA GLOBAL?

La diversité des organisations internationales tant dans leurs activités normatives qu'opérationnels, le changement constant de leur environment et de la politique quotidienne de leurs Etats Membres, les points d'interrogation qui se posent à propos d'une évolution prétendument positive de la cooperation traditionnelle vers l'idéal préconisé de l'intégration mal défini—voici quelques facteurs capables ou destinés à rendre une recherche avancée d'un schéma global, totalement efficace à comprendre et à diriger les relations complexes entre régionalisme, organisations internationales et intégration, largement illusoire.

Chaque schéma devrait reconnaître tôt ou tard ses propres limites inhérentes, que même une approche comparative comme celle de Schermers et Blokker n'est pas capable de dépasser.

Peut-être le meilleur service que les juristes de droit international pourraient rendre au « fonctionnement » des organisations internationales, consisterait à étudier et à analyser, de manière critique mais nuancée, les questions qui se posent, tant sur le plan normatif qu'au niveau opérationnel, dans les divers secteurs particuliers et tellement divers des activités des organisations.

L'agenda de recherche sur les organisations internationales pourrait, à mon avis, bénéficier d'une marche en avant d'une telle approche pragmatique et thématique.

Il n' y a pas mal de questions de ce genre que les rapporteurs, fidèles à leur tâche, n'ont pas pu soulever. D'où aussi provient mon souci, qu'il se peut fort bien, qu'après avoir étudié ces aspects pragmatiques et thématiques, le besoin d'essayer de « construire » une grande théorie sur notre sujet ne serait plus urgent.

Comme a conclu, à juste titre, Laurence, de la « géométrie variable » (des relations entre organisation universelle et régionales) résulte « la difficulté, voire l'impossibilité de systématiser les relations entre organisation universelle et régionales ».[25]

Et en plus, le résultat d'une approche pragmatique et thématique pourrait consister à témoigner de l'émergence de systèmes de valeurs internationales et régionales en tant que manifestation d'un ordre constitutionnel international en voie d'élaboration.[26]

[24] Voyez à cet égard les différends symposia qui ont été publiés par le *European Journal of International Law*.

[25] Boisson de Chazournes, *supra* n 1, 401.

[26] E De Wet, « The Emergence of International and Regional Values Systems as a Manifestation of the Emerging International Constitutional Order » (2006) 19 *Leiden Journal of International Law* 611–32.

L'observation par Virginia Leary va un peu dans le même sens : bien que les théories de régime, le concept du fonctionnalisme et de la spécialité sont bien capabales de nous faire mieux comprendre le fonctionnement des organisations internationales, « [they nevertheless] neglect the overarching international constitutional principles of the post-World War II international legal order ».[27]

[27] V Leary, « International Institutions: towards Coherent Multilateralism », dans L Boisson de Chazournes et V Gowland-Debbas (eds), *L'ordre juridique international, un système en quête d' équité et d'universalité, Liber Amicorum G Abi-Saab* (The Hague, Brill Nijhoff, 2001) 823–29, 824.

Part IV

Regionalism and Globalisation

12

L'impact de la globalisation sur la société internationale et son droit

ANA PEYRÓ LLOPIS*

LE DÉBUT DU XXIème siècle a souvent été perçu comme l'apogée de la globalisation. Au tournant de ce siècle, le puissant mouvement global semblait en effet bel et bien installé au cœur de la société internationale. A ses côtés, le régionalisme demeurait en tant que contrepoids qui accompagnait—sans remettre nullement en cause—cette globalisation. D'ailleurs, le triomphe de la globalisation semblait s'accompagner de la montée en puissance du régionalisme et, plus spécifiquement, des organisations régionales.

Or, ces dernières années, une série d'événements politiques, économiques et sociaux ont nettement remis en cause ce qui semblait pourtant être irréversible. En effet, si un sujet comme celui-ci—globalisation et régionalisme—avait été abordé les premières années du XXIème siècle, l'approche aurait probablement été différente. Or, depuis 2007, l'on perçoit plus clairement qu'auparavant la tension croissante entre la permanence des menaces d'étendue planétaire et la tentation de se replier sur des réponses de niveau étatique.

En effet, une réponse juridique universelle a pu apparaître, face aux défis contemporains, comme étant peu précise, floue, voire contradictoire.[1] En revanche, les systèmes juridiques internes, quoique souvent insuffisants face aux enjeux concernés, présentent du moins l'avantage pour les Etats d'avoir des contours bien dessinés et une réglementation concrète. En outre, les légitimités politiques restent des questions d'ordre interne, ce qui perpétue le dilemme de la protection par les Etats d'un intérêt général à portée universelle sans nuire pour autant à leurs intérêts nationaux respectifs en jeu.

Le droit international a également été bouleversé par les évolutions et changements que l'ordre mondial a connus ces dernières années. En effet, après l'euphorie liée notamment aux succès de la juridicisation et de la juridictionnalisation mondiales, le droit international connaît un certain ralentissement qui, en même temps, implique des transformations majeures.

* Chercheur Ramon y Cajal à l'Université Complutense de Madrid, Maître de conférences à l'Université de Cergy-Pontoise (en détachement).

[1] Mireille Delmas-Marty soulevait déjà ce dilemme et se référait à la nécessité d'un « pluralisme ordonné », un pluralisme qu'il conviendrait d'ordonner sans pour autant le supprimer. M Delmas-Marty, *Le pluralisme ordonné*, *Les forces imaginantes du droit*, tome 2 (Paris, Seuil, 2006).

A titre préliminaire, une question terminologique mérite d'être précisée dans la mesure où le terme globalisation, traditionnellement anglo-saxon (face au français mondialisation) commence à pénétrer également la langue française.[2] Les références à la globalisation ne répondent parfois qu'à l'usage d'un anglicisme, mais dans d'autres cas, il s'agit d'un emploi volontaire qui contient une dimension idéologique. En ce sens, la globalisation correspondrait à une mondialisation économique qui serait à l'origine de la déliquescence d'un ordre juridique mondial, compris en tant qu'ordre supraétatique.

Ainsi, dans la présente étude, les termes mondialisation et globalisation sont employés avec ces significations distinctes afin de tenir compte de l'impact de la globalisation sur la mondialisation. En effet, la vision économique de la mondialisation est au cœur de la question centrale qui va être ici analysée, à savoir, la déliquescence des organisations internationales traditionnelles, qu'elles soient à portée universelle ou régionale, face à des directoires oligarchiques et, de même, si non la paralysie, du moins un frein à la juridicisation de l'ordre juridique mondial face au développement des lois du marché.

La question qui se pose dès lors est l'incidence que cette nouvelle organisation de la société internationale a sur l'ordre juridique international dans le contexte mondial actuel. D'une part, d'un point de vue organique, il s'agit d'examiner l'impact de la globalisation sur la structure, l'organisation de la société internationale (I). D'autre part, cette fois-ci d'un point de vue matériel, l'on constate que la globalisation et ses oligarchies influencent également le droit international, face au déclin de la mondialisation et du régionalisme classique (II).

I. UNE NOUVELLE STRUCTURATION DE LA SOCIÉTÉ INTERNATIONALE GLOBALE

En ce qui concerne l'organisation de la société internationale, les nouveaux rapports de force qui se sont dessinés ces dernières années ne peuvent être ignorés. Ceux-ci mettent en exergue le déclin de la mondialisation des institutions (A) et, parallèlement, le renouveau des rapports de puissance, que ce soit dans le cadre de groupements flexibles, souvent régionaux, ou à travers le renforcement de relations bilatérales classiques (B).

A. Le Déclin des Institutions Mondiales : l'Ascension de l'Intergouvernemental de Puissance Face à l'Intergouvernemental Égalitaire

La globalisation de la fin du XXème et du début du XXIème siècle s'écarte ouvertement du réseau institutionnel tissé après la Seconde Guerre Mondiale (qu'il s'agisse du système onusien ou des institutions de Bretton Woods) pour se rallier

[2] Sur cette question, et notamment sur la terminologie en espagnol : A Remiro Brotóns, « Crisis global y respuesta mundial » (2010) 14 *Anuario de la Facultad de Derecho-Universidad Autónoma de Madrid* 23.

à des structures plus flexibles forgées autour de la puissance économique des Etats. Un rôle primordial est accordé de nos jours aux réunions des premières puissances économiques mondiales, notamment les sommets du G-8 et du G-20. Il s'agit là de structures plus flexibles que le réseau institutionnel tissé après la Seconde Guerre Mondiale, mais il s'agit surtout de nouveaux groupements d'Etats, construits autour de la puissance économique des Etats, qui prétendent non seulement gérer des questions qui concernent leurs membres, mais également réglementer pour l'ensemble des Etats de la société internationale.

Ainsi, les grandes réunions intergouvernementales ne sont désormais plus celles qui sont tenues sous les auspices de l'Organisation des Nations Unies (ONU) ou d'autres organisations internationales à portée universelle (Fonds monétaire international, Banque mondiale...), mais celles qui réunissent les premières puissances économiques mondiales, quitte à inviter également des organisations du désuet tissu institutionnel (notamment le FMI et les Banques centrales). Il suffit d'ailleurs de comparer la réunion du G-20, qui s'est tenue au Mexique les 18 et 19 juin 2012, avec le Sommet planète Terre (la Conférence de Rio+20), qui a paradoxalement eu lieu le lendemain (du 20 au 22 juin 2012), pour mettre en exergue les structures de pouvoir de la société internationale. La quasi-simultanéité des deux réunions montre de manière flagrante des niveaux de participation tout à fait inégaux, une importance politique et médiatique opposée et des résultats fort différents et ce malgré le fait que les Sommets planète Terre n'ont lieu que tous les dix ans.

Par ailleurs, d'autres institutions plus récentes ne se présentent pas aujourd'hui sous leur meilleur jour. C'est notamment le cas de l'Organisation mondiale du commerce qui se trouve dans l'impasse plus de dix ans après la Conférence ministérielle de Doha, cette dernière ayant alors alimenté de nombreux espoirs d'évolution de l'organisation.[3]

Une série de facteurs géopolitiques permettent d'expliquer cette remise en cause de l'organisation de la société mondiale. Il s'agit notamment des suivants :

(i) D'abord, après des années d'unilatéralisme de la part des Etats Unis, lié notamment à l'administration de Georges W. Bush, l'on assiste ces derniers temps à une sorte de désengagement des Etats-Unis sur la scène internationale et, dans tous les cas, à une volonté de partage des responsabilités au niveau international.

(ii) Ensuite, le centre des intérêts globaux a changé de région. En effet, il semblerait que la fin de l'hégémonie occidentale soit arrivée, avec, parallèlement, un décalage du centre planétaire. Celui-ci serait passé du méridien 0° au méridien 180° et se trouverait désormais au cœur du Pacifique.

(iii) En ce qui concerne strictement l'ordre financier global, celui-ci a démontré qu'il ne pouvait ni ne voulait être un système d'organisation de la société mondiale mais qu'il répondait à la logique des marchés et des puissances qui les contrôlent.

[3] Pour une analyse de l'échec de Doha, voyer notamment S C Schwab, « After Doha. Why the Negotiations Are Doomed and What We Should Do About It » (2011) 90 *Foreign Affairs* (www.foreignaffairs.com/articles/67719/susan-c-schwab/after-doha).

D'autres facteurs, tels que les dépendances énergétiques, les flux migratoires et encore bien d'autres mériteraient également d'être soulignés. Dans tous les cas, il s'agit toujours de facteurs qui s'éloignent des fondements de la société internationale de l'après Seconde Guerre Mondiale et des concepts classiques de l'organisation internationale tels que la souveraineté des Etats et l'égalité entre eux. Les Etats se regroupent désormais autour de centres d'intérêts concrets (ce qui n'est pas en-soi une nouveauté), tout en échappant à des structures trop institutionnalisées et susceptibles de limiter leur marge de manœuvre (s'éloignant par là de l'institutionnalisation progressive de la société internationale, notamment au niveau régional, de la seconde moitié du XXème siècle). En outre, ces nouveaux groupements d'Etats prétendent non seulement gérer des questions qui concernent leurs membres illustres mais également réglementer pour l'ensemble des Etats de la société internationale dans la mesure où la protection de leurs intérêts dépend souvent de l'action d'Etats tiers. L'on pourrait être tenté de penser que cela arrivait déjà dans une certaine mesure au sein des organisations internationales classiques, ce qui ne serait pas éloigné de la réalité. Mais avec la déstructuration de la société internationale, les Etats les plus puissants peuvent en outre se passer des contraintes qui découlent du fait d'être membres d'une organisation internationale reposant sur le principe de l'égalité souveraine.

B. Des Rapports de Puissance Hiérarchisés : du Régionalisme au Directoire

Face au déclin souligné de la société internationale, il convient de s'intéresser au rôle que le régionalisme joue ainsi qu'à la place réservée aux organisations régionales. Ces dernières n'ont en effet cessé de se développer parallèlement aux institutions à portée universelle. Parfois perçues comme un renforcement de l'organisation mondiale,[4] elles ont d'autres fois été en concurrence avec les institutions mondiales, pouvant être même à l'origine de la déliquescence de ces dernières. Et pourtant, elles se trouvent également dans l'impasse face à la flexibilité des nouvelles formes de regroupement des Etats. Quelle place alors pour le régionalisme dans ce contexte, dans cette nouvelle structuration de la société globale ? Il est encore difficile d'apporter une réponse à cette question qui en soulève d'autres :

i. En Premier Lieu, Pourrait-on Qualifier les « Directoires Oligarchiques » de Régionaux ?

Le régionalisme mérite d'abord d'être distingué des organisations régionales dans la mesure où le premier peut se manifester sous des formes autres que la structure rigide des organisations régionales. Le régionalisme s'éloigne donc du concept d'organisation régionale et peut être rapproché, tel que cela a été souligné précédemment, des réalités et des logiques de puissance, tout particulièrement en matière économique. Ainsi, des régionalismes non institutionnalisés et plus flexibles, avec des acteurs unis fondamentalement par des intérêts économiques, ou par le pouvoir

[4] Laurence Boisson de Chazournes, « Les relations entre organisations régionales et organisations universelles » (2010) 347 *Recueil des Cours de l'Academie de Droit International* 164.

de facto de leurs membres, se développent. Le régionalisme est alors compris en dehors des organisations régionales, en tant que solidarité d'intérêts entre certains pays qui souvent appartiennent à une même région mais qui d'autres fois n'en font pas partie.

S'agit-il encore de régionalisme malgré la provenance d'horizons géographiques éloignés ? Depuis longue date, rien ne semble s'opposer à envisager des régionalismes éloignés de la notion géographique de région. Par exemple, le chapitre VIII de la Charte des Nations Unies (limité, certes, aux organisations régionales amenées à intervenir dans le domaine de la paix et de la sécurité internationales) n'exige pas de condition de proximité pour qualifier un groupe d'Etats de régional. Il s'agit plus exactement de groupements partiels, en opposition à l'organisation mondiale.[5] H Kelsen considérait que l'article 52 de la Charte n'impliquait pas une proximité géographique mais simplement l'existence d'une « communauté d'intérêts ».[6] De même M. Virally disait-il que les organisations régionales se distinguent des universelles par le fait qu'elles « répondent aux exigences de solidarité restreintes, ressenties à l'intérieur d'un groupe limité d'Etats ».[7] Il insiste donc également sur l'existence d'intérêts communs restreints qui ne provient pas nécessairement de la proximité géographique. Ainsi propose-t-il d'opposer aux organisations universelles des organisations partielles ou restreintes, les organisations régionales n'étant alors « qu'une sous-catégorie à l'intérieur de la catégorie organisations partielles ».[8]

Des groupes d'Etats flexibles, tels que le G-8 ou le G-20, répondent à la définition de « communauté d'intérêts » ou d'exigences de solidarité restreintes bien qu'ils n'aient (bien entendu) jamais employé cette terminologie pour s'identifier. Heureusement, car il serait paradoxal de reprendre la terminologie de la communauté et de la solidarité pour se référer aux oligarchies dominantes. D'ailleurs, si l'on examine la Déclaration finale de la réunion du G-20 de juin 2012 (Mexique), après avoir reconnu le « large impact » de ses décisions, le G-20 déclare qu'il « continuera à faire des efforts avec les pays non membres, les organisations régionales et internationales, y compris les Nations Unies et d'autres acteurs ».[9] Une telle rédaction,

[5] Cette position est notamment défendue par : H Kelsen, *The Law of the United Nations* (Londres, Stevens & Sons Limited, 1951) ; M Virally, *L'Organisation mondiale* (Paris, Librairie Armand Colin, 1972) ; J Cardona Lloréns, « La coopération entre les Nations Unies et les accords et organismes régionaux pour le règlement pacifique des affaires relatives au maintien de la paix et de la sécurité internationales », *Boutros Boutros-Ghali Amicorum Discipulorumque Liber* (Bruxelles, Bruylant, 1998) 251 ; U Villani, « Les rapports entre l'ONU et les organisations régionales dans le domaine du maintien de la paix » (2001) 290 *Recueil des Cours de l'Academie de Droit International* 225. Elle a également été défendue par B Boutros-Ghali, en tant que Secrétaire général, *in* A/47/277-S/24111, du 17 juin 1992, *Agenda pour la paix. Diplomatie préventive. Rétablissement de la paix, maintien de la paix,* Rapport du Secrétaire général en application de la déclaration adoptée par la Réunion au sommet du Conseil de sécurité le 31 janvier 1992. *A contrario*, W E Beckett, *The North Atlantic Treaty, the Brussels Treaty and the Charter of the United Nations* (Londres, Stevens & Sons, 1950); P Vellas, *Le régionalisme international et l'Organisation des Nations Unies* (Paris, Pedone, 1948).

[6] H Kelsen, *The Law of the United Nations* (1951) 319–20 ; *Recent trends in the Law of the United Nations. A Supplement to the Law of the United Nations* (Londres, Stevens and Sons, 1951) 920.

[7] M Virally, « Les relations entre organisations régionales et organisations universelles », *Régionalisme et universalisme dans le droit international contemporain,* Colloque SFDI de Bordeaux (Paris, Pedone, 1977) 148.

[8] ibid 150.

[9] Déclaration de Los Cabos, Mexique, 19 juin 2012, para 83.

qui n'est pas exempte d'une bonne dose d'arrogance, est révélatrice de deux traits caractéristiques de ces nouvelles formes d'organisation de la société internationale. D'une part, elle reflète la place tout à fait secondaire réservée aux acteurs classiques de la société internationale, à savoir les Etats (non membres du G-20) et les organisations internationales (qu'elles soient à portée universelle ou régionale). D'autre part, elle indique clairement que les décisions du G-20 ne visent pas exclusivement ses membres mais cherchent à avoir un « large impact » sur la société internationale. Le G-20 s'éloigne par là, tel que cela a été souligné, des principes basiques de la société internationale reposant sur l'égalité souveraine des Etats et l'effet relatif des obligations internationales du droit des traités.

Cette déclaration peut d'ailleurs être comparée et confrontée à celle issue de la Conférence de Rio+20, dans laquelle les Etats soulignent le rôle crucial des organisations internationales, et notamment des organisations régionales :

> les organisations régionales et sous-régionales, y compris les commissions régionales des Nations Unies et leurs bureaux sous-régionaux, *ont un rôle majeur à jouer dans la promotion d'une intégration équilibrée des dimensions économique, sociale et environnementale du développement durable dans leurs régions respectives.*[10]

ii. Deuxième Question, ce « Nouveau Régionalisme », s'éloigne-t-il de la Structure de l'Organisation Régionale et se Rapproche-t-il également des Réalités et des Logiques de Puissance, tout Particulièrement en Matière économique ?

Au niveau européen, il convient de mettre en exergue le rôle que la Banque centrale européenne est en train de jouer actuellement face à d'autres institutions de l'Union européenne.

De même, force est de constater un renouveau des relations bilatérales et des mécanismes intergouvernementaux classiques, encore et toujours entre les Etats les plus puissants, avec un certain désengagement des institutions internationales et un repli sur des alliances bilatérales ou multilatérales restreintes.

iii. D'ailleurs, la Troisième Question que Soulève l'Analyse du Régionalisme dans le Contexte de la Globalisation Porte sur le Rôle et le Développement des Organisations Régionales plus Classiques

Le déclin des organisations internationales classiques et la montée en puissance des oligarchies s'accompagne de la stagnation des organisations régionales au sens strict du terme. L'Union européenne (UE) ne semble plus être le modèle ambitionné et suivi par d'autres régions en phase de construction institutionnelle. Le contexte économique actuel au sein de l'UE présage également un éloignement et des réticences chaque fois plus marquées vis-à-vis du modèle européen. Même des organisations régionales, à priori fondées sur le modèle européen, ont en réalité des institutions et modes de fonctionnement qui s'éloignent du modèle européen. En effet, le mode de

[10] A/66/L 56, 24 juillet 2012, Projet de résolution déposé par le Président de l'Assemblée générale, « L'avenir que nous voulons », para 100. Nous soulignons.

prise de décisions qui existe au sein de l'UE reste exceptionnel et, bien que d'autres organisations régionales et sous-régionales aient apparemment voulu suivre la formule d'intégration de l'UE, dans la pratique, leurs mécanismes de prise de décision restent intergouvernementaux, et ce malgré les similitudes institutionnelles qui existent entre elles. C'est notamment le cas de l'Union africaine qui, malgré une structure institutionnelle à l'image de l'UE (Conseil exécutif, Commission, Parlement panafricain, Cour de Justice ...), continue à adopter ses décisions par consensus (Conférence de l'Union et Conseil exécutif).

Toutefois, il convient de souligner que la stagnation de l'UE peut être opposée au renouveau d'un régionalisme de proximité, comme celui de la Ligue des Etats Arabes pour les conflits de la région. En effet, l'avènement du printemps arabe n'est pas exempt de conséquences sur l'organisation de la société internationale dans la mesure où l'on assiste au renouveau d'un régionalisme de proximité, prioritaire par rapport aux institutions à portée mondiale et notamment par rapport à l'ONU. Mais il ne faut pas se leurrer : il s'agit là d'une autre manifestation du désengagement au niveau mondial, justifié par la nécessité de compter sur l'accord des acteurs régionaux de la région concernée. Par exemple, l'on défend désormais que le soutien de la Ligue des Etats Arabes devrait être obtenu pour toute initiative dans la région, et *a fortiori* pour une intervention comme celle qui a eu lieu en Libye.

La société internationale connaît donc un moment d'effervescence qui l'éloigne des formules supraétatiques et qui, face à la permanence des enjeux mondiaux, se replie sur des solutions étatiques et interétatiques. Cette situation se ressent également, d'un point de vue matériel, sur son droit, le droit international public.

II. LA GLOBALISATION, LE RÉGIONALISME ET LEUR DROIT

La globalisation a également eu des effets sur le droit international. De la même façon que les institutions qui se sont forgées après la Seconde Guerre Mondiale ont dû faire face à des régionalismes flexibles, la globalisation a eu pour sa part des effets sur le droit international lui-même.

Le régionalisme qui s'est développé avec les organisations régionales du XXème siècle a contribué à l'essor du droit international et de ses institutions dans la mesure où il s'est inspiré des expériences universelles et est devenu « un outil de 'cristallisation' de l'universel ».[11] Face au déclin des institutions mondiales et des organisations régionales traditionnelles et à l'émergence d'autres formes d'organisation de la société internationale, autant l'ordre juridique mondial que celui régional ont connu un développement de règles plus flexibles et parfois non exemptes de dangers. En outre, le droit régional a une portée limitée face à des réalités globales dépassant l'ordre juridique régional, dans la mesure où les enjeux demeurent mondiaux, les moyens régionaux restent insuffisants et les Etats se replient, soit sur leurs ordres juridiques internes, soit sur des formes de coopération interétatiques classiques, soit sur des règles déterminées par le régionalisme flexible.

[11] Boisson de Chazournes, « Les relations entre organisations régionales » 164.

En effet, autant l'ordre juridique mondial que celui régional se trouvent confrontés aux défis posés par la globalisation, par ses nouveaux acteurs ainsi que par le développement de règles flexibles (*soft law*), souvent contestables, qui s'appliquent également à des Etats qui n'ont pas participé à leur formation. La globalisation serait alors, avant tout, un frein dans la progression du droit international supraétatique et se trouverait à l'origine du déclin de l'ordre juridique mondial (A). Le droit de la globalisation se présente alors comme un droit flexible et transnational, mais également un droit voyou qui s'écarte parfois des critères de légalité et de légitimité (B).

A. La Globalisation: Un Frein dans la Progression du Droit International Supraétatique

Ces dernières années, la formation d'un ordre juridique à portée universelle a connu un certain ralentissement. Cette tendance n'annonce pas pour autant l'avènement de la fin du droit international. Bien au contraire, l'on constate que celui-ci jouit d'une très bonne santé en tant que droit interétatique. C'est en tant que droit supraétatique qu'il aurait cessé de progresser. En effet, la plupart des développements des dernières décennies qui ont contribué à la formation d'un droit international supraétatique ne connaissent plus d'évolution majeure et sont même contestés.

Prenons quelques exemples afin de démontrer cette affirmation :

(i) Commençons par le domaine des droits de l'Homme, dans la mesure où il s'agit du domaine paradigmatique de la formation d'un droit de la communauté internationale et dans lequel le droit supraétatique a revêtu sa forme la plus claire, à travers les normes de *jus cogens* et l'existence d'obligations *erga omnes*.[12] Plus près de nous, vers la fin du XXème et le début du XXIème siècles, le domaine de la protection des droits de l'Homme a été en pleine effervescence avec l'émergence des interventions d'abord dites humanitaires puis de la responsabilité de protéger.[13] Or, depuis début 2011 et face aux différents mouvements dans une série d'Etats du monde arabe, l'on assisterait à une déliquescence de certaines de ces normes en formation de la communauté internationale. Ainsi, des Etats ayant défendu et réalisé des interventions humanitaires[14] seraient désormais plus réticents à de telles interventions, en avançant la notion de souveraineté des Etats et en rappelant les règles de la Charte des Nations Unies, bien que défendant en réalité des intérêts purement

[12] Voyer notamment M Ch Bassiouni, « International Crimes: Jus Cogens and Obligatio Erga Omnes » (1996) 59 *Law and Contemporary Problems* 63 ; E de Wet, « Jus Cogens and Obligations Erga Omnes », *The Oxford Handbook of International Human Rights Law* (Oxford, Oxford University Press, 2013).

[13] A/RES/63/308, du 7 octobre 2009. Voyer également, pour rappel, le Rapport « La responsabilité de protéger » de la Commission internationale de l'intervention et de la souveraineté (ICISS), instituée par le Gouvernement canadien en décembre 2001 (A/57/303, du 14 août 2002).

[14] Le Conseil de sécurité a adopté, avec des références explicites à la responsabilité de protéger des résolutions sur la situation en Libye (S/RES/1970 (2011)), Côte d'Ivoire (S/RES/1975 (2011)), Yémen (S/RES/2014 (2011)) ou le Soudan du Sud (S/RES/1996 (2011)). Il a néanmoins été bloqué par le véto de la Chine et de la Russie en ce qui concerne la situation en Syrie.

politiques et stratégiques ou économiques.[15] En outre, l'on perçoit un dangereux retour vers des doctrines relativistes qui tiendraient compte des différences culturelles, justifiant par là certaines violations des droits de l'Homme.[16] Enfin, l'intervention internationale en Libye, comparée à l'absence de réaction face à d'autres situations, montre qu'il continue à y avoir deux poids deux mesures dès lors qu'il s'agit de protéger les populations civiles.

En ce qui concerne les mécanismes universels de protection des droits de l'Homme, il existe certes d'une part un niveau élevé de ratifications des conventions internationales de protection des droits de l'Homme[17] et, en ce qui concerne le système des Nations Unies, l'Examen périodique universel (EPU) au sein du Conseil des droits de l'Homme des Nations Unies a également supposé une avancée dans le suivi des obligations des Etats en matière de droits de l'Homme. Mais d'autre part, le respect des recommandations formulées par les différents organes chargés du suivi des conventions de protection des droits de l'Homme reste limité, diminuant par là l'effectivité du système à portée universelle de protection des droits de l'Homme.

Face à cette stagnation—voire régression—au niveau universel de la protection des droits de l'Homme, fruit d'une globalisation qui ne s'y intéresse pas, la protection se renforce néanmoins au niveau régional, où la légitimité des Cours régionales de protection des droits de l'Homme (surtout européenne et interaméricaine) a été renforcée. Au niveau européen, une nouvelle étape a été franchie avec l'entrée du Traité de Lisbonne et la prévision de la future adhésion de l'Union européenne (UE) à la Convention européenne des droits de l'Homme,[18] dans la mesure où l'action de l'UE sera alors soumise au contrôle de la Cour européenne des droits de l'Homme.

(ii) Dans un tout autre contexte, celui de la juridictionnalisation de la société internationale, l'on constate également un repli du droit international supraétatique, et concrètement, de la soumission de certains crimes à portée internationale à des juridictions internationales. Face à la création et aux avancées de la Cour pénale internationale à la fin du XXème et début du XXIème siècles, l'on constate à présent un renouveau du rôle des tribunaux internes, des cours régionales ainsi que des formules hybrides à travers des tribunaux internes internationalisés.

La lutte contre la piraterie maritime illustre bien cette évolution. En effet, le Groupe de contact sur la piraterie au large des côtes somaliennes (et notamment son Groupe de travail n°2 sur les questions juridiques) avait envisagé au

[15] C'est notamment le cas du Royaume-Uni, de la France et des Etats-Unis qui, après les résultats de l'intervention en Lybie, voire en Irak pour les Etats-Unis, ont progressivement estimé qu'il n'était pas judicieux d'intervenir dans un conflit comme selui de la Syrie.

[16] M Delmas-Marty, « Le relatif et l'universel », *Les forces imaginantes du droit. Le relatif et l'universel* (Paris, Seuil, 2004) 65.

[17] Par exemple, pour simplement reprendre deux instruments emblématiques, le Pacte internationale relatif aux droits économiques, sociaux et culturels compte 164 ratifications et le Pacte international relatif aux droits civils et politiques 168 (état des ratifications consulté le 11 mars 2015).

[18] L'article 6.2 du Traité sur l'Union européenne dispose en effet que « [l]'Union adhère à la Convention européenne de sauvegarde des droits de l'Homme et des libertés fondamentales. Cette adhésion ne modifie pas les compétences de l'Union telles qu'elles sont définies dans les traités ».

départ autant la possibilité de demander l'inclusion de la piraterie dans le Statut de la Cour pénale internationale que la création d'une Cour internationale spécialisée en matière de piraterie (et qui aurait probablement été localisée en Afrique de l'Est). Les différentes options furent examinées dans le rapport du Secrétaire Général des Nations Unies sur les possibilités de concourir à la réalisation de l'objectif de poursuivre et d'emprisonner les personnes responsables d'actes de piraterie et de vol à main armée au large des côtes somalienne.[19] Or, les options visant des juridictions internationales furent rejetées pour se replier vers des solutions impliquant certaines juridictions nationales qui recevraient néanmoins une assistance internationale. L'accent est ainsi mis sur la nécessité de renforcer la coopération internationale (interétatique) et régionale en traduisant les pirates en justice auprès de juridictions nationales. Les juridictions visées ont été, dans un premier temps, celles du Kenya,[20] des îles Seychelles[21] et de l'île Maurice,[22] des Etats avec lesquels l'Union européenne a signé des accords de transfèrement. Dans un deuxième temps, les travaux menés au sein des Nations Unies incident sur la création de juridictions spécialisées en matière de piraterie maritime au sein de l'ordre juridictionnel somalien.[23] Parallèlement, tous les rapports demandent constamment aux Etats d'introduire dans leurs ordres juridiques internes respectifs des règles de droit pénal ainsi que la reconnaissance de la compétence de leurs tribunaux.[24]

En ce qui concerne les tribunaux internes internationalisés, la prolifération de ces juridictions hybrides ou mixtes (Cambodge, Sierra Leone, Kosovo, Timor Oriental, Liban, et pourquoi pas Irak, avec la mise en place du Tribunal pénal suprême irakien) sont des exemples de solutions qui s'éloignent des réponses intégralement supraétatiques. En effet, bien que ces tribunaux aient été créés internationalement, ils ont, de manière générale (il existe des différences importantes entre ces tribunaux) une composition mixte (juges internationaux et internes) et appliquent autant des règles de droit interne que de

[19] S/2010/394, du 26 juillet 2010, Rapport du Secrétaire général sur les différentes options possibles pour mieux parvenir à poursuivre et incarcérer les personnes responsables d'actes de piraterie et de vols à main armée commis au large des côtes somaliennes, y compris, en particulier, sur des options tendant à créer dans les juridictions nationales des chambres spéciales, éventuellement dotées d'éléments internationaux, ou à créer un tribunal régional ou encore à créer un tribunal international, et sur les accords correspondants en matière pénitentiaire, en tenant compte des travaux du Groupe de contact pour la lutte contre la piraterie au large des côtes somaliennes, des précédents en matière de création de tribunaux internationaux et de tribunaux mixtes, et du temps et des moyens nécessaires pour obtenir des résultats concrets et durables.

[20] Accord du 6 mars 2009.

[21] Accord du 10 novembre 2009.

[22] Accord du 14 juillet 2011.

[23] S/2011/360, du 15 juin 2011, Rapport du Secrétaire général sur les modalités de la création de juridictions somaliennes spécialisées pour juger les personnes soupçonnées de piraterie.

[24] Par exemple, dans le *Rapport du Secrétaire général sur les différentes options possibles pour mieux parvenir à poursuivre et incarcérer les personnes responsables d'actes de piraterie et de vols à main armée commis au large des côtes somaliennes [...]*, il y est souligné que « [l]es éléments nécessaires dans le cadre de la juridiction nationale pour engager des poursuites sont les suivants : infractions graves de piraterie et vols à main armée commis en mer; responsabilité pénale des personnes qui participent à la commission de telles infractions, ou tentent de les commettre; dispositions établissant une juridiction pénale nationale pour les infractions de piraterie commises en haute mer; et dispositions requises en matière de procédure et de preuve pour engager des poursuites » (S/2010/394, du 26 juillet 2010, par 17).

droit international. Il convient notamment de mettre en exergue la création, en mai 2007, du Tribunal spécial pour le Liban, mis en place afin de juger les responsables de l'assassinat de l'ex-premier ministre libanais Rafic Hariri, qui applique directement le code pénal libanais pour des crimes qui ne rentrent pas dans la catégorie de crimes internationaux au sens du statut de la Cour pénale internationale (terrorisme,...). Il convient d'ailleurs de rappeler à cet égard que toute tentative d'élargir la compétence *ratione materiae* de la CPI a été écartée.[25]

(iii) Dans le domaine du maintien de la paix et de la sécurité internationales, le désengagement des Nations Unies a également donné lieu à des réponses qui s´éloignent du cadre classique tel qu'il résulte du chapitre VII de la Charte des Nations Unies. Les organisations régionales ont souvent pris le relai et développé de nombreuses règles, parfois dans le cadre du chapitre VIII de la Charte, d'autres fois au-delà de celui-ci. Le régionalisme africain (et ses différents sous-régionalismes) mérite d'être placé au cœur de ces évolutions, de par le rôle qu'a été amenée à jouer notamment l'Union africaine dès sa création[26] et, plus récemment, la Ligue des Etats arabes, mais également d'autres organisations sous-régionales telles que la Communauté économique des États de l'Afrique de l'Ouest (CEDEAO). Parallèlement, toujours dans le domaine du maintien de la paix et de la sécurité internationales, il convient de rappeler que les décisions rendues d'abord par le Tribunal de l'Union européenne (ancien Tribunal de première instance), dans les affaires *Kadi* et *Yusuf*,[27] ont également été perçues comme un affaiblissement du système de sécurité collective de l'ONU, dans la mesure où des juridictions régionales pourraient désormais exercer un contrôle des décisions du Conseil de sécurité au regard du *jus cogens*.[28] En ce qui concerne la Cour de Justice de l'Union européenne (CJUE), elle a préféré souligner l'autonomie de l'ordre juridique régional par rapport aux résolutions du Conseil de sécurité. S'éloignant par là du Tribunal, la Cour a réalisé un « contrôle juridictionnel par rapport au seul acte communautaire ».[29]

A travers ces différents exemples, l'on constate que le désengagement mondial s'accompagne d'un repli vers d'autres niveaux d'action, considérés comme étant plus efficaces—parfois régionaux, souvent nationaux—pour des questions qui demeurent d'intérêt général pour la société mondiale.

[25] La Conférence de révision du statut de la Cour pénale internationale (Kampala, 2010) n'a même pas retenu cette question dans son ordre du jour. Les rapports du Secrétaire général (voy. notamment le rapport S/2010/394, du 26 juillet 2010) ne retiennent pas cette option.

[26] L'article 4.h) de l'Acte constitutif de l'Union africaine, du 11 juillet 2000, reconnaît « [l]e droit de l'Union d'intervenir dans un Etat membre sur décision de la Conférence, dans certaines circonstances graves, à savoir : les crimes de guerre, le génocide et les crimes contre l'humanité ».

[27] Arrêts du Tribunal de première instance Yusuf et Al Barakaat Foundation/Conseil, T-306/01 et Kadi/Conseil et Commission, T-315/01, du 21 septembre 2005 et arrêt de la Cour de justice de l'Union européenne Al Barakaat International Foundation, C-415/05 P et Yassin Abdullah Kadi, C-402/05 P, contre Conseil et Commission, du 3 septembre 2008.

[28] E Decaux, « Déclarations et conventions en droit international » (2006) 21 *Cahiers du conseil constitutionnel* 4. Boisson de Chazournes, « Les relations entre organisations » 356.

[29] Boisson de Chazournes, « Les relations entre organisations » 380.

Ainsi, la réponse à la défense des intérêts mondiaux se replie sur des solutions régionales et/ou étatiques. D'ailleurs, les droits internes ont connu des développements notoires ces dernières années, notamment afin de renforcer les mécanismes classiques de coopération interétatique, et ce aux côtés de l'acceptation d'une *soft law* transnationale.

B. L'Ordre Juridique Global : du Droit Transnational au Droit Mou

De la même façon que la société internationale se diversifie et que des groupements oligarchiques jouent désormais un rôle de premier ordre, les réponses juridiques aux défis relevés se flexibilisent parallèlement. En effet, dans la société globale, le droit international public est difficilement applicable aux acteurs concernés et aux actions qu'ils entreprennent. L'on songe avant tout bien entendu aux règles applicables aux acteurs privés économiques (notamment les entreprises transnationales) qui interviennent dans un marché global. Mais il s'agit également des règles pouvant contrer l'action de réseaux criminels transnationaux, parfois capables de créer de véritables structures parallèles à l'Etat, voire de les remplacer, notamment dans des régions en conflit ou post-conflictuelles. Face au défi de ces nouveaux acteurs globaux, ni l'ordre juridique mondial, ni celui régional, ni les ordres juridiques internes ont pu s'adapter à des phénomènes qui sont toujours et forcément plus rapides et agiles que les structures institutionnalisées.

Les réponses juridiques semblent s'orienter dans trois directions différentes :

(i) D'abord, vers la consolidation du droit transnational. En effet, celui-ci se présente comme un droit global, qui échappe souvent au carcan de la légitimité et qui s'adapte plus rapidement aux enjeux contemporains de la société internationale, dans le mesure où ses règles sont élaborées indépendamment des États et des organisations internationales. En suivant la formule de Philip Jessup, le droit transnational viserait tout type d'échanges à travers les frontières. Il ne se limiterait d'ailleurs pas à répondre aux besoins grandissants des acteurs du commerce international, tel qu'il a longtemps été perçu. La notion de droit transnational se développe également pour d'autres phénomènes transnationaux dont la caractéristique commune est d'aller au-delà des ordres juridiques internes, sans pouvoir pour autant être encadrés dans l'ordre juridique international.[30]

(ii) Ensuite, et en ce qui concerne les menaces transnationales, vers le repli sur des instruments de coopération juridique internationale entre Etats. D'après les Nations Unies, la criminalité transnationale est aujourd'hui l'une des principales menaces pour la sécurité humaine, quelle que soit son activité (terrorisme, piraterie, trafic de stupéfiants, traite d'être humains, blanchiment

[30] Voyer, par exemple, F Latty, *La Lex Sportiva: Recherche Sur Le Droit Transnational* (Leiden, Martinus Nijhoff Publishers, 2007). Ou dans un tout autre domaine, celui des migrations, E Decaux, « Du droit international au transnational » (2009) 252 *Accueillir* 18.

de capitaux ...).[31] Or, la Convention des Nations Unies contre la criminalité transnationale organisée de 2000, qui engage les Etats à prendre une série de mesures de lutte contre cette criminalité, se réfère fondamentalement au développement par les Etats de leurs ordres juridiques internes ainsi qu'au renforcement de leurs mécanismes de coopération juridique. Il s'agit notamment de l'inclusion des infractions pénales pertinentes dans les systèmes juridiques internes, de l'adoption de nouveaux cadres d'entraide judiciaire, de l'extradition et de la coopération entre les services de détection et de répression.[32]

(iii) Enfin, vers l'acceptation de règles élaborées par les directoires oligarchiques qui régissent—essentiellement d'un point de vue économique—la société internationale. Il s'agit là d'instruments juridiques flexibles de *soft-law*, mais qui ont cependant l'ambition de s'imposer à des Etats qui n'ont pourtant pas participé à leur élaboration. De telles règles, bien que non obligatoires, annoncent une tendance où le droit mou deviendrait, de par l'absence de légitimité, une sorte de droit voyou.

La globalisation semble avoir imprégné tout le tissu institutionnel et juridique international, qu'il soit à portée universelle ou régionale, au détriment de certains principes classiques de la société internationale, notamment l'égalité souveraine. C'est ainsi que, face aux développements de la société globale et de ses règles, il convient d'explorer les voies qui restent ouvertes pour tenter de reconduire et de forger une communauté internationale fondée sur une série de valeurs communes. Le régionalisme demeure une voie privilégiée pour renforcer les institutions mondiales, dans la mesure où, face à la globalisation, le régionalisme permettrait de consolider la sécurité humaine, que les Nations Unies invoquent face à la globalisation. La consolidation d'une diversité d'ensembles régionaux et sous-régionaux se présente alors comme une voie pour forger une véritable communauté à portée universelle. Le monde se présente en effet, plus que jamais, comme une diversité de mondes, tel que l'écrivain argentin Julio Cortázar le laissait entendre dans *Le tour du jour en quatre-vingts mondes*.[33]

[31] A/59/565, 2 juillet 2004, *Un monde plus sûr: notre affaire à tous. Rapport du Groupe de personnalités de haut niveau sur les menaces, les défis et le changement*, pp 12 et 26.

[32] Voyer notamment les articles 5 a 31 de la Convention des Nations Unies contre la criminalité transnationale organisée qui incluent tous ces éléments.

[33] J Cortázar, *La vuelta al día en ochenta mundos* (México, Siglo XXI Editores, 1967). Version français: *Le tour du jour en quatre-vingts mondes* (Paris, Gallimard, 1980).

13

New Regionalism and Global Constitutionalism: Allies, not Rivals

JOSÉ MANUEL PUREZA*

I. INTRODUCTION

THE BOOM OF regional intergovernmental institutions since the 1990s—a reality usually known as 'new regionalism'—raises several crucial questions about the nature of the current international system and about the role that international law plays in it. In this chapter, I will only deal with two of them. The first is the nature of the relations between the apparently contradictory processes of globalisation and regionalism. The second questions the type of connections—both formal and substantial—between two allegedly opposite trends taking place in the contemporary international legal order: global constitutionalism on one side, and regional fragmentation of international law on the other.

II. GLOBALISATION AND REGIONALISM: CONTRADICTORY PROCESSES?

We need to go beyond superficial common sense definitions to catch the disputable contents of both globalisation and international regionalism. Globalisation is far from being a neutral process. The prevalent belief, according to which globalisation is a linear, homogeneous and undisputed dynamic, masks extremely important elements, namely the close connection between globalisation, power and hegemony. From this point of view, it should be underscored that globalisation tends to reproduce, in each of the concrete fields it operates, the hierarchies of the world system and the asymmetries between core and peripheral societies. Therefore, standardisation of lifestyles or shortening of time-space are descriptions of globalisation that tend to diminish the real importance of disputes about different agendas and relations of hegemony. In keeping with Boaventura de Sousa Santos's admonition:

> ... it becomes clear that what we term globalization is, in fact, a set of different processes of globalization and, in the last instance, of different and sometimes contradictory globalizations. What we generally call globalization is, in fact, different sets of social relationships which give rise to different phenomena of globalization. In these terms there is not, strictly

* Professor at the School of Economics and Researcher at the Centre for Social Studies, where he co-coordinates the Humanities, Migrations and Peace Studies Working Group, University of Coimbra.

> speaking, one sole entity called globalization, instead there are globalizations; to be precise, this term should only be used in the plural. As they are sets of social relationships, globalizations involve conflicts and, therefore, winners and losers. The dominant discourse on globalization is the history of the winners, told by the winners.[1]

This focus on the conflicting nature of globalisation processes allows us to critically read the concrete meaning and scope of globalisation from economic and institutional points of view simultaneously. That critical reading clarifies that the current hegemony of the neoliberal ideology has robust strategies for emptying national regulations and replacing them with institutional and regulatory mechanisms, aimed at enforcing an uneven implementation of the principle of mobility, which is currently at the centre of real globalisation taking place nowadays. It is also applied to capital more than to labour, and to northern goods more than southern ones.

In the words of Philip Cerny, 'a growing tension between economic globalisation and embedded state/society practices increasingly constitutes the principal terrain of political conflict within, among, and across competition states'.[2] And the dominant result of that political conflict is diminishing the central position of the nation-state as a political institution, as a regulatory actor and as a key reference—a sort of 'natural scale'—for social sciences. Therefore, within the context of globalisation, a reshaping of both the theoretical and the political dimensions of the centrality of the nation-state is occurring with remarkable impacts on political action and political thought.

This is the framework in which the question concerning the concrete role of regional organisations must be read. Having this conflicting notion of globalisation in mind, the crucial question to be analysed is not an abstract opposition between universalism versus particularism or between the whole versus the fragment. In fact, one of the most relevant dimensions of globalisation is its work as a process of political structuring, which means that it 'involves reshaping political practices and institutional structures in order to adjust and adapt to the growing deficiencies of nation-states as perceived and experienced by such [state] actors'.[3]

Within this context, the really important question concerns the relevance of regional international organisations as re-shaped institutional structures—in their mandates and in their decision processes—by the dynamics of globalisation. That relevance is fundamentally revealed by the role given to regional normative and institutional structures in enabling and enforcing the ideological background of hegemonic globalisation, and its expression in different areas: political, economic, financial, cultural, and so on. Are they instruments of enforcement of that programme or are they instruments of resistance against it? In the words of James Mittelman,[4] 'is regionalism merely a way station toward neoliberal globalization, or a means toward a more pluralistic world order in which distinct patterns of socioeconomic organization coexist and compete for popular support?'

[1] B de Sousa Santos, 'Globalizations' (2006) 23 *Theory Culture and Society* 393–99, 395.

[2] PG Cerny, 'Paradoxes of the Competition State: The Dynamics of Political Globalization' (1997) 32 *Government and Opposition* 251–74, 251.

[3] ibid 253.

[4] JH Mittelman, *The Globalization Syndrome* (Princeton, Princeton University Press, 2000) 111.

Regionalism has been a continuous trend in the international order since the beginning of the twentieth century. However, it has gained specific features over time. This is why Mario Telò[5] talks about 'three waves of regionalism during the twentieth century': the 'malevolent regionalism' of the 1930s and beginning of the 1940s; the 'hegemonic regionalism' of the late 1940s and 1950s; and the 'post-hegemonic regionalism' of the 1990s. In turn, Mittelman[6] analyses the differences between the 'auto centric regionalism' of the 1930s and contemporary 'neoliberal regionalism'. As its main features, he points to the extroversion of neoliberal regionalism, its aim of diminishing the ability of states to control trade and monetary relations, and its defensive nature against further social disintegration ('degenerative regionalism').

The third wave of regional international organisations—the so-called 'new regionalism'—typical of the phase that started with the end of the Cold War, differs from the two former waves of regionalism (1945–65 and 1965–90) since its main feature is its instrumental function to neoliberal globalisation dynamics. In fact, the main role played by the most relevant regional organisations of our time (Asia-Pacific Economic Cooperation (APEC), Mercado Común del Sur (MERCOSUR), the Shanghai Cooperation Organization (SCO) or the redefined European Union) is above all to integrate their member states in a multidimensional global neoliberal order.

This brings about a crucial change in the purposes of regionalism: while the traditional forms of regionalism have been associated with protectionist strategies, the new regionalism is a privileged instrument of openness and adoption of the liberal creed. Why is that so? What has occurred that determined this important change? Following the neo-Gramscian approach suggested by Manuela Spindler,[7] I take the replacement of 'embedded liberalism',[8] as the ideological background of the world order, as being the crucial factor in the changing nature of regionalism. And, since theory is always for someone and for some purpose, it must be stressed that this change is the goal of specific social actors, namely global business actors. It is in their interest that the logic of the market is being infused into traditional regionalism, therefore creating both regionalised and globalised patterns of economic transactions, of political standards and of institutional formulae.[9]

According to John Ruggie, the international order that developed after the Second World War has mostly been concentrated on reaching a new balance between economics and politics, different from both economic nationalism and laissez-faire capitalism. For that purpose, it assumed the constraint of the market forces through legal-political intervention as a top priority, embedding liberalism in a state and interstate order, based upon the acceptance of a large space for public interventionism,

[5] M Telò, *European Union and New Regionalism. Regional Actors and Global Governance in a Post-hegemonic Era* (London, Ashgate, 2007) 2.

[6] Mittelman, *The Globalization Syndrome*, 112.

[7] M Spindler, 'New Regionalism and the Construction of Global Order', CSGR Working Paper No 93/02 (March, 2002), available at http://dspace.cigilibrary.org/jspui/bitstream/123456789/9242/1/New%20Regionalism%20and%20the%20Construction%20of%20Global%20Order.pdf?1.

[8] JG Ruggie, 'International regimes, transactions and change: embedded liberalism in the postwar economic order' (1982) 36 *International Organization* 379–415.

[9] Spindler, 'New Regionalism', above n 7, 4.

bringing together state regulation at the domestic scale and with international opening. In the words of Ruggie:

> this was the essence of the embedded liberalism compromise: unlike the economic nationalism of the thirties, it would be multilateral in character; unlike the liberalism of the gold standard and free trade, its multilateralism would be predicated upon domestic interventionism.[10]

Through this reconciliation between liberalisation in the external field and interventionism in the internal order, a compromise was sought as a solution in between the economic nationalism of the nineteen-thirties and contemporary liberal capitalism. This was the 'middle way capitalism', according to Jonathan Kirshner,[11] that would enable nation-states to both benefit from the free flow of goods and guarantee national social policies. In fact, embedded liberalism meant not only the safeguard of the adoption of public health or full employment as national goals, or the implementation of social policies as a crucial part of the social contract, but also the protection of national strategic industries or the establishment of controls on speculative transboundary movements of capital. In fact, as Eric Helleiner duly stresses, 'the overriding principle was restriction: states were given the explicit right to control all capital movements',[12] in contrast to the liberalisation of trade.

The role played by intergovernmental institutions at that moment, and especially the mandate given to regional international organisations, was precisely that of agreeing on limits to the dynamics of the market and therefore enabling the viability of robust and large social contracts within welfare states on the nation-state scale. This role was complemented at the international level by intergovernmental regulation that those organisations and intergovernmental platforms had adopted. In Spindler's view: '[T]he region of embedded liberalism is a protectionist region.'[13]

Now, what we are witnessing with this emergence of a third wave of regional organisations is a sort of Karl Polanyi's second move, on a global scale. The return of the hegemony of an unlimited market and therefore a deep change in the former balance of forces led by the *nébuleuse*—that is, the loose elite of local and global business actors, states and opinion makers, which produces the current canon of political and economic governance[14]—has placed embedded liberalism in a state of dramatic crisis. According to Hannes Lacher, this reversal of the former regulation is mostly due to the fact that it has never truly challenged 'the ultimate basis of the market as a disembedded institution itself: the commodification of human labor'.[15]

[10] Ruggie, 'International regimes', above n 8, 393.

[11] J Kirshner, 'Keynes, Capital Mobility and the Crisis of Embedded Liberalism' (1999) 6 *Review of International Political Economy* 313–37, 314.

[12] E Helleiner, *States and the Reemergence of Global Finance: From Bretton Woods to the 1990's* (Ithaca and London, Cornell University Press, 1994) 49.

[13] ibid 12.

[14] RW Cox, 'Democracy in Hard Times: Economic Globalization and the Limits to Liberal Democracy' in A McGrew (ed), *The Transformation of Democracy? Globalization and Territorial Democracy* (Malden, Blackwell Publishers, 1997) 49–72, 58.

[15] H Lacher, 'Embedded Liberalism, Disembedded Markets: Reconceptualizing the Pax Americana' (1999) 4 *New Political Economy* 343–60, 345.

The welfare state model has given way to the actual standard of the competitive state whose strategic goal is to strengthen the international and transnational competitiveness of national economic activities. At the core of this paradigmatic shift lies the replacement of the role of the state to keep certain areas out of the market by its role to increase the marketisation of more and more areas of economic activity, allegedly to improve the international competitiveness of national economies, following what Cerny calls the 'embedded financial orthodoxy'.[16] The relation between this replacement of the former welfare state model by the competitive state paradigm is a two-way process:

> the consolidation and expansion of the competition state is itself driving a process of political globalization which is increasingly relativizing the sovereignty of states and, indeed, forcing the pace of globalization in economic, social and cultural spheres too.[17]

Therefore, the neoliberal turn is far from being limited to the economic sphere. It involves a whole redefinition of governance and a redesign of the state itself. Apart from the adoption of strict financial discipline as a sort of *ultima ratio*, these changes include the adoption of an entrepreneurial culture within the state, namely through the implementation of market-based systems of incentives and through a new culture of competition between state agencies and the private sector for the supply of basic public goods.

Spindler argues that, within this changing context, regionalism itself has become 'part of the move towards the competition state, with market actors infusing old regionalism with a new logic, thus globalizing and marketizing regionalism.'[18] This reinforces the understanding according to which regional organisations have become instruments of the global neoliberal hegemony or, at least, intermediation mechanisms between the global neoliberal economic order and nation states and markets.

The 'new' in the new regionalism consists of a crucial difference in envisioning the nature of the global space. To explore this topic, I follow Wendy Larner and William Walters' contrast between two contemporary political rationalities concerning the conceptualisation of economic spaces.[19] The first is developmentalism. This conceptualises the global space as an international system of discrete self-contained units, separate parts of an international division of labour and with each one of them endowed with singular attributes expressed through the concept of comparative advantages. Against this aggregate notion of the global space, neoliberalism reads national and regional entities as sectors of a global space, which is understood as a space of investment flows and trade fluxes that cross all traditional delimitations.

There is, therefore, a clear similarity and a clear difference between those two political rationalities in what concerns the connection between states and the global space: the two conceptualise states as specific positions within the global space,

[16] PG Cerny, 'The Infrastructure of the Infrastructure? Toward "Embedded Financial Orthodoxy"' in the International Political Economy' in B Gills and R Palan (eds), *Transcending the State-Global Divide: A Neostructuralist Agenda in International Relations* (Boulder CO, Lynne Rienner, 1994) 223–49.

[17] Cerny, 'Paradoxes of the Competition State', above n 2, 252.

[18] Spindler, 'New Regionalism', above n 7, 16.

[19] W Larner and W Walters, 'The Political Rationality of "New Regionalism": Toward a Genealogy of the Region' (2002) 31 *Theory and Society* 391–432.

but whereas developmentalism sees the state as an autonomous bounded unit and regionalism as the aggregate result of a transfer of parts of that autonomy by different neighbour states, neoliberalism faces states as subordinate, non-autonomous units, whose only function is to facilitate at the local level the implementation of standardised policies for the whole global space. In these neoliberal terms, regionalism's role is no longer that of establishing protectionism. 'Regionalism presupposes a global economy', state Larner and Walters,[20] emphasising the continuity between the two levels and the hierarchical relation between them: regions (and their organisations) are not a compensatory mechanism for weakened nation states but rather an aid for the liberalisation of the national economic space.[21]

The current eurozone crisis gives us extremely clear signs of this new instrumental role of regional international organisations. Starting with the institutional partnership inaugurated for the enforcement of structural adjustment policies in highly indebted countries: the so-called 'Troika' is no more than an assemblage of the European Commission with the European Central Bank and the International Monetary Fund. Yet, more than this institutional dimension, it is the nature of the policies implemented by the Troika that evidences the self-representation of the European Union as an intermediary body between its member states and a global economic and financial order, whose contents are clearly contrary to the 'European social model', which for a long time have been based on indirect salaries, universal public services and social rights. The standard contents of austerity measures implemented in Greece, Ireland, Portugal and Spain, and all over the eurozone, follow an ideological script synthesised by Stephen Gill in five major components: sound policy, debt sustainability, surveillance and normalisation, attenuation of democracy, and prioritisation of market efficiency over equity and social solidarity.[22]

As João Rodrigues and José Reis[23] underscore, this script leads to the materialisation of neoliberal hegemony in the European context, as an expression of the power of the dominant transnational fraction of capital. The latter has been pushing for an integration process, based upon the expansion of market forces and the inherent sublimation of both the social democratic and neo-mercantilist traditions within a neoliberal understanding of European integration which has been inscribed in the institutional arrangements of the European Economic and Monetary Union (EMU). This dramatic process of change expresses the agency of what Gill calls 'a neoliberal transnational historic bloc'[24]—that is, 'a political synthesis of interests and identities drawn from across social classes and nations that mediates and seeks to coordinate national, regional and global dimensions of accumulation and legitimation'. Its agenda is focused on a restructuring of state policies so that they become interpreters of the priorities of the dominant forces of contemporary capitalism.

[20] ibid 408.

[21] B Donegan, 'Governmental Regionalism: Power/Knowledge and Neoliberal Regional Integration in Asia and Latin America' (2006) 35 *Millennium: Journal of International Studies* 23–51, 34.

[22] SR Gill, 'European Governance and New Constitutionalism: Economic Monetary Union and Alternatives to Disciplinary Neoliberalism in Europe' (1998) 3 *New Political Economy* 5–26, 15.

[23] J Rodrigues and J Reis, 'The Asymmetries of European Integration and the Crisis of Capitalism in Portugal' (2012) 16 *Competition and Change* 188–205, 189.

[24] Gill, 'European Governance and New Constitutionalism', above n 22, 11.

In clear contrast to the former political and institutional design of the European Communities, the model adopted since the 1990s has turned the European Union into a major example of what Bastiaan van Apeldoorn names 'embedded neoliberalism'.[25] On the one hand, the core of the European Union treaties enhances a free market orientation, namely through the constitutional status of the primacy of the principle of the free movement of capital, goods and services over social protection at the national level, or through the statutes of the European Central Bank, which excludes from its mandate all forms of direct funding of Member States and imposes supply-side policies to be adopted by them. On the other hand, this trend is not the object of any kind of balance through either market-correcting mechanisms or economic crisis management tools on the European scale, namely the EU budget.[26] The reshaping of the political mandate of the European Union embodies the contemporary co-existence and functional articulation between the transnational integration of capital and the regional varieties of capitalism.[27] To be more precise, the 1990s' turn has meant a shift of the European Union from a social market, or social-democrat, model of capitalism into a neoliberal and financially oriented one and, this shift reflects a strategy of reconciling regional integration with globalising forces.[28]

III. GLOBAL CONSTITUTIONALISM AND THE REGIONAL FRAGMENTATION OF INTERNATIONAL LAW

This leads us to the second question in this chapter. Within the context of the articulation between global and regional platforms, both of which serve the same hegemonic orientation, the traditional opposition between global constitutionalism and the regional fragmentation of international law has ceased to make sense. It is no longer a true opposition.

The concept of global constitutionalism has emerged in the last two decades, as a sort of upgrade, both normatively and institutionally, of the discourse on the role of international law within the globalisation process. Together with the mainstream discourse on global governance—that emphasises the failures and insufficiencies of traditional institutions and norms and takes that diagnosis as the basis for an exercise of institutional engineering in trying to responding to the regulatory challenges of the dominant agenda of globalisation—the narrative about global constitutionalism suggests that the international system is experiencing a crucial transformation. That transformation is leading global constitutionalism from the childhood of the Westphalian order to an adult international order, complete with mechanisms of differentiation, hierarchy and centralisation.

[25] B van Apeldoorn, *Transnational Capitalism and the Struggle over European Integration* (London, Routledge, 2002).

[26] Rodrigues and Reis, 'Asymmetries of European Integration', above n 23, 190–91.

[27] C Georgiou, 'The Euro Crisis and the Future of European Integration' (2012) 128 *International* Socialism, available at: www.isj.org.uk/?id=682.

[28] Gill, 'European Governance and New Constitutionalism', above n 22, 9–10.

From a normative perspective, the discourse of global constitutionalism is a means of overcoming the fragilities of traditional international law, namely its nature of contractual bric-à-brac.[29] The threefold differentiation in that traditional international legal order—concerning its sources, state obligations and mechanisms of international responsibility—has been subject to a hard process of conceptual critique that has resulted in the emergence of legal categories like *jus cogens*, obligations *erga omnes* and international crimes.

This is the conceptual framework within which the very idea of global constitutionalism has been able to emerge. It expresses the shared theorisation of liberal international legal scholars, who became the dominant points of reference for academic debate in the second half of the twentieth century. For them the increasing density of international law and the growing regulatory competences of international institutions have allowed for the emergence of a greater hierarchisation within the international order. As a result, the international order has acquired a constitutional nature, which has materialised with a superior set of norms and principles and a growing type of international organisations' deliberation, with binding effect.

However, these formal-legal and institutional understandings about global constitutionalism must be read within their political context. Danilo Zolo identifies four normative theses that lie at the core of the construction of what he calls 'legal cosmopolitanism', as follows:

> first, that of the primacy of international law and the progressive reduction of the sovereignty of states ...; second, that of jurisdictional centralism: ... the development of norms and centralized bodies for the verification and coercive application of the law; ... third, that of legal pacifism; ... and, finally, fourth, that of 'global constitutionalism which ... emphasizes the ability of centralized supranational institutions to safeguard the fundamental liberties of individuals which states have shown themselves incapable of protecting.[30]

Yet, the same author asks: 'Is it reasonable to entrust the defence of human rights to illiberal power structures?'[31] Zolo's question—and the critical distance it implicitly takes from the global constitutionalism discourse—places the political conditions and political contents of those norms and institutions at the very heart of the debate on global constitutionalism. This means that global constitutionalism is a contradictory and disputed field. It includes both the universal protection of human rights and universal standardisation of models of governance as well as the universal adoption of free markets and their (de)regulation.

In more concrete terms, this means that Zolo's definition of global constitutionalism is not comprehensive enough since it should include not only the notion that the real constitution of globalisation is unbalanced in terms of protection of human rights and liberties—giving absolute primacy to classical civil rights over social and economic rights—but also that there are other normative components of that constitution whose scope is the protection of the rights of the capital. Examples of the latter include the Organization for Economic Cooperation and Development's

[29] J Combacau, 'Le droit international: bric-à-brac ou système?' (1986) 31 *Archives de Philosophie du Droit* 85–105

[30] D Zolo, *Cosmopolis. Prospect for World Government* (Cambridge, Polity Press, 1997) 97.

[31] ibid.

(abandoned attempt at a) Multilateral Agreement on Investment, the General Agreement on Trade-in-Services (GATS), the Uruguay Round's Agreements on Trade-Related Intellectual Property Measures (TRIPS) and Trade-Related Investment Measures (TRIMS), minimalist regulation of the financial system, and so on.

It is in this sense that Gill uses the concept of 'new constitutionalism'.[32] Gill emphasises that new constitutionalism means, most of all, a set of principles—both legal and political—that separate economic policies from broad political accountability in order to make governments more responsive to the discipline of market forces and, correspondingly, less responsive to popular-democratic forces and processes. He concludes by saying that: '[n]ew constitutionalism is the political-legal dimension of the wider discourse of disciplinary neoliberalism'.[33] The most relevant contemporary regional organisations—including the North America Free Trade Agreement (NAFTA), APEC or the European EMU—are expressions of this new constitutionalism as they imposeneoliberal principles as undisputable priorities and therefore contribute to remove crucial areas of economic and social policies from the democratic dispute and correspondingly void elected governments from their competences in these areas.

This new global constitutionalism is therefore evidence that Martti Koskenniemi is absolutely right in pointing out that constitutionalism and empire go well together 'as testified both by 19th century European experience and today's American one'.[34] Under these circumstances, the traditional opposition between universal/global and particular/regional international law has lost a good part of its original meaning.

Koskenniemi's concept of 'managerialism'[35] could be a useful tool to analyse the current articulation between regional and universal international law. He uses the notion of managerialism to refer to a fragmentation of international normative and institutional regimes, used *à la carte,* to match subjects to their discipline—in his words: 'the world of legal practice is being sliced up in institutional projects that cater for special audiences with special interests and special ethos'.[36] Thus, the current international legal menu offers different closed boxes—international environmental law, international human rights law, international trade law, international security law, and so on—each with its specific institutions and norms, forming a sort of 'kaleidoscopic reality',[37] supported by states aimed at avoiding the potential costs of a single binding regime by operating through a multiplicity of regimes.

The dynamics of the fragmentation of international legal regimes and of enforcement mechanisms and institutions has been seen as something that 'generate[s] unwanted confusion' and 'distort[s] the operation of justice'.[38] In former ICJ Judge

[32] Gill, 'European Governance and New Constitutionalism', above n 22, 5.

[33] ibid.

[34] M Koskenniemi, 'The Politics of International Law—20 Years Later' (2009) 20 *European Journal of International Law* 7–19, 17.

[35] ibid 14–18.

[36] ibid 9.

[37] M Koskenniemi and P Leino, 'Fragmentation of International Law? Postmodern Anxieties' (2002) 15 *Leiden Journal of International Law* 553–79, 559.

[38] Speech by HE Judge Gilbert Guillaume, President of the International Court of Justice, to the UN General Assembly of the United Nations, 26 October 2000, available at www.icj-cij.org/court/index.php?pr=84&pt=3&p1=1&p2=3&p3=1.

Guillaume's view, 'the proliferation of international courts may jeopardize the unity of international law and, as a consequence, its role in inter-State relations'.[39] It is not only a certain understanding of international law that is questioned by the dynamics of fragmentation. More than that, it is a vision of the international sphere as a structure with a formal-legal hierarchy, at the top of which the United Nations governs, through public international law norms. As a result, the world of sovereign nations is radically undermined by this flexible and decentralised development of the international legal order. Within that traditional vision, the international order tended to be understood through the lens of what Koskenniemi calls 'a domestic analogy', which envisages treaties as playing the role of legislation, the rules and institutions that deal with the settlement of controversies as playing the role of adjudication and war, and counter-measures as playing the role of enforcement.[40]

Nowadays, the thematic approach to managerialism can also be articulated in a regional fashion: European regulation, American regulation, and so on. Yet, in contrast to Koskenniemi's belief that 'the proliferation of autonomous or semi-autonomous normative regimes is an unavoidable reflection of a 'postmodern' social condition and ... a beneficial prologue to a pluralistic community in which the degrees of homogeneity and fragmentation reflects shifts of political preference.'[41] I agree with Eyal Benvenisti and George Downs, who argue that

> while it is reasonable to argue that the proliferation of multilateral agreements has created an institutional environment that is less hierarchical than that which existed during the Cold War, it is not clear that resulting order is any more pluralistic with respect to the range or even the number of interests that it represents.[42]

The automatic correspondence between fragmentation and pluralism is a misleading one. The concrete reality of the contemporary international system is that fragmentation is promoted and used, most of all, by a handful of stronger states whose interest is not an enlargement of democracy and participation at the international level but rather a narrowing of the democratic egalitarian space and a sophisticated form of enhanced control, which does not explicitly assume an hierarchical form but which has that hierarchy as its final goal.

Within this context, I tend to acknowledge managerialism as a strategy of enforcement of the global hegemony of neoliberal politics. The deepening of the piecemeal approach is a deliberate strategy that favours the most powerful states, to the extent

[39] Speech by HE Judge Gilbert Guillaume, President of the International Court of Justice, to the General Assembly of the United Nations, 30 October 2001, available at www.icj-cij.org/court/index.php?pr=82&pt=3&p1=1&p2=3&p3=1. Koskenniemi and Leino ('Fragmentation of International Law?' 560) quote a preliminary survey conducted by the International Law Commission (ILC) in 2000 that prioritised the impacts of the fragmentation of international law in terms of 'endanger[ing] [international law's] stability as well as the consistency of international law and its comprehensive nature.' In the ILC survey, the absence of unity and hierarchy was interpreted as threatening the 'credibility, reliability and, consequently, authority of international law.'

[40] Koskenniemi and Leino, 'Fragmentation of International Law?', above n 37, 558.

[41] M Koskenniemi, 'What is international law for?' in MD Evans (ed), *International Law*, 3rd edn (Oxford, Oxford University Press, 2010) 32–57, 52.

[42] E Benvenisti and GW Downs, 'The Empire's New Clothes: Political Economy and the Fragmentation of International Law' (2007) 60 *Stanford Law Review* 595–631, 603.

that, benefiting from such a fragmented, issue-specific legal system, those states use it as a form of preserving or even enlarging their bargaining positions. This strategic use of fragmentation by powerful states is based on a cost-benefit analysis, characterised by Jonathan Charney in the following terms:

> Hierarchy and coherence are laudable goals for any legal system, including international law, but at the moment they are impossible goals. The benefits of the alternative, multiple forums, are worth the possible adverse consequences that may contribute to less coherence. This risk is low and the potential for benefits to the peaceful settlement of international disputes is high.[43]

It is therefore indisputable that powerful states use a twofold strategy to foster their dominant position: on the one hand, they claim their hierarchical superiority within multilateral institutions and regulatory frameworks; on the other hand, they promote institutional and regulatory fragmentation whenever it serves their political agendas.

This means that, in concrete situations and debates, the choice between regional and global legal and institutional constraints on national legal orders, so as to legitimise the implementation of neoliberal standards and goals, is precisely that: a choice, guided exclusively by a logic of maximum efficiency in binding local actors and convincing local public opinions. As Benvenisti and Downs point out: '[G]lobalization has put a premium on efficiency, and decentralized processes are simply more efficient than more formal, centralized ones.'[44] Koskenniemi himself acknowledges this ideological nature of the choice between different legal approaches to a specific problem.[45] In fact, those choices—between international human rights law and international trade law or between the European Convention on Human Rights and the EU Lisbon Treaty—reveal the true hierarchies that structure international law, well beyond the conceptual and natural construction of *jus cogens*. Following traditional constitutional theory, it could be said that the formal global constitution does not coincide with the material global constitution, the latter having gained practical primacy over the former.

Take the current euro crisis and its normative dimension. Fiscal and budgetary imperative limits have been imposed on the eurozone states that are justified in normative terms as a consequence of the EU constitutional norms adopted since the Maastricht Treaty of 1992. But those rules are themselves justified as expressions, at this specific regional level, of global regimes like those embodied in the WTO or the Bretton Woods system. So, this way of cascading, and thereby legitimising, neoliberal policies through either regional or global norms gives us a close-up view of the current instrumental role played by regional organisations, including at the level of normative production, when considering the global political and economic order.

[43] J Charney, 'The Implications of Expanding International Dispute Settlement Systems: The 1982 Convention on the Law of the Sea' (1996) 90 *American Journal of International Law* 69–75, 75.

[44] Benvenisti and Downs, 'The Empire's New Clothes', above n 42, 600.

[45] Koskenniemi, 'The Politics of International Law', above n 34, 11.

IV. CONCLUSION

The contemporary global order—institutional, economic and legal—is a regionalised one. Regional organisations are fabrics of the globally hegemonic codes of good governance and instruments for binding their member states to those codes. Within this context, international law is what it has always been: an ambivalent and disputed discourse that serves either as an instrument to enforce that hegemony or as an argument to resist it. That double nature of the international legal discourse (simultaneously apology and utopia)—and its corollary, the oscillation of dominant states between the instrumentalisation of international norms and regime and withdrawal from them[46]—puts all the emphasis on the concrete forms of the mobilisation of international norms, by whom and for what purposes. After all, just as Alexander Wendt[47] wrote about anarchy in international relations, international law is what states—and other social actors—make of it.

[46] N Kirsch, 'International Law in Times of Hegemony: Unequal Power and the Shaping of the International Legal Order' (2005) 16 *European Journal of International Law* 369–408, 381.
[47] A Wendt, 'Anarchy is what states make of it: the social construction of power politics' (1992) 20 *International Organization* 391–425

14

Commentaire sur Peyró et Pureza

ANTONIO REMIRO BROTÓNS*

I. MONDIALISATION ET GLOBALISATION

JE CONSIDÈRE QU'IL faut, d'abord, distinguer entre *mondialisation* et *globalisation*, deux phénomènes qui, tout comme souligne Ana Peyró, sont souvent confondus. La *mondialisation* représente un phénomène historique caractérisé dans sa dernière phase par les progrès réalisés en matière de transports, de microélectronique, des télécommunications et d'informatique. Le temps devient, alors, instantané et l'espace ubiquiste. La *globalisation,* quant à elle, va au-delà: c'est le classement de la *mondialisation* sur les bases néolibérales pour instaurer, après la chute du bloc socialiste, le royaume des *marchés financiers* en faisant des administrations publiques ses agents, avec des conséquences économiques, sociales et institutionnelles substantielles.

Dupes, ravagés, désorientés ou pris de panique, nombreux sont les pays du *Tiers Monde* qui, dans une sorte de *sauf qui peut,* ont consenti de rendre leurs étendards de combat pour un *Nouvel Ordre Économique International,* humaniste et solidaire, aux chefs de file du monde capitaliste néolibéral. La *globalisation* a transformé les *services publics* en *business* privés, a remplacé *l'État du bien-être* par le *bien-être des grandes sociétés financières et commerciales,* et fait prévaloir les intérêts particuliers des investisseurs étrangers sur les mesures régulatrices du marché qui répondent à un intérêt général. Dans ce contexte nous devons souligner que le soi-disant *nouveau constitutionnalisme* propose un système qui entreprend l'isolement des aspects clés de l'économie du contrôle populaire, afin de créer un mécanisme qui pousse aux États, dirigés par des gouvernements *dressés,* à livrer au *marché* des politiques, des biens et des services publics.

Sur cette toile de fond a émergé la crise d'octobre 2008. Il n'existe aucune nouveauté concernant le recours croissant aux *acteurs-non sujets* et aux *accords non juridiques* pour la gestion internationale des problèmes les plus sérieux. Dans ce contexte les organisations internationales et les obligations juridiques sont relégués au rôle d'instruments des engagements politiques des concerts informels. La nouveauté

* Professeur de droit international public, Universidad Autónoma de Madrid. Membre de l'Institut de Droit International.

relative à cet égard réside dans le fait que le G-8 a transféré au G-20 le *leadership* dans la réponse.

Nous sommes, en tout cas, face à des mécanismes de coopération informels qui, dénoués de toute infrastructure organique propre et de toute personnalité juridique, agissent comme une sorte de direction sélective, qui engage des accords de nature politique, sans la portée juridique obligatoire, préchauffées dans les réunions des hauts fonctionnaires, des ministres sectoriels et de gouverneurs de banques centrales. Cette direction sélective, pour ainsi dire, est reflétée dans les discours des chefs d'État et de chefs de gouvernement qui utilisent un langage promissoire relativement générique, où il ne manque pas une dose non négligeable de auto-complaisance. Et c'est ainsi qu'à partir du particularisme informel des plus puissants se reproduisent les vieux schémas de domination.

L'idée de profiter de la crise pour faire une réforme profonde des institutions financières internationales, et en faire des institutions plus participatives et démocratiques, n'a pas eu beaucoup de succès. Loin de réviser les fondements du système pour remplacer ses bases pour d'autres plus saines, on a accepté les présupposés de la *globalisation* et on a injecté une quantité immensurable d'argent public (c'est-à-dire, l'argent des citoyens) dans les circuits bancaires privés afin de les recapitaliser, sans une exigence simultanée de responsabilités individuelles ou corporatives. Les Nations Unies ont été marginalisées. Si l'on prend en compte la misère avec laquelle on gère les problèmes de la famine, de la santé ou encore de la préservation de l'environnement, la réponse a la crise financière souligne qui son les rois du monde et qui ses serviteurs. L'*agenda du Millenium* n'intéresse pas les globalisateurs au-delà du *lip-service;* elle ne semple pas prioritaire, non plus, pour les membres du G-20.

Dans un système où l'État est au service des marchés, la notion du bien commun et du service public est démembrée et les individus perdent la conscience d'appartenance à une société plurielle ; ils la transfèrent à une classe supra-étatique, la classe *globale,* qui s'approprie des institutions formellement représentatives. Et c'est le pas vers cette classe sociale transnational, la classe des *globalisateurs,* qui représente la nouvelle aspiration des serviteurs *globalisés.* Parler de *globalisation démocratique* est une *contradictio in terminis.* Une société globale ne peut être démocratique et une société démocratique ne peut être globale sans représenter un attentat contre soi-même. C'est, donc, manifestement malsain d'affirmer que la souche des misérables sera bien dans l'expansion de l'actuel modèle politique, économique et social *global.* Dans ce contexte on ne doit pas se surprendre d'identifier des partisans de se faufiler dans le chaos pour instaurer un nouvel ordre partant du néant au lieu de se résigner à une perverse injustice sociale planétaire, d'établir un modèle économique et social capable de répondre aux objectifs que ont occupé une place secondaire au niveau mondial jusqu'au présent.

J'ignore jusqu'à quel point l'adoption du même terme de *globalisation* pour se référer à d'autres sujets qui ne présentent qu'un lien marginal avec le concept que nous venons de considérer est sage. La *globalisation* offense certains droits économiques et sociaux et garde une image des droits civils et politiques des individus assez superficielle. À vrai dire, dans la *globalisation* ces droits sont exercés par le capital et ceux qui le possèdent.

II. UNIVERSALISME ET RÉGIONALISME

Le *régionalisme*, d'un point de vue historique, est en couple avec l'*universalisme.* La qualité universelle de la société et le droit international est relativement récente. Dans l'*universalisme* il y a certains principes que le mère *multilatéralisme* ne possède pas : pluralisme, non discrimination, égalité souveraine, libre détermination, droits de l'homme, développement, justice sociale internationale ... Ses racines sont dans la Charte des Nations Unies. L'ONU est une organisation universelle. Elle ne peut pas être, de par sa nature, un instrument de la *globalisation* et, si un jour, elle parvient à cette fin, elle perdra sa condition universelle. D'où le désir manifeste des *globalisateurs* de marginaliser l'ONU, de l'amoindrir même ou encore d'exclure les dissidents de l'*establishment.*

On devrait être exigeant sur la définition du *régionalisme,* en faisant sa distinction avec le *particularisme,* avec lequel on le confond souvent dans la pratique, et aussi avec d'autres formes de *multilatéralisme* qui ne sont plus que manifestations d'*unilatéralisme groupal* lorsqu'elles mettent en défi la légalité universelle.

À mon avis le *régionalisme* sollicite une certaine continuité territoriale des États impliqués, de l'identité et des intérêts communs et d'une distribution de pouvoir équilibrée, compatible avec l'existence de chefs de file (qui ne doivent pas être confondus avec les *hegémons*). Dans ce sens on pourrait dire que le *panaméricanisme* répondit à un modèle de subordination aux intérêts d'une grande puissance hégémonique, continentale, mais extrarégionale. L'UE par exemple peut être *régionalisme;* l'OTAN, *unilatéralisme groupal.* L'UE peut s'encadrer dans l'*universalisme;* l'OTAN peut être le sicaire politique et militaire de la *globalisation.*

Le *régionalisme* s'ajuste parfaitement dans l'*universalisme*, aussi bien d'un point de vue de la compatibilité des normes régionales que dans l'articulation des organisations. Le *régionalisme* ne se conçoit pas comme une forme d'auto-exclusion d'une société plus ample. Le *régionalisme* assume les problèmes propres à la région et se propose comme plateforme pour exprimer plus efficacement une position commune sur certains problèmes universels. Lorsque les organismes régionaux appliquent le principe de subsidiarité, elles représentent le meilleur complément de l'ordre et de l'organisation universelle. La région *défend son identité et ses intérêts communs dans un milieu universel dont le cosmopolitisme renforce.* On ne doit pas comprendre l'ordre normatif et institutionnel régional comme un ordre parallèle, autarcique. Les normes impératives de la société universelle protègent les membres les moins forts dans le faux *régionalismes hégémoniques,* aussi bien que la région en tant que telle face aux assauts de puissances extrarégionales.

III. GLOBALISATION ET RÉGIONALISME

La ferme opposition à la *globalisation* et à ses étendards des mouvements sociaux et ONG du *premier monde* suggère que la *globalisation* comme expression du *nouvel ordre capitaliste* n'aura un chemin aussi dégagé que la *civilisation* au XIXème siècle pour justifier l'exploitation coloniale et impérialiste. La *globalisation* est, dans sa conception même, conflictuelle, comme l'observe José Manuel Pureza. Le débat idéologique est loin d'être mort. Nombreux sont les instruments multilatéraux de la *globalisation,* tels que l'OMC, le FMI ou la Banque Mondiale, qui peuvent être utiles aux politiques revendicatives de certains groupes d'États qui ont le soutien et le *know-how* de membres innocents et non contaminés de la changeante *société civile internationale.*

Il est, par conséquent, difficile de conjuguer l'essence du *régionalisme* et la *globalisation.* Le *boom* du *régionalisme* des dernières décennies, souligné par Ana Peyró, va de pair avec la banalisation de son concept et une remarquable dispersion de ses objectifs. C'est ainsi que l'on parle d'un « nouveau régionalisme » dont la répercussion, aussi bien d'un point de vue normatif que d'un point de vue d'organisation international, est encore mise en question. Ana Peyró parle d'un « régionalisme oligarchique ». Pour José Manuel Pureza la question est de savoir si les organisations régionales seront-elles des instruments de médiation ou application de la *globalisation,* d'encadrement de ses membres dans l'ordre *globalisé,* ou bien elles se constitueront comme instances de résistance à cette *globalisation.* Je pense qu'on doit combattre les *régionalismes* et les *particularismes* qui s'offrent comme des chaînes de transmission de la *globalisation* et conserver, par contre, ceux qui soutiennent les normes constitutionnelles de la société universelle, ainsi que les institutions que la représentent. C'est dans ce sens qu'on peut parler de *globalisation* et *régionalisme* en tant que processus contradictoires. De nos jours, il serait même possible de s'interroger sur les probabilités de survie dans le *premier monde* des organisations régionales *globalisées* qui sont contestées par les citoyens.

La *globalisation,* loin de servir à l'universalité la ruine, jusqu'à point de parler d'un universalisme en décadence. La *globalisation* promue et profite, comme remarque José Manuel Pureza, la fragmentation de l'ordre international dans des divers régimes particuliers et, éventuellement, régionaux. Dans ce sens, c'est équivoque, à mon avis, prétendre que le « global constitutionalism » implique renforcer le rôle du droit international dans le processus de *globalisation.* De quel genre de droit s'agirait-il? Le droit des pays *civilisés* appliqué aux nouvelles technologies? Entre le *nouvel ordre de la globalisation* et le *chaos* nous devons revenir sur les principes de la Charte afin de les approfondir. Il faut renforcer les organisations internationales, universelles et régionales, pour le rendre plus représentatives et plurielles, sans préjudice d'être sensible à la réalité du pouvoir.

Part V

Allocating Interests: States' Legal Policies between Universalism and Regionalism

15

The Challenge for States of Universal and Regional Cooperation

ANDERS RÖNQUIST*

I. INTRODUCTION

IN ADDRESSING THIS topic I have been asked to analyse the legal and political problems that membership of regional and universal organisations poses for states, and their foreign policies, and how to cope with various problems that arise in respect of such membership. This covers a large agenda, of which I will only be able to provide a few examples. You will soon realise that I am not a professor of international law. I am a career diplomat who has from time to time had the privilege of working with human rights, international law and security policy. My contribution is therefore more from the point of view of a practitioner than that of an academic.

I would suggest that problems arise not so much between the states that are member of regional and of international organisations. Rather, the challenge is to solve the legal and political problems that are becoming more and more global due to active cooperation between the regional and global levels in the international order. Universal values must also be at the core of policy at the regional and sub-regional levels. In confronting present-day violent conflicts, often of an internal nature, the responsibility to protect is a responsibility of governments which must be pursued by regional and global organisations if states are unable or unwilling to shoulder their responsibilities. Common values are essential in pursuing these efforts.

II. UNIVERSALITY OF HUMAN RIGHTS

My opening remarks concern the universality of human rights and its impact on regional organisations. Related to this issue is the question of sovereignty, which is currently moving from the concept of a right to one of responsibility. Fortunately, the universality of human rights is now widely recognised.

The Universal Declaration of Human Rights[1] was drafted by experts from different regions and the subsequent, key UN human rights conventions have been ratified

* Ambassador, Director-General for Legal Affairs, Swedish Ministry for Foreign Affairs.

[1] Universal Declaration of Human Rights (adopted 10 December 1948), UNGA Res 217A (III), UN Doc A/810, 71 (1948).

by the great majority of states, as for example with the International Covenant on Civil and Political Rights (ICCPR),[2] the International Covenant on Economic, Social and Cultural Rights (ICESCR),[3] and the UN Convention on the Rights of the Child (UNCRC or CRC).[4] Yet, only a decade or two ago, arguments were put forward to diminish the value of these standards, by declaring them 'Western' as contrary to, for example, 'Asian values'. I remember well when, serving at our UN Mission in New York in the mid-1990s, I had the role of coordinating the yearly draft resolution on the human rights situation in Burma. One of the Asian ambassadors rebuffed arguments on Asian values, telling me: 'There are no Asian values. There are Chinese, Malaysian and Thai values.'

I also remember vividly the forceful statement by the Secretary-General of the UN, Kofi Annan, at the OAU (now AU) Summit in Harare in 1997, referring to arguments about human rights as an imposition from the West:

> I find these thoughts truly demeaning, demeaning of the yearning for human dignity that resides in every African heart. Do not African mothers weep when their sons or daughters are killed or maimed by agents of repressive rule? Are not African fathers saddened when their children are unjustly jailed or tortured? Is not Africa as a whole impoverished when even one of its brilliant voices is silenced?[5]

III. RESERVATIONS TO HUMAN RIGHTS TREATIES

Having established the universality of human rights, it is important to safeguard human rights standards and to ensure that they are not eroded, but upheld. Of specific concern in this regard is the need to monitor states when they are acceding to human rights conventions, to ensure that they do not make reservations that are incompatible with the object and purpose of the conventions. This can happen, for example, by making sweeping references to national or religious law in such reservations, and this has been especially so for the Convention on the Elimination of All Forms of Discrimination against Women[6] and the CRC. Sweden has been vigilant and made formal objections, invoking the severability doctrine[7] in such cases, which means that the reservation is considered null and void and, thus, is without legal effect. This doctrine is also applied by the respective treaty bodies. There was

[2] International Covenant on Civil and Political Rights, UNGA Res 2200A (XXI), 21 UN GAOR Supp No 16, 52, UN Doc A/6316 (1966) (adopted 16 December 1966, entered into force 23 March 1976) 999 UNTS 171 (ICCPR); there are 168 parties to the ICCPR.

[3] International Covenant on Economic, Social and Cultural Rights, UNGA Res 2200A (XXI), 21 UN GAOR Supp (No 16) 49, UN Doc A/6316 (1966) (adopted 16 December 1966, entered into force 3 January 1976), 999 UNTS 3 (ICESCR); there are 162 parties to the ICESCR.

[4] Convention on the Rights of the Child, UNGA Res 44/25, UN GAOR Supp No 49, 167, UN Doc A/44/49 (1989) (adopted 20 November 1989, entered into force 2 September 1990) 1577 UNTS 3, (CRC); there are 194 parties to the CRC.

[5] K Annan, 'A New Era Beckons Africa' (1997) 11(1) *Africa Renewal* 4.

[6] Convention on the Elimination of All Forms of Discrimination against Women, UNGA Res 34/180 (XXXIV), UNGAOR Supp No 46, 193, UN Doc A/34/46 (1979) (adopted 18 December 1979, entered into force 3 September 1981), 1249 UNTS 13.

[7] *Report of the International Law Commission on the Work of its 63rd Session*, UN doc A/66/10/Add1, 512–16.

an opportunity to revisit these issues when the United Nations General Assembly considered the comprehensive study by ILC Rapporteur Alain Pellet on reservations to treaties in 2012.[8]

Regional differences are also found in accepting that the universality of human rights means that it is legitimate for a state to require that common human rights undertakings are respected also by other states.

IV. THE INTERPLAY BETWEEN REGIONAL AND GLOBAL STANDARD-SETTING

The interplay between the regional and global levels can often have an important role in standard-setting negotiations. Let me mention a few examples.

In the 1980s a working group under the UN Commission on Human Rights made very slow process in drafting a declaration on minority rights—not least, because of the differences of opinion among Western countries. After the OSCE[9] managed to agree on a comprehensive set of minority norms in the Copenhagen Document of 1990[10] this inspired the UN, which managed to agree on a Minority Rights Declaration that was adopted in 1992.[11]

When the CRC was negotiated and adopted in 1989, Sweden and a large number of other countries fought to increase the protection for children from recruitment as child soldiers, from the age of 15, in line with the First Geneva Protocol,[12] to all children up to the age of 18. Such efforts were unsuccessful, due largely to the opposition of the United States. However, the African Charter on the Rights and Welfare of the Child,[13] which entered into force in 1999, established such a ban for all children up to the age of 18. And in 2000, following renewed efforts by Sweden and other countries, an Optional Protocol to the Convention on the Rights of the Child, setting an 18-year limit, was adopted.[14]

The death penalty has been abolished throughout Europe with the exception of Belarus. Resolutions on a moratorium on executions are steadily gaining more and

[8] Report of the Special Rapporteur, Alain Pellet, on 'Reservations to Treaties', *Report of the International Law Commission on the Work of its 63rd Session* (26 April to 3 June and 4 July to 12 August 2011), UN GAOR, 66th Sess, Supp No 10 (A/66/10 and Add 1) 12–49, paras 51–76. It includes the 'Guide to Practice on Reservations to Treaties'.

[9] The Organization for Security and Cooperation in Europe (OSCE) is the successor to the Conference on Security and Cooperation in Europe (CSCE), in respect of which the principles for security and cooperation in Europe were laid down in the Helsinki Final Act of 1 July 1975.

[10] See Document of the Copenhagen Meeting of the Conference on the Human Dimension of the CSCE, Copenhagen, 29 June 1990, available at www.osce.org/odihr/elections/14304, esp paras 30–39.

[11] Declaration on the Rights of Persons Belonging to National or Ethnic, Religious and Linguistic Minorities, UNGA Res 47/135 (18 December 1992) UN Doc A/RES/47/135.

[12] Protocol I Additional to the Geneva Conventions of 12 August 1949, and relating to the Protection of Victims of Armed Conflict (Protocol I) (done at Geneva 8 June 1977, entered into force 7 December 1978) 1125 UNTS 4, art 77, para 2.

[13] African Charter on the Rights and Welfare of the Child (ACRWC or Children's Charter) was adopted by the Organisation of African Unity (OAU) [now African Union (AU)] on 11 July 1990 (OAU Doc CABLE/LEG/24.9.49 (1990)); it entered into force on 29 November 1999.

[14] Optional Protocol to the Convention on the Rights of the Child on the involvement of children in armed conflict (adopted 25 May 2000, UNGA Res 54/263, entered into force 12 February 2002)) UN Doc A/RES/54/263 (2000), 2173 UNTS 222, art 38.

more support in the United Nations General Assembly. In 2010 there were 106 votes for the abolition of the death penalty and only 46 voting against.[15] But let us recall that the first country to abolish the death penalty was not European, but Costa Rica, in 1877.

V. THE INTERPLAY BETWEEN EUROPEAN COURTS

In Europe, each individual under the jurisdiction of any Council of Europe Member State can seek redress for human rights violations, which are not properly dealt with at the national level, at the European Court of Human Rights in Strasbourg, and the Court's judgments are binding on the state.

Institutions guaranteeing democracy, human rights and the rule of law are fundamental for adherence to the European Union, and the Court of Justice of the European Union in Luxembourg is becoming more and more involved in human rights matters. With the entry into force of the Treaty of Lisbon,[16] the European Union Member States decided that the Union shall accede to the European Convention for the Protection of Human Rights and Fundamental Freedoms.[17] Ongoing negotiations focus not least on the role of the Luxembourg Court in matters that will be dealt with by the Strasbourg Court.

VI. THE FIGHT AGAINST IMPUNITY AT THE GLOBAL, REGIONAL AND NATIONAL LEVELS

Talking of courts, I turn now to the fight against impunity at global, regional and national levels. The fight against impunity for gross violations of human rights and international humanitarian law has made remarkable progress with the establishment of the International Criminal Court (ICC)[18] and its wide acceptance, with now more than 120 ratifying states. A special challenge in this regard is to enhance the principle of complementarity,[19] ie to explore ways in which to enhance the capacity of national jurisdictions to investigate and prosecute serious crimes of international concern.

Is there also a role for regional organisations in such prosecutions? And would such a role enhance or risk undermining the ICC? I raise this question because the African Union (AU) launched the idea of expanding the jurisdiction of the African

[15] 'Moratorium on the use of the death penalty', UNGA Res 65/206 (LXV) (21 December 2010) UN Doc A/RES/65/206 (2011)

[16] Treaty of Lisbon amending the Treaty on European Union and the Treaty establishing the European Community, done at Lisbon on 13 December 2007 [2007] OJ C306, entered into force 1 December 2009 (Treaty of Lisbon).

[17] Convention for the Protection of Human Rights and Fundamental Freedoms as amended by Protocol 11 (done at Rome 4 November 1950, entered into force 3 September 1953) ETS No 5.

[18] Rome Statute of the International Criminal Court (ICC) (done at Rome 17 July 1998, entered into force 1 July 2002) 2187 UNTS 3; there are 122 parties to the Rome Statute.

[19] ICC Statute, ibid, Preamble and arts 17–20.

Court of Justice and Human Rights[20] to also include the prosecution of individuals for crimes including genocide, war crimes and crimes against humanity.[21] I note that in a letter[22] to the Justice Ministers and Attorney-Generals of African States Parties to the ICC a number of African NGOs raised pertinent questions. Would such reform risk undermining progress in the African human rights system? Would it divert resources from strengthening national prosecution? Would it discourage states from acceding to and cooperating with the ICC? I leave these as questions that merit further discussion and study.

And let me also refer to the judgment of the ICJ on the questions relating to the obligation to prosecute or extradite in the case of Belgium versus Senegal.[23] In the judgment, the Court refers to the object and purpose of the UN Convention against Torture[24] and the common interest and shared value of states parties to ensure that acts of torture are prevented and do not enjoy impunity.[25] The Court refers to these principles as obligations *erga omnes* and thus each state party has an interest in ensuring compliance.[26]

The Court goes on to say that Senegal's duty to comply with its obligations under the Convention cannot be affected by the involvement of the Economic Community of West Africa (ECOWAS) Court of Justice,[27] and that the referral of the matter to the AU cannot justify Senegal's delays in complying with its obligations under the Convention against Torture.[28]

VII. CONFLICT PREVENTION, THE RESPONSIBILITY TO PROTECT AND SOVEREIGNTY AS RESPONSIBILITY

Following the fall of the Berlin Wall there were impressive normative changes in the OSCE. In 1991, while it was still the CSCE, participating states agreed that issues concerning national minorities were matters of legitimate international concern, and

[20] African Union, Decision on the Protocol on Amendments to the Protocol on the Statute of the African Court of Justice and Human Rights, 1, Assembly/AU/Dec 427(XIX) (July 15–16, 2012), available at www.african-court.org/en/images/documents/Press_Docs/DECISIONS,%20DECLARATIONS,%20RESOLUTION%20of%20the%20AU%2019th%20Assembly.pdf.

[21] Merger of the African Court on Human Rights and Peoples Rights and the Court of Justice of the African Union to become the African Court of Justice and Human Rights, First Meeting of the Specialised Technical Committee on Justice and Legal Affairs, 15–16 May 2014, Addis Ababa, Ethiopia, STC/Legal/Min/7(1) Rev 1, with Annex—Statute of African Court of Justice and Human and Peoples Rights, Article 28A.

[22] Letter from 49 civil society organisations to the Justice Ministers and Attorneys General African states parties to the International Criminal Court, 3 May 2012, available at www.hrw.org/sites/default/files/related_material/Letter_on_African_Court_May_2012.pdf.

[23] *Questions Concerning the Obligation to Prosecute or Extradite* (*Belgium v Senegal*) (Judgment) (2012) www.icj-cij.org/docket/files/144/17064.pdf.

[24] Convention Against Torture and Other Cruel, Inhuman or Degrading Treatment or Punishment (adopted 10 December 1984, entered into force 26 June 1987) 1465 UNTS 85.

[25] *Questions Concerning the Obligation to Prosecute or Extradite* Judgment, above n 23, 68.

[26] ibid.

[27] The Court of Justice of the Economic Community of West African States (ECOWAS) was established by Protocol (A/Pl/7/91) to the Treaty of the ECOWAS (done at Abuja on 6 July 1991, entered into force 24 July 1993) (ECOWAS Court of Justice).

[28] *Questions Concerning the Obligation to Prosecute or Extradite* Judgment, above n 23, 112.

consequently did not constitute exclusively an internal affair of the respective state.[29] A principle that the following year was extended to all CSCE (later OSCE) principles on democracy, human rights and the rule of law in the Moscow Document.[30]

The right of intervention in case of war crimes, genocide and crimes against humanity has been accepted under the Constitutive Act of the African Union,[31] in an important move that has been described as one from non-interference to non-indifference.[32]

At the global level, developments in this regard have been slower. Nevertheless, significant progress was made in 2005 when the UN General Assembly adopted its landmark World Summit Outcome Resolution.[33] UN Members committed themselves to the principle of the responsibility to protect (R2P), by declaring that each individual state has a responsibility to protect its populations from genocide, war crimes, ethnic cleansing and crimes against humanity. It also declared that international community should, as appropriate, encourage and help states to exercise this responsibility.[34]

What is clear in the implementation of the responsibility to protect is the crucial role of cooperation between the United Nations and regional and sub-regional organisations. As highlighted in the UN Secretary-General's Report on R2P in 2011,[35] ECOWAS, AU and the OSCE were in the vanguard in developing both the principles of protection and the practical tools for achieving them. The Report goes on to stress the critical legal and political linkages between global and regional organisations, referring to Chapter VIII of the Charter.[36] It is thus not a question of a choice between regional and universal organisations when governments are at war with their own people. It is a question of choosing both and making them cooperate.

In 2002, I had the privilege of being Deputy Secretary-General of the Regional EU Conference Partners in Prevention in Helsingborg, Sweden. This was the first meeting of high officials from all European regional organisations and the UN to discuss joint work and collective challenges with regard to conflict prevention. It identified both the need to act on the basis of common values and the need for common action.[37] Events like the tensions in Macedonia in 2001 had shown how essential it is that regional organisations and the UN work hand in hand.

[29] Report of the CSCE Meeting of Experts on National Minorities, Geneva 19 July 1991, available at www.osce.org/hcnm/14588.

[30] Document of the Moscow Meeting of the Conference on the Human Dimension of the CSCE, 3 October 1991, available at www.osce.org/odihr/elections/14310.

[31] Constitutive Act of the African Union (done at Lomé, Togo, 11 July 2000, entered into force 26 May 2001) 2158 UNTS 33.

[32] B Kioko, 'The right of intervention under the African Union's Constitutive Act: From non-interference to non-intervention' (2003) 85/852 *Révue internationale de la Croix-Rouge/International Review of the Red Cross*, 805–25, 819.

[33] UNGA Res 10/1 2015 'World Summit Outcome' (LX) (16 September 2005).

[34] ibid, paras 138–39.

[35] UNGA Report of the Secretary General 'The role of regional and sub-regional arrangements in implementing the responsibility to protect' (2011) UN Doc A/165/877-S/2011/393 at para 4.

[36] ibid, paras 5 and 43.

[37] See 'Letter dated 19 September 2002 from the Permanent Representative of Sweden to the United Nations addressed to the Secretary-General' with attached 'Conclusions of the Chairman of the Regional European Union Conference on Conflict Prevention "Partners in Prevention", held in Helsingborg, Sweden, on 29 and 30 August 1992' (3 October 2002) UN Doc A/57/448-S/2002/1110.

For my own part, I learned this lesson when working with the OSCE High Commissioner on National Minorities in the early 1990s. In addressing often difficult questions regarding minority rights it is essential that solutions proposed by different organisations are coordinated and based on international norms. Otherwise there are risks of forum shopping and confusion, instead of consistent political messages.

VIII. CLIMATE CHANGE

More and more issues are nowadays rightly seen as global, requiring global solutions. Let me take as my first example climate change. During our last EU Presidency in the second half of 2009, Sweden made considerable efforts to reach a successful outcome of the Copenhagen Climate Conference.[38] The EU presented an ambitious position.[39] We were prepared to move to a 30 per cent reduction of greenhouse gas emissions, compared to 1990 levels, as our contribution to a global and comprehensive agreement, provided other developed countries committed themselves to comparable emission reductions. Similarly, developing countries needed to contribute adequately in accordance with their responsibilities and respective capabilities. It was not sufficient for the EU to be ambitious; rather climate needs global commitments and global action.

Sweden has for its part declared its ambition to reduce greenhouse emissions by 40 per cent by 2020. Yet, given the fact that Sweden's emissions amount to a mere 0.14 per cent of global emissions,[40] clearly we must work for global commitments. This is why it is so important that the Durban Climate Conference[41] resulted in a clear road map that would lead to a deal, which for the first time would legally bind all nations to curb emissions.

IX. FREE TRADE

Let me take another example, namely free trade. More open trade contributes to jobs and growth, when we need it the most. No country has ever managed to achieve long-term economic development by adopting protectionist policies, and we know that more openness to trade encourages job creation. Studies show that reducing trade barriers can significantly spur employment, productivity and wages.

[38] UNFCCC 'Report of the Conference on the Parties on its 15th Session, held in Copenhagen from 7 to 19 December 2009' FCCC/CP/2009/Add 1 (30 March 2010) 4 for the 'Copenhagen Accord' (Decision 2/CP 15).

[39] Council Conclusions on EU position for the Copenhagen Climate Conference (7–18 December 2009), 2968th Environment Council meeting, Luxembourg, 21 October 2009, available at www.consilium.europa.eu/uedocs/cms_data/docs/pressdata/en/envir/110634.pdf.

[40] The World Bank World Development Indicators on Environment 2013, available at www.wdi.worldbank.org/table/3.8.

[41] UNFCCC 'Report of the Conference on the Parties on its 17th Session, held in Durban from 28 November to 12 December 2011' FCCC/CP/2011/9.

Here again a global regime is what we should strive for. An ambitious conclusion of the Doha Round of Multilateral Trade Negotiations[42] constitutes the best option for the world trading system, global trade, and development. In the meantime, free trade agreements between individual countries and/or regional organisations should be seen as stepping stones to foster such a global accord.

X. DISARMAMENT

A third example is disarmament. I would like to present another type of dilemma by providing the example of the ban on cluster munitions. Sweden is among over 70 states that have ratified the Oslo Convention on Cluster Munitions[43] and are thereby obliged not to use, produce or transfer such weapons. At the same time, Sweden was very supportive also of a protocol on cluster munitions under the Convention on Certain Conventional Weapons.[44] The International Committee of the Red Cross (ICRC), the UN High Commissioner for Refugees (UNHCHR) and many States were opposed since they considered such a protocol would undermine the standards under the Oslo Convention. Sweden, on the other hand, thought it would supplement the Convention by including states that are the main users and producers of cluster munitions and therefore positively contribute to putting an end to the suffering and casualties caused by such weapons.

XI. THE EUROPEAN UNION: A COMMUNITY OF VALUES

Sweden has been a member of the European Union since 1995. The Union is founded on common values, including respect for human dignity, freedom, democracy, equality, the rule of law and respect for human rights, including the rights of persons belonging to minorities. If there is a clear risk of a serious breach by a Member State of these values rights deriving from the Treaties may be suspended. The enlargement process has been fundamental in promoting peace and democracy all over Europe since a rigorous scrutiny is made of the applicant country's performance on issues such as democracy, human rights and the rule of law.

With the entry into force of the Treaty of Lisbon in 2009, the Charter of Fundamental Rights of the European Union[45] acquired legally binding force. The Charter is largely inspired by the UN Declaration on Human Rights and the European

[42] The Doha Development Round of Multilateral Trade Negotiations was launched at the WTO Ministerial Conference, Fourth Session, Doha, 9–14 November 2001.

[43] Convention on Cluster Munitions (done at Dublin, 30 May 2008 and opened for signature at Oslo, 3–4 December 2008, entered into force 1 August 2010) (2009) 48 ILM 357.

[44] Convention on Prohibitions or Restrictions on the Use of Certain Conventional Weapons which may be deemed to be Excessively Injurious or to have Indiscriminate Effects (with Protocols I, II and III) (done at Geneva, 10 October 1980, entered into force 2 December 1983) 1342 UNTS 137 (Convention on Certain Conventional Weapons or CWC).

[45] Charter of Fundamental Rights of the European Union (done at Nice, 7 December 2000, entered into force 1 December 2009) [2010] OJ C83/309.

Convention for the Protection of Human Rights and Fundamental Freedoms. The Member States of the EU are all parties to the European Convention, and the rights therein constitute general principles of EU law. In addition, negotiations are ongoing to pave the way for the EU to accede to the European Convention on Human Rights.

At the same time, in accordance with the Treaty of Lisbon,[46] the Union's international action shall be based on the same principles which have inspired its own creation, development and enlargement. Under article 21, the EU shall build partnerships with third countries and international, regional and global organisations and promote multilateral solutions, in particular in the framework of the United Nations. Again, it is not a choice between regional and universal.[47]

The effectiveness and visibility of EU external action on human rights was considerably enhanced by the adoption of a strategic framework and action plan on human rights and democracy[48] and the decision in 2012 to appoint a special EU representative on human rights.[49]

XII. CLASHES BETWEEN REGIONAL AND UNIVERSAL COMMITMENTS

Of special interest, of course, is where membership of regional and universal organisations gives rise to conflicting obligations. A case in point is the question of sanctions regimes and the rule of law. First, let me underline that when it comes to sanctions, it is of course preferable that strong and targeted sanctions are decided by the Security Council and are binding on all states. Sanctions decided by a regional body like the European Union do not have the same impact. Commonly agreed international sanctions provide for a level playing field and send an important political signal. However, when the UN is blocked regional organisations must assume responsibility for peace and security.

Turning then to the question of sanctions and human rights, action by the UN Security Council under Chapter VII of the UN Charter is binding on the Members. According to article 103 of the UN Charter the obligations under the Charter shall prevail in the event of a conflict between the obligations of Members and obligations under any other international agreement. Much has been written on this dilemma since the ECJ judgment in September 2008 in the case of *Kadi & Al Barakaat International Foundation v Council and Commission*.[50] Clearly, the European jurisprudence has had the effect of pressuring the UN Security Council to enhance the protection of human rights.

[46] Treaty of Lisbon, above n 16.

[47] Consolidated Version of the Treaty on European Union [2008] OJ C115/13, para 1 of art 21, C115/28.

[48] EU Strategic Framework and Action Plan on Human Rights and Democracy, Luxembourg, 21 October 2009, 11855/12, available at www.consilium.europa.eu/uedocs/cms_data/docs/pressdata/EN/foraff/131181.pdf.

[49] Council Decision appointing the European Union Special Representative for Human Rights, 2012/440/CFSP of 25 July 2012 [2012] OJ L200/21.

[50] Joined Cases C402/05 P and C415/05 P, *Yassin Abdullah Kadi and Al Barakaat International Foundation v Council of the European Union and Commission of the European Community* [2008] ECR I-06351.

The Swedish approach has consistently been to work to ensure an enhanced rule of law protection in the UN sanctions regime, thereby also reducing the risk of conflicts between UN and EU obligations. As a result of such efforts the Security Council 1267 Regime[51] against al-Qaida and persons associated with it has been complemented with better criteria for listing, the right to humanitarian exemptions, a procedure for de-listing requests and a review of older lists.[52] An Ombudsperson was appointed, who is to act as a contact channel between the persons listed and the Sanctions Committee, and independently gather information about the case that is then submitted to the Committee for a decision. She has also been given the right of recommendation vis-à-vis the Sanctions Committee with regard to de-listing matters, ie a number of measures have been taken to strengthen the rule of law in this sanctions regime.[53] This is a process that has been spurred by the European Union and its Court.

Let me just briefly refer to the judgment delivered by the European Court of Human Rights in the case of *Nada v Switzerland*.[54] The Court observed that Switzerland could not simply rely on the binding nature of the Security Council resolutions but should have taken all possible measures, within the latitude available to it, to adapt the sanctions regime to the applicant's individual situation.[55] As the Court considered that Switzerland had failed to harmonise the international obligations that appeared contradictory, the Court found that there had been a violation of article 8, and also article 13, of the Convention.[56]

So, in conclusion, let me once again stress my basic message. Universal common values must be at the core of our efforts as states either we act at the national, regional or global level.

[51] The sanctions regime was first established by UNSC Res 1267 (15 October 1999) UN Doc S/RES/1267 (1999).

[52] UNSC Res 1730 (19 December 2006) UN Doc S/RES/1730 (2006).

[53] UNSC Res 1904 (17 December 2009) UN Doc S/RES/1904 (2009); UNSC Res 1989 (17 June 2011) UN Doc S/RES/1989 (2011); and UNSC Res 2083 (17 December 2012) UN Doc S/RES/2083 (2012).

[54] *Nada v Switzerland* App no 10593/08 [GC] ECHR, 12 September 2012.

[55] ibid, para 196.

[56] ibid, para 197.

16

Universalism and Regionalism—A Balance of Power Re-Struck

DAPHNA SHRAGA*

I. INTRODUCTION

THE RELATIONSHIP BETWEEN the United Nations, the foremost universal organisation, and regional organisations has been multifaceted and dynamic, vacillating from hierarchical to vertical and from cooperation to defiance. It has been a balance of power constantly re-struck at any point of time, organisation and field of activity. While in the area of human rights the regional has often 'led' the universal and shaped its policies, in international criminal justice it has defied it, and in peacekeeping operations both universal and regional organisations have partnered up to share the burden, quite often on conditions of parity. In all three areas, striking a balance between the universal and the regional has ultimately been about the power, authority and legitimacy of the Security Council.

II. HUMAN RIGHTS—THE REGIONAL LEADS THE UNIVERSAL

A. The Death Penalty

The establishment of the International Criminal Tribunal for the former Yugoslavia (ICTY) as a UN subsidiary organ[1] forced the United Nations to take a position on the application of the death penalty in the event of conviction for any of the crimes falling within its jurisdiction. Urged by most European states at the time of its establishment to exclude the death penalty from the statutory list of penalties, the UN Secretariat adopted the legal position advocated by the EU and applied it consistently to all subsequent UN-based tribunals. Non-imposition of the death penalty has since become a benchmark for UN cooperation with any national accountability

* Jerusalem and Tel-Aviv Universities, former Principal Legal Officer, Office of Legal Affairs, United Nations.

[1] UNSC Res 827 (25 May 1993) UN Doc S/RES/827 in which the Security Council established the International Tribunal for the Former Yugoslavia (ICTY) and adopted the Statute of the Tribunal, as annexed to the 'Report of the Secretary General Pursuant to Paragraph 2, Security Council Resolution 808 (1993), UN Doc S/25704'.

mechanism, where the mere existence of capital punishment on the books and the possibility of its imposition would have otherwise ruled out any UN cooperation.

While in the case of the death penalty the UN followed the EU lead out of conviction, in the case of the sanctions regime and due process rights, it was the threat to the viability of the sanctions regime that forced a compromise, however uneasy, between the universal and the regional.

B. Sanctions and Human Rights

The Security Council targeted sanctions regime, established in 1999 by SC Resolution 1267[2] as amended, was widely criticised for its lack of transparency and failure to comply with due process guarantees for individuals and entities on a designated list of Taliban, al-Qaida and their associates. Committed to ensuring fair and clear procedures for placing individuals and entities on the sanctions list, the Security Council has gradually introduced improvements in the listing and de-listing procedures; improvements that have done little to convince the critics.[3]

It was not until the European Court of Justice annulled in the *Kadi and Al-Barakaat* Case Regulation 881/2002[4]—the implementing European Community measure for the Security Council sanctions regime—for its failure to comply with international standards of due process,[5] that the Security Council was compelled to act. In its Resolution 1904 (2009), the Security Council took note of 'the challenges, both legal and otherwise to the measures implemented by Member States'.[6] In recognition of the serious threat that those challenges posed to the integrity of the sanctions regime, if not to the legitimacy of the Security Council, it established the Office of the Ombudsperson, with a mandate to receive requests from individuals and entities seeking removal from the Consolidated List.[7]

Notwithstanding this paradigm shift in the business of the Security Council, which for the first time ever accepted the scrutiny of an independent, non-judicial review

[2] The UN targeted sanctions regime was first established by UNSC Res 1267 (15 October 1999) UN Doc S/RES/1267.

[3] In subsequent resolutions it adopted humanitarian exemptions, enjoined designating states to provide detailed identifying information in support of the proposed listing, established a focal point to receive de-listing requests, requested the Sanctions Committee to notify the individual or entity of the listing, and to disseminate the summaries of the reasons for listing: (UNSC Res 1526 (30 January 2004) UN Doc S/RES/1526; SC Res 1617 (29 July 2005) UN Doc S/RES/1617; and SC Res 1735 (22 December 2006) UN Doc S/RES/1735; see JE Alvarez, 'Hegemonic International Law Revisited' (2003) 97 *American Journal of International Law* 874–78; B Fassbender, 'Targeted Sanctions Imposed by the UN Security Council and Due Process Rights: A Study Commissioned by the UN Office of Legal Affairs and Follow-up Action by the United Nations' (2006) 3 *International Organizations Law Review* 437.

[4] Council Regulation (EC) 881/2002 of 27 May 2002 imposing certain specific restrictive measures directed against certain persons and associated with Usama bin Laden, the al-Qaida network and the Taliban [2002] OJ L139/9.

[5] Notably the right to be heard, to be informed of the grounds for listing and the right to effective judicial remedy, Joined Cases C-402/05 and C-415/059, *Yassin Abdullah Kadi and Al Barakaat International Foundation v Council of the European Union and Commission of the European Communities*, Judgment of the Court (Grand Chamber) of 3 September 2008, paras 322–34.

[6] UNSC Res 1904 (17 December 2009) UN Doc S/RES/1904, ninth recital.

[7] UNSC Res 1904, ibid, Annex II.

mechanism, and engaged, however indirectly, with listed individuals, the institution of the Ombudsperson was dismissed by regional and national courts. In the view of courts of both types of jurisdictions the Office of the Ombudsperson had little effect on the deficient Sanctions Committee's procedures of listing and de-listing, for it could not be equated with an independent and impartial body or the provision of 'an effective judicial procedure for review of decisions of the Sanctions Committee'.[8]

In the conflict between the universal and the regional legal orders over the primacy of the UN Charter within the European legal space, the European Human Rights Convention—notwithstanding article 103 of the Charter—prevailed. European regional courts declined to review the lawfulness of Chapter VII Security Council resolutions, yet refused to grant their implementing Community Regulations 'immunity' from judicial review. Judging them not compliant with due process standards, they annulled the implementing Regulations, and in so doing rendered the Security Council resolutions effectively unenforceable in the European legal order.

The dialogue between the universal and the regional—a dialogue, in fact, between the political and the legal—has reached a standoff. For the Security Council, a process of reforms in the listing and de-listing procedures, culminating in the establishment of the Office of the Ombudsperson, was perhaps all that it was prepared to concede to due process standards. For regional courts, nothing short of 'an independent and impartial tribunal' within the meaning of article 14 of the International Covenant on Civil and Political Rights or article 6 of the European Convention on Human Rights could be considered to have met due process standards and render the Security Council decisions—through their implementing Regulations—enforceable within the European legal order.

A standoff of a different kind, but of equally serious consequences for the international legal order, has emerged in the field of international criminal justice between the UN Security Council and the African Union (AU) over the prosecutorial strategy of the International Criminal Court (ICC) and the African response.

III. INTERNATIONAL CRIMINAL JUSTICE: THE REGIONAL DEFIES THE UNIVERSAL

Of the nine situations currently before the ICC—all of which are African—the situations in Sudan[9] and in Libya[10] were referred to the Prosecutor by the Security Council under article 13 of the ICC Statute, and an investigation into the situations in Kenya and Côte d'Ivoire was initiated by the Prosecutor *proprio motu* under article 15 of the Statute.[11]

[8] Case T-85/09 *Yassin Abdullah Kadi v European Commission*, Judgment of the General Court (Seventh Chamber) of 30 September 2010, para 128; see also Report of the High Commissioner for Human Rights on the Protection of Human Rights and Fundamental Freedoms While Countering Terrorism, A/HRC/16/50 of 15 December 2010; Report of the Special Rapporteur on the Promotion and Protection of Human Rights and Fundamental Freedoms While Countering Terrorism, A/67/396 of 26 September 2012.

[9] UNSC Res 1593 (31 March 2005) A/RES/1593.

[10] UNSC Res 1970 (26 February 2011) A/RES/1970.

[11] The remaining four situations (in Uganda, the Democratic Republic of the Congo (DRC) the Central African Republic (CAR) and Mali) were self-referrals (the situation in the CAR was self-referred twice).

Considering itself unjustly targeted by the ICC in pursuit of an 'anti-African', 'biased' and 'discriminatory' judicial policy, the African Union requested the Security Council to exercise its authority under article 16 of the Statute and request the Court (in the cases of Sudan, Libya and Kenya) to defer investigation and prosecution for a period of 12 months. Faced with the Council's inaction, the AU decided on non-cooperation with the ICC in the execution of the arrest warrants against President al-Bashir and Colonel Qadhafi.[12] It then initiated a diplomatic campaign calling upon the General Assembly—in a move reminiscent of the 'Uniting for Peace' Resolution—to assume 'Article-16 authority' and request a deferral of an investigation or a prosecution, should the Council fail to act (positively) on the request. Its ultimate response, however, and the one intended as the final blow to the global justice system, was its decision to establish an African Criminal Court, as a third International Criminal Law Section in the African Court of Justice and Human Rights, having jurisdiction over the crimes of genocide, crimes against humanity and war crimes, among others.[13] In the standoff between the universal and the regional, the AU has not succeeded in forcing the Security Council to defer, but neither did the Council succeed in enforcing its decision to refer and compel members of the AU to cooperate.

IV. PEACEKEEPING OPERATIONS: THE REGIONAL AND THE UNIVERSAL (ALMOST ALWAYS) COOPERATE

The relationship between the UN and regional organisations in the field of peacekeeping has been a pattern of cooperation, partnership, but also one of defiance. For the UN, in an era of ever-expanding peacekeeping operations, insufficient financial and human resources and lack of political will or interest on the part of major powers to engage, 'regionalising peacekeeping' as a form of burden-sharing was a practical-imposed necessity.[14] For the regional organisations, participating in maintaining peace and security in their own regions was a test of their enhanced military capacity and a political statement of ownership of their regional affairs.

In the practice of UN operations, regional organisations and arrangements of military capacity were authorised under Chapter VII of the Charter to

[12] Decision on the Implementation of the Assembly Decisions on the International Criminal Court, Doc EX CL/670(XIX), African Union, Malabo, 30 June–1 July 2011, Assembly of the AU, 17th Ordinary Session (Assembly/AU/Dec 366 (XVII).

[13] Draft Protocol on Amendments to the Protocol on the Statute of the African Court of Justice and Human Rights, Meeting of Government Experts and Ministers of Justice/Attorneys, 7–11 and 14–15 May 2012, Addis Ababa, Ethiopia (Exp/Min/IV/Rev 7). In its 19th Ordinary Session on 15–16 July 2012, the Assembly of the Union decided to defer consideration of the draft Protocol until after a study of its financial and structural implications is presented to the AU organs in the summit, scheduled for January 2013. It was not until its 23rd Ordinary Session in June 2014 that the AU Assembly adopted the Protocol on Amendments to the Protocol on the Statute of the African Court of Justice and Human Rights, to try international crimes (Assembly/AU/Dec. 529(XXIII)). The African Criminal Court, however, is yet to be operationalised.

[14] Report of the Secretary-General pursuant to the statement adopted by the Summit Meeting of the Security Council on 31 January 1992, An Agenda for Peace, Preventive Diplomacy, Peacemaking and Peacekeeping, A/47/277–S/2411 (17 June 1992), para 64.

'use all necessary measures'—a codeword for the use of force—in support of a UN operation. NATO's Operation in Bosnia and Herzegovina in support of UNPROFOR,[15] the EU operations in support of the UN Operation in the Democratic Republic of the Congo (MONUC),[16] and the co-deployment of an EU and UN Operations in the border area between Chad and the Central African Republic,[17] are only a few examples of the way the regional assists the universal.

Cooperation of a different kind, particularly in Africa, has been the so-called 're-hatting', sequencing or transformation of a regional operation into a UN Mission. In Burundi, the AU Mission (AMIB) was incorporated into a UN command structure renamed ONUB, to be initially composed of existing AMIB forces,[18] in Mali, the African-led International Support Mission (AFISMA) was transformed into a UN Multidimensional Integrated Stabilization Mission in Mali (MINUSMA)[19] and in Sudan, the AU/UN Hybrid Operation in Darfur (UNAMID)—a first ever joint operation—was established by the Security Council.[20]

On three occasions, however, in the 1990s, regional organisations and arrangements conducted military operations in defiance of Security Council authority and in violation of Article 53(1) of the Charter. With the exception of the 1999 NATO (unauthorised) air-campaign in Kosovo, the military interventions of the Economic Community of West African States (ECOWAS) in Liberia and Sierra Leone were launched without a Security Council authorisation, but with its retrospective commendation.[21] And while there was little doubt that the retroactive 'authorisation' had legalised the operations, the question of whether it evidenced the emergence of a new norm whereby regional military operations could be legally launched on the expectation that they would be retroactively authorised, for a while at least, remained debatable. Subsequent practice of military interventions in Africa in the 2000s, however, did not substantiate the assumption of an emerging norm. In countries like Côte d'Ivoire,[22] Somalia[23] and Mali,[24] military interventions have been launched by the AU or ECOWAS, after having sought and being granted a Security Council authorisation.

[15] UNSC Res 770 (13 August 1992) A/RES/770.

[16] EU Operation, named Arthemis, authorised under SC Res 1484 (2003) of 30 May 2003, A/RES/1484, and EUFOR RD Congo authorised under UNSC Res 1671 (25 April 2006) A/RES/1671.

[17] UNSC Res 1778 (25 September 2007) A/RES/1778 approved the establishment of a 'multidimensional presence' composed of a UN operation (MINURCAT) and an authorised EU supporting operation under Chapter VII UN.

[18] UNSC Res 1545 (21 May 2004) A/RES/1545.

[19] UNSC Res 2100 (25 April 2013) A/RES/2100.

[20] UNSC Res 1769 (31 July 2007) A/RES/1769.

[21] UNSC Res 788 (19 November 1992) A/RES/788, para 1 and UNSC Res 1162 (17 April 1998) A/RES/1162, para 2.

[22] UNSC Res 1464 (4 February 2003) A/RES/1464.

[23] UNSC Res 1964 (22 December 2010) A/RES/1964, para 1; UNSC Res 2010 (30 September 2011) A/RES/201, para 1, and UNSC Res 2073 (7 November 2012) A/RES/2073, para 1.

[24] By resolution 2085 (2012), the Security Council authorized the deployment of an African-led International Support Mission in Mali (AFISMA) with a mandate to take all necessary measures to support the Malian authorities in recovering the regions in the north of the country under the control of terrorist groups. UNSC Res 2085 (20 December 2012) A/RES/2085, para 9.

V. CONCLUSION

In the complex and dynamic interplay between the universal and the regional, boundaries have been constantly redrawn, and in the process regional organisations have gained considerable power, legitimacy and clout. In the areas of human rights, international criminal justice and peacekeeping operations they have grown strong enough to determine the conditions of their cooperation but not enough to dictate them. Ultimately, however, there was no avoiding compromise, or else there would be a continuing standoff.

17

Human Security and Universal Human Rights of Undocumented Migrants: Transnational Vulnerabilities and Regional Traditions

DOROTHY ESTRADA-TANCK*

I. INTRODUCTION

HUMAN SECURITY IN its modern form emerged as a post-Cold War proposal under the United Nations Development Programme (UNDP) in 1994[1] and later by the Commission on Human Security Report entitled *Human Security Now* in 2003,[2] in order to confront threats that had been overlooked by conventional state-centred conceptions of national, military and territorial security. The UNDP Report sought to address the risks faced by individuals and communities, such as environmental hazards, poverty, global infectious diseases like HIV/AIDS, violent conflicts within states (not only between states), food and water scarcity, violence against women, and transnational organised crime. Building on the original 1945 objectives of the United Nations (UN) of people living free from fear and free from want, and free to live in dignity, and looking at the different types of threats people confront, the UNDP Report proposed seven main forms of human security: health security, economic security, environmental security, community security, political security, personal security, and food security.[3] The Report endorsed human rights as one of its core pillars and advocated for a person-cantered approach to dangers and harms that create mutual and interlinked vulnerabilities for persons around the world.[4]

Human Security Now built upon the 1994 UNDP Report, although it moved beyond the categorisation of the seven forms of human security. Instead, it proposed

* PhD in Law, European University Institute, Florence, Italy; Adviser, Case Matrix Network.

[1] UNDP, *Human Development Report 1993* and *Human Development Report 1994* (New York, UNDP, 1993 and 1994).

[2] Commission on Human Security, *Human Security Now* (New York, 2003).

[3] UNDP, *Human Development Report 1994*, above n 1, 23–25.

[4] S Fukuda-Parr, 'New Threats to Human Security in the Era of Globalization' in LC Chen et al (eds), *Human Insecurity in a Global World* (Cambridge MA, Harvard University Press, 2003) 1–13.

a definition in the form of a lens, or a framework of analysis, for examining human security and set criteria that were useful for reviewing different phenomena. The same approach will be employed in this chapter. The Report considered that:

> Human security means to protect the vital core of all human lives in ways that enhance human freedoms and human fulfillment. [It] means protecting fundamental freedoms—freedoms that are the essence of life ... protecting people from *critical (severe) and pervasive (widespread) threats* and situations. It means using processes that build on people's strengths and aspirations. It means creating *political, social, environmental, economic, military and cultural systems* that together give people the building blocks of *survival, livelihood and dignity*.[5]

In a complementary manner, the Second Report of the UN Secretary General on Human Security, of April 2012, reflects state consensus on a 'common understanding' of the notion of human security and highlights the fact that it 'makes *no distinction* between civil, political, economic, social and cultural rights and as a result addresses threats ... in a multidimensional and comprehensive manner'.[6]

On the basis of this definition, this chapter addresses the following questions. Can international human rights law and regional understandings of human rights, be enriched through the concept of human security, to face national and transnational threats that affect the human rights of undocumented migrants? Is the interpretation of human rights affected in the context of irregular migrant persons, especially those suffering structural vulnerability? How do modern liberal democracies, upholding the rule of law, understand the universal right of access to justice of undocumented migrants?

It will analyse these issues through the lens provided by the conceptual framework of human security, evaluated through some highlights from the main normative and judicial regimes in international human rights law, at the UN level, as well as regional developments within the Inter-American, European and African systems of human rights, with a focus mainly on the first of these two regions.

The thematic heart of the chapter will focus on the relationship between human security and the human rights of irregular migrants, considering that: a) migrants frequently face violations of their human rights; b) the sole state of legal irregularity is in itself a condition of vulnerability; and c) there are protection gaps in the existing international legal framework on the rights of migrants.

II. WHO IS AN UNDOCUMENTED MIGRANT?

According to current data, the International Organization for Migration (IOM) estimated in 2012 that that there were 214 million international migrants worldwide, that is, persons living and/or working in a country other than that of their birth or

[5] *Human Security Now*, above n 2, 4 (emphasis added).

[6] UNGA *Report of the Secretary General, Follow-up to General Assembly resolution 64/291 on human security* (2012) UN Doc A/66/763, para 26.

citizenship.[7] The total number of international migrants increased over a period of 10 years from an estimated 150 million in 2000 to 214 million persons in 2010; ie 3.1% of the world's population, or one of out of every 33 persons in the world today, are migrants. If considered in the aggregate, migrants would constitute the fifth most populous country in the world.[8] However, it is hard to provide an exact number for undocumented migrants, precisely because of their irregular legal status.

This chapter focuses on undocumented migrants, and to a certain extent asylum-seekers, and the human insecurities they confront as an issue that raises some novel questions for human rights and revisits questions under the new spotlight on the notion of human security. While the legal framework presents a definition of 'migrant worker'—applicable both to documented and undocumented migrant workers—it does not offer a more general definition of the migrant person, particularly for those migrants that are in an irregular situation regarding their entry to or residence in a given state. There is one notable exception, which is taken up in Advisory Opinion 18/03 of the Inter-American Court of Human Rights, *Juridical Condition and Rights of Undocumented Migrants*,[9] that defines a 'migrant' as 'any person who emigrates'—'leaves a state in order to transfer to another and establish himself there'—or 'immigrates'—'enters another State in order to reside there'.

Specifically with the words 'undocumented migrant', this text understands those persons without a residence permit authorising them to regularly stay or work in their country of destination. They may have been unsuccessful in the asylum procedure, have overstayed their visa or have entered the relevant country irregularly. The routes to becoming an undocumented migrant are complex, and at times the result of arbitrary policies and procedures over which the migrant has little or no control.

Regarding some of the receiving regions and countries in the developed world,[10] civil society actors addressing this field in Europe, for example, estimate that the majority of undocumented migrants enter Europe legally, but after a period of time experience difficulties and find themselves without the relevant permit for residence or employment. It has been stressed that 'irregularity is caused by an administrative infringement and not a criminal offence. It is often a process fuelled by exploitation, redundancy, misinformation and administrative delays'.[11] Civil society in the US has also highlighted immigrant rights as a means to test the condition of human rights

[7] International Organization for Migration, *World Migration Report 2011: Communicating Effectively About Migration* (2011), 49.

[8] See the International Organisation for Migration (IOM) at www.iom.int/jahia/Jahia/about-migration/facts-and-figures/lang/en.

[9] Inter-American Court of Human Rights, *Juridical Condition and Rights of Undocumented Migrants*, Advisory Opinion OC-18/03 (AO 18/03) requested by the United Mexican States, 17 September 2003, para 69(a) to (e).

[10] Possibly in contrast to popular perception, the receiving countries with the highest number of migrants, in terms of percentage of their total population, are not in the Global North. Countries with a high percentage of migrants include Qatar (87%), United Arab Emirates (70%), Jordan (46%), Singapore (41%), and Saudi Arabia (28%); see www.iom.int/jahia/Jahia/about-migration/facts-and-figures/lang/en.

[11] Platform for International Cooperation on Undocumented Migrants (PICUM) at www.picum.org/en/our-work/undocumented-migrants/; PICUM leads a 'network of concerned individuals and organizations committed to ensuring real sustainable change for undocumented migrants by informing and influencing policy makers'.

in society at large, by signalling that: '[W]hen the government has the power to deny legal rights and due process to one vulnerable group, everyone's rights are at risk'.[12]

Returning to legal definitions in the realm of UN instruments, the International Convention on the Protection of the Rights of All Migrant Workers and Members of their Families (CMW),[13] in article 2.1, offers a definition of 'migrant worker', as 'a person who is to be engaged, is engaged or has been engaged in a remunerated activity in a State of which he or she is not a national'. In article 5, the CMW clarifies that migrant workers and members of their families:

> (a) Are considered as *documented* or in a regular situation if they are authorised to enter, to stay and to engage in a remunerated activity in the State of employment pursuant to the law of that State and to international agreements to which that State is a party; and
> (b) Are considered as *non-documented* or in an irregular situation if they do not comply with the conditions provided for in subparagraph (a) of the present Article.

Let us now turn to analyse how the global and regional legal regimes have developed and interpreted international human rights standards, where human rights law intersects with human security, and the implications of this relationship.

III. THE INTERNATIONAL LEGAL FRAMEWORK FOR THE HUMAN RIGHTS OF MIGRANTS

A. The UN System

Based on the principles of equality and non-discrimination, the UN legal framework has consistently reaffirmed the human rights of *all* migrants and the prohibition of discrimination founded on national or social origin.[14] Only one of the nine core treaties in the whole UN human rights treaty system refers to migrants—specifically to migrant workers and their families. The 1990 International Convention on the Protection of the Rights of All Migrant Workers and Members of their Families, as its name suggests, refers to the rights of *all* migrant workers, ie both documented and undocumented migrant workers, and members of their families.[15] Part IV of

[12] See American Civil Liberties Union, 'ACLU's "Immigrants" Rights Project' at www.aclu.org/immigrants-rights/about-aclus-immigrants-rights-project.

[13] International Convention on the Protection of the Rights of All Migrant Workers and Members of their Families UNGA Res 45/158, annex, 45 UN GAOR Supp No 49, 262, UN Doc A/45/49 (1990) (adopted 18 December 1990, entered into force 1 July 2003) 2220 UNTS 3.

[14] See the general basis in arts 1(3) and 55 of the UN Charter and the specific mention in art 2 of the Universal Declaration of Human Rights (adopted 10 December 1948), UNGA Res 217 A (III), UN Doc A/810, 71 (1948).

[15] The Convention was drafted based on two prior instruments, the International Labour Organization (ILO) Migration for Employment Convention of 1949 (No 97) and the ILO Migrant Workers (Supplementary Provisions) Convention of 1975 (No 143), which together constitute what has been called the 'international charter on migration'; see P Taran, 'Clashing worlds: imperative for a rights-based approach to labour migration in the age of globalization' in vol II *Mondialisation, migration et droits de l'homme: le droit international en question/Globalization, migration and human rights: international law under review*, under the supervision of Vincent Chetail, Collection of the Geneva Academy of International Humanitarian Law and Human Rights (Bruxelles, Bruylant, 2007) 403, 421.

the CMW also provides for additional rights specifically for documented migrant workers.[16] It constitutes the only human rights treaty with universal aspiration that places existing human rights standards in the specific context of migration.

Other human rights treaty bodies have also consistently reaffirmed the applicability of all human rights—civil, political, economic, social and cultural—to migrant persons and the prohibition of discrimination based on national origin or immigration status.[17]

On the side of states, some of the concerns that are raised when human rights of undocumented migrants are brought forth are that they could restrict sovereign powers on immigration or endanger the economic stability and wellbeing of the national population. It has been argued that the human rights framework itself may offer an adequate balancing mechanism to allow for the exercise of state faculties, while at the same time promoting a coherent standard of respect and protection of fundamental human entitlements, central to constitutional democracies—many of which are receiving countries for migration. This 'human rights-sovereignty compromise' may shed light on ways of confronting the dilemma that anti-irregular immigration measures undoubtedly represent the idea of universal personhood and human dignity.[18]

In this respect, based on the legal framework, which has just been described, it must be reaffirmed that in speaking of the rights of migrants, the departing point in the debate is not—as is often purported—the national sovereignty of states and their ability to regulate territorial borders, but rather what the law, or different legal systems, have to say about such rights and the principles on which they are based. Indeed, the UN Special Rapporteur on the Human Rights of Migrants, Mr François Crépeau, has highlighted the tendency observed in some declarations by public officials and the mass media to consider migrants who arrive in states and have not been invited to come, or to enter, as somehow not enjoying the same rights as other people. Such a pattern has led to the creation of spaces of administrative discretion based on an underlying belief that there exist two kinds of human rights—those held

[16] Pt IV of the CMW, ibid.

[17] See art 27 of the International Covenant on Civil and Political Rights, UNGA Res 2200A (XXI), 21 UN GAOR Supp No 16, 52, UN Doc A/6316 (adopted 16 December 1966, entered into force 23 March 1976), 999 UNTS 171 (ICCPR) refers to ethnic, religious and linguistic minorities; art 30 of the Convention on the Rights of the Child, UNGA Res 44/25, UN GAOR Supp No 49, 167, UN Doc A/44/49 (1989) (adopted 20 November 1989, entered into force 2 September 1990) and art 5 of the Vienna Declaration and Program of Action, adopted by the World Conference on Human Rights, Vienna, 25 June 1993); Declaration on the human rights of individuals who are not nationals of the country in which they live, UNGA Res 40/144 (13 December 1985) UN Doc A/RES/40/144; UNHRC, 'General Comment 15 on the position of aliens under the Covenant' [ICCPR] (11 April 1986); UNHRC, General Comment 23, The rights of minorities (art 27) (1994), indicating that the rights of art 27 of ICCPR also apply to migrant workers; Committee on the Elimination of Racial Discrimination General Recommendation No 30, Discrimination against Non-Citizens (2004); Committee on the Rights of the Child General Comment No 6, Treatment of Unaccompanied and Separated Children Outside their Country of Origin (2005); and Committee on the Elimination of Discrimination Against Women General Recommendation No 26 on Women Migrant Workers (2008).

[18] See CM Rodríguez and R Rubio-Marín, 'The Constitutional Status of Irregular Migrants: Testing the Boundaries of Human Rights Protection in Spain and the United States' in MB Dembour and T Kelly (eds), *Are Human Rights for Migrants? Critical Reflections on the Status of Irregular Migrants in Europe and the United States* (Abingdon, Routledge, 2011) 73–98.

by citizens, and those of a second-class category, deserved by non-citizens. It must be underlined though, as UN Special Rapporteur Crépeau has clarified, that international law is firm in laying down the standard that all human rights are to be enjoyed by all human beings, the only exceptions being those that are allowed by international human rights law itself.[19] International law has been constructed, among other factors, precisely through the progressive understanding of state sovereignty as involving the responsibility of ensuring a series of values and living conditions for persons under the jurisdiction of states, *qua* persons with dignity, as a sufficient reason for the legal recognition and enjoyment of a set of rights.[20] In that sense, the first assertion that needs signalling is that *universal human rights* are, in principle, applicable to all migrants, whether regular or irregular.

As Morten Kjaerum, Director of the EU Fundamental Rights Agency, recently emphasised, 'You do not need a visa or a residence permit to qualify for human rights. Simply being born is your passport to human rights protection'.[21]

B. Regional Systems of Human Rights

Let us now take a brief look at some of the aspects that are worth highlighting in terms of the regional protection of universal human rights of undocumented migrants. Possibly the most notable and decided expression at the regional level is Advisory Opinion 18/03 of the Inter-American Court of Human Rights (IACHR) concerning *Juridical Conditions and Rights of Undocumented Migrants*, precisely because of its role in clarifying the legal human rights framework that is applicable to undocumented migrants, with a particular focus on migrant workers.

Although at the universal level, as I signalled above, the existing legal category for the protection of human rights in the context of migration is that of 'migrant worker', at the Inter-American level, there is a legal instrument that protects all migrants

[19] Statements by F Crépeau at the debate on 'The Management of the External Borders of the EU and its Impact on the Human Rights of Migrants: The Italian Experience. A Consultation between the UN Special Rapporteur on the Human Rights of Migrants, Mr François Crépeau, Civil Society, and Academia', organised by the Migration Policy Centre, Robert Schuman Centre for Advanced Studies of the European University Institute (EUI), with the support of the Open Society Foundations, and held at the EUI in Florence, Italy on 3 October 2012; details on file with the author. The event was held within the context of the Special Rapporteur's mission to Italy, as part of his year-long study of the human rights of migrants at the borders of the European Union (EU). Drawing on his experiences of similar visits, he developed a thematic study which was presented to the Human Rights Council in June 2013. The study analysed EU migration management in the context of border management, not only in light of the programmes and policies of the individual states visited but also considering the overarching EU migration policy framework, which focuses on its impact on the human rights of migrants. See press release, 'UN Special Rapporteur on the human rights of migrants concludes his third country visit in his regional study on the human rights of migrants at the borders of the European Union: Italy', Rome, 8 October 2012, available at www.ohchr.org/EN/NewsEvents/Pages/DisplayNews.aspx?NewsID=12640&LangID=E.

[20] In this sense, see A Cassese, *International Law*, 2nd edn (Oxford, Oxford University Press, 2005) 45.

[21] Speech by M Kjaerum, Director, European Union Agency for Fundamental Rights (FRA), 'Dignity and rights of irregular migrants', 4th Fundamental Rights Conference, Warsaw, Poland, 21–22 November 2011, p 2 (underscoring in the original), available at http://fra.europa.eu/fraWebsite/attachments/MK-Speech-FRC-NOV2011.pdf.

as such in their condition of 'structural vulnerability'.[22] Indeed, Advisory Opinion 18/03 of the IACHR, although non-binding, should be considered an authoritative legal source insofar as it is a judicial interpretation of the Inter-American human rights legal framework, basically the 1948 American Declaration on the Rights and Duties of Man (ADRDM) and the 1969 American Convention on Human Rights (ACHR).[23] It also analyses European human rights law as a comparative resource, as well as UN human rights law and international law more generally as binding sources for states in the Americas.

In AO 18/03 the Inter-American Court emphasised that:

> the fundamental principle of equality and non-discrimination forms part of general international law, because it is applicable to all States, regardless of whether or not they are a party to a specific international treaty. At the current stage of the development of international law, the fundamental principle of equality and non-discrimination has entered the domain of *jus cogens*. This in turn entails that the general obligation to respect and guarantee human rights binds States, regardless of any circumstance or consideration, including the migratory status of a person.

The Court further concluded that the migratory status of a person cannot constitute a justification for depriving him or her of the enjoyment and exercise of human rights, including those of a labour-related nature. When assuming an employment relationship, the migrant acquires rights that must be recognised and safeguarded because he or she is an employee, irrespective of the regular or irregular status of employment in the state where the person is employed. As the Court clarified, these rights are as a result of the employment relationship.[24]

In Europe, the response has been less categorical. At the normative level, the 1950 European Convention on the Protection of Human Rights and Fundamental Freedoms (European Convention), while not referring specifically to migrants, protects them insofar as it is applicable to all persons under a state's jurisdiction.[25] The 1961 European Social Charter (ESC) and the 1996 Revised European Social Charter (RESC) afford some degree of protection to undocumented migrants mainly through the right to non-discrimination in relation to different rights such as labour rights and guarantees of non-expulsion.[26] Also, through the supervisory bodies of both instruments, the European Committee on Social Rights and the European Court of

[22] AO 18/03, above n 9, paras 112, 113, 130, 131, 149 and 160; see also para 9 of Reasoned Concurring Opinion of Judge S García Ramírez to AO 18/03, as well as the *amicus curiae* presented by J Bustamante from Universidad Nacional Autónoma de México, who was UN Special Rapporteur on the Human Rights of Migrants from 2005 to 2011, ibid para 81.

[23] American Declaration of the Rights and Duties of Man (adopted April 1948), Organization of American States (OAS) Res XXX adopted by the Ninth International Conference of American States (1948) reprinted in *Basic Documents Pertaining to Human Rights in the Inter-American System* OEA/Ser L V/II 82, Doc 6 Rev 1, 17 (1992) (ADRDM); American Convention on Human Rights, (adopted 22 November 1969, entered into force 18 July 1978) OAS Treaty Ser no 36, 1144 UNTS 143 (ACHR).

[24] AO 18/03, above n 9, paras 4, 6 and 8.

[25] European Convention on the Protection of Human Rights and Fundamental Freedoms (adopted 4 November 1950, entered into force 3 September 1953) CETS No 005, 213 UNTS 1932 (European Convention), art 1.

[26] European Social Charter (adopted 18 October 1961, entered into force 26 February 1965) CETS No 035, 529 UNTS 89 (ESC); and European Social Charter (revised) RESC (adopted 3 May 1996, entered into force 1 July 1999) CETS No 163; see arts 18 and 19 of both instruments

Human Rights (ECtHR) respectively, the rights of migrants have to a certain extent been reaffirmed and protected. However, the usual approach of the ECtHR has been to underline the obligation of states to ensure the right to family life (article 8) and to non-discrimination (article 14) with respect to other rights in relation to non-nationals who are *lawfully* residing in their territory.[27] It is worth noting, though, some interesting developments by the ECtHR in recent years, such as the case of *MSS v Belgium and Greece*, which is especially illustrative, as will be seen in section V of this chapter.

Within the African human rights system undocumented migrants fall similarly under the general protection of the 1981 African Charter on Human and Peoples' Rights (ACHPR),[28] which sets forth the obligation of state parties to respect human rights of all persons under their jurisdiction. In the realm of human security concerns, as related to human rights, there have been evolutions in the African system concerning rights applicable to all women, including migrant women, in the form of the 'right to peace for women' and the 'right to food security', which are contemplated in the 2003 Protocol to the ACHPR on the Rights of Women in Africa.[29]

IV. APPLYING A HUMAN SECURITY LENS TO HUMAN RIGHTS OF MIGRANTS: LEGAL IRREGULARITY AS A SOURCE OF RISK

Migration across borders and different state jurisdictions poses questions as to the ways to better meet human rights obligations related to migrant persons, based on the existing standards reviewed in the previous section, but also thinking of creative interpretative methods to enhance such rights. As was mentioned above, the universal paradigm guiding human rights principles maintains that all persons are equal in dignity and rights, and will thus not be discriminated against on the basis of sex, gender, religion, culture, language, ethnicity, or national origin. However, the universality of human rights appears doubtful when faced with the conditions of migrant persons. Indeed, 'despite the theoretical universality of human rights law, in reality characteristics such as nationality or formal legal status can significantly affect the extent of rights an individual is actually accorded'.[30]

[27] See for example in the ECtHR *Gaygusuz v Austria*, App No 173/71/90 (1996) and *Poirrez v France*, App No 40892/98 (2003).

[28] African Charter on Human and Peoples' Rights (adopted 27 June 1981, entered into force 21 October 1986) Organization of African Unity, Doc CAB/LEG/67/3 rev 5, (1982) 21 ILM 58 1520 UNTS 217 (ACHPR).

[29] Protocol to the African Charter on Human and Peoples' Rights (adopted 13 September 2000, entered into force Nov 25, 2005), 2nd Ordinary Session of the Assembly of the Union, CAB/LEG/66.6 (Sept 13, 2000); reprinted in (2001) 1 *African Human Rights Law Journal* 40, arts 10 and 15 respectively.

In the Asian context, there is no institutional human rights system in place for the evolution of migrants' rights in the Association of Southeast Asian Nations (ASEAN), but see R Cholewinski, 'Labour migration management and the rights of migrant workers' in A Edwards and C Ferstman (eds), *Human Security and Non-Citizens: Law, Policy and International Affairs* (Cambridge, Cambridge University Press, 2010) 273, 287–88.

[30] J McAdam, *Complementary Protection in International Refugee Law* (Oxford, Oxford University Press, 2007) 12. See also more generally MJ Añón (ed), *La universalidad de los derechos sociales: el reto de la inmigración* (Valencia, Tirant lo Blanch, 2004) and A Solanes Corella (ed), *Derechos humanos, migraciones y diversidad* (Valencia, Tirant lo Blanch, 2010).

In fact, in many contexts, the strict enforcement of immigration law and increasingly restrictive policies have led to 'community insecurity' because of the deterrent effect on crime reporting that such enforcement entails.[31] Given that such enforcement increases the risk of deportment of undocumented migrants, some of them would rather remain clandestine than come forward to report crimes and cooperate with local police. This seems to echo other concerns regarding the detrimental effect on human rights of the progressively severe application of restrictions on immigration, which may and do leave persons outside the law or invisible to the law,[32] and therefore in a condition of vulnerability. Paradoxically, the rigorous and often arbitrary application of administrative immigration law is hindering the effective application and goals of human rights and labour law.

Although the heightened condition of vulnerability of asylum-seekers and refugees against this background and within the current economic crisis has been analysed,[33] less attention has been focused on the more general issue of undocumented migrants. Efforts are being made in this area, and the UN Committee on the Protection of the Rights of All Migrant Workers and Members of their Families—the body of independent experts in charge of monitoring compliance with the CMW (article 72)—plays a fundamental role in shedding light on such vulnerabilities and clarifying the concrete ways in which the human rights of migrant workers should be understood and applied. In its first *General Comment No 1 on Migrant Domestic Workers*, of 2011, the Committee noted that

> migrant domestic workers are at *heightened risk* of certain forms of exploitation and abuse ... These *risks and vulnerabilities* are further aggravated for migrant domestic workers who are *non-documented or in an irregular situation*, not least because they often risk deportation if they contact State authorities to seek protection from an abusive employer.[34]

In this sense, undocumented migrants often face a double victimisation, given that on the one hand, their irregular status places them at higher risk of violations of their human rights, and on the other hand, their human right of access to justice is also affected because of their fear of deportation.[35]

In its account of state obligations towards undocumented migrant domestic workers, especially women and children, the UN Committee qualifies the vulnerabilities

[31] See Center for Human Rights and Global Justice, *A Decade Lost: Locating Gender in US Counter-Terrorism* (New York, NYU School of Law, 2011) 102.

[32] See for example F Düvell and B Vollmer, 'European Security Challenges', *EU-US Immigration Systems 2011/07* (San Domenico di Fiesole, European University Institute, Robert Schuman Centre for Advanced Studies, 2011).

[33] See V Chetail and C Bauloz, 'The European Union and the Challenges of Forced Migration: From Economic Crisis to Protection Crisis?', *EU-US Immigration Systems 2011/07* (San Domenico di Fiesole, European University Institute, Robert Schuman Centre for Advanced Studies, 2011).

[34] Committee on the Protection of the Rights of all Migrant Workers and Members of their Families, *General Comment No 1 on Migrant Domestic Workers* (23 February 2011) UN Doc CMW/C/GC/1, para 7 (emphasis added).

[35] ibid, para 43. In this respect, see also arts 8 and 15 of the recently adopted ILO Convention Concerning Decent Work for Domestic Workers (No 189) (adopted 16 June 2011, entered into force 5 September 2013) refers to the state obligation of applying the provisions of the Convention also to *migrant* domestic workers and the duty to protect them from abusive practices, including those carried out by private employers.

they face as 'extreme'. Based on article 69 of the CMW it calls for states to take appropriate measures to address such vulnerabilities and to 'consider policies, including regularization programmes, to avoid or resolve situations in which migrant domestic workers are undocumented or are at risk of falling into irregular status.'[36]

The Committee reiterates these views in its *General Comment No 2 on the rights of migrant workers in an irregular situation and members of their families*, dedicated to the broader subject of irregular migrant workers altogether. In this comment, the Committee emphasises that

> migrant workers and members of their families in an irregular situation generally *live in fear* of being reported to the immigration authorities by public service providers or other officials, or by private individuals, which *limits their access to fundamental human rights, as well as their access to justice*, and makes them *more vulnerable* to labour and other types of exploitation and abuse.[37]

Restrictive laws have also enhanced the vulnerability of migrants and deepened their human insecurity. An example is the Alabama Immigrant Act, or 'Beason-Hammon Act', which entered into force on 28 September 2011. A report by Human Rights Watch noted that in the first two months alone that the law was in effect,

> local officials have used it to deny unauthorised immigrants access to everyday necessities such as water and housing in violation of their basic rights. The law also denies all unauthorized immigrants fundamental rights protections that should apply to everyone, not just citizens, making them *more susceptible to discriminatory harassment* and abuse by local authorities and ordinary people. They live in a *climate of fear and uncertainty*, which has had a particularly severe impact on children.[38]

Thus, I suggest that human security may play an integrative role as a concept in legal interpretation to fill these gaps and to act as a connecting bridge between the core content of human rights. Due to the actual vulnerability faced by migrant persons in an irregular situation, and increasingly so by migrant women and girls,[39] human security becomes relevant as a guiding notion to make visible these threats that affect the fundamental human rights of migrants and for such risk factors to be taken into account in the analysis of their human rights obligations.[40]

[36] The Committee on the Protection of the Rights of all Migrant Workers, above n 34, also highlights a similar exposure and a correlated fear which aggravates such risk, when it analyses 'women migrant domestic workers with irregular status, who are *especially vulnerable* during pregnancy, as they are often afraid to contact public health services out of *fear of deportation*', above n 34, para 52 (emphasis added).

[37] Committee on the Protection of the Rights of all Migrant Workers and Members of their Families, *General Comment No 2 on the rights of migrant workers in an irregular situation and members of their families* (28 August 2013) UN Doc CMW/C/GC/2, para 2 (emphasis added). See also paras 16, 46, 48, 71 and 79. On heightened risks for irregular migrants, see paras 21 and 50.

[38] Human Rights Watch, *No Way to Live. Alabama's Immigrant Law* (United States, Human Rights Watch, 2011), quote from the back cover of this publication (emphasis added).

[39] See the recent report of the UN Special Rapporteur on Violence Against Women, United Nations General Assembly A/66/215 (2011). The Special Rapporteur, Rashida Manjoo, reported for example that her visit in 2011 to the United States revealed the particular vulnerability of undocumented immigrant women to violence, including sexual harassment and abuse, in the workplace, paras 43–46.

[40] The idea of collective vulnerability to threats, due to structural discrimination that places certain groups and their members at risk, has already been used by human rights judicial bodies in cases of violence against women; see the cases of *Opuz v Turkey* App No 33401/02 (ECtHR, 2009), and *González et al ('Cotton Field') v Mexico* (IACHR, 2009).

V. ILLUSTRATIVE CASES OF A HUMAN SECURITY-BASED APPROACH TO THE HUMAN RIGHTS OF MIGRANTS

With its call to view widespread and systematic threats, which are often overlooked in traditional individualistic human rights analysis, the idea of a human security-sensitive outlook appears to have found its way as a useful tool in the matter of judicial interpretation.

Within the jurisprudence of the Inter-American Court of Human Rights, there is a significant case in which the Court revisited the same line adopted in its earlier Advisory Opinion 18/03. In the *Case of the Yean and Bosico Children v Dominican Republic*, the Court concluded that the Dominican Republic violated the right to the nationality of two girls of Haitian origin, who were daughters of undocumented migrants, since the Civil Registration Office refused to issue their birth certificates, even when they enjoyed this right according to the laws of the Dominican Republic itself.[41]

Drawing implicit links between the human security approach and the enjoyment of human rights by persons in vulnerable conditions, the Court analysed the situation. It considered the whole social setting in which the girls were placed and underlined the fact that 'the discriminatory treatment imposed by the State on the Yean and Bosico children is situated *within the context of the vulnerable situation* of the Haitian population and Dominicans of Haitian origin in the Dominican Republic, to which the alleged victims belong'.[42] Looking at the widespread character of these threats through the study of the individual experience of the girls, the Court emphasised the double situation of vulnerability of the victims, because of their lack of nationality and the fact that they were child girls.

The systemic character of these risks was taken up some years later by the UN Committee on Economic, Social and Cultural Rights (ESCR Committee) when it regretted that, regardless of the *Yean and Bosico* judgment, discrimination against Haitian children persisted in the Dominican Republic. Adopting the language of human security concerns, the ESCR Committee noted that the generalised situation of revocation of identity documents or non-renewal of residency documents, based on legal provisions in the Dominican Republic, had '*increased the exposure* of Haitian children and Dominican children of Haitian descent, especially, to *discriminatory practices*'.[43]

In a broader outlook concerning undocumented migrants in economic or labour terms, other non-citizens with an undefined legal status, such as asylum-seekers, have also faced severe human insecurities. In this respect, it is worth mentioning the case of *MSS v Belgium and Greece*, in which the ECtHR considered the transfer of an Afghan asylum-seeker from Belgium to Greece to be a violation by Belgium of article 3 of the European Convention. Notably, it did so by arguing that MSS was in a vulnerable situation, taking into account his individual distress and set against

[41] *Case of The Yean and Bosico Children v Dominican Republic* (IACHR, 2005).
[42] ibid, paras 168, 142 and 134 (emphasis added).
[43] UN Committee on Economic, Social and Cultural Rights, Concluding Observations of the report submitted by the Dominican Republic, E/C12/DOM/CO/3 (19 November 2010), para 11 (emphasis added).

the background of 'systemic conditions of material deprivation' faced in Greece by asylum-seekers, as a 'vulnerable population group in need of special protection'.[44] Based on those considerations, the Court found that the decision by Belgium to return the applicant to Greece amounted to a violation of the right under article 3 of the European Convention to be free from torture, inhuman or degrading treatment and the prohibition of removal to a country in which a risk of suffering such treatment could be faced (principle of *non-refoulement*). Likewise, it found that the living conditions of the applicant in Greece amounted to a violation of article 3 by that country.[45]

However, other examples can be given as to the consequences of not applying a human security perspective to the legal analysis of human rights violations, specifically in the area of the human rights of migrants. The earlier case of *N v United Kingdom*, decided by the ECtHR in 2008, involved a Ugandan woman who had arrived in the UK on a false passport and, although she did not know it at the time, was HIV-positive. In the UK she received life-sustaining medical treatment that would purportedly allow her to live 'for decades'. N had been rejected as an asylum-seeker, and if she were to be deported back to Uganda, there was strong evidence to suggest, due to the lack of anti-retroviral drugs in the Ugandan health system, that she would die within two years of her return. Nevertheless, the Court concluded that the removal of N to Uganda would not entail a violation of the *non-refoulement* obligation contained in article 3 of the European Convention.[46]

Regarding this case, Eve Lester has argued that a different result could have been reached by the Court had it applied a human security approach that emphasised the critical life-threatening risk that N faced, viewed in the light of the core content of the human right to the highest attainable standard of health. Moreover, 'judicial decisions that integrate human security into their analysis may compel states to translate their rhetoric into real deliverables which would increase accessibility and availability of anti-retroviral drugs in the developing world where the full burden of the HIV/AIDS pandemic is yet to be felt'.[47] Maybe such an outlook by the Court would have truly lived up to the commitment of guaranteeing N's human right to health and ultimately her right to life in the face of an imminent risk of losing it.

VI. SOME CONCLUSIONS

Assuring the human rights of migrants is one of the greatest challenges confronting international law. This is so both in theoretical terms as to the applicability of the

[44] *MSS v Belgium and Greece* App No 30696/09 (ECtHR, 2011) para 251; see also paras 232 and 233.

[45] ibid, points 10 and 5 of the dispositive part of the judgment. For a case following this same line of argumentation at the level of the Court of Justice of the European Union, see Joined Cases C-411/10 and C-493/10, *NS and ME and Others v Secretary of State for the Home Department and ME and Others v Refugee Applications Commissioner and Minister for Justice, Equality and Law Reform* (ECtHR, 2011).

[46] *N v United Kingdom* App No 26565/05 (ECtHR, 2008), see paras 18 and 19.

[47] For the detailed analysis of this case, as well as the similar case of *D v United Kingdom*, resolved in 1997 also by the ECtHR, but with a different outcome supportive of D's rights, see E Lester, 'Socio-economic rights, human security and survival migrants: Whose rights? Whose security?' in A Edwards and C Ferstman, above n 29, 314–56.

principle of the universality of human rights to migrant persons, and in practical terms because of the status of 'undocumented migrant' as one of the crucial sources of vulnerability and human insecurity in our world today.

Indeed, the human security of undocumented migrants constitutes a turning point in which some of the deep-seated roots of our societies, including liberal democracies, come into conflict: principles and institutions such as equality, citizenship and universal human rights appear to collide with evidence of discrimination, vulnerability and risk in which persons with an irregular migratory status are frequently placed. These conditions in the least grave scenario translate into de jure or de facto denial or limitation of access to rights, and in the worst-case scenario, which is not at all unusual, they may amount to life-threatening situations and harm to physical integrity and loss of life. When we are faced with such extreme cases, the ethical, political and legal frontiers to migratory norms and policies must be questioned if we wish to maintain a minimum coherence with the essentials of the rule of law and with international human rights law more generally.

In a nutshell, the human security lens can be valuable for a human rights analysis in a number of distinct ways. First, to identify threats to the human rights of undocumented migrants and to establish thresholds, and therefore criteria for red flags, as a trigger to activate a state's obligations, which cover the whole range of duties from prevention to protection and finally reparations for violations of fundamental human rights.

Second, as the cases in the previous section illustrate, the interpretative enhancement of a state's positive obligations may be achieved by utilising the human security perspective to analyse collective threats that facilitate human rights violations of individual persons and highlight the *interrelatedness* of conditions that would otherwise be analysed in an isolated manner. From a regional perspective, this seems to have been done more successfully at the Inter-American level, although the European human rights system offers some hopeful horizons.

And third, human security contributes to transcending the conceptual danger of viewing *non-citizens*, particularly undocumented migrants, as *non-persons*, and thus reaffirming the universality of all their human rights.

Part VI

Regionalism, Peace and Security

18

L'Union Africaine, une organisation régionale susceptible de s'émanciper de l'autorité du Conseil de Sécurité ? Opinio juris *et pratique récentes des Etats*

OLIVIER CORTEN*

ON SAIT QUE, en application de l'article 4h de son acte constitutif, l'Union africaine dispose d'un « droit d'intervenir dans un Etat membre ... dans certaines circonstances graves, à savoir : les crimes de guerre, le génocide et les crimes contre l'humanité », un amendement ajoutant le cas d'une « menace grave de l'ordre légitime ».[1] Cette disposition a donné lieu à un débat dès les lendemains de son adoption.[2] Selon plusieurs auteurs, cette disposition conférerait à l'Union africaine un véritable droit d'intervention humanitaire qui pourrait s'exercer, le cas échéant, sans autorisation du Conseil de sécurité.[3] L'idée sous-tendant le raisonnement est que rien n'empêche un groupe d'Etats de prévoir, pourvu que cela ne s'applique qu'aux Etats qui l'auraient acceptée, une règle assouplissant les conditions strictes subordonnant une action militaire à une autorisation du Conseil de sécurité (sauf le cas, dont il ne sera pas question ici, de la légitime défense). En ce sens, l'Union africaine aurait développé un régime juridique spécial qui, sans s'opposer formellement aux

* Université Libre de Bruxelles. Centre de droit international et de sociologie appliquée au droit international. Cet article a été finalisé en février 2014, et ne prend donc pas en compte les documents publiés postérieurement à cette date.

[1] Cet amendement est entré en vigueur le 4 janvier 2013; www.au.int/fr/ (pour le reste, l'ensemble des sources internet citées dans le cadre de cette contribution ont été consultées pour la dernière fois le 10 juillet 2012). V à ce sujet E Baimu and K Sturman, « Amendment fo the African Union's Right to Intervene. A shift from human security to regime security ? » (2003) 12 *African Security Review*.

[2] V. à cet égard mon ouvrage, *Le droit contre la guerre*, 2ème éd (Paris, Pedone, 2014), 563–571 ; trad. *The Law against War* (Oxford, Hart Publishing, 2010), 341–348).

[3] JI Levitt, « The Evolving Intervention Regime in Africa: From Basket Case to Market Place ? » (2002) *ASIL Proceedings* 142. V aussi, quoique de manière implicite, B Kioko, « The Right of Intervention Under the African Union's Constitutive Act : From Non-Interference to Non-Intervention » (2003) 852 *Revue internationale de la Croix-Rouge* 821 ; AA Yusuf, « The Right of Intervention by the African Union : A New Paradigm in Regional Enforcement Action ? » (2003) II *African Yearbook of International Law*, 3 et seq.

règles de la Charte des Nations Unies, s'en distinguerait par certains aspects. Un tel « droit d'intervention régional » se justifierait juridiquement sur la base du consentement des Etats membres de l'UA, sans préjudice du maintien des règles du *jus contra bellum* à un niveau général et universel.[4] D'un autre côté, certains auteurs ont dénoncé un tel raisonnement, en proposant une autre lecture de l'Acte constitutif de l'Union africaine.[5] Selon eux, les règles de la Charte sur la prohibition du recours à la force relevant du *jus cogens* (droit impératif), il serait inconcevable qu'un groupe d'Etats y déroge d'une quelconque manière. Le consentement ne constituerait donc pas une base juridique valide, ce qui s'explique si l'on prend en compte la circonstance que c'est la communauté internationale dans son ensemble (et non seulement les Etats ayant donné leur consentement) qui serait affectée par une modification, même purement régionale, des principes régissant l'usage de la force. L'article 4 de l'Acte constitutif est donc interprété de manière plus restrictive, comme attribuant spécifiquement une compétence à l'Organisation pour intervenir dans les situations précitées, mais moyennant le respect des règles de la Charte.[6] Une telle interprétation est confortée par certains éléments de texte, tel l'article 17 du protocole relatif à la création du Conseil de paix et de sécurité de l'Union africaine ou l'article 17a) du Pacte de non-agression et de défense commune de l'Union africaine, qui renvoient expressément au respect des dispositions du Chapitre VIII de la Charte.[7]

Au-delà de cette controverse qui entoure l'interprétation des termes de l'article 4h) ainsi que des autres instruments pertinents, on peut se tourner vers la pratique pour tenter de départager les deux tendances doctrinales. C'est en ce sens qu'a été conçue la présente contribution, qui a pour objet de démontrer que, au-delà des textes existants, aucun droit d'intervention de type régional n'a été mis en œuvre ni revendiqué, ni même évoqué, par l'Union africaine et ses membres. Dans un premier temps, on se tournera vers les débats qui ont eu lieu à ce sujet au sein de l'ONU, en particulier ces dernières années, jusqu'en 2012. On constatera ainsi que le schéma d'un droit d'intervention centralisé, mené sous l'égide du Conseil de sécurité est loin d'avoir été remis en cause au profit d'une tendance « régionaliste » à l'émancipation. Dans un deuxième temps, on se penchera sur le précédent l'intervention militaire menée en 2011 en Libye, qui confirme de manière particulièrement éclatante la faible autonomie de l'Union africaine sur le plan du recours à la force.

I. LA RÉAFFIRMATION DE L'AUTORITÉ DU CONSEIL DE SÉCURITÉ : LES DÉCLARATIONS DE PRINCIPE

Depuis le début des années 2000, on a reconnu, au sein des Nations Unies, la nécessité d'interpréter la Charte de San Francisco de manière dynamique, en tenant

[4] VG Gaja, *Quatrième rapport sur la responsabilité des organisations internationales*, 28 février 2006, 2 A/CN4/564, 18, par 47 et note 72.

[5] V le passage de mon ouvrage, précité, ainsi que R Kolb, « Article 53 » *in* JP Cot, M Forteau et A Pellet (dir), *La Charte des Nations Unies*, 3ème éd (Paris, Economica, 2005), 1422–23.

[6] L'effet utile de l'article 4h) serait ainsi de permettre à l'organisation, qui ne dispose que de compétences d'attribution, d'agir, y compris dans les conflits internes, dans le situations précitées, ce que ne pouvait par exemple pas faire l'Organisation de l'Union africaine.

[7] V le texte de ces instruments sur www.au.int/fr/.

compte de l'évolution des relations internationales depuis 1945. Dans ce contexte, on a insisté sur la nécessité de prendre en compte le phénomène de l'intégration régionale, spécialement dans le domaine de la sécurité.[8] Une articulation efficace entre l'échelle universelle et régionale a ainsi été recherchée, particulièrement dans le cas de l'Afrique, dont on a relevé qu'elle occupe en pratique la majeure part de l'ordre du jour des séances du Conseil de sécurité.[9] A-t-on, dans cette perspective, assisté à une amorce de décentralisation du pouvoir de recourir à la force au profit de l'Union africaine qui, en application de son acte constitutif et par le biais de son Conseil de paix et de sécurité, se serait vue investie d'un rôle similaire à celui du Conseil de sécurité ? Rien ne permet de le penser. Aucun schéma de décentralisation ne ressort en effet des très nombreux débats qui auraient pu susciter son ébauche et qui ont eu lieu à l'ONU depuis l'entrée en vigueur de l'acte constitutif de l'Union africaine. Le constat ressort d'une étude des discussions qui ont entouré la question de la réforme des Nations Unies, d'une part, et de celles plus spécifiquement relatives aux relations entre l'ONU et les organisations régionales, d'autre part.

A. Les Débats sur la Réforme du Système des Nations Unies : l'Insistance sur la Nécessité de Respecter le Schéma Traditionnel de la Charte

On s'est, dans le cadre de cette contribution, appuyé sur les compte rendus et les documents relatifs aux débats sur la réforme des Nations Unies, essentiellement entre 2000 et 2005. Ont spécialement été pris en compte les positions adoptées au sujet de la « responsabilité de protéger », concept qui aurait pu donner lieu à une reconnaissance d'une forme de droit d'intervention humanitaire au profit de l'Union africaine, sorte d'intermédiaire entre chaque Etat et l'Organisation des Nations Unies. En réalité, cependant, le seul document pouvant être interprété en ce sens est ce qu'on a appelé le « consensus d'Ezulwini » (juillet 2005), exprimant la position commune des Etats de l'UA sur la réforme des Nations Unies :

> [s]'agissant de l'usage de la force, il est important de respecter scrupuleusement les dispositions de l'article 51 de la Charte des Nations Unies qui autorisent l'usage de la force seulement dans le cas de légitime défense. En outre, l'Acte constitutif de l'Union africaine à son article 4h) autorise l'intervention dans des circonstances graves telles que le génocide, les crimes de guerre et les crimes contre l'humanité. En conséquence, tout recours à la force hors du cadre de l'Article 51 de la Charte des Nations Unies et de l'Article 4h) de l'UA, doit être prohibé.[10]

[8] V p ex la *Déclaration du millénaire*, annexée à la résolution 55/2, adoptée le 8 septembre 2000, § 9 ainsi que, déjà, la *Déclaration sur le renforcement de la coopération entre l'Organisation des Nations Unies et les accords ou organismes régionaux dans le domaine du maintien de la paix et de la sécurité internationales*, annexée à la résolution 49/57, adoptée le 17 février 1995, § 10.

[9] V les propos du représentant du Nigeria, S/PV6409, 22 octobre 2010, p 9.

[10] *Position commune africaine sur la réforme des Nations Unies. Le consensus d'Ezulwini'*, Ext/EX CL/2(VII), p 7, adopté par le conseil exécutif, 7ème session extraordinaire, 7–8 mars 2005, Ext/Ext CL/ Dec 1 (VII). Dans la *Déclaration de Syrte sur la réforme des Nations Unies*, les Etats de l'UA réaffirment leur « ferme attachement au consensus d'Ezulwini », qu'ils se déclarent « résolus à faire triompher » (Assembly/AU/Decl 2(V), 5 juillet 2005, disponible sur www.au.int/).

Ce texte pourrait être interprété comme exprimant la reconnaissance d'une nouvelle exception à l'interdiction du recours à la force au sens de la Charte des Nations Unies : le droit d'intervention de l'Union africaine en application de l'article 4h) de son acte constitutif.[11] Une telle argumentation se heurterait cependant à deux obstacles principaux.

D'abord, il serait bien difficile de montrer qu'une troisième exception aurait été reconnue par l'ensemble des Etats membres de l'ONU. Les termes du *Document final* adopté par les Etats membres de l'organisation à l'occasion de ses 60 ans sont loin de plaider en ce sens, comme l'illustre ce passage consacré à l'actualité des règles de la Charte relatives au *jus contra bellum*:

> Nous réaffirmons que les dispositions pertinentes de la Charte sont suffisantes pour faire face à l'ensemble des menaces contre la paix et la sécurité internationales. Nous réaffirmons aussi que le Conseil de sécurité dispose de l'autorité voulue pour ordonner des mesures coercitives en vue de maintenir et rétablir la paix et la sécurité internationales. Nous soulignons en outre l'importance d'agir conformément aux buts et aux principes consacrés dans la Charte.[12]

Nulle trace, à ce stade, d'un statut particulier pour l'Union africaine, ou plus généralement pour les organisations régionales. Ces dernières sont d'ailleurs mentionnées dans un autre passage du document, sans qu'il soit jamais fait mention d'une forme de droit d'intervention qui s'émanciperait du Conseil de sécurité :

> [c]onscients de la contribution importante que les organisations régionales apportent à la paix et à la sécurité, conformément au Chapitre VIII de la Charte des Nations Unies, et de l'intérêt que présente la mise en place de partenariats et d'arrangements structurés entre l'Organisation des Nations Unies et les organisations régionales, et notant en particulier, eu égard aux besoins spéciaux de l'Afrique, l'importance d'une Union africaine forte, nous sommes convenus : a) De soutenir les efforts que déploient l'Union européenne et d'autres entités régionales pour mettre en place des capacités telles que les dispositifs à déploiement rapide, les forces et moyens en attente et les dispositifs de soudure ...[13]

Absolument rien n'indique, tout au contraire, que le schéma retenu ouvre la voie à une décentralisation du droit d'intervention militaire, y compris en cas de violation grave du droit international humanitaire. Le passage de la résolution consacrée à la responsabilité de protéger ne fait que le confirmer, comme on le comprendra en en relisant les principaux extraits :

> Il incombe également à la communauté internationale, dans le cadre de l'ONU, de mettre en œuvre les moyens diplomatiques, humanitaires et autres moyens pacifiques appropriés, *conformément aux Chapitres VI et VIII de la Charte des Nations Unies*, afin d'aider à protéger les populations du génocide, des crimes de guerre, du nettoyage ethnique et des crimes contre l'humanité. Dans ce contexte, nous sommes prêts à mener en temps voulu une

[11] JI Levitt, « The Evolving Intervention Regime in Africa: From Basket Case to Market Place », *loc cit*, p 142; v aussi, de manière très prudente, KD Magliveras et GJ Neldi, « The African Union—A New Dawn for Africa ? » (2002) 51 *International & Comparitive Law Quarterly* 418.

[12] Document final du Sommet mondial de 2005, annexé à la résolution 60/1, adoptée le 24 octobre 2005, §79.

[13] Nous soulignons ; ibid, par 93 et par 139.

action collective résolue, *par l'entremise du Conseil de sécurité*, conformément à la Charte, notamment son Chapitre VII ...[14]

On reste dans un schéma où l'usage de la force relève en premier lieu de la souveraineté territoriale de chaque Etat, la « communauté internationale » ne pouvant intervenir qu'à titre subsidiaire et uniquement par l'entremise du Conseil de sécurité.[15] *A contrario*, aucune exception ni dérogation n'est envisagée pour les initiatives régionales, y compris en Afrique.

D'ailleurs, et on en arrive ici à un deuxième argument, les Etats africains eux-mêmes n'ont pas, à la suite du consensus d'Ezulwini, défendu une telle thèse. Tout au contraire, en tant que membres du mouvement des non-alignés ou du « groupe des 77 », ils ont été les plus fervents défenseurs du système de la Charte, et en particulier du maintien des prérogatives du Conseil de sécurité dans le domaine de la sécurité collective, spécialement lorsqu'on a traité de la question du droit d'intervention humanitaire.[16] La même position a été défendue lorsque les Etats africains se sont exprimés à titre individuel.[17] A ma connaissance, aucun d'entre eux n'a jamais prétendu qu'il fallait réserver ou adapter la Charte en ouvrant la voie à un droit d'intervention régional qui serait déduit de l'Acte constitutif de l'Union africaine. Au contraire, on constate une persistante insistance sur la nécessité de respecter l'autorité et les pouvoirs du Conseil du sécurité. Une insistance que l'on retrouvera, par ailleurs, dans les débats qui ont spécifiquement porté sur les relations entre l'ONU et les organisations régionales.

B. Les Débats sur les Relations entre l'ONU et les Organisations Régionales: le Maintien du Schéma Centralisateur

On s'est, à ce stade, appuyé sur les débats qui ont eu lieu, au sein de l'ONU, d'une part sur les relations entre l'ONU et les organisations régionales en général et, d'autre part, sur ceux qui ont plus spécialement porté sur le cas de l'Afrique ou de l'Union africaine. Ces débats se sont spécialement développé à partir de l'année 2003, et ont notamment donné lieu à des résolutions et déclarations du Conseil du sécurité, des résolutions de l'Assemblée générale ainsi qu'à des rapports du Secrétaire général. Or, et il s'agit là d'un enseignement hautement significatif en soi, la lecture de ces centaines de pages de documents ne révèle aucune prise de position de l'Union africaine ni d'un Etat africain qui aurait défendu la thèse d'un droit d'intervention décentralisé, s'émancipant du Conseil de sécurité.

[14] Nous soulignons ; ibid.

[15] O Corten, *Le droit contre la guerre*, op cit, pp 827–36.

[16] V not. Déclaration du « groupe des 77 » du 24 septembre 1999, par 69 et 70 (Declaration given on the occasion of the 35th anniversary of the creation of the « Group of 77 » (www.g77.org); *Déclaration du Sommet du sud*, adoptée par les chefs d'Etats et de gouvernement des pays membres du Groupe des 77 réunis à La Havane, 14 avril 2000, annexé à la lettre datée du 5 mai 2000, adressée au président de l'Assemblée générale par le Représentant permanent du Nigéria auprès de l'ONU ; A/55/74, 12 mai 2000, par 54. V aussi des déclarations du « Mouvement des non–alignés » (Final Document, Ministerial Conference, Cartagena (Columbia) 8–9 avril 2000, par 11; www.nam.gov.za/xiiiminconf/).

[17] V l'exposé détaillé des positions des Etats, dont il ressort qu'aucun Etat africain n'a défendu l'idée d'un droit d'intervention humanitaire ; Olivier Corten, *Le droit contre la guerre*, op cit, pp 832–36.

Au contraire, de nombreux passages des textes pertinents renvoient au respect du Chapitre VIII de la Charte, et plus spécifiquement de la responsabilité principale du Conseil de sécurité, comme peuvent illustrer les extraits suivants des résolutions adoptées sans vote ou à l'unanimité :

> *Soulignant* que la contribution croissante qu'apportent les organisations régionales en coopération avec l'Organisation des Nations Unies peut utilement compléter l'action menée par l'Organisation en matière de maintien de la paix et de la sécurité internationales, et soulignant à cet égard que cette contribution doit s'inscrire dans le cadre du Chapitre VIII de la Charte des Nations Unies ...;[18]

> Le Conseil de sécurité réaffirme que la Charte des Nations Unies lui a assigné la responsabilité principale du maintien de la paix et de la sécurité internationales;[19]

> Le Conseil affirme que, dans certains cas, il peut autoriser l'Union africaine à s'occuper des problèmes de sécurité collective sur le continent africain.[20]

Cette insistance sur le respect du chapitre VIII et de l'autorité du Conseil de sécurité se retrouve également dans un Communiqué conjoint adopté par le Conseil de sécurité et par le Conseil de paix et de sécurité de l'Union africaine.[21] La supériorité du Conseil de sécurité a aussi été réaffirmée par certains membres du Conseil, permanents (Etats-Unis,[22] Royaume-Uni,[23] France,[24] Chine,[25] Russie[26]), ainsi que par des organisations régionales comme la Ligue arabe,[27] l'Union européenne,[28] la CEI,[29]

[18] Nous soulignons : Résolution 1631 (2005), 17 octobre 2005, adoptée à l'unanimité, préambule, 7ème alinéa ; v aussi S/PRST/2007/7, 28 mars 2007, S/PRST/2007/42, 6 novembre 2007, résolution 2033 (2012), 12 janvier 2012, § 1.

[19] S/PRST/2007/42, 6 novembre 2007 ; v aussi Déclaration du Président du Conseil de sécurité, S/PRST/2009/3, S/PRST/2009/26, 26 octobre 2009, S/PRST/2010/1, 13 janvier 2010, S/PRST/2010/21, 22 octobre 2010, résolution 63/310 de l'Assemblée générale de l'ONU, Coopération entre l'Organisation des Nations Unies et l'Union africaine, adoptée sans vote le 14 septembre 2009, § 2, 65/274. Coopération entre l'Organisation des Nations Unies et l'Union africaine, 18 avril 2011, adoptée sans vote, § 2 ; Rapport du Secrétaire général sur la coopération entre l'Organisation des Nations Unies et l'Union africaine dans le domaine de la paix et de la sécurité, S/2011/805, 29 décembre 2011, p 1 § 3 ; Rapport du Groupe d'experts Union Africaine-ONU sur les modalités d'appui des opérations de maintien de la paix de l'Union africaine, p 7, § 6a) ; Lettres identiques datées du 24 décembre 2008, adressées au Président de l'Assemblée générale et au Président du Conseil de sécurité par le Secrétaire général, A/63/666–S/2008/813, 31 décembre 2008.

[20] S/PRST/2007/7, 28 mars 2007, 9ème alinéa.

[21] Rapport de la mission du Conseil de sécurité à Addis-Abeba, Khartoum, Accra, Abidjan et Kinshasa, du 14 au 21 juin 2007, S/2007/421*, 11 juillet 2007, annexe II, §§ 1 et 2.

[22] S/PV5776, 6 novembre 2007, p 3 ; S/PV6257, 13 janvier 2010, p 28 ; S/PV6702, 12 janvier 2012, p 17.

[23] S/PV6257, 13 janvier 2010, p 25 ; S/PV6702 (Resumption 1), 12 janvier 2012, p 10.

[24] S/PV5649, 28 mars 2007, p 17 ; S/PV5868, 16 avril 2008, p 21 ; S/PV6257, 13 janvier 2010, p 34.

[25] S/PV5007, 20 juillet 2004, p 14; S/PV5529, 20 septembre 2006, p 6 ; S/PV5868, 16 avril 2008, p 12 ; S/PV6092, 18 mars 2009, p 23 ; S/PV6702, 12 janvier 2012, p 25.

[26] S/PV4739, 11 avril 2003, p 24 ; S/PV5007, 20 juillet 2004, p 19 ; S/PV5282, 17 octobre 2005, p 19 ; S/PV5529, 20 septembre 2006, p 12 ; S/PV6092, 18 mars 2009, p 11 ; S/PV6306, 4 mai 2010, p 10 ; S/PV6702, 12 janvier 2012, p 29.

[27] S/PV4739, 11 avril 2003, p 17 ; S/PV5007, 20 juillet 2004, p 16 ; S/PV5649 (Resumption 1), 28 mars 2007, p 22 ; S/PV5776, 6 novembre 2007, p 27 ; S/PV5868 (Resumption 1), 16 avril 2008, p 22.

[28] S/PV4739, 11 avril 2003, p 32.

[29] S/PV5007, 20 juillet 2004, p 31.

l'Organisation du traité de sécurité collective,[30] l'ANASE[31] et l'Union africaine elle-même.[32] Lorsqu'ils se prononcent à titre individuel, les Etats africains rappellent fréquemment la nécessité de rester dans le cadre du chapitre VIII. A titre d'exemple, on peut évoquer l'Angola,[33] la Guinée,[34] le Bénin,[35] l'Algérie,[36] le Ghana,[37] l'Ouganda,[38] le Maroc,[39] l'Ethiopie,[40] le Congo,[41] l'Egypte,[42] le Soudan,[43] le Rwanda,[44] le Burkina Faso,[45] la Sierra Leone,[46] le Swaziland,[47] le Nigeria,[48] la Zambie,[49] le Sénégal,[50] la Libye,[51] le Gabon,[52] ou encore l'Afrique du sud.[53]

On pourrait peut-être répliquer que de telles déclarations n'excluent pas spécifiquement une interprétation novatrice ou originale du chapitre VIII de la Charte, laissent davantage de marge de manœuvre aux organisations régionales. Et, en effet, on peut aussi pointer certaines déclatations en appelant à une « interprétation dynamique et évolutive »,[54] « ambitieuse »,[55] « novatrice ou prospective »[56] ou « originale »,[57] en vertu de laquelle le Conseil de sécurité devrait faire preuve de davantage de « souplesse »[58] ou de « créativité ».[59] Il serait cependant excessif de déduire de ces termes une quelconque possibilité, pour l'Union africaine ou une autre organisation régionale, de s'arroger un droit d'intervention équivalent à celui dont dispose le Conseil de sécurité aux termes de la Charte. En ce sens, on peut citer cette déclaration

30 S/PV5529, 20 septembre 2006, p 35 ; S/PV5776, 6 novembre 2007, p 32.
31 S/PV5007, 20 juillet 2004, p 22 ; S/PV6257, 13 janvier 2010, p 9.
32 S/PV4739, 11 avril 2003, p 28 ; S/PV5007, 20 juillet 2004, p 7 ; S/PV5007 (Resumption 1), 20 juillet 2004, pp 13 et 14 ; S/PV5282, 17 octobre 2005, p 10 ; S/PV5529, 20 septembre 2006, p 18 ; S/PV5776, 6 novembre 2007, p 30 ; S/PV6092 (Resumption 1), 18 mars 2009, p 5 ; S/PV6206, 26 octobre 2009, p 5.
33 S/PV4739, 11 avril 2003, p 6.
34 S/PV4739, 11 avril 2003, pp 39–40.
35 S/PV5007, 20 juillet 2004, p 11 ; S/PV5282, 17 octobre 2005, p 6 ; S/PV5649 (Resumption 1), 28 mars 2007, p 17 ; S/PV5776 (Resumption 1), 6 novembre 2007, p 23.
36 S/PV5007, 20 juillet 2004, p 25 ; S/PV5282, 17 octobre 2005, p 14.
37 S/PV5776, 6 novembre 2007, p 20.
38 S/PV5649 (Resumption 1), 28 mars 2007, p 5 ; S/PV5868 (Resumption 1), 16 avril 2008, pp 25–26; S/PV6092, 18 mars 2009, p 13 ; S/PV6257, 13 janvier 2010, p 24.
39 S/PV6702 (Resumption 1), 12 janvier 2012, p 6.
40 S/PV5868, 16 avril 2008, p 24 ; S/PV6702 (Resumption 1), 12 janvier 2012, pp 6–7.
41 S/PV5649, 28 mars 2007, p 9.
42 S/PV5649, 28 mars 2007, p 29 ; S/PV6092 (Resumption 1), 18 mars 2009, p 7.
43 S/PV5649, 28 mars 2007, p 31.
44 S/PV5649 (Resumption 1), 28 mars 2007, p 18.
45 S/PV5868, 16 avril 2008, p 17 ; S/PV6092, 18 mars 2009, p 15.
46 S/PV5868 (Resumption 1), 16 avril 2008, p 6.
47 *Ibidem.*
48 S/PV5868 (Resumption 1), 16 avril 2008, p 8 ; S/PV6092 (Resumption 1), 18 mars 2009, p 16 ; S/PV6206, 26 octobre 2009, p 34.
49 S/PV5868 (Resumption 1), 16 avril 2008, p 9.
50 *Ibid.*, pp 9–10.
51 S/PV6206, 26 octobre 2009, p 17.
52 S/PV6409, 22 octobre 2010, p 21.
53 S/PV6409, 22 octobre 2010, p 31.
54 Algérie, S/PV5649 (Resumption 1), 28 mars 2007, p 20.
55 Algérie, S/PV5868 (Resumption 1), 16 avril 2008, p 3.
56 U.A., S/PV6702, 12 janvier 2012, p 9.
57 U.A., S/PV6409, 22 octobre 2010, p 6.
58 Etats-Unis, S/PV5776, 6 novembre 2007, p 3
59 U.A., S/PV6257, 13 janvier 2010, p 8.

particulièrement significative faite au nom du mouvement des non-alignés, dont on rappellera qu'il compte plus de 110 Etats, dont les Etats africains :

> Le Mouvement des pays non alignés est convaincu que l'ONU a la responsabilité fondamentale de garantir le maintien de la paix et de la sécurité internationales et que le rôle des accords régionaux devra être aligné strictement sur le Chapitre VIII de la Charte, qu'il ne *devra en aucune manière se substituer à celui de l'ONU* ...[60]

En ce sens, le Congo a signalé que « l'Union africaine s'est investie dans son rôle complémentaire, qui ne saurait se substituer à la primauté de l'ONU et de son Conseil de sécurité dans le maintien de la paix et de 1a sécurité internationales »,[61] tandis que l'Allemagne a prévenu qu'il était « impératif que les opérations de sécurité régionales se fassent sous mandat du Conseil si l'on veut maintenir la base juridique du système de sécurité internationale ».[62] Le refus d'envisager toute émancipation des organisations régionales lorsqu'il s'agit d'action coercitive a été répété par plusieurs membres du Conseil de sécurité. Le Royaume-Uni a rappelé qu'il ne pensait pas que « la coopération, quelle que bienvenue qu'elle soit en principe, doive se faire aux dépens de la primauté du Conseil de sécurité en matière de maintien de la paix et de la sécurité internationales »;[63] la France a affirmé que l'ONU « reste et doit rester au cœur du système de sécurité collective. Les organisations régionales appuient l'ONU mais ne s'y substituent pas »;[64] les Etats-Unis ont rappelé que le Conseil de sécurité « n'est subordonné à aucun autre organe, ni même aux calendriers ou aux capacités de groupes régionaux ou sous-régionaux »;[65] la Chine que les organisations régionales « peuvent prendre des mesures contraignantes uniquement avec l'assentiment du Conseil de sécurité »,[66] tandis que la Russie affirmait que l'autorisation du Conseil de sécurité « s'impos[e] quand le mandat de ces opérations comprend des mesures de recours à la force ».[67] On retrouve à travers ces déclarations le schéma classique d'une centralisation de l'usage de la force, ainsi que des traces du caractère impératif du système, auquel il ne peut en aucun cas être dérogé sur une base régionale.[68] En ce sens, l'Union africaine ne peut agir de manière autonome, mais uniquement « au nom de la communauté internationale »[69] ou du Conseil de sécurité.[70]

Mais que signifient, dans ce cas, les appels à une interprétation souple ou novatrice du chapitre VIII de la Charte ? Pour le comprendre, il faut sans doute faire le lien

[60] Nous soulignons ; S/PV6092, 18 mars 2009, p 30.

[61] S/PV6092 (Resumption 1), 18 mars 2009, p 11. V aussi les propos de l'Afrique du sud, S/PV6092, 18 mars 2009, p 9

[62] S/PV4739, 11 avril 2003, p 5.

[63] S/PV6702 (Resumption 1), 12 janvier 2012, p 10.

[64] France, S/PV5776, 6 novembre 2007, p 23.

[65] Etats-Unis, S/PV6702, 12 janvier 2012, p 17.

[66] S/PV5776, 6 novembre 2007, p 14.

[67] Russie, S/PV5776, 6 novembre 2007, p 18.

[68] V p ex. la déclaration du Royaume-Uni selon lequel « le Conseil de sécurité est évidemment responsable au premier chef de la paix et de la sécurité internationales et nul ne saurait déroger à cela. (Royaume-Uni, S/PV6092, 18 mars 2009, p 26).

[69] Communiqué conjoint adopté par le Conseil de sécurité et par le Conseil de paix et de sécurité de l'Union africaine, § 10 ; Rapport de la mission du Conseil de sécurité à Addis-Abeba, Khartoum, Accra, Abidjan et Kinshasa, du 14 au 21 juin 2007, S/2007/421*, 11 juillet 2007. V aussi l'Afrique du sud (S/PV5868, 16 avril 2008, p 5), le Botswana (ibid, p 28).

[70] UA, S/PV6409, 22 octobre 2010, p 7.

avec une certaine pratique, qui s'est développée depuis les années 1990, par laquelle certaines organisations régionales ont développé des opérations de maintien de la paix que l'on a parfois qualifié de « robustes ».[71] Que ce soit dans le cas du Libéria ou de la Sierra Leone, et ensuite de la Côte d'Ivoire, la CEDEAO est intervenue dans des conflits internes en s'appuyant formellement sur le consentement des autorités, mais parfois à l'encontre de la volonté de certaines parties au conflit.[72] Dans ce contexte, cette organisation régionale ne s'est manifestement pas sentie tenue de devoir requérir l'autorisation du Conseil de sécurité en vertu de l'article 53 de la Charte, qui n'exige une telle autorisation que pour des mesures « coercitives ». Si on suit cette logique, les mesures non coercitives que constituent par définition des actions menées avec le consentement de l'Etat, s'inscrivent plutôt dans le cadre de l'article 52 de la Charte, et peuvent être menée d'initiative par les organismes régionaux, le Conseil de sécurité n'intervenant, le cas échéant, qu'*a posteriori* pour appuyer l'opération de maintien de la paix. Un tel schéma, que l'on s'abstiendra d'évaluer ou de juger dans le cadre limité de cette contribution, se retrouve en tout cas en filigrane dans les débats qui ont été tenus au sein de l'ONU. Ainsi, le Conseil de sécurité « réaffirme son attachement au principe du règlement pacifique des différends, et reconnaît l'importance du rôle que les organisations régionales et sous-régionales jouent dans le règlement pacifique des différends d'ordre local et dans la diplomatie préventive ».[73] Dans le même sens, l'action des organisations régionales est souvent assimilée à des « opérations de maintien de la paix »[74] que ces organisations souhaitent placer sous l'égide des Nations, notamment pour des raisons de financement. Enfin, la seule disposition citée comme pouvant donner lieu à une interprétation souple est l'article 52, et non l'article 53, de la Charte.[75]

Rien n'indique donc, à la lecture de ces très nombreuses prises de position, que l'Union africaine ait revendiqué un droit d'intervention qui lui permettrait de s'émanciper des conditions énoncées dans la Charte, en tout cas lorsqu'on est dans le cas d'une action coercitive. Il est vrai que, à ce stade, on est resté dans le domaine du discours, tel qu'il s'est manifesté dans les enceintes feutrées des locaux de l'Organisation des Nations Unies. Si l'on choisit de se tourner vers la pratique, c'est-à-dire sur la manière donc ces discours se traduisent par des comportements sur le terrain, il n'est pas certain que le curseur se déplace vers une plus grande autonomie des organisations régionales vis-à-vis de l'ONU. C'est en tout cas cette thèse qui sera développée dans la deuxième partie de cette contribution.

[71] Russie, S/PV6409, 22 octobre 2010, p 13.

[72] Pour plus de détails, v Olivier Corten, *Le droit contre la guerre*, op cit, pp 568–83.

[73] S/PRST/2010/1, 13 janvier 2010 ; v aussi résolution 2033 (2012), 12 janvier 2012 ; v aussi Résolution 1809 (2008), 16 avril 2008, 15-0-0.

[74] Résolution 1809 (2008), 16 avril 2008, 15-0-0, § 4 ; Rapport du Groupe d'experts Union Africaine-ONU sur les modalités d'appui des opérations de maintien de la paix de l'Union africaine, p 8, § 11 ; Lettres identiques datées du 24 décembre 2008, adressées au Président de l'Assemblée générale et au Président du Conseil de sécurité par le Secrétaire général, A/63/666–S/2008/813, 31 décembre 2008. V la position de la CEDEAO (S/PV4739, 11 avril 2003, pp 36–37 ; S/PV5007 (Resumption 1), 20 juillet 2004, p 7), de la France (ibid, p 38), du Libéria (S/PV5649 (Resumption 1), 28 mars 2007, p 19 ; S/PV5868 (Resumption 1), 16 avril 2008, p 16), de l'Afrique du sud (S/PV5868, 16 avril 2008, p 6), du Burkina Faso ; S/PV6092, 18 mars 2009, p 15), du Royaume-Uni au nom de l'UE (S/PV5282, 17 octobre 2005, p 24).

[75] Nigeria, S/PV6561, 21 juin 2011, p 7 ; v aussi Colombie, ibid, p 13.

II. LA RÉAFFIRMATION DE L'AUTORITÉ DU CONSEIL DE SÉCURITÉ : L'ILLUSTRATION PAR LE PRÉCÉDENT EMBLÉMATIQUE DE LA LIBYE

Pour autant que l'on sache, il n'existe aucun précédent dans lequel l'Union africaine aurait mené ou décidé d'une intervention militaire pour faire cessez des crimes de guerre, des crimes contre l'humanité ou des actes de génocide conformément à l'article 4h) de son Statut. Le seul précédent connu est celui de l'affaire Hissène Habré, l'UA ayant invoqué cette disposition pour justifier son action—au demeurant relativement limitée—dans ce dossier.[76] On est donc, à ce stade, bien loin de pouvoir évoquer une pratique par laquelle une interprétation large du « droit d'intervention » ait été acceptée. Cela ne signifie pas qu'aucune occasion ne se soit jamais présentée. Dans les cas du Soudan ou de la Côte d'Ivoire, par exemple, la dénonciation de certains crimes internationaux n'a pas mené à l'invocation d'un droit d'intervention militaire dans le chef de l'UA, mais plutôt à des tentatives de médiation et le déploiement d'opérations de maintien de la paix avec l'accord des gouvernements concernés et sous l'égide du Conseil de sécurité des Nations Unies.[77] Dans le cas ivoirien, c'est celui-ci—et non un organe de l'Union africaine—qui a décidé d'une intervention pour mettre fin à la crise post-électorale, lorsque l'ancien président Gbagbo a refusé de céder le pouvoir au président élu, Alassane Ouattara.[78] Et cette intervention a été menée essentiellement par les forces des Nations Unies, ainsi que par la France, les organisations régionales africaines (UA et CEDEAO) étant réduites au rang de spectateurs.[79] Plus exemplatif encore du rôle limité de l'Union africaine est sans doute l'épisode de la Libye, que l'on détaillera dans les lignes qui suivent.[80] Dans ce cas, l'Union africaine a tenté de gérer la situation et de jouer son rôle dans le domaine du maintien de la paix. Cependant, loin de pouvoir invoquer ou exercer un quelconque droit d'intervention, elle a été rapidement marginalisée par le Conseil de sécurité de l'ONU, et plus spécialement par certains Etats agissant en son sein. Au final, la crise a été gérée non seulement sans, mais aussi à l'encontre des vœux, de l'Union africaine. C'est ce que l'on montrera en distinguant deux étapes du conflit : la première vise la manière dont la prise de décision de recourir à la force a été opérée, avec l'adoption de la résolution 1973 (2011) du Conseil de sécurité ; la seconde recouvre la manière dont cette décision a été mise en œuvre avec, là encore, une marginalisation manifeste des Etats africains.

[76] Conférence de l'UA, 7ème session ordinaire, Banjul, 2 juillet 2006, « Décision sur le procès d'Hissène Habré et l'UA », Doc Assembly/AU/3 (VII), disponible sur www.africa-union.org/Official_documents/Decisions_Declarations/fmDecisions_&_Declarations%20fr.htm.

[77] JI Levitt, « The Peace and Security Council of the African Union and the Security Council: The Case of Darfur, Sudan » *in* N Blokker and N Schrijver (eds), *The Security Council and the Use of Force. Theory and Reality—A Need for Change ?* (Leiden/Boston, Martinus Nijhoff, 2005) 229–36.

[78] Résolution 1975 (2011) du 30 mars 2011, § 6.

[79] V not *Kessing's Contemporary Archives*, 2011, pp 50381–82.

[80] V not les études suivantes: P Thielbörger, « The Status and Future of International Law after the Libya Intervention » (2012) 4 *GoJIL* 11–48 ; AJ. Bellamy and PD Williams, « The new politics of protection? Côte d'Ivoire, Libya and the responsibility to protect » (2011) 87 *International Affairs*, pp 825–50; MJ Domestici-Met, « Protecting in Libya on Behalf of the International Community » (2011) 3 *GoJIL*.

A. La Prise de Décision de l'Intervention: l'Union Africaine Ignorée

Pour bien comprendre comment la prise de décision a été opérée, il faut remonter aux débuts de la crise, et voir comment l'Union africaine et l'ONU ont géré l'évolution de la situation. On se rappellera que c'est le 15 février 2011 qu'ont débuté les manifestations populaires à Benghazi, la deuxième ville libyenne. Selon plusieurs organismes de défense des droits de l'homme, les autorités libyennes ont réagi brutalement, en utilisant la force contre les manifestants, en procédant à des arrestations massives et, apparemment, à des exécutions sommaires.[81] Les manifestations se répandent alors dans plusieurs villes du pays. Quelques jours plus tard, des pilotes de l'armée libyenne désertent à Malte, et déclarent qu'ils ont refusé de tirer sur des manifestants pacifiques. Plus généralement, la liste des défections de la part d'officiels libyens, particulièrement ceux qui sont en poste à l'étranger, s'allonge. Le 22 février, le colonel Kadhafi prononce un discours radio télévisé, dans lequel il dénonce un complot d'étrangers, fustige les manifestants comme des « rats », « drogués » et « alcooliques » dont l'attitude est passible de la peine de mort ; il affirme enfin qu'il combattra « jusqu'à la dernière goutte de sang ».[82]

C'est dans ce contexte que, le 23 février, le Conseil de paix et de sécurité de l'Union africaine publie un communiqué par lequel il

> [e]xprime sa profonde préoccupation face à la situation qui prévaut en Grande Jamahiriya arabe libyenne populaire et socialiste et condamne fermement l'utilisation indiscriminée et excessive de la force et des armes contre les manifestants pacifiques en violation aux Droits de I'Homme et au Droit international humanitaire, causant des pertes importantes en vies humaines et la destruction de biens ...[83]

Le Conseil décide aussi de dépêcher une mission en territoire libyen et de rester activement saisi de la question.[84] Le même jour, le président de la Commission de l'UA publie un communiqué similaire.[85] A ce stade, l'Union africaine semble affirmer son autorité pour assurer la gestion de la crise. Quelques jours plus tard, le 26 février, le Conseil de sécurité de l'ONU adopte sa résolution 1970 (2011), par laquelle est établi un embargo sur les armes, un gel des avoirs ainsi que des interdictions de voyager visant les hauts responsables du régime libyen, la situation étant par ailleurs déférée à la Cour pénale internationale pour investigation. Dans sa résolution, le Conseil ne se réfère qu'incidemment à l'Union africaine, en évoquant la condamnation opérée par le Conseil de paix et de sécurité, ainsi d'ailleurs que celle opérée par la Ligue arabe et l'Organisation de la Conférence islamique.[86] Lors des débats, le délégué de l'Afrique du sud estime que cette résolution « vient compléter » l'action de

[81] V not Human Rights Watch, *2012 Report* (www.hrw.org/world-report-2012) 595.

[82] http://afriqueactu.net/24277-discours-de-mouammar-kadhafi-le-22-fevrier-2011.

[83] Communiqué du CPS sur la situation en Libye, 261ème réunion 23 février 2011, § 2 (www.au.int/fr/content/communiqu%C3%A9-du-cps-sur-la-situation-en-libye).

[84] ibid, §§ 6 et 7.

[85] L'Union africaine profondément préoccupée par la situation en Libye, communiqué de presse, 23 février 2011, www.au.int/fr/content/lua-profond%C3%A9ment-pr%C3%A9occup%C3%A9e-par-la-situation-en-libye.

[86] Résolution 1970 (2011), préambule, 3ème considérant.

l'UA.[87] Plusieurs Etats semblent également envisager l'action des différentes organisations impliquées en termes de complémentarité.[88] Dès les lendemains de l'adoption de cette résolution, il est cependant devenu visible que les revendications en faveur d'une intervention militaires se sont fait de plus en plus vives, toujours de la part d'acteurs extérieurs à l'Union africaine. Dès le 28 février, le Royaume-Uni et les Etats-Unis se déclarent ainsi publiquement en faveur de l'établissement d'une zone d'interdiction de survol sur la Libye,[89] de même que la France qui, le 2 mars, affirme exclure à ce stade toute intervention militaire.[90] Le 10 mars, le Conseil de paix et de sécurité prend une nouvelle décision par laquelle, après avoir réitéré la condamnation « ferme et sans équivoque de l'UA de l'utilisation indiscriminée de la force et d'armes mortelles, d'où qu'elles viennent », de même que la « transformation de manifestations pacifiques en rébellion armée », il « réaffirme son ferme attachement au respect de l'unité et de l'intégrité territoriale de la Libye, ainsi que son rejet de toute intervention militaire étrangère, quelle qu'en soit la forme ».[91] Le Conseil estime aussi que « la situation actuelle en Libye appelle une action africaine urgente » et décide la mise en place d'un « comité *ad hoc* de haut niveau de l'UA sur la Libye comprenant cinq chefs d'Etat et de gouvernement, ainsi que le président de la Commission », chargé à la fois de faciliter le dialogue entre les parties libyennes et « d'interagir avec les partenaires de l'UA », dont l'ONU, en vue d'assurer la coordination.[92] Alors que l'Union africaine semble reprendre la main, la Ligue des Etats arabes se prononce, le 12 mars, pour l'instauration d'une zone d'exclusion aérienne en Libye. La France déclare qu'elle appuie cette proposition[93] et, après une réunion du G8,[94] le Conseil de sécurité se réunit le 17 mars pour adopter la résolution 1973 (2011). Dans cette résolution, on le sait, le Conseil autorise l'adoption de toutes les « mesures nécessaires », non seulement pour établir une zone d'exclusion aérienne mais aussi pour « protéger les populations et zones civiles menacées d'attaque », tout en « excluant le déploiement d'une force d'occupation étrangère sous quelque forme que ce soit sur n'importe quelle partie du territoire libyen ».[95] On semble à ce stade s'être radicalement écarté de la position africaine du « rejet de toute intervention militaire

[87] S/PV6491, 26 février 2011, p 3.

[88] V les représentants du Liban, de la Russie et du Brésil (ibid, pp 4 et 7).

[89] *Keesing's Contemporary Archives*, 2011, p 50310.

[90] Réponse du ministre d'état, ministre des affaires étrangères et européennes, Alain Juppé, à une question d'actualité à l'assemblée nationale (Paris, 2 mars 2011), www.diplomatie.gouv.fr/fr/pays-zones-geo/libye/la-france-et-la-libye/evenements-4528/article/libye-90266 ; v aussi Conférence de presse conjointe d'Alain Juppé avec le ministre d'Etat, ministre des Affaires étrangères du Royaume-Uni de Grande–Bretagne et d'Irlande du Nord, William Hague (Paris, 3 mars 2011), https://pastel.diplomatie.gouv.fr/editorial/actual/ael2/bulletin.asp?liste=20110303.html#Chapitre5.

[91] Communiqué de la 265ème réunion du Conseil de paix et de sécurité, 10 mars 2011, § 6; www.au.int/fr/content/le-conseil-de-paix-et-de-s%C3%A9curit%C3%A9-de-lunion-africaine-ua-en-sa-265%C3%A8me-r%C3%A9union-tenue-le-10—0.

[92] ibid, § 8.

[93] Résolution de la Ligue des Etats arabes. Déclaration d'Alain Juppé, 13 mars 2011, www.diplomatie.gouv.fr/fr/pays-zones-geo/libye/la-france-et-la-libye/evenements-4528/article/resolution-de-la-ligue-des-etats.

[94] Réunion des ministres des Affaires étrangères. Conclusions de la présidence, 14–15 mars 2011, www.diplomatie.gouv.fr/fr/enjeux-internationaux/affaires-economiques/g8/derniers-sommets-du-g8/le-sommet-du-g8-de-deauville-26-27/article/reunion-des-ministres-des-affaires-90642.

[95] Résolution 1972 (2011), §§ 4 et 8.

étrangère, quelle qu'en soit la forme ». La gestion par la crise de l'Union africaine a donc été largement ignorée, tout au plus le Conseil de sécurité ayant « pris note » du « communiqué du Conseil de paix et de sécurité africaine en date du 10 mars 2011 portant création d'un comité ad hoc de haut niveau sur la Libye » ainsi que de la décision d'envoyer un comité ad hoc sur place.

Il est vrai que la résolution 1973 (1973), votée par 10 voix pour et cinq abstentions, n'a pu être valablement adoptée que grâce au vote positif de trois Etats africains : l'Afrique du sud, le Nigeria et le Gabon. Comment expliquer que ces trois Etats africains aient accepté un texte qui contredisait directement celui adopté quelques jours plus tôt dans le cadre de l'Union ? Il est bien délicat de le déterminer. Seule l'Afrique du Sud a expliqué sa position officiellement lors des débats, et cette position est pour le moins ambiguë. Dans son exposé, le représentant sud-africain souligne en effet l'importance de l'envoi du comité *ad hoc* par l'Union africaine, puis affirme n'avoir voté en faveur de la résolution que moyennant des « réserves nécessaires aux fins de la préservation de la souveraineté et de l'intégrité territoriale de la Libye et du refus de toute occupation étrangère ou intervention militaire unilatérale sous quelque forme que ce soit ».[96] Si l'on s'en tient à une analyse des textes, il est bien difficile de comprendre cette position : la résolution 1973 (2011) contient indéniablement une autorisation de recourir à la force contre les autorités libyennes, ce que n'ont pas manqué de souligner plusieurs Etats lors des débats,[97] sans être contredits par l'Afrique du Sud. Dans ce contexte, on ne comprend pas quelles sont les « réserves » qui auraient permis de concilier le texte de cette résolution avec celle adoptée une semaine plus tôt par l'Union africaine, qui consistait essentiellement à promouvoir la voie pacifique en rejetant toute forme d'intervention militaire. On pourrait certes poser l'hypothèse que les trois Etats africains ont subi des pressions, ou se sont vus offrir des avantages, en vue d'obtenir leur vote, d'autant que ce dernier s'avérait tout à fait indispensable pour obtenir les neuf voix nécessaires, au vu de l'abstention de l'Allemagne, du Brésil, de la Chine, de l'Inde et de la Russie. Une autre hypothèse est que ces Etats auraient, au vu de l'évolution de la situation sur le terrain, été convaincus de la nécessité d'un changement de stratégie. Cependant, un tel scénario s'avère peu plausible au vu de l'interprétation qui a été donnée à la résolution 1973 (2011) par les Etats africains dès les lendemains de son adoption. La phase de la mise en œuvre de la résolution a en effet révélé une profonde division entre les Etats intervenants et leurs alliés, d'une part, et d'autres Etats, parmi lesquels les Etats africains, d'autre part.

B. La Mise en Œuvre de l'Intervention: l'Union Africaine Écartée

On ne reviendra pas, dans le cadre limité de cette contribution, sur les différentes étapes de l'intervention militaire en Libye, qui a débuté avec les bombardements français du 19 mars pour bientôt être placée sous l'égide de l'OTAN, l'opération

[96] S/PV6498, 17 mars 2011, p 10.
[97] ibid ; v les déclarations du Liban, des Etats-Unis, du Brésil et de la Russie.

« protecteur unifié » prenant officiellement fin le 31 octobre 2011.[98] Pour les besoins de notre réflexion, on pointera cependant deux éléments qui montrent que l'Union africaine a été manifestement écartée en tant qu'instance légitime de règlement du conflit. En réalité, le « droit d'intervention » énoncé dans la résolution 1973 (2011) a été interprété et mis en œuvre non pas sous l'impulsion mais à l'encontre, d'une part de la position, et d'autre part de l'action, de l'Union africaine.

Quant au premier point, qui concerne essentiellement l'interprétation de la résolution 1973 (2011), il faut commencer par exposer la position de certains Etats intervenants, lesquels ont progressivement élargi leurs objectifs militaires bien au-delà de ce que prévoyait, *stricto sensu*, le texte de la résolution. Dans un premier temps, la force militaire n'a ainsi été considérée comme « nécessaire » (selon le critère retenu par le Conseil de sécurité) qu'aux fins de protéger les civils d'une menace imminente d'attaque.[99] C'est ce qui a justifié les premières frappes contre les forces armées libyennes qui se dirigeaient vers Benghazi et d'autres localités du pays pour les reconquérir. Assez rapidement cependant, face à l'incapacité des forces rebelles à profiter de cette modification des rapports de force, l'objectif de l'intervention s'est élargi à la destruction de l'ensemble des infrastructure militaire et logistique du régime de Tripoli, destruction qui a été considérée comme nécessaire à la protection des civils.[100] En suivant cette logique, la France et certains de ses alliés ont progressivement affirmé que la résolution 1973 (2011) autorisait le renversement du gouvernement libyen par la force et, parallèlement, le soutien aux rebelles dans leur lutte pour la conquête du pouvoir.[101] Comme l'on pouvait s'y attendre, une telle interprétation est loin d'avoir fait l'unanimité au sein des membres des Nations Unies.[102] De nombreux Etats ont ainsi émis de sérieuses réserves, en relevant que le Conseil de sécurité n'avait jamais autorisé l'usage de la force pour réaliser un changement de régime. En ce sens, les Etats africains ont constamment défendu une interprétation restrictive de la résolution 1973 (2011), comme l'illustre notamment cet extrait du communiqué du Conseil de paix et de sécurité de l'UA, adopté le 26 avril 2011, à un moment où le basculement des objectifs de guerre de la stricte protection des civils vers le soutien aux rebelles libyens se manifestait de manière de plus en plus ostensible. Le Conseil :

> [r]étitère l'engagement de l'UA en faveur du respect de la résolution 1973 (2011). A cet égard, le Conseil souligne la nécessité pour tous les pays et organisations impliquées dans la mise en œuvre de la résolution 1973 (2011) d'agir de manière pleinement conforme à la

[98] See www.nato.int/cps/en/natolive/topics_71652.htm.

[99] V p ex l'interview de Mme Clinton de M. Gates, CBS, 27 mars 2011, www.state.gov/secretary/rm/2011/03/159210.htm.

[100] Interview de M. Juppé, Radio France internationale, 23 mai 2011, https://pastel.diplomatie.gouv.fr/editorial/actual/ael2/bulletin.asp?liste=20110524.html.

[101] V p ex la declaration conjointe des présidents Obama et Sarkhozi et du premier ministre Cameron le 1er avril 2011 (www.diplomatie.gouv.fr/fr/pays-zones-geo/libye/la-france-et-la-libye/evenements-4528/article/libye-tribune-conjointe-de-nicolas).

[102] V p ex Document final de la XVIe Conférence ministérielle du Mouvement des Non Alignés, NAM 2011/Doc 1/Rev 1, 23–27 mai 2011, p 84, www.kemlu.go.id/Documents/GNB%20ke-16/NAMDOC1-Rev1-Final%20Document-English-Final.pdf, ainsi que les positions de la Chine (www.mfa.gov.cn/eng/xwfw/s2510/2511/t820162.htm) et de la Russie (www.mid.ru/bdomp/brp_4.nsf/171aab5ddf3ec3c2c325 75d7004629c8/8a2f0895ae153061c32578810039399a!OpenDocument), de meme que d'autres Etats (v S/PV6531 et 6531 (Resumption 1), 10 mai 2011.

légalité internationale et aux dispositions de *cette résolution, dont l'objectif n'est autre que d'assurer la protection de la population civile*. Le Conseil demande instamment tous les acteurs impliqués de *s'abstenir d'actions, y compris d'opérations militaires visant de hauts responsables libyens et des infrastructures socio-économiques*, qui risquent d'aggraver davantage la situation et de rendre plus difficile un consensus international sur la meilleure voie à suivre.[103]

Dans le même sens, un représentant de l'Union africaine dénonce, au sein du Conseil de sécurité, « le précédent dangereux créé par des interprétations biaisées des résolutions de l'ONU et des conséquences qui en résultent pour la légalité internationale ».[104] Quant à l'Afrique du sud, elle précise que, en votant en faveur de la résolution 1973 (2011), elle visait la protection des civils, sans que l'on puisse nullement en déduire une « intention de procéder à un changement de régime ou de cibler certains individus ».[105] Sur le terrain, en dépit des protestations des Etats africains—ainsi d'ailleurs que de nombreux autres Etats—c'est au contraire une conception large de l'intervention qui a prévalu. La France et ses alliés, et dans une certaine mesure l'OTAN, sont donc parvenus à imposer leurs conceptions, le Conseil de sécurité étant, en raison précisément des divisions observées, incapable d'adopter une nouvelle résolution décidant de l'extension (ou au contraire de la réduction) des sanctions contre la Libye.

Si on se tourne, au-delà de ces prises de position de principe, sur l'action que l'Union africaine a tenté de mener, les mêmes conclusions s'imposent. L'organisation régionale principalement concernée a manifestement été écartée du processus de décision, comme on a pu s'en apercevoir dès les premiers jours qui ont suivi l'adoption de la résolution 1973 (2011).[106] Dans un communiqué de presse du 23 mars, le Conseil de paix et de sécurité de l'UA regrette que le comité *ad hoc* n'ait pas reçu l'autorisation des Nations Unies à se rendre sur place afin d'effectuer sa mission de médiation.[107] Il note avec satisfaction l'acceptation de sa feuille de route par le gouvernement libyen, et appelle à un cessez-le-feu immédiat.[108] On apprend ensuite que, deux jours plus tard, une réunion a été organisée à Addis Abeba, à laquelle s'est rendue une délégation du gouvernement libyen, mais aucun membre du Conseil National de Transition.[109] Le Comité y a engagé le CNT à une cessation « urgente et immédiate » des hostilités, conformément à sa feuille de route.[110] Comme on le sait, ces appels sont restés vains. Dans les semaines qui ont suivi, le Conseil de paix et de sécurité s'est félicité de l'acceptation de la feuille de route par le gouvernement en place, y compris la mise en œuvre d'un « mécanisme de surveillance efficace et

[103] Nous soulignons ; Conseil de paix et de sécurité, 275ème réunion, 26 avril 2011, PSC/MIN/COMM (CCLXXV), § 11.

[104] S/PV6555, 15 juin 2011, p 4.

[105] S/PV6566, 27 juin 2011, p 4.

[106] V Tom Kabau, « The Responsibility to Protect and the Role of Regional Organizations: an Appraisal of the African Union's Interventions » (2012) 4 *GoJIL* 73–74.

[107] Conseil de paix et de sécurité, 268ème réunion, 23 mars 2011, PSC/PR/BR.1(CCLXVIII), p 1.

[108] ibid. V aussi le Rapport du président de la Commission sur les activités du Comité *ad hoc* de haut niveau de l'UA sur la situation en Libye, 26 avril 2011, PSC/PR/2(CCLXXV), p 4.

[109] Communiqué de presse du 25 mars 2011, Addis Abeba.

[110] ibid.

crédible », tout en prenant note de l'absence d'accord du CNT.[111] Ce dernier, dans un contexte où s'intensifiaient les actions militaires sous l'égide de l'OTAN contre le régime, a exigé comme préalable à toute négociation le départ du pouvoir du colonel Kadhafi et de ses proches, une exigence condamnée, en vain, par les représentants de l'Union africaine.[112] En pratique, l'activité du comité *ad hoc*, dont on rappellera qu'il était composé de cinq chefs d'Etats et de gouvernements africains (Mauritanie, Mali, Nigeria, Ouganda, Afrique du sud), s'est révélée sans aucun effet.[113] La politique consistant à appuyer la voie politique en faisant pression à la fois sur le gouvernement et les rebelles a été écartée au profit d'une volonté de renverser le régime qui a été exprimé au sein d'autres cénacles que l'Union africaine, qu'il s'agisse de l'ONU, de l'OTAN, ou d'autres organismes informels.[114] Dans ce contexte, il n'est guère étonnant que, le 25 mai, le président de la Commission de l'UA se plaignait d'une « absence de coordination dans les efforts internationaux ».[115]

Finalement, on mesure la distance qui sépare l'interprétation extensive du droit d'intervention énoncé dans l'acte constitutif de l'Union africaine, d'une part, et l'observation des prises de position et actions dans la pratique récente, d'autre part. Loin de revendiquer un droit d'intervention qui pourrait l'émanciper de l'autorité du Conseil de sécurité, les Etats africains ont plutôt insisté sur la nécessité de maintenir le système centralisé de sécurité collective tel qu'il est énoncé dans le chapitre VIII de la Charte. Il en a spécialement été ainsi dans les années 2000, dans un contexte de la proclamation d'une « guerre contre le terrorisme » par l'administration Bush. Comme on le sait, les Etats non-alignés en général se sont opposés à toute tentative d'assouplissement des règles impératives prescrivant le non-recours à la force. Dans ce contexte, la revendication de la part des Etats africains d'une possibilité accrue de recours à la force, même limitée à leur continent, aurait semblé paradoxale. En pratique, on a d'ailleurs constaté que l'Union africaine avait préféré la voie non coercitive, en ne menant des opérations militaires que sur la base d'un accord de l'Etat concerné. Et, dans le cas de la Libye, on a vu comment cette organisation régionale restait impuissante à s'opposer à l'autorité du Conseil de sécurité et, au-delà, au pouvoir de certains acteurs qui se sont avérés en mesure d'imposer, sur le terrain, leur conception particulièrement extensive d'un droit d'intervention. Un exemple qui confirme, si besoin en était, que le discours juridique ne peut être compris et évalué qu'en le confrontant à son contexte politique d'édiction et d'application.

[111] Conseil de paix et de sécurité, 275ème réunion, 26 avril 2011, PSC/MIN/COMM(CCLXXV), § 6.

[112] ibid, § 9.

[113] V not le Rapport du président de la Commission sur les activités du Comité *ad hoc* de haut niveau de l'UA sur la situation en Libye, 26 avril 2011, PSC/PR/2(CCLXXV).

[114] V p ex le « groupe de contact » sur la Libye ; Conférence de Doha, 13 avril 2011, *Keesing's*, 2011, p 50427.

[115] Réunion du comité *ad hoc* de haut niveau de l'UA sur la Libye. Allocation de M le président de la Commission de l'UA, Addis Abeba, le 25 mai 2011, http://www.ausitroom-psd.org/Documents/2011 Fr.html.

19

Extraterritorial Application of the ECHR: A Relevant Contribution of Regionalism to Peace and Security?

ANA SALINAS DE FRÍAS*

I. INTRODUCTION

In 1990, on the occasion of German reunification and the end of the Cold War, events that signalled a new era, Michael Reisman declared that

> the challenge to international lawyers and scholars must be to clarify continuously the common interests of this ever-changing community, drawing on historic policies but bearing in mind that the constitutive and institutional arrangements that were devised to achieve them may no longer be pertinent or effective.[1]

Only two years after this major event, a bloody civil war erupted in the heart of Europe, making it necessary to resort once more to the use of armed force on the European continent. Perhaps Reisman was right when he predicted that the end of the Cold War meant only the reduction of one particular pattern of violence, but would not bring about peace or new international stability.[2]

Armed conflicts persist and, even today, constitute a direct threat to international peace and security. Increasing participation of contracting parties to the European Convention on Human Rights (ECHR)[3] in military operations—some extremely controversial—have pushed this regional system[4] to produce new case law

* Chair of Public International Law, International Relations and EU Law, University of Málaga. The presentation on which this chapter is based was delivered in 2012 since when there may have been developments in the case law of the ECtHR that have superseded some of the decisions cited here.

[1] See WM Reisman, 'International Law after the Cold War' (1990) 84 *American Journal of International Law* 859, 866.

[2] ibid, 863.

[3] European Convention on the Protection of Human Rights and Fundamental Freedoms (adopted 4 November 1950, entered into force 3 September 1953) CETS No 005, 213 UNTS 1932 (ECtHR).

[4] More specifically the Court stated: 'In short, the Convention is a multi-lateral treaty operating, subject to Article 56 of the Convention, in an essentially regional context and notably in the legal space (*espace juridique*) of the Contracting States ... The Convention was not designed to be applied throughout the world, even in respect of the conduct of Contracting States.' *Bankovic and Ors v Belgium and Ors*, App no 52207/99 (ECtHR, 12 December 2001), para 80. On criticisms of this concept of 'legal space', see R Wilde, 'The "Legal Space" or "Espace Juridique" of the European Convention on Human Rights: Is It Relevant to Extraterritorial State Action?' (2005) 10 *European Human Rights Law Review*, 115–24.

(albeit sometimes obscure)—showing how the European approach can contribute to international peace and security beyond the frontiers of Europe, through the extraterritorial application of some ECHR provisions, together with the legal and political constraints of such an application.

The European Court of Human Rights (ECtHR) has systematised potential extraterritorial application of the Convention into four different categories:[5] a) diplomatic, consular and flag jurisdiction cases;[6] b) cases where either states authorities act abroad or their actions produce extraterritorial effects;[7] c) extradition or expulsion cases involving the risk that an individual's rights could be violated once he leaves the territory of the signatory state; d) cases where a signatory state exercises 'effective overall control' over another state's territory. In this contribution we shall discuss the factual or potential extraterritorial application of the ECHR to situations where an effective control on the part of a state party to the Convention is carried out on a non-contracting state's territory. We shall also examine the effects it may have, in particular, on military operations where such control arguably exists, and, more specifically, regarding recent cases, where the Court has adjudicated concerning military operations involving ECHR contracting parties.

In this regard we shall analyse: first, the definition and scope of jurisdiction according to the case law initially developed by the ECtHR and its application to extraterritorial activities by contracting parties, mostly military occupation and humanitarian interventions; second, regression in the concept of jurisdiction on grounds of territorial control; third, regression in the concept of jurisdiction and international responsibility of inter-governmental organisations (IGOs); and fourth, recent positive steps opposing the restrictive approach of *Bankovic*.

It seems obvious that in order to analyse the application of ECHR standards out of Europe, jurisdiction becomes a key concept since it sets a limit on its application and effects. article 1 ECHR reads as follows: 'The High Contracting Parties shall secure to *everyone within their jurisdiction* the rights and freedoms defined in Section I of the Convention.'[8]

[5] See *Loizidou v Turkey* (Preliminary Objections) App no 15318/89 (ECtHR, 23 March 1995), Series A, no 310, para 62; *Bankovic* decision, ibid, paras 59–60; *Ilascu and Ors v Moldova and Russia*, App no 48787/99 (ECtHR, 8 July 2004), paras 312–18.

[6] Most of these cases were decided by the former European Commission of Human Rights and are related to decisions adopted by civil servants performing diplomatic or consular functions. Therefore, it is surprising that the Court insists on this category being an exceptional extraterritorial application of the ECHR, as this is one of the most ancient and traditional functional powers of the state, recognised by international law. The same reasoning can be applied to the so-called 'flag jurisdiction' cases; see, amongst other authorities, *X v Germany*, App no 1611/62 (Commission Decision, 25 September 1965); *X v United Kingdom*, App no 7547/76 (Commission Decision, 5 December 1977); *WM v Denmark*, App no 17392/90 (Commission Decision, 14 December 1992); *Ilse Hess v United Kingdom*, App no 6231/73 (28 May 1975); *Medvedyev and Ors v France*, App no 3394/03 (ECtHR, 29 March 2010).

[7] As the Court pronounced in the *Drozd and Janousek* case (*Drozd and Janousek v France and Spain*, App no 12747/87 (ECtHR, 26 June 1992)), concerning the condemnation of two individuals by a Court composed of French and Spanish judges, at a time when Andorra had not yet become an independent state, and either Spain and France were responsible for her administration: 'The term "jurisdiction" is not limited to the national territory of the High Contracting Parties; their responsibility can be involved because of acts of their authorities producing effects outside their own territory.' (para 91). However, there has been no other case grounded on this reasoning, despite the Court considering it still a different and individualised category of extraterritorial application of the ECHR.

[8] ECHR, above n 3, art 1.

However, the term 'jurisdiction' has not been further defined by the ECtHR, and its extraterritorial meaning has been discussed only in a limited number of cases. It is clear that jurisdiction exists when the state is able to exercise authority or control either over individuals (jurisdiction on grounds of personal link) or over territory (jurisdiction on grounds of a territorial link). It is clear that jurisdiction over a country's own territory, or over persons within it, does exist. However, it is not entirely clear that jurisdiction will continue to exist (apply) extraterritorially.

II. INITIAL DEFINITION AND SCOPE OF THE TERM 'JURISDICTION' IN THE CASE LAW OF THE ECtHR

There is a certain group of cases in which the de facto control over territories is such that, in these cases, 'jurisdiction' is unconditionally accepted within the meaning of article 1 ECHR. It has become a commonplace that the cornerstone for maintaining that the Convention can be applied extraterritorially is the *Loizidou v Turkey* case[9] and its progeny, in which the ECtHR dealt with the de facto occupation of North Cyprus by Turkey, and the support of this state by a puppet government there. The consequences of this military action were, amongst others, the deprivation of a number of fundamental rights to inhabitants of this part of Cyprus, amongst which was that of Mrs Loizidou and her right to private property. The Court, in an unprecedented and progressive approach clearly stated that it

> recalls that, although Article 1 sets limits on the reach of the Convention, the concept of 'jurisdiction' under this provision is not restricted to the national territory of the High Contracting Parties. According to its established case-law, for example, the Court has held that the extradition or expulsion of a person by a Contracting State may give rise to an issue under Article 3, and hence engage the responsibility of that State under the Convention ... In addition, the responsibility of Contracting Parties can be involved because of acts of their authorities, whether performed within or outside national boundaries, which produce effects outside their own territory.

It went on to say that:

> [B]earing in mind the object and purpose of the Convention, the responsibility of a Contracting Party may also arise when as a consequence of military action—whether lawful or unlawful—it exercises effective control of an area outside its national territory. The obligation to secure, in such an area, the rights and freedoms set out in the Convention derives from the fact of such control whether it be exercised directly, through its armed forces, or through a subordinate local administration.[10]

As widely accepted by academia, the departure point in dealing with the extraterritorial application of the Convention on grounds of a territorial link, has been a wide conception of the term 'jurisdiction' based on the key element of

[9] See *Loizidou v Turkey*, (Preliminary Objections), above n 5.

[10] ibid, para 62. The same idea is later underlined concerning a potential restrictive interpretation of arts 63.4, 25 and 46 of the European Convention as it stood at that time; see ibid, paras 86–89.

'effective control'.[11] Such control—that later turns into overall effective control[12]—might be inferred from the presence of a significant Turkish military contingent controlling territory in Cyprus, and from its back-up effect on a dependent and internationally delegitimised government. Certain key elements are present in the initial reasoning of the Court. They are as follows: situations when an extraterritorial application of the ECHR can be stated are either lawful or unlawful occupations; the discussion concerns jurisdiction being applied to a territory already under the Convention before the occupation since it belonged to one of the contracting parties; the element triggering jurisdiction according to the Court is the exercise of effective control over the given territory, whether it be lawful or unlawful, through that state's agents and/or military forces but also through a de facto subordinate local administration; and finally, the only criterion mentioned by the Court in order to construe the term 'jurisdiction' and to apply it extraterritorially, is the object and purpose of the Convention. The Court emphasised

> [T]hat the Convention is a living instrument which must be interpreted in the light of present-day conditions is firmly rooted in the Court's case-law ... Such an approach, in the Court's view, is not confined to the substantive provisions of the Convention, but also applies to those provisions ... which govern the operation of the Convention's enforcement machinery. It follows that these provisions cannot be interpreted solely in accordance with the intentions of their authors as expressed more than forty years ago ... In addressing this issue the Court must bear in mind the special character of the Convention as an instrument of European public order (*ordre public*) for the protection of individual human beings and its mission, as set out in Article 19, 'to ensure the observance of the engagements undertaken by the High Contracting Parties'.[13]

This reasoning was later applied again in the *Cyprus v Turkey* case[14] where the Court reinforced this reasoning, considering it to be 'framed in terms of a broad statement of principle as regards Turkey's general responsibility under the Convention for the policies and actions of the "TRNC" authorities.'[15]

These same key elements should be considered when assessing the Court's contribution to the extraterritorial application of the ECHR with regard to the military activities of the contracting parties. The Court's approach to the problem, although expressed in general terms, is in fact shaped by the particular circumstances surrounding each individual case. Present in all cases are the following circumstances: military activities/occupation on the territory of a contracting party to the Convention, and engagement in armed conflict with another contracting party. This situation

[11] Also in line with other human rights monitoring bodies such as the Committee Against Torture in its Concluding Observations, United States of America, UN Doc CAT/C/USA/CO/2, 25 July, para 15; or the UN Human Rights Committee in its Concluding Observations, United States of America, UN Doc CCPR/C/USA/CO/3/Rev 1, 18 December 2006, para 10. In this respect see SI Skogly, 'Extraterritoriality—Universal Human Rights without Universal Obligations?' in http://eprints.lancs.ac.uk/26177/1/Microsoft_Word_-_Monash_-_Extraterritoriality_-_Final_draft.pdf.

[12] See *Loizidou v Turkey* (Merits), App no 15318/89 (ECtHR, 18 December 1996), ECHR 1996-VI, 2216, para 56.

[13] See *Loizidou v Turkey* (Preliminary Objections), above n 5, paras 71, 93.

[14] The formula chosen by the Court in the case of *Loizidou v Turkey* (Preliminary Objections), above n 5, was later repeated in *Loizidou v Turkey* (Merits), above n 12, and in the case of case of *Cyprus v Turkey*, App no 25781/94 (ECtHR, 10 May 2001) ECHR 2001-IV, 1.

[15] *Cyprus v Turkey*, ibid, para 77.

may be interpreted as an 'internal' military conflict when applying the Convention, an interpretation the Court has already included as subliminal justification in subsequent cases where it has adjudicated on this matter.

Thus, contrary to this Court's analysis, when contracting parties' military activities have turned into occupation of a third state's territories or humanitarian intervention, ie, into situations external to the ECHR system, the Court has adopted a much more restrictive view and has toughened up on applicants' arguments[16] while at the same time accepting—sometimes literally—arguments of defendant governments against the extraterritorial application of the Convention to military activities abroad.[17]

III. REGRESSION IN THE CONCEPT OF JURISDICTION ON GROUNDS OF TERRITORIAL CONTROL

In 2001, the ECtHR was called on to adjudicate on a request on behalf of a number of civilians killed or injured by the NATO bombing of a Serbian television station as a consequence of the military intervention during the armed conflict in Kosovo. Controversy about this humanitarian intervention and how it was carried out is well known. The request was lodged against Belgium and another 16 states parties to the Convention, alleging a breach of articles 2, 10 and 13 ECHR. The Court, in its decision as to the admissibility, departed notably from its previous approach and finally decided to dismiss the request on the grounds of article 1 ECHR, accepting the reasoning given by the defendant states.

According to the reasoning of the Court, the first point to be decided is the ordinary meaning of the terms 'within their jurisdiction' in article 1. In order to do so, the Court makes resource to the elements it used in its previous decisions, not only reversing their importance, but also incorporating a series of nuances that alter completely the scope of the concepts previously recognised by the Court, such as 'the ordinary and essentially territorial notion of jurisdiction, other bases of jurisdiction being exceptional and requiring special justification in the particular circumstances of each case'.[18]

The Court finally dismissed the application, contrary to long-standing case law that considers the ECHR as, first, a living and evolving instrument to be construed in the light of present-day conditions; second, as a treaty intended to offer effective protection and not just illusory rights; third, as a treaty with a particular legal nature as a human rights treaty; fourth, as a treaty with a special character, taking into account its nature as an instrument of European public order for the protection of individual human beings; and fifth, as a treaty to be first and foremost interpreted according to its object and purpose. In dismissing the application, the Court took into account a number of facts, including the fact that

[16] The Court has even stated that: 'Indeed the applicants' approach does not explain the application of the words "within their jurisdiction" in art 1 and it even goes so far as to render those words superfluous and devoid of any purpose.' See *Bankovic*, above n 4, para 75.

[17] ibid.

[18] See *Bankovic v Belgium and Ors*, above n 4, para 61.

> [A]lthough there have been a number of military missions involving Contracting States acting extra-territorially since their ratification of the Convention ... no State has indicated a belief that its extra-territorial actions involved an exercise of jurisdiction within the meaning of Article 1 of the Convention by making a derogation pursuant to Article 15 of the Convention.[19]

This statement may reveal purely political motives by the Court, since when a contracting state is engaged in armed conflict outside its own territory and lodges a formal declaration under article 15 ECHR, this declaration may be seen as harbouring an intention to violate human rights with impunity in the course of military operations. States may prefer, therefore, not to make use of this declaration, which incites unfavourable public opinion. Additionally, article 15 only allows states to exceptionally derogate from article 2 ECHR in cases of lawful acts of war but the use of force, which is not in accordance with and cannot be justified under article 51 UN Charter, or has not been authorised by the UN Security Council under Chapter VII of the Charter, is not a legal basis for derogating from article 2. As rightly emphasised, in such a case it cannot be expected that states engaged in legally dubious military missions would make any derogations under article 15 ECHR, as it is likely to draw attention to the potential illegality of their actions.[20]

The Court also added that:

> the case-law of the Court demonstrates that its recognition of the exercise of extra-territorial jurisdiction by a Contracting State is exceptional: it has done so when the respondent State, through the effective control of the relevant territory and its inhabitants abroad as a consequence of military occupation or through the consent, invitation or acquiescence of the Government of that territory, exercises all or some of the public powers normally to be exercised by that Government.[21]

Nevertheless, the most important argument behind the decisive reasoning of the Court in seeking to narrow as far as possible the extraterritorial application of the ECHR, with regard to military operations out of Europe, was the following:

> In short, the Convention is a multi-lateral treaty operating, subject to Article 56 of the Convention, in an essentially regional context and notably in the legal space (*espace juridique*) of the Contracting States. The FRY clearly does not fall within this legal space. The Convention was not designed to be applied throughout the world, even in respect of the conduct of Contracting States. Accordingly, the desirability of avoiding a gap or vacuum in human rights' protection has so far been relied on by the Court in favour of establishing jurisdiction only when the territory in question was one that, but for the specific circumstances, would normally be covered by the Convention.[22]

Once decided that the ordinary territorial meaning of jurisdiction would make it applicable outside of the European space only in exceptional circumstances, the Court found that the air strikes on the Serbian television station causing deaths and

[19] ibid, para 62.

[20] See E Roxstrom, M Gibney and T Einarsen, 'The NATO bombing case (*Bankovic et al v Belgium et al*) and the limits of Western human rights protection' (2005) 23 *Boston University International Law Journal* 55–136, 118, 121.

[21] *Bankovic*, above n 4, para 71.

[22] ibid, para 80.

injuries were not equivalent to military ground control, that is, territorial control could only be attained through ground forces, and not through aerial domination. The case was, therefore, declared inadmissible, thus completely disregarding the effective control of the harmful operation itself, which means being in control of the decision to bomb or not, and, should a decision be taken to bomb, deciding up to what point.

Finally, as far as the methodology used by the Court in order to render such reasoning on the substance is concerned, the ECtHR has underlined the need to interpret the concept of jurisdiction of article 1 ECHR according to the ordinary meaning of the term in public international law. However, it has ignored the fact that jurisdiction under article 1 ECHR serves a completely different purpose from the purpose it serves under public international law. Article 1 ECHR makes it clear that jurisdiction is intended to regulate the relationship between the contracting parties and the category of persons to whom the state must provide the rights enumerated under the Convention.[23]

Equally, the new restrictive interpretation of jurisdiction from *Bankovic* includes inaccurate terms with widely differing meanings, as, for instance, when it states that 'the Convention applies *essentially* in a regional context, and *notably* in the legal space', two overly broad, open terms which may indicate that the Convention does not necessarily apply only in this area.[24]

Criticisms concerning this decision have been numerous and significant, mainly taking into account some very controversial statements made by the Court. In this vein, it has been said that the distinction made by the Court between aerial domination through the use of force and ground domination, even if the Court reiterates its insistence on the importance of effective control makes no sense nowadays, and that to regard air superiority as being a materially less 'effective' form of control would be incorrect in military terms. This is especially so, taking into account the sophistication of the types of weapons used, and the states' increasing preference for a means of warfare that, for the attacking state, diminishes the risk of their incurring casualties (eg drones). Moreover, it would cause major setbacks in the advancement of mechanisms for the protection of the civilians in war and assure the accountability of nation states, whilst creating inequality in favour of powerful states.[25]

[23] See A Orakhelashvili, 'Restrictive Interpretation of Human Rights Treaties in the Recent Jurisprudence of the European Court of Human Rights' (2003) 14 *European Journal of International Law* 529–68, 540; M Gondek, 'Extraterritorial Application of the European Convention on Human Rights: Territorial Focus in the Age of Globalization?' (2005) 52 *Netherlands International Law Review* 349–87, 367.

[24] See R Wilde, above n 4, 117; Roxstrom et al, above n 20, 60. Also, in a subsequent judgement the Court, when defining 'the territorial principle' has added some more open terms such as 'primarily territorial ... to be exercised normally ...'; see case of *Al-Skeini and Ors v United Kingdom* App no 55721/07 (ECtHR, 7 July 2011) 53 EHRR 18, para 131 (emphasis added).

[25] See M Kearney, 'Extraterritorial Jurisdiction of the European Convention on Human Rights' (2002) 5 *Trinity College Law Review* 126–57, 138; K Altiparmak, '*Bankovic*: an obstacle to the application of the European Convention on Human Rights in Iraq?' (2009) 9 *Journal of Conflict & Security Law* 213–51, 227.

Similarly, the way in which the Court interpreted article 1 in *Bankovic*, despite invoking the ordinary criteria of the treaty interpretation according to public international law, has been much criticised. This was due to the Court's misunderstanding of the meaning of both terms in public international law and in the framework of the Convention.[26] As suggested, such a wrong reasoning enables the Court to hide the true reasons of policy for its decision behind a veneer of respect for general international law.[27] Also, as rightly pointed out, the objective nature of a specific human rights treaty, and the consequences thereof, seem to be attributable to the character of the substantive obligations enshrined in the Convention and not to whether the treaty is universal or regional in scope.[28]

IV. REGRESSION IN THE CONCEPT OF JURISDICTION AND INTERNATIONAL RESPONSIBILITY OF IGOs

Six years later, and still with regard to the previous conflict in Kosovo, the ECtHR had to adjudicate on two applications dealing with different tasks assumed by the international forces serving respectively under the UN Interim Mission in Kosovo (UNMIK) and the Kosovo Force (KFOR). In the *Behrami* case[29] the Court was asked to decide on an application where, as a consequence of the failure to clarify a particular zone as being under the responsibility of KFOR—consisting of French and Norwegian forces—a cluster bomb exploded, resulting in one death and causing two young boys severe injuries. Contemporaneously, another application was lodged against the detention of Mr Saramati by UNMIK police, on suspicion of representing a threat to the security of KFOR and those residing in Kosovo. It is clear that both facts took place outside the 'European space' and that, as members of the international force on the ground, some contracting parties to the Convention were involved. The Court decided to join both applications, finally adjudicating on the inadmissibility of the case.

The final result, as in *Bankovic*, was also shadowed by political considerations and some fear to adjudicate on potential breaches of human rights by contracting parties engaged in military operations abroad. To begin with, the Court declared:

> The Court therefore considers that the question raised by the present cases is, less whether the respondent States exercised extra-territorial jurisdiction in Kosovo but far more centrally, whether this Court is competent to examine under the Convention those States' contribution to the civil and security presences which did exercise the relevant control of Kosovo.[30]

Doubts expressed by the Court clearly spoke of a worry concerning its role as any sort of potential last resource court for those persons whose human rights could

[26] See M Milanovic, 'From Compromise to Principle: Clarifying the Concept of State Jurisdiction in Human Rights Treaties' (2008) 8 *Human Rights Law Review* 411–48, 417–19.

[27] ibid, 436.

[28] See Orakhelashvili, above n 23, 532.

[29] *Behrami and Saramati*, App nos 71412/01 and 78166/01 (decision as to admissibility, 2 May 2007).

[30] ibid, para 71.

have been affected by military operations on third countries' territories, or anything close to a court with universal jurisdiction. Yet, instead of discussing the scope of the application of article 1 ECHR, the Court turned its attention to its competence to review acts in compliance with UNSC mandate:

> The question arises in the present case whether the Court is competent *ratione personae* to review the acts of the respondent States carried out on behalf of the UN and, more generally, as to the relationship between the Convention and the UN acting under Chapter VII of its Charter.[31]

The Court in *Behrami and Saramati* adopted its final decision with the following reasoning:

> In the present case, Chapter VII allowed the UNSC to adopt coercive measures in reaction to an identified conflict considered to threaten peace, namely UNSC Resolution 1244 establishing UNMIK and KFOR.
>
> Since operations established by UNSC Resolutions under Chapter VII of the UN charter are fundamental to the mission of the UN to secure international peace and security and since they rely for their effectiveness on support from member states, the Convention cannot be interpreted in a manner which would subject the acts and omissions of Contracting Parties which are covered by UNSC Resolutions and occur prior to or in the course of such missions, to the scrutiny of the Court. To do so would be to interfere with the fulfilment of the UN's key mission in this field including, as argued by certain parties, with the effective conduct of its operations. It would also be tantamount to imposing conditions on the implementation of a UNSC Resolution which were not provided for in the text of the Resolution itself.[32]

The Court, entering into the labyrinth of attributions of the given behaviour, avoided pronouncing on the responsibility of the contracting parties concerning breaches of the Convention. However, the attributability of the relevant acts and/or omissions to the UN does not prevent contracting parties to the Convention from incurring responsibility for the internationally wrongful conduct of KFOR and UNMIK, or even the possibility that the same conduct could be attributable to the respondent national states and might engage their international responsibility.

With such a narrow and evasive approach, the Court created the risk of removing all potential responsibility from civilian or military personnel contributed by ECHR contracting parties to any peace support operation. It was so even if the personnel who contributed should be able to exercise extra-territorial jurisdiction within the meaning of article 1 ECHR in the case of their behaviour or activities being in breach of the Convention and, therefore, attributable to their national states.[33]

[31] ibid, para 146.

[32] ibid, para 149.

[33] In fact, the Court has already relied on *Behrami and Saramati* as a precedent and has declared itself incompetent *ratione personae* in order to review the conduct of KFOR members as acts of states carried out on behalf of the UN. See *Ilaz Kasumaj v Greece* App no 6974/05 (ECtHR, 5 July 2007); *Slavisa Gajic v Germany* App no 31446/02 (ECtHR, 28 August 2007; *Dusan Beric and Ors v Bosnia and Herzegovina* App nos 36357/04; 36360/04; 38346/04; 41705/04; 45190/04; 45578/04; 45579/04; 45580/04; 91/05; 97/05; 100/05; 101/05; 101/05; 1121/05; 1123/05; 1125/05; 1129/05; 1132/05; 1133/05; 1169/05; 1169/05; 1169/05; 1169/05; 1172/05; 1175/05; 1177/05; 1177/05; 1180/05; 1180/05; 1185/05; 20793/05; 25496/05 (ECtHR, 16 October 2007).

However, the more reasonable approach of the Court in these cases would have been to examine every complaint concerning the conduct of national forces carrying out peace support operations, on a case-by-case basis, in order to decide whether or not the alleged breach was committed in a national or international capacity. This is because any act performed outside the scope of the international mandate of the operation, or outside its chain of command, should be considered to have been carried out in a national capacity and, consequently, to have created a sufficient jurisdictional link between the applicants and the respondent state such as to engage—if this be the case—its international responsibility under the ECHR.[34]

What is clear, however, is that the primacy of the UN Charter over the ECHR does not necessarily restrict the powers of the ECtHR over national contingents, as the decision to participate in operations authorised by the UNSC is voluntary. As correctly stated, the decision of the ECtHR to declare itself incompetent to review the conduct of personnel contributed by ECHR states to peace support operations, authorised under Chapter VII, is therefore not justified. Furthermore, it sends a wrong message to troop-contributing states, since these states could transfer operational command over their contingents to an international organisation, thus evading responsibility for any breaches of the ECHR committed by those forces on the territory of a third state, in alleging that their acts were performed in an international capacity.[35]

A clear conclusion can be drawn from the Court's reasoning. At a time when some contemporary judgments of the ECtHR on the extra-territorial application of the ECHR, on the grounds of a territorial link, were addressing the deeply criticised and restrictive judgment in *Bankovic*, in *Behrami and Saramati* the final decision of the Court constitutes a self-censorship justified by a sacrosanct respect for international law and, in particular, for the UN's role in keeping peace and security, the sole justification for this being the political—and not legal—consideration that:

> such acts may not have amounted to obligations flowing from membership of the UN but they remained crucial to the effective fulfilment by the UNSC of its Chapter VII mandate and, consequently, by the UN of its imperative peace and security aim.[36]

However, judgments of the Strasbourg Court, which have also concerned acts carried out by individual members of international contingents performing different missions on Iraq's territory, have sent more promising signals, as we shall see in the next section.

V. POSITIVE STEPS OPPOSING THE RESTRICTIVE APPROACH OF *BANKOVIC*

Continuing with its insistence on the territorial nature of jurisdiction, as highlighted in *Bankovic*, the Court added a new version of overall control of the territory of a third country when deliberating in *Ilascu v Moldova and Russia* on whether the

[34] See A Sari, 'Jurisdiction and International Responsibility in Peace Support Operations: The Behrami and Saramati Cases' (2008) 8 *Human Rights Law Review* 151–70, 166, 169.

[35] ibid, 168.

[36] See *Behrami and Saramati* decision, above n 29, para 149 *in fine*.

applicants' complaints fell under article 1 ECHR. The case dealt with the conviction and imprisonment of several sympathisers of the self-proclaimed independent Moldavian Republic of Transdniestria, which was in receipt of de facto economic, military and political support from the Russian Federation, but formally within Moldova's territory and under her jurisdiction. In *Ilascu v Moldova and Russia* the Court added, as an example of the possible extraterritorial application of the Convention, according to the criteria of 'overall control', the 'acts of war or rebellion, or the acts of a foreign State supporting the installation of a separatist State within the territory of the State concerned.'[37] However, despite its insistence on upholding the reasoning in *Bankovic*, the Court went back to the Cypriot cases, and to a wider approach, reinterpreting the term 'jurisdiction' in a more appropriate way. It expressed itself thus:

> the Court observes that, *although* in Bankovic and Others ... it emphasised the preponderance of the territorial principle in the application of the Convention, it has *also* acknowledged that *the concept of 'jurisdiction' within the meaning of Article 1 of the Convention is not necessarily restricted to the national territory of the High Contracting Parties.*[38]

The Court accepted that 'in exceptional circumstances the acts of Contracting States performed outside their territory, or which produce effects there, may amount to *exercise by them of their jurisdiction* within the meaning of Article 1 of the Convention.'[39]

Beyond the positive recovery of the wider concept of jurisdiction, as defined by the Court in pre-*Bankovic* applications, in *Issa and Ors v Turkey* it went one step further. In that case, under discussion was whether the application lodged by a group of Turkish applicants on behalf of their deceased relatives, all of them allegedly killed by Turkish officers on Iraqi soil, that is, beyond the Turkish-Iraqi border, was admissible under article 1 ECHR. The Court in *Issa v Turkey* not only declared the application admissible, but also in its judgment, on the basis of the territorial control criteria, admitted the possibility of a breach of the Convention, due to the extraterritorial application of article 2 in more flexible circumstances as far as control was concerned, as follows:

> The Court does not exclude the possibility that, as a consequence of this military action, the respondent State could *be considered to have exercised, temporarily, effective overall control of a particular portion of the territory of northern Iraq*. Accordingly, if there is a

[37] See *Ilascu and Ors v Moldova and Russia*, App no 48787/99 (ECtHR, 8 July 2004), para 312. Expanding on this concept, the Court later argued: 'In addition, the acquiescence or connivance of the authorities of a Contracting State in the acts of private individuals which violate the Convention rights of other individuals within its jurisdiction may engage the State's responsibility under the Convention. That is particularly true in the case of recognition by the State in question of the acts of self-proclaimed authorities which are not recognized by the international community.' Ibid, para 318.

[38] ibid, para 314 (emphasis added). See also *Isaak v Turkey* App no 44587/98 (ECtHR, 24 June 2008) concerning the killing of a Cypriot by a group of people, including civilians and some Turkish officers, in the UN buffer zone established in Cyprus, where the Court did not even discuss jurisdiction of the case and accepted a breach of art 2 of the Convention by Turkey, despite the deaths being caused only by civilians.

[39] ibid, para 314 (emphasis added); case of *Issa and Ors v Turkey* App no 31821/96 (ECtHR, 30 March 2005), para 68.

> sufficient factual basis for holding that, at the relevant time, the victims were within that specific area, it would follow logically that they were within the jurisdiction of Turkey...[40]

Although it may be that the final result was not satisfactory from a substantive point of view, since the Court returned a negative decision, due to the lack of sufficient evidence as to the presence of the Turkish officer on the precise date, the case has an important aspect. The Court not only accepted the extraterritorial application of the Convention on an exceptional basis but also the fact that occupation, domination or control need not be permanent; it can also be sufficient, in order to comply with this requirement, for such control to be only temporary. Nevertheless, it is also true that although the case involved a breach of the Convention on the territory of a non-contracting party to it (Iraq), the Court faced a 'traditional' case involving Turkey's war on Kurdish separatists, which remains far removed from military operations abroad, or any sort of humanitarian intervention.

Finally, a new line of cases inaugurated in 2010 constituted a far more significant contribution with regard to the review by the ECtHR of individual actions carried out by members of international contingents, potentially in breach of the ECHR's obligations. In three cases relating to the occupying forces in Iraq, not only did the ECtHR considered itself to be competent in the matter, or else that the facts fell within jurisdiction of article 1 ECHR, but the Court even condemned that behaviour as a breach of the Convention's obligations.[41]

The first case, *Al-Sadoon and Mufdhi v The United Kingdom*,[42] dealt with the hand-over of two Iraqi nationals detained on suspicion of having killed two British officers, and who were finally handed over to the Iraqi authorities, despite the reintroduction of capital punishment in the Iraqi criminal code for certain crimes, such as those of which the applicants stood accused. Applying the same doctrine inaugurated in the *Soering* case,[43] and obviating—despite allegations made by the United Kingdom—that the British forces were acting on a third country's territory in the framework of a multinational force, the Court had no doubt in considering such a surrender to be a breach of articles 2 and 3 ECHR.[44] For this they relied on a number of previous cases concerning any means of removal of a person, but also the *Bosphorus* case,[45] (specifically rejected in the *Behrami and Saramati* case)[46]

[40] *Issa and Ors v Turkey* ibid, para 74 (emphasis added).

[41] In this way, the Court established some important precedents that Fitzpatrick missed in order to support Theodor Meron's approach to this matter, who had earlier stated: 'there is no a priori reason to limit a state's obligation to respect human rights to its national territory. Where agents of the state, whether military or civilian, exercise power and authority jurisdiction, or de facto jurisdiction over persons outside national territory, the presumption should be that the state's obligation to respect the pertinent human rights continues. The presumption could be rebutted only when the nature and the content of a particular right or treaty language suggest otherwise.' See T Meron, 'Extraterritoriality of Human Rights Treaties (1995) 89 *American Journal of International Law* 78–82, 80–81; and see for this statement, J Fitzpatrick, 'Speaking Law to Power: The War Against Terrorism and Human Rights' (2003) 14 *European Journal of International Law* 241–64, 253.

[42] See *Al-Saadoon and Mufdhi v The United Kingdom* Appl no 61498/08 (ECtHR, 2 March 2010).

[43] *Soering v United Kingdom* (1989) Series A no 161.

[44] *Al-Saadoon and Mufdhi*, above n 42, para 143.

[45] See *Bosphorus Hava Yollari Tirizm ve Ticaret Anonim Sirketi v Ireland* App no 45036/98 (ECtHR, 30 June 2005).

[46] See *Behrami and Saramati*, above n 29, para 151.

and according to which the Court condemned the possibility of contracting parties acting in breach of the Convention's obligations because of their commitment to an international organisation (the UN). Nevertheless, it is also true that for the Court, in this case, there was one element that made an important difference: the fact that it was a multinational military operation led by the USA and the UK, and not a mission under the UN's mandate.

In the same vein, in *Al-Jedda v The United Kingdom*,[47] the ECtHR was called upon to adjudicate on an application lodged by an Iraqi/British national, detained by British troops in the British-run internment facility of Sha'aibah, Basrah, for a period of three years, in breach of article 5 ECHR (lack of judicial review). The British government contended that the Court did not have competence to adjudicate on the case, alleging that the internment was attributable to the UN and not to the UK and, therefore, the applicant did not fall within its jurisdiction according to article 1 ECHR. Alternatively, it argued that the internment had taken place pursuant to a UNSC mandate (SC Resolution 1546), which, according to article 103 UN Charter, had primacy over the Convention's obligations. The British government thus used the two main winning arguments presented in the *Bankovic* and *Behrami and Saramati* cases.

However, the ECtHR showed a wider approach, avoiding an automatic transposition of those arguments to this different case, stating first of all that:

> the Court is mindful of the fact that it is not its role to seek to define authoritatively the meaning of provisions of the United Nations Charter and other international instruments. It must, nevertheless, examine whether there was a plausible basis in such instruments for the matters impugned before it ... The principles underlying the Convention cannot be interpreted and applied in a vacuum and the Court must take into account relevant rules of international law... at the time of the invasion, there was no United Nations Security Council resolution providing for the allocation of roles in Iraq in the event that the existing regime was displaced ...

and furthermore:

> [T]he Court does not consider that, as a result of the authorisation contained in Resolution 1511, the acts of soldiers within the Multi-National Force became attributable to the United Nations or—more importantly, for the purposes of this case—ceased to be attributable to the troop-contributing nations ... Although the United States were requested to report periodically to the Security Council about the activities of the Multi-National Force, the United Nations did not, thereby, assume any degree of control over either the force or any other of the executive functions of the Coalition Provisional Authority.[48]

Again, the Court insisted on the difference between an operation under a UN mandate and the occupation of Iraq by means of a Multi-National Coalition of States, periodically reporting exclusively to the UN regarding their work on the ground.[49] Applying the doctrine of 'effective control', the Court went on to state that it

[47] See *Al-Jedda v The United Kingdom* [GC] App no 27021/08 (7 July 2011).
[48] ibid, paras 76–77, 80.
[49] ibid, para 83.

> considers that the United Nations Security Council had neither effective control nor ultimate authority and control over the acts and omissions of troops within the Multi-National Force and that the applicant's detention was not, therefore, attributable to the United Nations ... The internment took place within a detention facility in Basrah City, controlled exclusively by British forces, and the applicant was therefore within the authority and control of the United Kingdom throughout ...

In conclusion, the 'the internment of the applicant was attributable to the United Kingdom and that during his internment the applicant fell within the jurisdiction of the United Kingdom for the purposes of Article 1 of the Convention.'[50]

To summarise, a certain evolution appears to have taken place as far as military activities of contracting parties to the ECHR on third states' territories are concerned, although the new cases seem to insist on the self-restraint of the Court with regard to cases of military missions under mandate of the UN. Moreover, they have not clarified the question of discerning international responsibility of IGOs, troop-contributing states and national officers as far as those missions are concerned.

The same reasoning was followed by the Court in the *Al-Skeini* case,[51] concerning the killing of six Iraqi civilians in different situations by British soldiers—in particular one death during torture in a British-run internment facility in Iraq. In that case the Court found there to have been a breach of article 2 ECHR (right to life) under its procedural limb (duty to duly carry out an investigation on the deaths), and in so doing decided that the British soldiers implicated in the deaths were within jurisdiction of a contracting party according to article 1 ECHR. Noteworthy in *Al-Skeini* are some of the surprising allegations put forward by the respondent government of the United Kingdom, such as:

> the military action of the United Kingdom soldiers in shooting the applicants' relatives whilst carrying out military security operations in Iraq did not constitute an exercise of jurisdiction over them. No distinction could be drawn in this respect between a death resulting from a bombing and one resulting from a shooting in the course of a ground operation.[52]

However, this was precisely the main argument of those against the admissibility of the *Bankovic* application, namely that had it been a shooting instead of an aerial bombing, and thus, the application could have been declared admissible. Therefore, the main argument cannot serve one purpose and the opposite at the same time. This more generous approach by the ECtHR to jurisdiction is also evident in the way it considers article 56 ECHR:

> The existence of this mechanism [article 56 ECHR], which was included in the Convention for historical reasons, cannot be interpreted in present conditions as limiting the scope of the term 'jurisdiction' under Article 1. The situations covered by the 'effective control' principle are clearly separate and distinct from circumstances where a Contracting State has not, through a declaration under Article 56, extended the Convention or any of its Protocols to an overseas territory for whose international relations it is responsible.[53]

[50] ibid, paras 84–86.
[51] See *Al-Skeini and Ors*, above n 24.
[52] ibid, para 116.
[53] ibid, para 140.

This approach, together with the remark, phrased in broad terms, on the case law concerning Cypriot cases, namely that:

> The Court has emphasised that, where the territory of one Convention State is occupied by the armed forces of another, the occupying State should in principle be held accountable under the Convention for breaches of human rights within the occupied territory, because to hold otherwise would be to deprive the population of that territory of the rights and freedoms hitherto enjoyed and would result in a 'vacuum' of protection within the 'Convention legal space'... However, the importance of establishing the occupying State's jurisdiction in such cases does not imply, *a contrario*, that jurisdiction under Article 1 of the Convention can never exist outside the territory covered by the Council of Europe Member States. The Court has not in its case-law applied any such restriction.[54]

Finally, the Court decided that

> the United Kingdom, through its soldiers engaged in security operations in Basrah during the period in question, exercised authority and control over individuals killed in the course of such security operations, so as to establish a jurisdictional link between the deceased and the United Kingdom for the purposes of Article 1 of the Convention.[55]

VI. FINAL REFLECTIONS

As previously stated, the ability to hold governments of individual states accountable in international law, and to hold states responsible for their actions both at home and abroad, is of immense significance.[56] On this central point some key conclusions can be inferred from the Court's reasoning.

As far as extraterritorial jurisdiction concerning situations with a territorial link (effective control) is concerned, a very negative message, such as that in *Bankovic*, has been sent by the Court: human rights are universal and compulsory when powerful states, mainly Western states, so decide. In this vein the Court has dangerously followed, with complete obedience, the reasoning proposed by contracting parties both in *Bankovic* and *Behrami and Saramati* (use of force cases).

In addition, political motives appear to be behind these decisions reached by the Court[57] based, moreover, on an untenable argument[58] that the type of use of force employed to exercise control over a territory was by means of aerial strikes. However, as previously stated, although it may be said that the NATO alliance did not have control of the territory in as comprehensive a manner as Turkey had in

[54] ibid, para 142.
[55] ibid, para 149.
[56] See Kearney, above n 25, 136.
[57] See Wilde, above n 4, 119; Sari, above n 34, 170.
[58] Especially since the Court has evaluated completely differently the importance of control exercised by a population on a territory through aerial strikes in counter-terrorism cases, in particular in those cases concerning aerial bombing of Chechen villages by Russian armed forces. See, amongst other authorities, *Esmukhambetov and Ors v Russia* App no 23445/03 (ECtHR, 29 March 2011); *Khamzayev and Ors v Russia*, App no 1503/02 (3 May 2011); and *Kerimova and Ors v Russia*, App nos 17170/04, 20792/04, 22448/04, 23360/04, 5681/05 and 5684/05 (ECtHR, 3 May 2011).

Northern Cyprus, they exerted complete air dominance. Therefore, the question of choosing a specific kind of dominance, ie earth, air or sea, is mainly to do with casualties and risks, but has nothing to do with overall dominance or control, particularly when considering the level of sophistication of NATO air forces. In fact, modern warfare is reliant more upon air dominance (eg the Libyan intervention). Additionally, it has been rightly pointed out that to regard air superiority as being a materially less 'effective control' would not only be incorrect in military terms, but would also cause a major setback to the advancement of mechanisms for the accountability of Nation States and the protection of civilians in war.[59] Moreover, the absolute command and effective control of the bombing itself was in the hands of those states which were also contracting parties to the Convention.

The broad criteria set down by the Court in the Cypriot cases has been progressively narrowed, and in particular with regard to the use of force either by a coalition of states or under the auspices of an international organisation (UN, NATO). Accepting that the Court may not feel comfortable having to adjudicate on the activities accorded by the United Nations, this discomfort, when the breach is the consequence of armed activities of a coalition of states (Iraq), can only be explained when considering it as dependent upon the composition of the states comprising the coalition.[60]

Above all, given the centrality of human rights as a kind of secular unifying ideology for the global order, and in particular taking into account the centrality of human rights as the ideological nexus of European peoples and institutions, the Court should find jurisdiction over all territories in which states, subject to the Court's jurisdiction, are arguably complicit.[61] In a word, states cannot be allowed to do outside their territories that which they are conventionally prevented from doing within.

It has been argued that the obligations of the ECHR are culturally specific, and thereby inappropriate for application in situations taking place outside out of their cultural context. When the *Al-Skeini* case was discussed before the House of Lords, the Court raised the question of whether application of the ECHR to the United Kingdom in Iraq might involve inculcating 'the common spiritual heritage of the member states of the country of Europe' in a 'predominantly Muslim country'. In the same case, at a later stage, Lord Brown pointed out that unless an ECHR contracting state is within the area of the Council of Europe, 'it is unlikely ... to find certain of the Convention rights it is bound to secure reconcilable with the customs of the resident population', invoking Shari'a law as an example. However, Lord Brown perhaps failed to consider that the fight against impunity is a common value to any legal culture; the Convention, as it has been stated, cannot be said to be antithetical to the Iraqi or any other non-European culture per se.[62] Moreover, as has been pointed out, it might be that, if anything, subjecting the UK presence in

[59] See Kearney, above n 25, 138.

[60] See in this vein H King, 'The Extraterritorial Human Rights Obligations of States (2009) 9 *Human Rights Law Review* 521–56, 555.

[61] See Altiparmak, above n 25, 218.

[62] See T Thienel, 'The ECHR in Iraq. The Judgment of the House of Lords in *R (Al-Skeini) v Secretary of State for Defence*' (2008) 6 *Journal of International Criminal Justice* 115–28, 124.

Iraq to the regulation of human rights law would have the effect of mitigating, not exacerbating, the colonial nature of the occupation.[63]

States parties to the ECHR have taken part in all major recent conflicts, such as those in Yugoslavia, Iraq, Afghanistan, Libya, and also for many years, in the so-called 'war on terror'. Extra-territorial jurisdiction has been widely conceived and applied in some others situations, eg counter-terrorism cases, although it still remains unclear whether the Court will accept its responsibility in controlling breaches of the Convention by contracting parties occurring out of the 'European space', in situations including the use of force, although there appear to be some positive signals.

As previously suggested, perhaps the most regrettable restrictive approach in *Bankovic* was nothing more than the result of the ECtHR's concern, in its capacity of exercising regional human rights jurisdiction, that it would be perceived by third states as a Court exercising a sort of universal jurisdiction. Additionally, although the Court has paid a considerable price for its decision, so too have the victims, who, as a result of this decision suffer feelings of frustration and incomprehension.[64]

There is no doubt that this uncertainty and obscurity, in the case law concerning such a pressing legal and policy matter, risks undermining the Court's institutional credibility from an external point of view,[65] and that such doctrinal ambivalence could prevent contracting parties from accurately weighing the legal liabilities associated with particular extraterritorial actions, to the detriment of both human rights protection, security and finally peace. There is also the risk of the Court being overwhelmed by thousands of applications being filed before the Court. However, this would again be an overly simplistic, alarmist and risky way of explaining things, as we could not but hold that there is never too much of a risk in limiting the use of force or in protecting human rights.

Concerns about the success of military collective action by the international community are indeed important. Moreover, it is also worth keeping in mind the fear that

> anyone adversely affected by an act imputable to a Contracting State, wherever in the world that act may have been committed or its consequences felt, is thereby brought within the jurisdiction of that State for the purpose of Article 1 of the Convention.[66]

What is even more important, however, is the ability to guarantee that the rule of law applies during a humanitarian intervention, where the standards of human rights protection ought to be higher, in particular where there is no authorisation by the UN Security Council. And this can only be achieved through the accountability of those that carry out the intervention. This, of course, does not imply that humanitarian intervention should be treated differently to other extraterritorial acts. It merely

[63] See R Wilde, 'Triggering State Obligations Extraterritorially: The Spatial Test in Certain Human Rights Treaties' (2007) 40 *Israel Law Review* 503–26, 521.

[64] See G Cohen-Jonathan, 'Observations. La territorialisation de la juridiction de la Cour européenne des droits de l'homme' (2002) 52 *Revue Trimestrielle des Droits de l'Homme* 1055–82.

[65] See S Miller, 'Revisiting Extraterritorial Jurisdiction: A Territorial Justification for Extraterritorial Jurisdiction under the European Convention (2009) 20 *European Journal of International Law* 1223–46, 1229–30.

[66] *Bankovic*, above n 4, para 75.

emphasises that the more controversial the legality of an act, the more compelling the reasons for examining its compliance with human rights law become.[67]

Legal responses to both problems—use of force and countering terrorism—whether involving general or tailor-made solutions, necessarily imply making political options, all of which are grounded on moral assets, cultural inputs and the pursuit of community goals. It is assumed that the higher the political commitment among member states of a given system, the wider the cooperation and the more efficient mechanisms will ensure, resulting in the creation of a complete common system. It seems that, as a consequence of the exercise of power and the use of force outside each state's territorial limits, there is an emerging consensus on the extraterritorial application of human rights treaties.[68]

In the centre lies the ECtHR, since European states have taken a prominent part in military interventions, alongside other partners from within international organisations or among an international coalition of states. Its strong stand in favour of accountability of its contracting parties for any breach of rights protected by the ECHR either within or outside Europe reinforces the rule of law, human rights protection and, finally, peace and security beyond, and as a result of, the European system. This is perhaps one of the best possible contributions of European regionalism to international peace and security, preventing at least contracting parties to the ECHR from acting with impunity abroad. In the words of Judge Bonello: 'those who export war ought to see to parallel export of guarantees against the atrocities of war.'[69]

[67] See V Mantouvalu, 'Extending Judicial Control in International Law: Human Rights Treaties and Extraterritoriality' (2005) 9 *International Journal of Human Rights* 147–63, 159.

[68] For a detailed analysis of this aspect see: OA Hathaway et al, 'Human rights abroad: when do Human Rights Treaty Obligations Apply Extraterritorially? (2011) 43 *Arizona State Law Journal* 1–38.

[69] See *Al-Skeini* case, above n 24, Concurring Opinion of Judge Bonello, para 38.

20

Commentaire sur Corten et Salinas

MOHAMED BENNOUNA*

OLIVER CORTEN ET Ana Salinas ont traité deux aspects importants de l'impact du régionalisme sur la paix et la sécurité internationales, d'une part « le droit d'intervention » inscrit dans l'acte constitutif de l'Union africaine (UA) et, d'autre part « l'application extraterritoriale de la Convention européenne des droits de l'homme (CEDH) ».

En dehors de la recherche de la contribution des deux instances régionales, l'Union africaine et la Cour européenne des droits de l'homme, au maintien de la paix et de la sécurité internationales, les deux intervenants se sont posé la question cruciale des limites de ces contributions en relation avec l'action des Nations Unies et les valeurs universelles qu'elles incarnent. Il s'agit, à mon avis, d'une question centrale dans l'appréciation de l'apport du régionalisme à la paix et à la sécurité internationales, question qui revient à se demander si le régionalisme, arguant d'une spécificité donnée, peut se constituer en un ensemble fermé, recroquevillé sur ses propres valeurs et sa propre conception de la légitimité, au risque de retomber dans le modèle d'une sainte alliance, soumise à la domination des puissances du moment.

Certes, il ne s'agit pas là d'une question nouvelle, mais il est intéressant que les deux intervenants l'aient posée sous l'angle de deux pratiques différentes, qui ont pris place au sein des deux ensembles régionaux africain et européen. Pour les besoins de la discussion, je vais revisiter successivement les deux exposés que nous venons d'entendre.

Ce qui caractérise le droit d'intervention de l'Union africaine, prévu dans le nouvel article 4h) de son acte constitutif, c'est la possibilité offerte à cette organisation d'engager une action coercitive, par la force armée, dans l'un de ses Etats membres, à l'occasion de situations très graves telles que les crimes de guerre, le génocide et les crimes contre l'humanité. Apparemment, ce droit d'intervention, avec l'usage de la force, relèverait de la seule organisation régionale, sans autorisation préalable du Conseil de sécurité comme cela est prévu expressément au Chapitre VIII de la Charte. La responsabilité principale du Conseil dans le maintien de la paix et de la sécurité serait ainsi remise en cause.

Olivier Corten rappelle la controverse doctrinale suscitée par l'article 4h) de l'acte constitutif de l'Union africaine, les uns estimant que celui-ci peut faire exception au système de la Charte et les autres considérant qu'il ne confère des compétences à

* Juge à la Cour internationale de Justice. Membre de l'Institut de droit international.

l'UA que sous réserve du respect de la Charte des Nations Unies. Pour les départager, il a procédé, sur une base objective, à l'analyse de l'*opinio juris* et de la pratique récente des Etats, notamment africains. Le résultat de cette analyse n'est pas surprenant, l'Afrique ne bénéficie, en effet, d'aucune exception par rapport au principe de la centralisation, aux mains du Conseil de sécurité du recours à la force dans les relations internationales (en dehors du cas de légitime défense). Bien que je partage cette analyse, je ne suis pas persuadé, comme l'affirme Olivier Corten, que les opérations dites de maintien de la paix menées par la Communauté économique des Etats de l'Afrique de l'Ouest (CEDEAO) au cours de la décennie 90 dans certains pays africains, le Libéria et la Sierra Leone, avec le consentement des gouvernements concernés, ne relèvent pas de l'article 53 de la Charte (nécessité d'une autorisation du Conseil) mais de l'article 52 (règlement pacifique des différends). Il me paraît discutable que de telles opérations de maintien de la paix puissent échapper à l'exigence d'une autorisation préalable du Conseil de sécurité et à son contrôle. Surtout qu'il s'agit du recours à la force à la demande d'un gouvernement dont la légitimité a été remise en cause par sa propre population (on peut se reporter à ce sujet à la résolution adoptée par l'Institut de droit international, en septembre 2011, à la session de Rhodes). Quant à l'article 52, il réserve l'activité des organismes régionaux dans la mesure où elle est compatible avec les buts et principes des Nations Unies. C'est pour cela d'ailleurs que l'amendement de l'article 4h), afin d'y ajouter une « menace grave à l'ordre légitime », a suscité tant de controverses.

Il me semble que si une intervention militaire régionale pour le maintien de la paix devait se profiler au Mali, elle nécessiterait l'autorisation préalable du Conseil de sécurité. Les derniers développements dans cette affaire semblent le confirmer, puisqu'une demande dans ce sens a été adressée par le Mali au Secrétaire général des Nations Unies en septembre 2010.

Enfin, il faudrait également ne pas perdre de vue le concept de « responsabilité de protéger » introduit dans le document du sommet des Nations Unies de 2005 (par. 138 et 139). Il y est prévu en effet qu'en cas de défaillance de l'Etat à protéger ses propres populations du génocide, des crimes de guerre et des crimes contre l'humanité, « une action collective peut être menée par le Conseil de sécurité ... en coopération, le cas échéant, avec les organisations régionales » ; ce qui, clairement, ne permet pas une intervention autonome de celles-ci. D'ailleurs, relatant l'intervention armée en Libye, sur la base de la résolution 1973 (2011) du Conseil de sécurité, Olivier Corten souligne que l'Union africaine a été purement et simplement écartée de la mise en œuvre de cette résolution, laquelle a servi finalement au renversement du Gouvernement libyen par la force. L'UA a certes contesté l'interprétation qui a été faite de ce texte par des pays de l'Organisation du Traité de l'Atlantique Nord (OTAN), mais elle n'en a pas rejeté le principe.

Il reste que, dans cette affaire, l'OTAN n'a pas, jusqu'à présent, assumé ses responsabilités à l'égard des victimes civiles des frappes aériennes. La commission d'enquête internationale, créée par le Conseil des droits de l'homme de l'Organisation des Nations Unies, a demandé, en vain, à l'OTAN de mener les enquêtes nécessaires au sujet des victimes en question et de leur fournir, s'il y a lieu, les réparations adéquates.

Ana Salinas a considéré, précisément, en conclusion de son étude sur l'application extraterritoriale de la Convention européenne des droits de l'homme, qu'il s'agit là de la meilleure contribution du régionalisme européen à la paix et à la sécurité internationales. Celle-ci consiste en effet à empêcher les Etats parties à agir à l'étranger en toute impunité. En particulier, lorsqu'un Etat partie exerce un contrôle effectif sur un territoire étranger, la Cour européenne des droits de l'homme a considéré que son comportement, à l'égard des personnes qui s'y trouvent, relève de sa compétence conformément à l'article premier de la Convention. Mais alors, pourquoi la Cour, se demande Ana Salinas, n'a-t-elle pas accepté, dans l'affaire *Bankovic* en 2001, d'étendre cette interprétation de sa compétence aux bombardements aériens par l'OTAN de la Serbie ?

Je ne suis pas persuadé que le bombardement aérien d'un territoire puisse être assimilé au contrôle effectif de celui-ci. Je me demande si on ne se trouve pas tout simplement dans la situation de la mise en jeu de la responsabilité internationale d'un Etat à la suite du recours à la force armée contre un autre Etat. Quoiqu'il en soit, la question essentielle de l'étendue de l'application de la Convention européenne, en dehors de l'espace juridique européen, se pose.

Il en est ainsi, comme le relève Ana Salinas, de la participation des forces armées des Etats parties au sein d'une force multinationale à l'étranger, dans le cadre d'un mandat des Nations Unies, comme ce fut le cas, notamment, en ce qui concerne la Mission d'administration intérimaire des Nations Unies au Kosovo (MINUK).

Je serai là aussi en faveur de l'interprétation restrictive que la Cour a donnée de sa compétence, en refusant d'interférer dans la mise en œuvre de la résolution 1244 du Conseil de sécurité, autorisant l'intervention au Kosovo. Je rejoins par conséquent ceux qui pensent que le régionalisme trouve ses limites dans l'action de l'organisation universelle (voir l'affaire *Behrami et Saramati* (2007) devant la Cour européenne)[1]. Ceci étant, lorsque lesdites forces multinationales, comme en Iraq, échappent entièrement à l'autorité des Nations Unies, il est concevable que la Cour puisse se déclarer compétente à l'égard du comportement d'un Etat partie qui se trouverait dans cette situation (voir l'affaire *Al-Jedda et AlSkeini c. Royaume-Uni*(2011)),[2] et sur la base du critère du contrôle effectif. Nous nous retrouvons dans la situation déjà tranchée par la Cour internationale de Justice dans l'affaire de l'édification du mur dans le territoire palestinien occupé, soit celle d'une puissance occupante qui demeure responsable des violations de ses obligations en matière de protection internationale des droits de l'homme.[3]

En somme, si le recours à la force à l'échelle régionale est subordonné à l'autorisation du Conseil de sécurité, les Etats concernés, dans ces opérations, devraient répondre de leurs actes, notamment devant les cours régionales des droits de l'homme, lorsqu'ils exercent un contrôle effectif sur des territoires étrangers. Je conçois cependant que la notion d'effectivité et sa portée, en la matière, puissent faire l'objet de débats de la part de ceux qui souhaitent élargir le champ de protection des droits humains par delà l'espace territorial des conventions régionales.

[1] Cour européenne des droits de l'homme (Grande chambre), *Agim Behrami et Bekir Behrami c. France* (requête 74112/01) et *Ruzdhi Saramati c France, Allemagne et Norvège* (requête 78166/01), 2 mai 2007.

[2] Cour européenne des droits de l'homme (Grande chambre), *Al-Jedda c. Royaume-Uni* (requête n°27021/08) et *Al-Skeini et autres c. Royaume-Uni* (requête n°55721/07), 7 juillet 2011.

[3] *Conséquences juridiques de l'édification d'un mur dans le territoire palestinien occupé, avis consultatif,* CIJ Recueil (2004), p 178, par 106 et p 181, par 112.

21

Regionalism in the Field: The Case of South Sudan

JUAN JORGE PIERNAS LÓPEZ*

I. INTRODUCTION

THIS CONTRIBUTION AIMS at analysing the performance and interplay of the African Union, the European Union and United Nations in Sudan and South Sudan. In particular, the chapter examines the relationship between the two regional organisations and the universal organisation *par excellence* on the ground, and attempts to answer questions such as the following: how is the distribution of tasks between the three organisations carried out? Do any of them exercise a clear leadership? What are the principles that guide the relationship between the three organisations? Is it complementarity? Is it subsidiarity? Is there a hierarchy in place between the three organisations? Should there be one?

II. THE AU IN SUDAN AND SOUTH SUDAN

The African Union (AU) has been involved in Sudan, including Darfur, since shortly after its creation in 2002. In fact, the AU was the first organisation to intervene decisively in Darfur, ahead of the United Nations (UN) and the European Union (EU),[1] through the African Union Mission in Sudan (AMIS), a peacekeeping operation to ensure compliance and implementation of the N'Djamena Agreement on humanitarian ceasefire, signed in April 2004. This mission was subsequently endorsed by the UN Security Council (UNSC). Also in 2004, the Peace and Security Council of the AU extended the original mandate of AMIS to include, inter alia, the verification of compliance with the agreements reached between the parties subsequent to the

* LLD, European University Institute, Florence, Italy. Assistant Professor of EU and International Law at University of Murcia, Spain. This work results from the Spanish Ministry of Science and Innovation's Research Project, entitled 'La contribución del Derecho Internacional y sus instituciones (Organización de Naciones Unidas, Corte Penal Internacional y Unión Europea) a los intentos de solución de la crisis humanitaria de Darfur (Sudán)' ['The contribution of international law and its institutions (United Nations, International Criminal Court and the EU) to the attempts to solve the humanitarian crisis in Darfur (Sudan)'] (ref: DER2009-0739, 01/01/2010 to 31/12/2012).

[1] M Brossig, 'The Emerging Peace and Security Regime in Africa: The Role of the EU' (2011) 16 *European Foreign Affairs Review* 107–22, 117.

N'Djamena Agreement (AMIS II). More recently, in 2009, the AU established a High Level Panel for the implementation of the recommendations of the AU on Darfur and the Comprehensive Peace Agreement (CPA). The AU High Level Implementation Panel (AUHIP) is composed of the former presidents of South Africa, Nigeria and Burundi (Thabo Mbeki, Abdulsalami Abubakar, Pierre Buyoya, respectively).

With this background in mind, on 24 April 2012, the AU's Peace and Security Council adopted a communiqué including a roadmap towards the end of the hostilities and the restoration of dialogue between Sudan and South Sudan. This roadmap was subsequently endorsed by the UNSC, at the request of the African Union,[2] which made specific reference to it and displayed the bulk of its contents. Since the adoption of the roadmap, the AU Peace and Security Council has been monitoring its implementation and has adopted several communiqués urging Sudan and South Sudan to address their security issues and to comply with the terms of the roadmap.[3]

On 27 September 2012, an important event took place under the auspices of the AU, namely, the signing of a series of agreements between Sudan and South Sudan in Addis Ababa. These agreements, which are discussed below in section V, address some of the most important issues to be resolved between the parties in the post-conflict scenario.[4] The agreements are based on two principles: (i) establishing two viable states 'stable, secure and at peace with each other and their neighbours' and (ii) peaceful relations whereby '[T]he Parties affirm their commitment to respect the principles of the African Union Constitutive Act and the United Nations Charter concerning relations and cooperation between states and shall respect each other's sovereignty and territorial integrity.'[5]

The Cooperation Agreement also provides for the commitment of both parties to complete the negotiation of the outstanding CPA issue concerning the disputed and claimed border areas, and in assigning a particular role to the AUHIP in resolving the situation of the Abyei area. Finally, the same agreement establishes that both states will set up viable frameworks and mechanisms for bilateral cooperation. Unfortunately, important issues such as the final status of the Abyei area or the conflict in Southern Kordofan and Blue Nile remain outstanding. Nevertheless, the agreements represent a great achievement on the way towards the normalisation of the situation between the two countries.

[2] UNSC 2046 (2012) of 2 May 2012.

[3] See in this regard, for example, Communiqué PSC/PR/COMM (CCCXXIX) of 3 August 2012 or Communiqué PSC/MIN/COMM/3 of 2 May 2012.

[4] The series of agreements signed on September 27 include 'The Cooperation Agreement between the Republic of the Sudan and the Republic of South Sudan', 'The Agreement concerning Oil and related Economic Matters', 'The Framework Agreement on the Status of Nationals of the Other State', 'The Agreement on Border Issues (including Demarcation)', 'The Agreement on a Framework for Cooperation on Central Banking Issues', 'The Agreement on Trade and Trade-Related Issues', 'The Agreement on Certain Economic Matters: Division of Assets and Liabilities, Arrears and Claims and Joint Approach to the International Community', 'The Framework Agreement to facilitate Post Service Benefits (including pensions)', and 'The Agreement on Security Arrangements'. The texts of the various agreements can be found at: http://sites.tufts.edu/reinventingpeace/2012/09/27/sudan-and-south-sudan-full-text-of-agreements/.

[5] As referred to in the Cooperation Agreement between the Republic of the Sudan and the Republic of South Sudan, ibid, 3–4.

III. THE UN IN SUDAN AND SOUTH SUDAN

The UN has established four UN-only missions and one hybrid mission (with the AU) in Sudan. As for the UN-only missions, the first, the so-called UN Advance Mission in the Sudan (UNAMIS) was established under Resolution 1547 (2004) of the Security Council.[6] The mandate of UNAMIS was, in essence, to promote contact between the parties to the conflict and to prepare a future UN operation in support of peace. Subsequently, by means of Resolution 1590 (2005),[7] the Security Council established the so-called UN Mission in Sudan (UNMIS). The objective of this mission was to support the implementation of the CPA and to carry out humanitarian work and to promote and safeguard human rights. The mission terminated soon after the independence of South Sudan.

With the arrival of independence, the Security Council adopted a new resolution, Resolution 1996 (2011),[8] which established the UN Mission in the Republic of South Sudan (UNMISS). The main objective of the mission was to consolidate peace and security in the area and to help establish the conditions for development. Finally, by means of Resolution 1990 (2011),[9] the UNSC urgently authorised the establishment of the UN Interim Security Force for Abyei (UNISFA), made up of 4,200 soldiers, 50 police officers and civilian support, its main task being the monitoring and verifying of the redeployment of any Sudan Armed Forces, Sudan People's Liberation Army or its successor, from the Abyei Area as defined by the Permanent Court of Arbitration.

As for the hybrid mission, under Resolution 1769,[10] the Security Council established the hybrid African Union-UN in Darfur mission, known as UNAMID. The main objective of this mission was to protect civilians in Darfur and to monitor implementation of the agreements reached by the parties concerning this area. The mission also purported to monitor the borders with Chad and the Central African Republic.

Moreover, since 2010, the UN has a Special Representative of the Secretary-General for Sudan and South Sudan, Haile Menkerios, who became the UNSG's Special Envoy for Sudan and South Sudan on 27 July 2011. Together with the Special Envoy, the UN office works with the UN agencies that are active in Sudan.[11] In 2012 the Security Council called for greater coordination and coherence between the different UN actions and asked the Secretary General to report periodically to the Security Council on the implementation of this task.[12]

6 UNSC Res 1547 (11 June 2004) UN Doc S/RES/1547.

7 UNSC Res 1590 (24 March 2005) UN Doc S/RES/1590.

8 UNSC Res 1960 (8 July 2011) UN Doc S/RES/1960.

9 UNSC Res 1990 (27 June 2011) UN Doc S/RES/1990.

10 UNSC Res 1769 (July 31 2007) UN Doc S/RES/1769.

11 In particular, the Office for the Coordination of Humanitarian Affairs (OCHA), the Office of the High Commissioner for Refugees (UNHCR), the Office of the High Commissioner for Human Rights (OHCHR), the Food and Agriculture Organization (FAO) and the United Nations Children's Fund (UNICEF).

12 UNSC Res 2057 (5 July 2012) UN Doc S/RES/2057 'Calls upon UNMISS to coordinate with the Government of the Republic of South Sudan and participate in regional coordination and information mechanisms to improve protection of civilians and support disarmament, demobilization and reintegration efforts in light of the attacks by the Lord's Resistance Army (LRA) in the Republic of South Sudan and requests the Secretary-General to include in his UNMISS trimesterly reports a summary of cooperation and information sharing between UNMISS, the African Union/United Nations Hybrid Operation in

IV. THE EU IN SUDAN AND SOUTH SUDAN

The policy of the Council, the main actor in EU external relations before and after the Treaty of Lisbon, in Sudan has essentially been to support the negotiation and subsequent implementation of the CPA, and the AU's diplomatic efforts to resolve the conflicts that have arisen after the secession of South Sudan. Also, in relation to the humanitarian crisis in Darfur, the Council has reiterated its support for AU and UN efforts, through diplomatic, financial and civil support missions.[13] The civil and military support from the EU to AMIS, led by the AU, concluded in December 2007, when the mission was taken over by the joint AU-UN operation, UNAMID.

With regard to financial support, the Council decided, at its meeting back in 2003, and in response to a demand made by the AU, to establish a fund known as the African Peace Facility ('the Fund').[14] The Fund aims to support peacekeeping operations made by African countries in Africa. The Fund responds to the so-called principle of African ownership and is consistent with the idea that African countries and the AU are best placed and more legitimate to resolve and prevent conflicts in Africa.[15]

The Council has also adopted a comprehensive approach for Sudan, and since 2011, also for South Sudan, under which the Council undertakes, inter alia, to support the coexistence and development of two viable states and a peace agreement that solves the situation of Darfur. Moreover, for the sake of consistency, coordination and impact, the EU Member States have decided to develop a strategy of joint programming of development policies of the EU and its Member States in South Sudan.[16] The granting of development and humanitarian aid is one of the most

Darfur (UNAMID), the United Nations Organization Stabilization Mission in the Democratic Republic of Congo (MONUSCO), and regional and international partners in addressing the LRA threats.'

[13] See Joint Action 2005/557/CFSP of 18 July 2005 on the action of civil and military support of the European Union to the African Union mission in Darfur (AMIS II). For a critical analysis of the missions that the EU has been involved in Africa see, for example, A Vines, 'Rhetoric from Brussels and reality on the ground: the EU and security in Africa' (2010) 86 *International Affairs* 5, 1091–1108.

[14] Decision 2003/3 of the ACP-EC Council of Ministers of 11 December 2003 on the use of resources from the long-term development envelope of the ninth European Development Fund (EDF) for the creation of a Peace Facility for Africa [2003] OJ L345/108.

[15] The first AU mission that received assistance from the Fund was the mission to Darfur (AMIS). The Council also approved on 13 December 2004 the Guidelines for the implementation of peace support and security in Africa in the context of the European Security and Defence Policy. These Guidelines were based on the principle of respect for African ownership and full cooperation with the relevant international actors, notably the UN and the AU. See Council Joint Action 2005/557/CFSP of 18 July 2005 on the European Union civilian-military supporting action to the African Union mission in the Darfur region of Sudan [2005] OJ L188, 46, para 9.

[16] In this regard, in June 2012, the Council approved a Common Security and Defense Policy mission to strengthen aviation security at Juba international airport (EUAVSEC South Sudan), which is doubtless one of the first fruits of the new approach. The mission, which was requested by South Sudan, was due to start in September 2012 and to provide advice, mentoring, technical assistance, and training of security and law enforcement to the staff working at the airport; see further Council decision 2012/312/CFSP of 18 June 2012 on the European Union Aviation Security CSDP Mission in South Sudan (EUAVSEC-South Sudan), [2012] OJ L158/17. In the Preamble, the Council decision refers to UNSC Res 1996 (2011), adopted on 8 July 2011 that welcomed the establishment of the Republic of South Sudan on 9 July and 'underscored the need for forging stronger and well-defined partnerships among the United Nations, development agencies, bilateral partners, and other relevant actors, regional and sub-regional institutions

important policies of the EU in the field. In this regard, it has been noted that from as early as the foundational document of today's EU, namely the Schuman Declaration of 1950, the development of Africa has ranked as one of the main policies of the Union. In the terms of the Schuman Declaration:

> [W]ith increased resources Europe will be able to pursue the achievement of one of its essential tasks, namely, the development of the African continent.[17]

Furthermore, although the Council is the main actor in the Union's external relations, it is by no means the only one, and in this regard at least two more actors ought to be mentioned in this brief overview: the European Commission[18] and the European External Action Service.[19] One of the members of this latter body, Mr David O'Sullivan, signed in December 2011 the Establishment Agreement between the EU and the Republic of South Sudan. On the basis of this Agreement, which formally establishes diplomatic relations between the EU and the Republic of South Sudan, the EU Delegation in Juba undertook to help channel the EU's development aid to South Sudan, with a focus on five priority areas: the rule of law, health, education, water management, and food security.

Finally, another EU-related actor should be mentioned in this overview, namely the African, Caribbean and Pacific-European Union (ACP-EU) Council of Ministers. This body, created by the Partnership Agreement between the members of the African, Caribbean and Pacific Group of States, on the one part, and the European Community and its Member States, on the other part,[20] which was signed in Cotonou and subsequently amended (also known as the 'Cotonou Agreement'), approved the request of the Republic of South Sudan to accede to this Partnership. South Sudan had observer status until 20 November 2012 under the Cotonou Agreement, by

and the international financial institutions, to implement national strategies aimed at effective institution building, which are based on national ownership, the achievement of results, and mutual accountability.' Ibid, point 1.

[17] See AT Hengari, 'The European Union and global emerging powers in Africa: Containment, competition or cooperation?' (2012) 19 *South African Journal of International Affairs* 1–24, 1.

[18] The European Commission maintains bilateral relations with Sudan and South Sudan and manages EU financial instruments relating to these countries as well as the implementation of certain policies. Specifically, the Commission provides both humanitarian and development aid through several Directorate Generals (DGs). After the signature of the Comprehensive Peace Agreement in 2005, the Commission presented a Strategy Paper (Country Strategy Paper), which was signed on 25 January 2005. Another Country Strategy Paper has been drafted for South Sudan, following its independence, that foresees the joint programming of development and other policies.

[19] As for the European External Action Service (EEAS), the creation of this *sui generis* service and the transfer to it of staff from DG Development should allow for better coordination of the EU policies in Sudan and South Sudan. Since the commissioning of the EEAS, the programming of development policies is no longer the exclusive competence of DG Development and Cooperation—EuropAid (DEVCO), instead it became a joint responsibility of the EEAS and the Commission. See in relation to the potential impact that the EEAS may have on the UN-EU relationship, particularly from the standpoint of crisis management, the work of A Gonzalez, 'Las capacidades de gestión de crisis en el modelo de acción exterior' in LN Alonso González and A Garrido Muñoz (eds), *La Unión Europea Y El Multilateralismo Eficaz ¿Un compromiso consistente con Naciones Unidas?* (Madrid, Iustel/Monografías, 2011) 75–105.

[20] Partnership Agreement between the Members of the African, Caribbean and Pacific Group of States, of the one part, and the European Community and its Member States, of the other part, signed in Cotonou on 23 June 2000, as first amended in Luxembourg on 25 June 2005 and subsequently at Ouagadougou on 22 June 2010 [2010] OJ L287/3 (the 'revised Cotonou Agreement').

which date it had to deposit its Act of Accession with the Depositaries of the ACP-EU Partnership,[21] something that South Sudan had not yet done by September 2014.

In this regard, while South Sudan is still formally seeking accession to the Cotonou Agreement, Sudan is not. The revised version of the Cotonou Agreement includes a commitment to the establishment and effective functioning of the International Criminal Court, which constitutes an important development for peace and international justice.[22] This commitment has led the government of Sudan to reject the ratification of this instrument because its President, al-Bashir, has been the object of an arrest warrant issued by the International Criminal Court on charges of genocide, crimes against humanity and war crimes.

V. THE AU-EU-UN RELATIONSHIP IN SUDAN AND SOUTH SUDAN

The AU has sought to exercise leadership in the field of international action in Sudan, South Sudan, and particularly in the Darfur region. That leadership role has been recognised, to a large extent, by all stakeholders, particularly in relation to the situation in Darfur, and with regard to the involvement of the AUHIP, which was headed by President Mbeki, in the post-secession scenario. The issuance of the April 2012 Roadmap by the Peace and Security Council of the AU, which was accepted by the parties and endorsed by the UNSC is a clear example of that leadership.

The signing of the important agreements of 27 September 2012 is another example of the AU's leadership. Pursuant to the agreements, the parties (Sudan and South Sudan) recalled and affirmed

> the obligations arising from the decision of the African Union Peace and Security Council in its Communiqué of 24 April 2012, as endorsed by UN Security Council Resolution 2046 of 2 May 2012, and further reflected in the Communiqué of the African Union Peace and Security Council of 3 August 2012.[23]

In other words, the parties recognised the central character of the AU's communiqués for the resolution of their problems. In the same vein, the parties acknowledged 'with gratitude' the facilitation of the AUHIP, headed by President Mbeki in the first instance, followed by that of the UN, the Intergovernmental Authority on Development 'and other international and regional partners, and their indefatigable support and solidarity with the Parties' efforts to normalise their relations.'[24]

Similarly, the Cooperation Agreement signed on 27 September 2012 between Sudan and South Sudan assigned a prominent role to the AUHIP for the negotiation of the outstanding issues between the parties, since '[T]he AUHIP will continue to

[21] See Decision No 2/2012 of the ACP-EU Council of Ministers of 15 June 2012 concerning the status of the Republic of South Sudan in relation to the Partnership Agreement between the members of the African, Caribbean and Pacific Group of States, of the one part, and the European Community and its Member States, of the other part, Brussels, 15 June 2012 ACP/21/002/12, ACP-UE 2114/12.

[22] See in this regard the Preamble and art 7 of the revised Cotonou Agreement.

[23] Preamble to the Cooperation Agreement between the Republic of the Sudan and the Republic of South Sudan, 2.

[24] ibid, 3.

engage the issue of the final status of the Abyei Area through discussion with the AU Peace and Security Council, as well as the Parties.'[25]

Along the same lines, other agreements signed on 27 September 2012 also refer to the possibility of requesting the support of the AU, for example, to perform advisory functions in relation to the demarcation of the border between the two states.[26] Noteworthy is the fact that one of those agreements also provides for a 'Joint Approach to the International Community', according to which the parties *and* the AUHIP will constitute a joint delegation to seek assistance from the international community in relation to a number of subjects including, for example, the funding to carry out developmental programmes in South Sudan.[27] These agreements were complemented, also under the auspices of the AU, on 12 March 2013 with the adoption by both parties of an implementation matrix that forms an integral part of the Cooperation Agreement of 27 September 2012.[28] The role of the AUHIP will thus presumably go beyond the facilitation of the negotiation between the two states by contributing, on the basis of this agreement, to their obtaining the support of the international community on a number of important subjects.

The importance of the agreements and the crucial role played by the AU for their signature was soon applauded by the UNSC. In fact, in the press release published on the occasion of the signature of these agreements, the Security Council, after congratulating the parties for the agreements, urge them to address the outstanding issues concerning Abyei and the disputed areas and, in this regard '[T]he members of the Council look forward to President Mbeki's recommendations on these matters after he reports to the African Union Peace and Security Council and to the report of the Secretary General.'[29] Once more, the leadership of the AUHIP, under the chairmanship of President Mbeki in the post-secession arrangement, is undisputed.

Indeed, the performance of the AU in Sudan has been praised by the international community, particularly by the UN and the EU.[30] However, the view of some observers on the ground in Sudan has been less enthusiastic. The AU has in fact been criticised for being unable to produce concrete results, and for siding with the

[25] ibid, 6.

[26] See Agreement between the Republic of the Sudan and the Republic of South Sudan on Border Issues, at Part Five, para 10(2).

[27] See Agreement between the Republic of the Sudan and the Republic of South Sudan on Certain Economic Matters, at 8, point 6.

[28] The implementation matrix and the reactions of the parties and the African Union to its adoption are available at the website of the African Union, in particular at www.peaceau.org/en/article/adoption-of-implementation-matrix-by-the-republic-of-the-sudan-and-the-republic-of-south-sudan.

[29] UNSC Press Statement on Sudan/South Sudan issued by Council President Peter Wittig (Germany), on 28 September 2012, SC/1079-AFR/2456, available at www.un.org/press/en/2012/sc10779.doc.htm.

[30] See House of Lords, European Union Committee, *The EU and Sudan: on the brink of change*, 18th Report of Session 2010–12, House of Lords Papers 160 2010–12, The Stationery Office, 22 March 2012, p 29: 'We have been impressed by the increasingly assertive role of the African Union (AU) recently in Africa, in particular, in working successfully with both sides in Sudan towards the referendum in South Sudan. The EU should continue to support the efforts of the AU's High Level Implementation Panel under former President Mbeki, to resolve the outstanding areas of conflict.' A follow-up report was published in March 2012 in which the Committee signalled the increasing complexity of the situation in Sudan and South Sudan (related to South Sudan cutting off of the flow of its own oil to, and through, Sudan as well as cross-border military incidents). It called, inter alia, on the EU to work with the AU and the UN to use their influence to persuade both Sudan and South Sudan to return to the spirit of the CPA.

government of Sudan, following the issuance of the arrest warrant by the International Criminal Court against President al-Bashir on charges of genocide, crimes against humanity and war crimes.[31] Those critics remain however a minority when compared with the reaction of the international community generally.

The AUHIP has been working in liaison with the Special Envoy of the UNSG for Sudan and South Sudan, Haile Menkerios. In relation to this collaboration, a division of labour has been established. The UN concentrates on the correct implementation of the CPA,[32] thus coordinating the initiatives of the international actors that are involved in the CPA, while the AUHIP focuses on encouraging new agreements between Sudan and South Sudan, and thereby dealing with the African powers directly.

In this context, the UN has also mitigated the AU's military and logistical limitations on the ground, in particular those of AMIS in Darfur. Similarly, the UN has also exerted an international political leadership that neither the AU nor the EU could have exercised. The UN has managed to coordinate not only the two large regional organisations but also other international organisations, such as the Intergovernmental Authority on Development (IGAD), and high-profile international actors such as the US, China, or the UK in the development and implementation of the CPA. The UN's work in Sudan, particularly through the performance of the UNSG's Special Representative, Haile Menkerios, has been valued quite positively by most players in the field.[33]

In this regard, the UN's work has also been praised in relation to development aid and particularly rule of law assistance to South Sudan, the foregoing because the UN has a proven strength in this matter vis-à-vis the rest of international players.[34] According to some observers in discussions with the United Nations Development Program (UNDP) and others, it was made clear that the agency '(a) viewed its role in the rule of law area as central and pre-eminent, (b) felt that the expertise and experience in South Sudan of its personnel and subcontractors was superior to all others, and (c) wanted no interference or involvement of any other groups in the areas where it had established its programmes.'[35]

[31] See oral evidence given by Gill Lusk, a journalist who resided in Sudan for many years, in *The EU and Sudan: on the brink of change*, available at www.parliament.uk/documents/lords-committees/eu-sub-com-c/Sudan/SudanOralWritEvidence.pdf, 12.

[32] In fact, the UN mission in Sudan (UNMIS) seems to have played a key role in monitoring and implementing the CPA and in reducing military tensions in the area. See House of Lords Report, *The EU and Sudan: on the brink of change*, p 28, point 83.

[33] The EU representative in Sudan, Rosalind Marsden, has held that Mr Menkerios has exercised strong leadership in the area and has managed to use the good offices of UN to coordinate international action in the framework of the implementation of CPA. In fact, with more than 30,000 troops, UN presence in Sudan represents the largest UN deployment in the world. See written evidence from Dame Rosalind Marsden, EU Representative for Sudan, EEAS (SUD 7) in the context of *The EU and Sudan: on the brink of change*.

[34] Report by the International Legal Assistance Consortium, Pre-Assessment Mission, South Sudan, 6–13 December 2011, at www.ilac.se/download/reports_documents/mission-reports_documents/SOUTH-SUDAN_P-A_REPORT_120229.pdf, 18.

[35] ibid, 18.

As for the EU, this organisation has adopted a secondary role. Whether this role has been deliberately adopted, or whether it rather just reflects the limitations of the EU in exercising a greater political role, had been put into question.[36] In any event, the EU's political role in the field consists, essentially, in supporting the financial and military efforts of the AU. The EU thus recognises the main responsibility of the pan-African organisation on the ground, and seems satisfied with the policy coordination of the UN on humanitarian aid. Indeed, the EU's main role appears to be that of supporting the African Peace and Security Architecture (APSA) for the African states to be able to manage their own security problems.

The recognition of the crucial role played by the AU in the field of peace and security has been recognised in multiple policy documents,[37] yet remarkably has also been included in legal texts, particularly in the important revised version of the Cotonou Agreement of 2010. According to article 11 of the revised Cotonou Agreement: '[T]he Parties emphasize the important role of regional organizations in peace building and conflict prevention and resolution and in tackling new or expanding security threats with, in Africa, a key responsibility of the African Union.'[38]

Notwithstanding the foregoing, according to some authors, 'by paying excessive attention to the institutions that constitute the African Peace and Security Architecture, the Joint EU-Africa Strategy seems to have forgotten that the present crisis on the continent is the weakness of African states',[39] and this might be particularly important for a country that needs as much help as South Sudan. The performance of the EU has indeed been criticised, especially prior to the adoption of the EU's Joint Action of civil and military support to the AU mission in Darfur,[40] but also after.[41] Critics have mainly attacked the lack of EU leadership in the international response to the crisis in Darfur, and its refusal to consider it as genocide, as did the USA Government in July 2004.[42] Nevertheless, the action of the EU in terms of

[36] See oral evidence given by Roger Middleton, Consultant Researcher, Africa Programme, Chatham House, in an interview that was conducted in the framework of *The EU and Sudan: on the brink of change*, available at www.parliament.uk/documents/lords-committees/eu-sub-com-c/Sudan/SudanOral WritEvidence.pdf, Q 11, p 8.

[37] See, for example, Commission Communication, 'One year after Lisbon: The Africa-EU partnership at work' COM (2008) 61 final; and Commission Communication, 'On the consolidation of EU Africa relations' COM (2010) 634 final.

[38] See for the reference and a discussion of the revised Cotonou Agreement, S Bartelt, 'ACP-EU development cooperation at a crossroads?: One year after the second revision of the Cotonou Agreement' (2012) 17 *European Foreign Affairs Review*, 1–25.

[39] K Mpyisi, *How EU Support of the African Peace and Security Architecture Impacts Democracy Building and Human Security Enhancement in Africa* (Stockholm, International Institute for Democracy and Electoral Assistance, 2009) 3.

[40] One of the critics of the Joint Action 2005/557/CFSP of civil and military support of the EU to the African Union mission in Darfur with the greatest impact was an article by CWD Bock and LR Miller, 'Darfur: Where is Europe?' *The Washington Post*, 9 December 2004.

[41] See Human Rights Watch in 2007, *EU: Europe Should Assume Leadership Darfur Action—Not Words—Needed to End Darfur Crisis*, available at www.hrw.org. See also, regarding the involvement of the EU and the importance of the legal definition of the atrocities in Darfur, among others, K Mulaj, 'Forced displacement in Darfur, Sudan: Dilemmas of Classifying the Crimes' (2008) 46 *International Migration*, 27–48.

[42] US Ambassador RS Williamson delivered the following words to the then UN Human Rights Commission (now Committee) in Geneva in 2004, in an unsuccessful attempt to get greater EU commitment: 'ten years from now, the sixtieth Commission on Human Rights will be remembered for one thing

humanitarian aid and development cooperation has gained recognition, although it has encountered problems of coordination between the EU and other donors, and even between the EU and its member states.[43] The new comprehensive approach aims precisely at minimising coordination problems, at least within the EU.

In light of the foregoing, the interplay between the three international organisations covered by this chapter is based on the principles of subsidiarity and complementarity.[44] The strength of the system, which has led to the signing and implementation of the CPA and to the peaceful secession of South Sudan, is based more on *Autoritas* than on *Potestas*, in leveraging the strengths of each organisation on the ground. In other words, the interplay does not work in terms of strict hierarchy but rather in what has been coined the *hierarchy of influence*, according to which each organisation acts in the field in which it will probably have the greatest impact. In the words of a European stakeholder with experience on the field,

> if we talk about our posturing and our lead roles with various international organisations, we must understand the hierarchy of influence and know our position as European and where we fit in. We support those institutions primarily, rather than trying in any way to eclipse the role of others.[45]

In this regard, there is no substitute today for the international legitimacy and the good offices of the UN. The UN is, in all likelihood, the only organisation whose coordination is accepted (in different degrees) by all international actors, both states and international organisations. Similarly, among African leaders, the AU is more accepted than other international actors, including the UN. This regional comparative advantage has proved essential for the deployment of peacekeeping operations in the Sudan, whose president has rejected all non-African forces on its territory and has also proved essential for the carrying out of peace and post-conflict talks. For these purposes, it should be remembered that the AU has criticised the way in which the ICC prosecuted President al-Bashir of Sudan, and this has allowed him to travel and negotiate in different African states, despite the arrest warrant issued by the ICC. This has also happened despite the fact that members of the AU are also signatories of the revised Cotonou Agreement with the European Union, and this agreement provides, as mentioned above, for cooperation with the effective functioning of the ICC. In fact, acceptance at the national and supranational levels is considered

and one thing alone: Did we have the courage and strength to take strong action against the "ethnic cleansing" in Darfur? We will be asked, "Where were you at the time of the ethnic cleansing?" "What did you do?"'. See E Markussen and S Tottene (eds), *Genocide in Darfur: Investigating the Atrocities in the Sudan*, (New York, Routledge, 2006) 116.

43 See *The EU and Sudan: on the brink of change*, point 220, p 55. Similarly, other commentators have criticised the EU's action on rule of law assistance, which is precisely one of the fields where the EU should in principle be better able to provide a significant contribution. See in this regard the Report by the International Legal Assistance Consortium, Pre-Assessment Mission, South Sudan, 2011, p 18.

44 The need to work together for the common objective for supporting the African continent has even been noted in the relationship between some of the organisations working in Sudan, in particular the EU, with emerging powers such as China. See in this regard, AT Hengari, 'The European Union and global emerging powers in Africa'.

45 See oral evidence given by Paul Murphy, Director of Saferworld, who lived in Africa for over 20 years, in *The EU and Sudan: on the brink of change*, answer to Q90, p 41.

to be a determining factor in a regional organisation's role in peace and security,[46] and the AU is, for the reasons outlined, the best-suited organisation among the three reviewed to be accepted by both Sudan and South Sudan.

In this context, although the role of the EU appears to be subordinate, it is by no means unimportant. The EU has invested massively in the formation of the African Peace and Security Architecture (APSA), which has the AU at its core, and it enables the AU to carry out many of its tasks.[47]

Importantly, the above-described relations fit well with the system established by the UN Charter. In this respect, article 52 of the Charter, which falls under Chapter VIII on Regional Arrangements, states that

> [T]he Members of the United Nations entering into such arrangements or constituting such agencies shall make every effort to achieve pacific settlement of local disputes through such regional arrangements or by such regional agencies *before referring them to the Security Council.* [Emphasis added.]

Hence, this provision includes a clear preference for the peaceful settlement of local disputes through regional arrangements such as the AU, even prior to UNSC involvement. The problem arises when 'every effort' proves insufficient to prevent the escalation of violence and the massive violation of human rights, as has occurred in Darfur. In fact, the triangular AU-EU-UN system has been criticised for being too slow to respond to massive human rights violations. For example, the AU-EU partnership put in place under the AU's AMIS mission was insufficient to stop the atrocities in Darfur.[48] Indeed, a third international organisation, the North Atlantic Treaty Organization (NATO) had to intervene and, ultimately, the UN had to take over the mission under the AU-UN hybrid mission (UNAMID).

In the same vein, even UNAMID has been criticised. Commentators have pointed to the existence of ambiguities and of demands by both organisations to continue operational control of the mission in detriment to its effectiveness. Indeed, a US representative to the UN said in 2008 that the results of the hybrid mission suggested that it would not become a model for future collaboration between the AU and the UN.[49]

Against this background, with the recent memory of Darfur, and in the context of the complicated situation in Abyei, one may wonder whether the principles of subsidiarity and complementarity, which govern the AU-EU-UN relations for most subjects, should also apply to the issue of the use of force in order to prevent mass

[46] S Kingah and L Van Langenhove, 'Determinants of a regional organisation's role in peace and security: the African Union and the European Union compare' (2012) 19 *South African Journal of International Affairs* 201–22.

[47] See AU-EU Partnership the Africa-European Union Strategic Partnership, *Meeting current and future challenges together*, General Secretariat of the European Council, May, 2011, available at www.consilium.europa.eu/uedocs/cms_data/librairie/PDF/QC3111092ENC.pdf.

[48] International Crisis Group, *The EU/AU Partnership in Darfur: Not Yet a Winning Combination*, African report n° 99 (Nairobi/Brussels, International Crisis Group 25 October 2005), available at www.crisisgroup.org/en/regions/africa/horn-of-africa/sudan/099-the-eu-au-partnership-in-darfur-not-yet-a-winning-combination.aspx.

[49] See UN Press Release 084(08), April 16, 2008, 'Hopes for political solution in Darfur wilt under military action—says SG Ban in new UN report'.

violations of human rights. In other words, one may wonder whether unilateral intervention of the AU, which is more accepted than other actors by African powers, in addressing or avoiding a situation of grave humanitarian crisis should be allowed in case of UNSC inaction, ie should the hierarchy of influence also apply to this field. In this regard, and given the financial and logistical constraints affecting the AU, in the case of UNSC inaction, should current international law allow military intervention of the EU in support of the AU?

The issue of the possible unilateral use of force by the AU has been recently discussed by Judge Yusuf of the International Court of Justice, who in view of the wording of article 4(h) of the Constitutive Act of the AU,[50] which provides for the right of the AU 'to intervene in a Member State pursuant to a decision of the Assembly in respect of grave circumstances, namely: war crimes, genocide and crimes against humanity',[51] has held that

> should the UN Security Council fail to act, the grave circumstances in respect of which the African Organization is empowered to take military action, namely, genocide, war crimes and crimes against humanity, may sometimes require the adoption of emergency measures, including military action, aimed at saving human lives. Even in such a situation, the AU may still not be considered in breach of its international law obligations, so long as its action meets the conditions and criteria laid down in articles 52 and 54 of the Charter, as discussed above, and thus become eligible for an ex post facto endorsement or subsequent acquiescence by the Security Council.[52]

Judge Yusuf is by no means alone, as others have claimed the possible legality of such intervention[53] also reflects an emerging regional custom[54] although a majority still considers that article 53 of the Charter forbids such intervention.[55]

Similarly, in the EU context, although this organisation has proclaimed in its constitutional charter[56] its willingness to abide by the UN Charter's principles, some

[50] art 4(h), Constitutive Act of the African Union (done at Lomé, Togo, 11 July 2000, in force 26 May 2001) 2158 UNTS 33.

[51] See also the so-called Ezulwini consensus, African Common Position on the proposal of United Nations reform, African Union Executive Council, 7th Sess, Addis Ababa, 7–8 March 2005, according to which 'Any recourse to force outside the framework of Article 51 of the UN Charter and Article 4 (h) of the AU Constitutive Act, should be prohibited.'

[52] AA Yusuf, 'The Right of Forcible Intervention in certain conflicts' in AA Yusuf and F Ouguergouz (eds), *The African Union: Legal and Institutional Framework-A Manual on the Pan-African Organization* (Leiden, Martinus Nijhoff Publishers, 2012) 335–53, 347.

[53] See, for example, M Kunschak, 'The African Union and the Right to Intervention: Is there a need for UN Security Council Authorisation?' (2006) 31 *South African Yearbook of International Law* 209–23.

[54] See in this regard, J Cardona Llorens, 'La responsabilité de protéger: Le rôle des organisations internationales', *Colloque de la SFDI de Nanterre* (Paris, Éditions Pédone, 2008) 319–25, and A Abass and MA Baderin, 'Towards effective collective security and human rights protection in Africa: An assessment of the Constitutive Act of the new African Union' (2002) 46 *Netherlands International Law Review* 1–38, 22–23, cited by L Boisson de Chazournes in 'Les relations entre organisations régionales et organisations universelles' 347 *Recueil des Cours* (Hague Academy of International Law and Martinus Nijhoff Publishers, 2010) 292, fn 646.

[55] See, for example, Bautista Jimenez, 'Las relaciones triangulares entre Naciones Unidas, UE y UA' in Alonso González and Garrido Muñoz (eds), *La Unión Europea y el Multilateralismo Eficaz* (Iustel, 2012) 112–13, or B Kioko, 'The right of Intervention under the African Union's Constitutive Act: From non-interference to non-intervention' (2003) 85 *International Review of the Red Cross* 807–25, 821.

[56] See Treaty of Lisbon amending the Treaty on European Union and the Treaty establishing the European Community, done at Lisbon on 13 December 2007 [2007] OJ C 306/01, entered into force 1 December 2009, arts 3(5) and Declaration 13 to the Treaty of Lisbon.

have observed that the multilateralism to which the EU has agreed to adhere is an 'effective' one, thus not an unconditional multilateralism, but rather one that, in essence, 'opens up alternative ways of action in cases of perceived multilateral inefficiency'.[57]

Situations such as those that took place in Darfur ought not to happen again, and in this regard interpretations such as that advocated by Judge Yusuf are to be welcomed. At the same time, the risks of extending the legitimate use of force under international law should not be underestimated. In fact, even the authors suggesting a flexible interpretation of the Charter, in exceptional circumstances, prefer the prompt intervention of the UNSC under Chapter VII. In this regard, it has been argued that both article 4(h) of the Constitutive Act of the AU and the EU's reference to *effective* multilateralism should be interpreted as efforts to put pressure on the UNSC to properly exercise its responsibility, and not as an attempt to circumvent it.[58]

VI. CONCLUSIONS

The actions of the AU, the EU and the UN in Sudan and South Sudan allow us to observe the interplay between these three organisations on the ground. In this regard, it is submitted that the principles of subsidiarity and complementarity govern the relationship between them in Sudan and South Sudan when it comes to most subject matter, including diplomatic, political and humanitarian aid coordination. This relationship is based on a hierarchy of influence rather than a legal basis. It is more about *Autoritas* than *Potestas*.

The question remains whether this kind of relationship could be transposed to the issue of the use of force. As already discussed, there are good arguments on both sides defended by authoritative voices. The debate is in fact quite lively, as demands have already been made on behalf of the AU for the UNSC to take into account the principles of complementarity and subsidiarity, when it comes to the maintenance of international peace and security.

In this context, President Zuma of South Africa made clear before the UNCSC that

> [W]e are mindful of the fact that the UN Charter gives the UN Security Council the primary mandate and the responsibility for the maintenance of international peace and security,

[57] See in this regard P Cramér, 'Reflections on European Effective Multilateralism and the Use of Force' in M Evans and P Koutrakos (eds), *Beyond the established legal orders: Policy Interconnections between the EU and the Rest of the World* (Oxford, Hart Publishing, 2011) 225–47, 237. In the judicial field, the EU has already shown a critical approach to some parts of the functioning of the UN system, see the well-known Joined Cases C-402/05 and C-415/059, *Yassin Abdullah Kadi and Al Barakaat International Foundation v Council of the European Union and Commission of the European Communities*, Judgment of the Court (Grand Chamber) of 3 September 2008 [2008] ECR 635. See also, as to the particular role of the EU within international law, M Cremona, 'External relations and external competence of the European Union: the emergence of an integrated policy' in P Craig and G de Búrca (eds), *The evolution of EU Law*, 2nd edn (Oxford, Oxford University Press, 2011) 217–68, 267.

[58] See Boisson de Chazournes, 'Les relations entre organisations régionales et organisations universelles', 296, and Cramér, 'Reflections on European effective multilateralism and the use of force', 244.

> including in the African continent. At the same time, we are of the view that cognisance should be given to the fact that the Chapter encourages cooperation with regional bodies such as the AU in carrying out the UN mandate in line with the spirit of subsidiarity. It is our view that close cooperation with regional bodies has advantages. Regional bodies are closer to the situation, are familiar with the issues and often understand the dynamics of the conflict. Neighbouring countries also often bear the burden and consequences of conflict in their neighborhood. It is for this very reason that we support the principle of complementarity between the AU and the UN and their respective Security Councils.[59]

The answer of the UNSC to those demands has so far been negative.[60] It may be true that the importance and ambition of regional organisations, such as the AU, nowadays calls for a discussion as to whether Chapter VIII of the UN Charter remains the best framework to coordinate the roles of regional organisations and the UN for the sake of global peace and prosperity. Nevertheless, in the absence of an updated framework, caution should be observed as to the automatic transposition of the principles of complementarity and subsidiarity to the issue of the use of force for the grave consequences that such a use could entail. In this regard, it may be recalled that, as it happens in the EU context, the principle of subsidiarity should not apply to issues which fall under exclusive supranational competence, and the use of force is, still today and for good reasons, an exclusive competence of the UN Security Council, subject to the limited exceptions provided for in the UN Charter.

Having said that, as the UNSC itself has made clear in a recent statement, regional diplomacy is not restricted by the Charter, to the contrary as discussed above, the joint efforts of regional and universal international actors in South Sudan towards the normalisation of the relations between this new State and Sudan 'is a tribute to international and regional diplomacy and exemplifies the *true spirit of peace enshrined in the UN Charter*' (emphasis added).[61]

59 UNSC Verbatim Record (12 January 2012) UN Doc S/PV/6702, 3.

60 See SC Res 2033 (2012). An analysis of the speech by President Zuma and of the reaction of the UNSC can be found at http://blogs.cfr.org/patrick/2012/03/23/the-un-versus-regional-organizations-who-keeps-the-peace/.

61 UNSC Press Statement on Sudan/South Sudan issued by Council President Peter Wittig (Germany).

22

Regional Practices before the International Criminal Court: The Situations in Northern Uganda and Sudan

ALMA CORINA BORJAS MONROY*

I. INTRODUCTION

VARIOUS AFRICAN PEOPLES have special local reconciliation processes for achieving peace and justice. The question is whether these traditions should be considered by the Prosecutor of the International Criminal Court (ICC) in order to analyse cases or to forgo a prosecution in accordance with article 53 of the Rome Statute.[1] Having taken into consideration the traditional practices of the African peoples involved, could the Prosecutor decide that an investigation would not serve the interests of justice? This question is especially relevant because of the presumed existence or construction of a universal or global standard of criminal justice.

In addition to traditional practices, regional approaches to conflict resolution are becoming increasingly crucial in this context. Regional organisations and mechanisms for conflict resolution are often closer to the problems of the countries of a given region. They are more aware of the traditional mechanisms for conflict resolution in those countries, and in a better position to propose solutions that are adapted to local necessities.

In this sense, article 53 of the Rome Statute raises the possibility of a broad interpretation of the term 'interest of justice', which may allow the Prosecutor to consider other forms of the application of justice. For this reason, we take as an example the situations of Uganda and Sudan, in which the problem of regional practices and approaches for the solution of regional conflicts has been raised.

Finally, there will be a brief reflection on what should be the purpose of international criminal justice, analysing both the retributive and restorative views of justice.

* PhD candidate, Universidad Complutense de Madrid.

[1] Rome Statute of the International Criminal Court (adopted 17 July 1998, in force 1 July 2002) 2187 UNTS 90, art 53.

II. ARTICLE 53 OF THE ROME STATUTE: AN OPEN DOOR FOR REGIONAL PRACTICES?

Article 53 of the Rome Statute[2] gives the Prosecutor discretion to determine not to initiate an investigation based on the interest of justice. The question is how broad that discretion should be, and what are its limits? Is the concept of the interest of justice limited to retributive justice, or does it encompass wider considerations?

The article under discussion establishes that:

> 1. The Prosecutor shall, having evaluated the information available to him or her, initiate an investigation unless he or she determines that there is no reasonable basis to proceed under this Statute. At deciding whether to initiate an investigation, the Prosecutor shall consider whether:
>
> ...
>
> c) Taking into account the gravity of the crime and the interests of victims, there are nonetheless substantial reasons to believe that an investigation would not serve the interests of justice.

The debate around this article has focused on the issue of amnesties rather than on the 'discretionary power' given to the Prosecutor to determine whether to investigate a situation. The present analysis goes further by including in this discretionary power the possibility for the Prosecutor to take into consideration the regional practices of African people; these may include not only traditional practices but also regional approaches especially where a peace process is involved.

It has been argued that the role of political considerations should only fall within the powers of the Security Council (SC), as a political organ, and that is why the issue was included in article 16 in the Rome Statute.[3] Nevertheless, where the Prosecutor decides not to initiate an investigation on the grounds of the exercise of the alternative practice of justice that responds to regional traditions, it is not a political decision, nor is this contrary to the object and purpose of the Rome Statute. Instead, it is just the application of an alternative kind of justice.

When it comes to this possibility, the Office of the Prosecutor, in its policy paper on the Interests of Justice, has stated that:

> In relation to other forms of justice decided at the local level, the Office of the Prosecutor reiterates the need to integrate different approaches ... The pursuit of criminal justice provides one part of the necessary response to serious crimes of international concern which, by themselves, may prove to be insufficient ... As such, it fully endorses the complementary role that can be played by domestic prosecutions, truth seeking, reparation programs, institutional reforms and traditional justice mechanisms in the pursuit of a broader justice.[4]

Despite these considerations the policy paper also emphasises that the phrase 'interests of justice' is not synonymous with the interest of peace.[5]

[2] ibid.
[3] ibid, art 16.
[4] ICC-OTP-2007, Policy paper on the Interest of Justice, September 2007, pp 7–8.
[5] ibid.

Responding to this idea, different NGOs have pronounced strongly against this meaning. As part of the consultation proposal held by the Office of the Prosecutor on the 'Interests of Justice', Amnesty International (AI) concluded that the Prosecutor does not have the power to suspend an investigation, and even less if it is based on possible interference in political negotiations between warring factions to end an armed conflict. Furthermore, AI emphasised more generally that there is not the slightest suggestion that prosecutors should decline to investigate grave crimes or to prosecute them because some victims were personally opposed to their investigation or their prosecution.[6]

In the same sense, Human Rights Watch expressed the view that the only construction of 'interests of justice' that would be consistent with the preamble of the Rome Statute would be a narrow one that does not permit considerations of domestic amnesties, truth processes, traditional mechanisms or peace negotiations.[7] Both organisations built their arguments around a narrow interpretation of the object and purpose of the Rome Statute, and the fact that the political decision not to initiate an investigation is in the hands of the SC, in accordance with article 16 of the Rome Statute.

According to Kourabas there is a general consensus surrounding the interpretation of the Rome Statute's 'object and purpose', indicating that this puts an end to impunity. Therefore, given this consensus and the prosecution-heavy nature of the language in the Preamble, article 53 could not be interpreted as allowing the Prosecutor to refrain from an investigation or prosecution, since that would be in clear violation of the Rome Statute.[8]

Despite the previous arguments, the text of article 53 is clear with respect to such a possibility because it juxtaposes the traditional criminal justice considerations—the gravity of the crimes and the interests of the victims—with the broader notion of interests of justice and it clearly indicates that the latter might triumph over the former.[9] Since the Rome Statute has not defined the concept of interest of justice, no explicit position has been taken as to any of the so-called 'transitional justice' mechanisms.[10] Instead, this article grants wide discretion to the ICC Prosecutor to

[6] Amnesty International, 'Open letter to the Chief Prosecutor of the International Criminal Court: Comments on the Concept of the Interests of Justice' AI Index: IOR 40/023/2005, 17 June 2005, available at www.amnesty.org/en/library/asset/IOR40/023/2005/en/be106e8a-d4c0-11dd-8a23-d58a49c0d652/ior400232005en.html.

[7] Human Rights Watch, 'Policy Paper: The Meaning of "The Interests of Justice" in Article 53 of the Rome Statute', June 2005, available at www.hrw.org/news/2005/06/01/meaning-interests-justice-article-53-rome-statute.

[8] M Kourabas, 'A Vienna Convention Interpretation of the "Interests Of Justice" Provision of the Rome Statute, the Legality of Domestic Amnesty Agreements, and the Situation in Northern Uganda: A "Great Qualitative Step Forward", Or A Normative Retreat?' (2007) 14 *University of California Davis Journal of International Law & Policy* 59–94, 73.

[9] D Robinson, 'Serving the Interest of Justice: amnesties, truth commissions and the International Criminal Court' (2003) 14 *European Journal of International Law* 481–505, 488.

[10] J Wouters, S Verhoeven and B Demeyere, 'The International Criminal Court's Office of the Prosecutor: Navigating between Independence and Accountability?' in J Doria, H-P Gasser, M Cherif Bassiouni (eds), *The Legal Regime of the International Criminal Court. Essays in Honour of Professor Igor Blishchenko: in memoriam Professor Igor Pavlovich Blishchenko (1930–2000)* (Leiden, Martinus Nijhoff Publishers, 2009) 345–86, 364.

consider all matters pertaining to the interests of justice in deciding whether to move forward with an investigation.[11]

In any case, this determination is not merely a matter of prosecutorial discretion, since the Pre-trial Chamber may review the decision of the Prosecutor at the request of the state making a referral under article 14, or the UNSC may do so under article 13 and on its own initiative.[12] It is also preferable that the discretion not to initiate an investigation is in the hands of the Prosecutor, which can at least be subject to revision, instead of the UNSC, especially if one recalls the problems that the exercise of the power under article 16 of the Statute has already wrought in practice.[13]

In fact, such deferral could, for example, occur when there are politically viable and legally acceptable alternative justice mechanisms and amnesty-granting programmes.[14] No clear rules can be enunciated, but it is submitted that international recognition might be accorded where amnesty has been granted as part of a truth and reconciliation inquiry and each person granted amnesty has been obliged to make a full disclosure of his or her criminal acts as a precondition for amnesty, and the acts were politically motivated.[15]

III. SITUATIONS BEFORE THE ICC AND REGIONAL PRACTICES

A. The Northern Uganda Situation

In December 2003, in accordance with article 14 of the Rome Statute, the Government of Uganda referred to the Prosecutor the situation concerning the Lord's Resistance Army (LRA) in Northern Uganda. The Prosecutor decided to open an investigation into this matter on 29 July 2004, and on 5 July the situation was assigned to Pre-Trial Chamber II. Finally, on 8 July 2005, the Court issued its first public arrest warrants for five senior leaders of the LRA.

Despite the referral in the northern Uganda situation, as a solution to deal with the war, the Ugandan Parliament passed an Amnesty Act, which integrates the traditions of the Acholi community. The Amnesty Act of 2000 aimed to break the cycle of violence in northern Uganda, by encouraging combatants of various rebel groups to leave their armed groups without fear of prosecution.[16] The Acholi community expressed their concern about the impact of the ICC investigations and prosecutions,

[11] JD Ohlin, 'Peace, Security, and Prosecutorial Discretion' in C Stahn and G Sluiter (eds), *The Emerging Practice of the International Criminal Court* (Leiden, Nijhoff, 2009) 185–208, 188; SM Weldehaimanot, 'Arresting Al-Bashir: The African Union's Opposition and the Legalities' (2011) 19 *African Journal of International and Comparitive Law* 208–35, 234.

[12] Rome Statute, art 53(3)(a)(b); Robinson, 'Serving the Interest of Justice' 487.

[13] Rome Statute, art 16.

[14] J Wouters et al, 'The International Criminal Court's Office of the Prosecutor' 364.

[15] J Dugard, 'Possible Conflicts of Jurisdiction with Truth Commissions' in A Cassese and E Esser (eds), *The Rome Statute of the International Criminal Court—A Commentary*, Vol I (Oxford, Oxford University Press, 2002) 693–704, 700.

[16] C Rose, 'Looking Beyond Amnesty and Traditional Justice and Reconciliation Mechanisms in Northern Uganda: A Proposal for Truth-Telling and Reparations' (2008) 28 *British Columbia Third World Law Journal* 345–400, 353.

alleging that any prosecution would violate their traditions, and would prolong the war by making it too costly for the rebels to negotiate or surrender.[17]

> There appears to be a contradiction between the Amnesty Act, seen by many as an alternative to punishment, and the investigations and subsequent punishment by the ICC. Indeed, several delegations of Lango, Acholi, Iteso and Madi community leaders have prevailed upon the ICC to reconsider or at least to carefully consider its actions in light of the fact that the conflict is still ongoing and the ICC has no special powers of arrest.[18]

The amnesty was seen as being compatible with the Acholi dispute resolution mechanism known as *mato oput*. The Acholi believe that the bitterness of revenge does not solve a problem, and so it was easy for their people to accept the idea of amnesty, due to the entrenched idea of forgiveness. The Amnesty Act represents a contextual approach to ending violence and creating the conditions for sustainable peace. However, the Prosecutor did not consider the entire context when deciding to refer the situation in North Uganda.

The fact is, as was previously stated, broad grants of amnesty to the LRA rebels evoked traditional Ugandan processes of reconciliation and reintegration according to *mato oput*, even after others have been included. *Mato oput* is a traditional reconciliation ceremony, whereafter, the village welcomes the repentant back. It is not intended to provide a thorough explanation here of all the steps and rituals involved.[19] Such rituals have been 'used to reintegrate former LRA soldiers, despite their awful acts'.[20]

Some authors have offered a contrary interpretation, recalling that since the June 2007 agreement is based on the use of 'traditional justice mechanisms', such as *Mato Oput*, 'as a central part of the framework for accountability', it would not actually be a criminal sanction and therefore it would not fall within the concept of 'intent to bring to justice'.[21] Under this approach, these traditional methods do not meet the standards of justice required by the Rome Statute. Since the use of traditional justice mechanisms implies that criminal sanctions should not be taken into consideration under the ICC proceedings because of their inconsistency with the idea of bringing the accused to justice[22] the question is, what kind of justice are we talking about?

Furthermore, it has been argued that although Acholi chiefs have advocated the use of traditional mechanisms, and the Amnesty Commission created in Uganda has supported their use, such mechanisms may fall short of significantly promoting justice. Following this line of argument, Cecily Rose presents her reasons as to why

[17] KA Rodman, 'Is Peace in the Interests of Justice? The Case for Broad Prosecutorial Discretion at the International Criminal Court' (2009) 22 *Leiden Journal of International Law* 99–126, 111.

[18] Refugee Law Project Working Paper No 17, *Peace First, Justice Later: Traditional Justice In Northern Uganda*, July 2005, available at www.refugeelawproject.org, p 4.

[19] See Liu Institute for Global Issues, Gulu District NGO Forum, and Ker Kwaro Acholi, *Roco Wat I Acoli. Restoring Relations in Acholi-land: Traditional Approaches To Reintegration and Justice* (Vancouver, Canada, September 2005); Uganda Human Rights Commission and UN High Commissioner for Human Rights, *The Dust Has Not Yet Settled. Victims' Views on The Right to Remedy and Reparation. A Report from the Greater North of Uganda* (Kampala, Uganda, 2011).

[20] Kourabas, 'A Vienna Convention Interpretation of the "Interests of Justice"', 64.

[21] WW Burke-White and S Kaplan, 'Shaping the Contours of Domestic Justice: The International Criminal Court and an Admissibility Challenge in the Uganda Situation' (2009) 7 *Journal of International Criminal Justice* 257–79, 269.

[22] ibid, 274.

she considers as questionable the applicability of such ceremonies to the crimes committed by the LRA. Her reasons include the lack of knowledge among the Acholi of *Mato Oput,* the degree to which the Acholi's capacity to forgive has been overestimated, and also the unusually severe nature of this particular conflict.[23]

Despite these arguments, the communities are the ones who will have the final say on whether a method will work or not, especially if we take into account other experiences such as in South Africa and Rwanda. South Africa provides an example of how compensation may be tied to a larger truth commission, while alternatively Rwanda's *gacaca* tribunals show how a traditional justice mechanism may be codified and expanded to include compensation.

B. The Situation in Darfur, Sudan

In March 2005, the UNSC adopted Resolution 1593, referring to 'the prevailing situation in Darfur since 1 July 2002'.[24] The Prosecutor opened an investigation into this situation on 6 June and the case was allocated to Pre-Trial Chamber I. On 14 July 2008, the Prosecutor accused Sudanese President Omar al-Bashir of genocide, crimes against humanity and war crimes. The court issued an arrest warrant for al-Bashir on 4 March 2009 for war crimes and crimes against humanity, but ruled that there was insufficient evidence to prosecute him for genocide. Al-Bashir was the first sitting head of state to be indicted by the ICC.

The African Union (AU), the Arab League and many individual African states and leaders have strongly opposed the arrest warrant. The AU's Peace and Security Council (PSC) requested the UNSC to defer the process, initiated by the ICC, in accordance with article 16 of the Rome Statute, on the basis that such a prosecution may not be in the interest of the victims and justice.[25] They have stated that the AU was the most appropriate organisation to solve the problem.

In addition, the PSC invited the AU Commission to take all necessary steps for the establishment of an independent High-Level Panel, made up of distinguished Africans, to examine the situation in depth and to submit recommendations to the Council on how best the issues of accountability and combating impunity, on the one hand, and reconciliation and healing, on the other, could be effectively and comprehensively addressed,[26] thereby adding a regional dimension to the debate.[27] At its 12th Ordinary Session, not only did the AU Assembly endorse the decision of the PSC, passed during the 142nd meeting but it also expressed its deepest concern at the indictment made by the ICC Prosecutor.[28]

[23] Rose, 'Looking Beyond Amnesty', 365.

[24] UNSC Res 1593 (31 March 2005), UN Doc S/RES/1593 (2005).

[25] African Union, Communique of the 142nd Meeting of the Peace and Security Council, PSC/MIN/Comm (CXLII), para 11(i).

[26] ibid, para 11(ii).

[27] L Oette, 'Peace and Justice, or Neither? The Repercussions of the *al-Bashir* Case for International Criminal Justice in Africa and Beyond' (2010) 8 *Journal of International Criminal Justice* 345–64, 345.

[28] Assembly of the African Union, Decision on the Application by the International Criminal Court (ICC) Prosecutor for the Indictment of the President of the Republic of the Sudan, 12th Ordinary Session, 1–3 February 2009, Addis Ababa, Ethiopia, Assembly/AU/Dec 221(XII), para 1.

This was reiterated at its 13th ordinary session, that emphasised the unfortunate consequences that the indictment had had on the delicate peace processes underway in the Republic of Sudan and regretted that the request by the AU to the UNSC to defer the proceedings initiated against President al-Bashir, in accordance with article 16 of the Rome Statute, had neither been heard nor acted upon. Additionally in view of the fact that the request made by the AU has never been acted upon, the AU decided that its Member States should not cooperate, pursuant to the provisions of article 98 of the Rome Statute concerning the matter of immunities, in the arrest and surrender of President Omar al-Bashir of the Republic of Sudan.[29]

As can be seen, the UNSC and the ICC not only turned their backs on the possibility of a regional solution, ignoring the requests made by the AU but also this attitude resulted in the call to disobey the order for the arrest of President al-Bashir that undermines the integrity and credibility of the ICC. It is certainly a missed opportunity to apply 'African solutions to African problems'.

IV. INTERNATIONAL CRIMINAL JUSTICE: WHAT IS IT FOR?

Regional factors have been invoked to maintain that the use of international criminal prosecution is ignorant of African modes of justice and reconciliation. Therefore, international criminal tribunals, based on Western notions of justice, are inadequate, if not counterproductive, because they can do very little to re-establish a social balance in Africa.[30] Prosecution and punishment should not be viewed as the only, or even the most important, means to end impunity. If we confine ourselves to the courts in the struggle to guarantee human rights, we may ignore many other important initiatives designed to assist victims, rebuild societies and defend democracies.[31]

Justice is often classified according to two very distinct ideological perspectives: retributive and restorative. Retributivism holds that one who freely chose to victimise another deserves to suffer accordingly, and/or one who was victimised deserves rectification. When the victimisation is criminal, punishment usually has been taken to be the necessary means to accomplish this.[32] Retributive justice is most commonly associated with accountability and punishment, and focuses on forcing the perpetrator of a crime to 'pay' for the actions he took in the commission of that crime.

Restorative justice, conversely, is a process of active participation in which the wider community deliberates over past crimes. Under this approach the crime is viewed essentially as a violation of people and of relationships between people. Its

[29] Assembly of the African Union, Decision on the Abuse of the Principle of Universal Jurisdiction, 13th Ordinary Session, 1–3 July 2009, Sirte, Great Socialist People's Libyan Arab Jamahiriya, Assembly/AU/Dec 243(XIII) Rev 1, Doc Assembly/AU/1 I (XIII), para 4.

[30] Oette, 'Peace and Justice, or Neither?', 360.

[31] JK Yav, 'The relationship between the International Criminal Court and Truth Commissions: Some thoughts on how to build a bridge across retributive and restorative justices' (Centre for Human Rights and Democracy Studies, 2005), available at www.iccnow.org/documents/InterestofJustice_JosephYav_May05.pdf.

[32] E Blumenson, 'The Challenge of a Global Standard of Justice: Peace, Pluralism and Punishment at the International Criminal Court' (2006) 44 *Columbia Journal of Transnational Law* 801–74, 829.

primary objective is to correct such violations and to restore relationships. Therefore this process involves not only the perpetrator, the victims and survivors, but also the community in order to achieve a kind of justice that promotes reparation and reconciliation giving centre stage to both victim and perpetrator in a process that seeks to grant dignity and empowerment to the victim, with special emphasis placed upon contextual factors.[33]

As expressed in the Working Paper by the Refugee Law Project,

> [T]he traditional African sense of justice is not simply about isolating the retributive aspects of justice, as it is in the Western model. Instead, retribution is but one part of an overarching process that also encompasses rehabilitation, reconciliation, compensation, and restoration. In other words, it is not just that retribution equals justice. Indeed, justice itself is one component of restoring perpetrators back into harmony with the values of a community.[34]

Alternatively, there are those who consider that the foregoing analysis of the term's meaning suggests that 'justice' in the Rome Statute is meant to be retributive.[35] On this view, there would be no place for the type of interpretation that has just been presented. This factor notwithstanding, the objective of using criminal prosecution to re-establish social balance and to promote reconciliation, while laudable and rhetorically inspiring, is simply unattainable.[36] Eric Blumenson poses the question: what should happen when ICC non-intervention is important in ending a conflict?[37] We agree with his view that the obligation to do justice is not identical to, and does not always entail, a simple duty to prosecute and punish.[38]

Efforts to use criminal prosecution to modify behaviour and contribute to social balance rests on a failure to appreciate that the causes of conflict in Africa cannot be resolved through the criminal process, especially because the causes of deviant conduct reside not at the individual level but at the communal level. The main objective of criminal prosecution is punishing the guilty without providing a real remedy for social conflicts, which are at the root of the problem.[39] If this does not solve those problems then no matter how many convictions there are, they will never achieve the goal of peace.

The best summary of these ideas is expressed by the Refugee Law Project:

> [T]he implementers of retributive institutions see their task as mainly technical in nature, and often fail to consider contextual factors. This has been called 'global legalism from above' and is seen as one of the biggest difficulties of outside experts participating in the building of appropriate institutions in post-conflict societies. These programs are often 'one-size-fits-all' and therefore less effective than tailor-made solutions, since they target institutions and structures, rather than getting to the heart of the problem. In other words, while many of the ideals are good in theory, when applied to a complex conflict such as

[33] Yav, 'The relationship between the International Criminal Court and Truth Commissions'; Refugee Law Project Working Paper No 17, 'Peace First, Justice Later', 11.

[34] 'Peace First, Justice Later', ibid, 12.

[35] Kourabas, 'A Vienna Convention Interpretation of the "Interests Of Justice"', 74.

[36] O Oko, 'The Challenges of International Criminal Prosecutions in Africa' 31 *Fordham International Law Journal* (2008) 343–414, 349.

[37] Blumenson, 'The Challenge of a Global Standard of Justice', 834.

[38] ibid.

[39] Oko, 'The Challenges of International Criminal Prosecutions in Africa', 350.

> the one in northern Uganda, they look inadequate if applied in isolation. It is a mistake to assume that simply prosecuting and, hopefully, convicting Kony and a few of his senior commanders will satisfy the needs of justice in this context.[40]

We should not fall into the temptation of over-estimating and over-emphasising the role and impact of law in society. Despite the fact that the law and justice are fundamental pillars of society, these are not the only ones and there exists no single means of implementation either.

[40] Refugee Law Project Working Paper No 17, 'Peace First, Justice Later', 37.

Part VII

Regional Integration: Some Perspectives on Trade, Investment and Development

23

Public Interest in EU Foreign Investment Policy

IRENE BLÁZQUEZ-NAVARRO*

I. INTRODUCTION

TRADE AND INVESTMENT have historically been awkwardly coupled in the WTO. Moreover, the multilateral trading system still seems to be in a lasting abeyance when it comes to addressing the rapidlyevolving patterns of global trade. The relationship of investment law with trade law occurs in parallel and beyond the WTO. Together with bilateral investment treaties (BITs), states are increasingly concluding preferential trade agreements (PTAs) covering investment as well as other trade-related (and unrelated) issues and setting up their own far-reaching dispute-settlement mechanisms. A novel multi-dimensional regionalism is on the rise, with investment as one of its core flagships.

Within this regulatory framework, the advent of the European Union (EU), following the Lisbon Treaty, as the major global actor in the field of international investment law may influence many aspects of the future direction of this evolving regime of international law, which itself is presently embraced by a form of novel cross-cutting regionalisation.

This chapter discusses the increasing diversification of international economic law, and makes a statement concerning the interconnection of legal systems in this field, focusing on one aspect of fundamental and systemic importance in international investment law and arbitration: the search for increased consideration of the public interest.

It is submitted that the EU—itself an autonomous model of regional integration, which is under pinned by a solid construction of fundamentals or principles[1]—will normatively, and by adjudication, mediate to carve out the proper policy space for

* Senior Lecturer in Public International Law and European Union Law at the Autónoma University of Madrid (on leave). Currently and since October 2012, Head of the Strategic Affairs Office of the National Security Department at the Cabinet of the Prime Minister. All the views expressed in this chapter are strictly personal. I am most grateful for conversations with Ramón Vidal Puig (Legal Service of the European Commission). This chapter is framed within the Research Project on *Global Legal Goods* funded by the Spanish Ministry of Science and Innovation (DER2009-11436).

[1] Advocate General Cruz Villalón, 'Rights in Europe: The Crowded House' in J Díez-Hochleitner, C Martínez Capdevila, I Blázquez-Navarro and Frutos Miranda (eds), *Últimas tendencias en la Jurisprudencia del Tribunal de Justicia de la Unión Europea/Recent Trends in the Case Law of the Court of Justice of the European Union* (2008–2011) (Madrid, La ley/Wolters Kluwer, 2012) 1135–51.

the protection of legitimate public policy goods, and that this will affect the regime of international investment law.

The EU could, on the one hand, give content to classical investment treaty provisions—including the exception for public regulatory autonomy—and mediate in the legitimacy crisis that pervades investment arbitration[2] due to some 'egregious failures', such as the misuse of precedent, lack of internal consistency and minimalism.[3] Moreover, ideally, the minimum common standards of the future EU investment policy model could be multilateralised in the WTO as the basis for the regulation of investment by the WTO itself.[4] The engagement of the WTO,via this mode of assimilation, in twenty-first-century trade issues would contribute to saving the organisation from the risk of lethargy.[5]

In order to develop the aforementioned statement according to which the EU will promote a shift towards the wider protection of legitimate public policy goods, this chapter touches upon three issues, before concluding by drawing up a series of questions about investor-state arbitration mechanisms in EU international investment agreements.

First, the chapter looks at current trends in trade and investment policy. Second, it deals with the EU's competence to conclude PTAs covering investment and stand-alone investment agreements after the Lisbon Treaty, and explores the challenges of the EU's future investment policy. Third, it considers how the EU should define the balance between public and private interests that are at stake in international trade and investment agreements. It also looks at the role of the adjudicative branch in the final analysis to resolve the conflict between the protection of investors and the protection of public goods and the use by the adjudicator of the means-end scrutiny approach to achieving this end. Assuming that legal regimes interconnect mostly through adjudication, the chapter concludes with some remarks concerning future EU investor-state dispute settlement mechanisms.

II. CURRENT TRENDS IN TRADE AND INVESTMENT POLICY

Global trade and economy patterns are changing dramatically.[6] One of the most sweeping changes is 'the emergence of foreign direct investment as the main driver

[2] SD Frank, 'The Legitimacy Crisis in Investment Arbitration: Privatizing Public International Law through Inconsistent Decisions' (2005) 73 *Fordham Law Review* 1521–1625 and D Schneiderman, 'Legitimacy and Reflexivity in International Investment Arbitration: A New Self-Restraint?' (2011) *Journal of International Dispute Settlement* 471–95.

[3] F Ortino, 'Legal Reasoning of International Investment Tribunals: A Typology of Egregious Failures' (2012) 3 *Journal of International Dispute Settlement* 31–52.

[4] Journal Pauwelyn, 'Legal Avenues to "Multilateralizing Regionalism": Beyond Article XXIV' in R Baldwin and P Low (eds), *Multilateralizing Regionalism* (2009) 368–99 and J Pauwelyn, 'The WTO in Crisis: Five Fundamentals Reconsidered', paper submitted to the WTO Public Forum 2012 panel, *Is Multilateralism in Crisis?*, 24–26 September 2012, available at www.wto.org/english/forums_e/public_forum12_e/public_forum12_e.htm.

[5] H Gao and CL Lim, 'Saving the WTO from the Risk of Irrelevance: The WTO Dispute Settlement Mechanism as a "Common Good" for RTA Disputes' (2008) 11 *Journal of International Economic Law* 899–925.

[6] R Baldwin, '21st Century Trade and Global Trade Governance: The WTO's Future', paper submitted to the WTO Public Forum 2012, *Is Multilateralism in Crisis?*, available at www.wto.org/english/forums_e/public_forum12_e/public_forum12_e.htm.

of global integration and the re-configuration of much of world trade around cross-border production networks.'[7]

The WTO is ill-equipped both to cope with the emergence of this new kind of trade and to provide a normative response to the challenge it raises. There is a need for a WTO-plus multilateral trading system but, as has been emphasised, 'while the crisis continues to hit national systems hard, it will be very difficult to achieve high-standard multilateralism'.[8] In fact, the upward trend is forthe necessary governance to be provided mostly by preferential trade agreements (PTAs), accompanied by bilateral investment treaties (BITs).

The 2012 edition of the annual *World Investment Report* from the United Nations Conference on Trade and Development (UNCTAD) reflected this change in traditional investment treaty-making patterns. Thus, while BITs still dominate in quantitative terms, the proliferation of expansive PTAs (covering investment) has gained tremendous momentum as evidenced by the investment negotiations under way for the Trans-Pacific Partnership (TPP) Agreement, the conclusion of the trilateral investment agreement between China, Japan, and the Republic of Korea, the Mexico-Central America Free Trade Agreement (FTA) or the fact that the EU now has the power to conclude international agreements covering investment,[9] as witnessed by the Comprehensive Economic and Trade Agreement (CETA) with Canada.

Alongside the assertion of the last few decades, according to which 'regionalism is here to stay',[10] it has even been proclaimed that PTAs are now 'the only game in town'.[11] Moreover, adjudication of disputes through PTA-based dispute settlement mechanisms has come to reflect asymmetries of power in a way that the WTO dispute settlement has tried to prevent.

BITs play their part in this process of normative diversification beyond and outside the framework of the WTO. Despite the fact that the annual number of BITs has gradually decreased, they continue to be one of the most important sources of international investment law.

Recent global trends in investment policy are not only shifting to regionalism, but to a greater consideration of sustainable development objectives at the heart of investment promotion. This involves the balancing of the rights and obligations of investors and states towards the preservation of a space for the state to pursue legitimate public goods, and there is an increased concern about the necessary reform of investor-state dispute settlement mechanisms.[12]

[7] G de Jonquières, 'Wanted: A New Model for Multilateralism', paper submitted to the WTO Public Forum 2012, *Is Multilateralism in Crisis?*, ibid.

[8] P Lamy, speech at the Humboldt-Viadrina School of Governance in Berlin, 26 June 2012, available at www.wto.org/english/news_e/sppl_e/sppl239_e.htm.

[9] UNCTAD, *World Investment Report: Towards a New Generation of Investment Policies* (Geneva, UNCTAD, 2012) http://unctad.org/en/pages/newsdetails.aspx?OriginalVersionID=171&Sitemap_x0020_Taxonomy=World%20Investment%20Report.

[10] R Baldwin, 'Multilateralising Regionalism: Spaghetti Bowls as Building Blocs on the Path to Global Free Trade' (2006) 29 *The World Economy* 1451–518, 1508.

[11] J Bhagwati, 'The Broken Legs of Global Trade', paper submitted to the WTO Public Forum 2012, *Is Multilateralism in Crisis?*, available at www.wto.org/english/forums_e/public_forum12_e/public_forum12_e.htm.

[12] UNCTAD, *World Investment Report* (2012) 75–83.

The EU has broadly resorted to the use of article XXIV of the GATT 1994, which exceptionally allows a departure from the WTO's core most favoured nation principle (MFN), which requires that any trade concession by a WTO member must be extended immediately and unconditionally to every other WTO member.[13] The EU has concluded PTAs with third countries to such an extent that the EU's strict MFN regime applies to only a few WTO members.[14] MFN is no longer the rule of the EU's external trade relations—rather it has become the exception.[15]

With the entry into force of the Lisbon Treaty,[16] the EU acquired exclusive competence over foreign direct investment (FDI). Thus, despite some nuances, the EU has overall responsibility for the conclusion of international agreements on investment protection, whether BITS or PTAs, that provide for 'investor-state dispute settlement' mechanisms. The new exclusive competence of the EU on FDI will broadly influence EU policy concerning PTAs and BITs, and will have an impact on the investment-related international economic order. The political institutions of the EU have already taken positions on issues pertaining to international investment law. Comprehensive free trade agreements negotiations in which investment protection is being considered include the recently concluded EU-Canada FTA, or CETA, and negotiations with India and Singapore. Therefore, at least from the EU perspective,

[13] art XXIV of GATT 1994 permits the establishment of free trade areas and customs unions in the field of trade in goods derogating from the MFN clause. These PTAs have to avoid trade diversion and to promote trade creation and, as a result, guarantee the compatibility with the WTO regime. They should cover 'substantially' all trade, and the level of protection should not be higher than the average protection secured by national tariffs before setting up the regional agreement. The regional economic integration exception covering trade in services in PTAs is found in art V of the GATS while the special regime for PTAs, concluded among developing countries, is contained in para 2(c) of the Decision on Differential and more Favorable Treatment, Reciprocity and Fuller Participation of Developing Countries, 28 November 1979, called the 'Enabling Clause'. See WTO, *World Trade Report, The WTO and Preferential Trade Agreements: From Co-Existence to Coherence* (2011), particularly Part E 'The Multilateral Trading System and PTAs'.

On the proliferation of PTAs, and its impact on the multilateral system and related issues, see KC Bagwell and P Mavroidis (eds), *Preferential Trade Agreements—A Law and Economic Analysis* (Cambridge, Cambridge University Press, 2011); R Baldwin and P Low (eds), *Multilateralizing Regionalism* (Cambridge, Cambridge University Press, 2009); L Bartels and F Ortino (eds), *Regional Trade Agreements and the WTO Legal System* (Oxford, Oxford University Press, 2006); Y-S Lee, 'Reconciling RTAs with the WTO Multilateral Trading System: Case for a New Sunset Requirement on RTAs and Development Facilitation' (2011) 45 *Journal of World Trade* 629–51; P Mavroidis, 'WTO and PTAs: A Preference for Multilateralism? (or the Dog That Tried to Stop the Bus)' (2010) 44 *Journal of World Trade*, 1145–54 and P Mavroidis, 'Always Look at the Bright Side of Non-delivery: WTO and Preferential Trade Agreements, Yesterday and Today' (2011) 10 *World Trade Review* 375–87.

On the Decision of the General Council of the WTO concerning the Transparency Mechanism for Regional Trade Agreements, WTO Doc WT/L/671 of 18 December 2006, see S Shadikhodjaev, 'Checking RTA Compatibility with Global Trade Rules: WTO Litigation Practice and Implications from the Transparency Mechanism for RTAs' (2011) 45 *Journal of World Trade* 529–51.

[14] M Cremona, 'The European Union and Regional Trade Agreements' (2010) *European Yearbook of International Economic Law* 245–68.

[15] DC Horng, 'Reshaping the EU's FTA Policy in a Globalizing Economy: The Case of the EU-Korea FTA', (2012) 46 *Journal of World Trade* 301–26.

[16] Treaty of Lisbon amending the Treaty on European Union and the Treaty establishing the European Community, done at Lisbon on 13 December 2007, [2007] OJ C 306, entered into force 1 December 2009 (Treaty of Lisbon or Treaty on European Union or TEU).

it is a 'momentous development'[17] not only enhancing the coherence of EU foreign trade policy, but also developing much further the use of general principles in the global law of foreign investment.

III. THE EU'S COMPETENCE TO CONCLUDE PTAs COVERING INVESTMENT AND STAND-ALONE INVESTMENT AGREEMENTS

The European Economic Community (EEC) was not originally conceived as a single financial market. However, a progressive and complex normative design of EU financial policy has taken place over the years. In its external relations, the realisation and implementation of the EU's financial competences have been even more complex and blurred.[18]

Two main structural factors have favoured the regulation of direct investment through BITs concluded by memberstates and third states: first, the fact that the EEC did not establish obligations regarding financial relations beyond the Community; second, the lack of a multilateral international legal framework regulating direct foreign investment in a truly multilateral manner. The European Court of Justice (ECJ) stated clearly in its Opinion 1/94 that in the specific area of financial services the EU and its members had shared powers.[19]

In this context, although the EU's past mixed agreements[20] included an agenda on investment, it was a very narrow and limited one. Since 2006 and under the Global Europe strategy of 2006,[21] the EU has concluded comprehensive agreements including areas outside its exclusive competence and beyond WTO disciplines such as investment.[22] The EC-Chile Association Agreement and the EU-CARIFORUM Economic Partnership Agreement are both good examples of this strategy.[23] Moreover, the 'Minimum Platform on Investment' adopted on 27 November 2006 by the

[17] P Eeckhout, 'The European Union and International Law under the Treaty of Lisbon' *EJIL Talk!*, 15 October 2009, available at www.ejiltalk.org/the-european-union-and-international-law-under-the-treaty-of-lisbon/.

[18] LM Hinojosa Martínez, 'Las Relaciones Financieras de la UE con el Exterior' in A Remiro Brotóns and I Blázquez-Navarro (eds), *El Futuro de la Acción Exterior de la Unión Europea* (Valencia, Tirant lo Blanch 2006) 337–87.

[19] Opinion 1/94 [1994] ECR I-5267; according to the Court, the EU only had exclusive powers over investment related to trade under the Agreement on Trade-related Investment Measures (TRIMS), Annex 1A to the Agreement Establishing the World Trade Organization. The TRIMS forbids trade-related investment measures that distort international trade, such as local requirements for foreign investments that are deemed inconsistent with basic provisions of the GATT 1994.

[20] C Hillion and P Koutrakos, *Mixed Agreements Revisited—The EU and Its Member States in the World* (Oxford, Hart Publishing, 2010).

[21] 'Global Europe: Competing in the World. A Contribution to the EU's Growth and Job Strategy' COM(2006) 567 final.

[22] J Chaisse, 'Promises and Pitfalls of the European Union Policy on Foreign Investment—How Will the New EU Competence on FDI Affect the Emerging Global Regime?'(2012) 15 *Journal of International Economic Law* 51–84; T Eilmansberger, 'Bilateral Investment Treaties and EU Law' (2009) 46 *Common Market Law Review* 383–429, 387.

[23] See generally, http://trade.ec.europa.eu/doclib/docs/2012/june/tradoc_149622.jpg. For the current negotiating agenda of the EU, see Commission Staff Working Document on 'External sources of growth—Progress report on EU trade and investment relationships with key economic partners', available at http://ec.europa.eu/trade/policy/accessing–markets/investment/index_en.htm.

Council of the EU foresaw the systematic inclusion of investment chapters in the negotiation of PTAs.[24]

The Lisbon Treaty granted the EU new trade policy powers.[25] This is because the Treaty on the Functioning of the European Union (TFEU)[26] established for the first time the European Union's exclusive competence on foreign direct investment, as part of the EU's common commercial policy.[27]

Of special importance is the fact that the Lisbon Treaty equips the Common Commercial Policy with the general objectives of EU external action[28] and ensures that the European Parliament will play a prominent role in the trade policy of the Union because the ordinary legislative procedure applies for the adoption of internal acts.[29] The consent of the Parliament is needed for the conclusion of international trade agreements,[30] and the Commission has to report regularly to the special committee of the Parliament on the progress of trade negotiations.[31]

[24] Minimum Platform on Investment, adopted on 27 November 2006 by the Council of the European Union (unpublished Council document 15375/06), with revised version of 6 March 2009. See N Maydell, 'The European Community's Minimum Platform on Investment or the Trojan Horse of Investment Competence' in A Reinisch and C Knahr (eds), *International Investment Law in Context* (Utrecht, Eleven Publishing, 2008) 73–92. The Platform's scope of application was limited to 'measures affecting establishment'.

[25] The constitutional changes introduced by the Lisbon Treaty can be traced back to the Constitutional Treaty. See LN González Alonso, '¿Recomponiendo la figura?: el Tratado Constitucional y la competencia de la Unión Europea en materia de Relaciones Económicas Exteriores' in Remiro Brotóns and Blázquez Navarro (eds), *El Futuro de la Acción Exterior* 295–335; and M Krajewski, 'External Trade Law and the Constitution Treaty: Towards a Federal and More Democratic Common Commercial Policy?' (2005) 42 *Common Market Law Review* 91–127.

[26] See Consolidated version of the Treaty on the Functioning of the European Union [2012] OJ C 326/47 (Treaty on Functioning of European Union, or TFEU).

[27] art 207(1) and art 3(1)(e) TFEU. This is a topic of utmost concern in the academic literature. See R Vidal Puig, 'The Scope of the New Exclusive Competence of the European Union with Regard "Foreign Direct Investment"' (2013) 40 *Issues of Economic Integration* 133–62. See further, JA Bischoff, 'Just a Little BIT of "Mixity"? The EU's Role in the Field of International Investment Protection Law' (2011) 48 *Common Market Law Review* 1527–69; JN Calamita, 'The Making of Europe's International Investment Policy: Uncertain First Steps' (2012) 39 *Legal Issues of Economic Integration* 301–29; J Chaisse, 'Promises and Pitfalls' 56–62; A Dimopoulos, *EU Foreign Investment Law* (Oxford, Oxford University Press, 2011); M Krajewski, 'The Reform of the Common Commercial Policy' in A Biondi, P Eeckhout (eds) with S Ripley, EU *Law After Lisbon* (Oxford, Oxford University Press, 2011) 292–311, 301–04; N Lavranos, 'New Developments in the Interaction between International Investment Law and EU Law' (2010) 9 *The Law and Practice of International Courts and Tribunals* 409–41, 424–30; F Ortino and P Eeckhout, 'Towards an EU Policy on Foreign Direct Investment' in Biondi and Eeckhout (eds) with Ripley, *EU Law After Lisbon*, 312–27. See further 'Symposium on International Investment Law and European Union', KP Sauvant (ed), *Yearbook on International Investment Law & Policy 2010/2011* (New York, Oxford University Press, 2011).

[28] A Dimopoulos, 'The Effects of the Lisbon Treaty on the Principles and Objectives of the Common Commercial Policy' (2010) 15 *European Foreign Affairs Review* 153–70 and M Krajewski, 'The Reform of the Common Commercial Policy', ibid, 294–98.

Art 2 TEU establishes the Union's values and art 3 TEU sets its overall objectives. On the principles and objectives of the EU External Action, see M Cremona, 'External Relations and External Competence of the European Union: the Emergence of an Integrated Policy' in P Craig and G de Búrca (eds), *The Evolution of EU Law*, 2nd edn (Oxford, Oxford University Press, 2011) 217–68.

[29] art 207.2 TFEU.

[30] art218.6 (a) (i) to (v) TFEU.

[31] art 207.3 TFEU.

The exact scope of this new competence of the EU for the adoption of internal acts, according to article 207 TFEU,[32] is unclear. There is disagreement as to whether the EU has an implied exclusive competence regarding foreign portfolio investment, on the basis of the rules set by the chapter of the Treaty on capital and payments. Another controversial issue is whether article 207 TFEU covers investment liberalisation and investment protection; this is to say, market access for direct investment as well as measures concerning the standards or guarantees of protection for investments. It is submitted that the competence of the EU should be read narrowly as regards the first aspect, ie the substantive scope of the competence when it comes to foreign portfolio investment.

However, when it comes to direct investment in third countries, the EU powers in this field encompass both investment liberalisation and investment protection.[33] The Treaty speaks of FDI, which does not cover all forms of transnational investment and, particularly, the competence of the EU on FDI does not extend to short-term financial participation in undertakings. Instead, FDI implies a cross-border, long-term investment with the objective of establishing a lasting interest in an enterprise located in a foreign country, with a controlling stake in a business. Moreover, if one reads the caselaw of the ECJ correctly, it is hard to see how an implied exclusive competence on foreign portfolio investment can stem from the Treaty on the Functioning of the TFEU.[34] The competence of the Union is then confined to FDI but there are no further limitations on the powers of the EU in article 207 TFEU.[35] The EU is competent to conclude investment treaties, including the substantive treatment and protection of investment.[36]

What is clear is that Member States retain shared competences concerning investment. In the short and medium term, the competence of the EU in this domain is too restricted o include all forms of foreign investment. In consequence, investment negotiations will be conducted as part of broader *mixed* agreements,[37] aimed at the liberalisation of the market and at providing protection guarantees for investments.[38] The EU-Korea Free Trade Agreement, in force since 1 July 2011, may serve as a benchmark for future negotiations.[39] So too may the Canada-EU Free Trade Agreement (CETA), which was recently signed but is not yet in force.

[32] art 207.2 TFEU.

[33] Ortino and Eeckhout, 'Towards an EU Policy on Foreign Direct Investment' 318–19.

[34] Specifically based on arts 63 to 66 TFEU and art 4.2(a) TFEU.

[35] See further in detail art 207 TFEU.

[36] In my opinion, art 345 TFEU should not be seen as excluding from the EU's competence protection against expropriation. For a comparative analysis, see R Geiger, 'Regulatory Expropriations in International Law: Lessons from the Multilateral Agreement on Investment' (2002–2003) 11 *New York University Environmental Law Review* 94–109; H Ruiz Fabri, 'The Approach Taken by the European Court of Human Rights to the Assessment of Compensation for "Regulatory Expropriations" of the Property of Foreign Investors' (2002–2003) 11 *New York University Environmental Law Review* 148–73.

[37] See also Bischoff, 'Just a Little BIT of "Mixity"?'.

[38] See Commission, 'Towards a Comprehensive European International Investment Policy' COM(2010)343 final and 'Commission Staff Working Document on External sources of growth'. For an overview of FTA and other Trade Negotiations: http://ec.europa.eu/trade/creating-opportunities/bilateral-relations/agreements and http://trade.ec.europa.eu/doclib/docs/2012/june/tradoc_149622.jpg.

[39] For the EU–Korea FTA, see Horng, 'Reshaping the EU's FTA Policy'. Comprehensive free trade agreements negotiations in which investment protection has been considered include the Comprehensive

Both in trade *plus* agreements covering investment and BITs, mixity is here to stay in this new area of the Union's external action. Mixity should be managed according to the principles developed by the ECJ in its caselaw on the duty of loyal cooperation.[40] The Court has underlined the requirement (referred to as a principle for the first time in the *PFOS* case)[41] of unity in the international representation of the EU. In order to ensure that unity of representation, it is necessary to guarantee close cooperation between Member States and the Union, both in the process of negotiation and conclusion and in the implementation of the relevant agreement.

A future EU investment policy certainly requires cooperation and coordination among the Union and the Member State.[42] It remains to be seen whether Member States will carefully safeguard their retained national competences in the field of foreign investment, and how they will manage mixity alongside the EU institutions. It is not redundant to think that the Court will have to draw aline between exclusive and shared external investment competences by way of preliminary rulings, or in the exercise of its jurisdiction under article 218.11 TFEU. Besides, the responsibility for a breach of these mixed agreements that the EU and its member states might trigger needs to be addressed.[43]

Economic and Trade Agreement with Canada, for which negotiations concluded on 26 September 2014; EU–India negotiations towards a Broad-based Trade and Investment Agreement; EU–Singapore negotiations towards a Free Trade Agreement; and EU–Mercosur trade negotiations. Comprehensive free trade agreements have been recently concluded with Colombia and Peru and with Central America. According to the Commission, the EU should also consider under what circumstances it may be desirable to pursue stand-alone investment agreements. China and Russia may be candidates for an investment agreement covering all kinds of assets. See for an update on the state of negotiations, http://trade.ec.europa.eu/doclib/docs/2006/december/tradoc_118238.pdf.

[40] On the duty of loyalty and EU external relations law, see M Cremona, 'Defending the Community Interest: The Duties of Cooperation and Compliance' in M Cremona and B De Witte (eds), *EU Foreign Relations Law—Constitutional Fundamentals* (Oxford, Hart Publishing, 2008) 125–69; C Hillion, 'Mixity and Coherence in EU External Relations: The significance of the "duty of cooperation"' in Hillion and Koutrakos, *Mixed Agreements Revisited*, 87–115.

[41] On the *PFOS* case, see M Cremona, 'Case Comment on C–246/07, *CommissionvSweden (PFOS)*' (2011) *Common Market Law Review* 1639–66; A Delgado Casteleiro and J Larik, 'The Duty to Remain Silent: Limitless Loyalty in EU External Relations' (2011) 36 *European Law Review* 522–39; A Thies, 'Shared Competence and the EU Member States' Obligation to Refrain from Unilateral External Action: *PFOS* and Beyond' in J Díez-Hochleitner et al, *Últimas tendencias en la Jurisprudencia/Recent Trends in the Case Law*, 703–28; A Delgado Casteleiro, 'No More Mr Nice Guy: The Evolution of the Duty of Sincere Cooperation in EU External Relations Law' in ibid, 729–36.

On the BITs judgments of 2009, see C–205/06, *Commission vAustria* [2009] ECR I–1301 and C–249/06, *Commission v Sweden* [2009] ECR I–1335; and Case C–118/07, *Commission vFinland* [2009] ECR I-10889; see also J Díez-Hochleitner, 'El incierto futuro de los acuerdos bilaterales sobre protección de inversiones celebrados por los Estados miembros de la Unión Europea'(2010) 33 *Revista Española de Derecho Europeo* 5–43, also in (2010) 8*Spain Arbitration Review* 19–51; A Dimopoulos, 'The BITs-Casesand Their Practical and Doctrinal Implications' in Díez-Hochleitner et al, *Últimas tendencias en la Jurisprudencia/Recent Trends in the Case Law*, 737–58; P Eeckhout, 'Investment Treaties and EU Law', *EJIL: Talk!*, July 2009, available at www.ejiltalk.org/investment-treaties-and-eu-law/; N Lavranos, '*CommissionvAustria* Case C–205/06, Judgment, March 3, 2009, *CommissionvSweden*, Case C–294/06, Judgment, March 3, 2009: European Court of Justice Decisions on the Legal Status of Pre-Accession Bilateral Investment Treaties Between European Member States and Third Countries' (2009) 103 *American Journal of International Law* 716–22. See also Case C–264/09 *Commission v Slovakia* [2011] I–8065.

[42] See Calamita, 'The Making of Europe's International Investment Policy', for the different and sometimes conflicting views among the political institutions of the EU as regards future EU investment policy.

[43] For some concerns that the new EU competence, according to EU law, due to the legal status of existing BITs concluded by the Member States after the Lisbon Treaty and the obligations for Member

In the foreseeable future the EU will have to meet the challenge of definingthe substantive guarantees rather than standards for the protection of investments that the Union might seek to introduce into its agreements, such as according fair and equitable treatment, providing full protection and security, regulating rules on expropriation, observing contractual obligations undertaken with regard to investors, establishing dispute settlement procedures, and so on. In sum, the EU will have to give content to classical investment treaty provisions.

Although it is too early to make an accurate assessment of the policy of the EU on FDI, the EU may be expected to assume a distinctive role, taking into account its opening statements and positions as reflected, among others, in the Communication from the Commission of 7 July 2010.[44] This is particularly so in the Resolution of the European Parliament of 6 April 2011 on the future European international investment policy.[45] These documents highlight the fact that the EU's international investment policy should be guided by the principles and objectives of the Union's external action, including the promotion of the rule of law, human rights and sustainable development. The statements of the Commission and the Parliament also show that investment agreements should be consistent with the other policies of the Union and its Member States, and that the European investment policy will continue to allow the EU and the Member States to adopt and enforce measures necessary to pursue public policy objectives. This is one of the most important aspects where the EU could influence the regime of international investment law.

IV. PUBLIC VERSUS PRIVATE INTERESTS IN EU INTERNATIONAL TRADE AND INVESTMENT AGREEMENTS

It is not easy to take a stance on the balance that international investment law must strike between public and private interests.[46] This dialectic is permeated by the concept of international investment law either as a system of international law whose

States arising from art 351 TFEU, see M Burgstaller, 'The Future of Bilateral Investment Treaties of EU Member States' and JP Terhechte, 'Art 351 TFEU, the Principle of Loyalty and the Future Role of the Member States' Bilateral Investment Treaties' in Bungenberg et al, *International Investment Law and EU Law* 55–77 and 79–93, respectively; and the extensive contribution of Eilmansberger, 'Bilateral Investment Treaties and EU Law'.

44 Communication from the Commission, 'Towards a Comprehensive European International Investment Policy'.

45 European Parliament Resolution of 6 April 2011 on the Future European International Investment Policy (2010/2203(INI)). See Calamita,'The Making of Europe's International Investment Policy', which considers the Council's Conclusions on a Comprehensive European International Investment Policy of 25 October 2010 and the Commission's response to the Parliament's Resolution, adopted on 5 July 2011, in determining whether the EU will find the right balance for its own investment policy, which is distinct from the practice followed by the member states.

46 A Mills, 'Antinomies of Public and Private at the Foundations of International Investment Law and Arbitration' (2011) 14 *Journal of International Economic Law* 469–503 and A Mills, 'The Public–Private Dualities of International Investment Law and Arbitration' in C Brown and K Miles (eds), *Evolution in Investment Treaty Law and Arbitration* (Cambridge, Cambridge University Press, 2011). This issue and the openness of international investment law to related regimes are discussed in Schneiderman, 'Legitimacy and Reflexivity in International Investment Arbitration'.

internal rationality is the promotion and protection of foreign investment, or as a field informed by general international law.[47] I believe that international legal systems must share the principles of public international law and, as has been emphasised in the WTO cluster, they cannot be isolated.[48] While the stability, transparency, and predictability of the legal framework of the host state are essential conditions for investors, and states are not allowed to escape their contractual and conventional obligations, the interpretation that some investment arbitral tribunals have offered when it comes to exception clauses, provided for in BITs, leads to an unbearable freezing of host state sovereignty. International investment agreements must be interpreted in accordance with general international law, which recognises the rights (and obligation) of states to regulate for the benefit of the protection of legitimate public goals.

This is a hot topic that has increasingly been raised.[49] In the EU it will receive increased attention in the wake of the economic and financial crisis,[50] including sovereign debt,[51] and the fact that currently traditional capital-exporting states have also become capital-importing states.

[47] See LANM Barnhoorn and KC Wellens, *Diversity in Secondary Rules and the Unity of International Law* (The Hague, TMC Asser Instituut, 1995); A Remiro Brotóns, 'Desvertebración del Derecho internacional en una sociedad globalizada' (1997) I*Cursos EuromediterráneosBancaja de Derecho Internacional* 45–381; and B Simma and D Pulkowski, 'Of Planets and the Universe: Self-contained Regimes in International Law' (2006) 17 *European Journal of International Law* 483–529.

As regards the WTO regime, see X Fernández Pons, *La OMC y el Derecho internacional. Un estudio sobre el sistema de solución de diferencias de la OMC y las normas secundarias del Derecho internacional general* (Madrid/Barcelona, Marcial Pons, 2006); A Lindroos and M Mehling, 'Dispelling the Chimera of "Self-Contained Regimes": International Law and the WTO' (2005) 16 *European Journal of International Law* 857–77; and J Pauwelyn, *Conflict of Norms in Public International Law. How WTO Law Relates to Other Rules of International Law* (Cambridge, Cambridge University Press, 2003).

[48] G Marceau, 'A Call for Coherence in International Law. Praises for the Prohibition against "Clinical Isolation" in WTO Dispute Settlement' (1999) 33 *Journal of World Trade* 87–152.

[49] A Asteriti and CJ Tams, 'Transparency and Representation of the Public Interest in Investment Treaty Arbitration' in SW Schill (ed), *International Investment Law and Comparative Public Law* (Oxford, Oxford University Press, 2010) 787–816; CH Brower II, 'Obstacles and Pathways to Consideration of the Public Interest in Investment Treaty Disputes' in KP Sauvant (ed), *Yearbook on International Investment Law &Policy 2008–2009* (New York, NY, Oxford University Press, 2009) 347–78, 356; L von Markert, 'The Crucial Question of Future Investment Treaties: Balancing Investors' Rights and Regulatory Interests of Host States' in Bungenberg et al, *International Investment Law and EU Law* 145–64; P Muchlinski, 'Trends in International Investment Agreements: Balancing Investor Rights and the Right to Regulate: The Issue of National Security' in Sauvant (ed), *Yearbook on International Investment Law and Policy 2008–2009* 35–78; SA Spears, 'The Quest for Policy Space in a New Generation of International Investment Agreements' (2010) 13 *Journal of International Economic Law* 1037–75 and SA Spears 'Making Way for the Public Interest in International Investment Agreements' in C Brown and K Miles (eds), *Evolution in Investment Treaty Law and Arbitration* (Cambridge, Cambridge University Press, 2011); A van Aaken, 'International Investment Law Between Commitment and Flexibility: A Contract Theory Analysis' (2009) 12 *Journal of International Economic Law* 507–38; von Walter, 'Balancing Investors' and Host States' Rights—What Alternatives for Treaty-makers? (2011) *European Yearbook of International Economic Law* 141–44.

[50] Report of A Giardina to the 18th Commission of the Institut de Droit International, Session of Rhodes 2011, 'Legal Aspects of Recourse to Arbitration by an Investor Against the Authorities of the Host State under Inter-State Treaties' (2011) 74 *Yearbook of the Institute of International Law*.

[51] M Waibel, 'Opening Pandora's Box: Sovereign Bonds in International Arbitration' (2007) 101 *American Journal of International Law* 711–59; M Waibel, *Sovereign Defaults before International Courts and Tribunals* (Cambridge, Cambridge University Press, 2011).

The EU could encapsulate a new understanding of how the rights and obligations of investors and states should be re-balanced, with more deference being given to the state to adopt measures in the public interest, provided that investment disputes arise in public service sectors. The EU seems ready to meet the challenge of giving content to the so-called 'non-precluded measures clauses', ie exception clauses that protect legitimate public policy objectives, according to the statements and positions of the political institutions of the Union.[52] However, this is a highly controversial issue and there is a strong disagreement among member states. Besides, the EU cannot build on member states' practice because existing EU member states' BITs are not familiar with these exception clauses that preserve the regulatory power of the state.

Although the legislative branch of the Union will have an important say, when the protection of foreign investors and public interest clash, sensitive policy questions are likely to be submitted to adjudication and then interpreted and decided by the international investment dispute settlement authorities. To begin with, putting too much emphasison the adjudicative branch can be reasonably curtailed: the EU legislative branch should define the space for autonomous regulation by the state in future EU agreements.[53]

It is a beliefthat scrutiny in investment law has traditionally been done with very limited textual guidance. Few subtleties are spelt out in investment treaties. This is also the case in the WTO or in the EU domain. At most, measures must be 'necessary' to achieve the desired policy goal, and their application should not amount to arbitrary or unjustifiable discrimination, or a disguised restriction on movement or activity. Recent EU FTAs covering investment seem to have followed this trend of broadly referring to the circumstances that speak of an abuse or an inappropriate use and application of the exception, although the exception itself is more elaborate.[54]

Looking to the future, the EU can be expected to incorporate in its international investment agreements narrowly worded exception clauses, defining the notion of public interest as a *lex specialis* on the basis of core values, enshrined in the EU autonomous legal order, as interpreted by the ECJ. Reference to safeguarding the

[52] In the Communication from the Commission of 7 July 2010, emphasis was put on the need to 'clearly define the balance of the interests at stake, such as protection of investors against illegal expropriation or the right of each party to regulate in the public interest'. Significantly, in the Preamble of the Resolution of the European Parliament of 6 April 2011, similar concerns were expressed at the vagueness of language in agreements being left open for interpretation, particularly concerning the possibility of conflict between private interests and the regulatory tasks of public authorities (see in particular letter G and paras 23–26 of the aforementioned Resolution).

[53] A Roberts, 'Power and Persuasion in Investment Treaty Interpretation: The Dual Role of States' (2010) 104 *American Journal of International Law* 179–225.

[54] For example, art 8.3 of the FTA between the EU and its member states, of the one part, and the Republic of Korea, of the other part, regulates the exceptions concerning payments and capital movements. The wording of the article reads: 'Subject to the requirement that such measures are not applied in a manner which would constitute a means of arbitrary or unjustifiable discrimination between countries where like conditions prevail, or a disguised restriction on capital movements, nothing in this Chapter shall be construed to prevent the adoption or enforcement by either Party of measures: a) necessary to protect public security and public morals or to maintain public order; b) necessary to secure compliance with law and regulations which are not inconsistent with the provision of this Chapter including those relating to, among others, measures adopted or maintained to ensure the integrity and stability of a party's financial system, among others.'

public interest can be included as an objective in the agreement or in the preamble. National interests will be equally respected and preserved, since general principles of EU law are deeply rooted in the constitutional traditions of the member states.

Moreover, the EU could include interpretative statements in its agreements, attach reservations for certain sectors, leave out the *ex ante* state consent for an investor-state arbitration mechanism, give the fair and equitable treatment provision a specific content and make of it not only a standard of protection, refer to constitutional guarantees of due process and access to justice in a manner consistent with the right of states to regulate, or identify non-economic policy objectives in the preamble of investment agreements that reflect the general principles of EU external action.[55]

This fulfilment of public policy space in international investment law will work to the benefit of legal certainty and predictability and the preservation of global public goods. Normatively speaking, the EU understanding could lay some foundations concerning the proper balance between public and private interests that the law of investment currently and worryingly fails to strike.

And yet in the final analysis the adjudicator will have to resolve the conflict between the protection of investors and the protection of public goods, particularly in a crisis situation.[56] From the arbitral practice, it can be inferred that at least two options are possible when the protection of foreign investors and legitimate public policy interests clash. This will be the case provided that the treaty contains an exception clause, or the preamble language is legally sound: to first, widely preserve the regulatory autonomy of the state to apply these exception clauses precluding wrongfulness; and second, open the margin of review for arbitral tribunals to consider whether the measures adopted by the state were necessary to protect public policy objectives and what those objectives might be. The tribunals should use

[55] On the wide range of avenues to render investment agreements more flexible and deferent to the regulatory policies of the state see H Mann, 'Investment Agreements and the Regulatory State: Can Exception Clauses Create a Safe Haven for Governments', Issues in International Investment Law—Background Papers for the Developing Country Investment Negotiators' Forum, Singapore, 2007, available at www.iisd.org/pdf/2007/inv_agreements_reg_state.pdf.

[56] Of course the Argentinean economic crisis of 2001–02, and the emergency measures adopted by the government of the Argentine Republic in response to the systemic crisis, come to mind. For a complete survey and an extensive analysis of the Argentinean necessity cases, see JE Alvarez and T Brink, 'Revisiting the Necessity Defense: Continental Casualty v Argentina' in Sauvant (ed), *Yearbook of International Investment Law and Policy 2010–2011*, 31–62; D Kalderimis, 'Systemic Interpretation and International Investment Law—Some Practical Reflections', Society of International Economic Law, Third Biennial Global Conference, Singapore, 2012, Online Proceedings, Working Paper No 2012/46, available at www.ssrn.com/link/SIEL-2012-Singapore-Conference.html; J Kurtz, 'Adjudging the Exceptional at International law: Security, Public Order and Financial Crisis' Society of International Economic Law, Inaugural Conference, Geneva, 2008, available at www.ssrn.com/link/SIEL-Inaugural-Conference.html; J Kurtz, 'Delineating Primary and Secondary Rules on Necessity at International Law' in T Broude and Y Shany (eds), *Multi-Sourced Equivalent Norms in International Law* (Oxford, Hart Publishing, 2011) 231–58; A van Aaken and J Kurtz, 'Emergency measures and international investment law: How far can States go?' in KP Sauvant (ed), *Yearbook on International Investment Law & Policy 2009–2010* (New York, Oxford University Press, 2010) 505–53.

Apart from the fact that in general the tribunals have failed to give sufficient grounds for their decisions, some of these decision are fraught with a misinterpretation of the principle of systemic interpretation embedded in art 31.3(c) of the Vienna Convention on the Law of the Treaties (done at Vienna, 23 May 1969, entered into force 27 January 1980) 1155 UNTS 331.

the means-end scrutiny approach that can imply rationality review, proportionality assessment (cost benefit balancing), the 'less restrictive standard' (cost-effectiveness and necessity), the margin of appreciation doctrine, and so on.[57]

Although the first option is basically sound, it might carry the risk of clinical isolation of the international investment regime and it might be taken too far and disregard important aims in investment treaties. The means-end scrutiny approach is driven precisely by the concern about the potential for abuse of exception clauses. However, this alternative of adjudicative review is fraught with sensitive problems. In all its manifestations, it leads to a certain degree of supervising involvement in the state sovereignty.

The open questions as to the appropriate legal test to apply and the margin of discretion of the adjudicative branch that have arisen in the context of the WTO[58] or in the EU internal market[59] are likely to arise in the investment setting as its adjudicative branch becomes more mature and prone to apply a means-end approach for the resolution of hard cases such as the one we are dealing with.

I support the view that '[I]t remains to be seen which, of any, of these approaches will be taken up on a consistent basis by investor-state tribunals interpreting new-generation international investment agreements', and that

> given that the general exceptions provisions in new-generation international investment agreements are largely based on Article XX of the GATT and Article XIV of the GATS, the

[57] On the issue of embracing balancing and proportionality in investment arbitration, see WW Burke-White and A von Staden, 'Private Litigation in a Public Law Sphere: The Standard of Review in Investor–State Arbitration' (2010) 35 *Yale Journal of International Law* 283–346; T Kleinlein, 'Judicial Lawmaking by Judicial Restraint? The Potential of Balancing in International Economic Law' (2011) 12 *German Law Journal* (Special Issue, *Beyond Dispute: International Judicial Institutions as Lawmakers*) 1141–74; B Kingsbury and S Schill, 'Investor–State Arbitration as Governance: Fair and Equitable Treatment, Proportionality and the Emerging Global Administrative Law' in B Kingsbury et al (eds), *El Nuevo Derecho Administrativo Global en América Latina* (Buenos Aires, EdicionesRap SA, 2009), available at: www.iilj.org/GAL/documents/GALBAbook.pdf, 221–94; A Stone Sweet, 'Investor–State Arbitration: Proportionality's New Frontier' (2010) 4 *Law and Ethics of Human Rights* 47–76.

[58] Prima facie the less restrictive alternative is based upon a constitutional principle of the GATT system—the regulatory autonomy of the states to set the level of protection of their public goods—and the adjudicator must exercise self-restraint to determine whether there is an alternative measure to achieve the same level of protection. See also P Eeckhout, 'The Scales of Trade—Reflections on the Growth and Functions of the WTO Adjudicative Branch' (2010) 13 *Journal of International Economic Law* 3–26, 19; CP Bown and JP Trachtman, '*Brazil—Measures Affecting Imports of Retreaded Tyres*: A Balancing Act' (2009)8 *World Trade Review* 85–135; JJ Weiler, 'Comment. *Brazil—Measures Affecting Imports of Retreaded Tyres* (DS322). Prepared for the ALI Project on the Case Law of the WTO', ibid, 137–44; and D Regan, 'The Meaning of "Necessity" in GATT Article XX and GATS Article XIV: The Myth of Cost–Benefit Balancing' (2007) 6 *World Trade Review* 347–69.

[59] Although the ECJ has sometimes identified a less restrictive alternative, it has usually applied a proportionality test according to which a measure cannot be justified if it is more restrictive than necessary to achieve the legitimate objective. Recently, the Court has underlined the point that measures must be 'appropriate' to achieve their intended purpose, and that they must genuinely reflect a concern to attain their purpose in a consistent and systematic manner. In this respect see P Oliver, 'Recent Trends in the Case-Law of the Court of Justice of the EU: the Internal Market' in J Díez-Hochleitner et al (eds), *Últimas tendencias en la Jurisprudencia/Recent Trends in the Case Law* 769–91, 781–83. Critically, on the scrutiny of justification by the ECJ as regards the principle of proportionality, see C Barnard, 'Derogations, Justifications and the Four Freedoms: Is State Interest Really Protected?' in C Barnard and O Odudu (eds), *The Outer Limits of European Union Law* (Oxford, Hart Publishing, 2009) 273–305.

> WTO Appellate Body's approach to interpreting general exception clause probably provides the best indication of how investor-state tribunals will approach them.[60]

This approach, in my opinion, would be applicable to the public interest exceptions included in EU international investment agreements. I believe that the argument that the WTO is principally member-driven and international investment law is only about protecting investors is not convincing enough to criticise the recourse in investment cases to WTO jurisprudence. It seems to me that this is an excessively rigorous understanding of the ends that international investment treaties serve.

Clearly, to ensure states' regulatory autonomy in the investment arena is essential for the evolution of the discipline. Fine-tuning by adjudicators would be the master-key of international investment law. The question that remains open is by which dispute settlement mechanisms the EU and its member states will abide, in the field of investment law.

V. CONCLUSIONS

International law has always been diverse and constitutional legal systems of certain treaty regimes, such as the EU legal order, might be a model of change for other evolving regimes. The transfer of competence to the Union in the field of FDI is one of the major innovations of the Lisbon Treaty. It is of utmost importance because the influence of the EU as a new actor in the international investment arena suggests that we may in the near future witness an enhanced interconnection of legal systems in the field, led by the EU. In particular, the EU may promote a shift towards the wider protection of legitimate public policy goods.

I assume that legal regimes interconnect mostly by adjudication. Although the European Union has incorporated in its recent FTAs dispute resolution mechanisms to resolve cases arising between states (and the Union), it is an open question how future EU agreements, which include an investment chapter about both the liberalisation and protection of investment (or EU future stand-alone investment agreements), will define these mechanisms for investor-state dispute settlement.[61] It is more usual in investor-state arbitration to grant foreign investors the option to bring a direct claim against the host state before a compulsory international arbitration mechanism, with ICSID being the most popular forum.

Given the fact that the ICSID dispute resolution is not at present, and to a large extent, anoption for 'EU-plus member states' investment protection, because the ICSID Convention is only open to signature and ratification by states that are members of the World Bank and/or parties to the Statute of the International Court of

[60] Spears, 'The Quest for Policy Space', 1049 and 1062.

[61] The EU has taken steps to manage financial responsibility linked to investor–state dispute settlement tribunals; see Proposal of the Commission for a Regulation of the European Parliament and the Council establishing a framework for managing financial responsibility linked to investor–state dispute settlement tribunals established by international agreements to which the European Union is party, Brussels, 21 June 2012 (COM(2012) 335 final—2012-0163], available at: http://trade.ec.europa.eu/doclib/docs/2012/june/tradoc_149567.pdf.

Justice, and the EU qualifies under neither, the Commission underlines the fact that '[I]n approaching investor-state dispute settlement mechanisms, the Union should build on Member State practices to arrive at state-of-the-art investor state dispute settlement mechanisms.'[62]

These state-of-the-art investor-state dispute settlement mechanisms raise several questions of concern in both short and medium-term scenarios. Where will we find a concurring and supplementary mechanism to ICSID arbitration for investors that are not nationals of ICSID member states, or for investors seeking redress exclusively from the EU? Perhaps in the long term—provided in this latter scenario that the statute of the International Monetary Fund were modified, accepting the EU as a signatory.

Among the most important issues to deal with is whether there are obstacles for the EU to include investor-state arbitration mechanisms in EU international investment agreements with third states stemming from the jurisprudence of the ECJ, which would probably require a reform of EU primary law so that investment arbitral tribunals could be considered courts or tribunals of a member state under the remit of article 267 TFEU.[63]

Other important questions will be connected to the feasibility of including an umbrella clause in EU international investment agreements. These includethe necessity to incorporate coordination mechanisms that generally assure the consistency of tribunal awards, in particular, as regards the coherent interpretation of the provisions concerning both the liberalisation and the protection of investments, the interaction between investor-state dispute settlement mechanisms provided in EU international investment agreements and the WTO Dispute Settlement. The participation of the EU and its member states in investment arbitral mechanisms in the light of the division of competences in the field of investment, and the issue of responsibility for infringements of EU international investment agreements by member states are further matters to be considered.

[62] 'Towards a Comprehensive European International Investment Policy' COM (2010) 343 final.

[63] See M Burgstaller, 'Investor–State Arbitration in EU International Investment Agreements with Third States' (2012) 39 *Legal Issues of Economic Integration* 207–21.

24

Le régionalisme commercial africain

OUSSENI ILLY*

I. INTRODUCTION

LE RÉGIONALISME CONSTITUE aujourd'hui l'un des sujets brulants à l'OMC, qui attise parfois les passions et nourrit le débat, tant au niveau des Etats membres de cette organisation qu'au sein de la communauté scientifique s'intéressant aux questions des relations commerciales internationales. Conçu d'abord comme une exception à la libéralisation multilatérale des échanges, les accords commerciaux régionaux (ACR) ont connu, ces deux dernières décennies notamment, une explosion telle, que beaucoup en sont à s'inquiéter de l'avenir même du système commercial multilatéral (SCM). En effet, à la date du 8 janvier 2015, pas moins de 600 ACR ont été notifiés à l'OMC, dont 398 étaient en vigueur.[1] Plus des deux tiers de ces accords ont été notifiés après janvier 1995 (date d'entrée en vigueur de l'OMC). L'OMC donc, en quelques deux décennies d'existence, a connu deux fois de plus notifications d'accords que le GATT en 48 années d'existence ! Si ce rythme se maintient (cela semble être le cas, notamment depuis le blocage du Cycle de Doha), il est fort probable que l'on franchisse la barre du millier d'accords d'ici les deux prochaines décennies.

Le continent africain n'a pas été en reste de ce mouvement. Après l'euphorie pour le régionalisme dans les années 1960 et 1970 et l'accalmie observée dans les années 1980, on a assisté, au cours des années 1990 notamment, à un renouveau du régionalisme économique en Afrique. A tel point que l'on dénombre aujourd'hui 13 communautés économiques régionales (CER) sur le continent.[2] On peut ainsi noter parmi les plus connues, la Communauté économique des Etats de l'Afrique de l'Ouest (CEDEAO), la Communauté de développement de l'Afrique australe (SADC), l'Union économique et monétaire ouest-africaine (UEMOA), la Communauté économique et monétaire de l'Afrique centrale (CEMAC), le Marché commun de l'Afrique orientale et australe (COMESA), la Communauté de l'Afrique de l'Est (CAE), ou encore l'Union du Maghreb arabe (UMA). A ces communautés

* Professeur Assistant, Université Ouaga II, Burkina Faso.

1 Voyer site Internet de l'OMC, www.wto.org.

2 Voyer CEA (NU), *Etat de l'intégration régionale en Afrique* (2004) 41.

« sous-régionales », il faut ajouter le grand projet d'intégration à l'échelle du continent tout entier, à savoir la Communauté économique africaine (CEA).[3]

Les objectifs visés par ce régionalisme tous azimuts en Afrique sont multiples : développement économique du continent, sa meilleure insertion dans l'économie mondiale, pour ne citer que les deux principaux. La stratégie initiale consistant en la promotion d'une politique commerciale de substitution des importations et une déconnexion du système international semble abandonnée.[4] On parle maintenant plus volontiers d'un régionalisme ouvert dont l'un des objectifs majeurs serait l'apprentissage des règles de la mondialisation économique néo-libérale.

Les pays africains ne sont pas seulement impliqués dans un régionalisme intra-africain. Depuis la fin de la colonisation, beaucoup d'entre eux sont restés dans des liens économiques et commerciaux privilégiés avec l'ancienne métropole européenne, liens qui se sont poursuivis et développés avec le temps. C'est ainsi que l'on parle souvent de « régionalisme euro-africain » (ou plus généralement de « régionalisme Nord/Sud ») pour caractériser ces liens particuliers.[5] Aujourd'hui, avec la diversification des partenaires commerciaux de l'Afrique, on assiste au développement d'autres régionalismes transcontinentaux africains, en particulier de ce que l'on pourrait qualifier du « régionalisme afro-américain ». Depuis 2004 en effet, les Etats-Unis ont signé leur premier accord de libre-échange (ALE) avec un Etat du continent, en l'occurrence le Maroc. D'autres négociations dans le même sens se poursuivent, notamment avec les Etats membres de l'Union douanière d'Afrique australe—SACU (Afrique du sud, Botswana, Lesotho, Namibie, Swaziland).

Les termes « accords régionaux de commerce » (ou « accords commerciaux régionaux » : ACR) peuvent prêter à confusion. En effet, l'idée de « région » qui est au centre de l'expression peut faire croire que l'on se trouve en présence d'accords liant des Etats géographiquement proches, c'est-à-dire voisins. Il n'en est cependant rien, car la notion d'ACR est beaucoup plus souple dans le droit international du commerce et singulièrement à l'OMC. C'est ainsi que des accords liant seulement deux Etats, situés à des points diamétralement opposés du globe, peuvent recevoir cette qualification.[6] Ceci n'est cependant pas vraiment nouveau pour le droit international, puisque l'idée d'un régionalisme sans proximité géographique a toujours été défendue par d'éminents internationalistes, qui reconnaissent par-là même le caractère ambigu et complexe du phénomène dans les relations internationales.[7]

Les ACR ont toujours été une source de préoccupation pour le SCM. Depuis sa naissance en 1947, ce système n'a cessé de vouloir les placer sous son contrôle, à

[3] Voyer M Moise Mbengue and O Illy, "The African Economic Community", in AA Yusuf and F Ougergouz (eds), *The African Union: Legal and Institutional Framework. A Manual on the Pan-African Organization* (Leiden/Boston, Martinus Nijhoff Publishers, 2012) 187–2002.

[4] Voyer P Hugon, « Les économies en développement au regard des théories de la régionalisation » (2002) XLIII, n° 169 *Revue Tiers Monde* 9 ; également, DC Bach (ed), *Regionalization in Africa, Integration and Disintegration* (Oxford, J Currey, 1999) 1 et seq.

[5] Voyer JM Djossou, *L'Afrique, le GATT et l'OMC : entre territoires douaniers et régions commerciales* (Paris, L'Harmattan, 2000) 95.

[6] Exemple de l'ALE-Maroc- Etats-Unis dont nous venons de faire mention.

[7] Voyer J-C Gautron, « Le fait régional dans la société internationale », in SFDI, *Régionalisme et universalisme dans le droit international contemporain*, Colloque de Bordeaux (Paris, Pedone, 1977) 3–44.

défaut de pouvoir les interdire. De l'avis des défenseurs du multilatéralisme, les ACR sont dangereux pour l'économie mondiale en ce sens qu'ils réduisent le bien-être mondial,[8] et peuvent même être une source de menace pour la paix. Le principe de la non-discrimination qui est au cœur du SCM a été en effet institué, d'abord, il est vrai, pour lutter contre les errements protectionnistes de l'entre-deux-guerres, mais il l'a été aussi en quelque sorte pour atténuer les pratiques préférentielles discriminatoires qui ont jalonné les relations commerciales internationales au cours de cette période et qui ont été la source de nombreuses frustrations ayant contribué à exacerber la tension mondiale. L'ouverture des frontières et l'égalité de traitement entre les différentes nations à l'échelle mondiale étaient donc perçues comme un moyen de pacification des relations internationales et de promotion d'une paix durable.[9] A défaut donc d'interdire les ACR, il faudrait leur trouver une solution appropriée, qui évite qu'ils soient présentés, les uns envers les autres, en des blocs hostiles.

A côté de ces arguments anti-ACR, il y avait cependant d'autres arguments et d'autres réalités qu'il fallait également prendre en compte. D'abord, tous les économistes ne sont pas d'accord sur l'affirmation selon laquelle les ACR sont nuisibles au commerce mondial. Pour certains, ils sont même un sye complément nécessaire à la libéralisation multilatérale du commerce. Ensuite, les ACR—et surtout les préférences—ont précédé le SCM ; les interdire était donc politiquement difficile, voire impossible. Enfin, déjà à l'époque, beaucoup de juristes pensaient que les ACR—surtout les unions douanières—sont une exception coutumière à la clause de la nation la plus favorisée et donc en grande partie au SCM.[10]

Ce débat anti et pro ACR va donner naissance à l'article XXIV du GATT qui va tenter d'encadrer la conclusion et la mise en œuvre des ACR afin de ne pas entacher l'objectif multilatéral du GATT. Cet article sera complété par la suite par la Clause d'habilitation, qui va donner une certaine flexibilité aux pays en voie de développement (PVD) dans la conclusion d'ACR entre eux, puis par l'article V de l'Accord général sur le commerce des services (AGCS), qui régit la conclusion d'ACR dans le domaine du commerce international des services.

Le régionalisme africain, qui peut ainsi être scindé en deux principales catégories, à savoir le régionalisme intra-africain et le régionalisme extra-africain, soulève plusieurs interrogations quand à son appréciation par rapport au droit de l'OMC. S'agissant du régionalisme intra-africain, le sens commun voudrait que l'apprécie par rapport à la Clause d'habilitation, étant donné le caractère de PVD de tous les pays africains. Toutefois, le doute existe, en particulier compte tenue du débat qu'a

[8] Voyer J Bhagwati, *Termites in the Trading System. How Preferential Agreements Undermine Free Trade* (Oxford, Oxford University Press, 2008).

[9] Le slogan des Etats-Unis pendant l'ouverture des négociations du GATT en 1947 en dit long à ce sujet : « si les marchandises ne franchissent pas les frontières, les soldats le feront ». Voyer R Gardner, *Sterling-Dollar Diplomacy* (New York, McGraw-Hill Book Company, 1969) 9.

[10] Voyer D Vignes, « La clause de la nation la plus favorisée et sa pratique contemporaine : problèmes posés par la Communauté économique européenne » (1970) II *Recueil des Cours de l'Academie de Droit* 209–349, 213 ; v également B Knapp, « Le système préférentiel et les Etats tiers », Thèse de doctorat, Université de Genève (1959) 310 et seq.

suscité cette disposition quant à sa faculté à régir tous les types d'ACR entre PVD.[11] Le débat reste ouvert à ce niveau, comme nous le verrons par la suite.

Quant au régionalisme externe africain, elle a suscité beaucoup de controverses à travers notamment l'affaire Banane, qui a connu un dénouement il n'y a pas très longtemps.

Par ailleurs, le régionalisme africain ne doit pas être seulement lu dans une perspective de conformité au droit de l'OMC. En effet, un pan important de ce régionalisme concerne la participation au processus de l'OMC, notamment aux négociations commerciales. La plupart des ACR africains étant des unions douanières (ou ayant pour objectif de le devenir), leurs membres se sont accordés à mener une politique commerciale extérieure commune, ce qui représente à la fois un choix judicieux et un défi important.

Avant d'évoquer en profondeur ces questions, il est utile d'évoquer brièvement les différentes phases et les principales caractéristiques du régionalisme commercial africain.

II. LES DIFFÉRENTES PHASES ET LES PRINCIPALES CARACTÉRISTIQUES DU RÉGIONALISME AFRICAIN

A. Les Phases du Régionalisme Africain

Le régionalisme africain a connu trois grandes phases dans son développement. La première d'approche fédéraliste a commencé dans certains cas sous la période coloniale et s'est poursuivi après les indépendances jusqu'aux années 1970. A partir de cette période, la guerre froide et les idées du Nouvel ordre économique (NOI) aidant, et tenant compte de l'échec des premiers mouvements d'intégration, une nouvelle vision du régionalisme va s'imposer en Afrique. Les premiers mouvements qui pour la plupart avaient été démantelés vont être remplacés par de nouvelles organisations d'approche beaucoup plus autarcique. C'est ainsi que l'on a parlé de politique de substitution aux importations et de déconnexion du système international. Vers la fin des années 1980 cependant, vu la modestie des résultats atteints par cette politique et la crise de la dette suivie des programmes d'ajustements structurels réclamés par la Banque mondiale et le Fonds monétaire international, une nouvelle orientation de l'intégration va naître sur le continent. D'approche libérale, elle est destinée à préparer les pays africains à entrer dans la compétition mondiale.

i. L'Approche Fédéraliste de la Période Post-Indépendances

La période des indépendances (fin des années 1950—début des années 1960), a été marquée en Afrique par les idéaux du panafricanisme et d'unité africaine. D'abord

[11] Voyer *Communications des Etats-Unis et des Communautés européennes sur la modification de la notification au profit de la Clause d'habilitation par l'Arabie Saoudite de l'Union douanière du Conseil de coopération du Golfe (CCG)*, doc OMC, WT/COMTD/Add 1 (24 novembre 2008) et WT/COMTD/66/Add 2 (25 novembre 2008).

partagés par les mouvements de libération nationale sous la période coloniale puis par les jeunes Etats africains indépendants, ces idéaux variaient d'un groupe d'Etats à l'autre. Pour certains, le panafricanisme est porteur d'une exigence d'unité politique immédiate de l'Afrique ; pour d'autres, il est simplement porteur d'une solidarité entre des Etats souverains ; pour d'autres enfin, il est porteur d'un projet d'unité à long terme et par étapes des Etats africains.[12]

Le partisan le plus ardent du « panafricanisme-fédération » immédiat était l'illustre Chef de l'Etat ghanéen, le Docteur Kwame N'krumah, qui avait plaidé, au moment de la création de l'Organisation de l'Unité africaine (OUA) en 1963, la cause des Etats-Unis d'Afrique. En partant d'un constat, celui de la faiblesse économique, politique et diplomatique de la plupart des jeunes Etats indépendants, il estimait urgent de réaliser l'unité politique, car celle-ci était un préalable nécessaire à tout autre progrès sur le continent. Il rejette donc les démarches qui préfèrent procéder par étapes et par secteurs, en proposant immédiatement une forme fédérale d'organisation avec un gouvernement, un parlement, une défense, une diplomatie, une citoyenneté, une banque et une monnaie communes africaines.[13]

Ce projet, maximaliste, fut rejeté par la plupart des Etats africains. Néanmoins, à l'échelle réduite, quelques tentatives de fédéralisme vont voir le jour. C'est le cas de la Fédération du Mali, née de l'union entre le Sénégal et le Soudan (actuelle Mali) et proclamée dès le 4 avril 1959, alors que les deux pays étaient encore membres de la Communauté franco-africaine. La Fédération sera toutefois dissoute quelque temps après en 1960 lorsque les deux pays prirent leur indépendance.[14] Il y a également l'Union Ghana-Guinée (qui deviendra plus tard l'Union Ghana-Guinée-Mali avec l'entrée du Mali le 24 décembre 1960) formée en 1959, à l'initiative des Présidents Kwamé N'Krumah du Ghana et Sékou Touré de la Guinée. Cette Union tombera en désuétude avec la création de l'OUA en 1963. Enfin, on peut signaler en Afrique de l'Est, la Communauté de l'Afrique de l'Est, fondée en 1967 par le Kenya, l'Ouganda et la Tanzanie, et qui figure parmi les premières tentatives d'intégration réussies sur le continent.

Les groupements issus de ces premières expériences ont pour la plupart été démantelés ou modifiés. A partir des années 1970, on va assister à une nouvelle vague de mouvements régionaux en Afrique, avec une tendance beaucoup plus marquée à gauche.

ii. La Stratégie de Substitution aux Importations et de Déconnexion du Système International des Années 1970 et 1980

Les années 1970 ont été marquées dans les relations internationales par une contestation quasi-généralisée de l'ordre établi par les pays en développement. Cette contestation, qui s'est traduite en particulier par la revendication d'un nouvel ordre

[12] Voyer A Mahiou, « La Communauté économique africaine », *Annuaire Français Droit International (AFDI)*, (1993) 799.

[13] Voyer K N'Krumah, *L'Afrique doit s'unir* (Paris, Payot, 1964) 177 et seq.

[14] Voyer M Diouf, *Intégration économique : perspectives africaines* (Dakar, NEA, 1984) 68.

économique international (NOEI), a eu des répercussions dans la conduite de la politique économique dans les PVD y compris les pays africains.

Prenant note dès le milieu des années 1970 de l'échec du NOEI et de l'incapacité de la communauté internationale à trouver une solution à leurs problèmes de développement, les pays africains vont se relancer dans la coopération régionale en ravivant ou en créant de nouvelles organisations régionales. En Afrique de l'Ouest, trois communautés virent le jour en trois ans : la Communauté des Etats de l'Afrique de Ouest (CEAO) en 1973, l'Union du fleuve Mano en 1974 et la Communauté économique des Etats de l'Afrique de l'Ouest (CEDEAO) en 1975. En Afrique centrale, la Communauté économique des pays des grands lacs (CEPGL) voit le jour tandis que l'Union douanière des Etats de l'Afrique centrale (UDEAC) est complétée par la Communauté économique des Etats de l'Afrique centrale (CEEAC) en 1983.

Le point commun entre ces organisations régionales des années 1970 et 1980 est leur caractère marqué pour un régionalisme fermé, tourné vers la protection de la production locale. On a parlé ainsi de politique de substitution aux importations et de déconnexion du système international.

iii. L'Approche Libérale des Années Post-1990

Le bilan issu du régionalisme fermé des années 1970 et 1980 en Afrique n'a pas été à la hauteur des attentes : le revenu total de l'Afrique est resté insignifiant (inférieur à celui de l'Espagne par exemple), le produit intérieur brut (PIB) moyen par Etat était équivalent à celui d'une ville de 60 000 habitants d'un pays du Nord et l'ensemble du continent ne pesait que 3% des échanges mondiaux.[15]

Face à cette situation, de nouvelles stratégies vont être développées. Les Etats africains réalisent que le commerce international fait partie des instruments de développement et plutôt que de s'en exclure, il faut développer des stratégies pour y prendre une place de choix. On constatera cette nouvelle orientation dans les textes des nouveaux accords d'intégration économique du début des années 1990. Les pays africains y affirment plus volontiers leur option pour le libéralisme, et l'intégration régionale est perçue désormais comme une étape et un moyen pour affronter la compétition mondiale et non plus forcément comme un moyen de protection de la production nationale et régionale (théorie du protectionnisme éducatif).

Parmi les organisations de cette génération, on peut citer l'Union économique et monétaire ouest-africaine (UEMOA), créée en 1994, la Communauté économique et monétaire de l'Afrique centrale (CEMAC), créée également la même année, le Marché commun de l'Afrique orientale et australe (COMESA), créée en 1993. D'autres communautés vont voir également leurs textes révisés pour tenir compte de cette nouvelle vision de l'intégration. C'est le cas de la CEDEAO, dont le traité de

[15] *Cf* J Tenier, *Intégrations régionales et mondialisation : complémentarité ou contradiction?* (Paris, La documentation française, 2003) 86. Ces chiffres n'ont pas véritablement varié aujourd'hui et certains se sont même détériorés. C'est le cas des échanges mondiaux dans lesquels l'Afrique a vu sa part chuter de 4 à 2% entre 1970 et l'an 2000. Voyer P Hugon (dir), *Les économies en développement à l'heure de la régionalisation* (Paris, Karthala, 2003) 16.

1975 a été révisé en 1993, ainsi que de la Communauté de l'Afrique de l'Est (EAC), ressuscitée en 1999 après avoir été dissoute en 1977.

B. Les Caractéristiques Principales du Régionalisme Africain

Le régionalisme africain est marqué par quatre traits principaux à savoir, une approche « développementaliste » à travers une intégration approfondie, la tendance (mais encore hésitante) vers le supranationalisme, l'approche sous-régionale avec pour but ultime l'intégration continentale et enfin un extra-continentalisme de plus en plus marqué.

i. Un Régionalisme d'Intégration avec pour Principal Objectif le Développement Economique

Deux modèles dominants existent en matière d'intégration économique régionale : le modèle dit européen, qui privilégie l'intégration étroite par la définition de politiques communes aussi bien en matière économique que politique, et modèle dit américain, qui met l'accent sur le libre-échange, sans véritables politiques commerciales et économiques—encore moins sociales—communes.[16] Le régionalisme africain se rapproche plutôt la première conception. Le libre-échange fait certes partie des objectifs des différents accords régionaux mais il n'est pas l'objectif ultime. Le régionalisme est utilisé ici comme stratégie de développement.

A titre d'exemple, l'article premier du traité instituant la Communauté économique et monétaire de l'Afrique centrale (CEMAC) dispose que :

> La mission essentielle de la Communauté est de promouvoir un développement harmonieux des États membres dans le cadre de l'institution de deux Unions: une Union économique et une Union monétaire. Dans chacun de ces deux domaines, les États membres entendent passer d'une situation de coopération, qui existe déjà entre eux, à une situation d'union, susceptible de parachever le processus d'intégration économique et monétaire.

Par la suite, la Convention régissant l'Union économique de l'Afrique centrale (Convention annexe au Traité CEMAC), citera parmi les objectifs de l'Union, la coordination des politiques sectorielles nationales et la mise en œuvre d'actions et de politiques communes, notamment dans les domaines de l'agriculture, de l'élevage, de la pêche, de l'industrie, du commerce, du tourisme, des transports, des télécommunications, de l'énergie, de l'environnement, de la recherche, de l'enseignement et de la formation professionnelle.[17]

L'article 3 paragraphe 1 du Traité de la CEDEAO indique, quant à lui, que « la Communauté vise à promouvoir la coopération et l'intégration dans la perspective d'une union économique de l'Afrique de l'Ouest en vue d'élever le niveau de vie de ses peuples, de maintenir et d'accroître la stabilité économique, de renforcer les relations

[16] Voyer J-Y Morin, « Rapport introductif », in Société française de droit international (SFDI), *Perspectives convergentes et divergentes sur l'intégration économique* (Paris, Pedone, 1993) 31 et seq.

[17] Voyer Convention régissant l'UEAC, art 2, par d).

entre les États membres et de contribuer au progrès et au développement du continent africain ». Pour atteindre ce but, le paragraphe 2 du même article précise que l'action de la Communauté portera sur l'harmonisation et la coordination des politiques nationales et la promotion de programmes, de projets et d'activités, notamment dans les domaines de l'agriculture et des ressources naturelles, de l'industrie, des transports et communications, de l'énergie, du commerce, de la monnaie et des finances, de la fiscalité, des réformes économiques, des ressources humaines, de l'éducation, de l'information, de la culture, de la science, de la technologie, des services, de la santé, du tourisme, de la justice.

Le traité instituant la Communauté de l'Afrique de l'Est (CAE) va plus loin en stipulant qu'en vue d'atteindre les objectifs de la Communauté, qui sont, entre autres, l'élaboration de politiques et de programmes visant à accroître et à approfondir la coopération entre les États partenaires en matière politique, économique, sociale et culturelle, les États parties s'engagent à établir entre eux « une union douanière et un marché commun, puis une union monétaire et enfin une fédération politique ».[18]

Quant au traité instituant le Marché commun de l'Afrique orientale et australe (COMESA), il dispose en son article 3 que les objectifs du Marché commun sont :

a) la réalisation d'une croissance et d'un développement durables des États membres en favorisant un développement équilibré et plus harmonieux de leurs structures de production et de commercialisation;
b) la promotion d'un développement conjoint dans tous les domaines de l'activité économique et l'adoption conjointe de politiques et de programmes macroéconomiques en vue de relever les niveaux de vie des populations et de favoriser des relations plus étroites entre les États membres;
d) la promotion de la paix, de la sécurité et de la stabilité parmi les États membres en vue d'accroître le développement de la région; etc.

Les traités de l'UEMOA, de la SADC, de la SACU citent eux aussi parmi leurs objectifs, la coordination des politiques sectorielles nationales et la mise en place de stratégies communes de développement.[19]

Enfin, le traité établissant l'Union du Maghreb arabe (UMA) dispose que l'Union vise à renforcer des liens de fraternité qui unissent les États membres et leurs peuples les uns aux autres, à réaliser le progrès et la prospérité des sociétés qui les composent et la défense de leurs droits, à poursuivre une politique commune dans différents domaines, et enfin, à œuvrer progressivement à réaliser entre eux la libre circulation des personnes, des services, des marchandises et des travaux.[20]

ii. Un Régionalisme Institutionnel a Cheval entre Supranationalisme et Intergouvernementalisme

La distinction entre intergouvernementalisme (ou interétatisme) et supranationalisme dans la théorie de l'intégration régionale remonte aux origines de l'intégration

[18] Voyer Traité CAE, art 5, par 1 et 2.
[19] Voyer Traité UEMOA, art 4, par d), Traité SADC, art 5, par 2, Traité SACU (révisé de 2002), art 2, par e) et h).
[20] Voyer Traié établissant l'UMA, art 2.

européenne et a toujours entretenu le débat entre d'une part, les souverainistes et de l'autre, les partisans d'une Europe forte et unie face au reste du monde.[21]

Le supranationalisme implique la mise en place d'institutions régionales dotées d'un certain pouvoir autonome. Plus spécifiquement, le supranationalisme est lié à un système de droit régional qui prévaut sur les droits nationaux.[22]

L'interétatisme au contraire n'implique pas nécessairement la mise en place d'organisation régionale, et si une telle organisation est néanmoins instituée, elle est dotée de pouvoirs très limités (voire pas du tout). L'interétatisme implique une coordination des politiques nationales et le rassemblement de moyens par les Etats en vue de répondre plus efficacement à des besoins communs.[23]

L'intégration économique peut être poursuivie sous l'une ou l'autre approche selon les objectifs recherchés par les Etats. Les premiers mouvements africains d'intégration étaient dans leur ensemble d'approche intergouvernementale, en ce sens que les secrétariats des organisations régionales étaient dotés de très peu de pouvoirs (en dehors des tentatives éphémères de fédéralisme, voir supra). La deuxième génération d'ACR est quant à elle d'inspiration beaucoup plus supranationale avec cependant des survivances de l'intergouvernementalisme.

L'article 9 du Traité de l'UEMOA dispose par exemple que :

> L'Union a la personnalité juridique. Elle jouit dans chaque État membre de la capacité juridique la plus large reconnue aux personnes morales par la législation nationale. Elle est représentée en justice par la Commission. Elle a notamment capacité pour contracter, acquérir des biens mobiliers et immobiliers et en disposer. Sa responsabilité contractuelle et la juridiction nationale compétente pour tout litige y afférent sont régies par la loi applicable au contrat en cause.

L'article 16 du même traité met en place cinq organes chargés de la conduite des programmes et activités de l'organisation. Il s'agit de la Conférence des Chefs d'État et de gouvernement, du Conseil des ministres, de la Commission, de la Cour de justice et de la Cour des comptes. La Commission (dont le siège se trouve à Ouagadougou au Burkina Faso) est l'organe exécutif de l'Union. Le Traité de l'UEMOA ne donne pas de pouvoir supranational particulier à la Commission. Il lui est reconnu néanmoins le droit de recours en manquement devant la Cour de justice de l'Union pour amener les Etats qui ne respectent pas le Traité à se conformer à leurs obligations.[24]

Le Traité de la CEDEAO dispose quant à lui, en son article 88, que la Communauté possède la personnalité juridique internationale et jouit, sur le territoire de chacun de ses Etats membres, des privilèges et immunités nécessaires à l'accomplissement de sa mission. Le Secrétaire exécutif (maintenant Président de la Commission suite à la transformation du Secrétariat exécutif en Commission en 2006) représente la Commission dans ses relations extérieures (article 88.3).

[21] Voyer W Kennes, « African Regional Economic Integration and the European Union », in DC Bach (ed), *Regionalization in Africa, Integration and Disintegration* (Oxford, J Currey, 1999) 32.

[22] ibid.

[23] Voyer J-J Roche, *Théories des relations internationales* (Paris, Montchrestien, 2004) 106–07.

[24] Voyer art 5 du Protocole additionnel n° 1 relatif aux Organes de contrôle de l'UEMOA.

Le Traité CEMAC crée également une organisation internationale avec un Secrétariat exécutif basé à Bangui, en République Centrafricaine.[25]

Le traité instituant la CAE dispose pour sa part que « la Communauté a, dans chacun des États partenaires, qualité de personne morale ayant une succession perpétuelle et le pouvoir d'acquérir, de détenir, de gérer et d'aliéner des terrains et d'autres biens, et d'intenter des poursuites et d'être poursuivie en son nom propre. Elle a le pouvoir d'exercer n'importe quelle des fonctions qui lui sont conférées par le présent traité et de faire tout ce qui est nécessaire ou souhaitable, y compris des emprunts, pour assurer l'exécution de ces fonctions. »[26] La Communauté a établi un Secrétariat général dont le siège se trouve à Arusha en Tanzanie.

L'article 2 du Traité de la CEEAC indique pour sa part que : « Par le présent Traité, les HAUTES PARTIES CONTRACTANTES instituent entre elles une Communauté économique des États de l'Afrique centrale (CEEAC), ci-après dénommée la Communauté » et l'article 87 d'ajouter que « la Communauté jouit de la personnalité juridique et possède la capacité nécessaire de contracter, d'acquérir des biens meubles et immeubles indispensables à la réalisation de ses objectifs, d'emprunter, d'ester en justice, d'accepter les dons et legs et les libéralités de toutes sortes. » La Communauté dispose également d'un Secrétariat général basé à Libreville au Gabon.

Le Traité de la SADC va dans le même sens en disposant que: « SADC shall be an international organization, and shall have legal personality with capacity and power to enter into contract, acquire, own or dispose of movable or immovable property and to sue and be sued ».[27] La SADC dispose d'un Secrétariat dont le siège est basé à Gaborone, au Botswana.

Ce constat de l'institutionnalisation peut être fait pour le reste des ACR africains qui, dans leur ensemble, établissent des organisations régionales.[28] On est donc loin du nouveau régionalisme en cours à l'OMC, où en général les ACR ne créent pas d'institutions mais se contentent d'organiser la libre circulation des marchandises.

Ce régionalisme institutionnel cadre bien avec l'option d'intégration étroite choisie par les Etats africains, enthousiasmés qu'ils sont par le succès européen et espérant trouver ici les voies et moyens d'un décollage économique. Il comporte toutefois de nombreux inconvénients, en raison notamment du nombre élevé des ACR et des adhésions parallèles.[29]

iii. Une Approche Sous-Régionale avec pour but Ultime l'Intégration Continentale

Le régionalisme économique africain a connu un tournant important au début des années 1990. En effet, le 3 juin 1991, à Abuja au Nigéria, les 51 Etats membres de l'Organisation de l'Unité africaine (OUA) adoptèrent le traité lançant la

[25] Voyer Préambule et art 2 du Traité instituant la CEMAC. Le Secrétariat exécutif a toutefois été transformé en Commission récemment par l'Additif au Traité de la CEMAC du 25 avril 2007.

[26] Traité CAE, art 4.

[27] Voyer Traité établissant la SADC, art 3, par 1.

[28] Voyer art 186 du Traité COMESA, art 1er du Traité UMA, point 6 de la Déclaration du fleuve Mano instituant l'Union du fleuve Mano (MRU), art 33 de la Convention portant création de la CEPGL, etc.

[29] Voyer *infra*.

Communauté économique africaine (CEA). Ce traité, qui est entré en vigueur trois ans plus tard (le 12 mai 1994), marque le passage sur le continent africain, d'un régionalisme économique « sous-régional » vers un régionalisme économique continental. Désormais, les objectifs de l'intégration du continent ne se limitent donc plus au plan politique avec l'OUA (l'Union africaine aujourd'hui) mais concerne aussi l'économie, avec pour objectif sur le plan commercial, la mise en place d'un Marché commun africain, dont Kwame Nkrumah appelait déjà de ses vœux en 1964.[30] Également, les communautés régionales sont appelées à disparaître au profit de la communauté continentale à créer.

Cet évènement a été qualifié d'historique à l'époque mais force est de constater que deux décennies après le lancement de ce gigantesque projet, la CEA reste encore l'ombre d'elle-même et peine à trouver son chemin.[31]

iv. Une Dimension Intercontinentale

Un dernier élément caractérise le régionalisme commercial africain, à savoir son internationalisation. Depuis la fin de la colonisation, l'Afrique a gardé des liens commerciaux privilégiés avec ses ex-colonisateurs européens notamment, liens qui se sont transformés depuis les indépendances en un véritable « régionalisme afro-européen ». Les Conventions de Yaoundé puis celles de Lomé, de Cotonou et aujourd'hui la négociation des Accords de partenariat économiques (APE) sont la parfaite illustration de ces liens historiques et de ce régionalisme. Cette dimension internationale du régionalisme africain tend d'ailleurs à s'élargir vers d'autres continents avec, par exemple, la signature entre le Maroc et les États-Unis d'Amérique, le 15 juin 2004, du premier accord de libre-échange afro-américain. L'African Growth and Opportunity Act (AGOA) pourrait également être rangé dans ce registre, même si, pour l'instant, cet acte demeure un acte unilatéral américain.

Après l'analyse des caractéristiques du régionalisme africain, il est utile de voir à présent son interaction avec le système de l'OMC.

III. LE RÉGIONALISME AFRICAIN DANS LE CONTEXTE DE L'OMC

Trois problématiques se dégagent quand vient la question de l'appréciation des ACR africains par au droit et au système de l'OMC. Comme tous les autres accords liant les membres de cette organisation, les accords africains doivent être analysés d'abord sous l'angle de leur conformité au droit du régionalisme de l'OMC. Ensuite, et de façon plus spécifique peut-être à l'Afrique—ou du moins à un nombre limité d'ACR des Etats membres de l'OMC—, la question de la participation des communautés économiques régionales aux activités et au processus de l'OMC nécessite un examen. En effet, compte de la nature du régionalisme africain (mise en place d'unions

[30] K Nkrumah, *L'Afrique doit s'unir* (Paris, Payot, 1964) 191.

[31] Voyer O Illy, *L'OMC et le régionalisme : le régionalisme africain* (Bruxelles, Larcier, 2012) 211 et seq.

douanières et de marchés communs), la participation en tant que groupes aux négociations de l'OMC a été rendue nécessaire, voire indispensable, même si la pratique tarde à se concrétiser. Enfin, le processus de l'OMC a nécessairement un impact sur le régionalisme africain qu'il convient d'analyser.

A. La Question de la Légalité des ACR Africains par Rapport au Droit de l'OMC

Tous les ACR régionaux conclus par les Etats membres de l'OMC doivent en principe être soumis à l'organisation pour appréciation de leur conformité avec les dispositions sur le régionalisme de celle-ci. Bien que cette obligation n'ait jamais pu être réellement appliquée compte tenu en particulier des divergences d'interprétation que les parties du GATT puis les membres de l'OMC ont eues par rapport à l'article XXIV (pilier du droit du régionalisme),[32] il n'en demeure pas moins utile, ne serait-ce que par pure curiosité intellectuelle, de confronter les accords africains au droit de l'OMC.

Toutefois, avant une telle confrontation, il est nécessaire d'identifier le régime sous lequel devrait être appréciés ces accords. A cet égard, il faut distinguer selon que l'on a affaire au régionalisme interafricain ou au régionalisme intercontinental africain.

Le premier relève *a priori* de la Clause d'habilitation, qui régit la conclusion d'ACR entre PVD. Toutefois, compte tenu de l'imprécision de cette clause, des débats ont été soulevés, notamment quant à sa vocation à régir tous les types d'ACR liant les PVD. En effet, selon certains Etats membres de l'OMC, la Clause d'habilitation ne contient pas toutes les bases juridiques pour régir toutes les formes de régionalisme entre PVD. Prenant appui sur le fait que la Clause n'envisage l'abolition des barrières non-tarifaires dans le cadre des accords régionaux entre PVD que de façon exceptionnelle et dans des conditions à définir par les Etats membres de l'OMC[33], et qu'en outre, la Clause ne fait expressément exception qu'au seul article Ier du GATT, ils avancent que les ACR des PVD qui incluent la suppression des barrières non-tarifaires—ce qui est le cas des ACR africains—ne peuvent être régis que par l'article XXIV.[34]

[32] Il faut noter que de toute l'histoire du GATT de 1947, un seul rapport de conformité a pu être adopté en totalité. Il s'agit du *Rapport sur l'Union douanière entre la République tchèque et la Slovaquie*, adopté le 4 octobre 1994. Voyer doc GATT, L/7501. Les autres examens se sont toujours soldés par un échec quand vient le moment de leur adoption, chaque partie ayant sa propre interprétation de l'étendue des obligations de l'article XXIV. L'avènement de l'OMC n'a rien changé à cette donne, aucun rapport d'examen n'ayant pu être adopté depuis son entrée en fonction. L'examen des accords aux fins de leur conformité normative a même été suspendu suite à une décision du Conseil général de l'OMC intervenue en décembre 2006 (voy. OMC, WT/L/671, 18 décembre 2006).

[33] Le par 2 c) de la Clause d'habilitation s'intitule en effet : « Arrangements régionaux ou mondiaux conclus entre parties contractantes peu développés en vue de la réduction ou de l'élimination des droits de douane sur une base mutuelle et, *conformément aux critères ou aux conditions qui pourraient être prescrits par les PARTIES CONTRACTANTES, en vue de la réduction ou de l'élimination, sur une base mutuelle, de mesures non tarifaires*, frappant des produits que ces parties contractantes importent en provenance les unes des autres. » (Italiques ajoutés).

[34] Voyer *Communications des Etats-Unis et des Communautés européennes sur la modification de la notification au profit de la Clause d'habilitation par l'Arabie Saoudite de l'Union douanière du Conseil de coopération du Golfe (CCG)*, doc. OMC, WT/COMTD/Add 1 (24 novembre 2008) et WT/COMTD/66/ Add 2 (25 novembre 2008).

Sur les ACR interafricains, sept ont été notifiés à l'OMC. Il s'agit de la CEDEAO, de l'UEMOA, de la CEMAC, de la CAE, du COMESA, de la SADC et de la SACU.[35] Cinq accords, à savoir la CEEAC, la CEN-SAD, la CEPGL, la MRU ainsi que l'UMA ne sont pas sont pas notifiés. A ces accords, il faut ajouter la Communauté économique africaine (CEA). La notification étant une obligation, les Etats membres de ces accords sont en violation de l'Accord sur l'OMC.

Par ailleurs, si l'on s'en tient à leurs textes, la plupart des ACR africains sont en conformité avec l'obligation de libéralisation de l'essentiel des échanges prescrite par l'article XXIV. En effet, aucun des ACR africains n'exclut de son schéma de libération des produits ou un secteur économique particulier (en dehors des exceptions traditionnelles concernant les produits dangereux pour l'Homme et l'environnement).[36]

Quant au régionalisme intercontinental africain, il relève de l'article XXIV, comme l'attestent les décisions successives concernant les bananes dans le cadre des accords de Lomé entre l'Union européenne et les pays Afrique, Caraïbe, Pacifique (ACP).

B. La Participation des ACR Africains au Processus de l'OMC

La plupart des ACR africains font obligation à leurs membres d'agir en commun ou de coordonner leurs positions dans les instances de négociations commerciales internationales. Ceci parait logique, puisque la plupart d'entre eux mettent en place une politique commerciale extérieure commune, de sorte que cette politique pourrait être remise en cause si leurs membres agissaient sans coordination dans leurs relations commerciales avec les tiers.

L'article 50 du traité de la CEDEAO dispose par exemple que :

> Au niveau régional, la Communauté s'engage à promouvoir les échanges commerciaux par :
>
> ...
>
> e) la promotion de la diversification des marchés de l'Afrique de l'Ouest et de la commercialisation des produits de la Communauté ;
> f) la prise de mesures favorables à l'amélioration des termes de l'échange pour les produits ouest-africains et une plus grande facilité d'accès des marchés internationaux pour les produits de la Communauté ;
> g) *la participation, le cas échéant, en tant que groupe à des négociations internationales organisées dans le cadre du GATT, de la CNUCED ou de toute autre instance de négociation commerciale.*[37]

L'article 85 ajoute qu' « en vue de promouvoir et de sauvegarder les intérêts de la région, les Etats membres s'engagent à formuler et à adopter des positions communes au sein de la Communauté sur les questions relatives aux négociations internationales avec les parties tierces » et qu' « à cette fin, la Communauté prépare des

[35] O Illy, *L'OMC et le régionalisme : le régionalisme africain* (Bruxelles, Larcier, 2012) 147 et seq.
[36] ibid.
[37] Italiques ajoutés.

études et des rapports permettant aux Etats membres de mieux harmoniser leurs positions sur lesdites questions ».

Le traité de l'UEMOA quant à lui indique en son article 84 que « l'Union conclut des accords internationaux dans le cadre de la politique commerciale commune » et que « la Commission conduit ces négociations en consultation avec un Comité désigné par le Conseil et dans le cadre des directives élaborées par celui-ci ». L'article 85 poursuit en précisant que « si les accords mentionnés à l'article 84 sont négociés au sein d'organisations internationales au sein desquelles l'Union ne dispose pas de représentation propre, les Etats membres conforment leurs positions de négociation aux orientations définies par le Conseil à la majorité des deux tiers de ses membres et sur proposition de la Commission ».

Les traités des autres communautés du continent contiennent plus ou moins des dispositions similaires. L'article 21 de la Convention régissant l'Union économique de l'Afrique centrale (convention annexe au Traité CEMAC) stipule que « les Etats membres harmonisent leur position sur toutes les questions ayant une incidence sur le fonctionnement du marché commun traitées dans le cadre d'organisations internationales à caractère économique ». La Communauté peut conclure des accords avec les tiers dans le cadre de la politique commerciale extérieure commune et comme dans le cadre de l'UEMOA, les négociations sont menées par le Secrétariat exécutif.[38]

Quant à la CEA, l'article 94 de son traité dispose que « les Etats membres s'engagent à formuler et adopter des positions communes au sein de la Communauté sur des questions relatives aux négociations internationales en vue de promouvoir et de sauvegarder les intérêts de l'Afrique ».

Toutefois, ces engagements restent encore théoriques, puisque dans la réalité, les Etats africains participent largement encore à titre individuel aux négociations de l'OMC. Néanmoins, avec l'émergence du Groupe africain à l'OMC, une certaine harmonisation des positions des africaines se fait jour au sein de l'OMC.[39]

C. L'Impact de l'OMC sur le Régionalisme Africain

Ici encore, deux types d'impacts peuvent être identifiés selon qu'il s'agisse du régionalisme interafricain ou du régionalisme externe africain.

S'agissant du régionalisme interafricain, une crainte demeure et est liée à la distinction faite entre pays moins avancés (PMA) et PVD dans les négociations de Doha, les derniers étant soumis à une obligation de réduction de leurs tarifs beaucoup plus élevée que les premiers. Cette situation pourrait menacer certaines unions douanières sur le continent, du fait des tarifs extérieurs communs entretenus par ces unions.

L'impact de l'OMC a été beaucoup visible sur le régionalisme externe africain, en particulier le régionalisme afro-européen. Par le biais des condamnations répétées du régime de Lomé, elle a contraint en particulier les pays ACP et l'Union européenne à

[38] Voyer art 20 de la Convention régissant l'Union économique de l'Afrique centrale (UEAC).

[39] Voyer O Illy, *L'OMC et le régionalisme: le régionalisme africain* (Bruxelles, Larcier, 2012) 235 et seq.

redéfinir leur coopération commerciale en s'engeant dans la voie d'accords de libre-échange réciproques à travers les projets dits d'accords de partenariat économique (APE).

IV. CONCLUSION

L'Afrique est relativement épargnée par la frénésie régionaliste qui s'est emparée des Etats membres de l'OMC depuis le début des années 1990. Bien que le nombre d'ACR reste élevé sur le continent, il est sans commune mesure avec ce que l'on constate sur d'autres continents à l'échelle du globe. Sur les 604 accords notifiés à l'OMC au 8 janvier 2015, les Etats africains sont impliqués dans moins d'une trentaine.

Le régionalisme africain pose cependant des défis importants, liés à la nature particulière de ce régionalisme. Son caractère fortement institutionnalisé s'accommode peu de la multitude des accords et surtout des adhésions parallèles. Outre le problème complexe de l'administration des règles d'origine lié à toute prolifération d'accords préférentiels, il faut noter que tous les ACR d'Afrique—ACR internes—mettent en place, comme nous l'avons vu, des organisations régionales dotées d'organes permanents chargés de leur mise en œuvre et de leur gestion. Cela comporte bien des avantages et est même indispensable pour l'option de l'intégration renforcée qu'ont faite les Etats africains. Il emporte cependant des conséquences, rendues plus lourdes en raison du nombre élevé des accords et des adhésions parallèles et croisées. Le problème du paiement des cotisations, par exemple, est connu : beaucoup d'Etats africains ne mesurent pas toujours le poids de la charge financière qu'implique l'adhésion aux différents accords, de sorte qu'ils se retrouvent souvent incapables de payer régulièrement leurs contributions annuelles. Cette situation rend les organisations créées dépendantes assez souvent des subsides extérieures pour leur fonctionnement ; toute chose qui rend incertaine la conduite normale de leurs activités. Ensuite, il y a le problème de l'exécution, de la gestion et de la compatibilité des plans et programmes d'intégration des différents accords. Le problème technique délicat de l'appartenance à plusieurs unions douanières mérite ici d'être rappelé. Comme c'est connu, il est difficile, voire impossible pour un Etat d'appartenir à deux unions douanières à la fois (sauf dans le cas où un groupe formant une union douanière intègre ensemble une union plus large). Toutes les communautés économiques régionales africaines cherchant à établir des unions douanières, avec les adhésions multiples, croisées et individuelles, le résultat final risque d'être l'impossibilité de faire fonctionner correctement aucune des unions douanières sur le continent.

Annexe : ACR africains et leurs membres au 1er janvier 2015

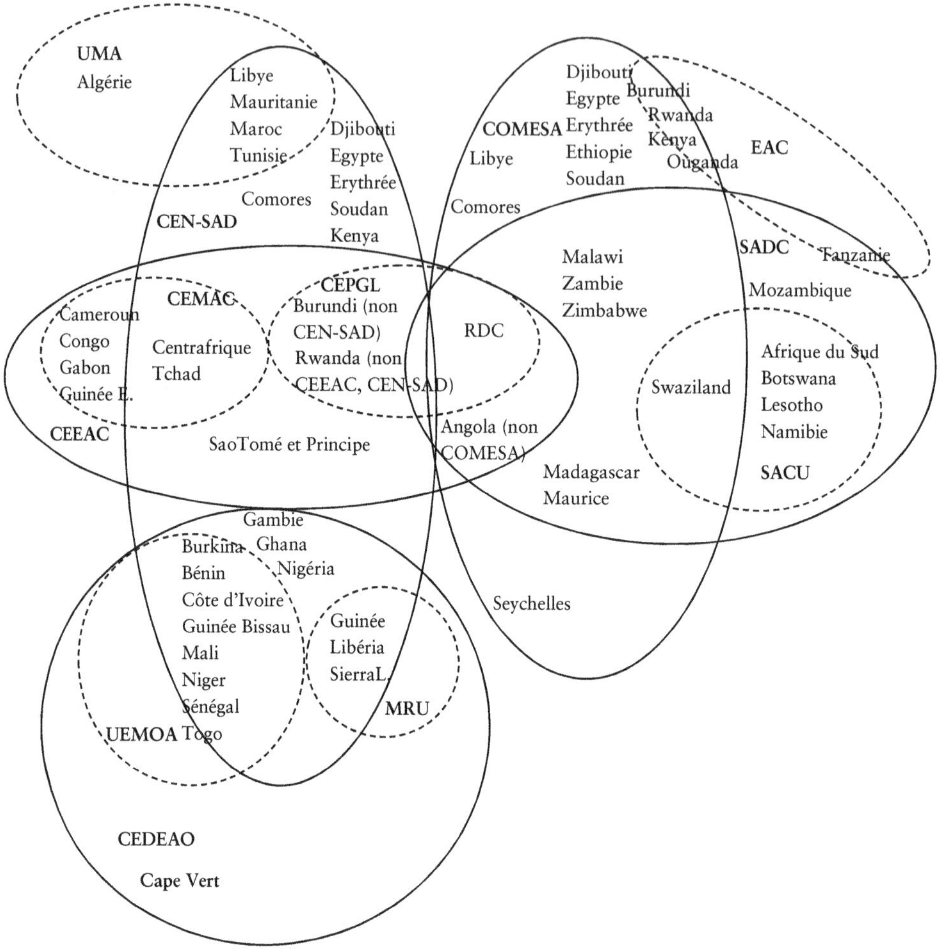

Source : O Illy, *L'OMC et le régionalisme : le régionalisme africain* (Bruxelles, Larcier, 2012) 210

25

Comments on Blázquez and Illy

GABRIELLE MARCEAU*

I. INTRODUCTION

JE TIENS D'ABORD à remercier mes amis de la SEDI de m'avoir invitée à participer à cette conférence sur un sujet qui me passionne and dans une très jolie ville, Valencia. Les deux papiers que l'on m'a demandé de commenter traitent du régionalisme interne et externe en Afrique et en Europe. J'ai beaucoup appris en les lisant et je pense qu'effectivement souvent les forums régionaux servent de laboratoires pour explorer des solutions qui peuvent souvent être exportées multilatéralement. Je ferai mes commentaires en anglais.

First, I will respond to one point each from each of the two panelists. Second, I will comment on the legal situation of regional trade agreements (RTAs) in the World Trade Organization (WTO), and point to a few issues for which research and negotiation is needed in order to clarify and improve our understanding of the implications of today's international law on regionalism. I conclude that the balance between regional and multilateral legal systems corresponds to the stage of our overall economic governance today.

I have learned a lot from Professor Irene's contribution to these proceedings. Irene Blázquez-Navarro, in her chapter titled 'Public Interest in EU Foreign Investment Policy, suggests that the manner in which (following the Treaty of Lisbon)[1] the EU is to deal with investment and trade matters internally will result in an EU-harmonised position that will influence the evolution of the WTO in that field. This would be the case *inter alia* with respect to the opportunity for investor-state dispute mechanisms.

I agree with her more general point that the internal evolution of the EU in its handling of trade and investment matters will impact the WTO. The EU is an important WTO player and it often brings about proposals to the WTO based on its experience

* Counsellor, Legal Affairs Division of the WTO Secretariat, Associate Professor at the Faculty of Law of the University of Geneva, Visiting Professor at the Graduate Institute on Law and Development (HEID) and President of the Society of International Economic Law (SIEL). I would like to thank Rohini Acarya, Maria Donner Abreu and Mary Footer for their useful comments. The views expressed in this chapter are personal to the author and do not bind the WTO Members or the WTO Secretariat. This chapter was written and completed in 2012, much before the circulation of the Appellate Body Report on Peru—Additional duty on Imports of Certain Agriculture Products (WT/DS/AB/R) adopted on 31 August 2015, which is so relevant to the issue of the relationship between RTAs and the WTO and their DSMs.

[1] Treaty of Lisbon amending the Treaty on European Union and the Treaty establishing the European Community, done at Lisbon on 13 December 2007, [2007] OJ C 306, entered into force on 1 December 2009.

within its own legal order. It may be true that governments have tried new trade approaches in their respective RTAs and have subsequently often tried to 'export' some of them to other negotiating forums, including the WTO. On other occasions, elements of existing RTAs are envied by WTO members outside such an RTA, and this may advance the need to include such elements on the WTO agenda. For example, the services coverage of the European Community treaty[2] may have encouraged other WTO members to press urgently for the negotiation of disciplines on trade in services during the Uruguay Round.[3]

I am not sure that I agree with Professor Irene's remark that in the WTO, the EU has benefited somehow from special treatment in terms of RTAs. This is because the EU is not an RTA in the WTO legal system; the EU is a full WTO member. The WTO does not have different types or categories of members. It is indeed peculiar that the EU states are WTO members, while the EU itself is also a WTO member. This arrangement arose as a political deal between the Geneva representatives of the EC (Apul Tran) and the US (Warren Lavorel), and the deal was not 'touched' by the legal group or even the US Congress.[4] A footnote in the WTO Agreement[5] provides that in case of voting, Europe would have no more votes than the number of EU states. Besides, only the EU member states, all of which are WTO members, contribute to the WTO budget—neither the EU as an international organisation nor any of its institutions does.

The chapter written by Ousseni Illy, titled 'Le Régionalisme Commercial Africain', is impressive, as was his PhD thesis, now published under the same title. Dr Illy's presentation was very informative on the extent of the relevance of regionalism in Africa. I would add that Africans have developed a special expertise in this field. Africa's experience with multiple overlapping RTAs—and their contradictory rules of origins—is a good example, and provides further evidence, that members need to negotiate an international agreement imposing disciplines on rules of origin.

II. GENERAL COMMENTS

A. The Institutional Place of RTAs in the WTO

Besides the EU, which is an original member, no RTA has become a WTO member and indeed accession to the WTO would not be open to RTAs.[6] In fact, the EU never

[2] Treaty Establishing the European Community (done at Rome, 25 March 1957) 298 UNTS 3, as subsequently revised and amended, expired by its terms 23 July 2002, and replaced by Treaty on European Union, 7 February 1992 [1992] OJ C191/1 (1992) 31 ILM 253.

[3] The Uruguay Round MTN was launched at the Ministerial Meeting held in Punta del Este, Uruguay; see Declaration of Punta del Este, Ministerial Meeting (20 September 1986) GATT 1987 BISD 33S/19.

[4] In the GATT forum, the EC member states had been coordinating matters under the EC treaty and speaking with a single voice since 1979.

[5] Marrakesh Agreement Establishing the World Trade Organization (WTO Agreement) (opened for signature 15 April 1994, entered into force 1 January 1995) 1867 UNTS 3, (1994) 33 ILM 1125, fn 2 to art IX:1.

[6] WTO Agreement, art XII on accession reads as follows:

> '1. Any State or separate customs territory possessing full autonomy in the conduct of its external commercial relations and of the other matters provided for in this Agreement and the

followed any process of accession; it simply signed the Final Act, as did the member states of the European Communities (EC), as the EU was previously known, which had acceded to the former GATT. As noted above, in the WTO legal system, the EU is not an RTA but is a full WTO member.

RTAs have no standing in WTO committees; nor do the rules on observers appear to provide for RTAs to request observership in any of the WTO committees.[7] An RTA cannot be party to a dispute, since the WTO dispute settlement mechanism (DSM) is reserved to WTO members.[8]

Of note, the WTO somehow encourages (perhaps not sufficiently) the grouping of small members for certain notification obligations, TPRM reports, as well as for the coordination of their positions in various institutional bodies. These efforts should help reduce the overall burden of such obligations on weaker countries; however, they also impose their own difficult coordination exercises. The general thinking is that the grouping of small countries should reduce the occurrence of frictions and facilitate the overall negotiation process. As noted by the Forum panel on 'Regionalism, International Organization and Integration', this perhaps is encouraged by economically stronger countries for this reason.

B. Evolution of the Way in Which the WTO (Members and DSM) have Dealt with RTAs

WTO rules do not deal with the daily internal functioning of RTAs, and international disputes in RTAs may not be relevant to the WTO Dispute Settlement Body (DSB). However, the WTO imposes conditions relating to both the internal and external

Multilateral Trade Agreements may accede to this Agreement, on terms to be agreed between it and the WTO. Such accession shall apply to this Agreement and the Multilateral Trade Agreements annexed thereto.

2. Decisions on accession shall be taken by the Ministerial Conference. The Ministerial Conference shall approve the agreement on the terms of accession by a two-thirds majority of the Members of the WTO.
3. Accession to a Plurilateral Trade Agreement shall be governed by the provisions of that Agreement.'

[7] RTAs do not have any right to become observers; however, there are rules allowing international governmental organisations (IGOs) to request observership. For example, the EFTA (Europe Free Trade Agreement) became an observer in July 1996, by means of para 4 of Annex 3 of the Rules of Procedure for Ministerial Conferences applicable to the General Council and other bodies, that states: 'Requests for observer status shall be considered on a case-by-case basis by each WTO body to which such a request is addressed, taking into account such factors as the nature of work of the organization concerned, the nature of its Membership, the number of WTO Members in the organization, reciprocity with respect to access to proceedings, documents and other aspects of observership, and whether the organization has been associated in the past with the work of the contracting parties to GATT 1947.' Given that EFTA's work fulfilled these conditions, it was granted observer status. See Rules of Procedure for Sessions of the Ministerial Conference and Meetings of the General Council, WT/L/161 (25 July 1996); in particular, the relevant annexes on observer requests do not refer to regional trade agreement bodies.

[8] See *United States—Import Prohibition of Certain Shrimp and Shrimp Products*, Appellate Body Report (adopted 6 November 1998) WT/DS58/AB/R para 101: 'It may be well to stress at the outset that access to the dispute settlement process of the WTO is limited to Members of the WTO. This access is not available, under the *WTO Agreement* and the covered agreements as they currently exist, to individuals or international organizations, whether governmental or non-governmental. Only Members may become

dimensions of RTAs *upon their formation*. An RTA's implementation and activities must continue to respect the relevant WTO requirements.

There are three main sources of WTO requirements for RTAs: article XXIV of the GATT 1994,[9] concerned with the trade in goods dimension of RTAs; article V of the GATS,[10] for the services dimensions of RTAs; and the Enabling Clause[11] for the trade in goods dimensions of RTAs between developing countries, if they so elect. An assessment of the WTO-consistency of RTAs with the parameters of article XXIV[12] allows members to refuse collectively the entry into force of a non-compatible RTA. However, in light of the positive GATT/WTO consensus practice, WTO members have never been able to reach a decision on the consistency or inconsistency of any RTA—even after the creation of the Committee on Regional Trade Agreements (CRTA), a new body responsible for the assessment of all RTAs. (Note, however, that RTAs notified under the Enabling Clause are examined in the Committee on Trade and Development that has traditionally been responsible for the monitoring of actions taken under the Enabling Clause since its inception in 1979.)[13]

On 14 December 2006, WTO Members adopted the Decision on RTA Transparency,[14] providing for expanded and harmonised notification and

parties to a dispute of which a panel may be seized, and only Members "having a substantial interest in a matter before a panel" may become third parties in the proceedings before that panel. Thus, under the DSU, only Members who are parties to a dispute, or who have notified their interest in becoming third parties in such a dispute to the DSB, have a *legal right* to make submissions to, and have a *legal right* to have those submissions considered by, a panel. Correlatively, a panel is *obliged* in law to accept and give due consideration only to submissions made by the parties and the third parties in a panel proceeding.' (Emphasis in the original, footnotes omitted.)

[9] art XXIV GATT 1994 in Annex 1A to the World Trade Agreement.

[10] art V GATS in Annex 1B to the World Trade Agreement.

[11] para 2(c), Differential and More Favourable Treatment, Reciprocity and Fuller Participation of Developing Countries (Enabling Clause), Decision of the Contracting Parties (28 November 1979) GATT Doc L/4903, GATT BISD 26S/203.

[12] art XXIV:7(c) GATT 1994 states:

> '(a) Any contracting party deciding to enter into a customs union or free-trade area, or an interim agreement leading to the formation of such a union or area, shall promptly notify the CONTRACTING PARTIES and shall make available to them such information regarding the proposed union or area as will enable them to make such reports and recommendations to contracting parties as they may deem appropriate.
>
> (b) *If, after having studied the plan and schedule included in an interim agreement referred* to in paragraph 5 in consultation with the parties to that agreement and taking due account of the information made available in accordance with the provisions of subparagraph (a), *the CONTRACTING PARTIES find that such agreement is not likely to result in the formation of a customs union or of a free-trade area within the period contemplated by the parties to the agreement or that such period is not a reasonable one*, the CONTRACTING PARTIES shall make recommendations to the parties to the agreement. *The parties shall not maintain or put into force, as the case may be, such agreement if they are not prepared to modify it in accordance with these recommendations.*
>
> (c) Any substantial change in the plan or schedule referred to in paragraph 5 (c) shall be communicated to the CONTRACTING PARTIES, which may request the contracting parties concerned to consult with them if the change seems likely to jeopardize or delay unduly the formation of the customs union or of the free-trade area.' (Emphasis added.)

[13] The WTO Committee on Trade and Development is a standing committee dating from the GATT era, set up in 1964, to oversee Pt IV of GATT 1947 and later also tasked with monitoring the Enabling Clause.

[14] General Council Decision, Transparency Mechanism for Regional Trade Agreements (14 December 2006) WT/L/671.

transparency disciplines. There is no reference to any assessment process, and in practice the CRTA no longer produces reports on the assessment of WTO-consistency of the notified RTAs. Instead, the WTO Secretariat produces a 'factual presentation' on each notified RTA (a modest copy of the Trade Policy Review Mechanism (TPRM)[15] report) that is circulated to members, rather than circulating the whole text of the RTA, thereby saving costs and time, increasing transparency, and arguably the chances of good exchanges between WTO members.[16] If a member is not satisfied, it can initiate the dispute settlement procedure.

So far, the implementation and operation of the Decision on RTA Transparency have proved beneficial, and members generally comply and participate in the new mechanism. Nonetheless, several issues arose when implementing the Decision with some existing RTAs. For example, the consideration of some agreements (the Gulf Cooperation Council (GCC), or the India-Korea and Korea-ASEAN Agreements) has been delayed as the goods aspects of these agreements have been notified under both article XXIV and the Enabling Clause. The Transparency Mechanism provides no guidance by which Committee (CTD or CRTA) should consider such 'dual notifications'. Unfortunately, some agreements are not notified by members even though they are in force.

Indeed, the problem of non-notified RTAs of course remains, despite the Decision on RTA Transparency. For instance, for some Latin American Integration Association (LAIA)[17] countries, notification requirements for RTAs under the LAIA framework are fulfilled, given that (i) the LAIA umbrella agreement has already been notified and (ii) periodical reports are submitted by the LAIA countries to indicate RTAs concluded among LAIA countries, briefly summarising them.[18] In addition, many members have difficulty submitting the statistical data required under the factual report process.[19] Delays are also experienced in receiving comments from parties to the draft factual presentations prepared by the Secretariat.

Finally, questions relating to the overlaps between the Decision on RTA Transparency and provisions of articles XXIV of GATT, V of GATTS and the Enabling Clause, remain—including whether and how a member can challenge the WTO consistency of an RTA (measure) during the operation of this new mechanism.

WTO law on RTAs is interesting to study because it confirms some of the more general statements made by the general panel on Regionalism—on the first day of this Valencia Conference. For example, formally the WTO members' right to form a preferential trade agreement is conditional, and it is for the member invoking the RTA exception to bear the burden of proving first that the concerned RTA is

[15] Trade Policy Review Mechanism, Annex 3 to the WTO Agreement.

[16] An important aspect of the factual presentation is that while RTA texts are structurally different, the factual presentation has the same structure for all agreements and therefore allows a comparison across RTA texts.

[17] Asociación Latino Americana de Integración (ALADI) in Spanish.

[18] Note that the G-20 countries in its their last statement (G-20 website) said that 'In order to strengthen the system of WTO surveillance of RTAs, we propose to discuss at the WTO making this mechanism permanent.' They also said: 'We urge WTO members to advance their discussions of the systemic implications of the increasing number of RTAs on the multilateral trading system.'

[19] Decision on RTA Transparency, paras 7–12.

WTO-consistent internally and externally, according to the requirements of the relevant WTO provision(s).[20]

However, all WTO members are members of at least one of the exisiting RTA and there are not many MFN trade relations in force world-wide. In fact the Appellate Body (AB) ruling in *Turkey—Textiles*, which prohibited panels from presuming the WTO-consistency of an RTA when a related measure is challenged by a party, was possibly too demanding. It seems to have been ignored or feared by WTO members. Since *Turkey—Textiles*, no member has ever directly challenged the WTO-consistency of any RTA per se, and in disputes concerning safeguard measures in the context of RTAs, defending countries have refused to engage in a demonstration of WTO-consistency of the RTA concerned.

Like Santiago Villalpando,[21] I would not suggest that the initial rule—the object of which may have been to maintain RTAs as 'exceptions' to be monitored by the membership—has been terminated. I believe that even if the evolution of states' practice goes towards a different balance of regionalism and multilateralism, possibly different from what the original drafters of article XXIV GATT had in mind, governments know that multilateralism often remains the best option, and sometimes the only effective means of dealing with some issues.

C. Why the Large Number of RTA Notifications throughout the History of GATT/WTO?

Given that there have been some 511 RTA notifications throughout the history of GATT/WTO, we might well ask why so many? Is the right to form RTAs a customary rule or practice within the multilateral trading system? In RTAs, WTO members have been able to address issues that are apparently too difficult to deal with in multilateral forums. For example, members have included in RTAs provisions on competition, investment, labour, human rights, or more elaborated remedies. Smaller groups of states mean less chance of conflicting interests. RTAs can be used as a step

[20] The Appellate Body in *Turkey—Restrictions on Imports of Textile and Clothing* Products (adopted 19 November 1999), WT/DS34/AB/R (*Turkey—Textiles*) [58]–[59] stated: 'Accordingly, on the basis of this analysis of the text and the context of the chapeau of paragraph 5 of Article XXIV, we are of the view that Article XXIV may justify a measure which is inconsistent with certain other GATT provisions. However, in a case involving the formation of a customs union, this "defence" is available only when two conditions are fulfilled. First, the party claiming the benefit of this defence must demonstrate that the measure at issue is introduced upon the formation of a customs union that fully meets the requirements of sub-paragraphs 8(a) and 5(a) of Article XXIV. And, second, that party must demonstrate that the formation of that customs union would be prevented if it were not allowed to introduce the measure at issue. Again, *both* these conditions must be met to have the benefit of the defence under Article XXIV.' We would expect a panel, when examining such a measure, to require a party to establish that both of these conditions have been fulfilled. It may not always be possible to determine whether the second of the two conditions has been fulfilled without initially determining whether the first condition has been fulfilled. In other words, it may not always be possible to determine whether not applying a measure would prevent the formation of a customs union without first determining whether there is a customs union. In this case, the Panel simply assumed, for the sake of argument, that the first of these two conditions was met and focused its attention on the second condition.

[21] See further S Villalpando in ch 10 of this volume.

or a stage toward the multilateral coordination of regional positions. For example, a solution to the trade and climate change deadlock could include taking trade-related climate change actions within RTAs. This would lead to more regionally harmonised practices that could eventually simplify the international negotiation process.

We also all know that some issues cannot be satisfactorily addressed in RTAs: for example, subsidies. It is not possible to maintain programmes for regional subsidies versus multilateral subsidies. In other words, it is not possible to control whether subsidies for chicken farming are actually provided only to chicken-farmers that export in a region or multilaterally. If a government provides subsidies to its farmers, they will export their subsidised chicken wherever they can, within that region and outside that region. Also prohibiting regional subsidies, when such farmers may have to compete outside the region with other farmers who will receive subsidies, would not appear fair. So disciplines on (regional) subsidies are generally never included in RTAs.

D. Need for Further Study of the Interactions of RTAs and WTO Law

The interactions of RTAs and WTO law need to be studied further in order to better understand the legal implications of states' practice in regional arrangements. For example, to what extent can an RTA justify discriminatory transit fees, regulations or transit restrictions? And to what extent can an RTA-consistent retaliation, between RTA parties and for RTA trade, include measures that might otherwise be WTO inconsistent? For example, can an RTA party suspend its obligations pursuant to the RTA retaliation provisions in a manner that would lead to the imposition of a GATT-inconsistent import quota, or tariffs above WTO bindings? Can it be argued that the application of article XXIV GAT must include 'effective' RTAs, and for an RTA to be considered 'effective' it needs to have a DSM which provides for retaliation mechanism? And is the answer the same in situations where the retaliation relates to a dispute concerned with non-WTO matters, such as competition, investment, human rights, labour considerations, and so on?

III. CONCLUSION

We need to better understand the relationship between regional and multilateral actions in today's governance. Clearly, regional actions have been able to respond to the needs expressed by governments, and some of those needs were not secured by international agreements and practices. Is the fact that in smaller groups, differences in interests are more limited, the only explanation?

RTAs are better suited for different types of international participations, from collaboration to cooperation. RTAs parties also bring together several areas of government responsibility, such as trade, investment, competition, human rights and others—each of which is part of a different legal system of rights and obligations.

Yet, as noted, some issues cannot be dealt with effectively in regional arrangements. This is true in all areas of regionalism, not only for RTAs. Even if the UN Charter includes a chapter on regional security arrangements, UN members agree that world peace requires world agreement(s). Moreover, states want to maintain international relational relations at multiple levels, and try to benefit from all of them.

Just as Santiago Villalpando, in his contribution on regionalism versus multilateralism in international law, spoke more generally about the evolution of the role of regional (security) arrangements within the UN system,[22] so I believe it is best to describe the evolution of RTAs within the GATT/WTO, as having followed a pragmatic and fluid migration from their initial role and responsibilities, rather than as having deviated from their original object and purpose.

Today, the balance between regional and multilateral relations corresponds to the evolutionary stage of our overall economic governance. In our efforts to improve world economic governance, we need to improve our understanding of the legal relationship of regional and multilateral agreements and practices, so as to better appreciate their mutual interaction and improve their design.

[22] See S Villalpando in ch 10 of this volume.

26

L'utilisation contemporaine du développement en Droit international des investissements: la méconnaissance des réalités régionales

NITISH MONEBHURRUN*

I. INTRODUCTION

CETTE CONTRIBUTION A surtout une visée méthodologique. Au-delà de son apport au niveau substantiel, l'article se focalise sur l'utilisation du concept du développement par les juristes. Si le domaine de l'étude est celui du droit international des investissements, sa portée est, quant à elle, plus générale. Ce qui y est présentée et, dans une certaine mesure, critiquée, c'est la méthode ou, plus exactement, l'absence de méthode qui colore très souvent l'invocation et l'utilisation du développement dans le domaine du droit international des investissements.

Cette branche du droit international est composée d'un arsenal normatif permettant la protection des investissements internationaux. Il existe, par exemple et entre autres, une protection accordée aux investisseurs internationaux contre un traitement injuste et inéquitable de la part de leur Etat d'accueil, contre une expropriation indirecte ou contre une discrimination en raison de la nationalité.[1] Cette protection se formalise juridiquement par le réseau grandissant des accords relatifs à la protection des investissements.[2] À côté des accords bilatéraux classiques et de quelques accords multilatéraux, se développent de plus en plus en sourdine des accords de libre-échange ayant en leur sein un chapitre consacré à la protection des investissements internationaux.[3] Un investisseur estimant que son Etat d'accueil a manqué à une des obligations ancrées dans un accord relatif aux investissements peut

* Docteur en droit international (École de droit de la Sorbonne, Paris), Professeur de droit (Centre Universitaire de Brasília), Professeur invité (Programme de Master en droit international, Universidad de la Sabana, Bogotá)

[1] P Julliard, « L'évolution des sources du droit des investissements » (1994) 250 *Recueil des Cours de l'Academie de Droit International* 9, 74–75; A Newcombe, L Paradell, *Law and Practice of Investment Treaties: standards of Treatment* (Alphen Aan Den Rijn, Kluwer Law International, 2009) 147–398.

[2] Les accords bilatéraux relatifs à la protection et à la promotion sur les investissements sont disponibles sur: www.unctadxi.org/templates/DocSearch____779.aspx (voir aussi: www.italaw.com/).

[3] Exemples d'États ayant constitué un réseau d'accords de libre-échange: États-unis, Canada, Chine, Malaisie, Australie, Japon, Chili, Singapour, l'Indonésie ou le Pérou.

demander la constitution d'un tribunal pour requérir d'éventuelles réparations lors d'une procédure arbitrale.

Cependant, la compétence du tribunal pour connaître de l'affaire dépend de certaines conditions, l'une d'entre elles étant l'existence d'un investissement.[4] La détermination de la compétence d'un tribunal est un point de procédure préliminaire fondamental.[5] L'article 25 de la Convention de Washington du 18 mars 1965 instituant le Centre International de règlement de différends relatifs aux investissements (CIRDI) énumère les conditions fondant la compétence d'un tribunal arbitral et précise dans ce sens que le différend doit être en relation directe avec un investissement.[6] Pour bénéficier d'une protection juridique, l'investisseur doit démontrer que son activité est un investissement. Ainsi, un tribunal constitué dans le cadre d'une affaire, doit avant toute chose et dans une procédure sur la compétence déterminer si l'activité litigieuse prend la forme d'un investissement afin de se dire compétent; c'est uniquement après cette étape qu'il pourra procéder à l'examen de la requête sur le fond.[7] La présence d'un investissement est une condition *ratione materiæ* de sa compétence.[8] Cependant, ni la Convention, ni le règlement d'arbitrage ne définissent l'investissement ou ne prévoient un faisceau d'indices en permettant l'identification.[9] Les tribunaux ont, conséquemment, dû en interprété le sens afin de déterminer leur propre compétence. C'est d'une interprétation contextuelle que la contribution au développement a été utilisée comme un critère de l'investissement. Le préambule de la Convention de Washington énonce, en effet, que les investissements privés internationaux jouent un rôle important dans la coopération internationale pour le développement économique.[10] Dans une logique inversée, certains tribunaux ont considéré que la contribution au développement économique est un critère de l'investissement.[11] Si le critère avait déjà été mis en avant par la

[4] EC Schlemmer, « Investment, Investor, nationality, and shareholders » in P Muchlinski, F Ortino, C Schreuer (eds), *The Oxford Handbook of International Investment Law* (Oxford, Oxford University Press, 2008) 62; C Schreuer, *The ICSID Convention: A Commentary* (Cambridge, Cambridge University Press, 2009) 82.

[5] J Gotanda, « An Efficient Method for Determining Jurisdiction in International Arbitrations » (2001) 40 *Columbia Journal of Transnational Law*, 12, 15 (note de bas de page omise).

[6] Convention de Washington instituant le Centre international pour le règlement des différends relatifs aux investissements, 18 mars 1965, article 25 (*disponible sur*: www.icsid.worldbank.org/ICSID/StaticFiles/basicdoc-fra/CRR_French-final.pdf).

[7] Voir par exemple: *Autopista Concesionada c Venezuela*, CIRDI n°ARB/00/5, Décision sur la compétence (27/09/2001), §96.

[8] EC Schlemmer, ci-avant note 4, 62.

[9] S Manciaux, *Investissements étrangers et arbitrage entre Etats et ressortissants d'autres Etats. Trente années d'activité du CIRDI* (Litec–CREDIMI, 2004) 43; voir aussi; C Schreuer, ci-avant note 3, 116.

[10] Voir: C Schreuer, U Kriebaum, « From Individual to Community Interest in International Investment Law » in U Fastenrath, R Geiger, DE Khan, A Paulus, SV Schorlemer, C Vedder (eds), *From Bilateralism to Community Interest. Essays in Honour of Judge Bruno Simma* (Oxford, Oxford University Press, 2011) 1081.

[11] Voir par exemple: *Patrick Mitchell c République Démocratique du Congo*, CIRDI n° ARB/99/7, Décision sur l'application d'annulation de la sentence (01/11/06) 29; *Abaclat et autres c Argentine*, CIRDI n° ARB/07/5, Décision sur la compétence et sur la recevabilité (04/08/2011) 349; *Romak SA c Uzbekistan*, CNUDCI, Sentence (26/11/2009) 198; *Malaysian Historical Salvors, SDN, BHD c Malaysia*, CIRDI n° ARB/05/10, Décision sur la compétence (17/05/07) 66; *Bayindir Insaat Turizm Ticaret Ve Sanayi AS c Pakistan*, CIRDI n° ARB/03/29, Décision sur la compétence (14/11/05) 137; *Abaclat et autres c Argentine*, CIRDI n° ARB/07/5, Décision sur la compétence et sur la recevabilité (04/08/2011), Opinion dissidente du Professeur George Abi-Saab du 28 octobre 2011, 49–50.

doctrine,[12] il a été affirmé pour la première fois[13] dans une affaire *Fedax c Vénézuéla*[14] avant d'être repris et confirmé dans une affaire *Salini c Maroc.* Le tribunal dans l'affaire *Salini* expliqua que:

> The doctrine generally considers that investment infers: contribution, certain duration of performance of the contract and a participation in the risks of the transaction ... In reading the Convention's Preamble, one may add the contribution to the economic development of the host State of the investment as an additional condition.[15]

Ce *dictum* de l'affaire *Salini* a marqué le contentieux sur la compétence. Dans le jargon du droit international des investissements, les termes « Salini test » ou critères « Salini » sont d'utilisation régulière et de compréhension familière.[16] Sur cette base, nombreux sont les tribunaux ayant eu recours au critère de la contribution du développement économique pour identifier un investissement et, ce faisant, pour déterminer leur compétence.[17] Ainsi, juridiquement, le développement n'est pas un objectif à atteindre : les dispositions des accords relatifs aux investissements n'encadrent pas—par leur teneur—la réalisation du développement mais la protection des investissements. Le développement se présente, quant à lui, comme un instrument. Et comme tout instrument, il a une fonction. Cette fonction se dédouble dans cette branche du droit: 1) le développement sert à identifier un investissement; 2) dans le but d'établir la compétence des tribunaux. Le développement est un outil ayant une fonction herméneutique. C'est là, une utilisation contemporaine de ce concept. Cette utilisation s'accompagne, cependant, d'une limite méthodologique: le développement n'est à aucun moment défini par les tribunaux qui considèrent

[12] GR Delaume, « Le Centre International pour le Règlement des Différends relatifs aux investissements » (1982) 4 *Journal du droit international* 775, 801; C Schreuer, « Commentary on the ICSID Convention », (1996) 11 *ICSID Review—Foreign Investment Law Journal* 320, 372; C Schreuer, ci-avant note 3, 128.

[13] ML Jaime, « L'apport des traités régionaux et multilatéraux à l'évolution du droit de l'arbitrage et du droit international des investissements » (Paris, Thèse de doctorat, Paris II, 2008) 443.

[14] *Fedax N. c Venézuéla*, CIRDI n°.ARB/96/3, Sentence sur la compétence (11/07/97) 43.

[15] *Salini Construtorri SpA and Italstrade SpA c Morocco*, CIRDI n° ARB/00/4, Décision sur la compétence (23/07/01) 52.

[16] E Gaillard, « Reconnaître ou définir ? Réflexions sur l'évolution de la notion d'investissement dans la jurisprudence du CIRDI » in JM Sorel (ed), *Le droit international économique à l'aube du XXIe siècle. En Hommage aux professeurs Dominique Carreau et Patrick Juillard* (Paris, Pédone, 2009) 18; A Reinisch, *Recent Developments in International Investment Law* (Paris, Pédone, 2009) 5.

[17] Voir par exemple: *Patrick Mitchell c République Démocratique du Congo*, CIRDI n° ARB/99/7, Décision sur l'application d'annulation de la sentence (01/11/06) 30, 33; *Phoenix Action, Ltd c République Tchèque*, CIRDI n° ARB/06/5, Sentence (15/04/09) 84; *Joy Mining Machinery Ltd c Egypt*, CIRDI n° ARB/03/11, Sentence sur la compétence (06/08/04) 53; *Malaysian Historical Salvors, SDN, BHD c Malaysia*, CIRDI n° ARB/05/10, Décision sur la compétence (17/05/07) 78; *Toto Costruzioni Generali SpA c République du Liban*, CIRDI n° ARB/07/12, Décision sur la compétence (11/09/09) 69; *Mytilineos Holdings SA c Serbie et Monténégro et République Serbe*, CNUDCI, Sentence sur la compétence (08/09/06) §115; *Pantechniki SA Contractors & Engineers c République d'Albanie*, CIRDI n° ARB/07/21, Sentence (30/07/2009) 36; *Noble Energy, Inc and Machalapower CIA LTDA c Equateur et « Consejo Nacional de Electricidad »* CIRDI n° ARB/05/12, Décision sur la compétence (05/03/08) 128; *Jan de Nul NC and Dredging International NC c Egypte*, CIRDI n° ARB/04/13, Décision sur la compétence (16/06/06) 91; *Bayindir Insaat Turizm Ticaret Ve Sanayi AS c Pakistan*, CIRDI n° ARB/03/29, Décision sur la compétence (14/11/05) 130; *Helnan International Hotels A/S c Egypte*, CIRDI n° ARB/05/19, Décision sur les objections à la compétence (17/10/06) 77.

qu'il s'agit d'un concept auto-explicatif, d'une évidence.[18] Ils ne précisent aucunement leur acception du développement ou les critères objectifs—et vérifiables—leur permettant de constater une contribution au développement d'un État. Cette lacune méthodologique caractérise, à vrai dire, plusieurs études faites sur le développement.[19] Ce faisant, c'est très souvent une idée préconçue du développement qui est utilisée et sa réalité est, elle, méconnue ou du moins, peu recherchée. Cette posture a plusieurs conséquences. D'une part, elle incite à la simplification d'un concept complexe en le déconnectant de la réalité où cette complexité s'étale et se diffuse—, et dont la compréhension scientifique implique nécessairement une étude approfondie, dépassant les seules limites du droit. Cette étape épistémologique est inexistante dans l'arbitrage relatif aux investissements internationaux. D'autre part, elle universalise et uniformise le concept du développement en considérant qu'il n'a qu'une forme, peu importe l'État, son économie, sa société, ses ressources, son environnement ou sa culture. Dans cette logique et par cet hymne universel, les réalités nationales et régionales du développement sont ignorées. La région est ici considérée comme le regroupement géographique d'États voisins mais aussi comme les différents découpages territoriaux composant l'organisation interne des États. Aussi est-ce dans ces réalités que se comprend le mieux le développement : chaque région et chaque État disposent de leurs propres paramètres de développement et ce qui vaut pour les uns n'est pas toujours transposables aux autres en raison des spécificités de chacun.[20] Dès lors, cette utilisation contemporaine du développement faite dans le droit international des investissements méconnaît souvent ces réalités régionales et *a fortiori* nationales. Par conséquent, c'est l'utilité même du recours au critère du développement pour identifier un investissement qui est mis en cause, et ce, en raison de la méconnaissance des réalités régionales et nationales par les tribunaux arbitraux.

Cette méconnaissance s'explique par la méthode des tribunaux qui ont recours au développement hors de sa technicité, en l'utilisant sans le définir au préalable (II) et elle est, par ailleurs, ancrée dans les accords relatifs aux investissements où le développement est présenté comme un concept universel (III).

II. LA MÉCONNAISSANCE DES RÉALITÉS RÉGIONALES PAR LES TRIBUNAUX: LE DÉVELOPPEMENT UTILISÉ COMME UN CONCEPT INDÉFINI

Les réalités régionales sont méconnues en raison de l'absence de méthode dans l'utilisation du développement par les tribunaux (A), qui le considère, à tort, comme étant un concept auto-explicatif (B).

[18] Vue la complexité qui l'entoure et qui le caractérise, le développement sera définie ci-bas lors de la première partie portant sur les définitions.

[19] G Azoulay, *Les théories du développement. Du rattrapage des retards à l'exception des inégalités* (Rennes, Presses Universitaires de Rennes, 2002) 30; H Sanson, « Le droit au développement comme norme métajuridique en droit du développement » in M Flory, A Mahiou, JR Henry (eds), *La formation des normes en droit international du développement* (Paris, Éditions du CNRS, 1984) 62.

[20] FMM Flory, « Inégalité économique et évolution du droit international » in *Pays en voie de développement et transformation du droit international* (Paris, Pédone, Colloque de la Société française de droit international d'Aix-en-Provence, 1974) 28.

A. L'Absence de Méthode Caractérisant l'Utilisation du Développement par les Tribunaux

Cette absence de méthode favorise le traitement du développement hors de sa complexité et de sa technicité (i) et exclue, dans cette veine, toute référence aux réalités régionales et locales qui caractérisent intrinsèquement le développement (ii).

i. L'Absence de Méthode Refoulant la Complexité du Développement

Le problème se situe dans la droite ligne de cette tendance qu'a parfois le droit international « à réglementer sans définir ».[21] Le Professeur Juillard se demandait, avec justesse, si « avant d'être tombé'malade de ses normes', le Droit international n'était-il pas déjà devenu infirme de ses définitions »?[22] En effet, pour affirmer que la contribution au développement d'un État est un critère valable de l'investissement, il faut que ce critère soit préalablement défini. La définition est l'étape préalable sine qua non avant le traitement scientifique d'une matière,[23] surtout lorsque cette dernière repose sur une grande complexité.[24] Par le cheminement que prend le développement dans le droit international des investissements, son utilisation devient paradoxale. Son utilité en tant qu'outil d'identification s'affaiblit si sa propre teneur n'est ni connue, ni comprise ou si elle est connue mais peu comprise, peu expliquée et peu mise en relation avec son objet.[25] Il y a une tendance à minimiser ou à ignorer cette étape méthodologique préliminaire qui consiste à présenter clairement le concept, à vérifier les possibilités de son utilisation avant d'en faire une application. Une des conséquences de cette négligence se remarque dans la confusion faite par plusieurs tribunaux entre « développement » et « développement économique » en se référant au préambule de la Convention de Washington.[26] Ce dernier, de même que les travaux préparatoires, mentionne clairement le terme « développement économique ». De deux choses, la première : d'une part, il ne serait ni novateur, ni révolutionnaire

[21] P Juillard, « Investissements privés » *in* D Carreau, FMM Flory, P Juillard, « Chronique de droit international économique » (1984) 30 *Annauire français de droit international* 773, 775.

[22] ibid, 781.

[23] R Descartes (dir E Lefranc), *Discours de la méthode* (Paris, Editions Classiques, 1866) 14; A Schopenhaueur, *O livre-arbitrio* (Rio de Janeiro, Nova Fronteira, 2012) 23.

[24] J Austry, *Le scandale du développement* (Genève, Slatkine, 1987) 26.

[25] HLA Hart, *Essays in Jurisprudence and Philosophy* (New York, Oxford University Press, 1983) 21.

[26] Voir par exemple: *Patrick Mitchell c République Démocratique du Congo*, CIRDI n° ARB/99/7, Décision sur l'application d'annulation de la sentence (01/11/06) cp 27–30; *Noble Energy, Inc and Machalapower CIA LTDA c Equateur et « Consejo Nacional de Electricidad »*, CIRDI n° ARB/05/12, Décision sur la compétence (05/03/08), cp 128, 132, 161; *Helnan International Hotels A/S c Egypte*, CIRDI n° ARB/05/19, Décision sur les objections à la compétence (17/10/06) cp 58, 59, 60, 77, 88; *Joy Mining Machinery Limited c Egypt*, CIRDI n° ARB/03/11, Sentence sur la compétence (06/08/04) cp 40, 53, 62–63; *Malaysian Historical Salvors, SDN, BHD c Malaysia*, CIRDI n° ARB/05/10, Décision sur la compétence (17/05/07) cp 44, 47, 66, 67, 68, 78, 111, 117, 122, 130, 136, 142, 143, 144; *Bayindir Insaat Turizm Ticaret Ve Sanayi AS c Pakistan*, CIRDI n° ARB/03/29, Décision sur la compétence (14/11/05) cp 130, 137; *Mytilineos Holdings SA c Serbie et Monténégro et République Serbe*, CNUDCI, Sentence sur la compétence (08/09/06) cp 116, 124.

Voir aussi: *Abaclat et autres c Argentine*, CIRDI n° ARB/07/5, Décision sur la compétence et sur la recevabilité (04/08/2011) Opinion dissidente du Professeur George Abi-Saab du 28 octobre 2011, cp 49, 50, 111, 114, 115.

que d'affirmer l'utilité du mot juste ou du terme exact dans l'interprétation et dans l'application d'un texte juridique.[27] La Convention de Vienne sur le droit des traités est on ne peut plus clair là-dessus. Les termes d'un accord doivent être conférés leur sens ordinaire.[28] D'autre part, les concepts de développement et de développement économique sont différents. Ils peuvent se rejoindre mais ils ne se confondent pas. Le développement économique est, certes, une forme ou une composante du développement mais il ne s'y confond pas car une contribution au développement économique n'implique pas toujours une contribution au développement d'un Etat.[29] Le développement économique est un processus par lequel la valeur réelle du revenu national d'un Etat croît sur un long terme.[30] Et une augmentation en termes de revenu n'est aucunement synonyme d'une contribution au développement. Les variations du produit intérieur brut d'un Etat ne sont en vérité qu'une mesure approximative de l'état du développement.[31] Tout dépend de ce qui est produit et de la politique de redistribution. La production d'équipement militaire n'a, par exemple, pas toujours un impact direct et positif sur le développement.[32] Et tout dépend aussi du coût de la production en question qui peut, par exemple, être faite en épuisant les ressources naturelles ou au détriment de la santé, de l'environnement et des droits humains. En effet, l'évaluation du développement se fait normalement selon une méthode holiste par laquelle plusieurs facteurs, dont le facteur économique, sont considérés simultanément.[33] Ayant plusieurs facettes, la matrice qui permet d'en saisir le sens est par essence pluridisciplinaire et tentaculaire. Le développement se compose d'éléments sociaux, structuraux, humains, environnementaux, économiques, juridiques, culturels, religieux, financiers, d'éléments de gouvernance[34] ...

[27] C Eisenmann, « Quelques problèmes de méthodologie des définitions et des claissifications en science juridique », in C Leben, *Ecrits de théorie du droit, de droit constitutionnelle et d'idées politiques* (Paris, Éditions Panthéon-Assas, 2002) 291.

[28] Art 31(1) de la Convention de Vienne sur le droit des traités.

[29] GM Meier, *The International Economics of Development: Theory and Policy* (New York, Harper & Row, 1968) 14; J Austry, ci-avant note 24, 74; G Azoulay, ci-avant note 19, 34; A Barrière, *Le développement divergent. Essai sur la richesse et la pauvreté des nations* (Paris, Economica, 1978) 4; JN Hyde, « Economic Development Agreements » (1962) 105 *Recueil des Cours de l'Academie de Droit International* 270, 277.

[30] C Furtado, *Développement et sous-développement* (Paris, PUF, 1966) 79; GM Meier, ci-avant note 29, 2.

[31] Voir, J Stiglitz, A Sen, JP Fitoussi, « Rapport de la Commission sur la mesure des performances économiques et du progrès social » (2009), voir notamment le Chapitre 1, p 23 et suivant (Le rapport est disponible sur: www.stiglitz-sen-fitoussi.fr/documents/rapport_francais.pdf); HW Singer, « La création de la CNUCED et l'évolution de la pensée contemporaine sur le développement » (1994) 35 *Revue Tiers Monde* 489, 490.

[32] GM Meier, ci-avant note 29, 7. Pour un argument contraire voir: WW Rostow, *Les étapes de la croissance économique* (Paris, Seuil, 1963) 91. L'auteur affirme que l'armement contribue potentiellement au démarrage des Etats en citant l'example de l'Allemagne, de la Russie ou du Japon tout en se gardant de préciser le rôle secondaire de ce secteur.

[33] World Bank Evaluation Department, *1999 Annual Review of Development Effectiveness*, n° 20180, novembre 1999, 1–4, disponible sur: www.go.worldbank.org/Z2M8K72ED0.

[34] I Adelman, *Teorias de desenvolvimento econômico* (Rio de Janeiro, Forense, 1972) 1; I Alechina, « The Contribution of the United Nations System to Formulating Development Concepts » in *Different Theories and Practices of Development* (Paris, UNESCO, 1982) 11, 22; G Azoulay, ci-avant note 19, 34; C Blake, « The World Bank's Draft Comprehensive Development Framework and the Micro-Paradigm of Law and Development » (2000) 3 *Yale Human Rights and Development Law Journal* 159, 160; CNUCED, *International Investment Agreements: Flexibility for Development*, UNCTAD/ITE/IIT/18, 2000, p 11; KE

et de liberté pour certains.[35] Dès lors, dans les éléments utilisés pour définir le développement, il est possible de retenir le processus structurel permettant, par une utilisation optimale des ressources, d'augmenter le niveau de vie d'une population sur un plan économique par une augmentation des revenus au plan micro et macro, dans un cadre équitable, dans le respect de l'environnement et des générations futures et selon une hygiène démocratique garantissant les droits et libertés fondamentaux.[36] Sa définition ne peut être monoculaire et encore moins réductrice. Ainsi, si le texte applicable mentionne spécifiquement le terme « développement économique », c'est ce dernier qui doit être utilisé car il a un sens précis. Cependant, les tribunaux ne font, eux, aucune différence terminologique. Développement et développement économique sont confondus, comme le sont les paramètres permettant de les dissocier. Mais que la confusion soit faite ou pas, les tribunaux n'examine aucunement chaque composante du développement ou du développement économique pour affirmer l'existence (ou non) d'une contribution ; cette démarche est absente de leur raisonnement. Dans le même cheminement, en ignorant ces paramètres, développement et/ou développement économique sont dépouillés de leur portée pratique et sont présentés dans le plus simple appareil sous une forme universelle, souvent très loin du réel et, conséquemment des réalités régionales.

Davis, MJ Trebilcock, « The Relationship Between Law and Development: Optimists versus Skeptics » (2008) 56 *The American Journal of Comparative Law* 895, 895–98; MD Varella, *Direito Internacional Econômico Ambiental* (Belo Horizonte, Del Rey, 2003) 7; P Hugon, « Droit, droits et économie du développement: Illustration à propos de l'alimentation » (2005) 1 *Monde en développement* 13, 14; JN Hyde, ci-avant note 29, 273–74; NG Lichtenstein, « Law in China's Economic Development: An Essay from Afar » (2000) 17 *ICSID Review-Foreign Investment Law Journal* 1, 1–20; GM Meier, ci-avant note 29, 14; JH Merryman, « Comparative Law and Social Change: On the Origins, Style, Decline & Revival of the Law and Development Movement », (1977) 25 *American Journal of Comparative Law* 457, W Paatii Ofosu Amaah, « Reforming Business-Related Laws to Promote Private Sector Development: The World Bank Experience in Africa » (2000) 15 *ICSID Review-Foreign Investment Law Journal* 1, 1–58; Singer, ci-avant note 31, 491.

[35] Voir notamment: G Azoulay, ci-avant note 31, 29; A Sen, *Development as Freedom* (New York, Anchor Books, 2000) 13–34; PNUD, *Rapport sur le développement humain. Durabilité et équité: un avenir meilleur pour tous* (New York, Publié par le Programme des Nations unies pour le développement, 2011) 1.

[36] Voir là-dessus : les objectifs du millénaire pour le développement (*disponible sur :* www.undp.org/french/mdg/basics.shtml); la résolution de l'Assemblée générale des Nations unies sur le droit au développement, n° 41/128, 14 décembre 1986 (*disponible sur :* www.un.org/french/documents/view_doc.asp?symbol=A/RES/41/128). Par ailleurs, La réglementation opérationnelle de l'Agence Multilatérale de Garantie des Investissements apporte aussi quelques éléments de définition dans le paragraph 3.06 de la Section II : « In determining whether an Investment Project will contribute to the development of the host country, the Underwriting Authority shall have due regard to such factors as the Investment Project's potential to generate resources for the host country; the contribution of the Investment Project to maximizing the host country's productive potential, and in particular to producing exports or import substitue and reducing vulnerability to external economic changes; the extent to which the Investment Project will diversify economic activities, expand employment opportunities and improve income distribution; the degree to which the Investment Project will transfer knowledge and skills to the host country ; and the effects of the Investment Project on the social infrastructure and environment of the host country. » (Disponible sur : www.miga.org/documents/Operations-Regulations.pdf.)

Voir aussi l'annexe de la Résolution A/RES/41/128, *Déclaration sur le Droit au développement*, du 4 décembre 1986, *disponible sur*: www.un.org/french/documents/view_doc.asp?symbol=A/RES/41/128.

ii. L'Absence de Méthode Excluant Toute Référence Régionale

Le développement est uniformisé et universalisé par les arbitres ; il devient une abstraction et un concept purement scolaire. Sa teneur, sa substance, ses implications, ses rouages et ses critères tels qu'ils existent et tels qu'ils sont ancrés au niveau régional,[37] au niveau national et au niveau local—ces diverses strates où il s'étend normalement—sont complètement ignorés. La réalité et les critères du développement d'un Etat de la région de l'Afrique du nord sont confondus avec ceux de l'Afrique sub-saharienne,[38] de la région de l'Amérique du sud,[39] de l'Asie du sud-est[40] ou de l'Europe de l'est. Or chacune de ses régions—et en leur sein, chaque État—, disposent d'une conjoncture qui détermine son niveau et son type de développement. La géographie, les ressources naturelles, la structure économique et sociale, la disponibilité de la main-d'œuvre, l'état de l'environnement, les politiques, les infrastructures, les institutions, la culture sont autant de facteurs qui varient d'une région à l'autre et d'un Etat à l'autre. Ainsi, ce qui est, par exemple, propice au développement d'une région riche en minéraux ne peut être érigé comme un principe applicable à toute région pour tout type de développement. De plus, la région en tant que territoire a une assise tant supra-étatique qu'infra-étatique. Plusieurs États ont un découpage territorial interne par région. Pour les grands États, les facteurs du développement varient facilement et très souvent d'une région à l'autre. Au Brésil, par exemple, les facteurs du développement de la région amazonienne diffèrent drastiquement de ce ceux de la région sèche du Sertão ou de la région montagneuse du Minas Gerais.[41]

Ce sont là autant de facteurs que les tribunaux arbitraux ne considèrent pas en utilisant le concept du développement ; ce dernier se trouve par conséquent dépourvu de tout réalisme. Il apparaît uniquement comme un outil de travail utilisé par les arbitres pour les besoin de l'interprétation. Dans cette mesure, les circonstances de son utilisation font douter de son efficacité et de son utilité. Ces lacunes caractérisant l'emploi du concept du développement peuvent être expliquées par au moins deux raisons: l'absence de définition du développement et la croyance par les arbitres qu'il s'agit d'un concept universel s'appliquant de manière uniforme en tout lieu et en tout

[37] P Hugon, « Les économies en développement au regard des théories de la régionalisation » (2002) 43 *Revue Tiers Monde* 9, 9–25; M Schiff, LA Winters, *Regional Integration and development* (New York, World Bank/Oxford University Press, 2003) 1–321.

[38] CNUCED, *Economic Development in Africa. South–South Cooperation: Africa And The New Forms of Development Partnership* (Genève, Nations unies, 2010) 116p; CNUCED, *Economic Development in Africa. Strengthening Regional Economic Integration for Africa's Development* (Genève, Nations unies, 2009) 115p; JS Omotola, « Globalization, New Regionalism and the Challenge of Development in Africa » (2010) 4 *Africana* 103, 103–36.

[39] J Beaujeu-Garnier, C Lefort, *L'économie de l'Amérique latine*, 9e édition (Paris, PUF, 1986) 127p; Programme des Nations unies pour le développement, *Regional Human Development Report for Latin America and the Caribbean 2010 Acting on the future: breaking the intergenerational transmission of inequality* (Genève, Nations unies, 2010) 206p.

[40] F Nicolas, « Mondialisation et régionalisation dans les pays en développement—les deux faces de Janus » (1997) 2 *Politiques internationales* 293, 293–307.

[41] CG Caubet, « Le traité de coopération amazonienne—régionalisation et développement de l'Amazonie » (1984) 30 *Annuaire français de droit international* 803, 803–18; C Droulers, M Broggio, « L'espace et le développement au Brésil : de la géophagie à la géosophie ? » (2001) 42 *Revue Tiers Monde* 673, 673–88; R Ordoñez, « Au Brésil, autant en rapporte le vent », *Courrier International*, 26/07/2012 (www.courrierinternational.com/).

temps. Cette constatation colore le droit international des investissements : pour plusieurs tribunaux, le développement est un concept auto-explicatif.

B. Le Développement Présenté Comme Un Concept Auto-Explicatif Par Les Tribunaux

Cette constatation résulte de l'étude des décisions et sentences arbitrales (i) même s'il existe quelques techniques juridiques permettant d'utiliser le concept du développement en considérant les réalités à la fois régionales et étatiques (ii).

i. Une Constatation Résultant de l'Étude des Décisions Arbitrales

Le concept du développement est tellement dilué dans les imaginations collectives[42] et fait tellement partie de l'actualité quotidienne que sa compréhension est prise pour acquise, loin la diversité qui le caractérise en fonction des régions et des États. En l'abordant, les tribunaux n'en apportent pas un grand éclairage car leur méthode est, à ce niveau, souvent imprécise et semble parfois relever de l'impressionnisme. Les arbitres livrent leurs impressions du développement plutôt que la réalité du développement. Comme mentionné, le développement est très éclectique dans sa conception et dans sa compréhension. Pour cette raison, son étude s'accompagne d'une dose de complexité. Il n'est pas possible de tirer des conclusions sérieuses affirmant l'existence d'une contribution au développement d'un État par une simple lecture ou par une simple vision des faits d'une affaire sans aucune étude concrète préalable. Certains tribunaux abordent cependant la question de manière plutôt brève en concluant, par une unique référence aux éléments factuels qui leur sont soumis, qu'une contribution au développement est bien présente. Ils considèrent le développement comme une évidence qui s'auto-définie. Ce faisant, le concept n'est abordé que de manière superficielle mais les conclusions qui en ressortent ont des implications sérieuses car elles influent grandement sur l'identification de l'investissement et sur la compétence des tribunaux. Des conclusions importantes découlent donc d'analyses légères. Dans une affaire *Jan de Nul c Égypte*, relative à l'élargissement et l'approfondissement de certaines parties sud du Canal de Suez, le tribunal arbitral devant examiner si l'activité en question pouvait être qualifiée d'un investissement affirma en ce qui concerne le critère du développement que « one cannot seriously deny that the operation of the Suez Canal is of paramount significance for Egypt's economy and development. »[43] Une position identique est visible dans l'affaire *Helnan c Égypte*.[44] Les conclusions dans ces deux affaires sont catégoriques et la méthode employée est peu convaincante; en vérité, il n'y a aucune méthode.

[42] RE Gordon, JH Sylvester, « Deconstructing Development » (2004) 2 *Wisconsin International Law Journal* 1, 3.

[43] *Jan de Nul NC and Dredging International NC c Egypte* CIRDI n° ARB/04/13, Décision sur la compétence (16/06/06) 92.

[44] *Helnan International Hotels A/S c Égypte*, CIRDI n° ARB/05/19, Décision sur les objections à la compétence (17/10/06) 77.

Les raisons expliquant cette conclusion n'apparaissent pas. Tout semble partir d'un préjugé où l'apparence d'un développement est considérée comme un développement. Le procédé est quelque peu tautologique car les arbitres semblent affirmer que le développement se définit comme le développement.

Le but ici n'est aucunement d'affirmer que les activités litigieuses dans ces deux affaires ont ou n'ont pas d'apport au développement de l'Etat égyptien. Les tribunaux n'ont aucune obligation d'utiliser le critère en question. Toutefois, si ils le font et si ils estiment que le critère du développement est d'une réelle importance, cela implique qu'ils se considèrent techniquement capables d'identifier et de définir ce critère. Dans le cas contraire, il existe un risque de se positionner hors du droit, le développement étant lui-même, souvent, à la limite du droit.[45] Cette configuration est apparue dans une affaire *Malaysian Historical Salvors c Malaisie*. Le juge unique nommé pour cette affaire a conclu qu'une activité de renflouage de navire n'était pas constitutif d'un investissement. En analysant le critère de la contribution au développement, l'arbitre se contenta d'affirmer que ce type d'activité ne contribuait pas de manière significative au développement de l'État d'accueil.[46] Dans sa conception, seules les activités impliquant des apports en infrastructures lourdes ou celles ayant des liens avec des services bancaires importants sont susceptibles de contribuer au développement d'un Etat et de revêtir, par conséquent, la qualification d'investissement.[47] Une fois de plus, cette position n'est nullement expliquée par l'arbitre; il ne fait aucunement ressortir pourquoi, mais surtout comment, uniquement certaines activités sont susceptibles d'avoir un effet positif sur le développement d'un État. Cela fragilise logiquement son raisonnement et sa construction juridique. Si cette décision a par la suite été annulée, la décision d'annulation fut accompagnée d'une opinion dissidente du Juge Shuhabuddeen. L'opinion se présente comme un véritable plaidoyer pour l'inclusion de la contribution au développement économique, précise le Juge, comme une véritable condition de l'investissement.[48] Cette opinion affirme que sans une contribution au développement économique, une activité ne peut recevoir la qualification d'investissement. Selon l'arbitre dissident, les parties peuvent, par leur volonté, définir l'investissement de manière très large. La compétence d'un tribunal est cependant configurée par des limites extérieures logiques[49] qui vont au-delà de leur volonté. Ces limites extérieures de la compétence sont déterminées par l'existence d'une contribution au développement économique de l'Etat d'accueil et

[45] Flory, « Introduction Générale » in M Flory, A Mahiou, JR Henry (eds), *La formation des normes en droit international du développement* (Paris, Éditions du CNRS, 1984) 9.

[46] *Malaysian Historical Salvors, SDN, BHD c Malaysia*, CIRDI n° ARB/05/10, Décision sur la compétence (17/05/07) 143; voir aussi, W Ben Hamida, « La notion d'investissement : La notion maudite du système CIRDI ? » (2007) *Gazette du Palais* 33, 37; D Vis-Dunbar, « Malaysian Historical Salvors Jurisdictional Award Annulled; Committee Split on Question of Economic Development as Criteria of ICSID Investments » (mai 2009) *Investment Treaty News* 1, 11 (disponible sur: www.iisd.org/itn/wp-content/uploads/2009/05/ITN-May-2009.pdf); JP Given, « Malaysia Historical Salvors Sdn, Bhd v Malaysia: An End to the Liberal Definition of 'Investment' in ICSID Arbitrations? » (2009) 31 *Loyola Los Angeles International and Comparative Law Review* 467, 467–500.

[47] *Malaysian Historical Salvors, SDN, BHD c Malaysia*, CIRDI n° ARB/05/10, Décision sur la compétence (17/05/07) 142.

[48] *Malaysian Historical Salvors, SDN, BHD c Malaysia*, CIRDI n° ARB/05/10, Décision sur l'annulation (16/04/09), Opinion dissidente du Juge Mohamed Shuhabuddeen, 4.

[49] ibid, §8.

cette contribution doit, selon lui, être substantielle.[50] Sans trop justifier sa position et utilisant peut-être son autorité, le Juge affirme qu'il va là d'une simple question de bon sens.[51] Il lui est difficile de comprendre comment une entité œuvrant uniquement dans le sens de la fructification de ses propres bénéfices et n'étant en rien lié au développement économique de l'Etat qui l'accueille puisse porter une affaire devant un tribunal CIRDI.[52] Comme plusieurs arbitres, il se réfèrent aussi au contexte de la Convention de Washington pour justifier la référence au développement économique qui figure aussi dans la trame des travaux préparatoires.[53] Il précise que les tribunaux tendent à minimiser cette question du développement.[54] Toutefois, ce que valorise le Juge Shuhabuddeen c'est surtout l'image du développement en général. Il bâtit, certes, une argumentation juridique pour justifier l'emploi de cette « condition » de l'investissement mais il n'explique pas quelles techniques et quelles méthodes doivent être utilisées par les tribunaux pour évaluer la contribution d'une activité.

ii. Les Techniques Juridiques Disponibles Pour Éclairer la Teneur et la Portée du Développement devant les Tribunaux Arbitraux

Concept polymorphe, le développement ne peut être réduit, sans être minimisé, à une simple description factuelle. L'objectif du développement peut être consensuel mais sa définition et ses implications ne le sont pas. Comme le souligne la Professeur Brigitte Stern, la création d'un grand magasin qui offre des prix très peu élevés aux consommateurs mais qui portent atteinte à l'activité des petites entreprises nationales ne constitue pas nécessairement un investissement propice au développement. Dans le même sens, elle se demande si les activités d'une mine d'or qui détruisent une forêt tropical ou la terre sacré d'un peuple indigène ou qui portent atteinte à l'environnement sont bénéfiques au développement. Elle en conclut que ces seules questions suffisent à soulever la difficulté que comporte l'incorporation de la dimension développementale à la définition de l'investissement.[55] Le calcul d'une contribution au développement nécessite l'utilisation de certains indicateurs[56] mais aussi—et cela apporte un élément de subjectivité—le choix de ces indicateurs; il implique aussi le choix d'une période de référence et il est, dans cette mesure, difficile d'évaluer la portée d'une activité car cette dernière peut-être positive pour le développement d'un Etat sur une durée donnée mais peut avoir des effets négatifs par la suite.[57] La question est d'une grande technicité et elle dépasse souvent la spécialité des tribunaux: l'évaluation de la contribution au développement ne se limite pas à une seule analyse juridique. Cependant, les tribunaux peuvent, s'ils le jugent utile, demander aux parties de présenter des éléments probatoires sur ces questions: ils peuvent faire

[50] ibid, §§33–38.
[51] ibid, §34.
[52] ibid, §§20–21.
[53] ibid, §14, §30.
[54] ibid, §23.
[55] B Stern, « The Contours of the Notion of Protected Investment » (2009) 24 *ICSID Review, Foreign Investment Law Journal* 534, 543; voir aussi: W Ben Hamida, ci-avant note 45, 36.
[56] S Manciaux, ci-avant note 10, 71.
[57] ibid.

citer des témoins ou entendre des experts du développement. C'est ce que permet par exemple l'article 34(2)(b) du Règlement d'arbitrage du CIRDI.[58] Le recours à des experts spécialisés en matière de développement est sans doute le meilleur moyen de rendre le concept compréhensible afin d'affiner et de raffiner sa fonction de critère de l'investissement. Leur expertise permettrait de rendre compte de la complexité du développement et en même temps, le concept serait abordé avec plus d'objectivité, en tenant compte de la réalité locale loin de tout universalisme et de tout uniformité vers lesquels il est souvent attiré. Dans ce cas, les tribunaux n'auraient pas pour tâche de juger scientifiquement le rapport d'expert mais devraient uniquement en apprécier l'objectivité, le sérieux et le bien fondé, notamment par la méthode utilisée. Ce procédé est par exemple utilisé lors de la présentation d'une expertise environnementale à un tribunal.[59] Il serait, certes, légitime de se demander si l'article 34(2)(b) mérite d'être appliqué pour le seul compte de l'éclaircissement d'un critère de l'investissement et si toute une mobilisation d'experts est justifiée à cet effet. Cela peut avoir l'air d'un « Much Ado About Nothing » dans un contentieux sur la compétence; mais si la référence au développement est pour certains tribunaux, fondamentale, il est difficile de comprendre pourquoi ils ne s'y attardent pas plus longuement pour que le critère soit étudié à sa juste valeur. Si le développement est une des raisons d'être du système de règlement des différends et de la relation entre investisseurs et Etats, il doit être traité le plus minutieusement possible. Dans le cas contraire, la démarche est douteuse et le critère s'enrobe lui-même d'un caractère douteux car s'il n'a qu'une portée théorique, son utilité peut-être questionnée. Et dans un tel cas de figure, il est plus pertinent d'éviter tout recours et toute référence au critère de la contribution au développement. Cela éviterait un usage erronée du concept. Les arbitres ne sont toutefois que le dernier maillon de cet usage générique et généralisée du développement. Bien en amont, les États négligent le eux-mêmes car en signant les accords relatifs aux investissements, ils lui accordent une acception et une valeur universelles.

III. LA MÉCONNAISSANCE DES RÉALITÉS RÉGIONALES PAR LES TEXTES: LE DÉVELOPPEMENT PRÉSENTÉ COMME UN CONCEPT UNIVERSEL DANS LES ACCORDS RELATIFS AUX INVESTISSEMENTS

Plusieurs accords se réfèrent au développement, notamment dans leur préambule, pour simplement affirmer que tel est l'objectif de la circulation et de la protection des investissements. Aucune définition du concept n'apparaît et aucune relation avec le contexte régionale et étatique des Etats signataires n'est visible. Toujours est-il que malgré cette absence de définition et de précision qui corrobore la méconnaissance

[58] Le Règlement est disponible sur: www.icsid.worldbank.org/ICSID/StaticFiles/basicdoc-fra/CRR_French-final.pdf.

[59] J Viñuales, *Foreign Investment and the Environment in International Law: An Ambiguous Relationship* (Geneva, Center for International Environmental Studies (Genève, The Graduate Institute, Research Paper no 2, 2010) 61–62. Voir aussi: *Chemtura Corporation c Canada*, CNUDCI, sentence (02/08/2010), 134–35.

des dimensions pratiques du développement (A), il existe quelques techniques juridiques parfois utilisées pour permettre une prise en compte du contexte régional et étatique (B).

A. La Négation des Réalités Régionales et Étatiques dans les Accords Relatifs aux Investissements

Si les accords relatifs aux investissements se présentent souvent comme des outils à double fonction, de protection des investissements et de promotion du développement, leurs dispositions sont rarement dirigées vers l'objectif du développement.[60] Substantiellement, un droit au développement ou un droit de réglementer dans le sens du développement n'y apparaît pas en tant que tel.[61] S'il serait cohérent qu'un Etat négocie de tels accords conformément à sa politique de développement,[62] il est aussi vrai que plusieurs pays en développement ne sont pas toujours techniquement armés afin d'aligner leurs objectifs dans les instruments de protection et de promotion des investissements.[63] L'aspect développemental des accords est surtout politique et cela se constate à sa présence marginale dans leur sein.[64] Cela est aussi lié à la négociation de ces accords: les pays en développement ont souvent un poids relativement faible lorsqu'il s'agit de négocier de tels accords[65] et, partant, à y inclure des dispositions relatives à la protection de leurs intérêts.[66] Ce faisant, ils peuvent difficilement faire ressortir leurs priorités de développement.[67] Ainsi, la référence au développement apparaîtra souvent dans un préambule, accompagnée d'un minimum de précision. Par exemple, le préambule de l'Accord sur la protection et la promotion des investissements du 22 décembre 1974 entre la France et l'Egypte précise que « l'encouragement et la protection des investissements sont propres à stimuler

[60] LE Peterson, *Bilateral Investment Treaties and Development Policy-Making* (International Institute for Sustainable Development, 2008) 4, 8 (disponible sur: www.iisd.org/pdf/2004/trade_bits.pdf).

[61] ibid, 4–5.

[62] CNUCED, *Development Implications of International Investment Agreements. IIA Monitor 2—International Investment Agreements* (Genève, UNCTAD/WEB/ITE/IIA/2007/2, 2007) 4 (disponible sur: www.unctad.org/en/docs/webiteiia20072_en.pdf).

[63] ibid, 5.

[64] CNUCED, *The development dimension of international investment agreements* (Genève, TD/B/C. II/MEM.3/2, 2008) 8; CNUCED, *Bilateral Investment Treaties 1995–2006: Trends in Investment Treaty Rule-Making* (Genève, UNCTAD/ITE/IIA/2006/5, 2006) 145.

[65] P Juillard, « Le système actuel est-il déséquilibré en faveur de l'investisseur privé étranger et au détriment de l'Etat d'accueil? » in C Leben (ed), *Le contentieux arbitral transnational relatif à l'investissement. Nouveaux Développements* (Paris, LGDJ, 2006) 191.

[66] K Fach Gomez, « Latin America and ICSID: David versus Goliath » (2011) 17 *Law and Business Review of the Americas* 195, 216–21; M Sornarajah, *The Settlement of Foreign Investment Disputes* (La Haye, Kluwer Law International, 2000) 9.

[67] EA Alexander, « Taking Account of Reality: Adopting Contextual Standards for Developing Countries in International Investment Law » (2008) 48 *Virginia Journal of International Law* 817, 823–24; N Monebhurrun, « Are Bilateral Investment Treaties Contemporary Unequal Treaties? » (2012) 1 *International Journal of Contemporary Laws* (disponible sur: www.ijcl.co.in/uploads/8/7/5/1/8751632/ijcl_vol.1_1_-_article_by_nitish.pdf).

le transfert de capitaux entre les deux pays, dans l'intérêt de leur développement économique. »[68] Des mentions similaires sont faites dans plusieurs accords modèles entre pays industrialisés et pays en développement.[69] Ceci étant dit, la question de la puissance économique et politique n'en est pas la seule cause. Les accords relatifs aux investissements entre les pays en développement sont eux-mêmes souvent très peu négociés et contiennent très peu de dispositions pouvant valoriser leurs intérêts. C'est souvent un modèle existant et provenant d'un pays industrialisé qui sera utilisé par un pays en développement dans ses relations économiques avec les autres Etats en développement.[70] Cela est dû à un manque d'expertise[71] mais aussi à un phénomène de « mode » où chaque Etat doit disposer de son arsenal d'accords; les accords qui sont proposés aux pays en développement par les pays développés sont souvent acceptés non seulement sans négociations préliminaires mais aussi sans réflexions préalables approfondies de la part des premiers. Il en résulte, par conséquent, une quasi-uniformisation de ces accords, et, dans la même veine, une méconnaissance du développement qui est présenté d'une manière quelque peu universel, comme un simple objectif, dépourvu de toutes les nuances profondes qui le caractérisent en pratique aux niveaux régional et national. Seuls quelques rares accords laissent transparaître une prise en compte du développement à ces niveaux et, cela est permis par l'utilisation de quelques techniques juridiques.

B. Les Techniques Juridiques de Prise en Compte des Impératifs Régionaux et Nationaux de Développement

Au-delà du préambule, et même si les accords sur les investissements peuvent limiter la marge de manœuvre des Etats dans la réalisation de leurs politiques individuelles,[72] au moins trois types de dispositions peuvent entretenir une relation avec le développement. Cette relation est indirecte mais c'est un moyen que les Etats utilisent ou qu'ils peuvent utiliser pour faire valoir leurs intérêts. Premièrement, la majorité des accords précise que les investisseurs ont l'obligation de conduire leurs activités

[68] L'accord est disponible sur: www.unctad.org/sections/dite/iia/docs/bits/egypt_france_fr.pdf. Dans le même sens, voir l'accord franco-indien (disponible sur: www.unctad.org/sections/dite/iia/docs/bits/france_inde_fr.pdf); l'accord Franco–algérien (disponible sur: www.unctad.org/sections/dite/iia/docs/bits/france_algeria_fr.pdf); l'accord franco-argentin (disponible sur: www.unctad.org/sections/dite/iia/docs/bits/france_argentina_fr.pdf).

[69] Voir par exemple, les accords modèles des États-unis, de la France, de la Colombie, du Canada, certains accords du Royaume uni, de la Chine ou des Pays-bas (disponible sur: www.italaw.com/investment-treaties.) Il s'agit bien entendu là d'une liste indicative.

[70] M Malik, « South–South Bilateral Investment Treaties: The Same Old Story? » (2011) *IV Annual Forum for Developing Country Investment Negotiators Background Papers*—New Delhi, publié par L'institut international du développement 1, 1–5 (disponible sur: www.iisd.org/pdf/2011/dci_2010_south_bits.pdf); KJ Vandevelde, « A Brief History of International Investment Agreements » (2005) 12 *University of California Davis Journal of International Law and Policy* 157, 170.

[71] M Malik, ci-avant note 70, 1–5.

[72] CNUCED, *International Investment Agreements: Flexibility for Development* (Genève, UNCTAD/ITE/IIT/18, 2000) 11.

conformément à la législation nationale.[73] Il appartient dans ce cas à la législation nationale des Etats de prévoir des dispositions pour la mise en œuvre de leurs impératifs de développement. Chaque Etat a des objectifs différents en matière de développement et il incombe à chaque Etat de formuler sa législation de manière à les réaliser. La difficulté qui se pose à ce niveau est le risque d'incompatibilité de la législation nationale avec les autres dispositions des accords relatifs aux investissements. Les dispositions nationales ne doivent pas être en contradiction avec celles des accords internationaux protégeant les investissements qui énoncent, pour la plupart, que les Etats s'engagent, dans le cadre de leur législation, à admettre et à encourager les investissements sur leur territoire.[74] L'admission et l'encouragement des investissements doit se faire conformément au droit national mais, en même temps, conformément aux accords bilatéraux. Par conséquent, le premier doit s'aligner sur les derniers et une législation nationale sur le développement ne peut pas entraver la protection due aux investissements aux termes d'un accord sur les investissements.

Toutefois, et c'est là le deuxième moyen, les parties peuvent émettre des réserves aux accords. La formulation d'une réserve à un traité est une possibilité que permet le droit international comme le confirme l'article 19 de la Convention de Vienne.[75] C'est ce qu'a fait, par exemple, le Vietnam dans le traité bilatéral d'investissement qui le lie au Royaume Uni. Certains secteurs et certaines matières sont exclus de l'application du traitement national. Les secteurs de presse, d'importation et de distribution de services, les services de télécommunication, les services du secteur touristique, bancaire et de l'assurance, l'exploitation du pétrole et du gaz ou de la pêche sont, par exemple, exclus du traitement national. Au niveau des matières exclues, figurent la propriété et l'utilisation des terres et des résidences, les subsides gouvernementaux et l'aide aux entreprises locales, les prix et les tarifs de certains produits et services sous contrôle étatique.[76] Des réserves similaires se retrouvent aussi dans l'accord anglo-panaméen du 7 octobre 1983 dans lequel le Panama a précisé dans une annexe que les secteurs économiques et les activités qui constituent une exception constitutionnelle et légale sont exclus du champ d'application de la protection due aux investisseurs britanniques. Ces secteurs et ces activités sont la communication, les banques, les sociétés privées d'utilité publique, la production énergétique, l'exploitation des ressources naturelles ou la production hydroélectrique.[77] Un procédé similaire est

[73] Voir par exemple, l'accord entre le Royaume Uni et le Chili du 8 janvier 1996, article 1(2), article 2(1) (disponible sur: www.unctad.org/sections/dite/iia/docs/bits/chile_uk.pdf); l'accord entre la France et le Cambodge du 16 juin 2000, article 1 (disponible sur: www.unctad.org/sections/dite/iia/docs/bits/france_cambodia_fr.pdf); l'accord entre la France et la Chine du 30 mai 1984, article 1 (disponible sur: www.unctad.org/sections/dite/iia/docs/bits/france_china_fr.pdf.)

[74] Voir par exemple: l'accord entre la France et la Chine du 30 mai 1984, article 2 (disponible sur: www.unctad.org/sections/dite/iia/docs/bits/france_china_fr.pdf); l'accord entre le Denmark et l'Ethiopie du 24 avril 2001, article 2 (disponible sur: www.unctad.org/sections/dite/iia/docs/bits/ethiopia_denmark.pdf); l'accord entre l'Allemagne et l'Algérie du 11 mars 1996, article 2 (disponible sur: www.unctad.org/sections/dite/iia/docs/bits/germany_algeria_fr.pdf).

[75] Voir l'article 19 de la Convention de Vienne.

[76] Voir Accord bilatéral entre le Royaume Uni et le Vietnam du 1e août 2002, annexe intitulée « Exceptions to the grant of national treatment to investments and returns of investments of nationals or companies of the United Kingdom » (disponible sur: www.unctad.org/sections/dite/iia/docs/bits/uk_vietnam.pdf).

[77] Voir l'annexe de l'accord entre Le Royaume Uni et le Paname, disponible sur: www.unctad.org/sections/dite/iia/docs/bits/uk_panama.pdf.

visible dans l'accord de partenariat économique entre l'Union européenne et le Cariforum.[78] Les Etats membres de l'Union européenne et ceux de la région caribéenne ont inséré plusieurs réserves au sein de cet accord, notamment, quant aux investissements, à la distribution de certains services et à la présence commerciale.[79] Étant plus en connexion avec leurs réalités régionales et locales, ces États et ces régions sont mieux placés pour connaître les priorités de leur développement. Ainsi, l'utilisation des réserves est un moyen pouvant être utile dans de tels accords bilatéraux ou régionaux afin d'adapter et de guider les investissements étrangers dans le sens d'un développement voulu. Il ne s'agit là que d'une forme de rationalisation des investissements vers le type de développement qui leur sied le mieux. Le troisième moyen obéit à un esprit similaire: il s'agit de l'utilisation des clauses d'exception à la protection des investissements. La clause de la nation la plus favorisée et celle du traitement national sont dans certains cas modulées pour prendre en considération les politiques de développement des Etats.[80] L'accord signé entre la Suisse et la Jamaïque dispose par exemple:

> Les incitations spéciales accordées par une Partie Contractante à ses seuls nationaux ou sociétés dans le cadre de sa politique de développement afin de stimuler la création d'industries locales, telles que celle des cottages, sont considérées comme étant compatibles avec le présent article, pour autant qu'elles n'affectent pas de façon significative l'investissement ou les activités des nationaux et sociétés de l'autre Partie Contractante en relation avec un investissement.[81]

Si ces techniques juridiques demeurent exceptionnelles dans le droit international des investissements, leur utilisation permet aux Etats et dans certains cas, aux intégration régionales, de valoriser leurs impératifs de développement respectifs d'une manière à la fois plus minutieuse et plus réaliste. Mais cette référence réaliste au développement demeure très rare.

IV. CONCLUSION

La présente conclusion prendra la forme d'une constatation et d'une proposition. Les deux ont déjà été présentées et il s'agit uniquement de les relever car elles constituent

[78] Accord de partenariat économique entre les États du Cariforum, d'une part, et la Communauté européenne et ses États membres, d'autre part, Bridgetown, 15 octobre 2008, disponible sur: www.eur-lex.europa.eu/LexUriServ/LexUriServ.do?uri=OJ:L:2008:289:0003:1955:FR:PDF.

[79] Accord de partenariat économique entre les États du Cariforum, d'une part, et la Communauté européenne et ses États membres, d'autre part, Bridgetown, 15 octobre 2008, article 66, article 69, Annexe IV.

[80] Voir l'article 3(4) de l'accord bilatéral concernant la promotion et la protection réciproques des investissements conclu le 11 décembre 1990 entre la Suisse et la Jamaïque (disponible sur: www.unctad.org/sections/dite/iia/docs/bits/switzerland_jamaica_fr.pdf); voir l'article 3(5) de l'accord bilatéral concernant la promotion et la protection réciproques des investissements conclu le 22 septembre 2000 entre les Pays-Bas et la Jamaïque (disponible sur: www.unctad.org/sections/dite/iia/docs/bits/netherlands_jamaica.pdf); voir l'article 3(3) de l'accord bilatéral concernant la promotion et la protection réciproques des investissements conclu le 20 janvier 1987 entre le Royaume uni et la Jamaïque (disponible sur: www.unctad.org/sections/dite/iia/docs/bits/uk_jamaica.pdf).

[81] Article 3(4) de l'accord bilatéral concernant la promotion et la protection réciproques des investissements conclu le 11 décembre 1990 entre la Suisse et la Jamaïque.

le cœur de cette réflexion. La constatation a été un *leitmotiv*: le développement est utilisé sans méthode et sans technicité convaincante; il est, partant, étudié loin de sa réalité régionale, étatique et locale pour être traité hors de tout procédé scientifique. De ce constat, la proposition se décompose en deux parties: il appartient premièrement aux États d'inclure dans leurs accords—nationaux ou régionaux—relatifs aux investissements ce qu'ils considèrent comme étant prioritaire pour leur développement. Ils sont dans la meilleure position pour juger ce qui contribue, ou pas, à leur développement. Deuxièmement, les tribunaux qui jugent utile de se référer au critère de la contribution au développement pour identifier un investissement, doivent le faire selon une démarche techniquement convaincante et pratiquement effective : pour ce faire, ils peuvent utiliser la possibilité que leur offre le droit d'avoir recours à des experts pour conforter et pour appuyer leur décisions.

Part VIII

Regionalism and Human Rights

27

The Judicial Activism of Regional Human Rights Treaty Bodies and the Sovereignty of States

THEODORE CHRISTAKIS*

I. INTRODUCTION

THERE ARE UNDOUBTEDLY many important topics to discuss in relation to the general theme of this ESIL Forum on 'Regionalism and Human Rights'. They include: the interesting relations between regionalism and universalism in the field of human rights; the spectacular disparities and contrasts in regional protection and, especially, the persistent absence of a regional system of protection in the Asia/Pacific region; the progressive normative convergence between the existing regional systems and the 'dialogue' between the regional organs of control or between the regional and the universal organs; and the 'exportation' and the influence of the European model of human rights.

In this chapter I prefer to focus on an important aspect of regionalism and human rights that concerns the dynamic methods of interpretation used by the European Court of Human Rights (ECtHR), the Inter-American Commission (IACHR) and Inter-American Court of Human Rights (IACtHR), but also progressively by the African Commission on Human and Peoples' Rights (ACHPR).[1] Following the path opened by the ECtHR, during the past two decades the Inter-American and African organs of protection have engaged with an impressive enterprise of 'rewriting' regional human rights treaties through dynamic interpretation of the original treaty provisions. This 'judicial activism'[2] has often raised the question of the legitimacy

* Professor of International Law, Director of the Centre for International Security and European Studies (CESICE), University of Grenoble Alpes, France. This chapter covers developments up to January 2013.

[1] The African Court of Human and Peoples' Rights (ACHPR) could adopt a similar attitude when and if this Court is finally able to function in an effective way. For the time being its case law is poor and its jurisdiction limited, as only five of the 26 states parties to the Protocol have made the declaration allowing direct access to the Court to NGOs and individuals.

[2] For reasons of convenience the term 'judicial activism' is used in order to describe not only activism by the three regional human rights courts noted in the text, but also the activities of non-judicial organs such as the regional Commissions. For a historical perspective and definition of the term 'judicial activism' in the theory of constitutional law, see KD Kmiec, 'The Origin and Current Meanings of Judicial Activism' (2004) 92 *California Law Review* 1441–77.

of such regional human rights treaty bodies (HRTB). It has also created the spectre of a 'Government of the Judges' who might extend states' obligations under human right treaties in an almost 'unlimited' way, thereby substituting themselves for policy makers and democratically elected parliaments in those states.

In this chapter I will first discuss to what extent regionalism encourages judicial activism by regional HRTB (II), before presenting the principal aspects of this activism by regional organs (III). I will then examine the main justifications for this judicial activism and the principal mechanisms put in place in order to 'reconcile' the regional systems with the sovereignty of states (IV). I will conclude by asking to what extent states react to the judicial activism of regional human rights organs (V).

II. TO WHAT EXTENT DOES REGIONALISM ENCOURAGE JUDICIAL ACTIVISM BY REGIONAL HUMAN RIGHTS TREATY BODIES?

It is well known that regionalism presents a lot of advantages for the development of human rights, when compared to similar developments at the universal level. These advantages can be summarised as follows. First, it is easier to get consensus among states that are often 'closer' from a cultural point of view and share relatively common national legal systems. This proximity may, nonetheless, also be counterproductive for the regional development of human rights, as demonstrated by the example of Asia. Here, despite the invitation of the UN Vienna Declaration and Program of Action of 1993 'to consider the possibility of establishing regional and sub-regional arrangements for the promotion and protection of human rights where they do not already exist',[3] there is still no effective mechanism, or regional human rights convention.[4]

Secondly, it is easier to negotiate and adopt human rights treaties, for the simple and practical reason that they relate to a restricted number of states participating in negotiations at the regional level. Thirdly, regional integration is an almost inescapable trend, especially in the economic field, and provides an opportunity to structure

[3] The Vienna Declaration and Programme of Action was adopted at the World Conference on Human Rights, 14–25 June 1993, Vienna, Austria, available at www.ohchr.org/en/professionalinterest/pages/vienna.aspx, para 37.

[4] The only progress has been the rather symbolic creation in September 2009 of the ASEAN Intergovernmental Commission on Human Rights (AICHR), which is just an ASEAN consultative body with no powers or functions similar to other regional human rights organs. The Asian states' devotion to the principle of non-interference and absolute state sovereignty (expressed by the ASEAN's self-identifying catch phrase, 'the ASEAN way') and the poor human rights record of some states in this region have contributed to an unwillingness on their part to establish an effective regional mechanism for the protection of human rights. The adoption by ASEAN members, during the November 2012 meeting in Phnom Penh, of an 'ASEAN Human Rights Declaration', which was drafted by the AICHR, did little to change this picture. This Declaration has, indeed, been heavily criticised by international human rights NGOs such as Amnesty International and Human Rights Watch as being 'fundamentally flawed' and as 'unquestionably fail[ing] to meet existing international human rights standards, let alone add value to them'. See further 'Civil society rejects flawed ASEAN Human Rights Declaration', Amnesty International Public Statement of 15 November 2012, available at: www.amnesty.org/en/library/asset/IOR64/005/2012/en/7eacdb53-76a6-49d8-9466-dc7fdaeccec7/ior640052012en.pdf.

civic activism and rights claims.[5] Fourthly, regional mechanisms offer the advantage of geographical accessibility for individuals presenting claims: it is easier for a Mexican to file a petition in Washington DC or to defend his case in San José than to go to Geneva. And sixth, regional interdependence and geographical proximity are also positive elements in achieving compliance with HRTB decisions, to the extent that neighbouring states and regional organisations can more easily request compliance and execution.

All these elements, and especially the first one, explain why regional HRTB are bolder than universal ones in their dynamic interpretation and application of human rights treaties.[6] Their willingness to contribute to the development of human rights law and, indeed, sometimes, to be ahead of their time, is bolstered by the feeling that relatively 'like-minded' states in the region are ready for these developments and will not oppose them. There is no surprise that the search for consensus is much easier to achieve at some specific, restricted regional and geopolitical levels than at the universal level. This is particularly true for some geographic regions like Europe, the Americas and even Africa, where efforts at regional integration have been remarkable during recent decades and have been followed by multiple claims for the promotion of democracy, human rights and respect for the rule of law.

Regionalism could nonetheless also provide an argument *against* the judicial activism of regional HRTB. It is well known in constitutional law theory that the debate concerning the legitimate limits to judicial activism and the power of constitutional judges to 'adapt' constitutive texts to new realities is often linked to the problem of the 'rigidity' of each constitution. If a constitution is very difficult to amend, this is used as a powerful argument in favour of the Supreme or Constitutional Court's power to interpret the constitution in a flexible and dynamic way.[7] In the field of human rights treaties it could be argued that the restricted number and the 'cohesion' of states in a particular region might facilitate the amendment of regional human rights treaties (and certainly more so than the amendment of universal human rights treaties). Indeed, the European Convention of Human Rights (ECHR) has been amended on a number of occasions using the process of the

[5] See eg, J Grugel, 'New regionalism, new rights? Latin American regionalism as an opportunity structure for civic activism', Doc de Trabajo n° 19, FLACSO/Argentina, 2009, available at http://rrii.flacso.org.ar/wp-content/uploads/2009/06/doc19.pdf.

[6] Of course we should not underestimate the bold techniques used by universal HRTB. Indeed, bodies such as the Human Rights Committee and other similar organs have often used an evolutive and dynamic interpretation in order to 'adapt' universal human rights treaties to present-day conditions. In doing so, they have also often clashed with individual states reluctant to accept these bold evolutions. The tensions between the Human Rights Committee and the United States concerning questions such as the application of the 'severability' doctrine in relation to invalid reservations or the extraterritorial reach of the ICCPR are good examples of this. For a general discussion of all these questions see T Christakis, 'Human Rights from a Neo-Voluntarist Perspective' in J Kammerhofer and J d'Aspremont (eds), *International Legal Positivism in a Post-Modern World* (Cambridge, Cambridge University Press, 2014) 421–50.

[7] See eg, E Chemerinsky, *Constitutional Law: Principles and Policies*, 3rd edn (New York, Aspen, 2006) 23 et seq, explaining that one of the basic arguments that 'non-originalists' use for an evolutive interpretation of the US Constitution is that the 'cumbersome amendment process' of this Constitution makes it impossible for it to meet the needs of a changing society. For a detailed analysis see DA Strauss, *The Living Constitution* (New York, Oxford University Press, 2010).

adoption of (amending) protocols.[8] If the contracting states can thus easily exercise their sovereign power of amending a regional human rights treaty by adopting protocols, which in the majority of cases do not need to be adopted by all member states in order to enter into force, then regional organs should not have the power to substitute themselves for states parties by deciding on important societal issues by way of 'evolutive interpretation'.

In reality, as we shall come on to see, this argument could also be used in exactly the opposite way: it could be argued that if states do not agree with the 'necessary' activism of regional HRTBs, they can always intervene in order to amend the regional conventions and 'undo' what those same regional HRTBs have tried to create, and to limit their powers.

III. WHAT ARE THE PRINCIPAL EXPRESSIONS OF THIS ACTIVISM BY REGIONAL ORGANS?

There are many different manifestations of the activism of these regional HRTBs. The most important of these is the constant use of 'evolutionary' or 'evolutive' interpretation. The constant recourse to the idea that human rights treaties are 'living instruments', the interpretation of which inevitably requires a dynamic process, gives the impression that regional HRTBs sometimes transform the original conventions by means of some kind of 'magician's hat' from which they can pull out an endless number of white rabbits, in the form of new obligations for states.

It is well known that the ECHR organs engaged with this path more than 30 years ago[9] and that the organs of the Inter-American system also eagerly adopted the 'living instrument' theory.[10] This is also the case of the ACHPR which, as some observers have noted, undertook under cover of dynamic interpretation, a major effort to 'rewrite the African Chapter'.[11] Indeed, it is well known that the African

[8] States are currently in the process of adopting Protocols 15 and 16 to the European Convention of Human Rights (ECHR), both of which are part of reform efforts aimed at realising effective implementation of the ECHR and ensuring viability of the ECHR mechanism. See Protocol No 15 amending the Convention for the Protection of Human Rights and Fundamental Freedom, opened for signature by the High Contracting Parties, Strasbourg, 24 June 2013, CETS No 213 (not yet in force) and Protocol No 16 amending the Convention for the Protection of Human Rights and Fundamental Freedoms opened for signature by the High Contracting Parties, Strasbourg, 2 October 2013, CETS No 214 (not yet in force).

[9] The ECHR first used the expression that 'the Convention is a living instrument which must be interpreted in the light of present-day conditions' in the famous early decision *Tyrer v United Kingdom*, (1978) 2 EHRR 1, which concerned outlawing punishment by 'caning' in a secondary school. Since then the expression has been used constantly in order to justify innovative solutions and readings of the Convention and even, sometimes, to bring about some spectacular reversals of the ECtHR's own previous judgments. One well-known example is the judgment in *Goodwin v United Kingdom* (2002) 35 EHRR 18 where the Court, taking into consideration societal evolutions, abandoned its previously settled case law, which consisted of refusing to secure postoperative transsexuals the right under art 8 ECHR to regularise their new gender by asking the Government to alter the initial official registers of births.

[10] See eg, *Mayagna (Sumo) Awas Tingni Community v Nicaragua*, Judgment of 31 August 2001, IACtHR, IACHR Ser C no 79, where the Court said: '[H]uman rights treaties are live instruments whose interpretation must adapt to the evolution of the times and, specifically, to current living conditions' (para 146).

[11] K Oteng Kufuor, *The African Human Rights System: Origin and Evolution* (New York, Palgrave Macmillan, 2010) 37 et seq.

Chapter presented some important flaws in its initial drafting and the African Commission decided to use evolutive interpretation in order to remedy those flaws—especially by 'nullifying' the 'clawback clauses' that were initially introduced by states into the African Convention in order to limit human rights protection.[12]

Another example of the bold techniques used by regional human rights organs comes mainly from the IACHR and the IACtHR, with the technique of elevating human rights to a *jus cogens* status, in order to crush any state resistance. The ability of the Inter-American organs to refer, directly or indirectly, to new rules of *jus cogens* is indeed impressive[13] and contrasts with the precautionary approach taken in this field by other jurisdictions such as the ECtHR—not to mention the ICJ or other universal organs.

One of the best examples of using the concept of *jus cogens* in order to annihilate states' resistance to the evolution of human rights norms is undoubtedly the 2002 decision of the IACHR in *M Domingues v United States.*[14] In this case the United States argued that it was not bound by any international norm prohibiting the execution of juvenile offenders. Specifically, the United States contended that it had consistently asserted its right to execute juvenile offenders by making reservations to treaties, filing briefs before national and international tribunals, and making public statements. Correspondingly, even if a norm of customary international law establishing 18 as the minimum age for the imposition of the death penalty had emerged, the US should be considered as a 'persistent objector' and thus considered as not bound by such a customary rule.

The IACHR made a big concession to state sovereignty by conceding that 'as customary international law rests on the consent of nations, a State that persistently objects to a norm of customary international law is not bound by that norm.'[15] However, immediately afterwards the IACHR explained that prohibition of the death penalty for juvenile offenders below the age of 18 years is now an international *jus cogens* norm and, as such, it 'binds the community of States, including the United States. The norm cannot be validly derogated from, whether by treaty or by the objection of a state, persistent or otherwise.'[16]

Other techniques used by regional human rights organs in order to promote human rights in a way that could conflict with the 'original intent' of states include: the introduction of a whole chapter on 'positive obligations', which was not previously guaranteed, on the basis of textualism;[17] the (almost) complete abandonment of any reference to the 'travaux préparatoires';[18] or the invalidation of reservations and the application of the 'severability' doctrine.[19] Another interesting technique

[12] ibid, 57 et seq.
[13] See C Maïa, 'Le *jus cogens* dans la jurisprudence de la Cour interaméricaine des Droits de l'Homme' in L Hennebel et H Tigroudja (eds), *Le particularisme interaméricain des droits de l'homme: en l'honneur du 40e anniversaire de la Convention américaine des droits de l'homme* (Paris, Pedone, 2009) 271–311.
[14] *Michael Domingues v United States,* Report no 62/02, Merits, 22 October 2002, 10 IHRR 1101 (2003).
[15] ibid, para 49.
[16] ibid, para 85.
[17] For an analysis, see Christakis, 'Human Rights', 428–29.
[18] ibid, 425–26.
[19] ibid, 433–34.

is the introduction of completely 'new' obligations by the transposition of external elements. We could think of the 'transposition' of solutions provided for in other regional systems. One example is the interaction and cross-fertilisation among regional human right treaties, which is a classical and old phenomenon of international human rights law that was highlighted by Judge AA Cançado Trindade back in 1987.[20] More puzzling though is the practice of taking into consideration other instruments, including treaties that have not been ratified by the responding state, and soft-law or non-binding instruments.[21]

IV. WHAT ARE THE LIMITS TO JUDICIAL ACTIVISM AND THE PRINCIPAL MECHANISMS OF RECONCILIATION WITH THE SOVEREIGNTY OF STATES?

Regional HRTBs often explain that the nature of human rights treaties requires dynamic and evolutive interpretation. Both the ECtHR and the IACtHR have constantly expressed the view that these treaties have an 'objective' character and that the aim of the drafting states has been to

> submit themselves to a legal order within which they, for the common good, assume various obligations, not in relation to other States, but towards all individuals within their jurisdiction.[22]

From this point of view the regional organs of control help states realise this objective by 'adapting' these old instruments to new realities in a constantly evolving world. Dynamic interpretation is thus perfectly legitimate, as the necessary means to realise the broader intention of states when drafting the ECHR, which was to put in place an effective system of regional protection of human rights.

At the same time these regional organs know that there are limits to this 'evolutive' interpretation of human rights, and must exercise self-restraint, fearing that otherwise they might lose their legitimacy.[23] This ranges from 'testing the water' and the reaction of states before proceeding to a new 'dynamic interpretation'[24] to a refusal

[20] AA Cançado Trindade, 'Co-existence and Co-ordination of Mechanisms of International Protection of Human Rights (at Global and Regional Levels)' (1987) 202 *Recueil des Cours* 101, where he states that 'Given the multiplicity of co-existing human rights instruments in our days, it comes as little or no surprise that the interpretation and application of certain provisions of one human rights treaty have at times been resorted to as orientation for the interpretation of corresponding provisions of another (usually newer) human rights treaty.'

[21] See Christakis, 'Human Rights', 430–31.

[22] *The Effect of Reservations on the Entry into Force of the American Convention on Human Rights*, Advisory Opinion OC-2/82, 24 September 1982, IACHR Ser A no 2(1982), para 29.

[23] As a couple of scholars have rightly observed: 'For legal institutions, no attribute is more important than legitimacy. Legitimacy provides courts authority; it allows them the latitude necessary to make decisions contrary to the perceived immediate interests of their constituents'. J Gibson and G Caldeira, 'The Legitimacy of Transnational Legal Institutions: Compliance, Support and the European Court of Justice' (1995) 39 *American Journal of Political Science* 459–89, 460.

[24] See eg ECHR, *Schalk and Kopf v Austria* (2011) 53 EHRR 20. 'Testing' the reaction of states in relation to the important question of same-sex marriage, the Court said that it 'would no longer consider that the right to marry enshrined in Article 12 must in all circumstances be limited to marriage between two persons of the opposite sex'. Nonetheless, it declined to find a violation of this article by the responding government by saying that 'as matters stand, the question whether or not to allow same-sex marriage

to proceed to a dynamic interpretation if the human rights body in question either considers that states are not ready for this[25] or that this could be at odds with some important rules of general international law that states have accepted at a universal level.[26] It is also important to highlight that the point that the evolutive interpretation technique is used not only in favour of an extensive reading of human rights but also, sometimes, in favour of the capacity of state parties to adopt derogations or restrictions to human rights.[27]

Two other important and interconnected mechanisms are increasingly used by the ECtHR in order to 'reconcile' its bold techniques of interpretation with the sovereignty of states. Interestingly, these techniques have not really been embraced by either the IACHR, the IACtHR or the ACHPR.

The first method is to refer more and more to states and the 'common denominator' among them in order to 'legitimise' the evolutive interpretation of the ECHR. It is well known that the existence of a 'European consensus' can facilitate the dynamic interpretation of the Convention by the ECHR, as for example in the landmark *Dudgeon*[28] or *Sunday Times*[29] cases, while lack of consensus may prevent a dynamic new reading of the Convention, as in the *Pretty* case.[30] The quest for consensus sometimes acquires such importance in the European system that HC Yourow has observed that '[t]he law of the Convention sometimes seems neither more nor less than consensus, or lack thereof, in the law and practice of the constituent State's parties.'[31]

The second method is to try to accommodate the great diversity of national traditions and practices in different areas by using the 'national margin of appreciation'

is left to regulation by the national law of the Contracting State.' For a critical approach to this judgment, see T Christakis, 'Interprétation évolutive ou confusion jurisprudentielle? Le risque de dilution de la notion de "droit" par le recours à la "marge nationale d'appréciation" dans l'arrêt Schalk and Kopf c./ Autriche du 24 juin 2010 de la CEDH', available at http://cesice.upmf-grenoble.fr/manifestations/interpretation-evolutive-ou-confusion-jurisprudentielle-le-risque-de-dilution-de-la-notion-de-droit-par-le-recours-a-la-marge-nationale-d-appreciation-dans-l-arret-schalk-and-kopf-c-autriche-du-24-juin-2010-de-la-cedh-par-t-christakis-106362.htm?RH=1265281047840.

[25] The famous judgment of the ECtHR in the case *Pretty v United Kingdom*, App no 2346/02 [2002] ECHR 423 (29 April 2002) is one of the best examples of this. The Court declined to recognise the existence of a 'right to die' under art 2 or a positive obligation upon states under art 3 to authorise assisted suicide of a terminally ill person. The Court said that 'While [it] must take a dynamic and flexible approach to the interpretation of the Convention, which is a living instrument, any interpretation must also accord with the fundamental objectives of the Convention and its coherence as a system of human rights protection.'

[26] See eg, *Al-Adsani v UK*, App no 35763/97 (ECtHR, 21 November 2001). Although the Court recognised that prohibition of torture was a *jus cogens* rule, it considered that this was not a reason to put aside the principle of sovereign immunity in international law, by virtue of which one state was not subject to the jurisdiction of another. The impossibility of instituting civil proceedings in the UK against a foreign state was thus not a violation of the applicant's right of access to a court under art 6, s 1 ECHR.

[27] See eg, F Tulkens, 'Les techniques interprétatives du juge de l'Union européenne– Discutant' (2011) 2 *Revue générale de droit international public* 533–40, 537 or A Orakhelashvili, 'Restrictive interpretation of Human Rights Treaties in the recent jurisprudence of the ECHR' (2003) 14 *European Journal of International Law* 529–68.

[28] *Dudgeon v UK* (1982) 4 EHRR 149.

[29] *Sunday Times v UK* (1979) 2 EHRR 245.

[30] For a detailed analysis see T Christakis, 'Human Rights', 440–42.

[31] HC Yourow, *The Margin of Appreciation Doctrine in the Dynamics of European Human Rights Jurisprudence* (The Hague, Martinus Nijhoff Publishers, 1996) 195.

doctrine. As the ECHR famously said in the *Handyside v United Kingdom* judgment of 1976:

> By reason of their direct and continuous contact with the vital forces of their countries, State authorities are in principle in a better position than the international judge to give an opinion on the exact content of these requirements as well as on the 'necessity' of a 'restriction' or 'penalty' intended to meet them.[32]

This doctrine has been used dozens of times since then, not only in relation to derogations and restrictions but also, more generally, in order to authorise states to give their own solutions concerning some important societal issues, such as the beginning of life, abortion, reproductive rights, same-sex marriage, assisted suicide and euthanasia and so on. The margin of appreciation doctrine, described by the Court itself as a 'tool to define relations between the domestic authorities and the Court'[33] is, in combination with the requirement of exhaustion of local remedies or the idea that national courts are the 'natural' judges of the ECHR, close to the broader principle of subsidiarity that reflects the idea that states have primary responsibility to protect the Convention rights domestically. These two principles of subsidiarity and margin of appreciation contribute greatly to the idea of a 'vital space' reclaimed by sovereign states. It therefore comes as no surprise that many European states are extremely attached to them, as shown by the Brighton Conference in 2012.

The national margin of appreciation doctrine has been greeted by some scholars as a practical solution which permits the Court to balance the need for regional protection of human rights and the different cultural, social, and historical identities of nation states. Indeed, some scholars have suggested that the transposition of this doctrine could constitute a kind of 'silver bullet' in order to put in place a protection of human rights in other regions of the world, such as the Pacific region.[34] The doctrine, according to these scholars, would allow a regional commission or court of human rights 'to take account of Pacific Island customs and traditions and/or their historic, cultural, and social "peculiarities"', which until now have constituted an obstacle to a regional system of protection.[35]

Nevertheless, it must be emphasised that other scholars have heavily criticised the national margin of appreciation doctrine and the 'moral relativism' it implies, fearing that, 'if applied liberally, this doctrine could undermine seriously the promise of international enforcement of human rights that overcomes national policies.'[36] It is

[32] *Handyside v United Kingdom* (1976) 1 EHRR 737, para 48.

[33] *A and Ors* v *United Kingdom* (2009) 49 EHRR 625.

[34] P Butler, 'Margin of appreciation—a note towards a solution for the Pacific?' (2008) 39 *Victoria University Law Review* 687–708. She argues (at 689) that the European doctrine of margin of appreciation 'would be a useful starting point to employ in a Pacific regional human rights instrument to find the appropriate balance between human rights protection ... and the treasuring of the traditions and customs of each individual Pacific Island society.'

[35] ibid, 708.

[36] E Benvenisti, 'Margin of Appreciation, Consensus, and Universal Standards' (1999) 31 *International Law and Politics* 843–54, 844. See also J Brauch, 'The Margin of Appreciation and the Jurisprudence of the European Court of Human Rights: Threat to the Rule of Law' (2004/2005) 11 *Columbia Journal of European Law* 113–50. Several other scholars (and sometimes even judges in their separate or

interesting to note that, although both the IACHR and IACtHR and the ACHPR have mentioned and applied the doctrine in some of their decisions and opinions, they have been reluctant to fully embrace it. These organs have also been reluctant to rely to 'regional consensus',[37] often putting the emphasis instead on universal standards and customs in the field of human rights.[38]

V. TO WHAT EXTENT DO STATES REACT TO JUDICIAL ACTIVISM?

Strong reactions of states to the methods used by regional HRTB and their 'avant-garde jurisprudence' could be the proof of the fact that judicial activism had crossed a 'red line'. It is nonetheless interesting to notice that states have reacted (at least up to now) in a rather limited way to judicial activism. Of course, states sometimes react strongly to *specific* decisions concerning them, but they only rarely take up arms against the *methods* used by HRTB and the general trends of 'dynamic interpretation' mobilised by them. States could, as a matter of fact, use at least three strategies in order to oppose the methods used by HRTB.

They could first of all withdraw, either alone or *en masse*, from human rights treaties. The weapon of withdrawal of human rights treaties is nonetheless rarely used.[39] Indeed, some states, like Switzerland after the *Belilos* judgment of 1988, or the UK after the *Hirst* judgment of 2005 and on other occasions, have considered the possibility of withdrawing from the European Convention, only to change their mind later. Throughout the history of the European Convention the only precedent for withdrawal has been (at least for the time being) the decision of the military regime in Greece to denounce the European Convention in 1969 in anticipation of the pending condemnation of the regime by the organs of the Council of Europe. In the Americas, however, denunciation has been used more frequently. Trinidad and Tobago withdrew from the IACHR in 1998, Peru tried unsuccessfully to withdraw from the IACtHR's jurisdiction in 1999,[40] and more recently, on 10 September 2012,

dissenting opinions) have criticised the margin of appreciation doctrine. As Letsas sums it up: 'Properly analysed, the doctrine of the margin of appreciation is at best redundant and at worst a danger to the liberal-egalitarian values which underlie human rights.' G Letsas, 'Strasbourg's Interpretive Ethic: Lessons for the International Lawyer' (2010) 21 *European Journal of International Law* 509–41, 531.

[37] According to M Killander, 'Regional consensus has played a negligible role in the jurisprudence of the African Commission and the Inter-American Court'; see M Killander, 'Interpreting Regional Human Rights Treaties' (2010) 7 *SUR International Journal on Human Rights* 145–69, 151. For a critique of the IACtHR and its insufficient regard for the consent of the regional community of states in the evolutive interpretation of human rights treaties, see G Neumann, 'Import, Export and the Regional Consent in the Inter-American Court of Human Rights' (2008) 19 *European Journal of International Law* 101.

[38] L Hennebel, 'The Inter-American Court of Human Rights: The Ambassador of Universalism' (2011) *Quebec Journal of International Law* (Special Edition) 57–97. See also more generally: L Hennebel and H Tigroudja (eds), *Le particularisme interaméricain des droits de l'homme* (Paris, Pedone, 2009).

[39] For a general view see the study by E Bates, 'Avoiding Legal Obligations Created by Human Rights Treaties' (2008) 57 *International Comparitive Law Quarterly* 751–88.

[40] The Inter-American Court declared Peru's 'purported withdrawal' inadmissible in two rulings on jurisdiction—the *Ivcher Bronstein Case*, Competence, Judgment of September 24, 1999, Inter-Am Ct HR (Ser C) No 54 (1999) and the *Constitutional Court Case*, Competence, Judgment of September 24,

the Bolivarian Republic of Venezuela gave notice of its intention to withdraw from the IACHR and subsequently did so.[41]

The second strategy that states, unhappy with the judicial activism of HRTB, could use is to adopt a 'systematic non-compliance' posture with the decisions of these bodies. However, this does not really seem to be the case either concerning the two major regional human rights courts that can adopt binding judgments. A study of the phenomenon concluded that the judgments of the IACtHR 'could be seen as effective regarding the modification of the Member States conduct in some areas.'[42] The effectiveness of the judgments of the ECtHR is also well known, and this despite a few contrary examples concerning especially non-compliance with (binding) interim measures under rule 39 of the Court.[43] It is also important to highlight that the major paradigm of the ECtHR demonstrates that a real 'dialogue' emerges sometimes between the human rights jurisdictions and domestic judges and national authorities.[44]

The third, and probably most important technique that states, unhappy with the judicial activism of HRTB, could use is to employ their treaty-making power and to amend constitutive treaties in order to restrict the powers of the relevant HRTB and to impose a more 'state-friendly' and less dynamic interpretation of human rights. The best example is the recent campaign against the ECtHR orchestrated by the UK and followed by some other states.[45] During the Brighton Conference of April 2012, the UK advanced some suggestions for amendments that would substantially limit the powers of the ECtHR. These suggestions met the resistance of many other state parties and were not adopted.[46]

1999, Inter-Am Ct HR (Ser C) No 55 (1999). According to the Court there is no provision in the Convention that expressly permits the states parties to withdraw their declaration of recognition of the Court's binding jurisdiction. The only avenue a state has to disengage itself from the Court's binding contentious jurisdiction is to denounce the Convention as a whole, which Peru declined to do in 1999; see www.cidh.oas.org/countryrep/Peru2000en/chapter3.htm.

[41] See OAS General Secretary Communicates Venezuela´s Decision to Denounce the American Convention on Human Rights, September 10, 2012, available at www.oas.org/en/media_center/press_release.asp?sCodigo=E-307/12.

[42] DA González-Salzberg, 'The effectiveness of the Inter-American Human Rights System: a study of the American States' compliance with the judgments of the Inter-American Court of Human Rights' (2010) 16 *Revista Colombiana de Derecho Internacional* 115–42.

[43] See for example, *Ben Khemais v Italy*, App no 246/07 [2009] ECHR 859 or *Mannai v Italy*, App no 9961/10 [2012] ECHR 150.

[44] See JP Costa, 'On the legitimacy of the European Court of Human Rights' judgments' (2011) 7 *European Constitutional Law Review* 173–82, 182. See also H Keller and A Stone Sweet (eds), *A Europe of Rights: The impact of the ECHR on national legal systems* (Oxford/New York, Oxford University Press, 2008).

[45] See eg, M Jacot, 'La Cour européenne des droits de l'homme menacée', *Le Monde*, 30 October 2011; M Boëton, 'Droits de l'homme: la Cour de Strasbourg sur la sellette', *La Croix*, 5 March 2012; and M Seno and S Delesalle-Stolper, 'La Cour des droits de l'homme en accusation', *Libération*, 17 April 2012.

[46] For a detailed analysis see N Hervieu, 'Préparatifs et discussions préliminaires à la Conférence de Brighton sur l'avenir de la Cour européenne des droits de l'homme' in *Lettre 'Actualités Droits-Libertés' du CREDOF*, 4 March 2012 and N Hervieu, 'Bilan contrasté pour la périlleuse conférence de Brighton sur l'avenir de la Cour européenne des droits de l'homme' in *Lettre 'Actualités Droits-Libertés' du CREDOF*, 23 April 2012; both articles are available at: http://combatsdroitshomme.blog.lemonde.fr/.

The Brighton Declaration nevertheless reflects the existing tensions between the Court and some states. It puts an emphasis on the margin of appreciation doctrine and the principle of subsidiarity when it states that the 'Conference therefore welcomes the development by the Court in its case law of principles such as subsidiarity and the margin of appreciation, and encourages the Court to give great prominence to and apply consistently these principles in its judgments.'[47] It also concludes that a reference to the principle of subsidiarity and the doctrine of the margin of appreciation, as developed in the Court's case law, should be included in the Preamble to the Convention,[48] despite the scepticism of the former President of the Court, Sir Nicolas Bratza, in this respect. While the ECtHR was able to 'cross the Brighton storm without sinking',[49] the sea is not yet calm. It remains to be seen to what extent some states will strengthen their resistance to the Court and it will also be interesting to observe to what extent the Court will try to appease this confrontational spirit by means of (excessive?) self-restraint.

An extract of a concurring opinion in which the Chair of this ESIL panel, Judge Cançado Trindade, joined in the 2003 Advisory Opinion of the IACtHR probably sums up the problem most effectively. According to him:

> It is not the function of the jurist simply to take note of what the States do, particularly the most powerful ones, which do not hesitate to seek formulas to impose their 'will', including in relation to the treatment to be dispensed to the persons under their jurisdiction. The function of the jurist is to show and to tell what the Law is ... This latter does not emanate from the inscrutable 'will' of the States, but rather from human conscience. General or customary international law emanates not so much from the practice of States (not devoid of ambiguities and contradictions), but rather from the *opinio juris communis* of all the subjects of International Law (the States, the international organizations, and the human beings). Above the will is the conscience.[50]

The message seems clear. *Lotus* is rolling over in its maritime graveyard! Of course, it goes without saying that other judges at the IACtHR or the ECtHR do not necessarily share this extreme *jus naturalis* vision of Judge Cançado Trindade.[51] But it is also clear that in the field of human rights, the old aphorism of Montesquieu according to which judges 'are no more than the mouth that pronounces the words of the law, mere passive beings, incapable of moderating either its force or rigour',[52]

[47] High Level Conference on the Future of the European Court of Human Rights, 18–20 April 2012, Brighton, Brighton Declaration, available at https://wcd.coe.int/ViewDoc.jsp?id=1934031, para 12 a.

[48] Brighton Declaration, ibid, para 12 b.

[49] N Hervieu, 'Bilan contrasté'.

[50] *Juridical condition and rights of the undocumented migrants*, Advisory Opinion OC-18/03, 17 September 2003, IACtHR, IACHR Ser A No 18/03 (2003), Concurring opinion, J Cançado Trindade, para 87.

[51] The recent book by Judge AA Cançado Trindade, *El ejercicio de la función judicial internacional: Memorias de la Corte Interamericana de Derechos Humanos* (Belo Horizonte, Del Rey Editora, 2011) offers a precious insight to his 14 years as a judge at the IACtHR and his vision of the Court and the inter-American system of protection in general.

[52] Montesquieu (Charles de Secondat, Baron de Montesqieu), *The Spirit of Laws*, 1748, (London, G Bell & Sons, 1914, translated by T Nugent, revised by JV Pritchard), Book XI (Ch VI).

simply has no place. The quest of the 'original intent' of states looks like a chimera because, as one scholar observed, it is almost absurd to argue that drafting states had 'intentions' regarding 'the almost infinite number of cases which may arise under the different Convention rights.'[53] Their real intention was to put in place an effective regime of protection of human rights that must necessarily evolve over time in order to adapt to new realities. Human rights judges and HRTB are just tools that states use in order to realise this objective, and judicial activism will be accepted by them in this particular field as long as these HRTBs do not cross the 'red line', thereby losing both their legitimacy and their effectiveness.

[53] G Letsas, 'Strasbourg's Interpretive Ethic', 523.

28

L'activisme judiciaire des organes de contrôle et la souveraineté des Etats: Commentaire sur Christakis

DJAMCHID MOMTAZ*

L'INTITULÉ CHOISI PAR le Professeur Théodore Christakis pour son intervention dans ce forum consacré au « régionalisme et droits humains » interpelle. Il a attiré notre attention sur la réécriture des conventions régionales de droits de l'homme par leurs organes de contrôle se substituant aux Etats parties, pratique qui contribua à brandir le spectre d'un « gouvernement de juges » et heurta les adeptes du volontarisme.[1] Sans pour autant dénier cette réalité, il n'en demeure pas moins qu'il faudrait relativiser ces propos. S'il est vrai que la souveraineté des Etats risque de se trouver menacée dans les cas où cette réécriture est fondée sur l'interprétation des instruments conventionnels au mépris des sources extérieures, une réécriture basée sur une interprétation extensive de la convention dont l'organe de contrôle a la garde, mieux accueillie par les Etats, a contribué au développement progressif du droit international des droits de l'homme au niveau universel.

I. L'INTERPRETATION DES CONVENTIONS DE DROITS DE L'HOMME AU MEPRIS DU DROIT INTERNATIONAL

Le recours des organes de contrôle à des sources extérieures pour interpréter les dispositions de l'instrument dont ils sont les gardiens est désormais une démarche banale. Par exemple, en vue de s'assurer que la mort n'a pas été infligée en violation des dispositions des instruments de droits de l'homme, les organes de contrôle ont été amenés à recourir au droit international humanitaire. Pour parvenir à cette conclusion que la situation au cours de laquelle il a été porté atteinte à la vie peut être qualifiée de conflit armé non international, la Cour interaméricaine s'est référée à la définition donnée par le protocole II du 12 juin 1977 additionnel aux Conventions

* Professeur à l'Université de Téhéran. Membre de l'Institut de droit international.

[1] H Tigroudja, « La Cour interaméricaine des droits de l'homme au service de l'humanisation du droit international public : propos autour des récents arrêts et avis » (2006) *Association Française de Droit de l'Informatique* 623.

de Genève avant de conclure qu'elle n'était pas arbitraire.[2] De même, la Cour européenne des droits de l'homme, longtemps réticente à se référer au droit international humanitaire comme source extérieure d'interprétation, y a consenti à son tour. Pour s'assurer que les personnes ayant perdu la vie au cours d'un conflit armé étaient des civils n'ayant pas participé de manière active aux hostilités et qu'elles jouissaient en conséquence de l'immunité contre l'attaque, la Cour s'est référée au Règlement de La Haye du 18 octobre 1907.[3] C'est uniquement au regard du droit applicable dans les conflits armés et non à la lumière des instruments de droits de l'homme pertinents que les organes de contrôle ont considéré que la privation de la vie dans le cas précis était arbitraire.

Le recours aux sources extérieures d'interprétation constitue une garantie pour le respect du principe de consensualisme, surtout quand l'instrument auquel les organes de contrôle se réfèrent est universellement ratifié ou que ses dispositions reflètent le droit international coutumier. La question peut néanmoins se poser lorsque l'organe de contrôle se réfère à un texte qui ne répond pas à ces qualificatifs. La Cour européenne s'est fondée sur le projet d'articles de la Commission du droit international pour préciser la portée du principe *restitutio in integrum*,[4] projet qui, il est vrai, a été favorablement accueilli par l'Assemblée Générale des Nations Unies et auquel la Cour internationale de justice a fait référence à de nombreuses reprises.

L'atteinte au consensualisme doit être considérée comme étant flagrante quand l'organe de contrôle applique une disposition de l'instrument de droits de l'homme en ignorant délibérément les normes bien établies de la *lex specialis* en la matière. Ainsi, les atteintes à la liberté d'expression et d'information dans la mer territoriale doivent s'apprécier à la lumière des dispositions pertinentes du droit de la mer. Il est regrettable que la Cour européenne des droits de l'homme ait condamné le Portugal pour avoir empêché le déroulement d'une campagne contre la prévention des maladies sexuellement transmissibles, le planning familial et la dépénalisation de l'interruption de grossesse, organisée à bord de navires étrangers dans sa mer territoriale. Cette décision a été prise au mépris de la règle bien établie en droit de la mer selon laquelle toute activité sans rapport avec le passage en mer territoriale perd son caractère inoffensif et peut être interrompue par l'Etat côtier.[5] De même, peut-on considérer qu'un Etat successeur est automatiquement lié par un instrument de droits de l'homme ratifié par l'Etat prédécesseur, ainsi que la Cour européenne l'a prétendu au mépris du principe du consensualisme dans les relations conventionnelles ?[6] Il est vrai que l'option de la table rase en matière de succession d'Etat aux traités, consacrée par la Convention du 23 septembre 1978, ne fait plus l'unanimité au sein de la doctrine pour ce qui est des instruments relatifs aux droits de l'homme, absence d'unanimité qui se reflète au sein des organes de contrôle des instruments universels des droits de l'homme.[7]

[2] Corte IDH, *Caso de las Masacres de Ituango c Colombia*. Arrêt du 1 juillet 2006, Serie C No 14.

[3] Arrêt du 15 juillet 2010: *Kononov c Lettonie* [GC], no 36376/04, ECHR 2010.

[4] Arrêt du 30 juin 2009: *Verein gegen Tierfabriken Schweiz (VgT) (no 2)* [GC], no 32772/02, ECHR 2009.

[5] Arrêt du 3 février 2009: *Women on Waves et autres c Portugal*, no 31276/05, ECHR 2009.

[6] Arrêt du 28 avril 2009: *Bijelić c Monténégro et Serbie*, no 11890/05, ECHR 2010.

[7] Réunion des présidents des organes de contrôle des conventions de droits de l'homme 29–23 septembre 1994. Doc NU A/49/537.

II. L'INTERPRETATION EXTENSIVE DES DISPOSITIONS DES CONVENTIONS DE DROITS DE L'HOMME

Contrairement à l'interprétation des instruments de droits de l'homme au mépris des règles bien établies du droit international et au risque d'entraîner une fragmentation de ce droit, l'interprétation extensive des dispositions de ces instruments a été mieux perçue par les Etats.

Les organes de contrôle des instruments régionaux ne sont pas les seuls à recourir à cette pratique. Le Conseil des droits de l'homme a été le premier, par ce moyen, à extraire de l'obligation de respecter les obligations conventionnelles celle de diligenter une enquête sur leurs violations.[8] La Cour interaméricaine parvient à une conclusion identique.[9] En effet, elle conclut, à l'instar du Comité des droits de l'homme,[10] qu'une loi d'amnistie générale et inconditionnelle, en excluant toute enquête sur les allégations de violations des droits de l'homme, serait incompatible avec les obligations contractées. Franchissant un pas supplémentaire, la Cour interaméricaine déclare l'amnistie nulle et non avenue et dépourvue de tout effet juridique, y compris sur le territoire de l'Etat qui l'a octroyée.[11]

La jurisprudence audacieuse de la Cour interaméricaine en la matière ne doit néanmoins pas être considérée comme une première. Le Tribunal pénal international pour l'ex Yougoslavie avait déjà abordé la question de la validité et de la non reconnaissance des amnisties et était parvenu à cette conclusion que celles couvrant les crimes de torture « n'auront pas la reconnaissance internationale ».[12] Par la suite, le Tribunal spécial pour la Sierra Leone refusera de donner effet à l'amnistie offerte par cet Etat.[13] Sur le plan interne, il est désormais acquis que l'amnistie octroyée par un Etat ne saurait priver un autre Etat du droit qu'il détient en vertu d'une clause de compétence universelle.[14] Ainsi, l'interprétation évolutive des organes de contrôle n'a fait qu'accentuer un mouvement déjà amorcé et auquel les Etats ont souscrit.

Il en va de même pour ce qui est de l'interprétation, considérée en son temps comme révolutionnaire, du droit à un procès équitable par la Cour européenne. D'après la Cour, ce droit implique un droit d'accès individuel aux tribunaux,[15] toute

[8] Communication du Comité des droits de l'homme émise le 21 juillet 1983. Le Comité relève l'obligation de l'Uruguay d'enquêter sur toute allégation de disparition et de déférer en justice le responsable de tels faits.

[9] Corte IDH, *Velásquez Rodríguez c Honduras*. Fond. Arrêt du 29 juillet 1988. Serie C No 4.

[10] Observation générale n° 20 émise le 10 mars 1992. Le Comité dénonce l'amnistie pour les actes de torture comme étant « généralement incompatible avec le devoir qu'ont les Etats d'enquêter sur de tels actes ».

[11] Corte IDH, *Caso Barrios Altos c Perú*. Fond. Arrêt du 14 mars 2001. Serie C No 75. Ce jugement a été interprété le 3 septembre 2001 par la Cour qui précise que le jugement « has generic effects » (Serie C No 83).

[12] Arrêt du 10 décembre 1998: *Procureur c Anto Furundziya*. Affaire No IT-95-17/1-T.

[13] Décision du 31 mai 2004: *Prosecutor c Charles Taylor*, Decision on Immunity from jurisdiction. Affaire No SCSL-2003-01-I.

[14] Décision du 23 octobre 2002 de la Chambre criminelle de la Cour de cassation. D'après la Cour, « au regard du principe de l'application de la loi nationale, seule peut être prise en considération l'amnistie décidée par les autorités françaises, sauf à priver de toute portée le principe de la compétence universelle ». Dans le même sens, *cf* le jugement rendu le 5 novembre 1998 par la Sala de la Penal de la Audicenca Nacional.

[15] Arrêt du 21 février 1975: *Golder c Royaume-Uni*, série A n° 18.

interprétation contraire ne faisant qu'accroître les risques d'arbitraire. La Cour interaméricaine va quant à elle jusqu'à qualifier le droit au juge de norme de *jus cogens.*[16] Si une telle qualification ne fait toujours pas l'unanimité, le droit au juge n'en a pas moins été considéré comme une « valeur commune de l'ordre public européen »[17] et certaines juridictions internes s'y sont référées pour refuser d'accorder l'immunité aux organisations internationales qui le méconnaissaient.[18]

III. CONCLUSIONS

Le rôle des organes de contrôle des instruments de droits de l'homme en tant que suppléants législatifs ne saurait être contesté. La Cour internationale de justice s'est récemment référée à la « jurisprudence interprétative » du Comité des droits de l'homme mais aussi à celle des Cours européenne et interaméricaine des droits de l'homme concernant les instruments conventionnels dont ces organes ont la garde. D'après elle, elle n'est nullement tenue, dans l'exercice de ses fonctions judiciaires, de se conformer à cette jurisprudence[19] mais « la nécessaire clarté », « l'indispensable cohérence du droit international » ainsi que « la sécurité juridique qui est un droit pour les personnes privées » l'amènent à en tenir compte.[20]

La contribution des organes régionaux de contrôle au développement progressif du droit international des droits de l'homme résulte aussi bien de l'homogénéité de leurs membres que de leur professionnalisme, toutes qualités qui les amènent à être plus à l'écoute de l'opinion publique des pays de la région, au risque de perdre toute crédibilité. A titre d'exemple, les réactions consécutives à la chute des dictatures en Amérique latine ont incontestablement joué un rôle primordial dans l'émergence de cette jurisprudence.

[16] Corte IDH, *Caso Goiburú y otros c Paraguay*. Fondo, Reparaciones y Costas. Arrêt du 22 septembre 2006. Serie C No 153, § 131. Il faut y voir l'influence du juge A Cançado-Trindade, ancien président de la Cour interaméricaine des droits de l'homme et actuellement juge à la Cour internationale de justice, qui, dans son opinion dissidente jointe à l'arrêt du 3 février 2012 de cette Cour dans l'affaire des immunités juridictionnelles de l'Etat précise : « Where there is no right of access to justice, there is no legal system at all. Observance of the right of access to justice is imperative ... We are in the domain of jus cogens ». *Immunités juridictionnelles de l'État (Allemagne c Italie; Grèce (intervenant))*, CIJ Rec (1012), § 219 de l'opinion.

[17] L Milano, « Les immunités issues du droit international dans la jurisprudence européenne » (2008) 76 *Revue trimestrielle des droits de l'homme* 1059, 1081.

[18] Arrêt du 25 janvier 2005 de la Chambre sociale de la Cour de cassation : *Banque africaine de développement c Degboe* ; et arrêt du 4 mars 2003 de la Cour de travail de Bruxelles dans l'affaire *Luchtmaja*. Ces deux décisions sont fondées sur l'arrêt du 18 février 1999 de la Cour européenne *Beer et Regan c Allemagne* qui privilégie le respect des droits fondamentaux, dont l'accès au juge, au détriment d'une conception extensive de l'immunité des organisations internationales (*Beer et Regan c Allemagne* [GC], no 28934/95).

[19] *Ahmadou Sadio Diallo (République de Guinée c République démocratique du Congo)*, CIJ Rec (2010) 639, 664, § 68.

[20] ibid, 665, § 66.

29

Quelques réflexions sur les systèmes régionaux dans le cadre de l'universalité des droits de l'homme

ANTONIO A CANÇADO TRINDADE*

I

CE FORUM 8 de la 5e Conférence générale de la Société européenne de droit international (2012), organisée à Valence, est consacré à un thème de grande actualité, comme en témoigne le nombre important de participants. En entamant la dernière partie de ce débat qui fera date, je tiens tout d'abord à remercier le professeur Theodore Christakis et le professeur Djamchid Momtaz pour leurs exposés et éminentes contributions. C'est un plaisir pour moi que de participer à ce forum à leurs côtés. Mon intention première n'était pas d'exprimer mon opinion personnelle sur certains points soulevés par les panélistes, mais comme quelques questions m'ont été aimablement posées, compte tenu de l'expérience que j'ai accumulée dans la magistrature internationale, tant au niveau régional qu'universel (à la Cour interaméricaine des droits de l'homme et à la Cour internationale de Justice), je les aborderai brièvement.

La première question, posée par mon collègue d'Amérique latine (Bogotá), a trait à l'activisme judiciaire face à la multiplicité des juridictions internationales (dans des domaines distincts du droit international), au niveau régional et universel. Pour ma part, je ne vois aucun risque de chevauchement de compétences. A cet égard, nous devons nous garder d'utiliser abusivement certains néologismes délétères, tels que les expressions « prolifération des juridictions internationales » ou « fragmentation du droit international ». Pareils néologismes dénigrants reposent en effet sur l'hypothèse erronée d'une délimitation de compétences, tout en passant à côté de l'essentiel : le développement de l'autorité judiciaire sur le plan international et l'accès à la justice internationale pour un nombre bien plus important de justiciables.

* Ancien président de la Cour interaméricaine des droits de l'homme ; juge à la Cour internationale de Justice ; professeur émérite de droit international à l'Université de Brasilia, Brésil ; professeur honoraire à l'Université d'Utrecht ; membre honoraire de l'Université de Cambridge (Sidney Sussex College) ; membre du *curatorium* de l'Académie de droit international de La Haye, et de l'Institut de droit international ; président de la Société latino-américaine de droit international.

À mon avis, les travaux des juridictions internationales doivent aujourd'hui être appréciés du point de vue des justiciables eux-mêmes,[1] et de la mission commune de *réalisation* de la justice qui est celle desdites juridictions. Leur multiplicité—signe de notre temps—se révèle rassurante et met en évidence les progrès considérables qui ont déjà été accomplis dans la réalisation de l'idéal de justice internationale. Chacune de ces juridictions voit sa compétence fondée sur une convention, un accord ou un instrument international distinct, et dispose de son propre droit applicable. Plutôt que de hiérarchie, il s'agit ici de complémentarité, sous la forme d'un réseau polycentrique de juridictions, affirmant et réaffirmant la capacité du droit international de régler les différends internationaux les plus divers, tant sur le plan interétatique qu'intraétatique.[2] C'est à chaque juridiction qu'il appartient—de concert avec les autres—d'apporter sa contribution effective à l'évolution constante du droit international, dans la quête de la réalisation de la justice internationale.

II

A mon sens, le meilleur moyen d'exercer durablement et harmonieusement cette mission réside dans un dialogue soutenu et respectueux entre juridictions internationales. A cet égard, je garde un excellent souvenir de la première réunion entre pareilles institutions qui s'est tenue à Luxembourg, les 3 et 4 décembre 2002, à l'occasion du cinquantième anniversaire de la Cour de justice des Communautés européennes (la Cour de l'Union européenne), ainsi que de la deuxième réunion de ce type qui s'est tenue à Managua, les 4 et 5 octobre 2007, à l'occasion du centenaire de la création de l'ancienne Cour centraméricaine de Justice (première juridiction internationale permanente des temps modernes).[3] Le dialogue doit se poursuivre, sans solution de continuité.

Le présent forum est tout à fait approprié pour se pencher sur cette question, puisqu'il rassemble, dans un même lieu, des participants issus des trois systèmes régionaux de protection des droits de l'homme, à savoir les systèmes européen, interaméricain et africain. En tant que président de la Société latino-américaine pour le droit international, je me dois d'exprimer ma gratitude aux organisateurs de cette Conférence de Valence—MM les professeurs Mariano J Aznar et Jorge Cardona Llorens—pour leur esprit d'ouverture, lequel permet de nourrir le dialogue entre juristes de différents continents, comme l'illustre la composition même de cette table

[1] AA Cançado Trindade, *Evolution du Droit international au droit des gens—L'accès des particuliers à la justice internationale : le regard d'un juge* (Paris, Pédone, 2008) 1–187 ; AA Cançado Trindade, *The access of Individuals to International Justice* (Oxford, Oxford University Press, 2011) 1–236 ; AA Cançado Trindade, *El Derecho de Acceso a la Justicia en Su Amplia Dimensión* (Santiago de Chile, CECOH/Librotecnia, 2008) 61–407 ; AA Cançado Trindade, *Le Droit international pour la personne humaine* (Paris, Pédone, 2012) 45–368.

[2] AA Cançado Trindade, « International Law for Humankind: Towards a New *Jus Gentium*—General Course on Public International Law—Part II » (2005) 317 *Recueil des Cours de l'Académie de Droit International de La Haye* 243–45 ; AA Cançado Trindade, « The Merits of Coordination of International Courts on Human Rights » (2004) 2 *Journal of International Criminal Justice* 309–12.

[3] Pour un compte rendu de ces deux réunions, *cf* AA Cançado Trindade, *Direito das Organizações Internacionais* (5ᵉ éd, Belo Horizonte/Brazil, édit Del Rey, 2012) 575–607 (ch XXVI).

ronde : le professeur D Momtaz, le professeur Th Christakis et moi-même venons de trois continents différents, mais nous nous comprenons fort bien, car depuis des années, nous nous intéressons à la même discipline, celle du droit des nations (le droit des gens).

III

La deuxième question m'a été posée par mon collègue scandinave (Oslo), et a trait à ce qu'il est désormais convenu d'appeler l'activisme judiciaire. Je suis d'accord pour dire que cette attitude s'est progressivement imposée dans le droit international contemporain. Mais j'irai plus loin : selon moi, le pire est l'inactivisme judiciaire. Il y a ceux qui craignent « de créer un précédent » ou « d'innover ». Si cette crainte était fondée, la justice pourrait être « administrée » par des machines ou des ordinateurs, de manière totalement mécanique. L'inactivisme judiciaire, en revanche, constitue un réel danger. Il y a quelques dizaines d'années, Gaston Morin, au sujet du droit privé,[4] a ainsi souligné la nécessité d'un réexamen constant des notions juridiques, faisant observer avec lucidité que les faits précédaient habituellement les normes et représentaient un défi permanent pour les personnes chargées de l'application desdites normes, celui de répondre à l'évolution des besoins en rendant la justice.

Dans cette mission ardue qui est la leur, les juges sont guidés par leurs propres raisonnements et convictions ainsi que par leur expérience, qui dépassent assurément le cadre du seul droit positif. Il y a plus d'un demi-siècle, Piero Calamandrei a rappelé que le terme *sententia* avait la même racine étymologique que le terme « sentiment », soulignant que « la sentence n'[était] l'œuvre ni de l'intelligence ni de la science, ce qui consisterait à connaître et à appliquer un élément préexistant, mais qu'il s'agissait d'une création empirique ... Même lorsque le juge recherche la solution d'un cas concret en se fondant sur certaines hypothèses générales, ... c'est en lui-même, dans sa conscience, qu'il la trouve ».[5] Il est des juges qui estiment que leur fonction se réduit à la simple ou stricte application du droit positif ; il en est d'autres (dont je fais partie) qui, par un effort d'interprétation—voire de recherche—du droit applicable, ouvrent un espace à la pensée créative. Selon moi, l'innovation et le développement progressif du droit sont inéluctables, à condition que nous soyons à la hauteur des principaux défis de notre époque.

IV

La troisième question m'a été posée par mon collègue, M le professeur Luigi Condorelli. Nous sommes d'accord pour considérer que le droit international humanitaire est, par essence, universel. De surcroît, certaines conventions des Nations Unies en matière de droits de l'homme, telles que la convention de 1989 relative aux droits de l'enfant, sont, elles aussi, devenues quasiment universelles. Dans le domaine du

[4] G Morin, *La révolte du Droit contre le Code—La révision nécessaire des concepts juridiques* (Paris, Libr Rec Sirey, 1945) 2, 6–7 et 109–15.

[5] P Calamandrei, *Proceso y Democracia* (Buenos Aires, Ed Jur Europa-América, 1960) 67.

droit international des droits de l'homme, des systèmes régionaux ont été créés (pour des raisons historiques que l'implacable contrainte de temps ne nous permet hélas pas d'examiner ici) parallèlement aux mécanismes des Nations Unies. Les juridictions régionales et les organes de contrôle ont conçu une interprétation téléologique commune des instruments de protection respectifs, conformément aux postulats de la règle générale d'interprétation des traités énoncée à l'article 31 des deux Conventions de Vienne sur le droit des traités (de 1969 et 1986).

Cette construction jurisprudentielle prétorienne des droits inhérents à la personne humaine est effectivement remarquable et s'est effectuée au sein des trois systèmes régionaux de protection dotés de juridictions internationales des droits de l'homme dans le cadre conceptuel de l'universalité de ces droits. Dans le système africain, la Commission africaine des droits de l'homme et des peuples avait déjà dûment pris en considération les dispositions pertinentes des traités relatifs aux droits de l'homme (tels que la Charte africaine des droits de l'homme et des peuples) *tout autant que* du droit international humanitaire, avant même que la Cour africaine des droits de l'homme et des peuples ait commencé à fonctionner (en 2006). Dans le système interaméricain, la Cour interaméricaine des droits de l'homme a développé une jurisprudence novatrice en matière de réparations et en ce qui concerne le droit fondamental à la vie[6] (comme comprenant les conditions de vie). Enfin, dans le système européen, la Cour européenne des droits de l'homme a développé une vaste et impressionnante jurisprudence, par exemple quant au droit à la liberté et à la sécurité de la personne et quant au droit à un procès équitable.

Cette construction jurisprudentielle prétorienne est tout à fait claire, même en cas de doute au sujet de la norme applicable, en ce qu'elle prévoit—en vertu et en application du principe général *pro persona humana*—que la norme qui trouve à s'appliquer est celle qui protège le mieux la personne humaine. Les Cours européenne et interaméricaine, qui, depuis 1999, entretiennent un dialogue fructueux sur une base permanente, se sont réunies pour la première fois avec la Cour africaine des droits de l'homme et des peuples récemment créée. Cette première réunion des trois cours internationales des droits de l'homme existant à ce jour, à laquelle j'ai participé, a eu lieu à Strasbourg, les 8 et 9 décembre 2008. Elle a été l'occasion d'instaurer un dialogue instructif[7] sur certaines questions d'intérêt commun telles que l'accès à la justice, les mesures conservatoires ou les différentes formes de réparation.

V

Enfin, et ce n'est pas le moins important, la multiplicité des traités et instruments internationaux et de protection des droits de la personne humaine est assortie d'un

[6] *cf* mon récent ouvrage à ce sujet : AA Cançado Trindade, *El Ejercicio de la Función Judicial Internacional—Memorias de la Corte Interamericana de Derechos Humanos* (Belo Horizonte/Brazil, Édit Del Rey, 2011) 1–340.

[7] *cf* AA Cançado Trindade, « Quelques réflexions à l'occasion de la première réunion des trois Cours régionales des droits de l'homme » (2009) 9 *Revista do Instituto Brasileiro de Direitos Humanos* 229; Ph Weckel, « La justice internationale et le soixantième anniversaire de la Déclaration Universelle des Droits de l'Homme » (2009) 113 *Revue Générale de Droit International Public* 5.

objectif commun fondamental et déterminant : la protection des droits inhérents à la personne humaine. Ces traités et autres instruments, au champ d'application universel ou régional, sont inspirés d'une source commune, à savoir la Déclaration universelle des droits de l'homme de 1948, véritable foyer d'irradiation des efforts visant la réalisation de l'idéal de l'universalité des droits de l'homme. Aussi n'est-il guère surprenant de retrouver des références à la Déclaration universelle dans les préambules de ces traités et instruments internationaux.

Dans le processus de généralisation de la protection des droits de l'homme, l'unité conceptuelle qui est la leur, en ce qu'ils sont tous inhérents à la personne humaine, a transcendé les différences dans la formulation desdits droits, tels que reconnus par les différents instruments. L'universalité ne signifie pas l'uniformité totale, mais elle constitue le cadre conceptuel du corpus juris en matière de protection des droits de l'homme, tant au niveau mondial que régional. Les particularités régionales viennent en réalité enrichir cette universalité, chaque système régional vivant son propre moment historique[8] et fonctionnant au sein de son propre espace géographique. Il n'en demeure pas moins que tous ces systèmes régionaux—tous—sont inspirés par l'universalité des droits de l'homme.

Les traités et instruments internationaux de protection des droits de l'homme ont été élaborés en *réponse* à toutes les formes de violation de ces droits, et ils comportent tous une dimension préventive. Leur application, au niveau universel ou régional, obéit à une herméneutique commune, qui met en exergue leur objectif commun, les valeurs supérieures qui les sous–tendent, le caractère objectif des obligations qu'ils énoncent ainsi que la nécessité avérée de réaliser leur objet et leur but. Puisse ce forum 8 de la 5e conférence générale de la Société européenne de droit international (2012) avoir contribué à clarifier ces questions.

[8] Prenons, par exemple, le système interaméricain des droits de l'homme : cinq étapes historiques peuvent être distinguées. La première étape, celle des antécédents du système, a été marquée par une panoplie d'instruments au contenu et aux effets juridiques variables (conventions et résolutions axées sur des situations ou des catégories de droits données). La deuxième étape, celle de la genèse du système interaméricain, s'est caractérisée par le rôle déterminant joué par la seule Commission interaméricaine des droits de l'homme et par le développement progressif de ses facultés. La troisième étape, celle de l'institutionnalisation conventionnelle du système, a débuté au moment de l'entrée en vigueur, en juillet 1978, de la Convention américaine relative aux droits de l'homme. La quatrième étape a été marquée par l'évolution de la jurisprudence de la Cour interaméricaine des droits de l'homme ainsi que par l'adoption des protocoles additionnels à la convention américaine et des conventions interaméricaines sectorielles. La cinquième étape, enfin, a été marquée par les efforts visant à renforcer le mécanisme de protection établi par la Convention américaine.

Part IX

Universal and Regional Responses to the Environment and Our Common Heritage

30

L'articulation des approches universelle et régionale en matière de protection du climat

GÉRAUD DE LASSUS SAINT-GENIÈS*

À PROBLÈME GLOBAL, réponse globale. En application de ce « mantra »[1] de la gouvernance internationale de l'environnement, le défi posé par les changements climatiques a conduit les États à mettre en place une coopération universelle au sein du cadre onusien, grâce à l'adoption de la Convention-cadre des Nations Unies sur les changements climatiques en 1992 (CCNUCC) et du Protocole de Kyoto en 1997 (PK).[2] Il est vrai que plusieurs arguments plaident en faveur du recours à une approche universelle en ce qui concerne la protection du climat.[3] Le plus pertinent d'entre eux est certainement le fait que l'atmosphère, qui détermine la qualité du climat, constitue un bien public mondial auquel tous les États ont un libre accès. Car le bénéfice environnemental issu du comportement vertueux d'un groupe d'États peut, en théorie du moins, être annihilé par l'action d'un seul autre État réfractaire à la coopération.

Un bref examen du droit international suffit pourtant à constater que le cadre onusien ne constitue pas l'unique *forum* au sein duquel se déroulent les discussions intergouvernementales relatives à la protection du climat et que l'Organisation des Nations Unies (ONU) ne dispose pas du monopole de la production normative en ce domaine. La gouvernance du climat se présente en effet sous la forme

* Docteur en droit, chargé de cours et Directeur adjoint de la Chaire de recherche et d'innovation Goldcorp en droit des ressources naturelles et de l'énergie, Faculté de droit de l'Université Laval.

[1] P Le Prestre, « Géopolitique régionale du climat et coopération internationale » (2009) 1 *Les Cahiers de l'Institut EDS* 4, 10.

[2] À l'alinéa 1 et 6 du préambule de la CCCNUCC, les États reconnaissent que « les changements du climat de la planète et leurs effets néfastes sont un sujet de préoccupation pour l'humanité toute entière » et, qu'en conséquence, « le caractère planétaire des changements climatiques requiert de tous les pays qu'ils coopèrent le plus possible ».

[3] L Boisson de Chazournes, « Le droit et l'universalité de la lutte contre les changements climatiques » dans *Cahiers Droit, Sciences & Technologies—Droit et Climat* (Paris, CNRS Éditions, 2009) 29.

d'une architecture qualifiée de « fragmentée »,[4] « transcalaire »,[5] « multi-niveau »,[6] au sein de laquelle coexistent, au côté de la coopération universelle, des initiatives de coopération plurilatérales (telles que le G8, le G20 ou le *Carbon Sequestration leadership Forum*), mais aussi régionales. En témoignent, pour ne mentionner que quelques exemples, l'action de l'Union européenne (UE) en matière de lutte contre les changements climatiques, dont les origines remontent à 1989,[7] la création en 2004 du *Iberoamerican network between climate change offices* (RIOCC) ainsi que le lancement en 2005 du Partenariat Asie-Pacifique pour le développement propre et le climat (PAP). Dans ce contexte de coexistence des approches universelle et régionale de protection du climat, la présente étude vise donc à analyser la façon dont s'articulent ces deux échelons de coopération.

La dispersion des lieux de production normative peut être génératrice d'interactions entre les différentes strates de l'environnement juridique mondial.[8] Tel est généralement le cas pour ce qui est des rapports qu'entretiennent les approches universelle et régionale en matière de protection du climat. L'observation de ces interactions révèle alors l'existence d'un modèle d'articulation dans lequel ces deux approches sont placées dans un rapport hiérarchique, chacune d'entre elles pouvant exercer, à tour de rôle, une influence sur l'autre niveau. Par l'effet de cette « hiérarchie enchevêtrée »,[9] ce modèle d'articulation garantit une certaine coordination et harmonie entre ces espaces distincts mais qui agissent dans un domaine de coopération identique (I). Or, depuis quelques années, un nouveau modèle d'articulation semble être apparu, sans pour autant avoir entraîné la disparition du précédent. Désormais, l'approche régionale peut également être autonome, déconnectée, affranchie, du cadre onusien et faire valoir des stratégies alternatives pour lutter contre les changements climatiques. En ce sens, cette nouvelle forme d'articulation relève davantage d'une logique horizontale, décentralisée, voire désordonnée, et laisse apparaître certaines tensions entre l'échelon universel et régional (II).

[4] F Biermann et al, « Fragmentation of Global Governance Architecture. The Case of Climate Policy » (décembre 2007) Global Governance Working Paper No 34 à la p 5, www.glogov.org/images/doc/WP34.pdf.

[5] D Compagnon, « Les défis politiques du changement climatique : de l'approche des régimes internationaux à la gouvernance transcalaire globale » dans C Cournil et C Colard-Fabregoule (éds), *Changements climatiques et défis du droit* (Bruxelles, Bruylant, 2010) 40.

[6] Subsidiary Body for Implementation, « Compilation and synthesis of fifth national communication. Executive summary » (20 mai 2011) à la p 9, FCCC/SBI/2011/INF.1. Le rapport note que « Parties are making broad use of multilevel governance—across multiple levels of government (e.g. local to regional) and non-governmental actors—when it comes to climate change issues ».

[7] Résolution du Conseil du 21 juin 1989 concernant l'effet de serre et la Communauté [1989] JO C 183/03.

[8] J-S Bergé, « Les interactions du droit international et européen, approche du phénomène en trois étapes dans le contexte européen » (2009) 3 *Journal du droit international* chron 4, para 1.

[9] Une « hiérarchie enchevêtrée » désigne « une interaction entre des niveaux dans laquelle le niveau supérieur redescend vers le niveau inférieur et l'influence tout en étant lui-même déterminé par le niveau inférieur ». D Hofstadter, *Gödel, Escher, Bach. Les brins d'une guirlande éternelle* (Paris, InterÉditions, 1985) 799.

I. LA PERSISTANCE DU MODÈLE VERTICAL

C'est historiquement dans le cadre de la relation entre l'espace onusien et communautaire que le modèle d'articulation verticale a été forgé puisque l'action de la Communauté européenne (CE) a constitué la première expérience régionale en matière de protection du climat. Le champ d'application de ce modèle s'est toutefois progressivement élargi pour couvrir d'autres initiatives régionales non communautaires. Ce modèle se caractérise principalement par deux éléments. L'approche régionale y apparaît tout d'abord comme un « relais »[10] de l'approche universelle (A), mais aussi, comme un espace de négociation du contenu de cette approche universelle (B).[11]

A. L'Approche Régionale comme Relais de l'Approche Universelle

i. Cas Communautaire

Conformément à la règle *pacta sunt servanda*, la ratification par la CE de la CCNUCC et du PK impliquait que cette organisation se conforme aux dispositions inscrites dans ces instruments. Tributaire de l'action de ses États membres pour assurer cette conformité, l'UE a donc élaboré un cadre juridique en matière de protection du climat destiné à faciliter la mise en œuvre de la CCNUCC et du PK sur son territoire. Dans cette optique, le droit communautaire a procédé à une « incorporation »[12] de certaines dispositions édictées au sein du cadre onusien. Ainsi, la décision 93/389/CEE[13] « transpose en droit Communautaire ... un certain nombre d'obligations générales découlant de la Convention-cadre des Nations unies sur les changements climatiques, afin de permettre à la Communauté de s'acquitter de ses obligations en tant que Partie contractante à celle-ci ».[14] En l'espèce, les obligations transposées sont celles énoncées aux Articles 4.1 a) et 4.2 a) et b) de la CCNUCC qui peuvent être considérées comme les obligations centrales de cet instrument dans la mesure où celles-ci portent sur les engagements en matière d'évaluation et d'atténuation

[10] Le Prestre, « Géopolitique régionale du climat et coopération internationale » (n 1) 2.

[11] Encore faut-il préciser que dans le cadre de l'articulation entre l'espace onusien et communautaire, ce modèle prend une forme particulière dans la mesure où, en tant qu'organisation d'intégration économique régionale, la CE est partie à la CCNUCC et au PK, en vertu des Articles 22 de la Convention et 24 du Protocole. L'existence de ce lien juridique contraint alors la CE à exécuter les normes universelles et l'autorise à participer comme membre à part entière aux négociations onusiennes. Voir : Décision 94/69/CE du Conseil du 15 décembre 1993 concernant la conclusion de la Convention-cadre des Nations unies sur les changements climatiques [1994] JO L 33/11. Également : Décision 2002/358/CE du Conseil du 25 avril 2002 relative à l'approbation au nom de la Communauté européenne du Protocole de Kyoto à la convention-cadre des Nations unies sur les changements climatiques et l'exécution conjointe des engagements qui en découlent [2002] JO L 130/1.

[12] L Gradoni, « Systèmes juridiques internationaux : une esquisse » dans H Ruiz Fabri et L Gradoni (éds), *La circulation des concepts juridiques : le droit international de l'environnement entre mondialisation et fragmentation* (Paris, Société de législation comparée, 2009) 46.

[13] Décision 93/389/CEE du Conseil du 24 juin 1993 relative à un mécanisme de surveillance des émissions de CO2 et des autres gaz à effet de serre dans la Communauté [1993] JO L 167/31.

[14] M Pallemaerts, « Le cadre international et européen des politiques de lutte contre les changements climatiques » (2004) 33–34 *Courrier hebdomadaire du CRISP* 1, 44.

des émissions de GES. En outre, le droit communautaire a également opéré un renvoi vers les règles onusiennes en demandant aux États membres de s'y conformer pour accomplir des obligations proprement communautaires. Cette pratique ressort notamment de la décision 2005/166/CE en vertu de laquelle les États sont tenus de respecter certaines lignes directrices adoptées par la Conférence des États Parties à la CCNUCC lorsqu'ils exécutent l'obligation communautaire qui consiste à transmettre à la Commission les informations permettant de démontrer qu'ils s'acquittent de leurs engagements inscrits dans le PK.[15] Ces exemples témoignent donc de « la très forte *imbrication* des sources internationales et européennes »,[16] puisque le droit communautaire facilite ici la mise en œuvre du droit universel au sein de l'UE, mais aussi de l'existence d'un phénomène de « *mimétisme* »[17] entre les règles universelles et régionales.

Par ailleurs, en tant que partie au PK, la CE fait également usage de certains des mécanismes qui sont inscrits dans cet accord. Conformément à l'Article 4, qui permet aux parties de remplir conjointement leur cible de réduction dans le cadre d'une organisation régionale d'intégration économique, la CE et ses membres ont pu inscrire un objectif unique de réduction dans le PK et répartir ensuite celui-ci de manière différenciée entre eux.[18] Enfin, il convient de mentionner la modification du système communautaire d'échange de quotas d'émission de gaz à effet de serre (SCEQE) apportée par la Directive 2004/101/CE. Cette modification était destinée à permettre la mise sur le marché communautaire des crédits d'émission obtenus par les réductions effectuées grâce aux mécanismes de projet du PK (mécanisme pour un développement propre et mise en œuvre conjointe).[19] Grâce à cette « linking directive »,[20] l'UE a ainsi créé une incitation pour encourager les opérateurs privés situés sur son territoire à faire usage des mécanismes de projets du PK.

ii. Autres Cas

Cette fonction de relais de l'approche universelle se retrouve également, quoique dans une moindre mesure et dans des formes plus diffuses, dans l'action d'autres

[15] Décision 2005/166/CE de la Commission du 10 février 2005 fixant les modalités d'exécution de la décision 280/2004/CE du Parlement européen et du Conseil relative à un mécanisme pour surveiller les émissions de gaz à effet de serre dans la Communauté et mettre en œuvre le protocole de Kyoto [2005] JO L55/57. Cette décision demande par exemple aux États de communiquer les informations à la Commission en se conformant aux « lignes directrices concernant la préparation des informations requises au titre de l'article 7 du protocole de Kyoto » énoncées dans la décision 22/CP7 de la Conférence des États Parties à la CCNUCC. Sur cet exemple voir : A-S Tabau, *La mise en œuvre du Protocole de Kyoto en Europe. Interactions des contrôles international et communautaire* (Bruxelles, Bruylant, 2011) 93–94.

[16] Bergé, « Les interactions du droit international et européen, approche du phénomène en trois étapes dans le contexte européen » (n 8) para 11.

[17] ibid.

[18] Le « partage des charges » a été effectué grâce à l'accord de Luxembourg adopté lors du Conseil du 15 et 16 juin 1998. Document 9702/98 du Conseil de l'Union européenne du 19 juin 1998 reflétant les résultats des travaux du Conseil « Environnement » des 16 et 17 juin 1998, annexe I.

[19] Directive 2004/101/CE du Parlement et du Conseil du 27 octobre 2004 modifiant la directive 2003/87/CE établissant un système d'échange de quotas d'émission de gaz à effet de serre dans la Communauté, au titre des mécanismes de projet du protocole de Kyoto [2004] JO L 338/18.

[20] M Rodi et al, « Implementing the Kyoto Protocol in a Multidimensional Legal System : Lessons from a Comparative Assessment » (2005) 16 *Yearbook of International Environmental Law* 3, 37.

initiatives régionales non communautaires. En témoigne notamment la RIOCC, une initiative de la Conférence des Nations Ibéro-américaines qui a permis d'instaurer un dialogue intergouvernemental entre 21 États sur les changements climatiques, et dont l'un des objectifs principaux consiste à favoriser « an effective implementation of the decisions of the United Nations Framework Convention on Climate Change ».[21] En outre, le programme de travail de cette initiative indique explicitement que le mécanisme pour un développement propre constitue l'un des domaines dans lequel elle a vocation à intervenir. Plus encore, la RIOCC a été reconnue par le Secrétariat de la CCNUCC comme un organisme partenaire pour assurer la mise en œuvre du Programme de Nairobi sur les impacts, la vulnérabilité et l'adaptation aux changements climatiques.[22]

Un autre exemple réside dans le Partenariat Afrique-UE sur les changements climatiques, lancé en 2007 dans le cadre du Partenariat stratégique entre ces deux continents. Les États parties à cette action régionale ont en effet indiqué que celle-ci « tiendra compte ... de la nécessité de mettre en œuvre et de continuer à développer les instruments liés au changement climatique, en particulier la convention-cadre des Nations unies sur les changements climatiques (CCNUCC) de 1992 et le protocole de Kyoto »[23] et ont mentionné parmi les résultats escomptés « la mise en œuvre ... des traités qui ont trait au changement climatique ».[24] Par ailleurs, les activités envisagées dans le cadre de ce partenariat sont destinées, entre autres, à faciliter la participation des pays africains au mécanisme pour un développement propre et il est précisé qu'elles pourront faire l'objet de financements en provenance des fonds établis dans le cadre de la CCNUCC et du PK (Fonds pour les pays les moins avancés, Fonds spécial pour les changements climatiques et Fonds d'adaptation).[25]

B. L'Approche Régionale comme Espace de Négociation de l'Approche Universelle

i. Cas Communautaire

Parce que la CCNUCC et la PK ont été ratifiés à la fois par la CE et ses États membres, ceux-ci participent côte à côte aux négociations internationales qui se déroulent au sein du cadre onusien.[26] Afin de préserver la cohérence et l'unité de leurs positions dans ces négociations, « the exclusive voice and the main external

[21] Iberoamerican Network of Climate Change Bureaus, « Introduction to RIOCC and PIACC » (septembre 2009) à la p 1, http//unfcc.int/adaptation/nairobi_work_programme/partners_and_action_pleges/items/5005.php. Voir également le « Programa de trabajo en 2005 de la Red Iberoamericana de oficinas de cambio climático » (décembre 2004), www.lariocc.es/es/reuniones-documentos.

[22] Voir le site internet de la CCCNUCC : http://unfccc.int.

[23] Partenariat Afrique-UE, « Premier Plan d'Action (2008–2010) pour la mise en œuvre du Partenariat Stratégique Afrique-UE » (2007) à la p 61, www.africa-eu-partnership.org.

[24] ibid.

[25] ibid, 63.

[26] T Delreux, « The European Union in International Environmental Negotiations: a Legal Perspective on the Internal Decision-making Process » (2006) 6 *International Environmental Agreements* 231.

representation of the EU in the formal UN negotiation »[27] est constituée par une institution informelle, la Troïka, composée de la présidence tournante de l'UE, de la future présidence et de la Commission. Cette configuration suppose alors que soient définies au préalable, dans le cadre de l'approche régionale, les positions de l'UE qui seront par la suite défendues dans le cadre onusien. La Troïka négocie donc au sein de l'enceinte universelle sur la base d'un « relatively strict mandate »[28] défini par le Conseil.

Ainsi, lors des préparatifs de la Conférence de Copenhague de 2009, la position de l'UE en matière d'atténuation des changements climatiques, soit un objectif de réduction des émissions de 30% pour les pays développés par rapport au niveau de 1990 d'ici 2020, a tout d'abord été inscrite dans le Paquet énergie climat adopté en décembre 2008,[29] un ensemble de mesures destinées à définir « l'architecture de la politique climatique européenne pour le post-2012 à la fois sur le plan interne et externe ».[30] Cette position a par la suite été confirmée au cours de plusieurs réunions du Conseil européen (mars, juin et octobre 2009) et c'est sur la base de ce mandat que l'UE a pris part aux négociations onusiennes.[31]

Certes, l'Accord de Copenhague ne constitue pas un succès diplomatique pour l'UE qui n'a pas véritablement réussi à imprimer sa marque sur le processus de négociations. Toutefois, cet accord marque le passage d'une approche *top down* à *bottum up* pour la définition des engagements de réduction qui favorise une internationalisation des politiques climatiques domestiques. Dans ce contexte, l'objectif déjà en vigueur dans l'UE en matière de réduction (20% d'ici à 2020 par rapport au niveau de 1990) constitue un élément central de l'approche universelle puisque c'est précisément cet objectif que l'UE et ses membres ont fait inscrire à l'Annexe I de l'Accord de Copenhague.[32] Par ailleurs, signe de la forte interaction entre les deux espaces, il convient de mentionner que cet objectif de réduction est assorti d'une « clause d'ajustement en fonction des résultats des négociations internationales »,[33] en vertu de laquelle l'UE pourrait, en cas d'accord international jugé satisfaisant, réduire ses émissions de 30% d'ici à 2020.

[27] S Oberthür, « The EU's Performance in the Climate Change Regime » (2011) 33 *Journal of European Integration* 667, 671.

[28] L Van Schaik et C Egenhofer, « Improving the Climate. Will the New Constitution Strengthen the EU's Performance in International Climate Negotiations? » (2005) 63 *Centre for European Policy Studies Policy Brief* 2, http://aei.pitt.edu/6588/1/1198_63.pdf. Voir également : S Afionis, « The European Union as a Negotiator in the International Climate Change Regime » (2011) 11 *International Environmental Agreements* 341, 343.

[29] Décision 406/2009/CE du Parlement européen et du Conseil du 23 avril 2009 relative à l'effort à fournir par les États membres pour réduire leurs émissions de gaz à effet de serre afin de respecter les engagements de la Communauté en matière de réduction de ces émissions jusqu'en 2020 [2009] JO L 140/137.

[30] S Maljean-Dubois et M Wemaëre, *La diplomatie climatique. Les enjeux d'un régime international du climat* (Paris, Pedone, 2010) 277.

[31] Iddri Climate Team, « Copenhagen: A Guide for Negotiations Where do we stand? Why are we there? What should we aim for? » (décembre 2009) Analyses No 4 à la p 4, www.iddri.org/ Publications/ Collections/Analyses/an_guide_negotiations_copenhagen_COP15.pdf.

[32] Union européenne, « Quantified economy-wide emissions targets for 2020 » (28 janvier 2010), http://unfccc.int/meetings/copenhagen_dec_2009/items/5264.php.

[33] Maljean-Dubois et Wemaëre (n 30) 297.

ii. Autres Cas

Qu'il s'agisse de la RIOCC ou du Partenariat Afrique-UE sur les changements climatiques, ces deux initiatives régionales constituent également des enceintes au sein desquelles les discussions peuvent porter sur des éléments de l'approche universelle. Dans le cas de la RIOCC, d'abord, son programme de travail indique explicitement que cette initiative a notamment pour objectif de contribuer au rapprochement des positions des États dans les forums de négociations internationales sur les changements climatiques. Ainsi, lors de la sixième rencontre annuelle de la RIOCC en juin 2009, les discussions ont notamment porté sur les préparatifs de la Conférence de Copenhague. Par ailleurs, la Commission des coordonnateurs de la RIOCC se réunit de manière informelle à chaque réunion de la Conférence des États Parties de la CCNUCC et de ses organes subsidiaires. En ce qui concerne le Partenariat Afrique-UE sur les changements climatiques, son premier objectif consiste à « renforcer le dialogue et les approches communes, y compris au niveau multilatéral, concernant les défis que pose le changement climatique en Afrique, en Europe et dans le reste du monde, notamment en vue des négociations relatives à la conclusion d'un accord mondial global sur le climat pour l'après-2012 ». L'élaboration d'une Déclaration conjointe Afrique-UE sur les changements climatiques en 2008 a ainsi donné lieu à des discussions relatives à la préparation de la conférence de Copenhague et à l'avenir du régime juridique onusien pour la période post-2012. Cette déclaration comporte d'ailleurs un paragraphe spécifiquement consacré au cycle de négociations en cours dans l'enceinte universelle.[34]

Au regard de ces divers éléments, il apparaît donc que l'articulation des approches universelle et régionale se caractérise, dans le cadre de ce modèle vertical, par une très forte imbrication, une résonance, entre ces des deux échelons de coopération. L'approche universelle influence l'approche régionale, laquelle peut permettre la formulation de positions susceptibles de peser sur le contenu de l'approche universelle.

II. L'ÉMERGENCE D'UN MODÈLE HORIZONTAL

Si l'articulation continue d'être marquée par l'existence de cette « hiérarchie enchevêtrée », celle-ci se double désormais d'une nouvelle figure fondée sur une logique non plus verticale, mais horizontale. En effet, les approches régionales tendent à s'autonomiser et à s'affranchir du système onusien pour incarner de véritables alternatives à l'approche universelle (A).[35] Cette évolution, qui ouvre inévitablement la voie à une possible concurrence entre les différentes enceintes multilatérales décentralisées, conduit ainsi à faire de la gouvernance climatique un nouveau terrain d'élection de la problématique de la coordination ou de la dissonance entre les cadres universel et régional de coopération (B).

[34] Déclaration conjointe Afrique-UE sur les changements climatiques (2 décembre 2008), www.africa-eu-partnership.org.

[35] H Van Asselt, « From UN-ity to Diversity? The UNFCCC, the Asia-Pacific Partnership, and the Future of International Law on Climate Change » (2007) 1 *Carbon & Climate Law Review* 17, 28.

A. L'Approche Régionale comme Alternative à l'Approche Universelle

L'idée selon laquelle l'approche régionale constituerait désormais une alternative à l'approche universelle en matière de protection du climat ressort particulièrement de trois exemples : le lancement du Partenariat Asie-Pacifique pour le développement propre et le climat (PAP) ; l'intégration de l'aviation civile dans le SCEQE ; la mise en place d'initiatives de réduction des émissions de GES entre divers démembrements des États du continent Nord-Américain.

Le 28 juillet 2005, six États de la région Asie Pacifique annonçaient le lancement d'un Partenariat « visant à mettre au point, déployer et transférer des technologies plus propres et plus efficaces ... pour répondre aux préoccupations nationales en matière de réduction de la pollution, de sécurité énergétique et de changement climatique ».[36] Si cette initiative, qui a pris fin en avril 2011, inaugurait un nouveau cadre régional de coopération pour lutter contre les changements climatiques, celle-ci n'ignorait toutefois rien du cadre onusien déjà existant. En effet, le texte portant création du PAP indiquait que ce partenariat serait « conforme et contribuera[it] aux efforts consentis par ses pays membres dans le contexte de la Convention-cadre des Nations Unies sur les changements climatiques » et s'inscrirait « dans le cadre des principes établis » par cet instrument.[37] *A priori* donc, cette référence laissait présager que l'articulation entre cette initiative et le cadre onusien s'effectuerait selon un modèle vertical.

Cependant, à plusieurs égards, le PAP n'apparaissait pas véritablement comme un relais de l'approche universelle. Ce partenariat ne contenait aucune disposition relative à la réduction des émissions de GES (il n'est que fait référence à l'atténuation « de l'intensité des GES » et à la « réduction de la pollution ») ou à l'adaptation aux effets néfastes des changements climatiques, deux domaines qui constituent pourtant les piliers de la stratégie universelle. En outre, il n'instaurait aucune forme de traitement préférentiel au bénéfice de certains États, contrairement à la dualité normative sur laquelle se fondent la CCNUCC et le PK.[38] Mais surtout, ce partenariat demeurait totalement déconnecté de toute la machine onusienne, comme les mécanismes de projet, les diverses sources de financement et les cycles de négociations en cours. En ce sens, la création du PAP paraissait bien marquer « the existence of an alternative climate change regime ».[39]

[36] Déclaration de principes de l'Australie, de la Chine, des États-Unis d'Amérique, de l'Inde, du Japon et de la République de Corée pour un nouveau Partenariat Asie-Pacifique sur le développement propre et le climat (28 juillet 2005) à la p 1, www.asiapacificpartnership.org/pdf/translated_versions/French_VisionStatement.pdf. Voir également : Charte du Partenariat Asie-Pacifique sur le développement propre et le climat, adoptée durant la réunion ministérielle inaugurale tenue à Sydney du 11 au 13 janvier 2006, modifiée durant la seconde réunion ministérielle tenue à New Delhi les 14 et 15 octobre 2007 (15 octobre 2007) à la p 1, www.asiapacificpartnership.org/pdf/translated_versions/French_APPCharter.pdf. Les États soulignent au deuxième alinéa du Préambule que « [l]es buts de ce Partenariat sont conformes aux principes consacrés par la Convention-cadre des Nations Unies sur les changements climatiques ».

[37] ibid.

[38] J McGee et R Taplin, « The Asia-Pacific Partnership on Clean Development and Climate: A Retreat from the Principle of Common but Differentiated Responsibilities? » (2009) 5 *Revue internationale de droit et de politique du développement durable de McGill* 11, 39.

[39] J McGee et R Taplin, « The Asia–Pacific Partnership on Clean Development and Climate: A Complement or Competitor to the Kyoto Protocol? » (2006) 18 *Global Change, Peace & Security* 173, 191.

La décision de l'UE d'intégrer les activités aériennes dans le SCEQE constitue un autre témoignage de l'apparition d'approches régionales affranchies du cadre onusien.[40] Si le secteur de l'aviation internationale est demeuré hors du champ d'application des objectifs de réduction inscrits dans le Protocole de Kyoto, l'Article 2.2 de cet instrument invitait toutefois les Parties visées à l'annexe I à limiter ou réduire les émissions provenant des transports aériens en passant par l'intermédiaire de l'Organisation de l'Aviation Civile Internationale. Or, en réaction à l'inaction de cette organisation, l'UE a adopté de manière unilatérale une directive qui impose à toutes les compagnies aériennes depuis le 1er janvier 2012 de couvrir 15% de leurs émissions de GES par des quotas d'émission.

Ce faisant, l'UE s'est affranchie du cadre onusien à double titre : d'une part, en passant outre le dispositif prévu à l'échelon universel ; d'autre part, en dérogeant à la logique de traitement différencié sur laquelle se fonde le régime du climat, puisque la directive produit des effets identiques pour l'ensemble des pays, qu'ils soient ou non visés à l'annexe I de la CCNUCC.[41] Sur cette question, l'UE montre ainsi sa capacité à faire valoir une autre voie pour son action régionale en matière de protection du climat que celle consistant uniquement à assurer la mise en œuvre des normes universelles auxquelles elle est partie.

Le troisième exemple qui témoigne d'une mutation du modèle d'articulation des approches universelle et régionale réside enfin dans la mise en place d'initiatives de lutte contre les changements climatiques entre les démembrements des États du contient Nord-Américain. En marge de l'action menée par le palier de gouvernement fédéral aux États-Unis et au Canada (qui est d'ailleurs marquée dans les deux cas par une certaine défiance à l'égard du processus onusien, notamment incarnée par le rejet du PK), les entités fédérées et provinciales élaborent depuis plusieurs années des mécanismes de coopération pour réduire collectivement leurs émissions de GES.[42]

Cette forme particulière de régionalisme peut être soit *intra*-étatique, telle que la *Regional Greenhouse Gas Initiative* qui regroupe uniquement des États américains, soit *inter*-étatique, telle que la *Western Climate Initiative*, une association créée en 2007 à laquelle sont parties plusieurs États fédérés et provinces canadiennes.[43] Dans ce dernier cas, la coopération vise à atteindre un objectif global de réduction de 15% des émissions par rapport au niveau de 2005 d'ici à 2020 à travers, entre autre, la création d'un marché commun qui permet l'échange des droits d'émission entre les divers partenaires.[44] La Californie et le Québec, seules entités à avoir pour

[40] Directive 2008/101/CE du Parlement européen et du Conseil du 19 novembre 2008 modifiant la directive 2003/87/CE afin d'intégrer les activités aériennes dans le système communautaire d'échange de quotas d'émission de gaz à effet de serre [2009] JO L 8/3.

[41] J Scott et L Rajamani, « EU Climate Change Unilateralism » (2012) 23 *European Journal of International Law* 469.

[42] D Comba, « Les mécanismes de marché des émissions. Expériences régionales et internationales » dans C Cournil et C Colard-Fabregoule (éds), *Changements climatiques et défis du droit* (Bruxelles, Bruylant, 2010) 106.

[43] H Selin et SD Van Deveer, « Climate Change Regionalism in North America » (2011) 28 *Review of Policy Research* 295, 298.

[44] Western Climate Initiative, « Cadre de mise en œuvre du programme régional de la Western Climate Initiative » (juillet 2010) à la p 12, www.westernclimateinitiative.org.

l'instant mis en place un marché du carbone au sein de leur juridiction, négocient actuellement les conditions visant à permettre la mise en commun de leur marché. Cette initiative, même si elle repose sur une utilisation du mécanisme *cap and trade* tel que prévu à l'Article 17 du PK, demeure toutefois totalement déconnectée du système onusien. Elle témoigne par ailleurs d'une conception différente de l'approche universelle en faisant des démembrements des États, donc du niveau local et non plus global, le moteur de la lutte contre les changements climatiques.

Ces trois exemples démontrent ainsi que l'approche universelle telle qu'incarnée par le régime onusien n'est plus « the only game in town »[45] en matière de protection du climat. Et les voies alternatives qu'incarnent désormais les initiatives régionales conduisent à faire de la gouvernance du climat un espace au sein duquel s'observe une certaine tension entre les échelons universel et régional.

B. La Gouvernance du Climat Saisie par la Tension entre l'Universel et le Régional

La CCNUCC et le PK ne contiennent aucune clause relative à la possibilité pour les États de conclure des accords plurilatéraux de lutte contre les changements climatiques en marge du cadre onusien. Cette situation, qui démontre que les États n'avaient sans doute pas prévu l'éventualité d'une régionalisation de cette question lors de l'élaboration des normes universelles, implique qu'il n'existe actuellement aucune règle susceptible de régir les rapports entre les approches universelle et régionale. Une telle absence contraste avec d'autres domaines de coopération tels que le commerce[46] ou la sécurité[47] dans lesquels les instruments universels définissent les conditions de la validité des ententes régionales, assurant ainsi leur primauté. Il est vrai que cette absence n'avait jusqu'à récemment guère était problématique dans le domaine de la protection du climat puisque le modèle d'articulation vertical garantissait une certaine coordination entre approches universelle et régionale.

Cela dit, l'apparition d'un régionalisme d'alternative ne compromet pas *ipso facto* la poursuite des objectifs de la CCNUCC et du PK et n'est pas nécessairement source de tensions. Les initiatives entre les démembrements des États Nord-Américains ne semblent pas par exemple concurrencer le modèle onusien. Au contraire, celles-ci paraissent même être favorablement accueillies par l'ONU, comme en témoigne la présence de Christiana Figueres, Secrétaire exécutive de la CCNUCC, au Sommet mondial des États fédérés et des régions organisé durant la Conférence de Rio + 20. En outre, rien n'exclut le possible développement, à terme, de synergies entre les deux échelons de coopération. Un projet financé dans le cadre du PAP pourrait par

[45] McGee et Taplin, « The Asia–Pacific Partnership on Clean Development and Climate: A Complement or Competitor to the Kyoto Protocol? » (n 39) 191.
[46] Voir par exemple Article XXIV du GATT.
[47] Voir par exemple Article 52 de la Charte des Nations Unies.

exemple générer des crédits dans le cadre du mécanisme de développement propre du PK.[48] Dans cette perspective le modèle d'articulation horizontal pourrait alors n'être qu'une étape pour l'approche régionale, avant son intégration dans une « hiérarchie enchevêtrée » avec le cadre onusien.

Cependant, pour l'heure actuelle, il semble quand même que cette évolution ait suscité l'apparition de certaines tensions entre les approches universel et régional, ce qui constitue un facteur de nouveauté dans la gouvernance du climat, et plus largement peut-être, dans le domaine du droit international de l'environnement où les stratégies universelles tendent à être privilégiées pour résoudre les questions d'environnement global. Ces tensions peuvent être observées à trois niveaux.

En premier lieu, certaines interrogations sont apparues quant à la compatibilité des normes régionales avec les normes universelles. Ainsi en est-il de la Directive 2008/101/CE qui intègre les activités aériennes dans le SCEQE dont l'incompatibilité avec l'Article 2.2 du PK a été soulevée dans le cadre d'une affaire introduite à la Cour de justice de l'UE.[49] Arguant d'une absence d'applicabilité directe du PK, cette juridiction s'est toutefois refusée à statuer sur le fond de cette question. Au-delà des aspects juridiques, cet arrêt illustre par ailleurs les tensions politiques entre les États qui peuvent résulter de l'émergence d'un régionalisme d'alternative.

En deuxième lieu, la décision du Canada de se retirer du PK mais d'adhérer au PAP a démontré qu'un phénomène de *forum shopping* pouvait exister en matière de protection du climat et donc qu'une concurrence pouvait s'instaurer entre les différentes enceintes. À la différence du cadre onusien, le PAP constituait un mode de coopération beaucoup plus souple et moins contraignant. Celui-ci reposait sur des initiatives volontaires des États ; il ne comportait aucun objectif chiffré de réduction des émissions avec un échéancier ; il ne prévoyait aucun système de contrôle (ni rapports, ni mécanisme d'observance).

Enfin, un troisième signe de tension réside dans le risque de voir l'efficacité de certains outils de protection du climat limitée par la multiplication des lieux de coopération. Le bon fonctionnement des mécanismes de projets, parce qu'il suppose des investissements, est tributaire de la confiance des opérateurs privés. Celle des opérateurs australiens a par exemple pu être ébranlée par les propos du Sénateur Campbell, alors ministre de l'environnement, lorsque celui-ci déclara à propos du lancement du PAP: « It's quiet clear that Kyoto Protocol won't get the world to where it want to go ... We've got to find something to works better. Australia is working on that whit partners around the world. »[50] Et même si les États membres du PAP firent par la suite plusieurs déclarations afin de préciser qu'il s'agissait d'un « complement, not an alternative »[51] à la CCNUCC et au PK, à considérer comme « not a competitor,

[48] Van Asselt, « From UN-ity to Diversity? The UNFCCC, the Asia-Pacific Partnership, and the Future of International Law on Climate Change » (n 35) 26.

[49] Affaire C-366/10 *Air Transport Association of America e. a. v Secretary of State for Energy and Climate Change* (CJUE, 21 décembre 2011).

[50] McGee et Taplin « The Asia–Pacific Partnership on Clean Development and Climate: A Complement or Competitor to the Kyoto Protocol? » (n 39) 174.

[51] ibid, 175.

but more an augmenter »[52] du processus onusien, la création de cette initiative a pu être interprétée comme une volonté d'affaiblir l'efficacité du processus onusien relancé après l'entrée en vigueur du PK.

III. CONCLUSION

Comme le rappelait récemment Christiana Figueres : « [g]overnments alone can not solve climate change ».[53] Est-ce à dire pour autant que la coopération des gouvernements doit nécessairement être universelle pour réussir ? Sur cette question, les avis divergent. Alors que certains auteurs considèrent que « a universal regime appears to be the most effective long-term polity model to tackle climate change »,[54] d'autres estiment au contraire que le régionalisme constitue un « atout »[55] pour la gouvernance du climat. Quoiqu'il en soit, l'apparition d'un régionalisme d'alternative constitue désormais une réalité internationale qui semble traduire un effritement de la confiance que les États placent actuellement dans les structures onusiennes pour protéger efficacement le climat, mais aussi, pour parvenir à faire coïncider les normes universelles avec leurs propres intérêts nationaux.

Face à cette double crise du cadre onusien, celle de son efficacité et de sa légitimité, le choix de certains États de se tourner vers d'autres horizons juridiques pour résoudre le défi climatique semble ainsi faire écho à ces propos énigmatiques formulés par Henri Michaux: « [e]n te méfiant du multiple, n'oublie pas de te méfier de son contraire, de son trop facile contraire : l'un. C'est toujours l'assouvissement l'unité. »[56] Reste à savoir si la dissonance qui se fait aujourd'hui entendre entre les voix universelle et régionale sera plus bénéfique pour la protection du climat que ne l'a été, jusqu'à récemment, leur unisson.

[52] ibid, 177.

[53] C Figueres, « Opening Speech by Christiana Figueres, Executive Secretary United Nations Framework Convention on Climate Change », discours prononcé lors de la 13e session du groupe de travail sur le Protocole de Kyoto et de la 11e session du groupe de travail sur l'action concertée à long terme (2 août 2010) à la p 1, http://unfccc.int/press/statements/items/5408.php.

[54] F Biermann et al, « Fragmentation vs Universalism? Assessing Options for the Polity of Post-2012 Global Climate Governance », communication présentée lors de la Conference on Human Dimensions of Global Environmental Change (24–26 mai 2007) à la p 20, www.2007amsterdamconference.org/Downloads/AC2007_BiermannEtAl.pdf.

[55] Le Prestre, « Géopolitique régionale du climat et coopération internationale » (n 1) 12.

[56] H Michaux, *Poteau d'angle* (Paris, Galimard, 1981) 27.

31

Are the Polar Regions Converging? A Study of the Evolution of the International Regime Governing the Arctic Region Compared to the Antarctic Treaty System

YOSHINOBU TAKEI*

I. INTRODUCTION

THE SIMILARITIES (FOR example, harsh climatic conditions and remoteness) of the Polar regions as well as their differences have prompted a number of scholars to compare these regions.[1] Geographical configurations (the Arctic Ocean is an ocean surrounded by continents, whereas Antarctica is a continent surrounded by an ocean) and other factors (for example, the absence of generally recognised territorial claims for Antarctica, as opposed to virtually undisputed territorial

* Associate Professor, World Maritime University, Malmö. I wish to express my sincere gratitude to Professor D Vidas and other participants in Agora 3 on 'Frozen Regions: Arctic & Antarctica in the New Millennium' as well as to Professor AG Oude Elferink, Professor EJ Molenaar and Professor Mary E Footer for their insightful comments. Research for this chapter was supported by funding from the Netherlands Polar Programme as well as the Cluster of Excellence 'The Future Ocean' funded by the German Research Foundation.

[1] See, for example, DR Rothwell and S Kaye, 'Law of the Sea and the Polar Regions: Reconsidering the Traditional Norms' (1994) 18 *Marine Policy* 41–48; DR Rothwell, *The Polar Regions and the Development of International Law* (Cambridge, Cambridge University Press, 1996); D Vidas (ed), *Protecting the Polar Marine Environment: Law and Policy for Pollution Prevention* (Cambridge, Cambridge University Press, 2000); T Koivurova, 'Environmental Protection in the Arctic and Antarctic: Can the Polar Regimes Learn From Each Other? (2005) 33 *International Journal of Legal Information* 204–18; E Lennon, 'A Tale of Two Poles: A Comparative Look at the Legal Regimes in the Arctic and the Antarctic' (2008) 8 *Sustainable Development Law & Policy* 32–36 and 65–66; T Blunden, 'The Legal Status of the Arctic under Contemporary International Law: An Antarctic Regime or Poles Apart?' (2009) 15 *Journal of International Maritime Law* 249–63; H Cohen, 'Some Reflections on Bioprospecting in the Polar Regions' in D Vidas (ed), *Law, Technology and Science for Oceans in Globalisation: IUU Fishing, Oil Pollution, Bioprospecting, Outer Continental Shelf* (Leiden, Martinus Nijhoff, 2010) 339–52; S Duyck, 'Drawing Lessons for Arctic Governance from the Antarctic Treaty System' (2011) 3 *Yearbook of Polar Law* 683–713; T Stephens, 'The Arctic and Antarctic Regimes and the Limits of Polar Comparativism' (2011) 54 *German Yearbook of International Law* 315–49; and EJ Molenaar, AG Oude Elferink and DR Rothwell (eds), *The Law of the Sea and the Polar Regions: Interactions between Global and Regional Regimes* (Leiden, Martinus Nijhoff Publishers, 2013).

claims in the Arctic; human populations residing in the Arctic region, as opposed to site visits by scientists and tourists in Antarctica) have led to the identification of two sets of international regimes. On the one hand, Antarctica is governed by a complex mixture of regional normative instruments and institutional arrangements developed within the Antarctic Treaty System (ATS), together with applicable global norms.[2] On the other hand, no comprehensive treaty specific to the Arctic region, comparable to the Antarctic Treaty, exists.

Land territory in the Arctic region is part of the territories of eight countries, where different domestic legal orders exist. In addition, the Arctic region is governed by a multiple set of norms, dealing with the region as a whole or sub-regions (eg, the Barents Sea and Nordic countries),[3] or global norms applicable to activities in the Arctic region (for example, fisheries, species protection and navigation). A good example of the latter for the marine area is the United Nations Convention on the Law of the Sea (UNCLOS) that establishes a legal framework for the oceans.[4] Its provisions are applicable globally, including in the Arctic Ocean, and are not specifically tailored to the Arctic Ocean (or the Polar regions) except for article 234 UNCLOS. The Arctic region is characterised by the lack of hierarchical order among the co-existing regional and sub-regional norms and institutions. For example, the Arctic Council, one of the few pan-Arctic cooperative arrangements, is not tasked with overseeing activities undertaken by other organisations dealing with the Arctic region.[5]

Melting sea-ice, together with political developments, drew the international community's attention to the Arctic as a 'region'. This has changed the foundation of our perceptions of the region, and its associated legal and institutional arrangements are in a process of change. Recent trends in the development of the international regime for the Arctic arguably suggest that it is becoming closer to the ATS in some respects.

[2] The elements of the ATS include 'the Antarctic Treaty, the measures in effect under that Treaty, its associated separate international instruments in force and the measures in effect under those instruments'; see further the Antarctic Treaty (done at Washington DC, 1 December 1959, entered into force 23 June 1961) 402 UNTS 71 and Protocol on Environmental Protection to the Antarctic Treaty (done at Madrid, 4 October 1991, entered into force 14 January 1998), 30 ILM 1455, art 1(e). Within the ATS, fisheries are managed by the Commission for the Conservation of Antarctic Marine Living Resources (CCAMLR), which was established by the Convention on the Conservation of Antarctic Marine Living Resources (CCAMLR Convention) (done at Canberra, 20 May 1980, entered into force 7 April 1982) 1329 UNTS 47, 19 ILM 841.

[3] Cooperation within the framework of the Nordic Council and the Nordic Council of Ministers is pursued by Denmark, Finland, Iceland, Norway, Sweden and the autonomous territories of the Faroe Islands, Greenland and Åland. See Norden, 'Countries and territories', available at www.norden.org/en/about-nordic-co-operation/countries-and-territories.

[4] United Nations Convention on the Law of the Sea (done at Montego Bay, Jamaica, 10 December 1982, entered into force 16 November 1994) 1833 UNTS 3. On the importance of the UNCLOS to the management of the Arctic Ocean, see eg, Ilulissat Declaration, Ilulissat, Greenland, 28 May 2008, available at www.arcticgovernance.org/the-ilulissat-declaration.4872424.html.

[5] The Arctic Council was established by a non-legally binding instrument as a high-level forum to address common issues for the Arctic, not as an international organisation with regulatory authority. Declaration on the Establishment of the Arctic Council, 19 September 1996, available at www.arctic-council.org/. Its activities during the first decade since its establishment in 1996 were mostly concerned with cooperation in environmental protection and sustainable development, in particular scientific assessments.

In particular, the adoption of the Arctic Search and Rescue (SAR) Agreement[6] and the Arctic Marine Oil Pollution Preparedness and Response (MOPPR) Agreement[7] indicates that the Arctic Council has started to serve as a forum for lawmaking.[8] In view of this, it is interesting to carefully analyze how the international regime for the Arctic region has been evolving in the light of developments within the ATS. This will assist in understanding what is meant by 'regionalism', and in determining whether it matters and how it operates in this context.[9]

This chapter considers if and how an international regime is being developed for the Arctic as a region, how it has been affected by the ATS and how the governance of the Polar regions is dealt with at the global level. The chapter covers three issues: the nature of the components of these regimes and their implications, the relationship between these regimes and their interactions with global forums. In so doing, it considers key developments that shed some light on these three issues. First, we discuss initiatives to strengthen the Arctic Council, including the implications of the adoption of the Arctic SAR Agreement and the Arctic MOPPR Agreement and various initiatives agreed at the recent Ministerial Meetings of the Arctic Council. Second, we discuss the influence of the ATS on the development of the international regime for the Arctic. We consider two topics: scientific research and seaborne tourism. Third, we review discussions about the Polar regions at the global level, focusing on the development of a Polar Code at the International Maritime Organization (IMO). The examination of those IMO discussions may reveal tensions between globalism and regionalism. The chapter concludes with some final remarks.

II. DEVELOPMENTS WITHIN THE ARCTIC COUNCIL

In this section, the chapter discusses the development of the governance system for the Arctic region, focusing on the strengthening of the Arctic Council and synergies between the ATS and the Arctic Council. The remainder of this section first discusses three issues in the light of recent developments within the Arctic Council which testify to its increasing importance and, in some cases, its resemblance to the ATS: first, the adoption of the Arctic SAR Agreement and the Arctic MOPPR Agreement;

[6] Agreement on Cooperation on Aeronautical and Maritime Search and Rescue in the Arctic (also known as the Arctic Search and Rescue Agreement or Arctic SAR Agreement) (done at Nuuk, Greenland, 12 May 2011, entered into force 19 January 2013) 50 ILM 1119.

[7] Agreement on Cooperation on Marine Oil Pollution Preparedness and Response in the Arctic (Arctic MOPPR Agreement) (done at Kiruna, Sweden, 15 May 2013, not yet in force), available at http://emeritus.lovdata.no/cgi-wift/udoffles?doc=tra-2013-05-15-007.txt&.

[8] See Y Takei, 'The Role of the Arctic Council from an International Law Perspective: Past, Present and Future' (2015) 6 *Yearbook of Polar Law* 349–74.

[9] Regionalism could mean a variety of concepts, such as specific attitudes towards the concept of international law in general, uniform positions in negotiations on certain issues, distinctive practices and so on. See the discussions on regionalism in the context of polar marine environmental protection in A Boyle, 'Globalism and Regionalism in the Protection of the Marine Environment' in Vidas (ed), *Law, Technology and Science for Oceans in Globalisation*, 19–33. In the context of this chapter, when we talk about 'regionalism', it could be 'polar' regionalism or 'Arctic' regionalism and 'Antarctic' regionalism. Whether 'frozen regions' are treated as a distinct region/issue or two regions will determine how international legal discourse plays a role in questions relating to these areas. On this issue, see also section III below.

second, the Arctic Ocean Review (AOR) project and related activities of the Protection of the Arctic Marine Environment Working Group (PAME); and third, the approval of the new Observer Rules.[10] These discussions are followed by an analysis of synergies between the ATS and the Arctic Council, in particular in scientific research and seaborne tourism.

A. Legally Binding International Instruments

One of the features of the evolution of the ATS is the adoption of treaties and legally binding decisions addressing specific issues within the framework of the ATS. In the Arctic region, there was only one regional treaty applicable to the entire Arctic Ocean until 2011, which was concluded by the five Arctic Ocean coastal states.[11] This situation, however, has changed following the adoption of the Arctic SAR Agreement in 2011.[12]

As previously mentioned, the Arctic SAR Agreement was the first legally binding instrument negotiated under the auspices of the Arctic Council, adopted in May 2011. Its importance lies both in the implications of its 'adoption' as well as the rights and obligations created by the Agreement.[13] The Arctic SAR Agreement establishes the meeting of states parties that will enable them to further cooperate, building upon the commitments made by the parties upon adoption of the Agreement.[14] While the Agreement emphasises non-prejudice to the delimitation of boundaries between states or their sovereignty, sovereign rights or jurisdiction, its delimitation of SAR regions and arrangements for entry into other parties' territory could help ease tensions relating to (primarily maritime) boundary disputes in the Arctic.[15]

At the 2011 Ministerial Meeting, the Arctic Council established a new Task Force to develop an international instrument on MOPPR.[16] Although the mandate did not explicitly refer to a 'legally binding' instrument, it was subsequently decided to aim for such an instrument.[17] This initiative is more ambitious and more closely linked

[10] In passing, it is noted that another element of the strengthening of the Arctic Council is the decision at the 2011 Ministerial Meeting to establish a permanent secretariat in Tromsø, Norway.

[11] Agreement on the Conservation of Polar Bears (done at Oslo, 15 November 1973, entered into force 26 May 1976) 13 ILM 13.

[12] Arctic SAR Agreement, above n 6.

[13] For details of the Arctic SAR Agreement, see Y Takei, 'Agreement on Cooperation on Aeronautical and Maritime Search and Rescue in the Arctic: An assessment' (2013) 2 *Aegean Review of the Law of the Sea and Maritime Law* 81–109. Some observers attach less importance to the obligations created by the Agreement; see, eg, S-M Kao, NS Pearre and J Firestone, 'Adoption of the Arctic Search and Rescue Agreement: A Shift of the Arctic Regime Toward a Hard Law Basis?' (2012) 36 *Marine Policy* 832–38, 837

[14] Arctic SAR Agreement, above n 6, art 10.

[15] As Stephens states, in 'The Arctic and Antarctic Regimes', p 334, the non-prejudice provision 'clearly has some parallels with Article IV of the Antarctic Treaty' but 'its scope is far more limited, in that it does not seek to limit in any way the assertion by States of sovereignty, sovereign rights or jurisdiction, whereas this restraint upon sovereignty is at the heart of the ATS'.

[16] Arctic Council, Nuuk Declaration on the occasion of the Seventh Ministerial Meeting of the Arctic Council, Nuuk, Greenland, 12 May 2011, available at www.arctic-council.org, under 07_nuuk_declaration_2011_signed.pdf, para 1 under the heading 'Arctic marine environment'.

[17] Meeting of Deputy Ministers, Stockholm, 15 May 2012, Final Report, available at www.arctic-council.org, under final_report_dm_meeting_15_may_2012.pdf, 2.

to the ongoing work of the Arctic Council in the sense that the Ministerial Meeting set up the Task Force and, at the same time, instructed the Emergency Prevention, Preparedness and Response Working Group (EPPR) to develop recommendations and/or best practices for the prevention of marine oil pollution.[18]

In addition, the Senior Arctic Officials (SAO) in 2012 approved the proposal by the MOPPR Task Force to request the EPPR to draft operational guidelines for the Task Force.[19] After several Task Force meetings, the Arctic MOPPR Agreement was adopted in 2013. Like the Arctic SAR Agreement,[20] the Arctic MOPPR Agreement is intended to implement a global instrument (ie, the International Convention on Oil Pollution Preparedness, Response and Co-operation)[21] at the regional level.[22] Together with the Arctic SAR Agreement, the Arctic MOPPR Agreement helps Arctic states address safety and environmental concerns arising from increasing activities in the Arctic.[23]

At the Nuuk Ministerial Meeting in 2013, Arctic Council member states did not decide on initiating negotiations for a new 'international instrument', but the Iqaluit Declaration adopted at the Ministerial Meeting in 2015 states that the member states decided to extend the mandate of the Task Force on Enhancing Scientific Cooperation in the Arctic, 'including to work towards a legally-binding agreement on scientific cooperation', with a view to completing its work no later than the next Ministerial meeting.[24]

In view of the increasing roles of the Arctic Council, one commentator has analysed its recent and ongoing activities using the concept of the 'Arctic Council System' inspired by the ATS.[25] Indeed, by virtue of the development of new legally binding instruments and institutions, the Arctic Council is gaining more and more importance as the cornerstone of the evolving international regime for the Arctic.[26]

[18] Senior Arctic Officials (SAO) Report to Ministers, Nuuk, Greenland, May 2011, 6–7. The EPPR is one of the six working groups of the Arctic Council. Working groups engage in their activities on a permanent basis whereas task forces are time-bound in their activities.

[19] Meeting of SAO, Stockholm, 28–29 March 2012, Final Report, 4–5.

[20] The Arctic SAR Agreement implements two global treaties: the 1944 Chicago Convention on International Civil Aviation and the 1979 International Convention on Maritime Search and Rescue.

[21] International Convention on Oil Pollution Preparedness, Response and Cooperation (done at London, 30 November 1990, entered into force 13 May 1995) 503 UNTS 51, 30 ILM 733.

[22] In the Arctic region, there are a number of bilateral cooperative arrangements on this issue. See EPPR, 'Arctic Guide', available at www.arctic-council.org/eppr/completed-work/oil-and-gas-products/arctic-guide/. Note that, in the case of the ATS the situation is different, art 15 and Annex IV, art 12 of the Environmental Protocol, provide a basis for such action.

[23] On the content and implications of these Agreements, see Takei, 'The Role of the Arctic Council'.

[24] Arctic Council, Iqaluit Declaration on the occasion of the Ninth Ministerial Meeting of the Arctic Council, Iqaluit, Canada, 24 April 2015, available at www.arctic-council.org, under oaarchive.arctic-council.org/handle/11374/662, para 44. See also SAO Report to Ministers, Iqaluit, Canada, April 2015, at 10, available at www.arctic-council.org, under oaarchive.arctic-council.org/handle/11374/494.

[25] EJ Molenaar, 'Current and Prospective Roles of the Arctic Council System within the Context of the Law of the Sea' (2012) 27 *International Journal of Marine & Coastal Law* 553–95, 567–73 in particular.

[26] On the contribution of the Arctic Council to the development of international law through the adoption of legally and non-legally binding international instruments, see Takei, 'The Role of the Arctic Council'.

B. Strategic Reviews and Planning

So as to maintain the effectiveness and adequacy of international regimes, it is essential to conduct regular strategic reviews and planning of their activities. For the Arctic region, most successful and influential outcomes from this type of exercise concern the marine component, namely the Arctic Marine Strategic Plan (AMSP) 2004[27] and the Arctic Marine Shipping Assessment (AMSA).[28] Furthermore, in response to a call by the AMSP for periodically reviewing the status and adequacy of international/regional agreements and standards that have application in the Arctic marine environment, the Arctic Council was engaged in the AOR project through PAME between 2009 and 2013.[29] The key objectives of the AOR project included analysing 'global and regional protection measures for environmental, economic and social/cultural outcomes' and developing 'a report addressing protection measures for the Arctic marine and coastal environment, including possible impediments to achieving a regionally integrated, sustainable development approach to the Arctic Ocean in light of current and emerging trends'.[30]

The second phase of the AOR project started in 2011, with the aim, inter alia, to '[a]nalyze potential opportunities in global and regional instruments and measures to achieving environmental, economic and socio-cultural outcomes' and to '[o]utline options to address potential opportunities to strengthen the conservation and sustainable use of the Arctic marine environment'.[31] The final report, which contained various useful recommendations, was presented to the 2013 Ministerial Meeting and its recommendations were approved by the Ministers.[32]

Like the AMSP and AMSA recommendations, which are currently contemplated in various bodies of the Arctic Council, the recommendations of the AOR project will give guidance to future policy options for Arctic states on matters within and beyond the Arctic Council.[33] With all of these instruments as well as the revision of the AMSP approved in 2015,[34] effective tools are already in place for the Arctic Council to periodically engage in strategic reviews and planning in the pursuance of its objectives as far as Arctic marine areas are concerned.

[27] The Arctic Marine Strategic Plan (AMSP), approved by the Ministerial Meeting in 2004, outlined, inter alia, goals, challenges and opportunities, as well as strategic actions relating to Arctic marine areas. For details of the AMSP, see www.pame.is/images/01_PAME/AMSP/AMSP_Nov_2004.pdf.

[28] For details of the Arctic Marine Shipping Assessment (AMSA), conducted under the auspices of the PAME, see www.pame.is/index.php/projects/arctic-marine-shipping/amsa.

[29] See AMSP, para 7.3.4.

[30] See SAO Report to Ministers, Tromsø, Norway, April 2009, at 59, available at www.arctic-council.org, under 10_SAO_report_to_ministers.pdf.

[31] 'Project Plan for AOR Phase II', in PAME 'PAME Work Plan 2011–2013', 26. See also the section on 'Scope and Approach', pp 26–27 and the section on 'Main components, Timeline and Major Milestones' at p 27 ('Develop new mechanisms as appropriate').

[32] Arctic Council, Kiruna Declaration on the occasion of the Eighth Ministerial Meeting of the Arctic Council, Kiruna, Sweden, 15 May 2013, available at www.arctic-council.org, under MM08_Final_Kiruna_declaration_w_signature.pdf, para 9, under the heading 'Protecting Arctic environment'.

[33] Indeed, the Kiruna Ministerial Meeting requested appropriate follow-up actions for AOR recommendations, ibid.

[34] Arctic Marine Strategic Plan 2015–2025, approved by the Ministerial Meeting in 2015, available at www.pame.is/images/03_Projects/AMSP/AMSP_2015-2025.pdf.

Building upon these and other related works, a project that may have broader implications for the future of the Arctic Council from a strategic viewpoint has been initiated, namely the assessment undertaken by the Task Force on Arctic Marine Cooperation, established at the Iqaluit Ministerial Meeting.[35] Its mandate is: 'to consider future needs for strengthened cooperation on Arctic marine areas, as well as mechanism (e.g. regional seas program, or other mechanism as appropriate), to meet these needs, and to make recommendations on the nature and scope of any such mechanisms'.[36] Its assessment of questions such as the geographic scope (eg the high seas area of the Arctic Ocean and/or (seabed) areas beyond national jurisdiction?), the relationship between the work of a cooperative mechanism and the work of other institutions or mechanisms serving similar functions in adjacent or overlapping areas, and the relationship to the Arctic Council (eg within the Arctic Council's existing structure or as a separate mechanism with a defined relationship to the Council?) will be of decisive importance for the future of the Arctic Council.[37]

C. Inclusiveness

One of the recurrent issues for an international regime is how to address third party challenges and to deal with external relations. In the case of the ATS, the Antarctic Treaty Consultative Meeting (ATCM) comprises both claimants and non-claimants interested in activities in Antarctica, successfully accommodating different interests among stakeholders. The legitimacy of the ATCM in the management of Antarctica has long been challenged, but accessions by countries such as Malaysia and Pakistan to the Antarctic Treaty signal that the ATS as it stands has gained greater recognition as a legitimate actor in the international community. In the fisheries context in particular, the CCAMLR Convention allows the involvement of states with different interests. For example, CCAMLR members are not limited to states engaged in fishing in the Southern Ocean but also include those engaged in research. In addition, the CCAMLR Convention also allows states (and regional economic integration organisations) party to the CCAMLR Convention which are not Antarctic Treaty parties to become members of CCAMLR.[38]

The problem of defining the contours of the international regime is more pressing for the Arctic region, especially given the increasing interest in activities in the Arctic expressed by non-Arctic states and entities such as China, India, Japan, the Republic of Korea and Singapore as well as the European Union. On the one hand, the Arctic Council is a closed club, in the sense that its membership is limited to the eight Arctic states, and participation by observer states in the activities of the

[35] See Iqaluit Declaration, above n 24, para 43 ('Establish a Task Force to assess future needs for a regional seas program or other mechanism, as appropriate, for increased cooperation in Arctic marine areas').

[36] SAO Report to Ministers Iqaluit, Canada, April 2015, above n 24, at 77.

[37] ibid, at 78.

[38] The EU and Namibia are CCAMLR members but are not parties to the Antarctic Treaty. There are three CCAMLR Convention parties which are not CCAMLR members and are also not party to the Antarctic Treaty.

Arctic Council is severely restrained. Negotiations in the above-mentioned two task forces—SAR and MOPPR (see previous section)—illustrate this aspect, although the participation of non-Arctic states to cooperate in search-and-rescue and marine oil pollution response operations upon request by parties is envisaged in both the Arctic SAR Agreement and the Arctic MOPPR Agreement. A further complicating factor is the relationship between the 'Arctic Eight' (the eight Arctic Council member states) and the 'Arctic Five' (the five Arctic Ocean coastal states). The membership of the former includes the other three Arctic states (Finland, Iceland and Sweden). In view of the controversy over the attempts by the 'Arctic Five' to form another forum to discuss marine issues, potential tension between the 'Arctic Five' and the 'Arctic Eight' could play a role in determining the shape and function of the future Arctic Council.[39]

On the other hand, as the Arctic states recognise, the law of the sea provides a framework governing the marine area of the Arctic region and, on that basis, both Arctic and non-Arctic states have rights and obligations in the region. Under UNCLOS, non-Arctic states have certain rights concerning various activities, which are currently conducted or contemplated, including navigation,[40] the laying of submarine cables,[41] fisheries[42] and marine scientific research.[43] Freedom of the high seas ensures the right of all states to engage in these activities under article 87 of UNCLOS and such freedom also applies in the EEZ for navigation and the laying of submarine cables under article 58. Furthermore, these states also have interests in the protection and preservation of the marine environment.[44] This would suggest that states other than the Arctic Council members may argue that the protection of the marine environment from oil and gas development activities in the Arctic region

[39] The tension appears to have peaked at the holding of the 2010 Arctic Ocean Foreign Ministers' Meeting held in Canada in March 2010. On this meeting, see Foreign Affairs, Trade and Development Canada, 'Minister Cannon Highlights Canada's Arctic Leadership at Arctic Ocean Foreign Ministers' Meeting', available at www.international.gc.ca/media/aff/news-communiques/2010/120.aspx. As analysed by Pedersen, the positions of the 'Arctic Five' on the role of the Arctic Council are not fixed; rather, they have changed their positions considerably in the period between 2008 and 2010. See further T Pedersen 'Debates over the Role of the Arctic Council' (2012) 43 *Ocean Development & International Law* 146–56, 150–54. In addition, in the context of fisheries, the 'Arctic Five' adopted a declaration, inter alia, containing interim measures for the single high seas portion of the central Arctic Ocean. Declaration concerning the Prevention of Unregulated High Seas Fishing in the Central Arctic Ocean, Oslo, Norway, 16 July 2015, available at www.regjeringen.no/globalassets/departementene/ud/vedlegg/folkerett/declaration-on-arctic-fisheries-16-july-2015.pdf.

[40] UNCLOS, above n 4, arts 17, 38, 58 and 87.

[41] UNCLOS, ibid, arts 58, 79, 87 and 112–15; there have been plans to lay submarine cables in the Arctic Ocean; see eg, 'Fibre optics to connect Japan to the UK—via the Arctic', *New Scientist*, 29 March 2012, available at www.newscientist.com/article/mg21328566.000-fibre-optics-to-connect-japan-to-the-uk--via-the-arctic.html.

[42] UNCLOS, ibid, arts 87 and 116–19.

[43] UNCLOS, ibid, arts 87, 143 and 256–57.

[44] See, eg ILC, 'Report of the International Law Commission on the Work of its 53rd Session' (23 April to 1 June and 2 July to 10 August 2001) concerning the adoption of 'Articles on Responsibility of States for Internationally Wrongful Acts' UN Doc A/56/10, YILC, vol I, Commentary on art 48, para 10; and *Responsibilities and Obligations of States Sponsoring Persons and Entities with Respect to Activities in the Area* (Advisory Opinion of the Seabed Disputes Chamber of the International Tribunal for the Law of the Sea 1 February 2011), ITLOS Reports 2011, paras 179–80.

is in their interest as well as in the interest of Arctic states. It is also noted that the OSPAR Commission, which includes non-Arctic states in its membership, has regulatory competence in part of the Arctic Ocean.[45]

Tensions between these two aspects could make the potential role of the Arctic Council controversial: the future approach toward non-Arctic states and entities will determine the legitimacy of its activities in terms of Arctic governance. In this regard, it is worth noting that the 2011 Ministerial Meeting of the Arctic Council adopted new observer rules. They abolished the distinction between ad hoc and permanent observers and established new criteria for admitting observers, including the recognition of the existing international legal framework.[46] In 2013, the Kiruna Ministerial Meeting admitted several states as new observers.[47] It remains to be seen how these rules are to be implemented, especially in relation to the European Union.[48]

Related to the above is the ongoing work of the Task Force on Arctic Marine Cooperation, which may address the questions of membership and participatory rights in a cooperative mechanism if such mechanism is decided to be negotiated.[49] Approaches to these questions, together with other important questions such as its geographic scope, the relationship between its work and that of similar mechanisms and its relationship to the Arctic Council, would profoundly affect the debate over the inclusiveness of the Arctic Council.

D. Synergies Between the ATS and the Arctic Council

A number of scholars, conducting comparative analyses of the Arctic and Antarctica regimes, have suggested that the Arctic states should improve governance of the region by learning from the experience in the ATS. Although direct cooperation between the ATS and the Arctic Council has scarcely been identified, some influence of the Antarctic experience is recognised in the field of scientific research and seaborne tourism.[50] This sub-section examines these two instances to determine the extent of such synergies between the ATS and the Arctic Council.[51]

[45] See Convention for the Protection of the Marine Environment of the North-East Atlantic (done at Paris, 22 September 1992, entered into force 25 March 1998) 32 ILM 1069, art 1(a).

[46] Criteria for admitting observers are stipulated in Annex 1 of the SAO Report for Ministers, Nuuk, above n 18, p 50.

[47] Kiruna Declaration, above n 32, para 5, under 'Strengthening the Arctic Council'.

[48] The Iqaluit Ministerial Meeting deferred decisions on pending observer issues with the goal of deciding on them at the Ministerial Meeting in 2017. Iqaluit Declaration, above n 24, para 51.

[49] SAO Report to Ministers Iqaluit, Canada, April 2015, above n 24, at 78.

[50] Safety and environmental protection concerning passenger ships used for tourism activities in polar waters has been extensively addressed in IMO conventions and the Polar Code, on which the next section of this chapter focuses.

[51] On other issues, with respect to which the AMSA report recommended the Arctic Council to follow the move of the ATS, see Arctic Council, 'Status on Implementation of the AMSA 2009 Report Recommendations', May 2011 (2011 Status Report), 5 and 9. In addition, the AMSA Report suggested coordination between the Arctic Council and the Antarctic Treaty Consultative Meeting (ATCM) to ensure continuity and standardisation concerning polar SAR, where appropriate. Arctic Council, Arctic Marine Shipping Assessment 2009 Report (AMSA 2009 Report), 174.

i. Scientific Research

Scientific activities are one of the primary activities taking place in Antarctica.[52] Article II of the Antarctic Treaty provides for a guiding principle for scientific activities in Antarctica as follows: 'Freedom of scientific investigation in Antarctica and cooperation toward that end, as applied during the International Geophysical Year, shall continue, subject to the provisions of the present Treaty.'[53] This principle is given effect by information exchange and other means stated in article III.[54] However, the impact of these provisions on marine scientific research in the Antarctic Treaty Area might be limited by virtue of article VI, which explicitly notes non-prejudice to the rights or the exercise of rights by any state under international law with regard to the high seas within that area.[55]

In the Arctic region, scientific activities on the land territory and in the territorial sea and internal waters of the Arctic states are, first and foremost, governed by the domestic laws and regulations of these countries.[56] In marine areas, a legal framework for marine scientific research is established by the law of the sea, which includes the extensive regulatory authority of coastal states in areas under their sovereignty and jurisdiction and freedom of scientific research enjoyed by all states in areas beyond national jurisdiction.[57]

In 2009, the Antarctic Treaty Consultative Parties (ATCPs) and Arctic Council member states held a joint meeting on polar science. They compared situations prevailing in both regions, encouraged developing coordinated research and suggested the strengthening of international cooperation.[58] In particular, the ATCPs and the Arctic Council member states

> *Call[ed] upon* IPY [the International Polar Year] participants to continue to make data collected under IPY 2007–2008 and its legacy programs available in an open and timely manner, recall[ed] the obligations related to exchange of scientific information to this effect in the Antarctic Treaty, and encourage[ed] the same spirit of scientific openness among Arctic researchers[.][59]

Although some influence of the ATS norm of scientific openness is found here, it is difficult to see concrete impacts on the practice of the Arctic Council. For example,

[52] The importance of scientific activities in Antarctica is suggested by the following provision in a resolution adopted by ATCM XXXII, which states that '[s]cientific research should be accorded priority in relation to all tourism activities in Antarctica' as one of the general principles of Antarctic tourism, Resolution 7 (2009)—ATCM XXXII—CEP XII, Baltimore, third recital.

[53] Antarctic Treaty, above n 2, art II.

[54] ibid, art III.

[55] See ibid, art VI, although the scope of the term 'high seas' in the Antarctic Treaty context could be subject to divergent interpretations. On marine scientific research in the Antarctic, see R Lefeber, 'Marine Scientific Research in the Antarctic Treaty System' in Molenaar, Oude Elferink and Rothwell (eds), *The Law of the Sea and the Polar Regions*, 323–41.

[56] Note, however, the special regime created by the Treaty of Spitsbergen. Treaty concerning the Archipelago of Spitsbergen (done at Paris, 9 February 1920, entered into force 14 August 1925), 2 LNTS 8.

[57] See eg UNCLOS, above n 4, arts 21(1)(g), 40, 56(1)(b)(ii), 87, 143 and Pt XIII.

[58] The Antarctic Treaty—Arctic Council Joint Meeting Washington Ministerial Declaration on the International Polar Year and Polar Science, Washington, 6 April 2009, available at www.state.gov/e/oes/rls/other/2009/121340.htm.

[59] ibid, para 3.

the Arctic Council has held discussions on how to maximise the legacy of the IPY and has considered the scoping study recommendation to improve access to scientific research in the Arctic through international action but the SAO decided to address this through actions at the national level.[60]

Interestingly, however, one of the recommendations contained in the 2013 AOR project report related to addressing barriers for scientific research in the Arctic.[61] Indeed, in response, the Arctic Council established a Task Force to enhance international cooperation in scientific research.[62] As noted earlier, the Arctic Council decided to develop a legally binding instrument under this Task Force.[63] It remains to be seen how this issue will be dealt with, in particular whether or not there will be convergence with the ATS on this issue.

An interesting issue in the context of scientific research is the ongoing debate over bioprospecting. On the one hand, the ATCM has been extensively debating this issue. While recognising that the ATS is the appropriate framework for managing the collection of biological material in the Antarctic Treaty area and for considering its use, the ATCM has discussed the relationship between article III(1) of the Antarctic Treaty and bioprospecting as well as the need for regulation by the ATCM.[64] On the other hand, UNCLOS is considered to provide the legal framework for bioprospecting for marine genetic resources.[65] In addition, the CBD and its Nagoya Protocol are applicable to genetic resources in areas under national jurisdiction, including its provisions on indigenous peoples.[66] In fact, Norway and Greenland (Denmark)

[60] Meeting of SAO, Final Report, 12–13 November 2009, Copenhagen, 11. See also B Baker and H Eicken, Marine Research Access in the Arctic Ocean: Background for Potential Guidelines in a Changing Arctic, 10 March 2010, at 5–6, available at www.iarc.uaf.edu/workshops/2009/4/MSR-10-3-2010-final.pdf.

[61] PAME, The Arctic Ocean Review Project, Final Report (Phase II 2011–2013), Kiruna, May 2013, available at www.pame.is/images/03_Projects/AOR/Reports/126082_pame_sept_2.pdf, 97.

[62] Kiruna Declaration, above n 32 para 13, under 'Strengthening the Arctic Council'.

[63] See SAO Report to Ministers, Iqaluit, Canada, April 2015, above n 24, at 10 ('In the course of these discussions, it became clear that addressing issues such as the movement of people and equipment across borders and access to research areas may require significant involvement from a wide range of government agencies and stakeholders that do not have a science mandate. It was agreed that resolution on these issues may benefit from the force of a legally binding agreement').

[64] See eg ATCM, Resolution 7 (2005)—ATCM XXVIII—CEP VIII, Stockholm 'Biological Prospecting in Antarctica'; ATCM, Resolution 9 (2009)—ATCM XXXII—CEP XII, Baltimore 'Collection and Use of Antarctic Biological Material'; ATCM, Resolution 6 (2013)—ATCM XXXVI—CEP XVI, Brussels 'Biological Prospecting in Antarctica'. For an overview of the consideration of the issue at the ATCM, see 'A Gap Analysis of the Antarctic Treaty System Regarding the Management of Biological Prospecting' (WP 26), submitted by the Netherlands, Belgium, Bulgaria, Finland, France, Germany, Spain and Sweden (2009). It should be noted that art III(1) of the Antarctic Treaty reads in part, as follows that '[i]n order to promote international cooperation in scientific investigation in Antarctica, as provided for in Article II of the present Treaty, the Contracting Parties agree that, to the greatest extent feasible and practicable: ... c. scientific observations and results from Antarctica shall be exchanged and made freely available.'

[65] In this context, it should be noted that the General Assembly decided to develop an international legally binding instrument under UNCLOS on the conservation and sustainable use of marine biological diversity of areas beyond national jurisdiction, negotiations for which will address, among other topics, marine genetic resources, including questions on the sharing of benefits. UN Doc A/RES/69/292, para 2.

[66] Convention on Biological Diversity (done at Rio de Janeiro, 5 June 1992, entered into force 29 December 1993) 1760 UNTS 79; Nagoya Protocol on Access to Genetic Resources and the Fair and Equitable Sharing of Benefits Arising From Their Utilization to the Convention on Biological Diversity (done at Nagoya, Japan, 29 October 2010, entered into force 12 October 2014), available at www.cbd.int/abs/doc/protocol/nagoya-protocol-en.pdf.

have adopted domestic laws and regulations for bioprospecting in areas under their national jurisdiction. On this issue, therefore, it is difficult to see any convergence among these two regions.

ii. Seaborne Tourism

In the ATS, regulation of tourism is, to a large extent, left to industry.[67] The International Association of Antarctica Tour Operators (IAATO) is an organisation founded in 1991 'to advocate, promote and practice safe and environmentally responsible private-sector travel to the Antarctic'.[68] It has produced a number of guidelines for companies and operators and has also been actively participating in the discussion on Antarctic tourism within the ATCM through its 'experts' attending meetings and the submission of its reports. Although it is a self-regulating system, its components have been occasionally 'codified' by the ATCM. One of the problems is how to regulate the activities of cruise ships operated by companies that are not members of the IAATO, ie the so-called 'free-rider problem'.[69]

Seaborne tourism in the Arctic is subject to national and international regulation; the latter includes a number of IMO conventions and non-binding guidelines concerning ship safety and marine environmental protection. If cruise ships in the Arctic depart from or arrive at ports in Arctic states, they are subject to their port states' jurisdiction as well as flag and coastal state jurisdiction.[70]

In recent years, the increase in tourism activities in the Arctic, and problems associated with it, have given rise to discussions within the Arctic Council. In connection with the recommendation on strengthening passenger ship safety in Arctic waters (Recommendation I(D)), the AMSA report stated as follows:

> [T]here are currently no common best practices for the circumpolar Arctic as there is in the Antarctic through the International Association of Antarctica Tour Operators. The Arctic's one cruise organization, the Association of Arctic Expedition Cruise Operators, is limited in scope with its geographic range in the Svalbard, Jan Mayen and Greenland area. Cooperation among cruise ship operators, in partnership with academic and regulatory bodies, is necessary to ensure more sustainable eco-tourism in the Arctic.[71]

[67] However, note the importance of the Environmental Protocol and steps taken by the ATCM in recent years. States are involved in the regulation of tourism in various capacities; see 'ATCM Review of Tourism Rules and Regulations' (WP 26), submitted by the United States, France, Germany, the Netherlands and New Zealand (2011), 3. Apart from the ATS, global instruments such as applicable IMO conventions regulate seaborne tourism in the Antarctic, as in the Arctic. See also discussion on the development of a mandatory Polar Code at the IMO in section III of this chapter.

[68] Information about the International Association of Antarctica Tour Operators (IAATO) is available at the IAATO's website: http://iaato.org/home.

[69] See '"Outstanding Questions" on Antarctic Tourism: An Inventory and Discussion' (IP 67), submitted by the Netherlands (14 May 2012), 13–14.

[70] See the map in Arctic Council, AMSA 2009 Report, above n 28, p 78. The substantial growth in the number of tourist vessels visiting the Arctic appears to relate to personal pleasure craft/yachts whereas the number of expedition vessels and large cruise ships is stable or declining in some regions. On trends in tourist vessels visiting the Arctic, see PAME, Arctic Marine Tourism Project (AMTP) Workshop Report, 18 and 19 March 2014, Ottawa, Ontario, Canada, available at www.pame.is/images/03_Projects/Arctic_Marine_Shipping/Arctic_Marine_Tourism_Project/AMTP_Workshop_Report_March_2014.pdf, 23–24.

[71] Arctic Council, AMSA 2009 Report, above n 28, 137; see also pp 99–100.

In response, the PAME work plan for 2011–13 included the taking of 'actions to encourage the Arctic cruise tourism industry to adopt new, or update existing, best practices for operations in the Arctic', in addition to the monitoring of and support for IMO initiatives to strengthen passenger vessel safety.[72] In addition, upon request by Denmark and the United States and within the framework of PAME, information concerning standards/guidance was compiled to be utilised for developing best practices for Arctic tourism cruises.[73] The information received includes standards and guidance for Antarctic tourism cruises, such as ATCM instruments. Overall, it is fair to say that experiences in the ATS were substantially taken into account in the case of seaborne tourism during these processes. Subsequently, the Arctic Marine Tourism Project (AMTP) Best Practice Guidelines were developed at PAME between 2013 and 2015, and approved by the SAO in March 2015.[74]

III. INTERACTIONS BETWEEN GLOBAL AND POLAR REGIMES: THE DEVELOPMENT OF THE POLAR CODE AT THE IMO

The linkage of the polar regimes is also found in the global discussions on certain issues common to the Polar regions. One such example is the development of the Polar Code within the IMO.[75] It is important to remember that international rules and standards for navigation shall be developed, inter alia, through the competent international organisation, ie, the IMO.[76] Since unilateral coastal state prescriptive jurisdiction is rather limited in this field, the IMO is the venue to discuss shipping regulations for the Arctic as well as the Antarctic, in cooperation with states outside the region and other stakeholders.[77]

The initial work of the IMO on this issue resulted in the Guidelines for Ships Operating in Arctic Ice-Covered Waters, adopted in 2002.[78] As the title suggests, they only applied to ice-covered Arctic waters because of the concern that special conditions of the Antarctic were not sufficiently taken into account. In view of the need to address the increase in cruise shipping in Antarctica, the IMO was requested

[72] SAO Report to Ministers, Nuuk, Greenland, May 2011, above n 18, 40.

[73] See Arctic Council, 2011 Status Report, above n 51, 6, which states: 'Denmark and the U.S. compiled existing international, national, industry and NGO standards and guidelines relevant to the operation of cruise ships in Arctic waters. Denmark agreed to submit the information contained in the joint U.S./Denmark I(D) paper to IMO. PAME requested its Chair to invite representatives of the Arctic cruise tourism industry to develop new, or augment existing, best practices in light of information contained in the joint U.S./Denmark I(D) paper as well as any other relevant information.'

[74] SAO Report to Ministers, Iqaluit, Canada, April 2015, above n 24, at 33. The Best Practice Guidelines are available at www.pame.is/images/03_Projects/Arctic_Marine_Shipping/Arctic_Marine_Tourism_Project/AMTP_Best_Practice_Guidelines.pdf.

[75] The mandatory Polar Code, as noted below, was recently adopted at the IMO. Other examples relating to the Polar regions include IMO Resolution A.999 (25), adopted on 29 November 2007, Guidelines on Voyage Planning for Passenger Ships Operating in Remote Areas.

[76] See, eg, UNCLOS, above n 4, art 211(1).

[77] In the context of the Arctic, UNCLOS, ibid, art 234 provides for an important exception to the limitation on unilateral coastal state jurisdiction in the EEZ.

[78] IMO, Guidelines for Ships Operating in Arctic Ice-Covered Waters, MSC/Circ 1056 & MEPC/Circ 399, 23 December 2002.

to expand their application to Antarctica while updating them. It adopted the Polar Guidelines in 2009.[79]

In 2009, the IMO decided to develop a mandatory Polar Code covering both the Arctic and the Antarctic. The Code was adopted at the Maritime Safety Committee in November 2014 and at the Marine Environment Protection Committee in May 2015; to make it mandatory under the International Convention for the Safety of Life at Sea (SOLAS) and the International Convention for the Prevention of Pollution from Ships (MARPOL), the relevant amendments of SOLAS and MARPOL were adopted at these Committees and they are expected to enter into force on 1 January 2017. While the final text of the Code does not include a non-prejudice clause with explicit reference to UNCLOS or the ATS, the Code should be interpreted in a manner consistent with the existing legal frameworks governing the Arctic and the Antarctic.[80] Consideration of this issue by the IMO has involved a wide range of stakeholders: both Arctic and non-Arctic states, including ATCPs; states interested in Arctic shipping and those interested in shipping in the Southern Ocean; as well as environmental NGOs, the Cruise Lines International Association (CLIA), the International Association of Classification Societies (IACS) and the shipping industry.

The Code serves different purposes simultaneously. On the one hand, it intends to impose strict requirements in the same manner for both polar waters: this is the prevailing emphasis in many provisions of the draft Code. As a matter of fact, the 2009 Polar Guidelines took this approach. Those guidelines state uniform requirements for the Arctic and Antarctic waters throughout the document, while recognising significant differences in these regions.[81] On the other hand, different conditions in the two regions have been taken into account in the regulations of the Code. The Code states as follows:

> While Arctic and Antarctic waters have similarities, there are also significant differences. Hence, although the Code is intended to apply as a whole to both Arctic and Antarctic, the legal and geographical differences between the two areas have been taken into account.[82]

Some provisions of the Code refer to only one of these regions; in some cases, they provide for different requirements taking into account different conditions in these regions.[83] The differentiation of Arctic and Antarctic waters, especially in the section dealing with environmental protection, was controversial. In fact, how to address

[79] IMO Resolution A 1024 (26), adopted on 2 December 2009, Guidelines for Ships Operating in Polar Waters.

[80] See Regulation 2 of SOLAS Chapter XIV (IMO Doc MSC 94/21/Add.1, Annex 7, at 4), which was added to make the Polar Code mandatory under SOLAS: 'Nothing in this chapter shall prejudice the rights or obligations of States under international law'. The Draft International Code for Ships Operating in Polar Waters, as found in Annex 3 of Sub-Committee on Ship Design and Construction, 1st session, Report to the Marine Safety Committee (IMO Doc SDC 1/26, 11 February 2014), in preambular para 8, stated as follows: 'Nothing in this Code shall be taken as conflicting with the United Nations Convention on the Law of the Sea, 1982, the Antarctic Treaty System and other international instruments applicable to polar waters.'

[81] See Guidelines for Ships Operating in Polar Waters, above n 79, para P-1.2.

[82] International Code for Ships Operating in Polar Waters, Resolution MSC.385(94), adopted on 21 November 2014, Annex, preambular para 6. See also para 3.2.

[83] See ibid, Part II-A and Part II-B.

the harmonisation and differentiation of Arctic and Antarctic shipping regulations has always been an important factor for consideration since the failed attempt to establish a Polar Code in the 1990s.

As witnessed by the support for early completion of the Polar Code negotiations, the ATCPs and Arctic states have cooperated in this initiative. However, this does not necessarily mean that they have taken a uniform approach in negotiations. For example, the Russian Federation has proposed to accord the regulatory competence of Arctic coastal states under article 234 of UNCLOS priority over the proposed Polar Code.[84] This vividly illustrates the difficulty encountered by the eight Arctic states in presenting a united front to the rest of the world.

IV. CONCLUDING REMARKS

While bodies within the ATS have been serving as the principal forum addressing issues affecting Antarctica, the Arctic Council cannot function in this way due to the fragmentation of authority to manage problems affecting the Arctic (most notably, territorial sovereignty and functional jurisdiction over maritime activities). The Arctic Council, however, is striving to become a centre for strategic policy-making on various Arctic-related issues, for example, through the development of legally binding instruments and the AOR project. This inevitably calls into question the legitimacy of such activities by the Arctic Council, due to its closed nature. The debates over observer admission (and beyond) may impact on the legitimacy of the Arctic Council; the current approach appears to give the impression that non-Arctic states will remain outside the important decision-making of the Arctic Council, as opposed to the ATS, even though this is not necessarily inconsistent with international law.

Interactions between the international regime for the Arctic region and the ATS are found both at the regional and global levels. The Arctic Council has been taking lessons from the ATS on issues such as seaborne tourism activities. Initiatives in these areas can also be a basis for maintaining consistency between the two regimes in addressing common challenges. At the global level, issues affecting both the Arctic and the Antarctic have been addressed on some occasions, most notably at the IMO. There, different interests are involved and wider stakeholders are participating in the discussion. Consistency of measures between the two regions has been contemplated in two ways: the application of the same measures to both regions; and upgrading of some measures for the Arctic to catch up with the Antarctic regulations. In some cases, stricter measures have been articulated for the Antarctic. Overall, it seems that the tendency towards convergence between the international regime for the Arctic region and the ATS is confirmed in some issue areas and regime structures but substantial and important differences remain between them (eg, the lack of a comprehensive treaty specific to the Arctic region).

[84] IMO Doc DE 55/12/23, February 2011, Procedure of accounting for national regulations: submitted by the Russian Federation, p 2. On a similar attempt by Canada, see IMO Doc DE 53/18/2, 20 November 2009, Proposed framework for the Code for ships operating in polar waters, submitted by Canada, Annex, para 2.11.

Regionalism, in the sense of a distinct region-wide approach to a particular problem in the Polar regions, is found for both the Arctic and the Antarctic, but it is expressed differently. In considering the possibility and limitation of regionalism in the Arctic region, it is important to remember that Arctic exceptionalism is largely constrained by the globally applicable norms of the law of the sea, while this global framework allows and, in some cases, suggests regional diversity in implementation.[85] Although common challenges and interactions are found in various ways, the Arctic and Antarctic regimes largely operate as two separate sets of regional regimes. One may even observe that, as opposed to the 'question of Antarctica', problems facing the Arctic region are, and will be, addressed through a complex mixture of rules and institutions at the regional level *as well as* global, sub-regional and national levels.

[85] Another factor restraining Arctic exceptionalism for marine areas may be the fact that Arctic Ocean coastal states are also Atlantic and/or Pacific coastal states at the same time.

32

The Delimitation Process in the Central Arctic Seabed: Sovereign Rights or a Condominium *or* Res Communis Omnium?

CLAUDIA CINELLI

I. INTRODUCTION

IN 2005 THE then chairman of the UN Commission on the Limits of the Continental Shelf (CLCS), Sir Peter Croker, affirmed during an interview for the BBC News that the Arctic is

> the only place where a number of countries encircle an enclosed ocean. There is a lot of overlap. If you take a normal coastal State, the issues are limited to adjoining States and an outer boundary. In the Arctic, it is quite different.[1]

[1] See for details of the interview, the report by P Reynolds, 'The Arctic's new gold rush' at http://news.bbc.co.uk/2/hi/business/4354036.stm. The Arctic region covers land areas and spans the Arctic Ocean. It encompasses territories belonging to eight states, commonly called the 'Arctic states', according to the Declaration on the Establishment of the Arctic Council: Joint Communiqué of the Governments of the Arctic Countries on the Establishment of the Arctic Council, Ottawa, Canada, 19 September 1996, available at www.arctic-council.org/. The eight states are: Canada, Denmark (for Greenland), United States (Alaska), Russian Federation, Norway, Finland, Sweden and Iceland.

On the one hand, five of them (Canada, Denmark (for Greenland), United States (for Alaska), the Russian Federation and Norway) are commonly classified as coastal states of the Arctic sea basin, while two of the remaining three (Finland and Sweden) are partly in the space delimited by the Arctic Circle but are land-locked in the corresponding Arctic sea basin.

On the other hand, Iceland is an island country in the North Atlantic Ocean, partly situated within the Arctic space defined by the tree-line, which is usually larger than the space defined by the Arctic Circle. It is not formally considered to be an Arctic coastal state because it is positioned outside the line of the Arctic Circle, which defines the Arctic sea basin. However, beyond the formal geographic line, and because of its proximity to the Arctic basin, Iceland is inevitably involved in issues regarding fisheries in the Arctic high seas as well as issues regarding the Arctic outer limits of the continental shelf.

Finally, the Arctic Ocean is the smallest of the Earth's five oceans, with the largest continental shelf, known commonly as the Siberian Shelf. There is no consensus yet on the exact definition of physical space that is the term 'Arctic Ocean'. For different options of geographical coverage of the Arctic (and, where relevant, different applicable law *ratione loci*), see the University of Arctic website, UArctic Atlas 'Defining the Arctic' at http://old.uarctic.org/AtlasTheme.aspx?m=642; International Maritime Organization (IMO) Guidelines for Ships Operating in Arctic Ice-Covered Waters, (23 December 2002) IMO Doc

Contrary to some academic legal theories,[2] what is happening in practice in the Arctic Ocean seems to be no different from any other ocean, ie, it is governed by the general international law of the sea, so there is not, nor does it seem there will be, an ad hoc regime that provides a specific solution to the exigencies of the changing Arctic Ocean. The increasing economic importance of the natural resources on the Arctic seabed in decades to come will essentially be determined by the level of accessibility to those resources in line with ongoing technological developments, which lower the cost of exploration and exploitation and increase the benefits in economic terms.

Whereas it is true that the Arctic contains approximately 25 per cent of the world's undiscovered oil and gas reserves,[3] in 2007 the planting of a Russian flag on the seabed—on the Lomonosov ridge, below the current position of the North Pole (4,261 m), was a sign hat the existence of rich deposits at relevant depths may not be of a purely theoretical nature. Several of the Arctic coastal states have strengthened their presence in the Arctic, moving towards a claim of sovereign rights over the North Pole. Even though the North Pole is just a geographical point situated in the Arctic Ocean, which is thought to change position progressively in accordance with terrestrial rotation, its importance is symbolic within the context of delimitation of the continental shelf beyond national jurisdictions.

It is important to underline the fact that the aim of this chapter is not to deal with the general study of the CLCS's legal nature and its functions, nor is it intended to be a study of any general definition of the continental shelf or general matters related to the establishment of the outer limits of the continental shelf beyond national jurisdictions or, alternatively, rules applicable to the International Seabed Area. Rather, it focuses briefly on the positions and practices of the Arctic coastal states within the ongoing process of delineation of the outer limits of their continental shelves in the Arctic seabed. In doing so, it takes into particular account the seabed under the North Pole (the Lomonosov ridge), which is rich with energy resources that stretch across the Arctic Ocean and separate the Amerasian Basin from the Eurasian Basin.

MSC/Circ 1056-MEPC/Circ 399; or the FAO Arctic Fisheries Zone: Zone No 18 at www.fao.org/fishery/area/Area18/en.

[2] The academic debate is marked by two opposing lines of thought. On one side, the proponents advocate an ad hoc regime for the Arctic (as distinct from the Antarctic regime); on the other side, their opponents support the application of the existing Law of the Sea framework, notably the 1982 UN Convention on the Law of the Sea (adopted 10 December 1982, entered into force: 16 November 1994), 1833 UNTS 3 (UNCLOS). In brief, the proponents argue that the '[the] UNCLOS cannot be seamlessly applied to the Arctic. The region's unique geographic circumstances do not allow for a neat application of this legal framework. The Arctic is home to a number of vexing problems that, taken in their entirety, make it a special case.' SG Borgerson, 'Arctic Meltdown: The Economic and Security Implications of Global Warming' (2008) 87 *Foreign Affairs* 63–77. The opponents—in accordance with the EU position—draw attention to the need for an extensive interpretation of the UNCLOS in light of the new conditions and specificities of the Arctic Ocean, without precluding any further work that may develop under some of the existing frameworks. This extensive interpretation takes into particular account the work of the EU and of the IMO as well as of specific international fora, such as the Arctic Council; see C Cinelli, *El Ártico ante el Derecho del Mar Contemporáneo* (Valencia, Tirant lo Blanch, 2012).

[3] Compare US Geological Survey at www.usgs.gov/ and for dissenting views of that data, see the following http://benmuse.typepad.com/arctic_economics/2008/07/how-much-oil-and-gas-in-the-arctic.html.

This chapter starts with a brief analysis of the 'Arctic question' and the applicable law thereto (section II). It then proceeds to study the current work of the CLCS on the Arctic seabed (section III), and concludes with some final reflections (section IV).

II. THE 'ARCTIC QUESTION' AND THE APPLICABLE LAW

The 'Arctic question' deals with a classical dilemma of international law: on the one hand, it addresses individual state interests in the Arctic, and on the other hand, it is concerned with safeguarding the Arctic commons. At present, priority is given to a selective application of international norms that secure particular interests.[4]

From an historic and contemporary perspective, the law of the sea has generally been applied to the Arctic Ocean. Indeed, some of the claims by Arctic states have been resolved by the International Court of Justice (ICJ),[5] while other solutions have been reached through international agreements.[6] Notable is the fact that both the 2008 Ilulissat Declaration[7] and the 2010 Chelsea ministers meeting[8] clearly reaffirmed the five Arctic coastal states' commitment to the international law of the sea. The former 'provides for important rights and obligations concerning the delineation of the outer limits of the continental shelf,' including an 'orderly settlement of any possible overlapping claims.'[9]

All Arctic states agreed to apply the existing framework of the international law of the sea, mainly codified by the 1982 United Nations Convention on the Law of the Sea (UNCLOS) to which all Arctic states, except for the United States, are state parties. However, none of the Arctic coastal states parties to the UNCLOS made a reference to any commitment to Part XI of UNCLOS and its Implementation Agreement regarding the common heritage of mankind regime in the Central Arctic Ocean in the event that the International Seabed Area is eventually delimited.[10]

[4] See M Byers, *International Law and the Arctic* (Cambridge, Cambridge University Press, 2014).

[5] For examples see: *Fisheries Case (United Kingdom v Norway)* (Judgment) [1951] ICJ Rep 3; *Fisheries Jurisdiction (United Kingdom v Iceland)* (Judgment) [1974] ICJ Rep 3; *Fisheries Jurisdiction (Federal Republic of Germany v Iceland)* (Judgment) [1974] ICJ Rep 175; and *Maritime Delimitation in the Area between Greenland and Jan Mayen, (Denmark v Norway)* (Judgment) [1993] ICJ Rep 38.

[6] Among the most recently reached agreements, on 15 September 2010 Norway and the Russian Federation signed the 'Treaty concerning Maritime Delimitation and Cooperation in the Barents Sea and the Arctic Ocean'. According to the law of the sea, and the rules and principles for maritime delimitation, the Treaty ensures the continuation of fisheries cooperation in the whole of the Barents Sea. The so-called 'Grey Zone Agreement', which covers fisheries control and enforcement in a specified area of the Barents Sea, will no longer apply once the Treaty comes into force. In addition, the Treaty ensures efficient and responsible management of hydrocarbon resource cases, should any single oil or gas deposit extend across the delimitation line; see www.regjeringen.no/en/dep/ud/campaign/delimitation.html?id=614002; see also C Cinelli, 'International Law of the Sea and the Arctic Ocean' (2011) 2/1 *Arctic Review on Law and Politics* 4–24.

[7] The text of the Ilulissat Declaration is available at www.arcticgovernance.org/the-ilulissat-declaration.4872424.html.

[8] See for details of the meeting of Arctic states at Chelsea, Quebec, 2010, www.international.gc.ca/polar-polaire/arctic-meeting_reunion-arctique-2010_index.aspx.

[9] Ilulissat Declaration, above n 7, second recital.

[10] UNCLOS, above n 2, Pt XI and the Agreement relating to the Implementation of Pt XI of the United Nations Convention of the Law of the Sea of 10 December 1982 (adopted on 28 July 1994, entered into force 28 July 1996) 33 ILM 1309 (1994), 1836 UNTS 4.

The applicable law in the Arctic Ocean should be the existing and comprehensive law of the sea framework, including any norms that do not rely on the geographic location of states. It should promote cooperation in protecting the general interests of the international community for 'the benefit of mankind as a whole'.[11]

A. The 'Soft Law' Approach to Common Concerns for the Arctic Ocean

Significant changes in the Arctic Ocean have led to the growing development of international cooperation at circumpolar and sub-circumpolar levels.[12] Here the prospect of common concerns among the Arctic States, and between them and other entities, has mainly been addressed by a 'soft law' approach. This is based on the establishment of specific new programmes for regulating the Arctic, but only two of them are legally binding.

First, in 2011 eight Arctic states concluded the Agreement on Cooperation on Aeronautical and Maritime Search and Rescue in the Arctic (also known as the Arctic Search and Research Agreement, or SAR Agreement)—the first binding treaty approved under the Arctic Council's auspices during the Nuuk ministerial meeting.[13] Two years later, during the 2013 Kiruna ministerial meeting, the second binding treaty was adopted, the Agreement on Cooperation on Marine Oil Pollution Preparedness and Response in the Arctic (MOPPR Agreement).[14] Both treaties reflect the growing relevance of the Arctic Council in filling specific legal gaps for the Arctic.

At the circumpolar level, cooperation has indeed materialised through the scientific and political role of the Arctic Council,[15] where the Council participates directly

[11] See, for example, UNCLOS, ibid, art 140 *in extenso*.

[12] At universal level, the Arctic has not yet given rise to any debate in the context of the UN but it is an object of attention—for different reasons—for various specialised agencies and other international bodies. These include: FAO, with regard to fisheries issues in some areas of the Arctic Ocean; IMO, with regard to the prevention and control of pollution from ships and the safety of navigation; UNEP, in relation to the implementation of multilateral environmental agreements (MEAs) and strategies for the preservation of the environment at the regional level; and UNESCO, due to the presence of some world heritage sites and the ability to create new ones.

Mention should also be made of the final Statement, adopted by the 2006 Arendal Seminar on *MEAs and Their Relevance to the Arctic* (organised by the UNEP, Key Polar Centre and the Standing Committee for Parliamentarians of the Arctic Region—SCPAR). It requested governments of Arctic states, and institutions of the European Union, to initiate an audit of existing legal regimes that impact the Arctic and to continue the discussion about strengthening or adding to them where necessary. See below Section B.

[13] Until 2011 there was one regional treaty applicable to the entire Arctic region which was signed by the five Arctic coastal states, ie the Arctic Search and Rescue Agreement, formally the Agreement on the Conservation of Polar Bears (Oslo, 15 November 1973, entered into force 26 May 1976). The Agreement on Cooperation on Aeronautical and Maritime Search and Rescue in the Arctic SAR (Nuuk, Greenland, 12 May 2011, entered into force 19 January 2013), following ratification by each of the eight signatory states—Canada, Denmark, Finland, Iceland Norway, Russian Federation, Sweden and USA. The text is available at www.ifrc.org/docs/idrl/N813EN.pdf.

[14] The text of the Agreement on Cooperation on Marine Oil Pollution Preparedness and Response in the Arctic (MOPPR Agreement) (Kiruna, 15 May 2013, not yet in force) is available at: www.state.gov/r/pa/prs/ps/2013/05/209406.htm.

[15] See, among other soft law activities within the Arctic Council, the Arctic Ocean Review Project by the Protection of the Arctic Marine Environment (PAME) Working Group at: www.aor.is/. The final report is available at: www.pame.is/images/03_Projects/AOR/Reports/126082_pame_sept_2.pdf.

and indirectly with sub-circumpolar Councils (particularly, the Nordic Council and the Barents Euro-Arctic Council).[16] According to Byers, 'regions dominated by realist thinking—as was the case in the Arctic during the Cold War—are susceptible to "*creeping cooperation*": a momentum-generating process of institutionalization and legalization.'[17]

Throughout the development of Arctic international cooperation, new techniques and tools for regulating the activities of various sectors of economic and social relevance have been implemented (in the pioneering fields of science, fishery management, maritime and air navigation, and hydrocarbons).[18] Increasingly they aim towards cross-sectorial activities from the perspective of environmental impact assessment and an integrated ecosystem approach.[19] The areas of cooperation within and across sectors are characterised by a disordered interaction between hard and/or soft law, which is applied when appropriate in the entire circumpolar area, or in specific sub-circumpolar areas.

This interaction leads to a legal impasse. On one hand, there is the existing patchwork of general hard law which, while binding, does not deal with the unique characteristics of the Arctic, and mostly supports state sovereignty, sovereign rights and jurisdiction. On the other hand, the impasse is embodied in the soft law approach to common concerns which, while specifically dealing with new conditions and needs of the Arctic Ocean and their impact at a global level, is not legally binding. And this impasse reflects the fact that the new international visibility of the Arctic encourages state self-interest, while leaving common interests and concerns in the shade.

However, despite the legal impasse, or perhaps because of it, the international significance of the soft law approach lies in the fact that it provides immediately different instruments for regulation which, to some extent, lead to the proliferation of international actors in the Arctic Ocean, including non-Arctic actors, *in primis* the European Union.

B. The Emerging Role of the European Union in the Arctic and the Strategic Importance of Developing Resources in the Arctic Seabed

In 1998, the EU opened an 'Arctic window' through the external actions of its Northern Dimension Policy. Today, the EU continues to be involved in these matters

[16] See for the Nordic Cooperation: www.norden.org/en; the Council of Baltic Sea States www.cbss.org/; and the Barents Euro-Arctic Council: www.beac.st/ respectively.

[17] M Byers, *International Law and the Arctic* (Cambridge, Cambridge University Press, 2013) 283.

[18] T Koivurova and EJ Molenaar, *International Governance and Regulation of the Marine Arctic. Overview and Gap Analysis* (Oslo, World Wildlife Fund, 2009); OR Young, 'The Arctic in Play: Governance in Time of Rapid Change' (2009) 24 *International Journal of Marine & Coastal Law* 423–42; OS Stokke, 'Protecting the Arctic Environment: The Interplay of Global and Regional Regimes' (2009) 1 *Yearbook of Polar Law* 349–71.

[19] As for environmental impact, see T Koivurova, *Environmental Impact Assessment in the Arctic: A Study of International Legal Norms* (Aldershot, Ashgate, 2002); T Koivurova 'The Regime of the Espoo Convention in the Arctic: Towards a Strategic Environmental Assessment Procedure' in T Koivurova, T Joona and R Shnoro (eds), *Arctic Governance* (Rovaniemi, Oy Sevenprint, 2004) 61–87. For an integrated ecosystem approach, see Norwegian, Danish, Swedish common objectives for their Arctic Council chairmanships 2006–12, Integrated Management Resources, available at http://arctic-council.org/

together with actively moving forward on other issues that have an internal dimension. Indeed, looking at the geopolitical consequences of Arctic warming, the EU has recently changed its Arctic Climate Change Policy into a challenge for its Integrated Maritime Policy.[20] Following the European Parliament resolution on 'Arctic governance', in 2008 the EU realised that awareness about the Arctic's importance in a global context needs to be raised further by delivering a stand-alone EU Arctic Policy.[21]

Furthermore, following another European Parliament resolution in January 2011 on a 'Sustainable EU policy for the High North', in June 2012, the European Commission and the EU High Representative for Foreign Affairs and Security Policy adopted the document, 'Developing a European Union Policy towards the Arctic Region: progress since 2008 and next steps',[22] which is accompanied by two other documents.

The first of these is 'The inventory of activities in the framework of developing a European Union Arctic Policy'[23] and the second is 'Space and the Arctic'.[24] The EU pillars of actions can be summarised in three words: 'Knowledge, Responsibility, Engagement' that support the *ratio* behind several initiatives, which contribute, inter alia, to research and sustainable development in the Arctic, and that promote environmentally friendly technologies, which could be used for sustainable activities, including oil and gas prospection, exploration and production.

In its 2008 Communication, the EU proposed, inter alia, actions in order to

> [a]ssess the effectiveness of Arctic-relevant multilateral agreements to determine whether additional initiatives or measures are needed. Closely follow the processes of maritime delimitation and of the establishment of the outer limits of the continental shelves to assess their impacts on EU interests.[25]

The aforementioned 2012 Joint Communication set out the case for increased EU engagement in Arctic issues, including in the Arctic Ocean central seabed. On 31 January 2013 in Rovaniemi (Finland), the European Economic and Social Committee (EESC) held a joint hearing with the Arctic Centre (University of Lapland)

article/2007/11/common_priorities. Currently the theme of Canada's chairmanship (2013–15) is 'development for the people of the North', with a focus on responsible Arctic resource development, safe Arctic shipping and sustainable circumpolar communities, available at www.arctic-council.org/index.php/en/about-us/arctic-council/canadian-chairmanship/735-canadian-chairmanship-program-2013-2015.

[20] Green Paper, 'Towards a future Maritime Policy for the Union: A European vision for the oceans and seas', COM (2006) 275 final, 14.

[21] P6_TA(2008)0474, Arctic Governance, European Parliament resolution of 9 October 2008 on Arctic governance, and Communication from the Commission of the European Union and the Council, the European Union and the Arctic Region, 20.11.2008, COM (2008) 763 final, respectively.

[22] European Commission and EU High Representative for Foreign Affairs and Security Policy, Joint Communication to the European Parliament and the Council, Developing a European Union Policy towards the Arctic Region: progress since 2008 and next steps, 26.06.2012, JOIN (2012) 19 final.

[23] European Commission and EU High Representative for Foreign Affairs and Security Policy, Joint Staff Working Document, The inventory of activities in the framework of developing a European Union Arctic Policy, 26.6.2012, SWD (2012) 182 final.

[24] European Commission and EU High Representative for Foreign Affairs and Security Policy, Joint Staff Working Document, Space and the Arctic, 26.6.2012, SWD (2012) 183 final.

[25] COM (2008) 763 final, 11, above n 21, p 11 (first recital under 'Proposals for action').

on the EU's Arctic policy.[26] This followed an application by the European Commission, on behalf of the EU, for permanent Observer status in the Arctic Council.[27]

During the Kiruna Ministerial Meeting, on 15 May 2013, the Arctic Council deferred a final decision on the EU's application until the Arctic ministers could agree by consensus, with Canada being the main obstacle to reaching agreement.[28] The EU bid included Canadian concerns about its ban on seal fur and other products from Canada.[29] Two years later at the Iqaluit Ministerial Meeting of 24–25 April 2015, the EU's application to join the Arctic Council was again deferred although this time it was Russia that blocked the consensus process.[30] The Observers are accredited to the Arctic Council proper,[31] ie by consensus of the Ministers of the Arctic Council, according to the seven new criteria adopted during the Nuuk Ministerial Meeting of the Arctic Council.[32] Their status continues for such time as consensus exists. Any Observer engaging in activities that are at odds with the Ottawa Declaration or with the Rules of Procedure, will have its Observer status suspended.[33]

Having stressed the above point, the Arctic Council appears to emphasise that the best way to solve circumpolar problems is to develop circumpolar cooperation, which creates limited access and roles for relevant and global actors, such as the EU.[34] Following the latest development, on 5 March 2014, the European Parliament

[26] European Economic and Social Council (EESC), 'On an Arctic Policy for the EU' Brussels, 1 February 2013, at http://europa.eu/rapid/press-release_CES-13-7_en.htm.

[27] Since 2008, when the Commission adopted its first Communication on the Arctic, the EU has established itself as a key supporter of the Arctic region, while considering the Arctic Council to be the primary forum for international cooperation in the region.

[28] Kiruna Declaration, on the occasion of the Eight Ministerial Meeting of the Arctic Council, Kiruna, Sweden, 15 May 2013, available at www.arctic-council.org/index.php/en/document-archive/category/425-main-documents-from-kiruna-ministerial-meeting.

[29] See, for example, N Sellheim, *Ruling on the EU Seal Products Trade Ban: Commentary on the Ruling of the European Court of Justice—General Court, Case T–526/10, April 27, 2013*, available at www.eu-arctic-forum.org/. The EU is also poised to restrict imports of oil produced in the Alberta tar sands; more information is available at: http://uk.reuters.com/article/2013/05/08/uk-eu-canada-oilsands-idUKBRE9470RP20130508

[30] Fernando Garcés de los Fayos, 'At a Glance: The outcome of the ninth Arctic Council ministerial meeting Directorate-General for External Policies, Policy department, European Parliament, DG EXPO/B/PolDep/Note/2015_171 EN, May 2015-PE 549.036 2, www.europarl.europa.eu/.../2015/.../EXPO_ATA(2015)549036_EN.pdf.

[31] Application for Observer status is directed to the Chairmanship. Observer status is open to non-Arctic states and approved by the Council at Ministerial Meetings that occur once every two years. The accreditation and review of Observers is in accordance with the provision set out in the Annex II (Accreditation and Review of Observers) to the Rules of Procedure, as adopted by the Arctic Council at the first Arctic Council Ministerial Meeting, held in Iqaluit, Canada, in 1998 and revised at the eighth Arctic Council Ministerial Meeting, held in Kiruna, Sweden in 2013. On this latter occasion, the distinction between ad hoc and permanent observers was abolished and new criteria for admitting observers were established. See art 1 of Annex II, which states that '120 days before a Ministerial meeting, the Chairmanship shall circulate, to all Arctic States and Permanent Participants, a list of entities that have applied for Observer Status.' An updated list of Observers is available on the Arctic Council website at www.arctic-council.org/index.php/en/.

[32] art 6 Annex II, Accreditation and Review of Observers, ibid.

[33] art 37 Rules of Procedure, above n 30.

[34] In the meantime, individual states' applications for permanent Observer status to the Arctic Council have been accepted. In contrast to previous ministerial meetings, the Kiruna Ministerial Meeting, which was held at Kiruna, Sweden, in May 2013, welcomed six new Observer states: China, India, Italy, Japan, Republic of Korea and Singapore.

adopted a resolution on the 'EU Strategy for the Arctic'[35] and, having regard to EU Directive 2013/30 on Safety of Offshore Oil and Gas Operations,[36] called on the EU to promote strict precautionary regulatory standards in the field of environmental protection and safety for oil exploration, prospection and production internationally.[37] Moreover, in the same document, the European Parliament called for a '*ban on oil drilling in the icy Arctic waters of the EU and the EEA* and for promotion by the EU of comparable precautionary standards in the Arctic Council and for Arctic coastal states' (emphasis added).[38]

There is no doubt that the EU has a vital interest in the Arctic continental shelves, ensuring maximum safety of offshore oil and gas operations and the protection of the environment. Nevertheless, the extent of the legal basis for such a ban is not yet clear. The European Parliament's approach also seems to differ from the European Commission's perspective, which proposed strengthening international cooperation on environmental standards for the extraction of Arctic hydrocarbons within *all* the region, according to the current international legal framework.

Moreover, the future EU Arctic policy should be consistent with the strategy of the Arctic Council and each Arctic state, so that Arctic governance can be developed and implemented on the basis of effective cooperation with countries and key partners. This seems also to be a concern of the European Commission. Indeed, there is a huge potential for EU governance innovation in the Arctic.

III. THE CURRENT WORK OF THE UN COMMISSION ON THE LIMITS OF CONTINENTAL SHELF IN THE ARCTIC SEABED

At the very beginning of the twenty-first century the CLCS—whose first election was in 1997—formally opened its doors for business when it took its first submission. It was presented by the Russian Federation in respect of, inter alia, the Central Arctic Ocean and, to some extent, it opened the premise for a 'new gold rush' in the Arctic, which was intensified by the successful outcome of the Arktika 2007 expedition.

Currently, the Russian Federation and Norway are the only two Arctic states that have presented their submissions to the CLCS; other Arctic states' submissions are partial and/or are still in progress.

A. The 2001 Russian Federation's Submission, the Reaction of other Arctic Coastal States and the Arktika 2007 Expedition

On 20 December 2001, the Russian Federation presented its submission to the CLCS in accordance with article 76(8) UNCLOS.[39] It contained information on

[35] European Parliament resolution of 12 March 2014 on the EU strategy for the Arctic, 2013/2595(RSP).

[36] Directive 2013/30/EU of the European Parliament and of the Council of 12 June 2013 on safety of offshore oil and gas operations and amending Directive 2004/35/EC Text with EEA relevance, OJ L 178/66, 28.06.2013, Preamble, p 2.

[37] European Parliament resolution on EU strategy for the Arctic, para 35.

[38] ibid.

[39] UNCLOS, art 76(8), above n 2.

the proposed outer limits of the continental shelf of the Russian Federation beyond 200 nautical miles from the baselines of which the breadth of the territorial sea is measured in four regions, among them, the Central Arctic Ocean.[40] The Russian Federation claimed a large extended continental shelf as far as the North Pole within the Arctic sector (about 1.2 million km^2) which includes the Lomonosov, Mendeleyev and Alpha ridges.[41] Once the UN Secretary-General gave due publicity to the Russian submission, Canada and Denmark—at that time not yet parties to UNCLOS—adopted a similar position, as their respective Diplomatic Notes show. Both of them clarified that they were unable to comment upon the Russian submission, specifying that their inability to do so was not to be interpreted as an agreement to, or acquiescence with, the Russian submission. In addition, they emphasised that any recommendations by the CLCS in response were without prejudice to the question of delimitation of the continental shelf between Canada and the Russian Federation, and Denmark and the Russian Federation, respectively.[42]

In the face of the Russian submission, American efforts to legally extend claims to the Arctic continental shelf may be complicated by the fact that the United States has yet to ratify UNCLOS. However, there may be no complication in the United States simultaneously implementing its continental shelf to the fullest extent of the outer limits permitted under general international law, while avoiding the CLCS procedure as set out by the UNCLOS.[43]

Nevertheless, in a more incisive manner than other Arctic coastal states, the United States affirmed in its Note Verbale, after the UN Secretary-General gave notice of the Russian submission to the CLCS, that '[t]he Russian submission is particularly complex and should be considered in a deliberate manner. A significant period of debate and reflection will be required for the Convention to be carefully applied in a manner to promote stability.' In addition, even though there was strong disagreement regarding the existence of the common heritage of mankind regime for the seabed, on this occasion the United States observed: '[i]nsofar as no applications to

[40] Commission on the Limits of the Continental Shelf (CLCS) Outer limits of the continental shelf beyond 200 nautical miles from the baselines: Submissions to the Commission: Submission by the Russian Federation 2001, 20 December 2001, Ref No CLCS01.2001.LOS, available at www.un.org/Depts/los/clcs_new/submissions_files/submission_rus.htm.

[41] See M Benith, 'Russia's claim in the Arctic and the vexing issue of ridges in UNCLOS' (2007) 11(27) *ASIL Insights*, 8 November 2007.

[42] See reaction of Canada and Denmark in respect of the submission of the Russian Federation to the CLCS (Note Verbale No 119N8 of the Permanent Mission of Denmark to the United Nations to the Secretary General of the United Nations of 4 February 2002 (reproduced as an attachment to the document CLCS.01.2001.LOS/DNK of 26 February 2002); Note Verbale No 0145 of the Permanent Mission of Canada to the United to the Secretary-General of the United Nations of 18 January 2002 (reproduced as an attachment to the document CLCS.01.2001.LOS/CAN of 26 February 2002) respectively. See also Norway's adoption of a similar position in Note Verbale of 20 March 2002 of the Permanent Mission of Norway to the United Nations to the Secretary-General of the United Nations (Doc CLCS.01.2001.LOS/NOR of 2 April 2002).

[43] See National Security Presidential Directive and Homeland Security Presidential Directive (adopted 9 January 2009), NSPD-66/HSPD-25, available at www.fas.org/irp/offdocs/nspd/nspd-66.htm, under section D Extended Continental Shelf and Boundary Issues.

explore or exploit the Area have been made or are likely to made in the Arctic for the foreseeable future, no prejudice is likely to result from a deliberative process.'[44]

In 2002 the CLCS, having carefully considered the Russian submission, declared it to be an improper document for lack of geodesic data and technical information, and the Russian Federation was asked to review its submission within a reasonable time.[45] Five years later, the discussion about who owns the North Pole was intensified by the Russian Arktika 2007 expedition. This was basically conducted in order to collect additional technical information and geodesic data for preparing a new submission, which it submitted to the CLCS on 3 August 2015, in support of their 2001 submission.[46]

The Russian flag dropped in the seabed under the North Pole is the clearest evidence of Russian ambition in the North Pole and reflects old tensions in the American-Russian relationship. Russians compare the success of Arktika 2007 with man's first step on the Moon: '[t]hat one small step for a man, one giant leap for mankind'[47] which was historically marked by the Apollo XII expedition and the planting of the American flag on the moon.[48]

Leaving aside the rhetoric about the common benefit for mankind and looking at the facts, the Russian flag appears to represent symbolic support for the 2001 Russian submission on the expanded continental shelf towards the North Pole. Its importance lies in the fact that it encompasses a very extensive zone, which is extremely rich in natural resources and which would be fully under the sovereign rights of the Russian Federation.

B. Norwegian Arctic Outer Continental Shelf and other Developments

At the international level, Norway is the only Arctic coastal state which has defined its Arctic outer continental shelf. In March 2009, the CLCS made its recommendations regarding the 2006 Norway submission, in which it accepted, with some refinements, the outer continental shelf limits that Norway had proposed, including those related to the continental shelf of Svalbard.[49] That has raised new discussions

[44] United States of America: Notification Regarding the Submission Made by the Russian Federation to the Commission on the Limits of the Continental Shelf, Ref No CLCS.01.2001.LOS/USA, 18 March 2002.

[45] Statement by the Chairman of the Commission on the Limits of the Continental Shelf on the progress of work in the Commission—Tenth session, CLCS/32 12 April 2002.

[46] See Russian Federation submitted to the Commission on the Limits of the Continental Shelf, in accordance with Article 76, paragraph 8, of the Convention, 3 August 2015, www.un.org/Depts/los/clcs_new/submissions_files/submission_rus_rev1.htm.

For the latest development, see http://barentsobserver.com/en/arctic/2014/08/putin-russia-must-strengthen-position-arctic-29-08.

[47] 'C'est comme le premier pas sur la lune! Il n'est pas peu fier, le géologue Artur Chilingarov...', 'La Russie mène la ruée vers l'or noir de l'océan Arctique' *Tribune de Genève,* 3 August 2007.

[48] Among other commentators and critics was the Canadian Foreign Affairs Minister, Mr Peter MacKay, who affirmed '[T]his isn't the 15th century. You can't go around the world and just plant flags and say "We're claiming this territory"', *BBC News*, 2 August 2007.

[49] Summary of the Recommendations of the Commission on the limits of the Continental shelf in regard to the submission made by Norway in respect of areas in the Arctic Ocean, The Barents Sea and the Norwegian Sea on 27 November 2006. No legal Act on the outer limits of the Norwegian continental

between Norway and other states, both Arctic and non-Arctic (Spain, for example)[50] states concerning implementation of the Svalbard Treaty of 1920[51] in the continental shelf of the archipelago of Svalbard in light of contemporary international law of the sea.[52]

However, according to the CLCS recommendations, the part of the Norwegian continental shelf in the High North extending beyond the 200-mile zone covers some 235,000 km;[2] it does not lie anywhere near the North Pole. Therefore, the CLCS recommendations have clarified that, in the words of the Norwegian Foreign Minister Jonas Gahr Støre: 'In the discussion about who owns the North Pole—it's definitely not us.'[53]

While the United States is not a party to UNCLOS, some states that are parties have submitted claims, including Denmark and Iceland (both in 2009) and Canada (in 2013). As far as Denmark and Iceland's submissions are concerned, the work of the CLCS is being developed in the submarine area situated beyond 200 nautical miles from the baselines of Norway, the Faroe Islands, Iceland, Jan Mayen, Greenland and the Svalbard archipelago, in accordance with the submissions presented on 29 April 2009 by Iceland and Denmark in conjunction with the government of the Faroe Islands.[54]

These submissions were made in implementing the previous Agreed Minutes of 20 September 2006, as adopted by Norway, Denmark and Iceland, which set out an agreed procedure for determining future delimitation lines in the aforementioned submarine area.[55] On 14 March 2014 the CLCS endorsed the entire area claimed by the Government of Denmark together with the Government of the Faroes, and recognised the sovereign rights of Denmark/Faroes on this area in accordance with the UNCLOS. Currently, Denmark/Faroes and Norway are still awaiting the completion of the submission of Iceland, which is pending, in order to finalise the three bilateral delimitation agreements on the submarine area situated beyond 200 nautical miles

shelf has been adopted yet, but a White Paper to the Norwegian Parliament for delineating them in accordance with the CLCS Recommendations is in progress.

[50] See, Spanish Note Verbale, dated 3 March 2007and Norwegian Note Verbale, dated 28 March 2007 referring to the Spanish Note Verbale. Both are available at www.un.org/Depts/los/clcs_new/submissions_files/submission_nor.htm; see C Cinelli, 'Spain in the Arctic' (2010) 16 *Spanish Yearbook of International Law Online* 1–17.

[51] Svalbard Treaty (done at Paris, 9 February 1920, entered into force 14 August 1925), 2 LNTS 7.

[52] *Mutatis mutandis*, it reflects the old discussion over the Fisheries Protection Zones around Svalbard, for which see, G Ulfstein, *The Svalbard Treaty: From Terra Nullius to Norwegian Sovereignty* (Oslo, Scandinavian University Press, 1995); T Pedersen, and T Henrisken, 'Svalbard's Maritime Zones: The End of Legal Uncertainty?' (2009) 24 *International Journal of Marine & Coastal Law* 141–61.

[53] 'Limits of Norway's Arctic seabed agreed', *Barents Observer*, 16 April 2009, available at www.barentsobserver.com.

[54] See CLCS, Outer limits of the continental shelf beyond 200 nautical miles from the baselines: The Icelandic Continental Shelf, Partial Submission to the Commission on the Limits of the Continental Shelf pursuant to article 76, paragraph 8 of the United Nations Convention on the Law of the Sea in respect of the Ægir Basin area and Reykjanes Ridge; and The Partial Submission of the Kingdom of Denmark together with the Government of the Faroes to the Commission on the Limits of the Continental Shelf: The Continental Shelf North of the Faroe Islands, respectively, 29 April 2009. See also Doc CLCS/64, 1 October 2009.

[55] The text of the Agreed Minutes is available at www.regjeringen.no/en/dep/ud/documents/Laws-and-rules/retningslinjer/2006/Agreed-Minutes.html?id=446839.

from the baselines of Norway, the Faroe Islands, Iceland, Jan Mayen, Greenland and the Svalbard archipelago. According to the 2006 Agreed Minutes, the definitive demarcation of the limits should be determined by three bilateral agreements which will then be signed after each concerned state requests the CLCS to consider them and to make its recommendations.

Finally, on 6 December 2013, Canada submitted a partial claim to the CLCS related to the limits of the continental shelf beyond 200 nautical miles from the baselines from which the breadth of the territorial sea is measured in the Atlantic Ocean (the Labrador Sea, the Grand Banks and Nova Scotia).[56] It also declared that it intends to submit information at a later date on the limits of the continental shelf beyond 200 nautical miles in the Arctic Ocean.[57]

IV. CONCLUSION

Claims are purely subjective because states can make whatever claim they decide upon, including a discretional division into converging sectors of the Arctic seabed, which is the result of states' considerations of convenience. It is sufficient to look at the Russian sector whose apex is currently characterised by the white, blue and red Russian flag over the seabed under the North Pole, or the ambitions of the Danish and/or Canadian explorations, or those of the United States that might aim to reach the North Pole.[58]

The overlapping claim areas do not always correspond to the area of overlapping entitlements. Following, *mutatis mutandis*, the argument presented by Vaughan Lowe before the ICJ in the case concerning *Maritime Delimitation in the Black Sea (Romania v Ukraine)*, a correct approach to the delimitation of the Arctic seabed would be to look at the area of possible overlapping entitlements (rather than claims) of states' sovereign rights.[59]

The distinction between overlapping entitlements and overlapping claims is important in order to determine correctly the relevant maritime area in the Central Arctic Seabed for the purposes of delimitation in accordance with article 76 UNCLOS. Generally speaking, the basic premise for delimitating the continental shelf is the entitlement of the state to the relevant maritime area that constitutes a natural prolongation of its land territory into, and under, the sea which exists by virtue of its sovereignty over the land. Equally, it is an extension of the exercise of its sovereign rights for the purpose of exploring the seabed and exploiting its natural resources.

Reviewing and analysing the geographical and morphological features of the Arctic seabed beyond national jurisdiction on the bases of states' submissions is the

[56] The text of the Canadian submission is available at www.un.org/depts/los/clcs_new/submissions_files/can70_13/es_can_en.pdf.

[57] ibid, p 3.

[58] See the map elaborated by the International Boundaries Research Unit at Durham University in the United Kingdom at www.dur.ac.uk/ibru/resources/arctic/.

[59] *Maritime Delimitation in the Black Sea* (*Romania v Ukraine*) ICJ, Verbatim Record, 5 September 2008, para 45 ff, at p 61 et seq.

primary task of the CLCS, without prejudice to the question of delimitation of the continental shelf between states with opposite or adjacent coasts.

It is to be expected that a long time will pass before the CLCS will complete its work on the Arctic seabed. Similarly, the delimitation of the continental shelf between states with opposite or adjacent coasts will be affected by agreements, on the basis of international law, in order to achieve an equitable solution.

The final question is not 'who owns the North Pole', but whether any seabed beyond national jurisdiction is left in the Central Arctic Ocean. Far from being fully delimited, one can imagine three different scenarios for the Arctic seabed beyond national jurisdiction and under the North Pole. First, that there is just one Arctic coastal state—the Russian Federation, Denmark, Canada or USA—which is entitled to its sovereign rights on the seabed of the Central Arctic Ocean, including the part under the North Pole where the Russian flag has been planted. Second, the seabed under the North Pole is effectively an area of overlapping entitlements in so far as it creates a situation that may lead to a sort of joint exploitation reached by an agreement, by a judgment of the ICJ or perhaps a condominium. Third, the application of all the norms of the UNCLOS, including those related to the common benefit of mankind, and the overlapping entitlements approach to the delimitation of the outer limits of the Arctic continental shelf, leaves open the possibility for thinking about the potential existence of an Arctic Area, ie *res communis omnium*. However, if it is finally delimitated, it would be a very small area.

Back in 1995 Russian Rear Admiral Valery Aleskin affirmed that 'whoever controls the Arctic controls the world'. However, it is to be hoped that it will be the International Seabed Authority who 'controls the Arctic', pursuant to the implementation of the common heritage of mankind regime in the Arctic Area, by becoming a vehicle for the equitable distribution of the Arctic seabed wealth in line with its use exclusively for peaceful purposes.[60]

[60] See the original idea for such a regime in general terms, A Pardo, *The Common Heritage—Selected Papers on Oceans and World Orders: 1967–74* (Malta, University of Malta Press, 1975).

www.ingramcontent.com/pod-product-compliance
Lightning Source LLC
Chambersburg PA
CBHW081124180926
51611CB00004B/45